Virtual Technology Innovations in Education

Seyfullah Gökoğlu
Bartın University, Turkey

Fatih Erdoğdu
Zonguldak Bülent Ecevit University, Turkey

IGI Global
Scientific Publishing
Publishing Tomorrow's Research Today

Vice President of Editorial	Melissa Wagner
Managing Editor of Acquisitions	Mikaela Felty
Managing Editor of Book Development	Jocelynn Hessler
Production Manager	Mike Brehm
Cover Design	Phillip Shickler

Published in the United States of America by
IGI Global Scientific Publishing
701 East Chocolate Avenue
Hershey, PA, 17033, USA
Tel: 717-533-8845
Fax: 717-533-8661
Website: https://www.igi-global.com E-mail: cust@igi-global.com

Library of Congress Cataloging-in-Publication Data

Names: Gökoğlu, Seyfullah, 1985- editor | Erdoğdu, Fatih, 1987- editor
Title: Virtual technology innovations in education / Edited by Seyfullah Gökoğlu, Fatih Erdoğdu.
Description: Hershey, PA : IGI Global Scientific Publishing, [2025] | Includes bibliographical references and index. | Summary: "This book aims to inspire educators, administrators, and policymakers to embrace the potential of virtual innovations, ultimately contributing to a more adaptive, inclusive, and forward-thinking educational environment"-- Provided by publisher.
Identifiers: LCCN 2024053083 (print) | LCCN 2024053084 (ebook) | ISBN 9798369360309 hardcover | ISBN 9798369360316 paperback | ISBN 9798369360323 ebook
Subjects: LCSH: Educational innovations | Virtual reality in education | Artificial intelligence--Educational applications | Virtual exchange (Education)
Classification: LCC LB1027 .V573 2025 (print) | LCC LB1027 (ebook) | DDC 371.1001/9--dc23/20250214
LC record available at https://lccn.loc.gov/2024053083
LC ebook record available at https://lccn.loc.gov/2024053084

British Cataloguing in Publication Data
A Cataloguing in Publication record for this book is available from the British Library.

Table of Contents

Detailed Table of Contents

The integration of virtual reality (VR) into educational settings is poised to revolutionize the way students interact with learning materials. This chapter explores the burgeoning role of VR in education, assessing its current applications, the advantages it offers, and the challenges it presents to educators. It also examines the potential for VR to shape the future of educational practices. The educational landscape is experiencing a technological renaissance, with VR emerging as a transformative tool. It offers an immersive learning experience that can enhance student engagement and facilitate a deeper understanding of complex subjects. VR's potential is expansive, enabling students to engage with course materials in novel and interactive ways, such as through virtual field trips to historical sites or the simulation of surgical procedures in medical education. The Impact of Virtual Reality in Education hence has to be further explored.

The COVID-19 pandemic has dramatically impacted global education, necessitating the development of more adaptable and innovative learning paradigms. Immersive technologies such as Augmented Reality (AR), Virtual Reality (VR), and Mixed Reality (MR) present substantial potential for enhancing educational experiences by making learning more interactive and accessible. These technologies are transforming various fields, including vocational education, medical training, and the Architecture, Engineering, and Construction (AEC) sector. This paper explores the benefits and challenges of integrating VR into educational settings, highlighting its role in bridging the gap between theoretical and practical learning, improving student engagement and motivation, and offering cost-effective training solutions.

The findings suggest that while VR is not a complete replacement for traditional education, it is a valuable supplementary tool that can significantly enhance learning experiences and outcomes.

In this chapter, the features of virtual robotic simulations designed in accordance with physical robotic kits are examined from different perspectives. Nowadays, with the spread of online education, virtual robotic simulations are preferred as alternative and supportive tools to physical robotic kits. Simulations include challenges, activities, games and competitions organized in parallel with the curriculum of grades K-12. Challenges related to daily life and designed from simple to complex aim to improve students' STEM (Science, Technology, Engineering, Mathematics) knowledge and skills. In this section, online platforms including Lego Mindstorms, VEX, Arduino and Mbot virtual robotic tools used in classroom activities or international competitions around the world are examined. Simulations on the platforms are evaluated according to their physical properties, difficulties involved and usability in educational environments. In addition, studies in the literature on simulations are included and examples of the usability of simulations in educational environments are presented.

The study aims to identify the types of e-learning embraced by the higher education institutions (HEIs) in Bangladesh, schemes offered to catch up with the trend of e-learning, features of LMS suitable for learners in a developing country, and to understand learners' attitudes towards e-learning. The study used 316 learners' data collected from 16 HEIs in Bangladesh. Descriptive statistics show that HEIs are equipped with eleven types of platforms and are always ready to deal with uncertainties in the new normal and onward. In addition, HEIs put forward several progressive schemes easing up the process of conducting classes in a hybrid mode combining face-to-face and online instructions. Fifteen features of LMS are in use and are the most demanded by users in a developing country. The learners are aware of the benefits of e-learning and have mastery of it and it is entirely within their control. Learning online is also likable to the learners as it enhances the scope of learning.

This book chapter examines the integration of virtual reality and artificial intelligence technologies in the field of education. While the integration of AI-based content, analysis, and feedback systems into educational VR environments presents a significant opportunity, it also brings various challenges, including privacy, data security, social equity, and ethical issues. The chapter addresses the effects of AI-supported VR applications on teacher-student interactions and pedagogical outcomes across different educational levels. Additionally, it evaluates predictions and potential scenarios for the future use of these technologies in education. Finally, the chapter provides strategic recommendations to address the challenges encountered in the integration of AI and VR in education, offering guidance on the ethical and effective use of these technologies. By providing a comprehensive guide for educators, policymakers, and developers, this chapter offers valuable insights into managing digital transformation processes and utilizing these technologies to enhance learning experiences.

Continuing advancement in technology provides an opportunity for institutions of higher education to enhance electronic learning experiences for students. Virtual Reality (VR) technologies have been developed for a wide range of applications in education, but further research is needed to establish appropriate and effective learning techniques and practices to promote meaningful learning. By creating an immersive and interactive learning environment, VR offers a novel approach to education that can enhance engagement, improve understanding of abstract concepts, and provide teaching experiences that the traditional lecture method cannot. Using VR immerses the student in the topic at hand without distraction from real-world events. VR in the classroom can provide innovative and engaging learning experiences that encourage students to approach the subject matter from alternative perspectives. This chapter examines the potential use of VR systems for education, examining its benefits, applications, challenges and prospects.

Digital transformation is a requisite for dealing with equity, access, quality, and sustainability issues in higher education. Understanding the challenges faced during the rapid transition to online learning amid the pandemic would provide valuable insights into digital transformation in higher education. Therefore, this chapter presents the challenges faced during the rapid transition to online learning, the first year of the pandemic, and the implications for digital transformation. The synthesized findings from the reviewed articles published during the rapid transition period were presented and discussed with the example empirical studies. The identified challenges were classified into four categories: (1) challenges faced by learners, (2) challenges faced by instructors, (3) challenges faced in online teaching, and (4) challenges faced in management and organization. Based on these challenges, the implications for digital transformation in higher education, a requisite for the institutions' resilience for equity, access, quality, and sustainability, were presented.

In recent times, with the advent of digitalization of higher education virtual mobility has emerged more clearly as a new model in the domain of internationalization of higher education. This more inclusive mobility model offers meaningful and multilateral interaction for the wider youth and offers the opportunity to build greater intercultural understanding of different societies and thus expands their worldwide view. However, despite the growth in virtual mobility opportunities in the current scenario, there is sparse research on the theoretical and empirical analysis of such programmes on human capital or career development outcomes. In this context, the prime aim of this article is to provide the conceptual underpinning of Virtual mobility. The strengths and weaknesses of virtual mobility model have been analyzed in contrast to traditional physical mobility model. Lastly, this paper sheds light on the potential effects of this new model of mobility and thus raised important concerns.

Virtual technology-driven environments (VTD) are widely used in education and training due to their positive impact on cognitive, affective, and psychomotor skills. However, measuring and evaluating the effectiveness of these environments poses challenges, including technological complexity, diverse user behavior, and data collection methods. Researchers and practitioners employ various methods to address these issues, such as self-report measurements and objective methods that assess user experiences during system interactions. This book chapter examines physiological, physical and behavioural measures used to assess user responses, cognitive competencies and task performance in VTDs. The chapter offers an overview of existing methods, discusses their applications across different fields, and highlights future developments. The aim is to provide a comprehensive perspective on the challenges of measurement and evaluation in virtual environments.

Artificial intelligence is also used to transfer knowledge and culture about the past to future generations. Thus, the improvement of students' history education processes and the innovations that artificial intelligence can bring to history education can be discussed. Historical research is an important discipline that helps us understand the evolution of humanity by examining past events. Traditionally, historians access and interpret information by manually analyzing documents, archives and other sources. However, with the development of artificial intelligence technologies in recent years, new possibilities in historical research are emerging, and AI has great potential in historical research. In the future, AI technologies are expected to help us understand our historical knowledge in a deeper and more comprehensive way. In this study, as well as answering the question of what artificial intelligence is, the question of how artificial intelligence can be used in history education is also answered.

Preface

The education landscape is undergoing a significant transformation as virtual technologies continue redefining how knowledge is delivered, accessed, and applied. "Virtual Technology Innovations in Education" is a comprehensive exploration of this transformation, offering educators, administrators, and policymakers the insights and practical tools to incorporate these innovations into educational settings effectively. This book covers a range of virtual technologies, from e-learning platforms to augmented reality (AR), virtual reality (VR), artificial intelligence (AI), and even the metaverse, each contributing uniquely to the evolving digital framework of education. By analyzing the impact of these technologies on teaching and learning, the book provides a structured guide for integrating virtual innovations, enhancing the educational experience, and expanding learning opportunities.

In today's world, the shift towards digital integration in education is no longer a mere enhancement but a critical necessity catalyzed by global events such as the COVID-19 pandemic. Traditional educational structures have encountered considerable challenges in adapting to the needs of a digitally oriented society. As remote learning became necessary, the urgency for accessible, flexible, and innovative virtual solutions became evident across all levels of education, from K-12 to higher education and professional development. Against this backdrop, Virtual Technology Innovations in Education addresses these shifts, providing readers with strategies to navigate and leverage virtual technologies for an effective, resilient educational landscape.

The target audience for this book includes educators, school administrators, higher education leaders, policymakers, and researchers keen to understand and utilize the transformative potential of virtual technologies in educational contexts. This book also serves as a valuable resource for instructional designers and technology developers who seek to align their innovations with the evolving demands of education. By focusing on integrating digital solutions into traditional practices, the book meets the diverse needs of its audience, ensuring that the insights presented are both relevant and applicable to various educational contexts.

The book comprises 14 carefully curated chapters, each addressing a unique aspect of virtual technology integration in education:

Chapter 1 examines the potential of Virtual Reality in education to increase student engagement and transform learning experiences.

Chapter 2 discusses the potential for technologies such as VR and MR to supplement traditional methods by increasing interactivity in post-pandemic education.

Chapter 3 evaluates the impact of virtual robotic simulations on developing STEM skills in education.

Chapter 4 analyzes e-learning adaptation processes and student attitudes in higher education institutions in Bangladesh.

Chapter 5 evaluates the opportunities offered by AI-supported VR applications with ethical and safety issues in education.

Chapter 6 examines the potential of using VR headsets in the classroom to enhance attention and comprehension.

Chapter 7 provides theoretical and practical knowledge about the use of augmented reality applications in mathematics education.

Chapter 8 examines the integration and use of a local enterprise system in a higher education institution in Ghana.

Chapter 9 analyzes the challenges of transitioning to online learning during the pandemic and the impact of this experience on digital transformation.

Chapter 10 addresses the advantages and challenges of the virtual mobility model to promote internationalization in higher education.

Chapter 11 examines the objective measurement methods used to evaluate virtual technology-supported environments and areas for future development.

Chapter 12 discusses how integrating artificial intelligence into history education can transform the processes of transmitting historical knowledge.

Chapter 13 examines how integrating neural networks and metacognitive strategies can improve learning processes.

Chapter 14 places the transformational impact of virtual technology in education in a historical context, examining its evolution from its academic origins to the present day, together with technological advances and the contributions of pioneers.

By presenting a holistic view of the opportunities and challenges associated with virtual technology integration, Virtual Technology Innovations in Education contributes to education by providing a valuable resource for fostering meaningful digital transformation. The diverse range of perspectives and case studies included in this book address the current state of virtual technologies in education and set a foundation for future advancements. This book aims to inspire educators, administrators, and policymakers to embrace the potential of virtual innovations, ultimately contributing to a more adaptive, inclusive, and forward-thinking educational environment.

In conclusion, this book is a crucial contribution to the body of knowledge on educational innovation, addressing both the strategic and ethical considerations of virtual technology use. Through its actionable insights and comprehensive scope, Virtual Technology Innovations in Education is poised to guide educators and institutions toward impactful, sustainable changes in the digital age.

Acknowledgments

We sincerely thank all our authors, researchers, and colleagues from the academic community for their invaluable support and contributions to the preparation of this book, titled Virtual Technology Innovations in Education. Each chapter of this book, which aims to expand knowledge and understanding of virtual technology innovations in education, has been enriched through our contributors' meticulous research and dedicated efforts of. The 14 chapters in this volume, authored by academics and practitioners who are experts in their fields, offer a comprehensive perspective on the role of virtual technologies in education. We would also like to express our gratitude to the IGI Global publishing team for their professionalism and support throughout the editorial process. Additionally, we are thankful to our reviewers, whose insights and feedback have significantly enhanced the academic quality of this work. Finally, we extend our heartfelt thanks to our families and colleagues for their moral support and the students and researchers who inspired us. We hope that this book, developed to foster a deeper understanding of the impact of virtual technologies in education, will serve as a valuable resource for policymakers, educators, researchers, and students alike.

Chapter 1
Exploring the Impact of Virtual Reality in Education

Goh Ying Yingsoon
https://orcid.org/0000-0002-6654-2887
Universiti Teknologi MARA, Malaysia

Nurul Ajleaa Abdul Rahman
Universiti Teknologi MARA, Malaysia

Zhang Haiyan
https://orcid.org/0009-0007-3245-9552
Jining Normal University, China

ABSTRACT

The integration of virtual reality (VR) into educational settings is poised to revolutionize the way students interact with learning materials. This chapter explores the burgeoning role of VR in education, assessing its current applications, the advantages it offers, and the challenges it presents to educators. It also examines the potential for VR to shape the future of educational practices. The educational landscape is experiencing a technological renaissance, with VR emerging as a transformative tool. It offers an immersive learning experience that can enhance student engagement and facilitate a deeper understanding of complex subjects. VR's potential is expansive, enabling students to engage with course materials in novel and interactive ways, such as through virtual field trips to historical sites or the simulation of surgical procedures in medical education. The Impact of Virtual Reality in Education hence has to be further explored.

DOI: 10.4018/979-8-3693-6030-9.ch001

INTRODUCTION

Virtual reality (VR) has emerged as a transformative technology with the potential to revolutionize education, promising to enhance learning experiences and improve knowledge retention. Since the 1990s, the concept of VR has gained traction, leading to numerous studies exploring its application in educational settings. One such study examined the impact of using augmented reality/virtual reality (AR/VR) on science knowledge retention, highlighting the benefits of immersive learning environments. (Lege & Bonner, 2020). However, despite the progress made, challenges remain in integrating VR into mainstream education, including the need for affordable technology, teacher training, and accessibility for all students. Nonetheless, the promise of VR in education continues to inspire researchers and educators, with the potential to create personalized and engaging learning experiences that traditional mode of education can't offer

Virtual reality has the potential to create immersive and interactive learning experiences that can\'t be replicated with traditional teaching methods. In this chapter, we will explore how VR can be used to create more engaging and effective learning experiences for students.

While this book chapter does not focus on a single subject, it does emphasize the transformative role of VR in language education and science education, showcasing how these technologies can enhance learning experiences across the curriculum. In language education, VR creates authentic and interactive environments that facilitate language immersion and practice, while in science education, it allows students to conduct virtual experiments, explore abstract concepts, and visualize phenomena that are otherwise difficult to demonstrate in a traditional classroom setting. The versatility of VR in these fields serves as a testament to its potential to enrich educational practices across all disciplines.

Current State of VR in Education:

We will begin by discussing the current state of VR in education, including the types of VR technologies that are currently being used, the subjects that are being taught using VR, and the feedback from educators and students on the use of VR in the classroom.

Virtual reality (VR) technologies have demonstrated a remarkable versatility in their application across various academic disciplines. Whether it is immersing students in historical reenactments, allowing them to explore the human body in biology, or simulating complex chemical reactions in chemistry, VR has the potential to revolutionize the way different subjects are taught. This adaptability makes VR particularly suitable for teaching a wide range of disciplines, from the arts to the sciences. In this book chapter, we specifically hone in on the use of VR in language acquisition and psychology, two fields where the immersive and interactive nature of VR offers unique educational benefits that traditional teaching methods may not provide.

The terms "Metaverse" and "Simulacra" both relate to the concept of virtual reality, but they have different meanings and implications. (Rospigliosi, 2022). The Metaverse is a term that has become popular recently, particularly with the rise of companies like Meta (formerly Facebook) and their push into virtual reality and augmented reality technology. The Metaverse refers to a virtual reality space where users can interact with a computer-generated environment and other users, often through avatars. On the other hand, Simulacra refers to a copy or imitation of something that is authentic or original. In the context of virtual reality, simulacra could refer to virtual environments that simulate real-life situations or experiences. Both concepts are relevant to the use of virtual reality in education. For example, platforms like Roblox and Minecraft can be seen as simulacra because they simulate real-life situations or environments, such as building structures or solving problems. These platforms can also be considered part of the Metaverse, as they are virtual spaces where users can interact with each other and the environment. As for examples of using virtual reality in education, here are a few: Virtual field trips, remote learning, and simulation and training.

A systematic literature review and bibliometric analysis on virtual reality (VR) and education provides a comprehensive understanding of the current state of research in this field. (Rojas-Sánchez, et al, 2023). This review involves identifying and analyzing relevant studies from various sources, such as academic journals, conference proceedings, and grey literature, to extract valuable insights into the application of VR in educational settings. The bibliometric analysis, on the other hand, focuses on quantitatively evaluating the growth, patterns, and trends of the VR and education literature. By examining key factors such as the number of publications, collaboration networks, funding sources, and research gaps, this analysis sheds light on the evolving landscape of VR in education. Together, these approaches contribute to a richer understanding of how VR is being utilized, trends on research and development and its potential impact on teaching and learning experiences.

Table 1. Current State of VR in Education

Theme	Main concern	Researchers
1	Creating VR learning environments	Geng et al. (2021) (Rospigliosi, 2022).
2	Using VR in various fields of knowledge	Osti et al. (2021) Schmidt and Glaser (2021)
3	Learning with VR apps, devices or games	Chen and Hsu (2020) Zhang et al. (2018) Sood and Singh (2018)
4	Learning processes using simulation	Makransky et al. (2020)
5	Creating avatar for VR learning experiences Interacting with a computer-generated VR environment and other users, often through avatars	(Rospigliosi, 2022).

The current state of virtual reality (VR) in education is multifaceted, with various themes and concerns emerging from recent research (refer table 1). Geng et al. (2021) highlighted the challenge of creating VR learning environments, emphasizing the need for teachers to understand and effectively integrate this technology into their pedagogical practices. Additionally, Osti et al. (2021) and Schmidt and Glaser (2021) explored the application of VR in diverse fields of knowledge, demonstrating its potential for enhancing learning experiences across different subjects. Chen and Hsu (2020), Zhang et al. (2018), and Sood and Singh (2018) focused on the use of VR apps, devices, or games as tools for learning, examining their effectiveness in engaging students and facilitating educational outcomes. Lastly, Makransky et al. (2020) investigate learning processes using simulation, particularly immersive virtual reality (IVR) laboratory simulations, assessing gains in self-efficacy and physical outcome expectations among students. These studies collectively contribute to a comprehensive understanding of VR's role in education, identifying both opportunities and ongoing challenges in its integration and utilization.

Benefits of VR in Education

Next, we will explore the potential benefits of using VR in education. This will include a discussion of how VR can create more engaging and immersive learning experiences, how VR can help students to better understand complex concepts, and how VR can provide students with hands-on experience with virtual objects and environments.

Jensen and Konradsen's (2018) study aims to provide an updated understanding of the application of head-mounted displays (HMDs) in educational and training settings. They highlight the significance of acquiring various skills through HMDs, including cognitive skills such as memory, comprehension, and spatial and visual knowledge. Additionally, they emphasize the importance of visual exploration or observation. Furthermore, they underscore the relevance of affective skills, which pertain to emotional control and response to virtual reality-based instructions. This research highlights the multifaceted benefits of incorporating HMDs in education and training, enabling a more immersive and interactive learning experience.

Virtual reality (VR) has emerged as a transformative educational tool, offering a host of benefits that enhance learning experiences. One of the most significant advantages of VR in education is its ability to create immersive and engaging environments that can significantly improve student performance. (Allcoat, & von Mühlenen, 2018). By simulating real-world scenarios and allowing students to interact with the virtual environment, VR can facilitate better understanding and retention of information. Furthermore, the hands-on nature of VR learning often leads to increased student motivation and emotional investment in the material, as it allows for a level of interactivity and exploration that traditional teaching methods cannot match. This heightened emotional engagement can result in more positive emotional responses, increased curiosity, and a greater desire to learn. Moreover, VR can also offer a safe space for students to practice and repeat tasks, fostering a sense of autonomy and self-efficacy. Overall, the integration of VR into educational settings holds the potential to revolutionize learning by enhancing performance through immersive experiences, heightening emotional connections to the content, and boosting overall engagement.

Concrete examples of VR-supported contents are abundant. In a history class, students can virtually walk through ancient civilizations, such as exploring the streets of Pompeii before its destruction, providing an immersive learning experience that traditional textbooks cannot replicate. For science education, VR-supported content allows students to perform interactive simulations of complex biological processes, like DNA replication, offering a hands-on approach to understanding intricate scientific concepts.

Osti et al. (2021) conducted a study that demonstrates the potential of virtual reality (VR) in enhancing training programs, particularly in the construction industry. By utilizing a novel VR system, the researchers created a simulated virtual training site and provided participants with a 3D training video, which was experienced through a VR head-mounted display (HMD). A second group was presented with a simpler 2-D instructional video for comparison. The results revealed that the group utilizing the VR HMD exhibited better retention, task performance, learning speed, and overall participation. This study highlights the practical application of VR as a highly effective teaching and learning tool, offering an immersive and interactive experience that can significantly enhance training outcomes in various fields.

Schmidt and Glaser (2021) explored the use of virtual reality to teach skills to adults on the autism spectrum, utilizing 360-degree video modeling and headset-based VR. Their research aimed to investigate the acquisition of skills related to safety and the appropriate use of public transport. The findings suggested a very positive learning experience, indicating that the intervention was not only feasible but also relevant to the unique needs of individuals with autism. This study underscores the potential of VR to provide a supportive and engaging environment for individuals with special needs, offering a promising approach to skill development and learning in a safe and controlled virtual environment.

Chen and Hsu (2020) investigated the effectiveness of a VR game-based English mobile learning application, examining its impact from both cognitive and psychological perspectives. They found that the interaction with the VR application and the challenges presented by the game-based design facilitated the entry into a state of flow, a highly focused and immersed state of consciousness, thereby enhancing students' motivation to learn. This study highlights the potential of VR in fostering an engaging and effective learning experience, as it allows students to fully immerse themselves in a virtual environment, making learning more enjoyable and efficient.

For examples, in a math class, students engage with a VR game that challenges them to navigate a maze by solving algebraic equations, turning abstract concepts into a fun, interactive challenge. For language learning, a VR role-playing game immerses students in a virtual world where they must communicate in the target language to advance, thereby enhancing their speaking and listening skills in a practical context.

Sood and Singh (2018) discussed the potential of educational games for electroencephalography (EEG) in improving the cognitive and learning skills of students. They proposed that the combination of VR and computing can provide accessible e-learning education worldwide. By utilizing VR in educational games, students can engage in interactive and immersive learning experiences that promote critical thinking, problem-solving, and overall cognitive development. This integration of technology holds great promise in transforming traditional educational methods and making education more accessible and engaging for students worldwide.

Makransky et al. (2020) conducted two studies to explore the benefits of using immersive virtual reality (IVR) laboratory simulations in science education. The first study involved an IVR laboratory safety simulation and utilized a pre- and post-test design to assess changes in participants' self-efficacy and physical outcome expectations. The second study compared the effectiveness of IVR simulation with video simulation for learning the topic of DNA analysis. The results revealed significant gains in self-efficacy and physical outcome expectations in both groups, indicating that the simulations were beneficial for learning. However, the increases in career aspirations and personal outcome expectations did not reach statistical significance.

These findings suggest that IVR laboratory simulations can be valuable tools in science education, enhancing students' confidence and expectations related to scientific concepts and practices.

Geng et al. (2021) investigated the pedagogical potential of Interactive Spherical Virtual Reality (ISVR) based on video in geographic education, with a specific focus on the perspective of teachers. The researchers introduced this technology to teachers, exploring their acceptance, creation, and experience with it. The aim was to acquaint teachers with the potential of ISVR technology for teaching and learning purposes. The study found that the main concerns revolved around the integration of this technology into pedagogy, with the need for more professional development highlighted as crucial for designing and refining this innovative teaching methodology. The request for additional training in the use of technology suggests that there may be a level of change adversity that needs to be addressed for successful implementation of VR in educational settings.

Table 2. Benefits of virtual reality in education

Benefit	Key points	Researchers
1	Pedagogical potential	Geng et al. (2021)
2	Changes in participants' self-efficacy and physical outcome expectations	Makransky et al. (2020)
3	Improvement in the cognitive and learning skills of students	Sood and Singh (2018)
4	Enhancing students' motivation to learn	Chen and Hsu (2020)
5	Providing a supportive and engaging environment for individuals with special needs	Schmidt and Glaser (2021)
6	Offering an immersive and interactive experience that can significantly enhance training outcomes	Osti et al. (2021)
7	Heightening emotional connections to the content, and boosting overall engagement	(Allcoat, & von Mühlenen, 2018)
8	Acquiring various skills including cognitive skills such as memory, comprehension, and spatial and visual knowledge	Jensen and Konradsen's (2018)

The integration of virtual reality (VR) into educational settings offers a myriad of benefits that enhance the overall learning experience. Research by Geng et al. (2021) highlights the pedagogical potential of VR, suggesting that it can revolutionize how knowledge is imparted and absorbed. Makransky et al. (2020) note significant changes in participants' self-efficacy and physical outcome expectations, indicating that VR can empower learners by boosting their confidence in their abilities and improving their expectations of positive outcomes. Sood and Singh (2018) found improvements in the cognitive and learning skills of students, showcasing that VR can refine critical thinking and retention capabilities. Moreover, Chen and Hsu (2020) underscore the ability of VR to enhance students' motivation to learn, creating an engaging environment that captures their interest. VR also caters to individuals with special needs, providing a supportive and inclusive space for learning as observed by Schmidt and Glaser (2021). Osti et al. (2021) emphasize the immersive and interactive nature of VR, which can significantly enhance training outcomes by simulating real-life scenarios. Allcoat and von Mühlenen (2018) highlight the emotional resonance that VR can foster, heightening connections to the content and boosting overall engagement. Lastly, Jensen and Konradsen (2018) discuss the acquisition of various skills, including cognitive abilities such as memory, comprehension, and spatial and visual knowledge. In summary, VR in education offers a multifaceted tool that promotes effective learning, inclusivity, and cognitive growth, making it a transformative technology with immense potential in the classroom (refer table 2).

Challenges of VR in Education

While VR has many potential benefits, there are also challenges associated with implementing VR in the classroom. In this section, we will discuss some of the challenges of using VR in education, including the cost and availability of VR technology, the need for specialized training for educators, and the potential for VR to create feelings of discomfort or motion sickness in some users.

Addressing the challenges to the implementation of VR in education is of paramount importance. Despite its potential to revolutionize teaching and learning, barriers such as high costs, technical issues, limited content, and the need for teacher training can hinder widespread adoption. Overcoming these hurdles is crucial to ensuring that the transformative benefits of VR are accessible to educators and students across all fields, and to the overall advancement of educational technology.

Zhang et al. (2018) explored the recent developments in game-based VR educational laboratories, acknowledging the inherent disadvantages that prevent the widespread deployment of VR in the educational field. These disadvantages include the unrealistic representation of certain concepts, the lack of customization and flexibility, as well as the financial feasibility and the physical and psychological discomfort experienced by users. While these challenges exist, the authors emphasize the need for further research and development to address these issues and enhance the overall user experience, ultimately aiming to integrate VR more effectively into educational settings.

In light of the challenges identified by Zhang et al. (2018), it is imperative that the educational community, developers, and policymakers work collaboratively to mitigate these barriers. This involves not only advancing the technology to improve realism and customization but also investing in the creation of diverse, high-quality content that aligns with curriculum standards. Additionally, efforts to reduce costs and improve accessibility, along with comprehensive training programs for educators, are essential to integrate VR into classrooms effectively. By addressing these challenges, we can ensure that VR becomes a valuable tool that enriches the educational experience for all students, regardless of their field of study.

The adoption of virtual reality (VR) as a teaching aid in education has garnered significant interest due to its immersive and interactive nature, which has the potential to enhance learning experiences (Alfalah, 2018). However, there are several challenges that need to be addressed. Firstly, the high cost associated with acquiring VR technology, including hardware and software, can be a barrier for educational institutions with limited budgets. Additionally, the need for specialized training for educators to effectively integrate and use VR in the classroom is crucial. Furthermore, the availability of suitable VR content that aligns with the curriculum and meets the diverse learning needs of students is another challenge. Lastly, concerns regarding the potential for student addiction to the immersive virtual environments and the impact on their physical and mental health need to be considered. Despite these challenges, the benefits of VR in IT education, such as improved retention, engagement, and practical skill development, make it a promising teaching aid worth exploring.

To address the challenges of implementing VR in education, a multifaceted approach is required. For the issue of cost, exploring partnerships with technology companies, grants, and shared resource models among institutions could make VR more affordable. To tackle the training gap, professional development programs should be established to equip educators with the necessary skills to integrate VR effectively. Content creation can be fostered through collaborations between educators and developers to ensure that VR experiences are both educational and engaging. Moreover, ongoing research into the health and psychological impacts of VR use can guide the development of best practices and safety protocols to mitigate potential risks. By systematically addressing these challenges, the educational community can harness the full potential of VR, ensuring it becomes a sustainable and beneficial addition to the teaching toolkit.

The methodology of Implementing virtual reality (VR) in education for Industry 4.0 and sustainability is a multi-faceted approach that requires careful planning, integration, and evaluation. (Paskiewicz, et, 2021). Firstly, it is crucial to identify the specific educational needs and objectives that VR can address, such as enhancing understanding of complex systems, improving skills training, or fostering innovation. Next, the selection and development of VR content should be aligned with these goals, ensuring that it is accurate, engaging, and interactive. The integration of VR into the curriculum must be seamless, with educators receiving proper training to effectively utilize the technology and guide students throughVR experiences. Additionally, considerations for sustainability include ensuring the VR solutions are energy-efficient, have a minimal carbon footprint, and promote the reuse or recycling of hardware components. Challenges in understanding the methodology may arise due to the novelty of VR in educational settings, the need for ongoing technological advancements, and the potential costs associated with implementation. Addressing these challenges requires ongoing professional development for educators, collaboration with technology experts, and the development of best practices within the educational community.

To effectively address the challenges of VR implementation in education, concrete steps must be taken. Educators should be provided with continuous professional development opportunities, including workshops and online courses, that focus on VR integration strategies, content creation, and classroom management. Institutions can foster collaboration with technology experts through partnerships, which can lead to the co-development of VR applications tailored to educational needs. Additionally, the establishment of a community of practice within the educational sector can facilitate the sharing of best practices, case studies, and resources. This community can also work together to create guidelines for the safe and ethical use of VR, ensuring that the technology is deployed in a manner that maximizes learning outcomes while minimizing potential drawbacks.

Virtual reality (VR) in education presents both exciting opportunities for interactive learning and significant challenges. (Cruz-Neira, et al, 2018). While the immersive nature of VR can make learning experiences more engaging and memorable, it also tends to be more time-consuming than traditional teaching methods. The creation and setup of VR scenarios or games can be complex and require substantial planning, resources, and technical support. Moreover, students may require time to adjust to the VR environment, which can further impact the overall time commitment. Educators must balance the benefits of immersive learning with the need to cover curriculum within set timeframes, necessitating careful curriculum design and possibly adjustments to the traditional pace of instruction.

Immersive virtual reality (VR) has shown significant promise in education due to its ability to create personalized and engaging learning experiences (Marougkas, et al, 2024). By allowing students to enter virtual environments that simulate real-world scenarios or abstract concepts, VR can enhance understanding and retention. However, challenges exist in terms of access, cost, and technical requirements, which can limit the widespread adoption of VR in education. To personalize learning, VR can be customized to cater to individual students' needs, interests, and learning styles. This can be achieved through adjustable difficulty levels, choice of virtual environments, and interactive elements that cater to different learning preferences. Overall, VR has the potential to revolutionize education by providing a highly effective and immersive learning experience that caters to the unique needs of each student.

To personalize learning through VR, educators can start by conducting initial assessments to understand each student's needs, interests, and learning styles. Using this data, they can then select or design VR experiences that offer adjustable difficulty settings, allowing students to progress at their own pace. Teachers should also provide a range of virtual environments and interactive elements that appeal to various preferences, such as visual, auditory, or kinesthetic learning. Furthermore, incorporating adaptive learning algorithms within VR programs can dynamically adjust the content and challenges based on the student's performance and engagement, ensuring a tailored and responsive educational experience.

In language arts education, VR can be employed in a variety of ways to enhance learning. For instance, students can engage in virtual role-playing scenarios where they assume characters from classic literature, allowing them to explore the settings and events of the story from an immersive perspective. Additionally, VR can facilitate interactive poetry workshops where students can manipulate virtual objects to represent themes and metaphors in their writing, or even travel to historical locations that inspired famous poems. Furthermore, VR can simulate real-world scenarios for language practice, such as conducting interviews in a foreign language or participating in a virtual debate, thereby providing a practical and engaging approach to language arts education.

In physics education, VR offers a range of applications that can bring abstract concepts to life. For example, students can use VR to explore the solar system, manipulating planets and their orbits to understand gravitational forces firsthand. VR can also simulate complex experiments, such as building and testing virtual circuits to learn about electricity and magnetism, or conducting virtual collisions to study the principles of momentum and energy conservation. Additionally, VR allows students to explore atomic structures and molecular bonding in 3D, providing a spatial understanding that is difficult to achieve through traditional 2D diagrams and models.

Virtual reality (VR) has the potential to significantly enhance the quality of students' learning experiences in various subjects, including non-science fields like business and language education. By creating immersive and interactive environments, VR can make complex concepts more tangible and easier to understand. For instance, in business education, VR can simulate real-world scenarios, allowing students to practice decision-making in a risk-free environment. (McGovern, et al, 2020). In language education, VR can provide students with the opportunity to practice speaking and listening skills in a virtual setting that simulates real-life situations, thus improving their language proficiency. However, implementing VR in education also comes with challenges, such as the high cost of equipment, the need for specialized training for educators, and the potential for student distraction. Despite these challenges, the benefits of VR in enhancing students' learning experiences make it a promising technology worth exploring further in education.

To tackle the potential for student distraction in VR environments, educators can implement several strategies. Firstly, setting clear learning objectives and guidelines before entering the VR session can help students stay focused on the educational goals. Secondly, designing VR experiences with built-in mechanisms that limit non-essential interactions and provide gentle reminders of the task at hand can help maintain engagement. Additionally, monitoring student progress through real-time analytics can allow teachers to intervene when students stray from the lesson. Finally, incorporating breaks and transitions between VR activities can prevent fatigue and reorient students' attention to the educational content.

In language arts education, VR can be leveraged to create immersive and interactive learning experiences that enhance comprehension and engagement. For instance, students can step into the pages of a novel by virtually visiting the settings depicted in the text, such as walking through the streets of Victorian London in a virtual recreation of a scene from "Oliver Twist." VR can also enable students to engage in interactive storytelling, where they become characters in a narrative and make decisions that affect the plot, thereby deepening their understanding of character development and narrative structure. Another example is the use of VR to practice public speaking; students can deliver speeches in a virtual auditorium, complete with an audience that provides real-time feedback on their performance, helping to build confidence and oratory skills. When students become distracted during VR language arts activities, educators can take proactive steps to refocus their attention. For example, they can pause the VR experience to provide a quick reminder of the learning objectives or to pose a relevant question that redirects the students' thoughts back to the task. Additionally, educators can incorporate interactive elements within the VR environment that prompt students to actively participate, such as requiring them to solve a puzzle or make a decision that advances the story, thereby re-engaging them with the content. Monitoring student progress and providing immediate, constructive feedback can also help maintain their focus and ensure they remain on track with the educational goals of the VR session.

In physics education, VR can transform abstract concepts into tangible experiences, but distractions can still occur. When students are distracted during a VR physics lesson, such as exploring the laws of motion in a virtual laboratory, educators can employ several strategies to re-engage them. For instance, they can introduce a new challenge within the VR environment, like asking students to design and test a Rube Goldberg machine that demonstrates energy transfer. If students are losing focus during a virtual exploration of the solar system, the teacher might initiate a guided discussion about the characteristics of each planet as they virtually fly by. Furthermore, incorporating gamification elements, such as earning points for correctly identifying physical phenomena or solving problems, can incentivize students to stay on task. Educators can also use the VR platform's built-in tools to provide real-time prompts or to adjust the difficulty level of the activity, ensuring that the experience remains both stimulating and educational.

Preservice teachers' intention to use immersive virtual reality (IVR) in education can be attributed to several factors. (Bower, et al, 2020). Firstly, IVR offers a highly engaging and interactive learning experience, which can significantly enhance students' motivation and interest in the subject matter. The immersive nature of VR allows preservice teachers to create dynamic and interactive lessons, enabling them to better cater to diverse learning styles and individual needs. Additionally, IVR provides preservice teachers with the opportunity to develop essential digital literacy skills, which are increasingly important in today's technology-driven educational landscape. Furthermore, the potential of IVR to foster collaboration and communication among students is another compelling reason for preservice teachers to incorporate it into their teaching practices. However, there are several challenges associated with the use of virtual reality in education. Firstly, the high cost of purchasing and maintaining VR equipment can be a significant barrier, particularly for schools with limited resources. Additionally, the need for specialized training and professional development to effectively integrate VR into the curriculum can be a challenge for preservice teachers. Furthermore, concerns regarding the potential for student addiction and the negative impact of extended VR use on vision and physical health are important considerations. Lastly, the availability of suitable VR content that aligns with educational standards and objectives can also be a limiting factor. Despite these challenges, the potential benefits of IVR in education may outweigh the drawbacks, making it a promising tool for preservice teachers to explore.

If preservice teachers find that their school lacks VR equipment, they should consider alternative approaches to incorporate immersive learning experiences. They can start by advocating for the acquisition of VR technology through grant applications, partnerships with local businesses, or educational foundations that support innovative teaching methods. In the meantime, preservice teachers can explore low-cost or no-cost alternatives such as mobile-based VR solutions, which are more affordable and accessible. Additionally, they can collaborate with other educators to create shared VR resources or establish a rotational schedule for using VR equipment borrowed from another institution. Furthermore, preservice teachers can focus on developing lesson plans that incorporate other forms of technology or hands-on activities that simulate the immersive and interactive aspects of VR, thereby still providing engaging and diverse learning opportunities for their students.

Table 3. Challenges in using virtual reality in education

Challenges	Key points	Researchers
1	Concerns regarding the potential for student addiction and the negative impact of extended VR use on vision and physical health	(Bower, et al, 2020)
2	The high cost of equipment, the need for specialized training for educators, and the potential for student distraction	McGovern, et al, 2020
3	Access, cost, and technical requirements, which can limit the widespread adoption of VR in education	Marougkas, et al, 2024
4	Creation and setup of VR scenarios can be complex and require substantial planning, resources, and technical support	Cruz-Neira, et al, 2018
5	The need for ongoing technological advancements, and the potential costs associated with implementation	Paskiewicz, et, 2021
6	The high cost associated with acquiring VR technology, including hardware and software, can be a barrier for educational institutions with limited budgets	Alfalah, 2018
7	Training costs	Alfalah, 2018
8	The unrealistic representation of certain concepts, the lack of customization and flexibility, as well as the financial feasibility and the physical and psychological discomfort experienced by users	Zhang et al. (2018)

In sum, despite its numerous benefits, the implementation of virtual reality (VR) in education is not without challenges. Bower et al. (2020) raise concerns about the potential for student addiction and the negative impact of extended VR use on vision and physical health. The high cost of VR equipment, the need for specialized training for educators, and the potential for student distraction are also issues highlighted by McGovern et al. (2020). Marougkas et al. (2024) point out access, cost, and technical requirements as barriers that can limit the widespread adoption of VR in education. The creation and setup of VR scenarios are complex and require substantial planning, resources, and technical support, as Cruz-Neira et al. (2018) and Paskiewicz (2021) note. Ongoing technological advancements are necessary, and the associated costs can be a significant obstacle for educational institutions with limited budgets, as Alfalah (2018) emphasizes. Additionally, the high cost of acquiring VR technology, including hardware and software, and the need for training costs are significant barriers. Zhang et al. (2018) also highlight the unrealistic representation of certain concepts, the lack of customization and flexibility, as well as the financial feasibility and the physical and psychological discomfort experienced by users. These challenges must be carefully considered and addressed to ensure the responsible and effective integration of VR in educational settings (Refer table 3).

Future of VR in Education

Finally, we will look to the future of VR in education and discuss some of the potential developments and trends that we can expect to see in the coming years. This will include a discussion of the continued growth of VR in education, the development of new and improved VR technologies, and the potential for VR to be integrated with other educational technologies, such as artificial intelligence and augmented reality.

Virtual reality (VR) has the potential to revolutionize education by providing immersive and interactive learning experiences that go beyond traditional teaching methods. By simulating real-life scenarios and environments, VR can make learning more engaging and effective. For instance, students can virtually visit historical sites, explore outer space, or dissect virtual organisms, enabling them to better understand complex concepts. Moreover, VR can facilitate personalized learning by adapting the content according to individual learning styles and pace. It also allows for practical skill development, such as virtual surgery simulations, where students can practice medical procedures in a risk-free environment. As technology advances, the integration of VR in education is expected to expand, offering more diverse and innovative learning opportunities. (Yoo & Brownlee, 2020).

Augmented, mixed, and virtual reality-based head-mounted devices have emerged as innovative tools in the field of education, offering an immersive and interactive learning experience. (Barteit, et al, 2021). These devices are designed to provide students with a more engaging and cost-effective alternative to traditional teaching methods. By incorporating virtual elements into the real world, they enable students to visualize complex concepts in a more intuitive manner. Furthermore, these devices promote collaboration and communication among students, fostering a sense of community in the classroom. As they continue to become more affordable and accessible, they have the potential to revolutionize the way education is delivered and enhance learning outcomes for students worldwide. Development of these equipment and facilities are hence essential fir future use of virtual reality in education.

Creating augmented and virtual reality applications involves a multi-step process that requires expertise in various technologies and design principles (Ashtari, et al, 2020). It begins with understanding the project's goals and target audience, which helps in determining the scope and requirements of the application. Once the objectives are defined, the next step is to design the user interface and experience, keeping in mind usability and interactivity. After that, developers need to choose the right hardware and software platforms that best suit the project's needs.

For examples, in an architecture class, students utilize a VR application to design and test 3D models of buildings, allowing them to experience spatial relationships and structural integrity in a virtual environment. For medical education, a VR application enables students to practice surgical procedures on virtual patients, providing a realistic training ground without the risks associated with real-life practice.

Developers then proceed to program the application, using specialized tools and programming languages such as Unity or Unreal Engine. (Bazavan, et al, 2021). They must also create 3D models, animations, and interactive elements that will be part of the AR or VR environment. Additionally, integrating sensors and tracking systems to capture user input and reactions is crucial for a immersive experience. Once the development is complete, rigorous testing is conducted to ensure the application is bug-free and provides a seamless user experience across different devices. Finally, the application is launched and marketed to reach the target audience, with continuous updates and improvements based on user feedback to enhance its functionality and appeal.

In conjunction to this, Virtual reality (VR) software serves as an indispensable tool for preparing oral presentations by offering an immersive and interactive learning environment. By utilizing VR technology, learners can engage in virtual settings that closely resemble real-world scenarios, enabling them to practice and refine their presentation skills with a reduced fear of consequences. This form of technology also caters to different learning styles, making it accessible to a wider audience. Furthermore, VR platforms provide opportunities for collaboration, feedback, and self-assessment, fostering an enhanced learning experience that conventional methods may lack. As such, understanding and incorporating VR software in education is crucial for educators and learners alike, empowering them to embrace new possibilities in preparing for oral presentations and fostering confident speakers. (Alsaffar, 2021).

In the realm of language arts education, virtual reality software has become an invaluable asset, transforming the way students prepare for and engage with oral presentations. For instance, VR programs can simulate a virtual auditorium, allowing students to practice public speaking in front of a large, animated audience, thereby helping to overcome stage fright. Additionally, language arts students can use VR to explore literary settings, such as walking through the streets of Victorian London to better understand the context of a Dickens novel or engaging in a virtual Socratic seminar where participants debate themes from a Shakespeare play in an immersive, historical classroom setting. This technology also enables collaborative writing projects where students from different locations can co-author a story within a shared virtual space, providing immediate feedback and editing in real-time. These examples illustrate how VR is not only enhancing the learning experience for language arts students but also equipping them with the confidence and skills necessary for effective communication.

In physics education, virtual reality software offers students immersive experiences that bring complex concepts to life. For example, students can use VR to explore the solar system, navigating through space to understand the scale and motion of planets, or even landing on a comet to investigate its composition. VR also allows students to simulate particle collisions in a virtual Large Hadron Collider, providing a detailed view of subatomic particles and the forces at play, which is not possible in a traditional classroom setting. Furthermore, VR can be used to demonstrate the principles of classical mechanics, such as observing the trajectory of a projectile in a frictionless environment or experiencing the effects of gravity in different planetary conditions. Additionally, students can engage in interactive labs where they manipulate virtual objects to explore concepts like electricity and magnetism, or they can dismantle and reassemble virtual machines to understand the underlying physics of mechanical systems. These VR experiences not only make abstract physics theories more tangible but also encourage curiosity and critical thinking among students.

The future of virtual reality (VR) in education is promising, with ongoing advancements in technology poised to further integrate this immersive tool into various learning environments. (Bonetti, et al, 2018). As VR continues to evolve, it is likely to offer even more personalized and adaptive learning experiences, tailoring the educational content and pace to individual students' needs. This personalization can help address diverse learning styles and abilities, making education more inclusive. Additionally, with the rise of open-source platforms and decreasing costs of VR equipment, more institutions and educators will be able to adopt VR, expanding its reach and impact. Collaborative VR spaces may also emerge, allowing for shared learning experiences that transcend geographic boundaries. Moreover, the integration of VR with other emerging technologies, such as artificial intelligence and machine learning, could lead to even more sophisticated learning systems that can predict and adapt to students' learning patterns in real-time. The future of VR in education seems to be deeply intertwined with the goal of creating more effective, engaging, and accessible learning experiences for everyone.

The adoption and adaptation of Virtual Reality (VR) in education is poised to revolutionize the way knowledge is imparted and absorbed. (Marks & Thomas, 2022; Noghabaei, et al, 2020). With its immersive and interactive capabilities, VR is increasingly being recognized as a powerful tool that can enhance learning experiences. It enables students to explore complex concepts in a more intuitive and engaging manner, allowing for a deeper understanding of abstract ideas. For instance, medical students can practice surgical procedures in a virtual environment, providing them with a risk-free way to develop their skills. Moreover, VR can facilitate remote learning, making education accessible to students regardless of their location, and can cater to different learning styles, making education more inclusive. As technology continues to advance, the future holds immense potential for the integration of VR in education, offering personalized, immersive, and collaborative learning experiences that cater to the needs of the students of tomorrow.

In language arts education, the integration of VR can transport students into the worlds of classic literature, allowing them to interact with characters and settings in ways that deepen comprehension and spark imagination. This technology also empowers students with diverse learning styles to engage with texts through immersive storytelling, fostering a more inclusive and dynamic learning environment.

In physics education, VR adoption allows students to visualize and manipulate complex physical phenomena in three-dimensional space, bridging the gap between theory and practical understanding. This technology opens up new avenues for interactive simulations, enabling learners to conduct virtual experiments that would be otherwise impossible or unsafe in a traditional lab setting.

The trend analysis of Virtual Reality (VR) in education indicates a promising future where it is anticipated to become an integral part of the learning process. (Noghabaei, et al, 2020). As technology advances, VR is increasingly being recognized for its potential to revolutionize education by providing immersive and interactive learning experiences. It allows students to visualize complex concepts in a more tangible and engaging manner, making learning more enjoyable and effective. Furthermore, VR enables personalized learning experiences, as students can learn at their own pace and in their preferred environment. This is particularly beneficial for students with different learning styles and those in remote areas without access to traditional educational resources. As a result, the future use of VR in education is expected to expand significantly, with more schools and universities adopting it as a standard tool to enhance teaching and learning. Additionally, VR has the potential to bridge the gap between theoretical knowledge and practical application by providing realistic simulations for practical training in various fields, such as medicine, engineering, and aviation. This trend highlights the transformative power of technology in shaping the future of education.

Virtual reality (VR) technology has shown great potential as an educational and intervention tool for special educational purposes, such as children with Autism Spectrum Disorder (ASD), offering a controlled and adaptable environment that can help them practice social skills, overcome anxiety, and improve their cognitive abilities. (Zhang, et al, 2022). The immersive nature of VR allows individuals with ASD to engage in activities that might be challenging in real-life settings, fostering learning and progress at their own pace. As VR technology continues to evolve, future directions in its use for educational purposes include even more personalized and adaptive learning experiences tailored to the unique needs of students with ASD. Advanced algorithms can monitor and adjust the learning environment in real-time, providing immediate feedback and support. Moreover, the integration of VR with other assistive technologies and neurofeedback mechanisms could further enhance its effectiveness. Additionally, research is ongoing to explore the potential for VR to simulate real-world scenarios for vocational training, preparing individuals with ASD for employment opportunities. The continued development and refinement of VR as an educational tool promise to empower students with ASD, providing them with new avenues for growth and success.

The role of virtual reality (VR) and artificial Intelligence (AI) in education is rapidly expanding, offering innovative ways to enhance learning experiences and cater to individual student needs. (Gandedkar, et al, 2021). VR provides an immersive and interactive environment that can simulate real-world scenarios, making complex concepts more tangible and engaging for students. AI, on the other hand, leverages data and machine learning algorithms to personalize learning experiences, adapt to student performance, and provide real-time feedback. In the future, the integration of VR and AI in education is poised to revolutionize the way knowledge is imparted and acquired. With advancements in technology, we can expect more sophisticated AI systems that can analyze student behavior and learning patterns to tailor VR experiences even further. This could involve creating dynamic and adaptive virtual classrooms, where the curriculum and teaching methods are continuously optimized to suit each student's strengths and weaknesses. Moreover, AI-driven VR could simulate personalized scenarios for project-based learning, enabling students to explore and experiment in virtual environments that are uniquely crafted for their individual goals and interests. This convergence of VR and AI has the potential to make education more accessible, engaging, and effective for all learners, regardless of their backgrounds or abilities.

Virtual reality (VR) has shown great promise in education, offering an immersive and interactive learning experience that can enhance student engagement and improve learning outcomes. Over the past few years, there has been significant progress in the integration of VR into educational settings, with schools and universities increasingly adopting this technology to create more dynamic and personalized learning experiences for their students. However, despite its potential, VR in education also faces several challenges, including the high cost of equipment, the need for specialized training for educators, and the potential for student distraction. (Lege & Bonner, 2020). In the future, as these challenges are addressed and VR technology continues to advance, it is likely that VR will become an even more prevalent tool in education, offering students unique and innovative learning opportunities that go beyond the traditional classroom setting. These innovative VR applications in language arts and physics education will enable students to engage in interactive historical reenactments and hands-on explorations of quantum mechanics, transcending the limitations of textbooks and physical labs.

Virtual reality (VR) has revolutionized various fields, including education and professional training, and neurosurgery is no exception (Fiani, et al, 2020). In recent years, VR technology has been increasingly utilized in neurosurgical education and training, offering a novel and immersive approach to enhance skills and professional development. By simulating complex neurosurgical procedures, VR enables trainee neurosurgeons to practice in a highly realistic and interactive environment, promoting better understanding and retention of the subject matter. Furthermore, VR has the potential to provide a platform for remote training and collaboration, allowing trainee neurosurgeons from different locations to access high-quality educational resources and expertise. As the technology continues to advance, VR is poised to become an invaluable tool in neurosurgical education and training, empowering professionals to deliver optimal patient care.

Table 4. Suggestions for future use of virtual reality in education

Suggestions	Key aspect	Researchers
1	Affordable VR facilities, gadgets, equipment and accessories	Yoo & Brownlee, 2020 Barteit, et al, 2021
2	Software in developing VR applications	Bazavan, et al, 2021
3	Pedagogical Approaches Educational principles and instructional design	Ashtari, et al, 2020
4	Functionality of VR in education	Alsaffar, 2021
5	Adoption and adaptation of VR in education	Marks & Thomas, 2022; Noghabaei, et al, 2020
6	Trend analysis of Virtual Reality (VR) in education	Noghabaei, et al, 2020
7	VR as assistive technology	Zhang, et al, 2022
8	VR with AI AI driven VR in education	Gandedkar, et al, 2021
9	Addressing the challenges	Lege & Bonner, 2020
10	Educational skills training and professional training	Fiani, et al, 2020

Table 4 presents ten suggestions for the future use of virtual reality (VR) in education, eachlinked to key aspects and researchers. These suggestions encompass a range of important considerations for the integration of VR in educational settings. The first recommendation emphasizes the need for more affordable VR facilities, gadgets, equipment, and accessories to make the technology accessible to a wider audience. This is supported by Yoo & Brownlee (2020) and Barteit, et al. (2021). The second suggestion highlights the importance of developing suitable software for VR applications in education, as highlighted by Bazavan, et al. (2021). The third suggestion focuses on pedagogical approaches, advocating for the integration of educational principles and instructional design, as emphasized by Ashtari, et al. (2020). Furthermore, the table suggests exploring the functionality of VR in education and analyzing the adoption and adaptation of VR in educational settings. This is supported by Alsaffar (2021), Marks & Thomas (2022), and Noghabaei, et al. (2020). Additionally, the table emphasizes the significance of trend analysis of VR in education and its potential as an assistive technology. Zhang, et al. (2022) support the use of VR as an assistive technology, while Noghabaei, et al. (2020) highlight the importance of trend analysis. The table also suggests considering the integration of VR with artificial intelligence (AI) to enhance educational experiences, as supported by Gandedkar, et al. (2021). Moreover, addressing the challenges associated with VR in education is crucial, as highlighted by Lege & Bonner (2020). Lastly, the table emphasizes the potential of VR for educational skills training and professional training, as supported by Fiani, et al. (2020). Overall, these suggestions provide a comprehensive framework for the future use of VR in education, encompassing various aspects and perspectives from prominent researchers in the field. The authentic application of VR in language arts and physics education realizes the full potential of immersive learning, aligning with expert insights to create a multifaceted and engaging educational landscape.

The integration of virtual reality (VR) into educational settings represents a transformative leap forward in the way knowledge is imparted and absorbed. By creating immersive, interactive learning environments, VR has the potential to revolutionize education by making complex concepts more accessible and engaging. (Kuna, et al, 2023). Students can now explore historical events, intricate scientific structures, or distant planets with a level of realism and depth that traditional teaching methods alone cannot achieve. Moreover, VR fosters empathy and understanding by allowing learners to experience different cultures or perspectives firsthand, thus bridging gaps in learning and promoting a more inclusive educational ecosystem. As technology continues to evolve, the future of education is set to be reshaped by VR, offering a limitless landscape of learning possibilities that transcend the confines of traditional classrooms.

CONCLUSION

The use of virtual reality in education has the potential to create more engaging and effective learning experiences for students. However, there are also challenges associated with implementing VR in the classroom. In this chapter, we will explore the current state of VR in education, the potential benefits and challenges of using VR, and the future of VR in education.

Virtual reality (VR) has emerged as a transformative technology with the potential to revolutionize education. By creating immersive and interactive learning experiences, VR has the ability to enhance student engagement and facilitate deeper understanding of complex concepts. (Calabuig-Moreno, et al, 2020). It allows students to explore virtual environments, conduct experiments, and engage in virtual simulations, providing a level of realism and interactivity that traditional teaching methods cannot match. Furthermore, VR has the potential to break down geographical barriers, making education more accessible and equitable. However, there are also challenges associated with VR implementation, such as the need for expensive equipment, technical limitations, and potential health risks. Nonetheless, as VR technology continues to advance and become more accessible, it is poised to play a significant role in shaping the future of education.

REFERENCES

Alfalah, S. F. (2018). Perceptions toward adopting virtual reality as a teaching aid in information technology. *Education and Information Technologies*, 23(6), 2633–2653. DOI: 10.1007/s10639-018-9734-2

Allcoat, D., & von Mühlenen, A. (2018). Learning in virtual reality: Efects on performance, emotion and engagement. *Research in Learning Technology*, 26(0). Advance online publication. DOI: 10.25304/rlt.v26.2140

Alsaffar, M. J. (2021). Virtual reality software as preparation tools for oral presentations: Perceptions from the classroom. *Theory and Practice in Language Studies*, 11(10), 1146–1160. DOI: 10.17507/tpls.1110.02

Ashtari, N., Bunt, A., McGrenere, J., Nebeling, M., & Chilana, P. K. (2020, April). Creating augmented and virtual reality applications: Current practices, challenges, and opportunities. In *Proceedings of the 2020 CHI conference on human factors in computing systems* (pp. 1-13). DOI: 10.1145/3313831.3376722

Barteit, S., Lanfermann, L., Bärnighausen, T., Neuhann, F., & Beiersmann, C. (2021). Augmented, mixed, and virtual reality-based head-mounted devices for medical education: Systematic review. *JMIR Serious Games*, 9(3), e29080. DOI: 10.2196/29080 PMID: 34255668

Bazavan, L. C., Roibu, H., Petcu, F. B., Cismaru, S. I., & George, B. N. (2021, September). Virtual reality and augmented reality in education. In 2021 30th Annual Conference of the European Association for Education in Electrical and Information Engineering (EAEEIE) (pp. 1-4). IEEE. DOI: 10.1109/EAEEIE50507.2021.9531005

Bonetti, F., Warnaby, G., & Quinn, L. (2018). Augmented reality and virtual reality in physical and online retailing: A review, synthesis and research agenda. In *Augmented reality and virtual reality* (pp. 119–132). Springer., DOI: 10.1007/978-3-319-64027-3_9

Bower, M., DeWitt, D., & Lai, J. W. (2020). Reasons associated with preservice teachers' intention to use immersive virtual reality in education. *British Journal of Educational Technology*, 51(6), 2215–2233. DOI: 10.1111/bjet.13009

Calabuig-Moreno, F., González-Serrano, M. H., Fombona, J., & García-Tascón, M. (2020). The emergence of technology in physical education: A general bibliometric analysis with a focus on virtual and augmented reality. *Sustainability (Basel)*, 12(7), 2728. DOI: 10.3390/su12072728

Chen, Y. L., & Hsu, C. C. (2020). Self-regulated mobile game-based English learning in a virtual reality environment. *Computers & Education*, 154, 103910. DOI: 10.1016/j.compedu.2020.103910

Cruz-Neira, C., Fernández, M., & Portalés, C. (2018). Virtual Reality and Games. *Multimodal Technologies and Interaction*, 2018(2), 8. DOI: 10.3390/mti2010008

Fiani, B., De Stefano, F., Kondilis, A., Covarrubias, C., Reier, L., & Sarhadi, K. (2020). Virtual reality in neurosurgery:"can you see it?"–a review of the current applications and future potential. *World Neurosurgery*, 141, 291–298. DOI: 10.1016/j.wneu.2020.06.066 PMID: 32561486

Gandedkar, N. H., Wong, M. T., & Darendeliler, M. A. (2021, June). Role of virtual reality (VR), augmented reality (AR) and artificial intelligence (AI) in tertiary education and research of orthodontics: An insight. [). WB Saunders.]. *Seminars in Orthodontics*, 27(2), 69–77. DOI: 10.1053/j.sodo.2021.05.003

Geng, J., Chai, C. S., Jong, M. S. Y., & Luk, E. T. H. (2021). Understanding the pedagogical potential of Interactive Spherical Video-based Virtual Reality from the teachers' perspective through the ACE framework. *Interactive Learning Environments*, 29(4), 618–633. DOI: 10.1080/10494820.2019.1593200

Jensen, L., & Konradsen, F. (2018). A review of the use of virtual reality head-mounted displays in education and training. *Education and Information Technologies*, 23(4), 1515–1529. DOI: 10.1007/s10639-017-9676-0

Kuna, P., Hašková, A., & Borza, Ľ. (2023). Creation of virtual reality for education purposes. *Sustainability (Basel)*, 15(9), 7153. DOI: 10.3390/su15097153

Lege, R., & Bonner, E. (2020). Virtual reality in education: The promise, progress, and challenge. *The JALT CALL Journal*, 16(3), 167–180. DOI: 10.29140/jaltcall.v16n3.388

Lege, R., & Bonner, E. (2020). Virtual reality in education: The promise, progress, and challenge. *The JALT CALL Journal*, 16(3), 167–180. DOI: 10.29140/jaltcall.v16n3.388

Makransky, G., Petersen, G. B., & Klingenberg, S. (2020). Can an immersive virtual reality simulation increase students' interest and career aspirations in science? *British Journal of Educational Technology*, 51(6), 2079–2097. DOI: 10.1111/bjet.12954

Marks, B., & Thomas, J. (2022). Adoption of virtual reality technology in higher education: An evaluation of five teaching semesters in a purpose-designed laboratory. *Education and Information Technologies*, 27(1), 1287–1305. DOI: 10.1007/s10639-021-10653-6 PMID: 34257511

Marougkas, A., Troussas, C., Krouska, A., & Sgouropoulou, C. (2024). How personalized and effective is immersive virtual reality in education? A systematic literature review for the last decade. *Multimedia Tools and Applications*, 83(6), 18185–18233. DOI: 10.1007/s11042-023-15986-7

McGovern, E., Moreira, G., & Luna-Nevarez, C. (2020). An application of virtual reality in education: Can this technology enhance the quality of students' learning experience? *Journal of Education for Business*, 95(7), 490–496. DOI: 10.1080/08832323.2019.1703096

Noghabaei, M., Heydarian, A., Balali, V., & Han, K. (2020). Trend analysis on adoption of virtual and augmented reality in the architecture, engineering, and construction industry. *Data*, 5(1), 26. DOI: 10.3390/data5010026

Osti, F., de Amicis, R., Sanchez, C. A., Tilt, A. B., Prather, E., & Liverani, A. (2021). A VR training system for learning and skills development for construction workers. *Virtual Reality (Waltham Cross)*, 25(2), 523–538. DOI: 10.1007/s10055-020-00470-6

Paszkiewicz, A., Salach, M., Dymora, P., Bolanowski, M., Budzik, G., & Kubiak, P. (2021). Methodology of implementing virtual reality in education for industry 4.0. *Sustainability (Basel)*, 13(9), 5049. DOI: 10.3390/su13095049

Rojas-Sánchez, M. A., Palos-Sánchez, P. R., & Folgado-Fernández, J. A. (2023). Systematic literature review and bibliometric analysis on virtual reality and education. *Education and Information Technologies*, 28(1), 155–192. DOI: 10.1007/s10639-022-11167-5 PMID: 35789766

Rospigliosi, P. A. (2022). Metaverse or Simulacra? Roblox, Minecraft, Meta and the turn to virtual reality for education, socialisation and work. *Interactive Learning Environments*, 30(1), 1–3. DOI: 10.1080/10494820.2022.2022899

Schmidt, M., & Glaser, N. (2021). Investigating the usability and learner experience of a virtual reality adaptive skills intervention for adults with autism spectrum disorder. *Educational Technology Research and Development*, 69(3), 1–35. DOI: 10.1007/s11423-021-10005-8

Sood, S. K., & Singh, K. D. (2018). An Optical-Fog assisted EEG-based virtual reality framework for enhancing E-learning through educational games. *Computer Applications in Engineering Education*, 26(5), 1565–1576. DOI: 10.1002/cae.21965

Yoo, J., & Brownlee, E. A. (2020). The past, present, and future of virtual reality in higher education. In *Handbook of Research on Adult Learning in Higher Education* (pp. 633–657). IGI Global. DOI: 10.4018/978-1-7998-1306-4.ch024

Zhang, M., Ding, H., Naumceska, M., & Zhang, Y. (2022). Virtual reality technology as an educational and intervention tool for children with autism spectrum disorder: Current perspectives and future directions. *Behavioral Sciences (Basel, Switzerland)*, 12(5), 138. DOI: 10.3390/bs12050138 PMID: 35621435

Zhang, M., Zhang, Z., Chang, Y., Aziz, E. S., Esche, S., & Chassapis, C. (2018). Recent developments In game-based virtual reality educational laboratories using the microsoft kinect. [IJET]. *International Journal of Emerging Technologies in Learning*, 13(1), 138–159. DOI: 10.3991/ijet.v13i01.7773

ADDITIONAL READING

Bower, M., DeWitt, D., & Lai, J. W. (2020). Reasons associated with preservice teachers' intention to use immersive virtual reality in education. *British Journal of Educational Technology*, 51(6), 2215–2233. DOI: 10.1111/bjet.13009

Calvert, J., & Abadia, R. (2020). Impact of immersing university and high school students in educational linear narratives using virtual reality technology. *Computers & Education*, 159, 104005. DOI: 10.1016/j.compedu.2020.104005

Di Natale, A. F., Repetto, C., Riva, G., & Villani, D. (2020). Immersive virtual reality in K-12 and higher education: A 10-year systematic review of empirical research. *British Journal of Educational Technology*, 51(6), 2006–2033. DOI: 10.1111/bjet.13030

Jang, J., Ko, Y., Shin, W. S., & Han, I. (2021). Augmented reality and virtual reality for learning: An examination using an extended technology acceptance model. *IEEE Access : Practical Innovations, Open Solutions*, 9, 6798–6809. DOI: 10.1109/ACCESS.2020.3048708

Liu, R., Wang, L., Lei, J., Wang, Q., & Ren, Y. (2020). Effects of an immersive virtual reality-based classroom on students' learning performance in science lessons. *British Journal of Educational Technology*, 51(6), 2034–2049. DOI: 10.1111/bjet.13028

Luo, H., Li, G., Feng, Q., Yang, Y., & Zuo, M. (2021). Virtual reality in K-12 and higher education: A systematic review of the literature from 2000 to 2019. *Journal of Computer Assisted Learning*, 37(3), 887–901. DOI: 10.1111/jcal.12538

Tai, T. Y., Chen, H. H. J., & Todd, G. (2022). The impact of a virtual reality app on adolescent EFL learners' vocabulary learning. *Computer Assisted Language Learning*, 35(4), 892–917. DOI: 10.1080/09588221.2020.1752735

Villena-Taranilla, R., Tirado-Olivares, S., Cózar-Gutiérrez, R., & González-Calero, J. A. (2022). Effects of virtual reality on learning outcomes in K-6 education: A meta-analysis. *Educational Research Review*, 35, 100434. DOI: 10.1016/j.edurev.2022.100434

Wu, B., Yu, X., & Gu, X. (2020). Effectiveness of immersive virtual reality using head-mounted displays on learning performance: A meta-analysis. *British Journal of Educational Technology*, 51(6), 1991–2005. DOI: 10.1111/bjet.13023

KEY TERMS AND DEFINITIONS

Augmented Reality (AR): A technology that overlays digital information or virtual objects onto the real world, enhancing the user's perception and interaction with their environment.

Collaborative VR: A virtual reality setting that enables multiple users to interact with each other and work together within the same virtual environment, fostering communication and teamwork skills.

Immersive Learning: A teaching method that utilizes virtual reality to provide students with an interactive and engaging learning experience, allowing them to feel as if they are part of the simulated environment.

Interactive Simulations: Computer-based programs that enable students to practice and apply their knowledge in a virtual environment, often used to teach complex concepts or skills.

Virtual Field Trips: Educational excursions conducted through virtual reality, enabling students to explore and learn about various places, cultures, and historical events without physically traveling.

Chapter 2
Navigating the Virtual Classroom With Virtual Reality:
Revolutionizing Education Through Immersive Experiences

Seema Yadav
https://orcid.org/0000-0002-8477-5895
Bhopal School of Social Sciences, India

ABSTRACT

The COVID-19 pandemic has dramatically impacted global education, necessitating the development of more adaptable and innovative learning paradigms. Immersive technologies such as Augmented Reality (AR), Virtual Reality (VR), and Mixed Reality (MR) present substantial potential for enhancing educational experiences by making learning more interactive and accessible. These technologies are transforming various fields, including vocational education, medical training, and the Architecture, Engineering, and Construction (AEC) sector. This paper explores the benefits and challenges of integrating VR into educational settings, highlighting its role in bridging the gap between theoretical and practical learning, improving student engagement and motivation, and offering cost-effective training solutions. The findings suggest that while VR is not a complete replacement for traditional education, it is a valuable supplementary tool that can significantly enhance learning experiences and outcomes.

DOI: 10.4018/979-8-3693-6030-9.ch002

INTRODUCTION

Knowledge transfer has been a defining feature of civilization from the dawn of time, and education is seen as the fundamental building block of a civilized society. Effective methods to improve the speed, ease of use, and dependability of information flow are constantly being sought after. Better technical learning has been made possible by digital technologies. Education is undergoing a significant transformation in the era of digital technology, with traditional teaching and learning methods, approaches, and resources giving way to more contemporary ones (Chimakurthi, 2018). Despite education being a basic human right for all residents of the world, there is still educational inequality within and across nations. Many children still have difficulty obtaining and receiving high-quality education nowadays. Thus, there is a need to pay close attention to bridging the gap between urban and rural education systems to maximize the benefits of immersive technology in raising social competence and perceived social support for children living in remote areas of the world, decreasing inequality, and enhance the quality of education (X. Wang et al., 2023). It should be noted that immersive Creative technologies have huge potential in education because they make subjects interactive and easier to learn (Davydova et al., 2023). Immersion Technology was a popular movement in intriguing technology for imitation, demonstration, and presentation. These methods might be applied to medical education. Augmented Reality (AR), Virtual Reality (VR), and Mixed Reality (MR) comprise the field of Immersion Technology (Srikong & Wannapiroon, 2020).

Rapid technological advancements have an impact on daily life and present new opportunities, changes, and relationships. This article will discuss immersive technology. Assessment tools and connections have also been developed, and the use of multiple instruments in the classroom to simulate 3-dimensional graphics has helped to promote virtual learning (Srikong & Wannapiroon, 2020). Learners are compelled to analyze, solve problems, and improve abilities when virtual technology is used in the classroom, particularly when it comes to Immersive Technology for Medical Education (Srikong & Wannapiroon, 2020). The integration of Immersive Technologies (ImTs) into building process workflows is still a relatively new concept, with limited knowledge of specific possibilities and methods. This is due to the novelty of ImTs concerning Digital Twin (DT), Virtual Reality (VR), Augmented Reality (AR), and Mixed Reality (MR) in the metaverse and its rapid and ongoing development in Building Information Modelling (BIM) (Liu et al., 2023). Immersion technology involves simulating real-world scenarios with virtual instruments on a computer screen. Mixed Reality (MR), Augmented Reality (AR), and Virtual Reality (VR) are all applied using this technology. It can produce a striking experience to draw in viewers so they can respond and take charge of this immersive environment (Srikong & Wannapiroon, 2020).

An effective technique to solve subpar occupational safety and health (OSH) performance through worker education and training is through the use of immersive technologies (Babalola et al., 2023). Information is now more easily accessible thanks to digital technologies and services, which have also greatly expanded the possibility for technology users to obtain individualized services and for marketers to deliver targeted advertisements (R. Wang et al., 2023). In certain contexts, such as online gambling and shopping, the ideas of immersive technology, online marketing, and persuasive technology may be used to promote profitable outcomes that could be harmful by encouraging addictive-like behaviors. Addictions may be indicated by excessive use of technology and participation in specific online activities (R. Wang et al., 2023). Travel destinations that have been underperforming recently may see an increase in interest and use thanks to immersive technologies like augmented reality and virtual reality. In addition to utilizing cutting-edge VR technology that is becoming more widely accessible in the consumer market, it is hoped that this study will encourage more research on applying this technology to fresh situations (Pratisto et al., 2022). Through the use of highly interactive objects in a virtual environment, virtual reality (VR) mixes technologies to create an immersive presence while stimulating users' senses to make them feel as though they are in an almost natural setting. Virtual reality (VR) has gained popularity recently as a tool for training, teaching, and learning through 3D simulation and the visualisation of course material in a virtual environment (Agbo et al., 2021). Knowledge transfer has always been crucial to the advancement of civilization, and education is a fundamental pillar of a civilized society. In the digital era, traditional educational methods are being replaced by modern, technology-driven approaches. Despite education being a basic human right, educational inequality persists both within and across nations. Many children, especially in rural areas, still struggle to access high-quality education. Immersive technologies, such as Augmented Reality (AR), Virtual Reality (VR), and Mixed Reality (MR), hold great potential to make education more interactive and accessible, thereby helping to bridge this gap and improve the quality of education.

Immersive technologies are being explored in various fields, including medical education and occupational safety, to enhance learning experiences and outcomes. These technologies create virtual environments that simulate real-world scenarios, encouraging problem-solving and skill development. In the building industry, the integration of immersive technologies with Building Information Modelling (BIM) is still emerging, offering new possibilities for project workflows. Furthermore, immersive technologies are transforming how information is accessed and services are personalized, influencing behaviors in contexts such as online gambling, shopping, and travel. They provide highly interactive and engaging experiences that can be both beneficial and potentially addictive. Overall, the rapid advancement of immersive technologies is reshaping education, training, and various other sectors, presenting new opportunities and challenges.

UNDERSTANDING VIRTUAL REALITY IN EDUCATION

Over time, there hasn't been much of an evolution in students' learning patterns. The swift advancement of digital technology has prompted a concentrated investigation into methods to enhance the quality of instruction through the use of artificial intelligence (AI), virtual reality (VR), and additional technologies (Lin et al., 2024). Virtual reality science games aim to provide students with a positive mental experience in a calm and natural setting, in addition to aiding in the development of inquiry abilities. The game should be presented as succinctly and precisely as feasible and shouldn't be overly complicated or fancy because of the limited budget for VR game creation (Lin et al., 2024). In education, imparting knowledge has always involved teaching the truth. Boredom arises from trying to view history through the lens of a traditional textbook, studying for tests, and attending classes. Conversely, virtual reality (VR) has allowed for more remarkable, efficient, and captivating ways for kids to learn (Chimakurthi, 2018). The creation of the physical world and the animation that may be worked on in the real world as if we were a part of it are what make up the seemingly perplexing concept of physical reality. In technical terms, virtual reality is the creation of visual simulations using computer and device technology (Chimakurthi, 2018). Considering how to employ artificial intelligence (AI), virtual reality (VR), and other technologies to enhance the quality of instruction has garnered significant attention in light of the rapid advancement of digital technology (Lin et al., 2024). Embodied learning, or learning that unites the body and mind, will introduce new learning experiences in the age of digital-intelligence integration. It suggests approaches for these games from the perspectives of environment design, interaction design, and content design. From the standpoint of embodied cognition, game design still has a lot of issues that need to be resolved (Lin et al., 2024). From directly experiencing real-world situations to immersing oneself in an immersive simulated environment, virtual reality (VR) exists on an experiential continuum. Utilizing a head-mounted display (HMD) device, virtual reality entails using a computer to provide an immersive and interactive experience that makes the user feel as though they are a part of the simulated or virtual world (Cochrane, 2016).

VR as a teaching tool will actively engage students and have good cognitive and pedagogical effects when used in conjunction with traditional and e-learning (Soliman et al., 2021). Utilizing virtual reality technology, people can receive more thorough training and learn about the realities of murder. To provide subscribers with a better experience, they fabricate a setting that appears realistic. Through the employment of a wireless system linked to a virtual reality training screen that mimics the movement of real-world objects, a virtual reality landscape that is integrated with real-time gadgets is created (Chimakurthi, 2018). The definition of a virtual reality (VR) system is a highly interactive 3D digital media environment that uses the user's touch, hearing, and vision to create a simulated reality and an immersive experience. In essence, it gives people the impression that they are in a different virtual environment (Hong & Wang, 2023). Persuasive technology refers to a variety of technological resources that are used in daily life to influence users' beliefs, attitudes, and actions. These resources include websites, mobile phones, tablets, and smart devices. Through the use of computer-generated simulation, immersive technology simulates the physical environment and produces Mixed Reality (MR), Augmented Reality (AR), and Virtual Reality (VR) experiences (R. Wang et al., 2023). Virtual reality (VR) has been more and more popular as a teaching tool in the past several years, especially in vocational education, where it enables students to obtain practical experience in a secure setting. Nonetheless, there is a lack of studies on the difficulties and potential applications of VR in classroom vocational education (Ravichandran & Mahapatra, 2023). Virtual reality (VR) has become a potent tool for vocational education, offering a distinct and successful learning environment. One of VR's primary advantages for vocational education is its capacity to offer a secure and regulated learning environment, letting students hone their practical abilities without worrying about the repercussions of their actions in the real world (Ravichandran & Mahapatra, 2023).

Virtual reality (VR) is a technology that enables users to fully immerse themselves in a virtual environment (VE). Instead of spending more money on other pricey devices, users can enjoy AR and VR effects with their own handheld devices. However, using the AR/VR application requires users to hold and touch handheld devices, which makes it challenging to multitask (Tan et al., 2022). Virtual reality (VR) technologies promise authentic learning experiences in formal and informal learning spaces through new forms of visual representations, perceptual engagement, and physical participation. These technologies have the potential to fundamentally change astronomical education practices (Kersting et al., 2023). The primary benefit of virtual reality (VR) lies in its exceptional capacity to build intricate, multidisciplinary learning environments that incorporate both digital and physical objects.

This allows for the development of critical thinking abilities like problem-solving, communication, and critical thinking through interactive interaction tests (Chimakurthi, 2018). The immersive and embodied learning experiences that virtual reality (VR) technology offers make complex topics more approachable, and so create great prospects to improve astronomy education (Kersting et al., 2023). To increase reliability and lower direct exposure of humans to hazardous procedures, the development of high-power computers and information technology has greatly improved the digitalization of fundamental processes within various industries. Industry 4.0 is one of the most notable platforms for these kinds of digital revolutions (Babalola et al., 2023). Immersion technologies, when combined with other industry 4.0 technologies, have become a potent means of addressing subpar occupational safety and health (OSH) performance in the construction industry (Babalola et al., 2023).

Virtual reality (VR) is a medium made up of interactive computer simulations that recognize a user's position and activities and substitute feedback to one or more senses, creating the impression that the user is physically present or mentally immersed in the simulation (van der Linde-van den Bor et al., 2022). An innovative method for improving the utilization of intricate 3D graphics and visualization environments is provided by virtual reality (VR) technology (K. Li & Wang, 2021). Experiential VR models that are tailored to each subject of knowledge will be included as a result of trends in VR type and application in various disciplines of knowledge. The goal is to develop instructional tools that improve students' knowledge acquisition in particular subject areas (Rojas-Sánchez et al., 2023). It will become more crucial than ever to prepare educators to use these tools within a coherent curriculum that can be modified to fit the needs of various academic fields. In this way, the effectiveness of VR in education going forward will mostly depend on how motivated students become and how well they can recognize the qualities required to get a sufficient level of learning through VR (Rojas-Sánchez et al., 2023). A computer-simulated environment that allows the user to interact and change their perception through a combination of sensory data transmitted to the brain is known as virtual reality (VR) (Soliman et al., 2021). A new technique in medical science is virtual technology. Situations that are infrequently encountered in clinical trials will be replicated by this technology. Before users become experts and handle problems in accordance with medical ethics, they must practice this complex skill for a considerable amount of time. Operating room physicians will have greater confidence. Remarkably, the speed at which hardware, software, and programming skills for immersive media are developing can make it easier for doctors to conduct their jobs. In real-time, patients can provide feedback, which physicians can use to inform their research in all areas of medicine (Srikong & Wannapiroon, 2020).

The majority of other virtual reality educational programs concentrated on a single ecosystem scenario or catered to certain student populations, and the majority of them reported improvements in academic performance and learning interests (Ruan, 2022). Over time, students' learning patterns have evolved little, but the rapid advancement of digital technology, particularly artificial intelligence (AI) and virtual reality (VR), is revolutionizing education. VR games in science education offer engaging, calm environments that enhance inquiry skills without the boredom of traditional methods. VR creates immersive, interactive experiences that make learning more captivating and effective, blending digital and physical realities. This technology is especially beneficial in vocational training, providing safe, practical learning environments. Despite the challenges in integrating VR into curricula, its potential to enhance critical thinking and problem-solving skills is immense. The ongoing development of VR and other immersive technologies holds promise for transforming various educational fields, including medical and astronomical education, by making complex topics more accessible and engaging.

VIRTUAL REALITY AND ITS RELEVANCE IN EDUCATION: DIFFERENT TYPES OF VR TECHNOLOGIES AND THEIR APPLICATIONS IN EDUCATIONAL SETTINGS

VR offers an engaging and dynamic learning environment that boosts motivation and engagement, which increases knowledge retention and skill acquisition. Virtual reality (VR) simulations can also be tailored to meet specific learning objectives, offering individualized and flexible learning opportunities (Ravichandran & Mahapatra, 2023). Virtual reality (VR) possesses the capacity to transform vocational education by offering a novel and efficient method of skill development, enhancing learning results, and eventually equipping learners for actual career obstacles (Ravichandran & Mahapatra, 2023). The architecture, engineering, and construction (AEC) business is paying more and more attention to the uses of augmented and virtual reality (AR/VR) technologies thanks to updated equipment and maturing technology. An increasing number of academics are experimenting with AR/VR technologies, particularly in education and training, to give students or learners an immersive, interactive, and visual environment (Tan et al., 2022). High standards for information comprehension and application skills are always present in the architecture, engineering, and construction (AEC) industry's educational program (Tan et al., 2022). Virtual reality (VR) technologies have the potential to revolutionize astronomy education by providing learners with immersive and unique visual learning environments that encourage cooperation and communication (Kersting et al., 2023). Virtual reality has enormous potential to enhance classroom and remote learning interactions between educators and students. To collaborate and share knowledge with classmates, virtual reality (VR) boosts student motivation (Chimakurthi, 2018). Disconnecting the user from the outside world and giving them a sensation of being/presence in the virtual world is a popular definition of immersion, which is a crucial component of a VR experience (Soliman et al., 2021). It is important to investigate how virtual reality might support inclusive and differentiated learning in agricultural classrooms. VR has the potential to support accessibility and accommodate a variety of learning styles, which could result in more individualised and inclusive teaching strategies (Greig et al., 2024).

The advantages of the VR lab extend beyond the university or organization to include the students' educational experience, teaching, and cognitive processes. The potential and excellence of VR technology in education are demonstrated by evidence from numerous study articles that designed and used VR applications and labs (Soliman et al., 2021). The rapid advancement of computer and medical technology has resulted in a dramatic alteration of nursing professional skills training. Virtual reality (VR) has become a cutting-edge technical support technology in nursing education, and its creative application has drawn attention as a very effective way to improve the quality of nurse training (Hong & Wang, 2023). With the development of VR technology, people may now experience "immersive" Reality from the comforts of their home, providing the most lifelike visual and tactile experience. It enables users to engage in some activities that are impossible in reality with VR technology. Thirdly, it facilitates the development of abstract thought processes. Abstract thinking must be embodied since many abilities required for human production and practical activities cannot be learned by pure imagination (C. Li & Li, 2020).

In a modern classroom, the utilisation of Augmented Reality (AR), Virtual Reality (VR), and Gamification has been greatly aided by interactive and immersive technologies. These technologies claim to provide an improved user experience and can be used both offline and online. Because these gadgets provide interactive content during class, their use also increases student involvement (Kaur et al., 2022). Virtual reality (VR) offers an engaging and dynamic learning environment that enhances motivation and engagement, leading to improved knowledge retention and skill acquisition. VR simulations can be customized to meet specific learning objectives, providing personalized and flexible learning opportunities. In vocational education, VR presents an innovative method for skill development, preparing learners for real-world challenges. The architecture, engineering, and construction (AEC) industry is increasingly utilizing AR/VR technologies to create immersive, interactive, and visual learning environments. VR also has significant potential in astronomy education, fostering cooperation and communication through unique visual experiences. By disconnecting users from the outside world and creating a sense of presence, VR enhances classroom and remote learning interactions, boosting student motivation. The use of VR labs extends educational benefits beyond traditional settings, supporting cognitive processes and teaching methods. In nursing education, VR's application has revolutionized professional skills training, improving the quality of nurse training. Overall, the advancement of VR technology supports abstract thinking, interactive learning, and increased student involvement, making it a valuable tool in modern education.

EXEMPLIFYING VR INTEGRATION IN EDUCATION

With the use of sophisticated visual and aural design, immersive and multimodal learning technology draws kids in with a three-dimensional approach, making for a very captivating and unforgettable learning experience (Ravichandran & Mahapatra, 2023). In both teacher education and teaching and learning research, classroom films are frequently utilized to watch and evaluate the quality of instruction. 360-degree films, which offer a more realistic and immersive classroom experience and may have an impact on teaching-quality evaluations, have been added to traditional video environments more frequently in recent years (Daltoè et al., 2024).

To improve immersive learning experiences, virtual reality (VR) is a tool that is becoming more and more popular in vocational education. Through realistic simulations of real-world situations, virtual reality (VR) offers training participants a secure setting in which to hone their practical abilities (Ravichandran & Mahapatra, 2023). With virtual reality (VR), learners can immerse themselves in a variety of situations and settings that could be challenging or impossible to recreate with conventional teaching techniques. Virtual reality (VR) is a potentially effective teaching tool for vocational education. It offers learners immersive experiences that can improve their practical skill acquisition and better equip them to face real-world issues (Ravichandran & Mahapatra, 2023). By giving pupils the chance to practice real-world situations in a secure setting, virtual reality (VR) can boost their confidence and inspire them for their future careers. By offering a virtual reality (VR) learning environment that is immersive, interactive, and game-like, VR in vocational education can improve student engagement and motivation (Ravichandran & Mahapatra, 2023). Students can explore stellar remnants, measure objects using virtual tools, and interact with stars in an immersive virtual reality setting (Kersting et al., 2023). Since virtual reality simulates travel without really visiting a location, it can be helpful. Pupils can study the various facets and perspectives of the location while also gaining a better understanding of it by looking at genuine photographs. Without ever leaving the classroom, all of this is achievable (Chimakurthi, 2018). Games and other leisure activities could be used in a whole new way for learning and knowledge building if virtual reality is implemented. Its effectiveness in increasing motivation and interaction makes this learning approach effective. This efficaciousness can be increased by visual reality. Incorporating drama and theatre into their studies has allowed teachers to notice that virtual reality games and activities do more than just entertain students; they also encourage their participation in class activities, which helps them meet learning objectives (Chimakurthi, 2018).

VR is becoming more and more popular as a way to simulate a real-world setting. Therefore, we advise travel agencies to use virtual reality (VR) to introduce the destination. Users can explore the virtual trip's route. Travel agencies can incorporate virtual reality (VR) information about their locations into their applications so that users can experience the place in virtual reality (Pratisto et al., 2022). As VR technology progressed, research and commercial interest shifted from the gaming business to education and training because of its increased processing power, lower cost, and smaller form factor (Soliman et al., 2021). With a decrease in form factor and an increase in features and power, virtual reality (VR) technology has advanced significantly over time. The technology is becoming more and more popular in the domains of education, training, and healthcare, but its appeal in gaming platforms is well-established these days (Soliman et al., 2021). Given its cognitive and learning advantages over traditional learning methods, virtual reality (VR) is a great tool for engineering education when used in a mixed-learning environment (Soliman et al., 2021).

Virtual reality (VR) application for the Great Wall of China, asserting that VR is still lagging in these areas that are important for engineering education. Visualizing such old structures is a crucial educational tool that amply demonstrates the possibilities of virtual reality technology (Soliman et al., 2021). One effective way to raise pupils' environmental literacy is through environmental education. The use of virtual reality (VR) technology in education is becoming more common as a result of its strong sense of immersion and involvement. As multimedia technologies advance, so does the approach to environmental education in colleges and universities (Ruan, 2022).

Virtual reality is a new technology that replicates real-world situations. It is an interactive, dynamic, three-dimensional virtual environment created by a computer that combines a range of data. In contrast to standard HCI devices, virtual reality technology may imitate scenes that are not physically touchable in addition to giving users sharp vision and sound (C. Li & Li, 2020). An area of study that stems from artificial intelligence networks is virtual reality technology. A new chapter in the study of the physical education model has been opened by the use of virtual reality technology in sports training and physical education. It significantly alters the conventional face-to-face teaching approach, boosts student initiative, guides students through a prepared sports training environment using virtual reality technology, increases students' enjoyment of sports, and facilitates the efficient execution of sports training (C. Li & Li, 2020).

Positive expectations, vision, optimism, and optimistic thinking about the future are all fostered by virtual surroundings. Enhanced sense of presence is the key to positive thinking and the main benefit of VR for cognitive reorganization (Drigas et al., 2021). Individuals with special education needs can quickly adopt states of mind that reduce implicit bias, encourage positive behavior, and support academic success by using neuro-linguistic programming. VR has been proven to be consistent with the NLP technique, which helps to reduce unintentional bias, develop users' flexibility in changing perspectives, foresee a bright future, and perceive themselves more realistically with fewer depressive symptoms (Drigas et al., 2021). The ability to create and share user-generated material via mobile devices, social media, head-mounted displays, and mobile VR cameras is mapped by an ecosystem of resources, offering the chance to create real VR learning environments. Networked student-centered pedagogies inform the creation of these virtual reality learning experiences (Cochrane, 2016). To facilitate participant-active, authentic learning experiences, (Cochrane, 2016) investigated the potential of mobile virtual reality (VR) for designing learning environments. They also presented a framework for student-generated mobile VR projects that makes use of an ecology of resources and triggering events made up of a collage of freely available mobile social media tools and students' smartphones.

Medical science is adopting a new tactic: virtual technology. With the use of this technology, scenarios that are uncommon in clinical trials will be replicated. It's a challenging skill that requires a lot of practice before users become proficient in solving issues in a way that upholds medical ethics (Srikong & Wannapiroon, 2020). In an operation, doctors will have greater confidence. By the way, doctors' jobs can be made easier by the quick development of immersive media technology, software, and programming skills. Patients have the option to respond in real-time, and physicians can use these answers to inform their research in all areas of medicine (Srikong & Wannapiroon, 2020).

Immersive and multimodal learning technology, including virtual reality (VR), is transforming education by providing sophisticated visual and aural experiences that captivate students and enhance knowledge retention and skill acquisition. In vocational education, VR offers realistic simulations of real-world situations, allowing learners to practice skills in a safe, controlled environment, which boosts confidence and motivation for future careers. The technology's application extends beyond vocational training, with significant impacts in fields like architecture, engineering, construction, astronomy, and environmental education, where it provides unique, interactive learning experiences that traditional methods cannot. VR is also being used in travel, enabling virtual tours that help users explore destinations without leaving the classroom. The technology has advanced significantly, making it more accessible for education and training, and offering cognitive and learning benefits over traditional methods. In medical education, VR simulates rare clinical scenarios, enhancing doctors' skills and confidence. Additionally, VR supports special education needs by fostering positive behavior and reducing bias through immersive experiences. Overall, VR's potential to create engaging, interactive, and immersive learning environments is revolutionizing educational practices across various fields.

CHALLENGES AND CONSIDERATIONS IN USING VIRTUAL REALITY IN EDUCATION

Immersion technologies are not without problems in this industry, and there is little proof of how well these technologies address the sustainability problems in fashion (Mesjar et al., 2023). It would seem costly to produce apparel in a sustainable manner. The industry's problem is to provide equal chances for sustainable manufacturing to all parties, especially smaller businesses; nonetheless, the operation of digital technologies like immersive applications can be costly and technologically demanding. By looking into ways to bring down the cost of these new technologies, the industry as a whole might use these newer digital tools to potentially increase innovation and sustainability (Mesjar et al., 2023).

Virtual reality (VR) is a potentially useful teaching technology for career education, but it is not without drawbacks. The initial expense of purchasing the required hardware and software is one of the main obstacles. VR development and maintenance also call for a high degree of technological know-how, which can be quite difficult for vocational schools with little funding. One possible drawback of virtual reality (VR) is its excessive immersion, which could cause learners to become disoriented or experience motion sickness (Ravichandran & Mahapatra, 2023). For career education, virtual reality (VR) is a potentially helpful teaching tool. One of the biggest challenges is the initial cost of buying the necessary gear and software. VR maintenance and development also require a high level of technological expertise, which might be challenging for vocational institutions with limited funds. The extreme immersion of virtual reality (VR) has the potential to be a disadvantage since it might make students dizzy or queasy (Ravichandran & Mahapatra, 2023).

The degree to which skills can be transferred to the real workplace may be hampered by VR simulators' inability to accurately mimic the physical characteristics of a real-world vocational context. It might take a lot of time and resources to create VR content of a high caliber. There's also a chance that students would rely too much on VR simulations, which would prevent them from getting any practical experience. VR is a technology that is worth investigating and further developing because of its advantages in vocational education, even despite these difficulties (Ravichandran & Mahapatra, 2023). The staging of experiences and the co-creation of value are being redefined and revolutionized by immersive technologies, which have implications for the management of customer encounters. Nevertheless, the function of immersive technology within the customer experience management (CXM) process has not been extensively studied (Tom Dieck & Han, 2022). Immersion technologies, including virtual and augmented reality, are becoming more and more popular among consumers (Tom Dieck & Han, 2022). Technological developments change the power dynamics in a variety of industries, including retail, tourism, and education, from enterprises to customers (Tom Dieck & Han, 2022). Virtual reality (VR) has several drawbacks despite its many advantages in the fields of training and education. Virtual reality (VR) as a technology consumes human interaction and causes social and communication problems among learners (Chimakurthi, 2018).

The challenging world can be replicated using virtual reality technology, which can also overcome the constraints of the traditional physical education curriculum regarding sports facilities, gear, safety, and other areas. The graphic representation of intricate and abstract sports theory may give students precise, scientific direction and increase their technical understanding. VR technology is capable of more than just simulating sports scenes through the creation of VR panoramas when compared to traditional sports teaching methods (C. Li & Li, 2020). VR is a fully immersive technology that immerses the user in a computer-generated virtual world. As a result, it eliminates any true connection to the actual world or minimal engagement. This technology blends computer-generated virtual objects with the real environment through three-dimensional (3D) registration and real-time interaction (Baroroh & Agarwal, 2022).

Immersion technologies, such as virtual reality (VR) and augmented reality (AR), offer significant potential in education and various industries but are not without challenges. In fashion, these technologies could drive innovation and sustainability, but their high costs and technological demands make them less accessible, especially for smaller businesses. Similarly, in vocational education, VR's potential as a teaching tool is tempered by high initial costs, the need for technical expertise, and issues such as motion sickness and over-reliance on simulations. Moreover, VR simulators often struggle to accurately replicate the physical nuances of real-world environments, which can hinder the transfer of skills to actual workplaces. Despite these hurdles, the advantages of VR in enhancing educational experiences and practical training make it a valuable area for further exploration and development. In customer experience management, immersive technologies are revolutionizing how experiences are staged and value is co-created, although their roles are not yet fully understood. These technologies are becoming increasingly popular among consumers and are shifting power dynamics in industries like retail, tourism, and education, from businesses to customers. However, the use of VR in education and training also poses social and communication challenges, as it can consume human interaction and lead to isolation. In physical education, VR can overcome limitations related to sports facilities and safety by providing scientific guidance and enhancing technical understanding through immersive simulations. Nonetheless, the immersive nature of VR can also disconnect users from the real world, limiting genuine interaction. Overall, while VR and other immersive technologies offer promising advancements, they require careful consideration of their drawbacks and strategic implementation to maximize their benefits in education and other fields.

STRATEGIES FOR OVERCOMING BARRIERS AND MAXIMIZING THE POTENTIAL OF VR IN EDUCATIONAL CONTEXTS

The location of technology implementation needs to be reevaluated in the context of emerging immersive technologies that have the potential to impact consumer experiences at various touchpoints during a customer journey (Tom Dieck & Han, 2022). The decision to use virtual reality (VR) in the classroom is based on weighing the advantages and disadvantages of the technology. VR integration in a traditional classroom ought to be done with greater caution. To identify the stakeholders, justifications, and difficulties associated with using virtual reality (VR) in higher education, (Jin et al., 2022) conducted a qualitative investigation in this paper that involved two rounds of interviews and a participatory design workshop and saw the university as a connecting body of relationships among various stakeholders.

The integration of virtual reality (VR) into university curricula has tremendous potential pedagogical and economic benefits, particularly when taking into account the additional benefits to the learning process and the possible cost savings and expansion in terms of experimental offerings (Soliman et al., 2021). One technology that can improve user involvement is immersive; it does this by offering pertinent information and enhancing the system's attractiveness, interactivity, and informational value. It is separated into multiple categories, with varying implementations, such as VR, AR, and MR (Baroroh & Agarwal, 2022). Immersive technologies, including VR, AR, and MR, are reshaping consumer experiences and educational practices. In customer experience management, these technologies impact various touchpoints along the customer journey, requiring a reevaluation of their implementation. In education, integrating VR offers significant pedagogical and economic benefits, such as enhanced engagement, cost savings, and expanded experimental offerings. However, incorporating VR in traditional classrooms necessitates careful consideration of its advantages and drawbacks. Immersive technology can improve user involvement by providing relevant information and enhancing system interactivity and attractiveness. While promising, the integration of these technologies must account for the stakeholders, justifications, and challenges to maximize their effectiveness.

FUTURE DIRECTIONS AND OPPORTUNITIES: POTENTIAL FUTURE APPLICATIONS OF VR IN ADDRESSING EVOLVING EDUCATIONAL NEEDS

Because virtual reality technology provides dynamic and realistic simulations of real-world instruction within a virtual learning environment, it holds great promise for enhancing vocational education. The drawbacks of traditional skill training include high costs, high risk, low returns, prolonged training, inefficiency, pollution, and issues with reproducibility. These problems can be resolved by combining virtual reality and vocational education (Ravichandran & Mahapatra, 2023). Virtual reality (VR) in vocational education has a bright future because the technology is getting better and more widely available. One of VR's many applications in vocational education is the creation of lifelike work environment simulations, which give students a secure environment in which to hone their practical abilities. Additionally, by enabling trainees to collaborate on projects and acquire experience working in teams, technology can support collaborative learning (Ravichandran & Mahapatra, 2023).

Increased uniformity and standardization in vocational training could come from the growing usage of VR, which would produce a workforce that is more competent and skilled. With the potential for immersive learning and enhanced skill development, as well as implications for more efficient evaluation and a more trained workforce, VR in vocational education appears to have a bright future (Ravichandran & Mahapatra, 2023). With the application of new technologies that are relevant to them, it is feasible to design and visualize potential customer journey scenarios through virtual scenario-based developments that pique curiosity and encourage participation. To create future scenarios that are dynamic, and economical, and enable the visualization and interaction of computer-generated information by numerous stakeholders, scenario visualization can be done through the use of AR, VR, or MR (Tom Dieck & Han, 2022). It is hardly hyperbole to suggest that virtual reality (VR) will probably have the biggest impact on education given how quickly the world is developing. Indeed, we expect to see more of it from our wonderful readers. In the realm of education, the reality has given students and teachers new opportunities (Chimakurthi, 2018). When compared to traditional techniques, the existence of technology is so widespread and multifaceted that its benefits are genuinely remarkable, which highlights the importance of education and learning. The enormous potential to improve the coherence and usefulness of learning further enriches this. Professionals now find that, in many situations, live performances and training sessions are safer than traditional training (Chimakurthi, 2018).

Virtual reality (VR) has drawn more attention as a teaching tool, and many believe it may eventually impact teaching methods, particularly with the rise of the Metaverse. The majority of earlier studies on VR education focus on programs or platforms created with specific training or educational goals in mind (Jin et al., 2022). Supporting AR/VR prototyping at the early to intermediate stages, customizing AR/VR authoring tools according to domain knowledge, and incorporating learning resource access into implementation workflows are impactful. Similar techniques can be applied in an educational setting to assist instructors in creating VR applications. These techniques include offering VR prototype or template tools, allowing instructors to customize tools according to their areas of expertise, and integrating learning resources or features that enable users to locate institutional help rapidly (Jin et al., 2022). By physically interacting with the models and immersing themselves in the virtual world, virtual reality (VR) allows the user/student to actively study and develop knowledge. Additionally, students are participating in an interactive learning environment and using the knowledge they have learned in the classroom to solve problems or validate theories in models in a virtual setting, which generally complies with constructivist learning theory (Soliman et al., 2021). Virtual reality is a cutting-edge educational technology that has the potential to completely change the system. Instead of being a revolutionary approach to education, the usage of virtual reality (VR) is an extra tool whose worth is likely to become much more apparent in the years to come, given the current COVID-19 Pandemic, the need for social distancing, and distant learning (Soliman et al., 2021).

VR technology can more accurately replicate sporting activities that call for expensive instructional resources and sporting venues, reflecting the humanized design of the learning environment. To accomplish the objectives of physical education and sports training reform, the integration of virtual reality technology into physical education might comprise top-notch apparatus and spaces, enabling pupils to genuinely enjoy exercise and operation (C. Li & Li, 2020).

To ensure that people are not uncomfortable when wearing VR, the technology must get over its current technical obstacles. Aside from that, in order to effectively employ VR technology in the classroom, educators must adhere to a set of guidelines and work towards reforming traditional physical education while maintaining a reasonable standard for VR equipment use (C. Li & Li, 2020). The interaction of content, psychological, cognitive, behavioral, and technological elements in relation to user adoption of immersive technology and successful technology deployment. Furthermore, not all user experiences with AR/VR devices are favorable. The variables that contribute to unpleasant user experiences were identified by the suggested framework as motion sickness, cognitive overload, physical discomfort, and distraction. The negative consequences that immersive technology use can have on user experiences should be minimised by system designers. Notably, individual differences influence how users' cognitive and affective responses are shaped by technical and content inputs. Therefore, one possible way to mitigate the negative effects of using immersive technology could be to better understand user characteristics (Suh & Prophet, 2018).

Virtual reality (VR) technology holds significant promise for vocational education by providing dynamic, realistic simulations that address the high costs, risks, and inefficiencies of traditional training methods. The growing accessibility and advancements in VR technology enable lifelike work environment simulations, allowing students to safely practice practical skills and collaborate on projects, potentially leading to a more skilled and standardized workforce. Immersive technologies like AR, VR, and MR can enhance customer journey scenarios by creating engaging, interactive, and cost-effective visualizations. This capability can also enrich educational experiences by enabling students to interact with and learn from virtual models, supporting constructivist learning theories. VR's potential in education is vast, offering new opportunities for both students and teachers. It provides a safer, more effective training method compared to traditional approaches and has garnered attention for its role in the evolving Metaverse. Early-stage AR/VR prototyping and customized authoring tools can further support educational initiatives by helping instructors create tailored VR applications and integrate learning resources seamlessly. While VR technology can revolutionize physical education by simulating expensive sports activities and enhancing the learning environment, technical challenges such as motion sickness and cognitive overload need to be addressed. Understanding user characteristics and minimizing negative experiences can improve VR adoption and effectiveness in both educational and consumer contexts. Overall, VR is an additional tool in education with the potential to transform learning experiences, particularly in the wake of the COVID-19 pandemic and the shift towards remote learning. Its integration requires careful consideration of both technological and pedagogical factors to maximize its benefits and address potential drawbacks.

EMERGING TRENDS AND ADVANCEMENTS IN VR TECHNOLOGY AND THEIR IMPLICATIONS FOR EDUCATION

The impact of COVID-19 on education has been enormous on a global scale. It is critically necessary for researchers and academic research organizations to draw lessons from the COVID-19 pandemic. Higher education recipients want to consider how to develop a paradigm for learning that is more adaptable and innovative. The potential for implementing AR/VR technology in education and training is indicated by the industry's rapid expansion in the AEC sector (Tan et al., 2022). Several effective case studies have demonstrated VR's potential as a teaching tool in career education. To train their mechanics, for example, automakers like Ford and Volvo have used VR simulators, allowing them to practice practical skills in a secure setting. Similar to this, airlines like Qantas and Lufthansa have trained their pilots using virtual reality (VR), giving them access to real-world events and emergencies so they can hone their decision-making abilities (Ravichandran & Mahapatra, 2023). VR is a useful tool for Ohio Technical College welding students to practice their techniques as it minimizes safety concerns and the requirement for costly materials. By offering students realistic and captivating simulations that enable them to gain practical skills safely and economically, these excellent case studies show how VR may improve vocational education (Ravichandran & Mahapatra, 2023). It was determined that the VR solution was a workable and efficient learning tool after it was assessed and refined iteratively in response to input from instructors and students. The study also emphasized how VR technology may be used for internal training programs and virtual site inspections (Ravichandran & Mahapatra, 2023). Virtual reality (VR) can serve as a link between theoretical and practical learning scenarios, which can significantly improve and consolidate related declarative memory. Effective pedagogical design suggests a balanced mix of VR and non-VR learning representations. To compare interactive 3D learning content on tablets with virtual reality experiences over an extended duration, more research is required (Ravichandran & Mahapatra, 2023).

VR has demonstrated significant promise as an instructional tool for career education. By offering a simulated environment that replicates real-world circumstances, virtual reality (VR) can improve practical learning by allowing learners to gain hands-on experience without incurring risks or costs. By enhancing motivation and engagement, virtual reality (VR) can also make learning more dynamic and immersive (Ravichandran & Mahapatra, 2023). Students in remote locations with little infrastructure will benefit from it. Even though there are still certain obstacles and restrictions related to the use of virtual reality in the classroom, successful case studies and best practices can direct teachers towards the successful integration of VR in vocational education. VR technology is a viable and exciting instrument for future pedagogy since it opens up new possibilities for vocational education as it develops (Ravichandran & Mahapatra, 2023). The use of AR and VR in the AEC sector for training and education has some restrictions. Lastly, an analysis of the present issues surrounding AR/VR for training and education in the AEC sector. (Tan et al., 2022) sheds light on potential developments in AR and VR for training and education in the AEC sector. (Steinbauer, 2024) suggests using virtual reality (VR) as an educational tool to inform pupils about harassment at work.

Virtual reality is a cutting-edge educational technology that has the potential to completely change the system. Instead of being a revolutionary approach to education, the usage of virtual reality (VR) is an extra tool whose worth is likely to become much more apparent in the years to come, given the current COVID-19 Pandemic, the need for social distancing, and distance learning. Utilizing technology such as virtual reality (VR) will play a major role in the race to provide university students with an optimal continuum of an amazing education. Early adopting colleges will have an advantage and can guarantee their students an excellent education (Soliman et al., 2021).

Using virtual reality technology to reform teaching techniques is one of the primary strategies in modern education. In my nation, physical education plays a significant role in school. Students' excitement for studying can be significantly increased by using VR technology to create online VR panoramas and VR films (C. Li & Li, 2020). Through VR visualization, sports venues, equipment, safety, and other limitations of traditional sports courses can be broken down into complex environments that VR technology can simulate. It can also provide complex and abstract sports theoretical knowledge, giving students accurate and scientific guidance to gain more skills and knowledge (C. Li & Li, 2020). One of the most important tools in teacher education is video-based reflection on one's own instruction (Westphal et al., 2024).

The COVID-19 pandemic has had a profound global impact on education, prompting a critical need for more adaptable and innovative learning paradigms. AR/VR technology has shown significant potential in education, particularly highlighted by its rapid adoption in the AEC sector. Case studies have demonstrated VR's effectiveness in career education, such as training mechanics and pilots in secure, realistic simulations. VR minimizes safety risks and material costs for vocational students like welders at Ohio Technical College, enhancing practical skill acquisition economically. Research emphasizes VR's role in bridging theoretical and practical learning, improving declarative memory through balanced pedagogical designs. Despite challenges, VR enhances engagement and motivation in vocational education, making learning dynamic and immersive, particularly beneficial for students in remote areas with limited resources. AR/VR applications in the AEC sector face constraints but show promise for future developments in training and education. Looking forward, VR is positioned as a transformative educational tool, especially amid current challenges like social distancing and distance learning. Its integration into teaching methods, including physical education, offers new avenues for engaging students through virtual environments and simulations. Overall, VR's evolution in education holds promise for enhancing learning experiences and preparing students for future challenges. (Greig et al., 2024) recommended for implementing and assessing professional development programs for teachers on VR use and agricultural literacy using the VRFARM framework, as well as encouraging more research on the long-term effects, diversity of educational settings and geographic locations, and inclusivity of VR in agricultural classrooms. The classroom can now use immersive learning systems that use consumer-grade virtual reality (VR) goggles and software. Virtual reality (VR) is a significant advancement in contextual learning, providing students with authentic experiences that mimic various material kinds as they would be encountered in real life. The three-dimensional effect provides an immersive element that can immerse the learner in a special setting that is closely related to the course material. Virtual reality experiences can be beneficial in educational environments, but they also need to meet the needs of the individual students as well as the course's learning objectives (Cecotti et al., 2024). Increasing the visibility of incorporating VR technology into the classroom, fostering an environment that encourages its adoption, and making VR technology more enjoyable are all factors that can support instructors' intention to use VR technology in the classroom going forward (Du & Liang, 2024). One effective way to help student instructors deal with stress is to teach them to reflect on their teaching by using more reciprocity and putting more distance between them and difficult classroom circumstances. A promising approach to support student teachers' professional vision, well-being, and stress-resistance is to integrate mindfulness-based practices, reappraisal, and video-based reflection on one's own teaching (Westphal et al., 2024).

ROLE OF VR IN FOSTERING COLLABORATION, CREATIVITY, AND CRITICAL THINKING SKILLS IN LEARNERS, PREPARING THEM FOR THE DEMANDS OF THE 21ST-CENTURY WORKFORCE

VR material has a great retention rate because of its immersive aspect, which guarantees less distraction. Students are exposed to real-world situations through three-dimensional representations in experiential learning. A virtual tour of a farm, for instance, can be used to learn about different farming techniques and offers an interactive educational experience. Through immersive and gamified activities, virtual reality education offers an enjoyable learning experience that improves students' critical thinking skills. It also offers a safe environment, eliminating the possibility of any waste from experiments physical, chemical, or biological (Ravichandran & Mahapatra, 2023). Accessibility and affordability are two benefits of employing virtual reality (VR) as a teaching tool in vocational education. Through the use of virtual reality (VR), students can access experiences that would not be possible without it. For instance, in a secure setting, trainees can practice operating on hazardous machinery, conducting surgeries, and flying airplanes (Ravichandran

& Mahapatra, 2023). Training becomes more economical and scalable when virtual reality replaces costly facilities or equipment like heavy machinery or airplane simulators. For vocational education facilities on a tight budget or looking to cut training expenses without sacrificing quality instruction, this makes virtual reality an appealing choice (Ravichandran & Mahapatra, 2023). A careful design that aligns with the curriculum, learning objectives, and course outcomes is necessary for the VR application/lab. To optimize the learning experience, cognitive abilities, and skills of the students, it is imperative that the design include learning theories and methodologies (Soliman et al., 2021). It is determined that using VR is advantageous for both the university and the students. Students' performance and grades rise as a result of their pedagogical and cognitive gains. This is directly related to the VR application design, which integrates learning theories and is centered on the learning objectives. Additionally, active student participation using VR is a component of BLA and a student-centered approach, which is preferable to traditional, passive learning methods (Soliman et al., 2021). Fostering student teachers' professional vision, well-being, and ability to handle stress may be achieved by combining video-based reflection on one's own teaching with reappraisal and mindfulness-based techniques (Westphal et al., 2024).

CONCLUSION

The integration of immersive technologies like VR in education holds immense potential for transforming learning experiences across various disciplines. VR's ability to create engaging, interactive, and safe learning environments can significantly enhance student engagement, motivation, and knowledge retention. It is particularly beneficial in vocational education, where it allows for the practical application of skills in a controlled, risk-free setting. Despite the challenges and limitations, the successful case studies and ongoing research underscore VR's viability as a supplementary educational tool. As technology continues to evolve, early adopters in higher education and vocational training stand to gain a competitive edge by providing superior educational experiences. The COVID-19 pandemic has accelerated the adoption of such technologies, underscoring their importance in maintaining educational continuity and preparing students for future challenges. In conclusion, the integration of immersive technologies, particularly Virtual Reality (VR), Augmented Reality (AR), and Mixed Reality (MR), holds transformative potential for education. These technologies enhance learning by providing immersive, interactive experiences that bridge theoretical knowledge with practical applications. From vocational training to higher education, VR facilitates safe, cost-effective simulations that improve skill acquisition and engagement while reducing traditional barriers such as access to specialized equipment. AR complements learning by overlaying digital information onto real-world environments, enhancing understanding and interaction. As educational paradigms shift towards more adaptable and innovative models, the strategic implementation of immersive technologies aligned with pedagogical goals becomes essential. This evolution not only addresses current educational challenges exacerbated by the COVID-19 pandemic but also sets the stage for a more inclusive, dynamic approach to learning that prepares students for the complexities of the modern world. As research and development in immersive technologies continue to advance, their role in education is poised to expand, offering new avenues for personalized, effective learning experiences across diverse fields and settings.

REFERENCES

Agbo, F. J., Sanusi, I. T., Oyelere, S. S., & Suhonen, J. (2021). Application of Virtual Reality in Computer Science Education: A Systemic Review Based on Bibliometric and Content Analysis Methods. *Education Sciences*, 11(142), 1–23. DOI: 10.3390/educsci11030142

Babalola, A., Manu, P., Cheung, C., Yunusa-Kaltungo, A., & Bartolo, P. (2023). A systematic review of the application of immersive technologies for safety and health management in the construction sector. *Journal of Safety Research*, 85, 66–85. DOI: 10.1016/j.jsr.2023.01.007 PMID: 37330902

Baroroh, D. K., & Agarwal, A. (2022). Immersive Technologies in Indonesia Faces "New Normal" COVID-19. *International Journal of Technology*, 13(3), 633–642. DOI: 10.14716/ijtech.v13i3.5220

Cecotti, H., Huisinga, L., & Peláez, L. G. (2024). Fully immersive learning with virtual reality for assessing students in art history. *Virtual Reality (Waltham Cross)*, 28(33), 1–15. DOI: 10.1007/s10055-023-00920-x

Chimakurthi, V. N. S. S. (2018). Emerging of Virtual Reality (VR) Technology in Education and Training. *Asian Journal of Humanity. Art and Literature*, 5(2), 157–166. Advance online publication. DOI: 10.18034/ajhal.v5i2.606

Cochrane, T. (2016). Mobile VR in education: From the fringe to the mainstream. *International Journal of Mobile and Blended Learning*, 8(4), 44–60. DOI: 10.4018/IJMBL.2016100104

Daltoè, T., Ruth-Herbein, E., Brucker, B., Jaekel, A. K., Trautwein, U., Fauth, B., Gerjets, P., & Göllner, R. (2024). Immersive insights: Unveiling the impact of 360-degree videos on preservice teachers' classroom observation experiences and teaching-quality ratings. *Computers & Education*, 213, 104976. Advance online publication. DOI: 10.1016/j.compedu.2023.104976

Davydova, D., Gil'vanov, R., Kukushkina, Y., & Romanova, I. (2023). Immersive Technologies in Higher Education. *Proceedings of Petersburg Transport University*, 20(1), 120–132. DOI: 10.20295/1815-588X-2023-1-120-132

Drigas, A., Mitsea, E., & Skianis, C. (2021). Neuro-Linguistic Programming, Positive Psychology & VR in Special Education. *Scientific Electronic Archives*, 15(1), 31–39. DOI: 10.36560/15120221497

Du, W., & Liang, R. Y. (2024). Teachers' Continued VR Technology Usage Intention: An Application of the UTAUT2 Model. *SAGE Open*, 14(1), 1–17. DOI: 10.1177/21582440231220112

Greig, J. A., Colclasure, B., Rampold, S., Ruth, T., & Granberry, T. (2024). Enhancing agricultural education through virtual reality: Facilitation, application, reflection, and measurement in the classroom. *Advancements in Agricultural Development*, 5(2), 64–80. DOI: 10.37433/aad.v5i2.353

Hong, C., & Wang, L. (2023). Virtual Reality Technology in Nursing Professional Skills Training: Bibliometric Analysis. *JMIR Serious Games*, 11(e44766), 1–15. DOI: 10.2196/44766 PMID: 37603389

Jin, Q., Liu, Y., Yarosh, S., Han, B., & Qian, F. (2022). How Will VR Enter University Classrooms? Multi-stakeholders Investigation of VR in Higher Education. *CHI Conference on Human Factors in Computing Systems*, 1–17. DOI: 10.1145/3491102.3517542

Kaur, D. P., Kumar, A., Dutta, R., & Malhotra, S. (2022). The Role of Interactive and Immersive Technologies in Higher Education: A Survey. *Journal of Engineering Education Transformations*, 36(2), 79–86. DOI: 10.16920/jeet/2022/v36i2/22156

Kersting, M., Bondell, J., Steier, R., & Myers, M. (2023). Virtual reality in astronomy education: Reflecting on design principles through a dialogue between researchers and practitioners. *International Journal of Science Education. Part B. Communication and Public Engagement*. Advance online publication. DOI: 10.1080/21548455.2023.2238871

Li, C., & Li, Y. (2020). Feasibility Analysis of VR Technology in Physical Education and Sports Training. *IEEE Access : Practical Innovations, Open Solutions*, 20, 1–8. DOI: 10.1109/ACCESS.2020.2995063

Li, K., & Wang, S. (2021). Development and application of VR course resources based on embedded system in open education. *Microprocessors and Microsystems*, 83(103989), 1–6. DOI: 10.1016/j.micpro.2021.103989

Lin, X., Li, R., Chen, Z., & Xiong, J. (2024). Design strategies for VR science and education games from an embodied cognition perspective: A literature-based meta-analysis. *Frontiers in Psychology*, 14(January), 1–14. DOI: 10.3389/fpsyg.2023.1292110 PMID: 38259582

Liu, Z., Gong, S., Tan, Z., & Demian, P. (2023). Immersive Technologies-Driven Building Information Modeling (BIM) in the Context of Metaverse. *Buildings*, 13(1559), 1–30. DOI: 10.3390/buildings13061559

Mesjar, L., Cross, K., Jiang, Y., & Steed, J. (2023). The Intersection of Fashion, Immersive Technology, and Sustainability: A Literature Review. *Sustainability (Basel)*, 15(3761), 1–22. DOI: 10.3390/su15043761

Pratisto, E. H., Thompson, N., & Potdar, V. (2022). Immersive technologies for tourism: a systematic review. In *Information Technology and Tourism* (Vol. 24, Issue 2). Springer Berlin Heidelberg. DOI: 10.1007/s40558-022-00228-7

Ravichandran, R. R., & Mahapatra, J. (2023). Virtual Reality in Vocational Education and Training: Challenges and Possibilities. *Journal of Digital Learning and Education*, 3(1), 25–31. DOI: 10.52562/jdle.v3i1.602

Rojas-Sánchez, M. A., Palos-Sánchez, P. R., & Folgado-Fernández, J. A. (2023). Systematic literature review and bibliometric analysis on virtual reality and education. *Education and Information Technologies*, 28(1), 155–192. Advance online publication. DOI: 10.1007/s10639-022-11167-5 PMID: 35789766

Ruan, B. (2022). VR-Assisted Environmental Education for Undergraduates. *Advances in Multimedia*, 2022, 1–8. DOI: 10.1155/2022/3721301

Soliman, M., Pesyridis, A., Dalaymani-Zad, D., Gronfula, M., & Kourmpetis, M. (2021). The application of virtual reality in engineering education. *Applied Sciences (Basel, Switzerland)*, 11(6), 1–14. DOI: 10.3390/app11062879

Srikong, M., & Wannapiroon, P. (2020). Immersive technology for medical education: Technology enhance immersive learning experiences. In *Siriraj Medical Journal* (Vol. 72, Issue 3, pp. 265–271). DOI: 10.33192/Smj.2020.36

Steinbauer, R. (2024). Teaching Students About Workplace Harassment by Letting Them Experience it in a Virtual Reality Environment. *Journal of Management Education*, 48(4), 671–707. DOI: 10.1177/10525629231225735

Suh, A., & Prophet, J. (2018). The state of immersive technology research: A literature analysis. *Computers in Human Behavior*, 86, 77–90. DOI: 10.1016/j.chb.2018.04.019

Tan, Y., Xu, W., Li, S., & Chen, K. (2022). Augmented and virtual reality (AR/VR) for education and applications. *Buildings*, 12(10), 1529–1553. DOI: 10.3390/buildings12101529

Tom Dieck, M. C., & Han, D. (2022). The role of immersive technology in Customer Experience Management. *Journal of Marketing Theory and Practice*, 30(1), 108–119. Advance online publication. DOI: 10.1080/10696679.2021.1891939 van der Linde-van den Bor, M., Slond, F., Liesdek, O. C. D., Suyker, W. J., & Weldam, S. W. M. (2022). The use of virtual reality in patient education related to medical somatic treatment: A scoping review. In *Patient Education and Counseling* (Vol. 105, Issue 7). DOI: 10.1016/j.pec.2021.12.015

Wang, R., Bush-Evans, R., Arden-Close, E., Bolat, E., McAlaney, J., Hodge, S., Thomas, S., & Phalp, K. (2023). Transparency in persuasive technology, immersive technology, and online marketing: Facilitating users' informed decision making and practical implications. *Computers in Human Behavior*, 139(October), 1–15. DOI: 10.1016/j.chb.2022.107545

Wang, X., Young, G. W., Plechatá, A., Mc Guckin, C., & Makransky, G. (2023). Utilizing virtual reality to assist social competence education and social support for children from under-represented backgrounds. *Computers & Education*, 201(104815), 1–18. DOI: 10.1016/j.compedu.2023.104815

Westphal, A., Richter, E., Lazarides, R., & Huang, Y. (2024). More I-talk in student teachers' written reflections indicates higher stress during VR teaching. *Computers & Education*, 212, 1–15. DOI: 10.1016/j.compedu.2024.104987

KEY TERMS AND DEFINITIONS

Augmented Reality (AR): - Technology that overlays digital information on the real world, enhancing real-world experiences.

Educational Technology: - Tools and resources used to improve teaching and learning processes through technological innovations.

Immersive Technologies: - Technologies that create engaging, interactive environments, including VR, AR, and MR.

Mixed Reality (MR): - A blend of physical and digital worlds, enabling interaction with both real and virtual objects.

Pedagogical Design: - The planning and structuring of educational experiences, incorporating various teaching methodologies and technologies like VR.

Vocational Education: - Training that equips learners with practical skills for specific trades or professions, often enhanced by VR simulations.

Virtual Reality (VR): - A technology that creates a simulated environment for users to interact with, enhancing learning through immersion.

Chapter 3
Use of Virtual Environments in Educational Robotics

Servet Kılıç
https://orcid.org/0000-0002-1687-3231
Ordu University, Turkey

ABSTRACT

In this chapter, the features of virtual robotic simulations designed in accordance with physical robotic kits are examined from different perspectives. Nowadays, with the spread of online education, virtual robotic simulations are preferred as alternative and supportive tools to physical robotic kits. Simulations include challenges, activities, games and competitions organized in parallel with the curriculum of grades K-12. Challenges related to daily life and designed from simple to complex aim to improve students' STEM (Science, Technology, Engineering, Mathematics) knowledge and skills. In this section, online platforms including Lego Mindstorms, VEX, Arduino and Mbot virtual robotic tools used in classroom activities or international competitions around the world are examined. Simulations on the platforms are evaluated according to their physical properties, difficulties involved and usability in educational environments. In addition, studies in the literature on simulations are included and examples of the usability of simulations in educational environments are presented.

DOI: 10.4018/979-8-3693-6030-9.ch003

INTRODUCTION

A robot can be defined as a vehicle that detects the external environment thanks to sensors, obtains certain data, interprets the codes written by people who write programs through microcontrollers, and reacts by making some analyzes. Robotics is a multidisciplinary branch of science that deals with the design, production and use of robots. Building robots with robotics education kits is a fun, educational and creativity-enhancing activity that can be used to develop students' construction, programming and design skills (Gerecke & Wagner, 2007). Programmable bricks or similar structures with microcontroller features enable the control of many mechanical and electronic parts through programming, as well as the realization of daily events in a laboratory environment (Resnick et al., 1996). Today's robotics kits offer a more accessible graphics-based programming environment for users who want to program complex robotic behaviors. For this reason, if activities related to daily life problems are designed with robotics and students are offered the opportunity to apply them, students' critical thinking and computational thinking (CT) skills can be improved (Chen et al., 2017). During robotics applications, students take an active role in problem-solving processes, learn by exploring and collaborating with their peers, and thus help their peers develop basic mental skills (Atmatzidou & Demetriadis, 2016).

It is possible to find educational robotic kits at different levels for every level, from pre-school to higher education. In many countries of the world, robotics programming course within the scope of computer science is included in education curricula at the K-12 level (Bocconi et al., 2016). It is preferred as an elective course in higher education institutions, especially in departments focusing on Science, Mathematics and Technology. In addition, private schools that provide education at the K-12 level and have high financial income prepare students for national or international competitions by establishing robotic laboratories. While students in such educational institutions may have the opportunity to work with physical robotic kits, especially in schools located in rural areas, students may not have access to robotic kits due to financial limitations. Some robotic kits, such as Arduino, are advantageous in terms of usability due to their lower costs (Junior et al., 2013; Mozo et al., 2017). However, in crowded and small classes, it may be difficult for students to carry out robotic activities both individually and in groups. Although students can access the kits in the classroom, their access to these kits outside the classroom is very limited. Virtual educational robotics platforms have a structure that can overcome these limitations in the application of physical robotic kits in classrooms (Berland & Wilensky, 2015; Shoop et al., 2016).

The use of virtual robotics is becoming increasingly widespread due to reasons such as easy configuration, efficient use of time, easy creation of learning activities, teachers and students being able to access these environments outside the classroom, providing faster feedback on problems that occur, and low cost (Shoop et al., 2016; Witherspoon et al., 2017). The use of virtual environments in the field of robotics programming is an important tool that enables students and developers to learn robotic concepts and develop their applications. Virtual environments can be used to develop programming skills without a physical robot and can also be used to simulate complex scenarios. After the pandemic that affected the whole world in 2020, education at many education levels, from pre-school to higher education, was provided remotely through virtual classes for a certain period of time. Therefore, the importance of virtual educational robotic environments has become more evident in this process (Jent et al., 2024). Students had the opportunity to access these environments online both in and outside of class. There are also some obstacles and limitations in the applicability of robotic simulations. Alsoliman (2022) mentioned that there are some obstacles due to web-mediated cultural norms and educational policies regarding virtual learning. Although it is less costly to obtain than physical kits, the fact that some students do not have a computer and internet limits the use of virtual robotic simulations. Some simulations are used online via the web. Therefore, the lack of internet access is an important limitation. The fact that robotic programming is newly included in the curriculum or is not included in some curricula can create limitations in the integration of robotic simulations into courses and in terms of the robotic programming knowledge of educators (Harter et al., 2023; Kılıç & Çakıroğlu, 2023). In addition, the educational content in some simulations may not be compatible with the curriculum in schools. In real classroom environments, students can keep their motivation and interest high by touching physical robots and making their own designs (Alimisis, 2013). This situation can be seen as a limitation in virtual robotic simulations.

There are virtual platforms developed for free or for a fee so that many different physical robotic kits can be used online. A detailed examination of educational robotic kits and virtual platforms will make it easier for educators and students to access and use these environments. In this context, the following headings will be included in this section.

BACKGROUND

Educational Robotics

Today, while robots perform different tasks in many different areas, the number of robots and the jobs they perform are gradually changing. While humanoid robots usually come to mind when talking about robots, there are actually many different types of robots used in different fields. According to application areas; They differ such as industrial robots, home robots, medical robots, service robots, military robots, entertainment robots, space robots, hobby and competition robots. As can be seen, robots are preferred to make life easier in different areas of daily life. In recent years, robots have become an indispensable part of science and engineering education (Cameron, 2005). In this way, robotics have a wide range of usage in education; It has begun to be used as a teaching tool in different disciplines such as STEM (Science, Technology, Engineering, Mathematics), programming, machinery and electrical-electronics (Foss et al., 2019; Şimşek, 2019). While it can be used in different age groups in formal education, it is also used outside of school in various courses, workshops, competitions, festivals, projects or maker works. Programming plays a very important role in organizing and designing robotics as desired. It can be said that the diversity and development of programming tools directly affects the developments in the field of robotics. Therefore, it can be said that the historical development of educational robotics is directly related to the development of programming tools.

The period when the first robotics kits and programming tools were developed for educational purposes dates back to the mid-20th century. The studies carried out by Papert and his friends in the 1960s to understand how children think and learn led to the emergence of the Logo programming language (Papert, 1993). The emergence of the Logo programming language and the Turtle robot, which contributed to applications in the field of mathematics, laid the foundation for the use of different tools, including robotics, today. The first works of Logo in education began to be seen in the 1980s. Since this date, educational robotics studies have continued to develop as an accepted important field (Benitti, 2012). Additionally, robotics competitions and events became popular during this period.

The basic theory of Educational Robotics (ER) is based on Constructivism and Constructionism approaches (Papert, 1993). Within the framework of the constructivist approach, Piaget (1974) sees children not as passive receivers in the world but as active receivers who constantly interact with their environment. With this understanding, Papert started working with Piaget in the 1950s (Ackermann, 2001). Papert proposed the Constructionism approach, inspired by some important points of the constructivist approach (Papert & Harel, 1991). Papert emphasized that in the process of building knowledge in the individual's mind, the internal structure should be supported by structures in the outside world, including the use of computers (Rogers & Portsmore, 2004). An individual can reveal knowledge by building a sand castle on the beach with his peers or by designing a robot and programming it functionally (Kafai & Resnick, 1996). ER applications, which are seen as materials suitable for the Constructionism approach, play an important role in attracting students' attention and increasing motivation (Eguchi, 2010), in the development of problem solving and creative thinking (Karim et al., 2015), in gaining programming skills (Numanoğlu & Keser, 2017), and in the development of CT and STEM skills (Becker et al., 2017).

ER kits used for educational purposes generally include electronic sensors such as touch, color, ultrasonic, light and gyroscope, while mechanically they include motors, wheels, gears, arms, feet, connections and other parts used for design purposes. ERs, which can be designed for different purposes, can be programmed as block, text or icon based. In particular, the widespread use of environments with block-based programming interfaces increases the use of ERs (Atmatzidou & Demetriadis, 2016; Chen et al., 2017). Block-based programming environments have features such as a useful interface and ease of use, debugging feature, multimedia support and design-based structure, making these environments preferable (Brennan & Resnick, 2012). Interfaces that allow text-based coding enable programming at a more complex level. Many robots used in different fields other than ERs have text-based programming interfaces. Therefore, having text-based programming knowledge can make it easier to program many robots related to daily life. While icon and block-based coding interfaces are generally used by primary and secondary school students, text-based coding interface is used by students studying at high school or higher levels. In other words, while students who are at the novice level prefer icon or block-based coding environments, students who have gained a certain amount of experience prefer the text-based coding interface.

Robotics Types and Virtual Environments

Lego

Papert thought that it would be more useful to use the Logo programming language with Lego toys in order to make it concrete. Lego-Logo collaboration began by considering the different design features of Lego and the programmable feature of Logo. In the late 1980s, Lego began producing sets that taught students robotics and programming skills using the Logo programming language. In the late 1990s, Lego introduced the RCX series, the first of the Mindstorms series. In 2006, it launched the NXT series, which includes a programmable brick, microprocessor, software with an icon-based graphic interface, sound, color, distance and touch sensors, as well as other mechanical parts, and the set was updated as NXT 2.0 in 2009. With this series, a new era has begun in Lego robotics. Following the NXT 2.0 series, which was widely used until 2013, the EV3 series, which has similar features but consists of more advanced components, was launched. In addition to having a more advanced programmable brick compared to its previous versions, the programmable brick is more functional than others in terms of memory and processing speed. Apart from the Mindstorms series, WeDo and SPIKE kits, which are more suitable for use by primary and secondary school students, have been developed. Figure 1 shows Lego's robotic kits.

Figure 1. Lego Mindstorms robotics kits

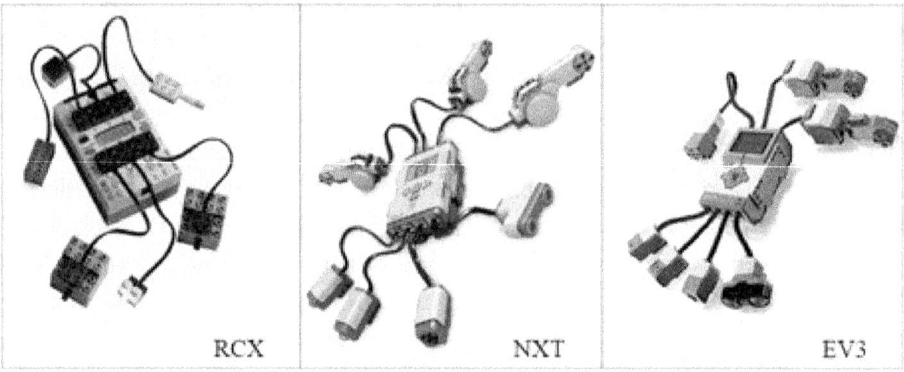

NXT and in recent years EV3 kits have been widely used to improve students' computational thinking and problem-solving skills (Atmatzidou & Demetriadis, 2016; Yildiz & Seferoğlu, 2021). EV3 is an educational robot kit that is widely preferred around the world (Benitti, 2012; Berland & Wilensky, 2015) and used in international competitions (First Lego League, First Robotics Competition etc.). These kits are especially preferred in private educational institutions other than public schools. Due to the limited financial resources of some public schools, there may be limitations in the supply of these kits. For this reason, in recent years, virtual Lego robotic environments have been recommended as an alternative to physically used kits (Berland & Wilensky, 2015; Kılıç & Gökoğlu, 2022).

Robot Virtual Worlds

The robot virtual worlds (RVW) platform includes games, competitions and a virtual robot programming curriculum (VRP-C) that allows the use of VEX, NXT and EV3 kits (Robot Virtual Worlds, 2024). VRP-C was developed in collaboration with Carnegie Mellon University and Robomatter. It includes activities from simple to complex that enable the use of different programming structures (basic movement blocks, operators, variable definition blocks, mathematical and logical operation blocks, loop blocks, decision structures, arrays) for the use of motion action components, distance, color, tour, gyroscope and touch sensors (Figure 2)

Figure 2. VRP-C interface

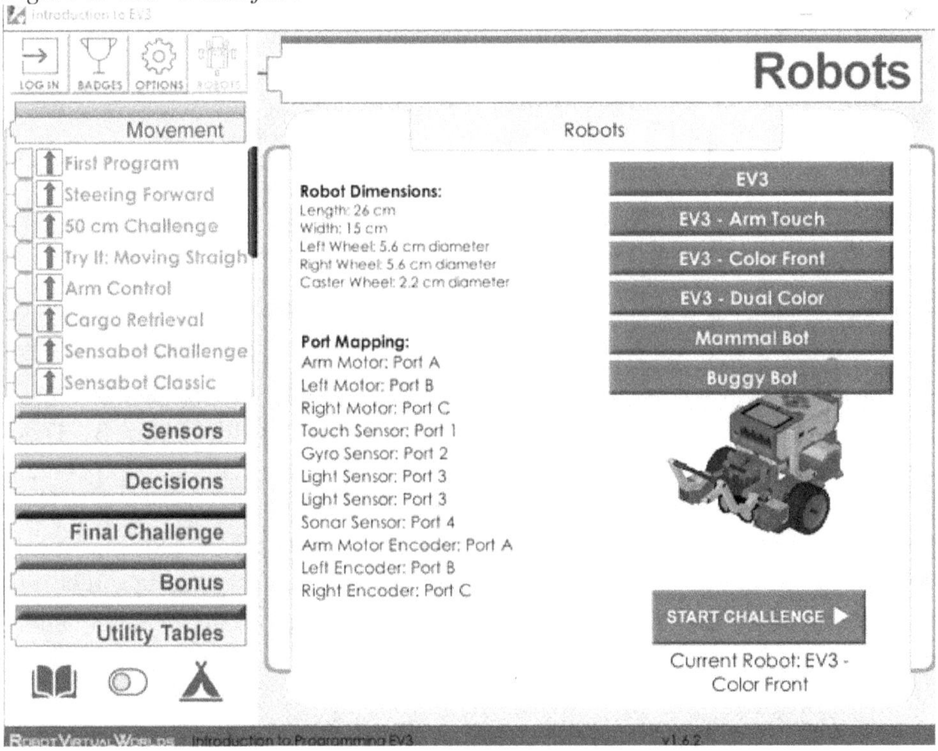

As seen in Figure 2, different robot designs can be chosen according to the achievements in the activities. Port information and measurement information for the selected robot design are provided. VRP-C includes different activities, from simple activities in which the basic movements of the robot are provided to complex activities in which different sensors are used together. VRP-C also allows students to learn individually (Mistretta, 2022; Witherspoon et al., 2017; Witherspoon &

Schunn, 2019). The progress of students logging into the system is recorded in the CS-STEM network (Cs2n.org, 2020). The system gives students badges for each challenge completed. Thanks to these badges, which are among the elements of gamification, students can track their progress and receive certificates. Teachers can create classes through this network and follow the development of students in the class. Table 1 lists the unit titles, topics and activity numbers in VRP-C.

Table 1. Units, topics and activities in VRP-C

Unit Name	Activity	Topics Covered
Movement	8	Forward, backward, rotation movements Arm movements Dimensioning, lap and degree calculations
Sensors	14	Use of touch, gyroscope, ultrasonic, color and tour sensor Equations with inequalities Boolean logic Decision structures (if-else, wait-until, Switch-case), loops
Decisions	10	Complex activities where different sensors are used together (touch, ultrasonic, light, gyro, motor rotation sensors) Complex activities using different programming structures (math blocks, arrays, loop, variable definition, decision structures)
Final Challange (Search and Rescue)	1	The competition section, which requires the use of all learned sensors and programming structures and consists of 4 different challenges (passing through the untidy room, firefighting, passing through the empty room, and human rescue).

The activities in VRP-C are structured from basic activities to complex activities. Activities are designed in relation to three-dimensional daily life (Figure 3). There are videos that reveal the relationship of some activities to daily life and contain some instructions. These videos are short-term promotional materials that contain task-related explanations while relating problems to daily life. Videos play a role in focusing on the subject by reducing cognitive load and encouraging students to solve problems by considering attention, interest and motivation (Witherspoon et al., 2017).

Figure 3. Sample activities included in VRP-C

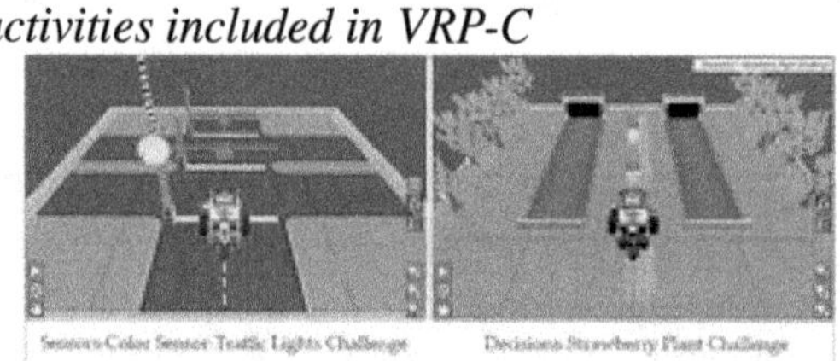

The activity on the left in Figure 3 involves the task of a robot to move correctly at traffic lights. The activity on the right addresses the problem of distinguishing strawberries according to their freshness and loading them onto the appropriate moving belts. The activities in VRP-C can be programmed with the text-based ROBOTC programming language, ROBOTC block-based and icon-based EV3-G software (Figure 4).

Figure 4. Text (a), graphical (b) and icon-based (c) programming techniques in VRP-C.

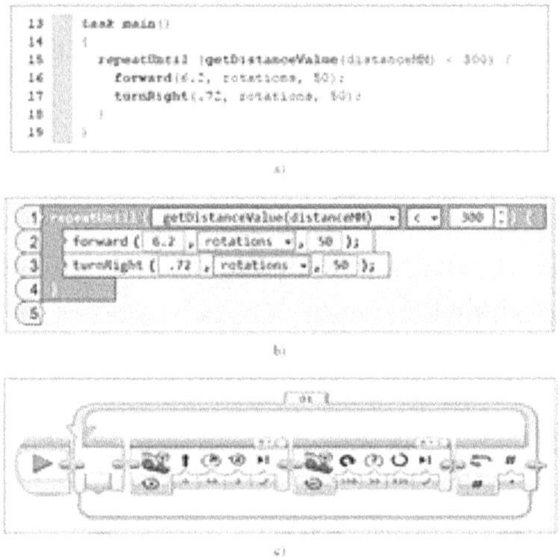

ROBOTC text is a C-based programming language used for programming robots. ROBOTC graphics allow the use of programming structures in blocks (Witherspoon et al., 2017). There are data sets on the blocks that allow values such as number of turns, rotation speed and angle to be entered. EV3-G software has a free, easy-to-use and icon-based programming interface developed by Lego. This environment was originally designed for programming physical Lego robotics kits. Connection with VRP-C can be achieved via virtual programmable brick. Virtual bricks are supplied from the RVW platform for a fee. However, virtual bricks do not impose much financial burden on schools compared to physical robot kits (Witherspoon et al., 2017).

There are studies on VRP-C in the literature. Witherspoon et al. (2017) tried to reveal how VRP-C affects students' CT skill development. ROBOTC graphic-based programming language was used. Post-test scores of secondary school students who progressed by doing more activities through VRP-C differed significantly from their pre-test scores. Kılıç and Gökoğlu (2022) investigated the usability of VRP-C for teaching robotic programming. Robotics programming training was given to computer science (CS) teacher candidates using VRP-C within the scope of a scientific education activity. After the research, it was revealed that VRP-C is compatible with robotic programming curricula in schools and that prospective CS teachers are willing to use VRP-C in their lessons in terms of content, functionality and cost. Additionally, compatibility, visual design, feedback, time management, editing and gamification are shown as features that increase the usability of VRP-C. Kılıç and Çakıroğlu (2023) examined the pedagogical content knowledge development of CS teachers to increase students' CT skills through robotic programming. Within the scope of the research, an educational model was created using VRP-C and CS teachers were trained within the framework of this model. After the research, CS teachers' content knowledge about robotics and CT and their pedagogical content knowledge on integrating CT into robotics have improved sufficiently. Seeing CK as a combination of CT and robotics has provided important clues in organizing training in the context of the integration of CT into robotics teaching. In addition, it was stated that structuring the activities in VRP-C from simple to more complex and preparing the activities in relation to daily life would contribute to teachers' ability to structure the course within the framework of CT. Studies have shown that VRP-C is a tool that can be used in robotics programming courses or out-of-class activities. Designing the tool from simple to complex in accordance with a curriculum can contribute to individual students learning robotic programming. Creating a class and registering students allows the teacher to monitor students' progress. Giving badges after successful completion of activities can be seen as an important element in keeping students' motivation alive and motivating them. Having activities related to daily life may be effective in ensuring students' CT development. Including videos that explain the activities and relate them to daily life can facilitate the integration of VRP-C into the course.

Virtual Robotics Toolkit

Virtual Robotics Toolkit (VRT) is a physics-supported robotics simulator platform that enables the use of virtual Lego Mindstorms EV3 and NXT robotic vehicles (Virtual Robotics Toolkit, 2024). This platform is a paid environment that offers students the opportunity to learn robotic programming and design. By having a real robotic experience, users can improve their coding skills, test robots' behavior, and develop strategies to solve various tasks. VRT provides support for ultrasonic sensor, color sensor, touch sensor, IR sensor, touch sensor, gyroscope Sensor, infrared sensor and compass sensor. Educators can use this platform to get students practicing and improving their STEM skills. Simulation deals with physical concepts such as force and motion in environments designed to suit real life. With toolkits, virtual robots can be designed and programmed in a similar way as the parts used in the physical robot. Codes written for the simulated robot can also be used in real environments with physical robots. Robots designed with various CAD tools such as LEGO Digital Designer, LDraw, MLCAD or LDCad can be transferred to the virtual environment (Figure 5). In this way, different functional robots can be designed based on imagination by using different mechanical and electronic robot parts together. Thanks to the simulator's advanced physics engine, robots are designed to move in a manner similar to real-world conditions. When performing activities with robots, variables such as friction force or gravity are taken into account and changes can be made to these values.

Figure 5. Transferring the robot designed with LEGO Digital Designer software to VRT

VRT, which started as a tool for researchers and engineers in the 2010s, has undergone significant development with the birth of the Cogmation simulator. Cogmation Simulator is a robotic simulation software developed by Cogmation Robotics. This simulation software enables the design, simulation and testing of various robotic systems and platforms. It is designed specifically for those developing robotics projects, allowing them to see how designs will behave in the real world before creating robotic prototypes. The Cogmation Simulator can simulate various types of robots and sensors. Using the software, users can program the robots' movement, test their interactions with objects in their environment, and develop codes that can perform various tasks. In this way, it is possible to prevent errors that can be made in the real world and optimize designs more efficiently. Cogmation Simulator is a preferable option for those working in the field of robotic programming and design, for industrial robotic projects or for hobby purposes.

VRT is a paid membership platform. The paid membership includes seven sample ready-made projects of different challenges, including a user sumo and football. The challenges are structured from simple to difficult to gain new skills and sensors. Line-following robot to navigate in the maze, vacuum cleaner robot to organize messy rooms, and demolition robot for unnecessary construction are among the activities carried out individually. Users program robots to pass challenges using the features of the environment and robots presented to them. After gaining experience in basic projects, you can compete with other players in multiplayer competitions. Users have the task of programming robots that do more than one job at the same time. In football, sumo and other multi-player events, users can have the opportunity to use different sensors and gain more complex programming knowledge and skills. In addition to challenging tasks, the main activities in the projects are designed in accordance with the First Lego League (FLL) and World Robot Olympiad (WRO) competitions held around the world (Figure 6). The field mats used for football and sumo competitions at VRT are updated every year based on the competition.

Figure 6. Project window in VRT

WRO brings together students from different countries to develop students' creativity and problem-solving skills through challenging and educational robotic tasks. Each year, a new set of themes is created that encourages students to create and code robots that will solve tasks of specific challenges. VRT updates the projects at regular intervals, taking into account the themes. FLL is one of the largest robot competitions held worldwide, with participation from dozens of countries and thousands of teams. The competition encourages participants to design and program their own robots to perform the tasks given each year in minimum time and to reach maximum points. VRT simulated the challenges given in both competitions in 2016 in its own projects. Figure 7 gives examples of activities included in VRT.

Figure 7. VRT sample tasks

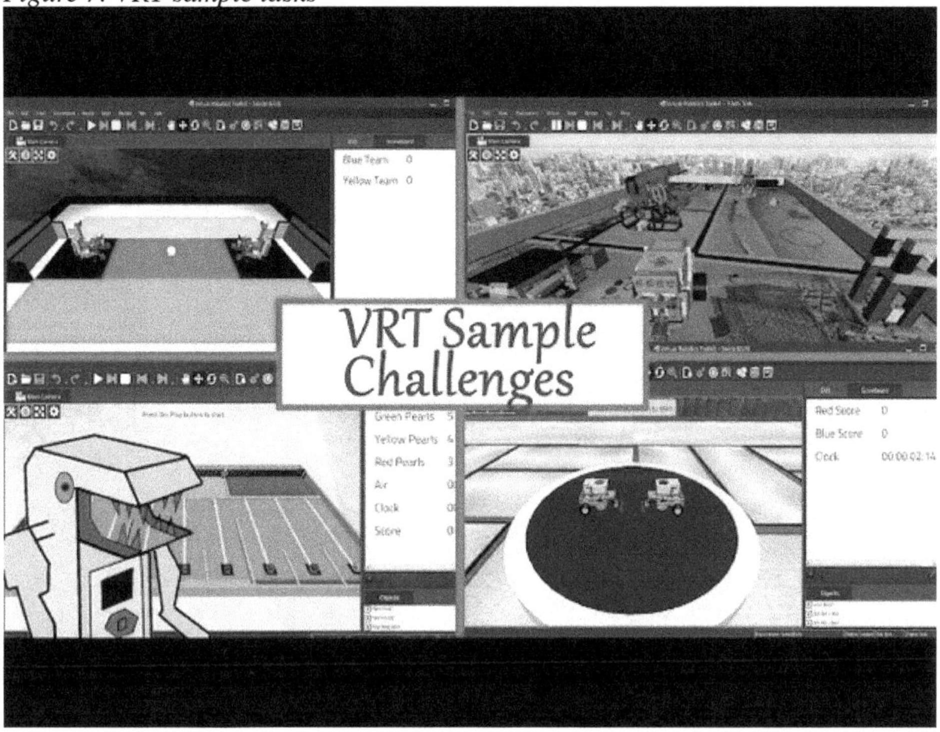

The platform includes support learning materials for novice, intermediate and expert users. There is also tutorial material that explains the installation, use and programming interface of the VRT, as well as instructions for importing EV3 programming and tools designed in CAD programs. While NXT and EV3 robots can be programmed with their original icon-based coding interface, robots can also be programmed as block-based or text-based. In this way, students of different age groups can meet the challenges using different interfaces depending on their programming experience. Figure 8 shows an example of VRT's icon-based coding interface.

Figure 8. VRT's icon-based coding interface

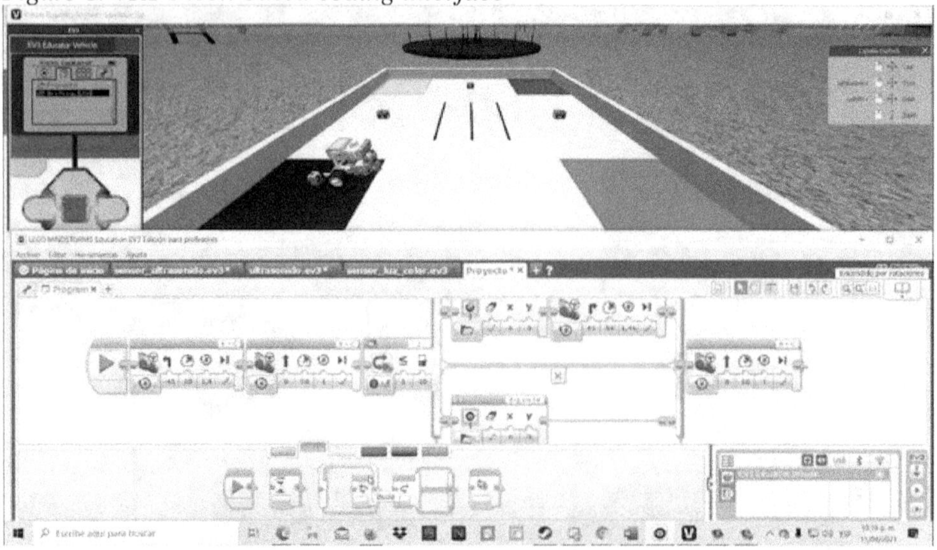

There are studies conducted using VRT in the literature. While some of these studies examined VRT theoretically, some of them examined VRT practically. Souza et al. (2020) used the VRT platform to evaluate the reality gap between virtual robot simulation and physical robots. The aim of the study is to reveal the effects of the gap that may occur in VRT and the effects of differences that may occur while testing the algorithms. Researchers also aimed to suggest strategies to reduce the reality effect. Three tests were carried out on two different robots, both in the real world and in simulation, using different design models of EV3. During the testing process, data were collected via tachometer, infrared, gyroscope and light sensor and comparisons were made. The results revealed that in terms of time to complete the task, the two robots had similar values with a small standard deviation in both scenarios. Later, when the standard deviation values were taken into account, it was observed that there were some gaps between the simulation and real-life actions. Researchers have made some suggestions to fill the gaps. Alsoliman (2022) investigated the effects of robotic simulations on STEM teaching and learning by using both Lego's physical robot and VRT platform together. The study was conducted within the scope of STEM studies of five different eighth grade students in different K-12 schools. The study included the opinions of both teachers and students. The study results revealed that the use of virtual classrooms is acceptable to many educational institutions and is an effective platform in online education. In addition, teachers stated that VRT is a suitable tool for STEM learning and teaching. VRT has environments designed for both regular events and international competitions.

In some schools, robotics clubs are established to prepare students for competitions. In this respect, VRT can provide an alternative for educators. Transferring robots designed with CAD software to VRT can allow students to focus on the development of their design skills. VRT may be a suitable tool especially for preparation for FLL competitions where robot designs come to the fore.

VEX Robotics

VEX Robotics kit is a tool designed to develop STEM skills of students in different age groups (VEX Robotics, 2024). VEX Robotics includes a modular robotic platform that includes various mechanical parts, motors, sensors and other electronic components. Kits designed for different groups allow users to design, build, program and test their own robots. In addition to being suitable for STEM education, VEX aims to develop collaboration, creativity, teamwork, task sharing, leadership, CT and problem solving. Many competitions are organized for VEX, such as the robotics world championship, artificial intelligence robotics competition and international competitions for different sets. VEX robotics competitions are one of the fastest growing educational robotics competitions for middle school and high school students worldwide (Sullivan & Bers, 2019). It is included in special sets and platforms for competitions. VEX robotic kits include sets suitable for different age groups such as VEX 123, VEX GO, VEX IQ, VEX EXP and VEX V5. VEX 123 is a set that is suitable for beginners to understand the basics of computer science, learn mathematics and develop their thinking skills. VEX GO is a set that enables activities such as research, repair, debugging, discovery and trial and error to support STEM activities adapted for primary school students. VEX IQ is a robotics system designed for middle school students to challenge advanced users. With VEX IQ, student teams taking part in the Challenge can design suitable robots to play with other teams in a game-based engineering challenge. VEX EXP is a set designed to promote STEM education and support curriculum for high school, college and adults. VEX V5, on the other hand, contains many elements that provide unlimited design opportunities for experienced users, including adults from high school level, and are suitable for use in both classrooms and competitions. Figure 9 shows a robot designed with the VEX IQ set.

Figure 9. A robot designed with the VEX IQ set

A STEM laboratory is included in the web platform to increase the use of VEX robotic kits in K-12 classes. STEM Labs function as add-on courses that can fit into existing curricula. Applied learning activities are included to create an expanded learning experience suitable for the use of different robotics kits in classrooms. Created mainly to support educators, STEM laboratories consist of free applied courses that are compatible with education standards, fun, easy to follow, and support collaboration and exploratory learning. Again, for educators to both support their learning and become educational technology leaders; Certified trainings, seminars, conferences and camps are organized. A comprehensive network of professional development resources is also provided to all educators within the framework of Professional Development (PD+). Videos, course plans, sample activities, seminars and conferences are among the resources offered in this network.

VEX robotic kits can be programmed as block-based and text-based with VEXcode software. Additionally, thanks to the Visual Studio code extension, users can program their VEX hardware to be compatible with different platforms using both C++ and Python languages. Block-based coding can be converted into an instant text-based code interface (Figure 10). In this way, the transition process from block-based coding to text-based is facilitated for beginner users. Text-based code structures can also be used with the drag-and-drop method. There are sample projects that users can access within the VEX platform. Construction templates and codes of the projects are shared with the project. In this way, students have the opportunity to experience ways to use the mechanical and electronic parts of the robot more professionally.

Figure 10. VEXcode software interface

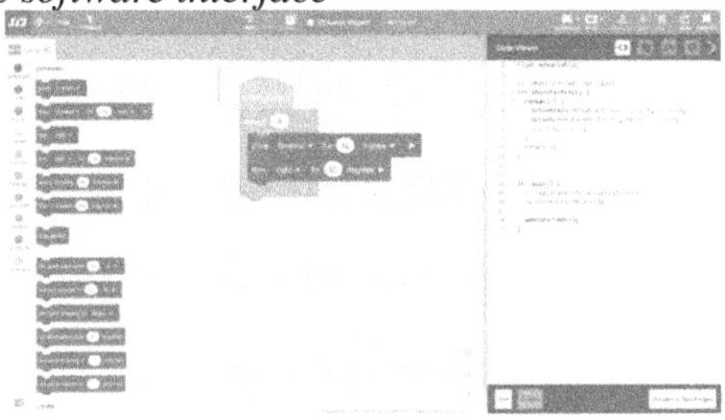

In the literature, studies carried out with VEX robotics kits can be found. Stewardson et al. (2019) investigated whether participation in VEX robotics competitions was associated with student self-efficacy and educational choices. After passing certain stages, the results revealed a positive correlation between participation in competitions and improved student self-efficacy. Furse (2019) again tried to determine the self-efficacy levels of students participating in VEX robotics competitions. It has been stated that the self-efficacy of secondary school students participating in the competition is primarily affected by biological gender and the number of seasons in which they participate in the competitions. It has also been revealed that there is a significant relationship between self-efficacy and competition participants' preference for real STEM departments. As can be seen, VEX robotic kits are among the widely preferred tools in international competitions. Therefore, VEX robotic kits can be preferred to increase students' motivation and improve their STEM skills and self-efficacy through competitions.

VEXcode VR

VEXcode VR is a platform that enables virtual programming of VEX robots to improve students' STEM and programming skills through specific challenges and games (VEXcode VR, 2024). There are challenges, games and activities at different levels that are in line with the curriculum and related to daily life at the K-8 grade level. While a certain number of block-based games can be accessed for free, access to more comprehensive events and games is provided in advanced and premium paid memberships. Especially in the Premium membership category, there are playgrounds that simulate VEX competitions for GO, IQ and V5 robots. VEXcode VR creates fun and engaging environments for students' creativity, programming strategies and problem-solving skills through challenges, games and competitive events at different levels. When logging into the platform online, it does not require any installation or logging in with a student account. Just like the VEX physical robotic coding interface, VEXcode VR can be programmed with both a block-based and text-based coding interface with Python (Figure 11). Coding interfaces can be used separately, or you can instantly switch from block-based coding to text-based.

Figure 11. VEXcode VR coding interfaces

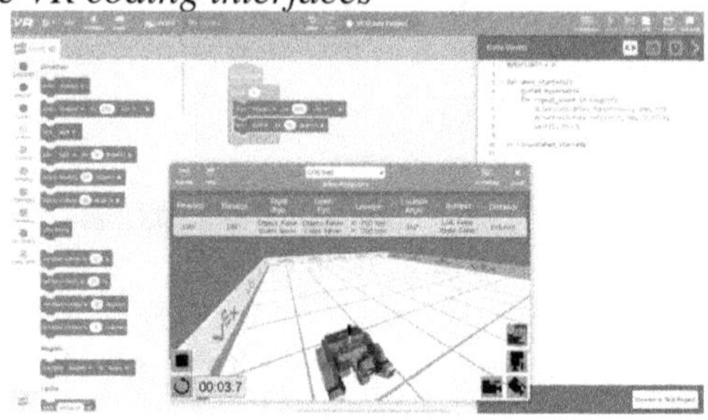

There are courses, educational resources and guides so that educators and students can use VEXcode VR effectively. In the courses, basic concepts for robot components and algorithm development such as moving robots back and forth, rotating at different angles, cyclic movements, bumper sensor, distance sensor, location sensor, eye sensor are discussed. In addition, the text-based coding course also explains the use of basic programming structures such as loops, conditionals, operators and data structures in various difficulties. The platform includes activity laboratories that aim to improve students' STEM skills by addressing different disciplines. All activities in the laboratories are designed for students. Students can interact with each other in activities focused on different fields and structured in accordance with the curriculum. There are game areas and coding challenges that concern different disciplines, such as navigating a maze, the life of living things, underwater ocean cleaning, drawing pictures and creating constellations (Figure 12).

Figure 12. Laboratory STEM activities

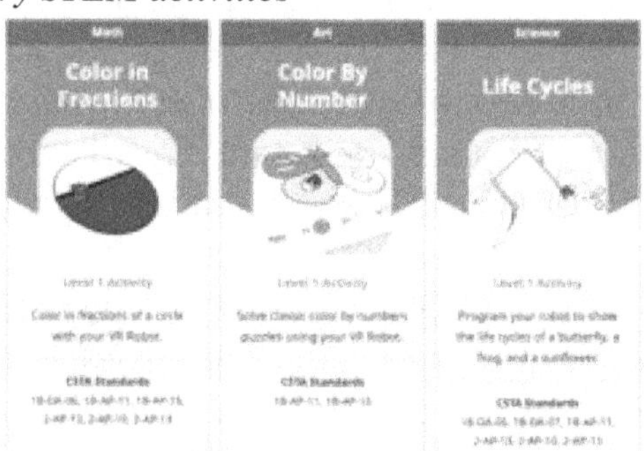

When logging into the VEXcode VR platform, two separate profiles can be preferred: educator or student. Students can register for classes through the class code provided by educators. The teacher can keep track of students' work, completed activities and games they play, and share information with students. Students can carry out projects individually or with their friends. In this process, students do not encounter any problems such as software installation, cabling or compiler errors. Sensor data can be viewed in real time with features such as the control panel. Students can share their projects in class, email them, or upload them to learning management systems such as Google Classroom, Canvas, and Schoology. Teachers can review shared project files by opening them in the VEXcode VR environment.

There are studies conducted using VEXcode VR in the literature. Lin et al. (2023) aimed to introduce Switch mode, a design strategy to support students' transition from block-based programming to text-based programming. Switch mode allows students to write text-based commands within a block-based program. It has been stated that the key mode used through the VEXcode VR tool will provide users with basic algorithm and programming skills on a block-based basis and will facilitate the transition to more complex and powerful text-based programming. Stoffova and Hyksova (2023) examined virtual robotic platforms including VEXcode VR to teach the design and programming of robots to primary school students through distance education. In the study, which presents some examples and reveals the possibilities, it is emphasized that virtual robotic platforms are seen as an urgent solution for robot programming today, when online education has become quite widespread. As can be seen, studies indicate that VEXcode VR is an effective tool in teaching robot programming in online environments. The inclusion of different challenges and games related to different disciplines and daily life makes the platform stand out for the development of STEM skills. Having suitable playgrounds and activity areas for international VEX robotics competitions makes it possible for students to prepare for competitions based on collaboration outside the classroom. Educators' ability to create classes and include students in classes can make it easier to track and monitor students outside the classroom. Activities and games at different difficulty levels can enable students to progress individually according to their own learning pace and keep their motivation alive.

Arduino

Arduino is an open-source, open-source platform that is developed to be accessible to everyone and is an easily accessible platform where hardware and software processes are used together (Ocak & Efe, 2018). Arduino was developed in 2005 by a group working at the Ivrea Design Institute in Italy. This group specifically aimed to develop a cost-effective and flexible electronic prototyping platform that students could easily access and use. Arduino has spread rapidly around the world thanks to its open source and cost-effective structure. The software can be downloaded free of charge, and since it supports Mac OS X, Windows and Linux, applications can be developed without any problems compatibility with the operating system. It can be frequently used to develop prototypes and design home-type projects in fields such as education, art and engineering. Apart from these, those who are interested in electronics and programming can choose Arduino due to its low cost, ease of access to resources and usefulness (Akbıyık, 2019). Arduino allows programming of many components thanks to its libraries. Thanks to analog and digital inputs, analog and digital data can be processed. With the help of sensors, many data from the outside world can be processed and used in output operations. The core component of the Arduino platform is a printed circuit board (Figure 13), which is available in a variety of models and usually includes a microcontroller.

Figure 13. Arduino Uno Board

There are many types of printed circuit boards. The Uno card shown in Figure 13 is among the preferred models for beginners. Apart from Uno, there are many types of cards with microcontrollers, such as the Mega card for projects that need more input/output pins and memory, the Nano card used for smaller-sized projects, and the Leonardo, which can emulate devices such as a keyboard or mouse via a USB connection. Since Arduino is open source, clone boards that perform similar functions are produced and used in many countries. LED, potentiometer, button, buzzer, digital display, LCD display, rain sensor, light sensor, temperature sensor, gas sensor, ultrasonic sensor, motion sensor, fever sensor, alcohol sensor, servo motor, DC motor, stepper motor, bluetooth module, WIFI module and GPRS module are among the components used. There is a development environment called Arduino IDE (Integrated Development Environment) that users can access free of charge, program and install software on the boards (Figure 14). The Arduino IDE development environment allows text-based coding.

Figure 14. Arduino IDE development environment

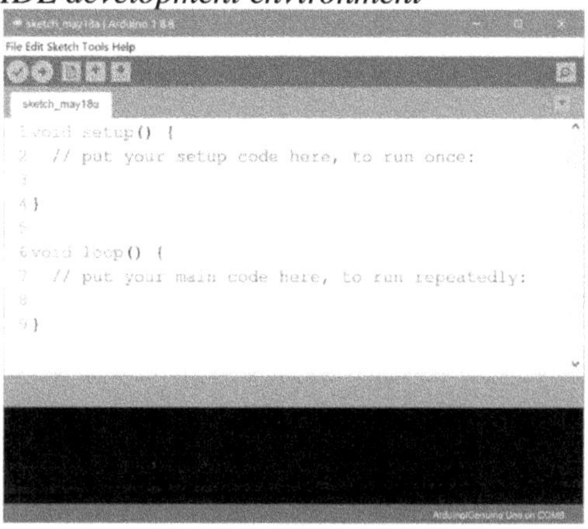

Arduino has been widely used in both online learning environments and face-to-face formal or informal learning environments, especially in recent years (Oluk & Korkmaz, 2018). In the literature, it is possible to come across studies in which Arduino is used on robotics-related subjects. Akbıyık (2019) investigated the effect of Arduino microcontroller applications on students' self-efficacy and problem-solving skills in programming education. In the study conducted on 11th grade students of vocational high school, it was revealed that Arduino improved the students' self-efficacy and problem-solving skills. García-Tudela and Marín-Marín (2023) conducted a systematic review to analyze Arduino's usage areas and its success at the primary education level. After the research, it was stated that Arduino is a tool that can be used in problem-based learning environments in the context of STEM subjects. Başaran (2018) stated that by using Arduino in electrical experiments in the physics course at the university level, there were positive developments in students' attitudes towards the physics laboratory and information communication technologies. Güven (2020) carried out activities to measure air and water resistance, light transmittance, wearable technology and earthquake severity using Arduino in a secondary school science class. It was stated that after the activities, students' attitudes towards science lessons and the use of technology in lessons increased.

Tinkercad

Tinkercad is a free online platform where three-dimensional modeling and designs are made through coding using objects and electronic circuit elements (Tinkercad, 2024). The platform first started operating in 2011 as a three-dimensional modeling tool that can work with WebGL-enabled browsers. The program can be used offline on desktop computers, as well as online via mobile devices such as tablets and phones. With Tinkercad, developed by Autodesk, different modeling can be made using ready-made objects. Many models can be created with pieces consisting of geometric shapes, such as items used in many areas of daily life, architectural decorative designs and vehicles. These designs can be made directly by drag-and-drop method, or they can be converted into process animations through block-based coding (Figure 15). Graphical code blocks can be named according to different languages. Blocks contain basic programming structures such as variables, loops, operators, mathematical expressions, and data.

Figure 15. Designing three-dimensional objects via block-based coding

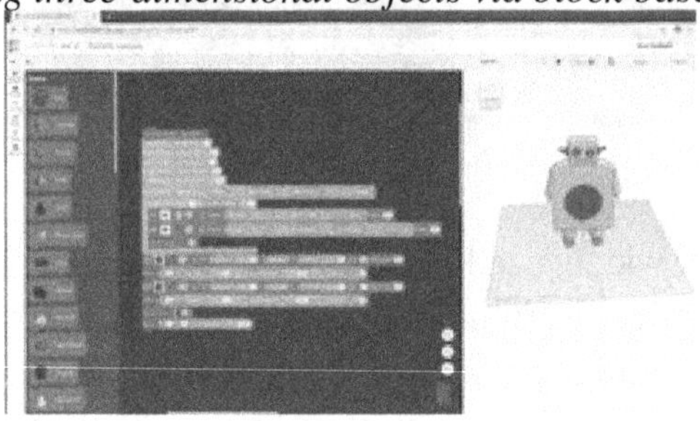

Circuits can be designed and robots can be programmed using electronic circuit elements created virtually through Arduino and Micro:bit simulations. Many basic components used with Arduino can be used within the platform. There are output units such as LED, resistor, 7 segments, buzzer, LCD display and motors. There are also input units such as buttons, potentiometers, ultrasonic, light, temperature, gas, pressure, humidity and force sensors. The platform allows robot programming in both interfaces, block-based and text-based (Figure 16).

Figure 16. Circuit design and coding interfaces

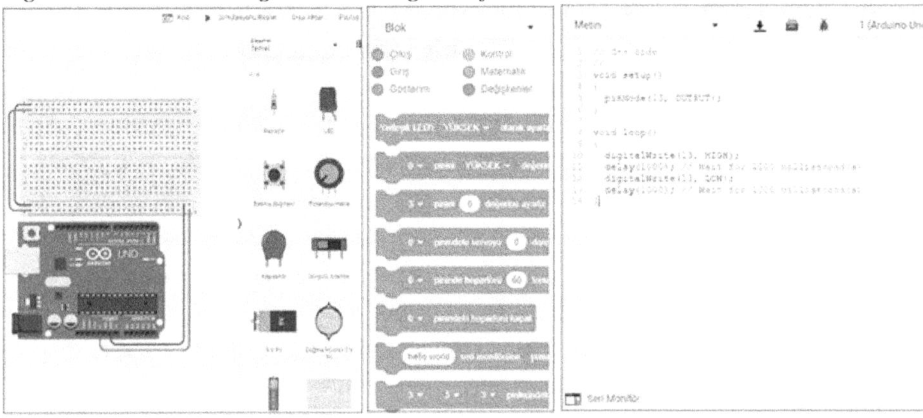

The application can be used offline on desktop computers, as well as online via mobile devices such as tablets and phones. When logged into the system online, it is necessary to register to the system to use more powers and features offered by the platform. The system offers two profiles: student and educator. When logged in to the account as an educator, the system allows creating a virtual classroom. For courses conducted online, educators can create classes and include students in classes via class codes. Students can be given out-of-class tasks by creating activity plans. Within these classes, students can share the activities or projects they have done. They can carry out joint project studies based on cooperation with each other. Educators can access shared documents, edit documents, and provide feedback to students. When students join classes, they can see the documents and notifications shared by the educator. In both ways, when the user logs into the system, the designed models, circuits and coding are saved in the profile. While items registered in the profile can be shared with other users, items shared by other users can also be easily accessed.

Tinkercad can be used in both in-class and extracurricular activities in the robot programming course. While the block-based interface can be used for younger students and students who are new to programming, more advanced students can use the text-based interface. Thinkercad can be used as a virtual laboratory environment and the experiences students gain in a face-to-face laboratory environment can be imparted to students in this environment (Shalannanda, 2020). In the three-dimensional design course conducted with university students, students can learn to use Thinkercad in a short time and design complex objects using long code blocks (Diaz et al., 2019). Students studying in technical high schools can learn the working principle and coding methods of microcontrollers through Thinkercad (Juanda & Khairullah, 2021). In addition to computer science, students can be helped to explore STEM subjects.

Force, motion, energy, pressure, gas, humidity, temperature, light, etc. It can be used to teach subjects in courses such as Physics or Chemistry (Başaran, 2018; Güven, 2020). For example, by creating an LED-supported circuit, the structure, operation and circuit elements of the electrical circuit can be shown. Some formulas can be concretized by measuring the voltage and current in the circuit with devices such as multimeters. The values obtained from the temperature and humidity sensor can be transferred to the LCD screen and the heat and temperature issue can be displayed. Applications related to the concept of pressure can be made by using a pressure sensor. In this way, many different topics related to physics such as electricity, pressure, force, motion, energy and gas can be conveyed to students with Thinkercad applications. Unlike programming, the Thinkercad program can be used to display molecules and similar structures that have three-dimensional properties.

MBot

MBot is a robotics kit that is generally used to attract young students' interest in STEM fields and improve their programming skills. The kit has been prepared to enable students to develop their manual skills in mechanics, increase their experience in computer systems, and understand the logic of robotic systems from an early age. MBot includes basic components and features such as light sensor, ultrasonic sensor, color sensor, infrared, button, buzzer and RGB LED. The mCore card on mbot is Arduino supported. In this way, the robot can be uploaded by writing programs with Arduino's IDE or other programming platforms. It can be controlled with smart devices such as mobile phones and tablets. MBot is also compatible with LEGO parts and can be used with LEGO parts through compatible connections on the box containing the circuit board. In this way, it can also be used with parts of advanced kits such as LEGO Mindstorm EV3. Updates were made to mBot in the following years, and mBot2 was released.

Thanks to CyberPi's integrated sensors and WIFI communication capabilities integrated into the MBot2 system, it enables application in computer science, STEAM, robotics, internet of things, data science and artificial intelligence curricula in connection with other fields such as Mathematics, Physics and Engineering. MBot2 can be coded block-based with mBlock software, which has a Scratch-based interface, or text-based with Python (Makeblock, 2024). By switching between both coding interfaces, students can establish the relationship between the two languages. MBlock can also integrate with hardware such as Arduino and Raspberry Pi, so users can develop physical applications. Figure 17 shows the mBot2 robotic kit and coding interface.

Figure 17. MBlock software interface and MBot2 robotics kit

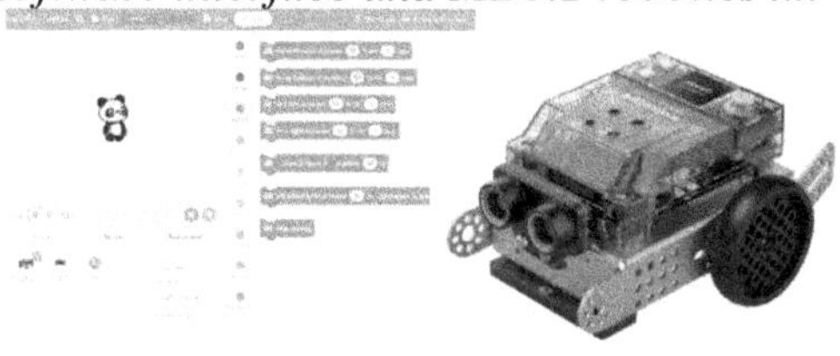

MBlock software includes blocks of programming structures such as loops, condition structures, functions, operators, variables, lists and arrays. MBlock is designed for preschool, primary and secondary school student levels. It is aimed to develop students' high-level thinking and coding skills through training organized within its own organization. The development of critical thinking and problem solving is encouraged, along with teaching resources and detailed programming projects. A robotic simulation has been developed that works integrated with MBlock software and enables online use of the mBot kit (Simulator mBot, 2024). While the simulator is available for a fee, some applications with limited access can also be used free of charge (Figure 18)

Figure 18. MBot Simulator interface

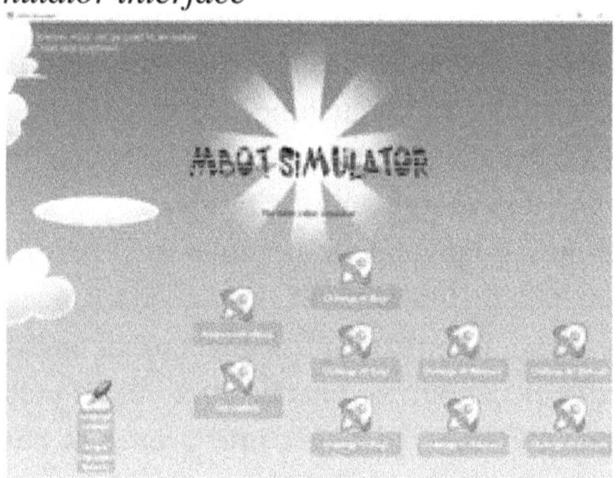

As seen in Figure 18, challenges designed for different levels can be accessed free of charge. The interface is supported with different languages, especially English. When any difficulty is selected, the simulator automatically establishes synchronization with the MBlock software (Figure 19). Tasks performed with the simulator include activities related to daily life such as obstacle detection, line tracking, maze solving, linear object tracking, turning on RGB LED lights, parking a vehicle, installing radar, burglar alarm and height meter.

Figure 19. MBot simulation and its connection with mBlock

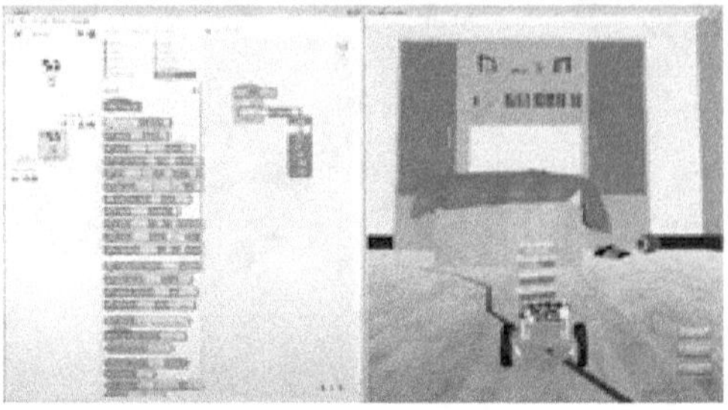

While there are no studies carried out with mBot simulation in the literature, studies carried out using the physical mBot robotic kit are quite common. Numanoğlu and Keser (2017) aimed to determine the usability of mBot and the STEM Educational Robot Kit platform in teaching programming. Using the MBlock programming environment, sample applications containing basic programming concepts were developed and experiments were carried out on the kit. The result of the research revealed that loops, condition structures, functions, operators, variables, lists and arrays can be easily learned and applied in programming teaching through mBlock and mBot. Pisarov and Mester (2019) investigated how primary school students use Scratch and mBlock graphics software packages for programming in computer science classes. After the research, students were able to grasp the basic concepts of programming through various interesting examples such as working with blocks, mathematical formulas, linear programming and branching structures, loop instructions and logical operations. Sáez-López et al. (2019) designed an educational environment that integrates programming and robotics in the fields of science and mathematics by using a visual programming language to improve students' understanding of logic and mathematical elements. In this context, it is aimed to understand computational concepts in primary education and to ensure student participation and loyalty. Within the framework of active pedagogical practices that instill motivation, enthusiasm, commitment, fun and interest, significant improvements have been achieved in students' understanding of computational and mathematical concepts.

The fact that the MBot robotics kit is compatible with widely used robotic kits such as Arduino, Raspberry Pi and Lego Mindstorms, and that the MBlock software allows the programming of these kits, provides the opportunity to use this kit to support the K-12 curriculum. Scratch supported block-based coding interface can contribute to students in the K-8 category learning programming while having fun. With the Python-supported text-based coding interface, students' transition from visual to text-based coding can be facilitated. With its compatibility with Arduino and Raspberry Pi, educational environments can be designed to develop students' STEM skills. MBot simulator can be preferred to support students' out-of-class work. Depending on the economic situation, the simulator's facilities can be used and robotic coding training can be given to students in the younger age group through the demo version.

CONCLUSION

Virtual simulations of physical robotic kits such as Lego Mindstorms, VEX, Mbot and Arduino are widely used around the world in curricular and extracurricular activities focused on developing students' STEM skills or to prepare for international competitions. Platforms are created in accordance with robotic programming curriculum for student groups of different ages. Thanks to curriculum, students at different levels, from pre-school to higher education, can learn subjects from simple to complex and in a certain order, individually or as a group. The fact that the difficulties on the platform are related to daily life and that there are written and visual materials explaining the difficulties can increase the motivation level of the students. Challenges, games and competitive activities created at different levels can be effective in helping students learn while having fun and developing their problem-solving skills. Additionally, gamification elements are included in the simulations. In some simulations, students are given badges, awards or points after successfully passing the challenges. While these reinforcements are added to the students' profiles, they can also keep their motivation alive. While ready-made robots can be used on some platforms, students can import robots they have designed themselves into some platforms. This feature, which is effective for the development of students' design and creativity skills, is very suitable for preparing for competitions such as FLL. Some simulation environments, especially Lego Mindstorms and VEX, are designed for competitions such as FLL and WRO. Difficulty and competition mats used on the platforms are updated at regular intervals. Therefore, teachers can choose these platforms to prepare for competitions every year. Virtual robots can be programmed using both block-based and text-based coding interfaces. While the block-based coding environment is preferred for students who are new to programming or at the K-8 level, experienced and older students prefer the text-based coding interface. By synchronizing both interfaces, students' transition from block-based to text-based can be facilitated.

There are some studies in the literature for the simulation environments examined in this section. Researchers can conduct application-based research to support distance education or face-to-face learning using the mentioned simulations. Researchers can use simulations to determine the effect of the flipped classroom method in robotics education. Collaborative and project-based studies can be conducted outside of school using different features of simulations. Students can be trained within the framework of international competitions using virtual VEX robotics kits and their interest, perception, motivation and higher-order thinking skill development can be examined. Researchers can examine the effects of Arduino, Lego and VEX virtual robotics kits suitable for STEM education on students' STEM and academic development in different interdisciplinary fields. In recent years, artificial intelligence-supported virtual robotics platforms have been developed. Platforms such as CoppeliaSim, Blockly for LEGO Mindstorms and RoboDK have features such as programming robot simulations, testing algorithms, providing machine learning support and developing solutions to some problems. However, these platforms are still new to provide integration into robotics education environments. Researchers can contribute to the development of students' robotic programming, algorithm development and design skills by conducting studies on these platforms and applications. The results obtained can provide concrete information for teachers to integrate virtual robotics into their classrooms or use them in distance education. Teachers can support students' development with both in-class and out-of-class activities and monitor students' performances by creating classes. Researchers can examine the effects of simulations on teachers' development of robotics programming pedagogical content knowledge through practice-based research. Policy makers can take new steps to accelerate teachers' professional development in robotics programming and the integration of robotics programming into curriculum at different levels.

REFERENCES

Ackermann, E. (2001). Piaget's constructivism, Papert's constructionism: What's the difference. *Future of Learning Group Publication*, 5(3), 438.

Akbıyık, N. (2019, October*).The effects of using Arduino microcontroller in programming education on high school student's self-efficacy and problem solving skills.In* SETSCI-Conference Proceedings (pp. 99-105).

Alimisis, D. (2013). Educational robotics: Open questions and new challenges. *Themes in Science and Technology Education*, 6(1), 63–71.

Alsoliman, B. S. H. (2022, July). Virtual robotics in education: The experience of eighth grade students in STEM. [). Frontiers Media SA.]. *Frontiers in Education*, 7, 950766. DOI: 10.3389/feduc.2022.950766

Atmatzidou, S., & Demetriadis, S. (2016). Advancing students' computational thinking skills through educational robotics: A study on age and gender relevant differences. *Robotics and Autonomous Systems*, 75, 661–670. DOI: 10.1016/j.robot.2015.10.008

Başaran, B. (2018*). Investigation of the effect of integration of arduino to electrical experiments and preparation of experiment reports in poster type on the attitudes of science teacher candidates towards physics laboratories, technology and information and communication tecnology* (Unpublished Master's thesis). Kocaeli University, Institute of Science and Technology, Kocaeli.

Becker, S. A., Cummins, M., Davis, A., Freeman, A., Hall, C. G., & Ananthanarayanan, V. (2017). *NMC horizon report: 2017 higher education edition*. The New Media Consortium.

Benitti, F. B. V. (2012). Exploring the educational potential of robotics in schools: A systematic review. *Computers & Education*, 58(3), 978–988. DOI: 10.1016/j.compedu.2011.10.006

Berland, M., & Wilensky, U. (2015). Comparing virtual and physical robotics environments for supporting complex systems and computational thinking. *Journal of Science Education and Technology*, 24(5), 628–647. DOI: 10.1007/s10956-015-9552-x

Bocconi, S., Chioccariello, A., Dettori, G., Ferrari, A., Engelhardt, K., Kampylis, P., & Punie, Y. (2016). *Developing computational thinking in compulsory education* (Policy Report). Spain: European Commission

Brennan, K., & Resnick, M. (2012, April). New frameworks for studying and assessing the development of computational thinking. In Levine, F. J. (Ed.), *Proceedings of the 2012 Annual Meeting of the American Educational Research Association* (pp. 1-25). Vancouver: The University of British Columbia.

Cs2n.org. (2020). The CS-STEM Network. Retrieved from https://www.cs2n.org/

Cameron, R. G. (2005). *Mindstorms robolab: Developing science concepts during a problem based learning club (Yayımlanmamış yüksek lisans tezi)*. The University of Toronto.

Chen, G., Shen, J., Barth-Cohen, L., Jiang, S., Huang, X., & Eltoukhy, M. (2017). Assessing elementary students' computational thinking in everyday reasoning and robotics programming. *Computers & Education*, 109, 162–175. DOI: 10.1016/j.compedu.2017.03.001

Díaz, L. M., Hernández, C. M., Ortiz, A. V., & Gaytán-Lugo, L. S. (2019, October). *Tinkercad and Codeblocks in a summer course: An attempt to explain observed engagement and enthusiasm. In 2019 IEEE Blocks and Beyond Workshop (B&B)*. IEEE.

Eguchi, A. (2010, March). What is educational robotics? Theories behind it and practical implementation. In D. Gibson (Ed.), *In Society for Information Technology & Teacher Education İnternational Conference* (pp. 4006-4014). Waynesville: Association for the Advancement of Computing in Education Foss, A., Wilcoxen, C., & Rasmus, J. (2019). The academic and behavioral implications of robotics in the classroom: An elementary case study. *Technology & Innovation, 20*(3), 321-332. DOI: 10.21300/20.3.2019.321

Furse, J. S. (2019). Measuring the self-efficacy of students participating in VEX robotics competitions (Doctoral dissertation, Utah State University).

García-Tudela, P. A., & Marín-Marín, J. A. (2023). Use of Arduino in Primary Education: A systematic review. *Education Sciences*, 13(2), 134. DOI: 10.3390/educsci13020134

Gerecke, U., & Wagner, B. (2007). The challenges and benefits of using robots in higher education. *Intelligent Automation & Soft Computing*, 13(1), 29–43. DOI: 10.1080/10798587.2007.10642948

Güven, E. (2020). *Using of Arduino assisted robotics coding activities in science teaching on 5th grade secondary school* (Unpublished Master's thesis). Muğla Sıtkı Koçman University, Institute of Educational Sciences, Muğla.

Harter, L., McKenna, J., & Van Campenhout, R. (2023, March). Teacher Perceptions of an Educational Robotics Professional Development Program. In *Society for Information Technology & Teacher Education International Conference* (pp. 2062-2068). Association for the Advancement of Computing in Education (AACE).

Jent, J. F., St. George, S. M., Agosto, Y., Rothenberg, W. A., Howe, E., Velasquez, C., & Natale, R. (2024). Virtual robotic telepresence early childhood mental health consultation to childcare centers in the aftermath of COVID-19: Training approaches and perceived acceptability and usefulness. *Frontiers in Psychology*, 15, 1339230. DOI: 10.3389/fpsyg.2024.1339230 PMID: 38903468

Juanda, E. A., & Khairullah, F. (2021, February). Tinkercad Application Software to Optimize Teaching and Learning Process in Electronics and Microprocessors Subject. In *6th UPI International Conference on TVET 2020 (TVET 2020)* (pp. 124-128). Atlantis Press. DOI: 10.2991/assehr.k.210203.101

Junior, L. A., Neto, O. T., Hernandez, M. F., Martins, P. S., Roger, L. L., & Guerra, F. A. (2013). A low-cost and simple Arduino-based educational robotics kit. Cyber Journals: Multidisciplinary Journals in Science and Technology. [JSRC]. *Journal of Selected Areas in Robotics and Control*, 3(12), 1–7.

Kafai, Y. B., & Resnick, M. (2012). *Constructionism in practice: Designing, thinking, and learning in a digital world*. Routledge. DOI: 10.4324/9780203053492

Karim, M. E., Lemaignan, S., & Mondada, F. (2015, June). A review: Can robots reshape K-12 STEM education? In O. SwanteeIn (Ed.), *International Workshop on Advanced Robotics and its Social Impacts (ARSO)* (pp. 1-8). London: Institute of Electrical and Electronics Engineers.

Kılıç, S., & Çakıroğlu, Ü. (2023). Design, implementation, and evaluation of a professional development program for teachers to teach computational thinking via robotics. *Technology. Knowledge and Learning*, 28(4), 1539–1569. DOI: 10.1007/s10758-022-09629-3

Kılıç, S., & Gökoğlu, S. (2022). Exploring the usability of virtual robotics programming curriculum for robotics programming teaching. *Informatics in Education*, 21(3), 523–540. DOI: 10.15388/infedu.2022.20

Lin, Y., Weintrop, D., & Mckenna, J. (2023, June). Switch Mode: Building a middle ground between Block-based and Text-based programming. In *Proceedings of the 2023 Symposium on Learning, Design and Technology* (pp. 114-118). DOI: 10.1145/3594781.3594803

Makeblock. (2024). About. Retrieved from https://www.makeblock.com/

Mistretta, S. (2022). Virtual robotics in hybrid teaching and learning. *New Updates in E-Learning*, 1-15.

Mozo, J. R., Quintero, H. M., & Ariza, H. M. (2017). Educational robotics: Algorithm logic learning comparison. *International Journal of Applied Engineering Research: IJAER*, 12(24), 15470–15474.

Numanoğlu, M., & Keser, H. (2017). Robot usage in programmıng teachıng - mBot example. *Bartın University Journal of Faculty of Education*, 6(2), 497–515.

Ocak, M. A., & Efe, A. (2018). *Coding and microcontroller applications with Arduino*. Anı Publishing.

Oluk, A., & Korkmaz, Ö. (2018). Opinions of information technology teachers on the use of educational robots [Bilişim teknolojileri öğretmenlerinin eğitsel robotların kullanımına yönelik görüşleri]. *Pegem Citation Index*, 0, 215–224.

Papert, S. (1993). *The children's machine: Rethinking school in the age of the computer*. Basic Books, Inc.

Papert, S., & Harel, I. (1991). Situating constructionism. *Constructionism*, 36(2), 1–11.

Piaget, J. (1974). The future of developmental child psychology. *Journal of Youth and Adolescence*, 3(2), 87–93. DOI: 10.1007/BF02215168 PMID: 24414238

Pisarov, J., & Mester, G. (2019, December). Programming the mbot robot in school. In *Proceedings of the International Conference and Workshop Mechatronics in Practice and Education, MechEdu* (pp. 45-48).

Resnick, M., Martin, F., Sargent, R., & Silverman, B. (1996). Programmable bricks: Toys to think with. *IBM Systems journal, 35*(3.4), 443-452.

Robot Virtual Worlds. (2024). Robot virtual worlds. Retrieved from https://www.robotvirtualworlds.com/

Robotics, V. E. X. (2024). The VEX ecosystem. Retrieved from https://www.vexrobotics.com/

Rogers, C., & Portsmore, M. (2004). Bringing engineering to elementary school. *Journal of STEM Education: Innovations and Research*, 5(3), 17–28.

Sáez-López, J. M., Sevillano-García, M. L., & Vazquez-Cano, E. (2019). The effect of programming on primary school students' mathematical and scientific understanding: Educational use of mBot. *Educational Technology Research and Development*, 67(6), 1405–1425. DOI: 10.1007/s11423-019-09648-5

Shalannanda, W. (2020, November). Digital Logic Design Laboratory using Autodesk Tinkercad and Google Classroom. In *2020 14th International Conference on Telecommunication Systems, Services, and Applications (TSSA* (pp. 1-5). IEEE. DOI: 10.1109/TSSA51342.2020.9310842

Shoop, R., Flot, J., Friez, T., Schunn, C., & Witherspoon, E. (2016). Can computational thinking practices be taught in robotics classrooms. Retrieved from https://www.cmu.edu/roboticsacademy/PDFs/Research/CTP_RoboticsClassrooms.pdf

Şimşek, K. (2019). *Investigation of the effects of robotic coding application on science achievement and scientific process skills of 6th grade students in science course matter and heat unit* (Unpublished master's thesis). Marmara Üniversity, İstanbul.

Simulator MBot. (2024). About us. Retrieved from https://en.iraifrance.com/a-propos-de-nous

Souza, J. D., Silva, P. J., Pinto, A. H., Monteiro, F. F., & Teixeira, J. M. (2020, November). Assessing the reality gap of robotic simulations with educational purposes. In *2020 Latin American Robotics Symposium (LARS), 2020 Brazilian Symposium on Robotics (SBR) and 2020 Workshop on Robotics in Education (WRE)* (pp. 1-6). IEEE. DOI: 10.1109/LARS/SBR/WRE51543.2020.9306947

Stewardson, G. A., Robinson, T. P., Furse, J. S., & Pate, M. L. (2019). Investigating the relationship between VEX robotics and student self-efficacy: An initial look. *International Journal of Technology and Design Education*, 29(4), 877–896. DOI: 10.1007/s10798-018-9461-4

Stoffova, V., & Hyksova, H. (2023, October). Education Robotics in Virtual Environment. In *Proceedings of the Future Technologies Conference* (pp. 479-496). Cham: Springer Nature Switzerland.

Sullivan, A., & Bers, M. U. (2019). VEX Robotics Competitions: Gender differences in student attitudes and experiences. *Journal of Information Technology Education*, 18, 18. DOI: 10.28945/4193

Tinkercad. (2024). About. Retrieved from https://www.tinkercad.com/

VEXcode VR. (2024). Expanding the VEXcode VR universe. Retrieved from https://www.vexrobotics.com/vexcode/vr

Virtual Robotics Toolkit. (2024). About. Retrieved from https://www.virtualroboticstoolkit.com/discover

Witherspoon, E. B., Higashi, R. M., Schunn, C. D., Baehr, E. C., & Shoop, R. (2017). Developing computational thinking through a virtual robotics programming curriculum. [TOCE]. *ACM Transactions on Computing Education*, 18(1), 4–24.

Witherspoon, E. B., & Schunn, C. D. (2019). Teachers' goals predict computational thinking gains in robotics. *Information and Learning Science*, 120(5/6), 308–326. DOI: 10.1108/ILS-05-2018-0035

Yildiz, T., & Seferoğlu, S. S. (2021). The effect of robotic programming on coding attitude and computational thinking skills toward self-efficacy perception. *Journal of Learning and Teaching in Digital Age*, 6(2), 101–116.

KEY TERMS AND DEFINITIONS

FLL: First Lego League, which includes students between the ages of 9 and 16; The competition aims to increase young people's interest in engineering and coding.

STEM: Science, Technology, Engineering, Mathematics

VEX: Educational robotics kit used for students at K-12 level

WRO: World Robot Olympics aims to increase young people's interest in robots and science

Chapter 4

Integrating E-Learning Into Traditional Educational Practices in a Developing Country: Post-COVID-19 Era

Md.Khaled Amin
https://orcid.org/0000-0002-3929-3088
Department of Marketing, American International University-Bangladesh, Dhaka, Bangladesh

Vichayanan Rattanawiboonsom
Faculty of Business, Naresuan University (NU), Thailand

ABSTRACT

The study aims to identify the types of e-learning embraced by the higher education institutions (HEIs) in Bangladesh, schemes offered to catch up with the trend of e-learning, features of LMS suitable for learners in a developing country, and to understand learners' attitudes towards e-learning. The study used 316 learners' data collected from 16 HEIs in Bangladesh. Descriptive statistics show that HEIs are equipped with eleven types of platforms and are always ready to deal with uncertainties in the new normal and onward. In addition, HEIs put forward several progressive schemes easing up the process of conducting classes in a hybrid mode combining face-to-face and online instructions. Fifteen features of LMS are in use and are the most demanded by users in a developing country. The learners are aware of the benefits of e-learning and have mastery of it and it is entirely within their control. Learning online is also likable to the learners as it enhances the scope of learning.

DOI: 10.4018/979-8-3693-6030-9.ch004

INTRODUCTION

Conducting academic activities online is relatively new for developing countries like Bangladesh. The community experienced unprecedented growth in online education in the wake of the outbreak in 2020 and this trend continued up to 2021. The concept of e-learning was quite disputed in Bangladesh before the outbreak; therefore, the academic degrees earned online were not considered competitive by the job market, and the graduates holding online degrees were not appreciated by society.

During the outbreak, the community started recognizing the importance of e-learning in all aspects. The acceptance of online education in Bangladesh was levitated during the pandemic when the government began to provide technical support to several higher education institutions (HEIs) amidst the crisis, despite limited resources. During the Covid-19 period, government policies were found to be strongly associated with digital transformation specifically at the tertiary level in Bangladesh (Abbas, Ar, & Hosseini, 2024). The transition was even more accelerated by the prompt initiatives put forward by some private HEIs, resulting in a huge boost in remote learning. Initially, educators and learners were provided limited online hands-on training on the functionality. Educators were briefed about the assessment criteria in a tech-mediated learning environment. HEIs arranged online workshops and seminars to raise aspiration among the educators and boost usage. The acceptance and use of e-learning have been amplified by the spread of diseases leaving HEIs with no alternatives but to incorporate technologies into education (Poddubnaya et al., 2021).

In the new normal era, HEIs were instructed by the government to continue with academic activities with a recommendation to adopt the globally recognized blended mode of education, combining online and face-to-face on-site instruction. Transitioning to blended mode requires huge technological support from both ends: institutions and personal initiatives.

Unlike other technological advancements, e-learning provides enormous benefits and meets some challenges in the new normal. Flexibility and accessibility (Smith, 2020), cost-effectiveness (Jones, 2021), and personalized learning experience (Brown, 2019) are some of the benefits that e-learning provides. Conversely, technological barriers (Garcia, 2020), lack of social interaction (Chen et al., 2022), and motivational issues (Wang & Baker, 2020) are labeled as the challenges of e-learning to overcome. In addition to that, e-learning adoption is also influenced by several determinants: technological infrastructure (Al Lily et al., 2020), digital literacy (Chao et al., 2021), and socioeconomic factors (Selwyn, 2020).

Existing literature discusses the barriers and challenges of e-learning (Ahmed et al.,2021), the benefits of online education, the role of e-learning (Rahman and Hassan, 2020), online learning amidst the pandemic (Haque et al.,2020), factors affecting behavioral intention to adopt e-learning tools, etc., but lacks clarity in the new normal.

It has been claimed that e-learning in developing countries is not customized to the needs of students and educators in those countries, as it was originally designed for and by developed countries where e-learning is not an emerging issue. It has been urged to produce a smoother version of e-learning making the system friendly and effective for developing countries (Shahryar, 2021). The scholar also raised concerns over the functionality and accessibility of the system adopted by HEIs as keeping the learners engaged was a laudable task (Khatun, 2020).

Focusing on the above concerns, the study aims to identify the types of tools/systems/platforms incorporated by the institutions in Bangladesh in imparting knowledge remotely, investigate the facilities and schemes offered by the institutions to expedite online education in the new normal, identify useful features of LMS suitable for learners in a developing country, and understand factors that may affect e-learning adoption in developing countries.

The study can be an important blueprint for the key decision-makers thinking about implementing e-learning mechanisms and for the e-learning vendors wishing to branch out into Southeast Asia. During the survey, we also found some motivating factors influencing the learners to embrace e-learning in the post-pandemic era with which we wish to expand the work further. The effectiveness of e-learning in imparting knowledge is also on our checklist. However, the carriage of e-learning needs to be pulled by horses. Growth and acceptance somewhat hinge on the following criteria: platforms, facilities and schemes, digitalization in education, and cultural factors.

E-Learning Platforms in Remote Education

The notion of e-learning has become an integral part of education across the globe during the pandemic and even in the new normal, despite obstacles. As such, HEIs globally embraced several tools to impart knowledge during and after the pandemic. We begin by portraying some of the tools used by institutions globally. Various learning management tools (LMS), such as Moodle, Canvas, and Blackboard gained much attention due to their widespread features and functionalities (Wang and Baker, 2020). The tools, embedded with video conference features, such as Zoom, Microsoft Teams, and Google Meet, had revolutionized the education system in synchronous modes speeding up real-time interaction between educators and learners during the pandemic (Ramsey, 2020).

Apart from the LMS and video conferencing tools, there were some content-creating platforms: Articulate Storyline, Adobe Captivate, and H5P embedded with gamification elements parallelly empowered by the educators in designing educational content attuned to the needs of the learners in hopes of providing a personalized learning experience (Hämäläinen and Vähäkangas, 2021). Learning environments augmented with virtual reality (VR) and augmented reality (AR) technologies: EngageVR, AltspaceVR, and ClassVR were found to be operative in delivering complex concepts, particularly in science and engineering disciplines (Dalgarno et al.,2020). Mobile-based learning services provided by Khan Academy, Duolingo, and Coursera simultaneously accelerated self-directed and micro-learning, and offered flexible learning opportunities catering to the needs of modern learners ahead of their learning journey (Al-Samarraie et al.,2021).

Literature also sheds light on the learners' perceptions of e-learning as understanding their attitude towards it is crucial in formulating remote education strategies. Despite several challenges encountered by learners, both technical and psychological during the transition period, learners eventually adopted the new mode of education. Due to its advanced features, e-learning was positively received by learners globally. It has been found that learners having prior experience in e-learning showed a strong positive attitude towards remote learning (Luo et al., 2021; (Alam, Hassan, & Ogawa, 2023). In some cases, the learners were frustrated with e-learning as there were a lot of technical issues with the connectivity that made it difficult for them to stay motivated and focused (Al Lily et al., 2020).

During the COVID-19 pandemic, government policies were more inclined to digital transformation at the tertiary level offering establishing initiatives to support transition during the crisis ensuring desirable learning outcomes through digital means while mitigating the health crisis (Abbas, Ar, & Hosseini, 2024).

Range of Facilities and Schemes Offered by HEIs to Expedite Online Education

During the outbreak, many institutions provided learners with digital devices with subsidized internet connectivity to ensure smooth connectivity (UNESCO, 2020). Several institutions provided educators with learning support in the form of training, workshops, and symposiums to aid them in adopting teaching tools (UNE-

SCO, 2020). Some institutions provided educators support to upload asynchronous lectures to meet the learners' diverse learning needs (Al Lily et al., 2020).

Many HEIs provided access to digital libraries, e-books, and academic journals (Garcia, 2020). Various innovative schemes and facilities, such as tech support and help desks (Taylor et al., 2020), financial assistance and scholarships (Adams & Williams, 2020), mental health and well-being services (Jones, 2021), virtual classrooms (Johnson, 2020) were introduced by HEIs to facilitate remote learning across the globe. The above-demonstrated facilities and schemes signify HEIs' commitment to ensure quality in remote learning, regardless of challenges.

Digitalization and Globalization in Education

The integration of digital technologies in education has gained much attention over the past few decades, particularly accelerated by the pandemic despite digitalization and globalization, which are mainly the two sides of the same coin. To catch up with global trends in education with digital technologies has always been instrumental in ensuring continuity in education. The HEIs are increasingly incorporating digital technologies to ensure a smooth impartation of knowledge. The implementation of digital technologies in a limited form has been recognized as the major movement towards digitalization in Bangladesh during the pandemic.

As a result, e-learning platforms and digital content have been introduced at primary, secondary, and tertiary levels of education in Bangladesh. Globalization has significantly influenced the use of digital technologies in education. The need for integrating global resources into traditional systems has been triggered by globalization making education more acceptable globally, which eventually increased the use of massive open online learning resources (Islam, Hossen, & Ali, 2022). Globalization has facilitated collaboration between local and foreign universities allowing students access to global resources (Ahmed, 2021).

Social Interaction, Cultural Factors and the Roles of Instructors in Fostering Techno Mediated Learning Environment

The effectiveness of e-learning heavily depends on the scope of communication and interaction between educators and learners (Hrastinski, 2009), and this can be pursued using the features, such as discussion boards, group projects, and real-time messaging embedded in the platforms (Moore, 1989). Social interaction established a common ground for the two parties: educators and learners with which a sense of community among learners can be developed for a better retention rate (Dawson, 2006).

The role of an instructor in fostering e-learning is unparalleled. Instructors play pivotal roles in a techno-mediated learning environment due to their diverse roles: facilitators, mentors, and content creators to support critical thinking and personalized learning path (Bates, 2015). Instructors continuously upgrade their digital literacy skills to support the changes and promote engagement and collaboration (Kumar & Daniel, 2016). According to Vygotsky (1978), learning is rooted in social interaction and culture facilitates learning with tools for communication and thoughts. Culture affects the mediated learning process (Mercer, 1995). As suggested by Bourdieu (2020), learners from cultural backgrounds may vary in access to resources, social norms, and practice depending on how they engage with mediated learning tools.

Features of E-learning

In the wake of the pandemic, a few HEIs started to develop customized e-learning platforms. As a result, a platform named 'buX' was introduced by BRAC University allowing learners access to videos, documents, discussion boards, and assignments online in hopes of making learning interactive and lively ("About | buX," n.d.). VUES (Virtual University Expert System), a customized e-learning introduced by AIUB, was in full swing integrating learners and educators to create a virtual university. The above platforms were designed in such a way that a user can have access to the resources through mobile devices.

Considering the vast use of mobile devices, e-learning should be compatible with mobile devices ensuring the accessibility of the educational content whenever needed (Al Lily et al., 2020). Incorporation of interactive elements, such as quizzes, discussion forums, and multimedia may enhance learner engagement and encourage active participation online (Means et al., 2013). Integration of video conferencing, chat, and multimedia messaging options promotes active interaction and participation between learners and educators (Al Lily et al., 2020). Needless to mention, e-learning should have methods for assessing work, including quizzes, assignments, and project work handed in by learners online accompanied by feedback to support learners' growth (Means et al., 2013).

Challenges of E-learning

The notion faced several challenges, such as limited access to technology, educators' perception in dealing with the transition, lack of understanding of technicalities, and environmental and psychological issues when the rate of acceptance hiked during and even in the post-pandemic periods. One of the notable challenges was to ensure equal access to technologies in all areas, including rural, urban, and suburban in Bangladesh. Learners from rural areas confronted difficulties when accessing documents as they were provided with limited resources (UNESCO, 2021). The subsequent challenge arose also from the educator's side. Educators raised serious concerns over the transition difficulties. The raised ethical issues slowed down the educators from reaping the benefits as they were concerned over the quality and transparency of education (Hodges, Moore, Lockee, Trust, & Bond, 2020). Poor internet connectivity, incompatibility in devices, delayed transition time, and frustration refrained the educators and learners from using the system eventually impacting negatively users' mental health and wellbeing (Loades et al., 2020; Means & Neisler, 2020)

Factors Affecting Users to Adopt E-learning in the Post-Pandemic Era

Among the other variables, e-learning adoption in developing countries was highly influenced by information quality, service quality, digital literacy, and computer anxiety (Tyagi & Krishankumar, 2023). Applying an extended TAM, a study confirmed the significant and direct impact of subjective norms, technical support, computer anxiety, perceived enjoyment, hedonic motivation, and course content on perceived ease of use and perceived usefulness. In contrast, subjective norms had a direct significant positive impact on the intention to use e-learning (Obaid et al., 2023). Students' continuance intention to use e-learning was explored by applying the UTAUT 3 model in which performance expectancy and social influence were confirmed as the most important indicators (Maisha & Shetu, 2023). In the areas where technological infrastructure and accessibility are robust, the e-learning adoption rate was found to be higher (Adedoyin & Soykan, 2023). Facilitating conditions and learning value were found to have impacted directly the actual use behavior of an e-learning system (Zacharis & Nikolopoulou, 2022). Students' intention to use e-learning was determined by perceived enjoyment, experience, computer anxiety, and self-efficacy (Siron, Wibowo, & Narmaditya, 2020). System quality, information quality, and service quality had a combined influence on system use and user satisfaction, excluding the impact of information quality on user satisfaction (Ali, Abdullah, Hassan, Abdullahi, & Mohamed, 2024).

Perceived ease of use, usefulness, perceived daily routine, perceived critical mass and perceived self-efficacy had an impact on the post-acceptance of e-learning through the mediating effect on fear of vaccination (Al-Maroof, Alhumaid, Akour, & Salloum, 2021).

E-learning in Bangladesh

E-learning has gained substantial attention as a viable alternative to traditional education. In- Bangladesh, it has been well accepted by educators and learners as they found e-learning useful in watching lessons, reading materials, taking part in forums, etc.(Sarker, Mahmud, Islam, & Islam, 2019). Bangladesh is such a country where opportunities are centralized in the capital city, named Dhaka. Access to quality education depends on how smartly one overcomes the two barriers: geographical and financial (Rafa, 2024). In Bangladesh, in response to the crisis pushed by COVID-19, e-learning plays a mediating role in bridging the gaps between urban and suburban or rural regions. The Edu-tech available in Bangladesh before the pandemic was web-enhanced where only the course materials and syllabi grades used to be posted online. During the pandemic, the country experienced synchronous online education where courses were taught online. As of late, the country's HEIs are experiencing blended mode combining online and face-to-face teaching.

E-learning is likable to most students as they find it functional and are willing to spend a substantial amount of time on LMS attending lectures, viewing course information, and completing assignments regularly (Sarker et al., 2019). However, learners encountered difficulties as the materials were poorly designed and the learning was disrupted by the poor internet connection (Sarker et al., 2019). Several pitfalls can be mitigated by providing extensive training to the users to enrich their knowledge and skills (Akter, Munira, & Amin, 2017). The researcher highly stressed the development of quality content and user-friendly systems to enhance asynchronous interaction between the educator and learners in hopes of reaping benefits from e-learning technologies in Bangladesh (Sarker et al., 2019). However, the overall attainment can be hampered by the digital divide as it was identified as the challenge of e-learning system adoption in developing countries (Eltahir, 2019). Also, In Bangladesh, students' attitudes were influenced significantly by gender, prior exposure to digitalization, and socio-economic background (Alam et al., 2023).

Parallelly, the notion of m-learning is also stressed in the literature disclosing the competitive aspects of the mode. Students' perception of m-learning is positive in Bangladesh as they think that m-learning is a useful tool in mitigating the study gap in the wake of the pandemic (Biswas, Roy, & Roy, 2020). System quality, information quality, and service quality are identified as influential in measuring user satisfaction with online learning (Uddin, Ghosh, & Isaac, 2019). In the post-pandemic era, students' intention to use e-learning was influenced by common variables: performance expectancy and social influence (Maisha & Shetu, 2023).

Methodology

The descriptive study analyzed data from 326 learners aged between 18 and 34 years, who were selected purposely (Homogeneous) from private, public, and international institutions in Bangladesh, covering sixteen higher education institutions. The study's respondents were active learners studying in different HEIs in Bangladesh. Approximately 68% of the respondents were male and the remaining 32% were females. Half (41%) of the respondents were from Technical, i.e., Science and Engineering backgrounds. One-third (39%) of the respondents were from non-technical backgrounds, i.e., business economics, law, and social science. The remaining 19% were from the departments offering both technical and non-technical education, e.g., Business and Technology Management (BTM) to the learners. Almost half of the respondents (55%) accessed learning content through personal computers, but an adequate number of learners (44%) used smartphones to get access to the uploaded content.

An instrument forming statements adopted from prior studies published on similar themes was designed to collect data to understand the trend. The items to measure the variable 'facilitating condition' were adopted from (Venkatesh, Morris, Davis, & Davis, 2003). Information quality was measured by four items largely adopted from (DeLone & McLean, 2003). Performance expectancy and effort expectancy were reflected by five items each and the items were adopted from (Venkatesh et al., 2003). Items to measure Social influence and self-efficacy were (Venkatesh et al., 2003). Policies and initiatives were retrieved from the literature that was discussed in the earlier parts of the chapter.

The link to the questionnaire was shared on different social media platforms for responses. The researcher also hired an enumerator to collect responses, who personally invited the respondents to fill out the paper-based questionnaire. The online form designed with MS Form was posted on June 1, 2022, and was active for a month. The study ensured the voluntary participation of the respondents in all phases of data collection as no monetary benefits were provided to the respondents in any form at any stage of data collection. The following headings of the chapter were written in line with the objective set in the earlier section.

Educational Tools/Platforms Used in Bangladesh

Figure 1 shows diverse types of tools that were in use to impart knowledge both in synchronous and asynchronous modes. These platforms vary in price, features, content quality, and methods. Survey data revealed that the majority (two-thirds) were encouraged to use e-learning tools and platforms, e.g., Google Classroom, which were offered free of cost or at a reduced rate. Often, these tools have limited functionality, but one can avail of them with limited effort. Free or licensed video conferencing mobile-based applications, such as Zoom, and Google Meet were also on the list of one-third of the users. Almost half of the learners embraced various social media platforms, such as Facebook and YouTube to attend classes asynchronously.

Figure 1. Types of e-learning platforms

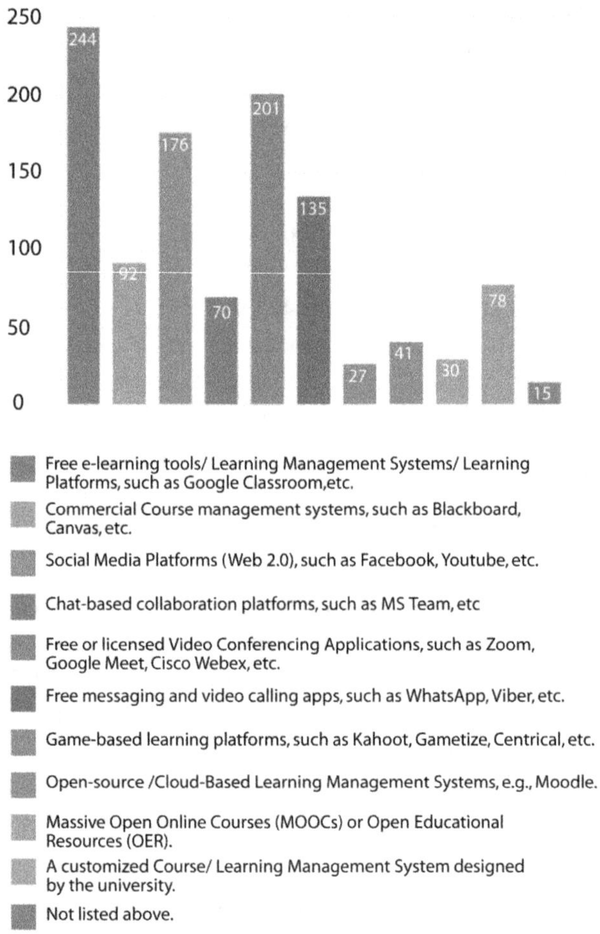

Source: Survey result.

Few HEIs have incorporated commercial course management systems, such as Blackboard and Canvas into traditional education providing a rich and competitive learning experience. Due to their functionality and benefits, Chat-based, e.g., MS Team, and game-based, e.g., Kahoot educational platforms were also in high demand. Learners also had experience dealing with the massive open online courses and open educational resources. The use of some of the customized tools with advanced features designed by the HEIs was in use. Concisely, tools, such as Moodle, Google Classroom, Zoom, Microsoft Team, EdX and Coursera, Blackboard, and Adobe Connect provide comprehensive features and user-friendly interfaces; hence, widely appreciated by the learners in Bangladesh. In Bangladesh, literature also shows evidence of the use of Google Classroom (Rahman and Hassan, 2020), Moodle (Chowdhury et al.,2019), Zoom (Khan et al.,2021), MS Team (Islam and Haque,2020), Coursera (Haque et al., 2020), Khan Academy (Kabir et al.,2019), Blackboard (Rahman et al., 2017), Adobe Connect (Ahmed et al.,2021), Schoology (Hasan et al., 2020).

Facilities or Schemes Offered by the Institutions in Bangladesh to Facilitate Remote Learning

Figure 2. Schemes to ease remote learning.

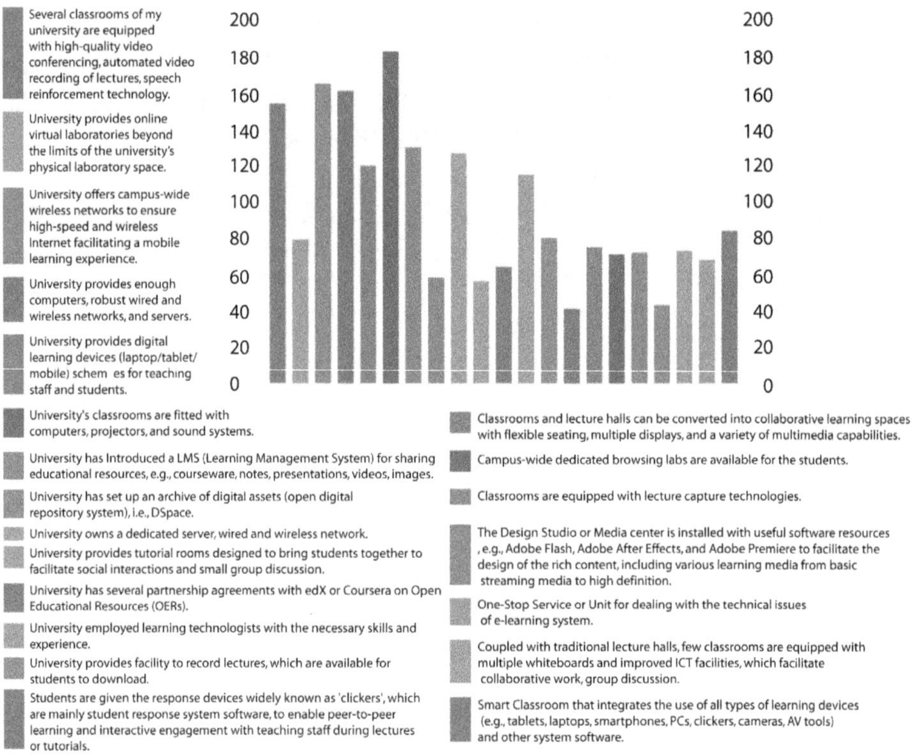

Source: Survey result.

The tidal wave of remote learning has been well diverted by the barrage of progressive schemes allowing the HEIs to run e-learning in full swing. During the pandemic, the HEIs in Bangladesh implemented various facilities and schemes to support learners and educators to cope with the transition. The HEIs provided virtual classrooms, and access to digital resources, such as online databases, and libraries, to ease remote learning, allowing learners and educators to reap the benefits. Many HEIs offered grants, reduced tuition, tuition installment plans, financial aid, and packages to the learners so they could continue their education without unwanted financial constraints. In the new normal, universities invested heavily in ICT infrastructure development, including the upgradation of bandwidth, proliferating Wi-Fi connectivity, and providing necessary software and hardware to support remote.

To familiarize users with the features and benefits of e-learning, universities have started recognizing the need for arranging workshops, seminars, and talk shows that are on e-learning. To ensure effective delivery, initiatives to equip faculty members with online teaching techniques and tools were also taken by several HEIs. Recognizing the wide range of use of mobile devices, several institutions came up with mobile-friendly e-learning platforms, allowing students to access the resources virtually. Universities have established dedicated help desks to provide users with round-the-clock support. Many institutions signed MOUs or partnered with various Edu-tech companies to leverage their resources and experience in developing innovative learning solutions to enhance the overall e-learning experience. The above facilities and schemes were introduced to ensure continuity in education in the pandemic and post-pandemic eras. Briefly, the HEIs in Bangladesh have been structured in such a way that they can sustain academic activities in a pandemic situation.

Out of twenty-one schemes and policies depicted in Figure 2, four items were mostly opted for by the respondents. Most of the universities' classrooms in Bangladesh are fitted with computers, projectors, and sound systems, through which lectures can be delivered remotely whenever needed. Universities offer dedicated Wi-Fi networks to foster a mobile learning experience. Universities have heavily invested in infrastructure development, such as providing enough computers, setting up wired and wireless networks, and acquiring servers to support e-learning. Most universities' classrooms are fitted with high-quality video conferencing technology.

Features of LMS Suitable for learners in a Developing Country

Figure 3. Features of Learning Management System

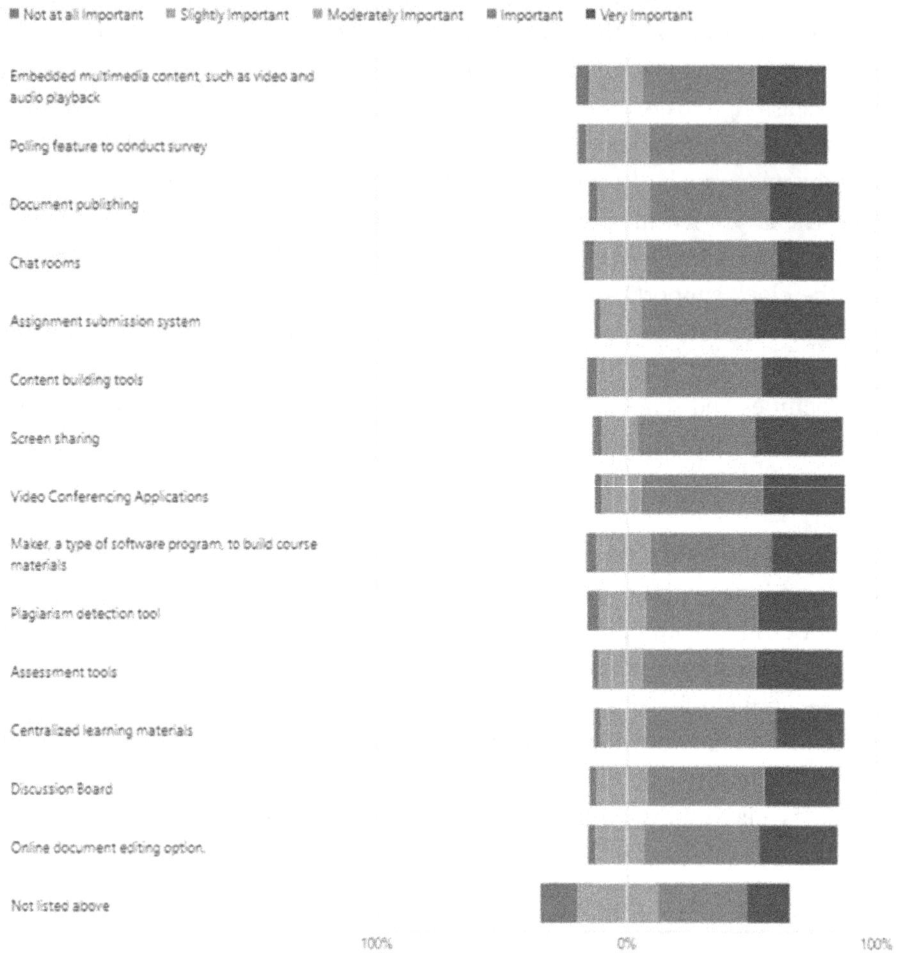

Source: Survey result.

Figure 3 shows a list of features of a standard LMS. From the literature, we listed several features of LMS that are highly appreciated globally. The majority have consented to prioritize the following features: document publishing, chat room, assignment submission system, content-building tools, screen sharing, video conferencing applications, plagiarism detection, assessment tools, centralized repository to store materials, discussion board, and online document editing option. The features, such as polling and embedded multimedia content were less prioritized by the learners in Bangladesh.

Key Influential Factors

Facilitating Conditions

"Facilitating condition is the degree to which users perceive that the technology and organizational resources, such as knowledge, resources, and opportunities may ease the use of a particular system." (Venkatesh et al., 2003). It has been reported that the facilitating conditions are the key factor in the formation of users' behavioral intention to use certain technologies (Taylor & Todd, 1995).

A learner describes in an open comment section how he managed to attend online classes despite having limited resources, "online-based classes were not effective for all of us. We are living in an underprivileged area, and it is difficult to attend online classes with a poor internet connection."

In a study, facilitating conditions were reflected by network coverage and operating system (Mahardika, Thomas, Ewing, & Japutra, 2019).

Figure 4. Facilitating Conditions

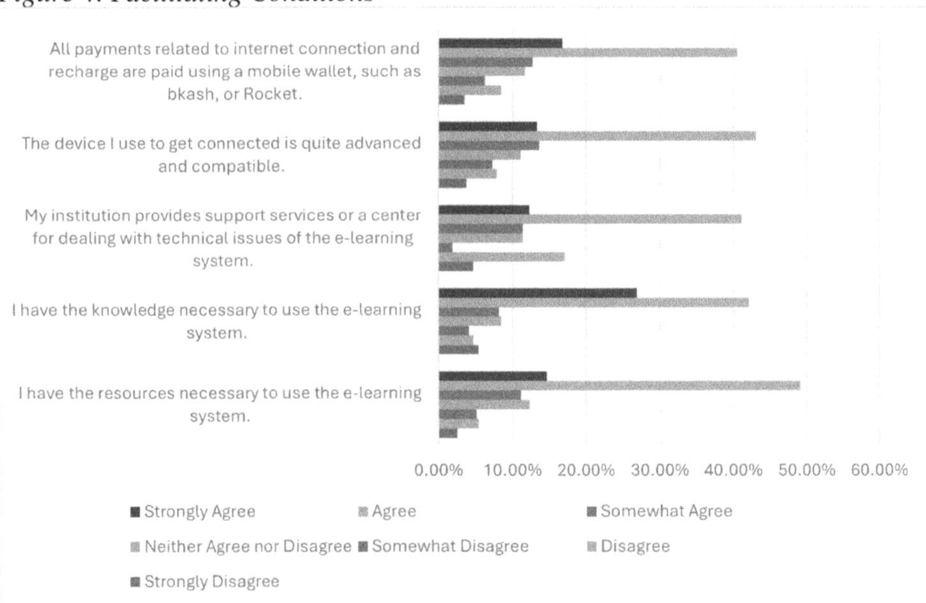

Source: Survey result

Figure 4 portrays items and scales to measure facilitating conditions for e-learning usage in Bangladesh. The respondents were asked questions related to several dimensions of facilitating conditions. The first two questions were asked to know about the availability of resources and knowledge necessary to deal with the e-learning system in Bangladesh. Most respondents shared that they retained the resources and expertise to use the system. By asking the third question, we wanted to know the degree of support provided by the institution that they were enrolled in. Around 65% of the respondents said that adequate support service was provided by the institutions. We wanted to know about the configurations of the devices learners utilized to connect. The result confirmed that the devices they used to get connected to the system were quite advanced and compatible, and approximately 70% of the respondents shared this. Around 68% of the respondents shared that they used countries' various mobile wallet services, such as bKash and Rocket, to pay all payments related to connectivity, recharge, etc. In conclusion, the use of e-learning in Bangladesh was facilitated by the institutions.

Information Quality

"Information quality refers to the quality of information produced by a system." (DeLone & McLean, 2003). Information quality is theorized as the process of storing and providing information in such a way that is accessible to the users, has ease of operation, and is secure (Lee, Strong, Kahn, & Wang, 2002). In a study, it was found that the information quality is positively influenced by system quality (Gorla, Somers, & Wong, 2010).

Figure 5. Information quality

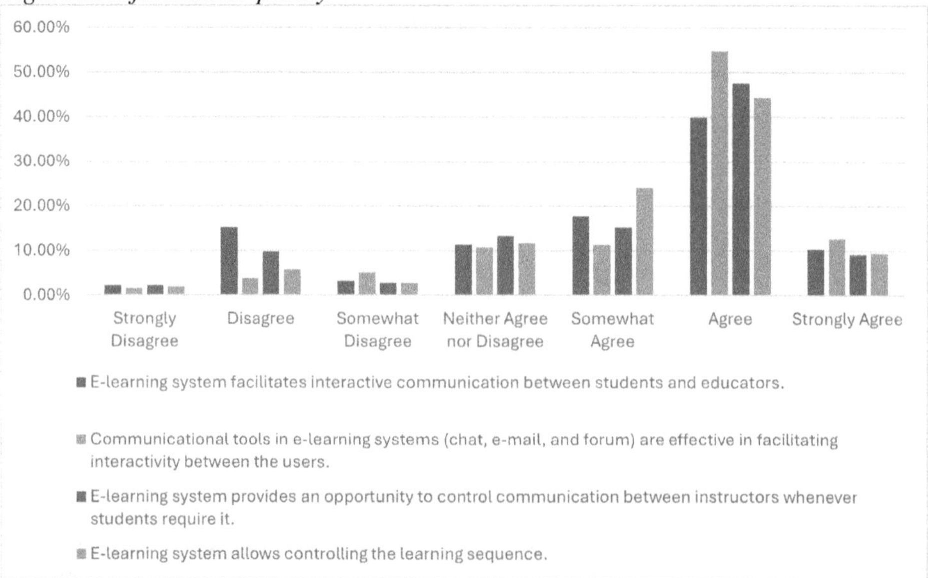

Source: Survey result

Figure 5 comprises four items to measure the information quality of a system used in Bangladesh. By asking the first question, we wanted to know the degree of ease users enjoy when interacting. The result shows that almost two-thirds of learners agreed the system was flexible and was not difficult to interact with. Interaction between learners and educators took place with less difficulty. The second question was asked to measure the effectiveness of the learning management tool in easing interaction. The majority (80%) confirmed that those tools, such as chat, e-mail, and forum were much more effective in expediting interaction. 70% of the respondents said that e-learning provided the opportunity to control communication between instructors whenever students require it. E-learning allowed the users to control the sequence and was confirmed by 80% of the respondents. In conclusion, accessibility was not an issue in using e-learning in Bangladesh. The system provided enough support in dealing with academic activities.

Performance Expectancy

"Performance expectancy is the degree to which users believe that using technology will help him or her to attain goals."(Venkatesh et al., 2003). The variable perceived usefulness was conceptualized as performance expectancy in various studies (Utomo, Kurniasari, & Purnamaningsih, 2021).

Figure 6. Performance expectancy

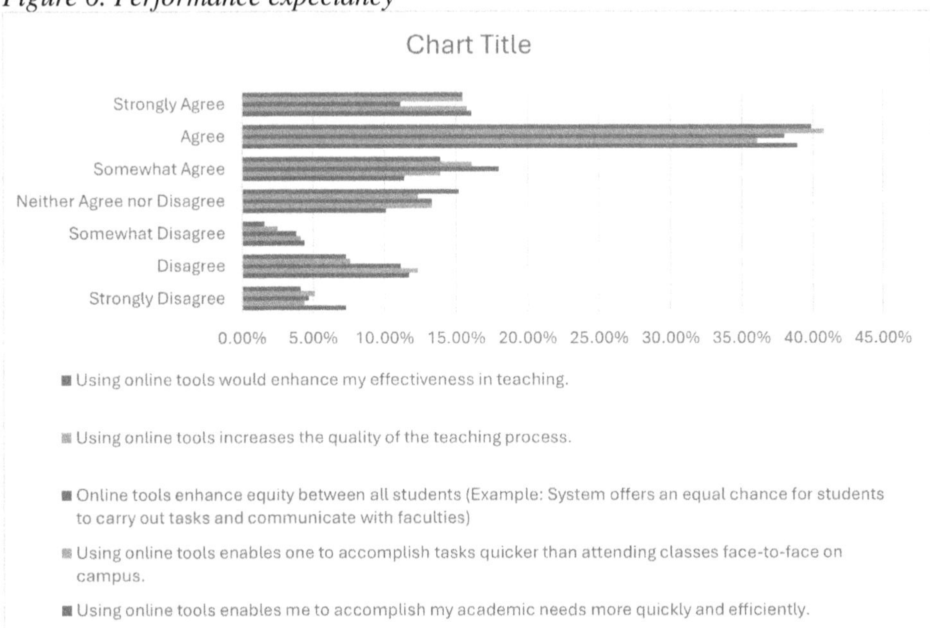

Source: Survey result

Performance expectancy is the degree to which people perceive that using related technology will help them to reap more benefits.

According to a learner, "An online education system is a tremendous way to mitigate the digital divide, it will be helpful for most of the students who have problems with affordability in urban areas. Besides, it will also help me gain more knowledge at the academic and corporate levels."

To measure the performance expectancy of e-learning, we asked the respondents a range of questions. As shown in Figure 6, the majority (70%) said that the tools enabled them to accomplish their academic needs more quickly and efficiently. 65% of the respondents shared that e-learning tools enabled them to accomplish academic tasks quicker than attending classes held face-to-face on campus. In terms of maintaining equity, online tools were proven much more effective offering an equal chance for students to carry out tasks and communicate with faculties, and this was shared by 70% of the respondents. Online tools increased the quality and learning process and tools would enhance the effectiveness of learning, shared by almost 70% of the respondents. In conclusion, the benefits of using e-learning were well understood by the users.

Effort Expectancy

"Effort expectancy is the degree to which users think that using technology will be easy and free from hassle." (Venkatesh et al., 2003). It is the level of sophistication a user expects when using a system, which may lead to higher acceptance (Utomo et al., 2021).

Table 1. Effort expectancy

	Strongly Disagree	**Disagree**	**Somewhat Disagree**	**Neither Agree nor Disagree**	**Somewhat Agree**	**Agree**	**Strongly Agree**
Learning to operate the e-learning tool (e.g., MS Team, Google Classroom, Moodle) is easy for me.	2.8%	3.2%	1.6%	10.1%	13.3%	44.0%	25%
My interaction with the tool (e.g., MS team) is clear and understandable.	3.5%	3.2%	1.3%	7.6%	12.7%	50.0%	28.8%
I would find the systems easy to use.	3.5%	3.5%	1.3%	8.9%	11.4%	49.7%	21.8%

continued on following page

Table 1. Continued

	Strongly Disagree	Disagree	Somewhat Disagree	Neither Agree nor Disagree	Somewhat Agree	Agree	Strongly Agree
It is easy for me to become skillful in using the systems	2.8%	4.7%	1.9%	10.8%	14.2%	45.9%	19.6%
I would find it easy to get the online systems to do what I want it to do.	3.2%	8.5%	2.2%	11.4%	11.6%	46.5%	13.6%

Source: Survey result

We wanted to know the level of sophistication one had when the system was in use by the users. Almost 85% of the respondents shared that it was easy for them to learn the technicalities.

According to the respondent, "The online education system is increasing day by day and its importance is highly recognized. Many students became confident and experts in using the system as it can build a sense of confidence among the students."

As shown in Table 1, the majority (90%) of the respondents said that their interaction with the tool was clear and understandable. Around 80% of the respondents found the system easy. Learners became skillful in using the system and they found it easy to go online to do what they wanted to do. In conclusion, learning to use the system was easy for the users.

Social Influence

"Social influence is the degree to which users prioritize the viewpoints of other users when using a system." (Venkatesh et al., 2003). A study identified that social influence is directly associated with behavioral intention to use a system (Abbad, 2021).

Figure 7. Social influence

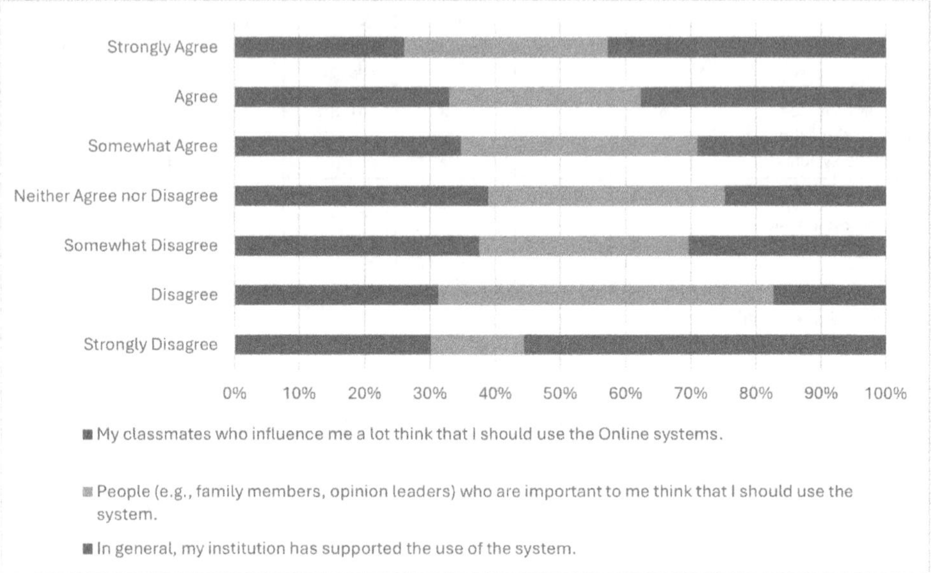

Source: Survey result

As illustrated in Figure 7, the social influence of a community was measured by three statements. The respondents were influenced by the members of the reference groups classified as primary or secondary. The majority (65%) of the respondents said that they were influenced by their classmates to use the online system. Half of the respondents opined that they were induced by family members with whom they had more interaction. 75% of the respondents stated that they were supported by their institutions in all aspects, such as providing training facilities and dedicated support services, arranging user-friendly and industry-standard e-learning tools, availing data packages at a reduced rate, etc. In conclusion, society was quite supportive of using e-learning as users received positive support from the community.

Self-efficacy

The presence of technical knowledge is sometimes referred to as self-efficacy. "Self-efficacy is the degree to which an individual believes that she or he can perform a specific job using computer or mobile devices." (Venkatesh, Thong, & Xu, 2012).

Figure 8. Self-efficacy

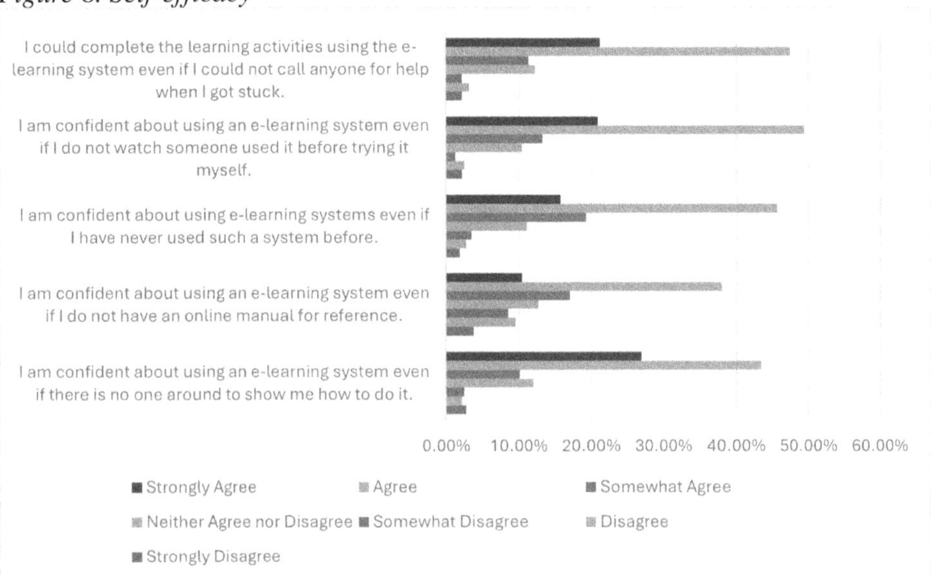

Source: Survey result

The community was found to be highly active as the level of confidence in dealing with the system was measured high. 80% of the respondents argued that they would use the system if no one was around them to show how to use the system.

> *A learner commented that "an online education system or e-learning system is appreciable. A dull student can enrich his skills and knowledge on a subject by interacting online with peers and embedded features."*

As shown in Figure 8, most of the respondents (60%) stated that they would run the system if there was no online manual or book to inform them about the functionality of the system. In conclusion, computer and mobile phone self-efficacy had a tremendous impact on the adoption of e-learning.

CONCLUSION

The transformative impact of e-learning in developing countries has been incredible. HEIs embraced various tools, platforms, and initiatives to facilitate e-learning. What was once disputed has now become an integral part of Bangladeshi education. The transition was even fueled by initiative-taking measures, such as investing in ICT infrastructure, faculty training programs, and partnerships started by several private HEIs along with the initiatives imposed by the government. Unlike other countries, the pandemic taught Bangladeshi HEIs how to impart knowledge in a pandemic situation where educational institutions are forced to shut down on-campus operations. Various platforms of e-learning ranging from free options to more sophisticated commercial platforms played pivotal roles in ensuring accessibility and engagement providing rich and personalized learning. At one extreme, those applications ease the way of teaching, while at the other extreme, applications empower people. Moreover, HEIs offered a range of facilities and schemes to hasten the transition. Despite challenges, such as technical and economic challenges brought about by the pandemic, learners showed a resilient attitude towards e-learning.

Learners had essential knowledge and skills in dealing with e-learning tools because they had been exposed to computers and mobile phones. Learners possess an elevated level of self-esteem in dealing with technicalities without any intervention. Learners' interactions with the tools were clear and understandable, which supported self-paced learning. The penetration rate is triggered by the initiatives adopted by internet service providers (ISPs) providing flawless speedy internet connection at a reduced rate. Also, learners used advanced devices that were compatible, and the issues, such as subscription and recharge managed by the convenient mobile wallet platforms. Due to its benefits and accessibility, learners are committed to using e-learning in the future.

The combined initiatives enforced the widespread adoption of e-learning tools and platforms across the country. In addition, the inclusion of mobile-friendly solutions and round-the-clock support services has propelled the adoption of e-learning in Bangladesh. However, the establishment requires ongoing investment in technology, pedagogical innovation, support services, and continued collaboration between HEIs and industry partners. From the lessons learned during the pandemic, the HEIs can continue to harness the power of remote learning to propel a more sustainable and inclusive education system. The study proposes the following policies for implementation in the new normal in hopes of enhancing the retention rate in Bangladesh.

1. A proper culture of conducting and attending classes online should be cultivated within the institution to support learning online.
2. HEIs should invest heavily in the infrastructure development that supports online education.
3. Online education becomes effective when the HEIs supply the necessary tools, such as devices, connectivity, and software.
4. The more interesting and engaging the content is, the easier it is for students to understand and learn.
5. E-learning systems should be dynamic so that learners can get a chance to add creativity to this system.
6. Every classroom should have the necessary hardware so students can access resources shared online.

7. Seminars and workshops on e-learning usage should be arranged regularly.
8. Sufficient support services should be provided to support the continuity of learning online.
9. The organization's mission and vision should be attuned to e-learning to reap the maximum benefits.
10. A portion (at least 25%) of the course content should be taught online to support e-learning.

REFERENCES

Abbad, M. M. M. (2021). Using the UTAUT model to understand students' usage of e-learning systems in developing countries. *Education and Information Technologies*, 26(6), 7205–7224. DOI: 10.1007/s10639-021-10573-5 PMID: 34025204

Abbas, A., Ar, A. Y., & Hosseini, S. (2024). A global perspective of government initiatives to support higher education during the COVID-19 pandemic: A systematic review of literature. *Research in Globalization*, 8, 100202. DOI: 10.1016/j.resglo.2024.100202

About | buX. (n.d.). Retrieved June 30, 2024, from https://bux-home.bracu.ac.bd/about

Adedoyin, O. B., & Soykan, E. (2023). Covid-19 pandemic and online learning: The challenges and opportunities. *Interactive Learning Environments*, 31(2), 863–875. DOI: 10.1080/10494820.2020.1813180

Ahmed, M., Hasan, M., & Haque, A. (2021). Exploring the Challenges and Opportunities of E-Learning Platforms in Bangladesh. *Asian Journal of Multidisciplinary Studies*, 9(1), 111–120.

Ahmed, M. T. (2021). Online education in Bangladesh during Covid-19: An empirical study. *The International Journal of Social Sciences (Islamabad)*, 4(5), 172–188.

Akter, A., Munira, S., & Amin, K. (2017). Key influencing factors for adopting e-learning platforms of private University Students' in Bangladesh. *Journal of Business and Economic Development*, 2, 94–98.

Al-Emran, M. A. Al-Sharafi, & K. Shaalan (Eds.), *International Conference on Information Systems and Intelligent Applications* (pp. 227–242). Cham: Springer International Publishing. https://doi.org/DOI: 10.1007/978-3-031-16865-9_19

Al Lily, A. E.. (2020). Academic domains as political battlegrounds: A global enquiry by ninety-nine academics in the fields of education and technology. *Information Development*, 36(2), 198–223.

Al Lily, A. E., Ismail, A. F., Abunasser, F. M., Alqahtani, R., & Alabdulkareem, S. A. (2020). Distance education as a response to pandemics: Coronavirus and Arab culture. *Technology in Society*, 63, 101317. DOI: 10.1016/j.techsoc.2020.101317 PMID: 32836570

Al-Maroof, R. S., Alhumaid, K., Akour, I., & Salloum, S. (2021). Factors That Affect E-Learning Platforms after the Spread of COVID-19: Post Acceptance Study. *Data*, 6(5), 49. DOI: 10.3390/data6050049

Al-Samarraie, H., Ghazal, S., & Saeed, N. (2021). Mobile Learning Applications: A Systematic Literature Review. *Education Sciences*, 11(1), 12.

Ali, A. F., Abdullah, R. H., Hassan, A. A., Abdullahi, H. O., & Mohamed, M. M. (2024). COVID-19 Pandemic Impact on E-Learning Adoption and Its Utilization at Higher Education: A Comparative Analysis of Institutions and Students' Perspectives. *Ingénierie Des Systèmes d Information*, 29(2), 447–457. DOI: 10.18280/isi.290206

Bates, A. W. (2015). *Teaching in a digital age: Guidelines for designing teaching and learning*. BCcampus. Retrieved from https://openlibrary-repo.ecampusontario.ca/jspui/handle/123456789/276

Biswas, B., Roy, S. K., & Roy, F. (2020, June 13). *Students Perception of Mobile Learning During COVID-19 in Bangladesh: University Student Perspective* [SSRN Scholarly Paper]. Rochester, NY. Retrieved from https://papers.ssrn.com/abstract=3667908

Brown, A. (2019). *Personalized e-learning: The future of education*. Routledge.

Chao, L. N.. (2021). Digital literacy and the digital divide: The role of organizational digital citizenship and social support. *Computers in Human Behavior*, 115, 106637.

Chen, L.. (2022). The impacts of e-learning on social interactions among students: A systematic review. *Computers & Education*, 174, 104345.

Chowdhury, N. H., Hossain, M. S., & Ahmed, S. (2019). Challenges of E-Learning in Higher Education: Evidence from Bangladesh. *International Journal of Education and Development Using Information and Communication Technology*, 15(3), 144–155.

Dawson, S. (2006). A study of the relationship between student communication interaction and sense of community. *The Internet and Higher Education*, 9(3), 153–162. DOI: 10.1016/j.iheduc.2006.06.007

DeLone, W., & McLean, E. (2003). The DeLone and McLean Model of Information Systems Success: A Ten-Year Update. *Journal of Management Information Systems*, 19(4), 9–30. DOI: 10.1080/07421222.2003.11045748

Eltahir, M. E. (2019). E-Learning in developing countries: Is it a panacea? A case study of Sudan. *IEEE Access : Practical Innovations, Open Solutions*, 7, 97784–97792. DOI: 10.1109/ACCESS.2019.2930411

Garcia, M. (2020). Addressing the digital divide: Strategies for equitable access to e-learning. *Journal of Educational Technology & Society*, 23(3), 179–191.

Garcia, M. (2020). Collaborative Approaches to Online Education: Lessons from the COVID-19 Pandemic. *Higher Education Research & Development*, 39(5), 987–995.

Gilleard, C. (2020). Bourdieu's forms of capital and the stratification of later life. *Journal of Aging Studies*, 53, 100851. DOI: 10.1016/j.jaging.2020.100851 PMID: 32487342

Gorla, N., Somers, T. M., & Wong, B. (2010). Organizational impact of system quality, information quality, and service quality. *The Journal of Strategic Information Systems*, 19(3), 207–228. DOI: 10.1016/j.jsis.2010.05.001

Hämäläinen, T., & Vähäkangas, M. (2021). Creating Interactive Video Lectures with H5P: A Tool for Enhancing Active Learning in Online Courses. *International Journal of Information and Communication Technology Education*, 17(1), 32–43.

Haque, M. Z., Sadeek, M. A., & Rahman, M. M. (2020). Online Learning Amidst COVID-19 Pandemic: A Case Study of Higher Education in Bangladesh. *Journal of Education and e-learning Research*, 7(3), 247–258.

Hasan, M. M., Hossain, M. S., & Rahman, M. M. (2020). E-Learning Platforms in Higher Education: A Case Study of Bangladesh. *Journal of Management and Science*, 7(2), 98–107.

Hodges, C. B., Moore, S., Lockee, B. B., Trust, T., & Bond, M. A. (2020). *The difference between emergency remote teaching and online learning*.

Hrastinski, S. (2009). A theory of online learning as online participation. *Computers & Education*, 52(1), 78–82. DOI: 10.1016/j.compedu.2008.06.009

Islam, M. R., & Haque, M. M. (2020). Integrating Microsoft Teams in Higher Education: An Experience from Bangladesh. *Journal of Education and Practice*, 11(15), 19–27.

Islam, R., Hossen, M. M., & Ali, S. Y. (2022). STUDENTS' PERCEPTION ABOUT ONLINE LEARNING IN THE EDUCATION SECTOR DURING COVID-19: A STUDY ON THE DIFFERENT EDUCATIONAL INSTITUTIONS OF BANGLADESH. *Journal of Business Studies*, 199.

Jones, R. (2021). Cost-effectiveness analysis of e-learning versus traditional classroom learning. *International Journal of Educational Technology in Higher Education*, 18(1), 1–15.

Kabir, M. H., Chowdhury, M. T., & Roy, M. K. (2019). Exploring the Role of Khan Academy in Improving E-Learning in Bangladesh. International Journal of Management. *IT and Engineering*, 9(3), 401–414.

Khatun, F. (2020, July 27). Making Online Education Effective. The Daily Star.

Kumar, S., & Daniel, B. K. (2016). Integration of learning technologies into teaching within Fijian Polytechnic Institutions. *International Journal of Educational Technology in Higher Education*, 13(1), 36. DOI: 10.1186/s41239-016-0036-8

Lee, Y. W., Strong, D. M., Kahn, B. K., & Wang, R. Y. (2002). AIMQ: A methodology for information quality assessment. *Information & Management*, 40(2), 133–146. DOI: 10.1016/S0378-7206(02)00043-5

Loades, M. E., Chatburn, E., Higson-Sweeney, N., Reynolds, S., Shafran, R., Brigden, A., Linney, C., McManus, M. N., Borwick, C., & Crawley, E. (2020). Rapid systematic review: The impact of social isolation and loneliness on the mental health of children and adolescents in the context of COVID-19. *Journal of the American Academy of Child and Adolescent Psychiatry*, 59(11), 1218–1239. DOI: 10.1016/j.jaac.2020.05.009 PMID: 32504808

Luo, J., Deng, L., & Wan, J. (2021). The Influence of COVID-19 on Chinese College Students' Attitudes toward Online Learning. *Educational Technology Research and Development*, 69(2), 783–803.

Mabey, C., & Ramsey, J. (2020). Teaching and Learning Online with Zoom. *Journal of Chemical Education*, 97(9), 3257–3259.

Mahardika, H., Thomas, D., Ewing, M. T., & Japutra, A. (2019). Experience and facilitating conditions as impediments to consumers' new technology adoption. *International Review of Retail, Distribution and Consumer Research*, 29(1), 79–98. DOI: 10.1080/09593969.2018.1556181

Maisha, K., & Shetu, S. N. (2023). Influencing factors of e-learning adoption amongst students in a developing country: The post-pandemic scenario in Bangladesh. *Future Business Journal*, 9(1), 37. DOI: 10.1186/s43093-023-00214-3

Means, B., & Neisler, J. (2020). *Suddenly online: A national survey of undergraduates during the COVID-19 pandemic*. Digital Promise. Retrieved from Digital Promise website:https://digitalpromise.dspacedirect.org/bitstream/20.500.12265/98/3/DPSuddenlyOnlineReportJuly2020.pdf

Means, B., Toyama, Y., Murphy, R., Bakia, M., & Jones, K. (2013). *Evaluation of Evidence-Based Practices in Online Learning: A Meta-Analysis and Review of Online Learning Studies*. US Department of Education.

Mercer, N. (1995). *The guided construction of knowledge: Talk amongst teachers and learners*. Multilingual matters. DOI: 10.21832/9781800418288

Moore, M. G. (1989, January 1). Editorial: Three types of interaction [Editorial]. DOI: 10.1080/08923648909526659

Poddubnaya, T. N., Zadneprovskaya, E. L., Voevodina, S. S., Ilyinova, N. A., Khatit, F. R., & Panina, E. A. (2021). Distance Learning Experience in the Context of Globalization of Education. *Journal of Educational Psychology - Propositos y Representaciones, 9*. Retrieved from https://eric.ed.gov/?id=EJ1299286

Rafa, A. T. (2024, February 18). Paving way for a more inclusive Bangladesh. Retrieved May 4, 2024, from The Daily Star website: https://www.thedailystar.net/anniversary-supplement-2024/innovate-educate-elevate/news/paving-the-way-more-inclusive-bangladesh-3545126

Rahman, M. M., Hossain, M. S., & Islam, M. R. (2017). An Assessment of E-Learning Readiness in Higher Education: Evidence from Bangladesh. *International Journal of Engineering and Science Invention*, 6(3), 30–35.

Sarker, M. F. H., Mahmud, R. A., Islam, M. S., & Islam, M. K. (2019). Use of e-learning at higher educational institutions in Bangladesh: Opportunities and challenges. *Journal of Applied Research in Higher Education*, 11(2), 210–223. DOI: 10.1108/JARHE-06-2018-0099

Selwyn, N. (2020). The digital divide: Beyond access. The International Encyclopedia of Digital Communication and Society, 1-11.

Shahryar, S. S. (2021, April 21). The realities of online education in Bangladesh. The Daily Star.

Siron, Y., Wibowo, A., & Narmaditya, B. S. (2020). Factors affecting the adoption of e-learning in Indonesia: Lesson from Covid-19. *Journal of Technology and Science Education*, 10(2), 282. DOI: 10.3926/jotse.1025

Smith, J. (2020). The benefits of online learning: A comparative analysis. *Journal of Online Learning and Teaching*, 16(2), 1–12.

Taylor, S., & Todd, P. (1995). Decomposition and crossover effects in the theory of planned behavior: A study of consumer adoption intentions. *International Journal of Research in Marketing*, 12(2), 137–155. DOI: 10.1016/0167-8116(94)00019-K

Tyagi, S. K., & Krishankumar, R. (2023). Examining interactions of factors affecting e-learning adoption in higher education: Insights from a fuzzy set qualitative and comparative analysis. *Journal of Science and Technology Policy Management, ahead-of-print*(ahead-of-print). https://doi.org/DOI: 10.1108/JSTPM-02-2023-0022

Uddin, M. M., Ghosh, A., & Isaac, O. (2019). Impact of the system, information, and service quality of online learning on user satisfaction among public universities students in Bangladesh. [IJMHS]. *International Journal of Management and Human Science*, 3(2), 1–10.

UNESCO. (2020). COVID-19 Educational Disruption and Response. Retrieved from https://en.unesco.org/covid19/educationresponse

UNESCO. (2021). Education in the time of COVID-19—UNESCO Digital Library. Retrieved April 23, 2024, from https://unesdoc.unesco.org/ark:/48223/pf0000374075_eng

Utomo, P., Kurniasari, F., & Purnamaningsih, P. (2021). The effects of performance expectancy, effort expectancy, facilitating condition, and habit on behavior intention in using mobile healthcare application. *International Journal of Community Service & Engagement*, 2(4), 183–197. DOI: 10.47747/ijcse.v2i4.529

Vygotsky, L. S. (1978). *Mind in society: The development of higher psychological processes* (Vol. 86). Harvard university press.

KEY TERMS AND DEFINITIONS

Asynchronous Learning: A type of learning where learning does not occur in real-time allowing learners to access content, to participate in discussions at their schedule.

Blended Learning: An instructional mode combining traditional face-to-face and techno-mediated learning aiming to optimize the learning experience through direct and digital engagement.

Content Creation Platforms: Content creation platforms, such as Articulate Storyline, Adobe Captivate, and H5P are designed to support educators in designing interactive and gamified educational content aspiring student involvement and motivation in a techno-mediated learning environment.

Learning Management System (LMS): LMS platforms, such as Moodle, Canvas, Blackboard, etc. are engagement-based progress-tracking tools through which users can manage, track, and deliver educational content online.

Mobile Bases Learning: A training software, i.e., Khan Academy, Duolingo, and Coursera that provides flexible on-demand learning solutions on mobile devices encouraging self-directed and micro-learning mechanisms.

MOOC (Massive Open Online Course): A type of open access and free resources, such as Coursera, edX, Udemy, etc. that supports large-scale online participation and is offered to a wide audience.

Synchronous Learning: A type of techno-mediated learning in which learners and educators get involved in lectures (live), interactive discussions, and other activities at the same time in real-time mode

Video Conferencing Tools: Video conferencing tools, such as Zoom, Microsoft Teams, and Google Meet enable synchronous and real-time interaction between learners and educators.

Chapter 5
AI-Supported VR in Education:
Learning Analytics, Interactions, and Ethical Bias

Ali Geris
https://orcid.org/0000-0003-2136-5490
Manisa Celal Bayar University, Turkey

Baris Cukurbasi
https://orcid.org/0000-0002-2856-2676
Manisa Celal Bayar University, Turkey

ABSTRACT

This book chapter examines the integration of virtual reality and artificial intelligence technologies in the field of education. While the integration of AI-based content, analysis, and feedback systems into educational VR environments presents a significant opportunity, it also brings various challenges, including privacy, data security, social equity, and ethical issues. The chapter addresses the effects of AI-supported VR applications on teacher-student interactions and pedagogical outcomes across different educational levels. Additionally, it evaluates predictions and potential scenarios for the future use of these technologies in education. Finally, the chapter provides strategic recommendations to address the challenges encountered in the integration of AI and VR in education, offering guidance on the ethical and effective use of these technologies. By providing a comprehensive guide for educators, policymakers, and developers, this chapter offers valuable insights into managing digital transformation processes and utilizing these technologies to enhance learning experiences.

DOI: 10.4018/979-8-3693-6030-9.ch005

INTRODUCTION

The implementation of Virtual Reality (VR) technologies in education has been growing, offering students immersive and interactive learning experiences. VR's interactive capabilities facilitate the understanding of complex concepts and ideas that are challenging to physically demonstrate, while also accelerating cognitive processes (Marougkas et al., 2023; Han, 2023). Recent research shows that VR significantly enhances student motivation, learning outcomes, and engagement (Algerafi et al., 2023; Esposito et al., 2023). Pedagogical approaches such as constructivist learning, experiential learning, and problem-solving have been effectively integrated into VR applications to improve learners' knowledge acquisition (Marougkas et al., 2023). However, challenges like access to VR technologies, high costs, and ethical considerations remain (Lai et al., 2021). Successfully integrating these technologies into educational settings with appropriate approaches is crucial for enhancing student motivation (Han, 2023).

The integration of VR environments in education, combined with the rapid development of Artificial Intelligence (AI)-supported content analysis and feedback systems, marks a significant advancement in educational technology. While AI has the potential to deliver personalized learning experiences, the strategies for integrating AI with VR present substantial challenges. AI-based VR environments must be adaptable to assess individual student needs and provide suitable content while also being versatile in data collection, analysis, and feedback processes (Vassigh et al., 2023). Developing AI-supported adaptive learning systems using machine learning (ML) algorithms involves challenges in complex data processing and content creation (Wang, 2023). It is imperative for educators and developers to correctly integrate pedagogical strategies and align the technology with learning objectives (Amin et al., 2023). Moreover, addressing data privacy, accessibility, and ethical principles is paramount in integrating AI-based content into educational VR environments (Tiwari, 2023). Despite these challenges, AI-supported educational VR environments offer a significant opportunity to revolutionize learning experiences.

AI-supported VR environments have the potential to significantly transform teacher-student interactions and pedagogical practices by increasing student engagement and personalizing learning processes. However, delivering AI-based content and feedback systems to students is a complex task. These technologies significantly contribute to students' learning processes, necessitating that teachers develop new strategies. Studies examining the pedagogical outcomes of AI-supported VR environments across various educational levels indicate that the technology generally enhances learning outcomes and increases motivation.

Research at the higher education level shows that personalized course content provided through AI-VR can be tailored to students' interests and needs, thereby enhancing learning outcomes and satisfaction (Yu & Xu, 2022; Geriş & Özdener, 2024). Consequently, the topic of learning analytics in creating adaptive learning environments is highlighted. The potential of AI-VR environments to personalize content according to the user and facilitate self-directed learning is undeniable. Additionally, AI-VR is recognized as an effective tool for enhancing students' imagination and fostering creative thinking (Rong et al., 2022). Despite the increased interest and motivation towards VR experiences among students, further research is needed to ascertain the long-term effects of these technologies (Jiang & Fryer, 2023). Moreover, it is essential to provide pedagogical guidance to educators on integrating AI-VR technologies in alignment with learning outcomes.

In summary, this book chapter provides an in-depth analysis of the integration of AI and VR technologies in the educational, examining their pedagogical impacts and interactions while addressing the challenges and opportunities these technologies present. The chapter also investigates fundamental issues related to privacy, data security, social equity, accessibility, and ethics in AI and VR integration, offering strategic solutions to these challenges. Predictions and potential scenarios for the future use of these technologies in educational settings are evaluated in the context of current research and practices. This chapter aims to provide educators, policymakers, and technology developers with insights and guidance on maximizing the potential of AI and VR technologies in education. Thus, readers will gain a deeper understanding of how to use AI and VR technologies ethically and effectively and how to manage digital transformation processes in education.

Aim

The primary aim of this book chapter is to explore the integration of AI and VR technologies in educational settings, emphasizing their potential to enhance education. This chapter seeks to comprehensively address the pedagogical impacts of AI and VR technologies, their influence on teacher-student interactions, and fundamental issues such as ethics and data security. Additionally, it evaluates future potential usage scenarios. In line with these objectives, the chapter investigates the integration strategies for AI-based content analysis and feedback systems within educational VR environments. It examines the impacts of AI-based VR on pedagogy and teacher-student interactions, evaluates the pedagogical outcomes of AI-supported VR applications across different educational levels and disciplines, and analyzes predictions and potential usage scenarios for AI-supported VR technologies in educational settings over the coming years. Furthermore, it identifies fundamental issues related to privacy, data security, social equity, accessibility, and ethics in AI and VR integration, offering relevant recommendations. By achieving these aims, this book chapter aspires to provide insights and strategic guidance to enhance the understanding of AI and VR technology integration in education. It seeks to equip educators, policymakers, and technology developers with the knowledge necessary to effectively and ethically manage the digital transformation processes in education.

INTEGRATION OF AI AND VR TECHNOLOGIES IN EDUCATION

Integration of Educational VR Environments in Education and Data Collection Processes

The incorporation of VR technologies into educational settings has become increasingly widespread, providing students with interactive and immersive learning experiences. These technologies enhance the understanding of complex concepts and ideas that are difficult to physically demonstrate, thereby accelerating cognitive processes and improving learning outcomes (Marougkas et al., 2023; Han, 2023). Effective integration of VR into education requires strategic approaches and efficient management of data collection processes, which are crucial for maximizing the potential advantages of VR in educational contexts.

One essential strategy for integrating VR into educational environments is the adoption of constructivist learning paradigms. Constructivist learning emphasizes the significance of active student participation in the knowledge construction process, a principle that VR technologies inherently support. By employing experiential learning and problem-solving pedagogies, VR can create interactive and engaging educational experiences (Marougkas et al., 2023). For instance, research in healthcare education has demonstrated VR's effectiveness in developing practical skills and providing a safe learning environment (Kyaw et al., 2019). Additionally, social constructivist approaches, which aim to enhance empathy and social interactions, can be integrated into VR environments to cultivate these competencies among students (Muravevskaia & Gardner-Mccune, 2022).

Constructivist learning approaches leverage students' active involvement in their educational journeys. This methodology encourages learners to construct new knowledge based on their prior experiences, facilitating meaningful learning. VR technologies serve as powerful tools in this endeavor. For example, in history education, VR enables students to experience historical events in a virtual setting, fostering a deeper understanding of the subject matter. Furthermore, collaborative learning environments facilitated by VR promote collective knowledge construction among students (Fox-Turnbull & Snape, 2011).

Data collection within educational VR environments is crucial for analyzing and enhancing learning processes. Utilizing head-mounted displays (HMDs) and other sensors, educators can gather real-time interaction data from students engaged in VR activities (Prakash & Rajendran, 2022). This data provides valuable insights into student behaviors and learning patterns, enabling educators to tailor instructional strategies and improve educational outcomes. Hence, effective data collection mechanisms are critical for the successful integration of VR in education. To ensure the effective integration of VR into educational settings, several strategic considerations must be addressed:

1. Alignment with Pedagogical Goals: VR technologies should be seamlessly integrated with pedagogical goals and learning outcomes. This alignment ensures that the use of technology enhances the educational experience and fulfills the intended learning objectives (Amin et al., 2023).
2. User-Centered Design: VR applications must be designed to accommodate the diverse needs and learning styles of students. Incorporating feedback loops and adaptive learning systems can significantly enhance user experience and educational effectiveness (Vassigh et al., 2023).
3. Accessibility and Ethical Considerations: It is crucial to increase the accessibility of VR technologies and address ethical concerns such as data privacy and security. Ensuring equitable access to these technologies for all students is essential for their widespread adoption and success (Tiwari, 2023).
4. Long-Term Impact Research: Extensive research is needed to understand the long-term impacts of VR technologies in education. This research will help develop sustainable and effective VR-based educational practices (Jiang & Fryer, 2023).

The integration of educational VR environments and the meticulous management of data collection processes hold significant potential to enhance student engagement and learning outcomes. By implementing appropriate strategies and ensuring efficient data collection, educators can maximize the benefits of VR in educational contexts (Pugachova, 2023). Collaboration among educators, researchers, and technology developers is essential to fully realize the transformative potential of VR technologies in education.

Integration of AI into VR Content and Feedback Systems

The integration of AI into VR environments holds substantial promise for enhancing educational experiences through personalized content delivery and advanced feedback mechanisms. This section explores the current state of AI integration in VR, focusing on the impact of AI on content creation and feedback systems, strategies for effective integration, and potential future developments in this field.

AI has revolutionized content generation in VR by utilizing ML and reinforcement learning (RL) algorithms to create adaptive and personalized educational materials. Procedural content generation (PCG) methods enhanced by AI can automatically produce both textual and non-textual content, such as practice questions, quizzes, and immersive VR learning environments (Wang, 2023). These AI-driven techniques significantly improve the efficiency and effectiveness of educational interventions by tailoring content to individual learner needs (Wang, 2023). The application of natural language processing (NLP) and ML algorithms in generating educational VR content has shown promising results, although challenges in developing high-quality and effective content persist. Additionally, it is crucial to consider technical parameters such as frames per second (FPS), latency, and batch values, which significantly influence the performance and user experience in VR environments (Geris et al., 2024).

The integration of AI in VR feedback systems enhances the learning experience by providing real-time personalized feedback to learners. Traditional feedback mechanisms often suffer from delays, limiting their effectiveness in facilitating immediate improvement. AI-powered systems, however, deliver instant feedback, allowing learners to quickly identify and correct mistakes, thereby enhancing their performance and engagement (Rakya, 2023). Studies have demonstrated the benefits of AI in providing nuanced feedback that adapts to the learner's progress and needs, promoting a more supportive and responsive learning environment (Rakya, 2023).

Effective integration of AI into VR content and feedback systems requires strategic approaches that consider the unique capabilities and limitations of these technologies. Key strategies include:

1. Personalization and Adaptivity: AI algorithms should be designed to analyze learner data and adapt content and feedback in real-time. This ensures that the educational material is always relevant and challenging, meeting the specific needs of each student (Wang, 2023).
2. Interactivity and Immersion: Combining AI with VR's immersive capabilities can create highly interactive learning experiences. For example, AI can generate dynamic scenarios based on learner interactions, enhancing the sense of presence and engagement (Inkarbekov et al., 2023).
3. Ethical Considerations and Data Privacy: Integrating AI in educational VR environments necessitates careful consideration of ethical issues and data privacy. Systems must be designed to protect sensitive learner information and ensure that AI algorithms are transparent and fair (Lim, Gottipati & Cheong, 2023).

4. Multimodal Feedback: Leveraging AI to provide multimodal feedback—combining visual, auditory, and haptic cues—can significantly enhance the learning experience. Studies have shown that incorporating haptic feedback in VR environments improves skill acquisition and retention, particularly in fields like medical training (Yin et al., 2020).

Recent research highlights the potential of AI to transform VR education through innovative content generation and feedback systems. For instance, AI-driven VR applications in healthcare education have successfully created realistic and adaptive training environments that improve learning outcomes (Ghaednia et al., 2021). Additionally, the integration of AI in VR gaming has provided deeper immersion and interactivity, which can be translated into educational contexts to make learning more engaging (Xi, 2020).

Looking ahead, future research should focus on refining AI algorithms to produce even higher-quality educational content and exploring new applications of AI in VR. Developing more sophisticated models and addressing current challenges such as high data complexity and ethical concerns will be crucial for advancing this field. Moreover, fostering collaboration between educators, technologists, and policymakers can help ensure that AI-powered VR systems are effectively integrated into educational practices (Bassyouni & Elhajj, 2021).

The integration of AI into VR content and feedback systems represents a significant advancement in educational technology. By personalizing learning experiences and providing real-time adaptive feedback, AI enhances the effectiveness of VR as an educational tool. Strategic integration, combined with ongoing research and ethical considerations, will be essential for maximizing the potential of these technologies in transforming education.

Development of AI-Supported VR Learning Systems

The integration of AI into VR learning systems signifies a substantial advancement in educational technology. AI-supported VR learning systems enhance the educational experience by providing personalized content, adaptive feedback, and immersive learning environments. Systematic design approaches to VR-based learning activities have shown that interactive and participatory presentation of teaching materials can significantly boost students' knowledge acquisition and learning motivation (Heinemann, 2022). This section delves into the importance of

AI-VR integration, its benefits, current implementations, and future development pathways for these systems.

AI-supported VR learning systems are pivotal for several reasons. Primarily, they offer personalized learning experiences by adapting content to meet individual learner needs. AI algorithms, such as ML and reinforcement learning (RL), analyze learner data and adjust the VR environment, accordingly, ensuring that each student receives tailored educational content (Wang, 2023). Additionally, these systems enhance engagement and motivation by creating interactive and immersive learning experiences that surpass traditional methods (Oliveira et al., 2021).

The integration of AI in VR learning systems brings numerous benefits. Personalized content delivery is among the most significant advantages, as AI can generate adaptive learning materials that cater to the unique needs of each learner. This customization can significantly improve learning outcomes by addressing individual strengths and weaknesses (Wang, 2023). Moreover, AI-driven feedback systems provide real-time, nuanced feedback that helps learners continuously correct mistakes and improve performance (Rakya, 2023).

Furthermore, AI-supported VR systems can simulate complex scenarios and environments that are challenging to replicate in traditional educational settings. This capability is particularly beneficial in fields such as medical and technical education, where practical experience is crucial (Ghaednia et al., 2021). The immersive nature of VR, combined with the adaptive intelligence of AI, creates a rich learning environment that enhances both cognitive and practical skills.

Several studies have explored the integration of AI and VR in educational contexts. For instance, in healthcare education, AI-driven VR systems have been used to create realistic training environments that improve students' practical skills and knowledge retention (Kyaw et al., 2019). In language learning, AI algorithms analyze learner interactions to provide personalized feedback and adaptive content, enhancing language acquisition and cultural understanding (Rebolledo Font de la Vall & González Araya, 2023).

The use of AI in VR gaming also provides insights into educational applications. AI can analyze players' physiological and psychological responses to tailor the game environment, improving engagement and learning outcomes (Xi, 2020). These applications demonstrate the versatility and potential of AI-supported VR systems across various educational fields. To develop effective AI-supported VR learning systems, several factors must be considered:

1. Advanced AI Algorithms: Developing sophisticated AI algorithms that can accurately analyze learner data and adapt the VR environment in real-time is essential. This includes improving NLP and ML techniques to generate high-quality educational content (Wang, 2023).

2. Interactivity and Immersion: Enhancing the interactivity and immersion of VR environments through AI-driven simulations can create more engaging learning experiences. This involves integrating advanced VR engines and sensors to effectively capture and respond to learner interactions (Inkarbekov et al., 2023).
3. Ethical and Privacy Considerations: Addressing ethical issues and ensuring data privacy is crucial for the widespread adoption of AI-supported VR systems. Developers must implement robust data protection measures and ensure that AI algorithms are transparent and fair (Tiwari, 2023).
4. Collaboration and Research: Fostering collaboration between educators, technologists, and researchers can drive innovation in this field. Continuous research is needed to refine AI algorithms and explore new applications of VR in education (Bassyouni & Elhajj, 2021).

AI-supported VR learning systems represent a significant advancement in educational technology, offering personalized, immersive, and adaptive learning experiences. By leveraging advanced AI algorithms and VR technologies, these systems can enhance engagement, improve learning outcomes, and provide practical training in complex environments. Future development should focus on refining AI techniques, ensuring ethical considerations, and fostering collaboration to maximize the potential of AI-supported VR systems in education

PERSONALIZED LEARNING AND LEARNING ANALYTICS

Pedagogical Impacts and Teacher-Student Interactions

The integration of learning analytics and personalized learning in VR environments has profound pedagogical impacts, particularly in enhancing teacher-student interactions and improving educational outcomes. This section examines the existing literature on the pedagogical effects of personalized learning and learning analytics in VR environments, highlighting key findings and implications for educational practice.

Personalized learning in VR environments leverages AI and ML algorithms to tailor educational content and experiences to individual learners' needs. This approach enhances the effectiveness of VR as an educational tool by providing customized pathways that cater to each student's strengths and weaknesses. The design and evaluation of VR content creation platforms are crucial to ensuring that users have effective and interactive learning experiences. Studies have shown how VR content creation platforms can be supported by learning analytics and how user experience can be enhanced through these methods. Monitoring student performance and providing feedback using analytical tools are essential in this context. The application of personalized learning frameworks in VR has demonstrated significant improvements in student engagement and motivation, as learners receive content directly relevant to their learning goals.

The pedagogical impacts of personalized learning in VR environments are multifaceted. One significant benefit is the enhancement of declarative knowledge acquisition. Research indicates that immersive VR-based learning environments can significantly improve knowledge retention compared to traditional lecture-based instruction. The tailored nature of VR content allows for a more in-depth understanding of complex subjects, as students can interact with the material in a more meaningful way. Additionally, personalized VR learning environments promote higher levels of cognitive engagement. By adapting to individual learning styles and preferences, these systems create a more engaging and immersive educational experience. This engagement is crucial for deep learning, where students not only acquire information but also develop the ability to apply it in various contexts.

The integration of learning analytics in VR environments enhances teacher-student interactions by providing real-time insights into student performance and learning behaviors. Teachers can use these insights to tailor their instructional strategies and provide targeted support to students. The ability to monitor and analyze student interactions within the VR environment allows educators to identify areas where students may be struggling and intervene promptly. Moreover, AI-driven feedback systems in VR environments offer personalized feedback that is immediate and specific to the learner's actions. This feedback is crucial for reinforcing learning and helping students correct mistakes in real-time. The continuous loop of action and feedback in VR environments fosters a more dynamic and interactive learning process, enhancing the overall educational experience.

Several studies have highlighted the successful implementation of personalized learning and learning analytics in VR environments. For instance, in healthcare education, AI-driven VR systems have been used to create realistic training scenarios that improve practical skills and knowledge retention. These systems provide immediate feedback and adapt to the learner's performance, ensuring that training is both effective and engaging. Another example is the use of personalized VR environments in language learning, where AI algorithms analyze student interactions to provide customized feedback and adaptive content, enhancing language acquisition and cultural understanding. These implementations demonstrate the versatility and potential of personalized learning in VR across different educational fields. To further enhance the pedagogical impacts of personalized learning in VR environments, several recommendations can be made:

1. Advanced AI Algorithms: Continued development of sophisticated AI algorithms that can accurately analyze learner data and adapt VR environments in real-time is essential. This includes improving ML techniques to generate high-quality educational content (Wang, 2023).
2. Ethical Considerations and Data Privacy: Ensuring data privacy and addressing ethical issues in the use of AI in VR environments is crucial. Developers must implement robust data protection measures and ensure transparency in AI algorithms (Tiwari, 2023).
3. Interactivity and Engagement: Enhancing the interactivity and immersion of VR environments through AI-driven simulations can create more engaging learning experiences. This involves integrating advanced VR engines and sensors to capture and respond to learner interactions effectively (Inkarbekov et al., 2023).
4. Collaboration and Research: Fostering collaboration between educators, technologists, and researchers is vital for advancing this field. Ongoing research is needed to refine AI algorithms and explore new applications of VR in education (Bassyouni & Elhajj, 2021).

The integration of personalized learning and learning analytics in VR environments has significant pedagogical impacts, enhancing teacher-student interactions and improving educational outcomes. By leveraging advanced AI algorithms and VR technologies, educators can create immersive and adaptive learning experiences that cater to individual student needs. Future developments should focus on refining AI techniques, ensuring ethical considerations, and fostering collaboration to maximize the potential of these technologies in education

The Role of Learning Analytics in Adaptive VR Learning Environments

Learning analytics (LA) is integral to the enhancement of adaptive VR learning environments, providing critical insights into learner behaviors and optimizing educational interventions. This section delves into the integration of LA in adaptive VR settings, underscoring its importance, current applications, and future directions. Learning analytics encompasses the measurement, collection, analysis, and reporting of data to optimize learning processes. In adaptive VR environments, LA is pivotal in customizing educational experiences to meet individual learners' needs by continuously monitoring and analyzing their interactions within the VR space. This personalized approach ensures that content and activities are both relevant and suitably challenging for each student, thereby enhancing learning effectiveness and engagement.

An advanced method for adaptive VR-based training integrates real-time kinematic and kinetic data, along with physiological metrics from users, to customize the training experience. This method ensures alignment with the user's capabilities and performance, significantly enhancing learning outcomes. Such frameworks have been successfully implemented across various domains, including military training and healthcare education, yielding substantial improvements in learner performance and engagement. Studies indicate that VR training environments augmented with multisensory cues can notably enhance user experience and task performance. For instance, incorporating additional sensory cues in VR training heightens the realism and immersion of the learning experience, resulting in better retention and application of learned skills in real-world scenarios.

Research into the emotional value of immersive VR in education reveals that high levels of immersion positively impact learners' emotional and cognitive processes. Immersive VR fosters a sense of presence and motivation, which are crucial for effective learning. Structural equation modeling studies highlight affective and cognitive pathways through which immersion influences learning outcomes, emphasizing the need for designing VR environments that enhance these pathways. Additionally, a comprehensive study on students' textual analyses of VR content demonstrated how text analytics can be integrated into the learning process to improve performance. The study revealed that learning progress can be monitored and individualized feedback provided by automatically analyzing the texts created by students. Instructional analytics in VR environments, supported by techniques such as ML, data mining, and AI, offer significant adaptability and contributions to learning.

Further evidence from virtual classroom studies underscores the effectiveness of well-designed instructional strategies in enhancing student motivation and educational outcomes. Cukurbasi and Kiyici (2021) found that such environments significantly increase student engagement and achievement. Regal (2023) also demonstrated that the integration of VR and AI in educational applications markedly improves student performance and enriches the learning experience, with personalized and adaptive learning experiences boosting motivation and academic success.

Future research should aim to integrate more advanced learning analytics techniques, such as ML and data mining, to analyze complex learner behaviors and provide deeper insights into the learning process. As the use of LA in VR environments expands, addressing ethical issues and ensuring data privacy becomes essential. Robust data protection measures and transparent, ethical use of learner data must be implemented. Collaborative efforts among educators, technologists, and researchers are crucial for advancing adaptive VR learning environments. Interdisciplinary research can foster innovative solutions and more effective educational technologies. Additionally, more longitudinal research are necessary to evaluate the long-term effects of adaptive VR learning environments on educational outcomes, assessing not only immediate learning gains but also the retention and transfer of knowledge and skills over time.

Learning analytics is pivotal in the development and optimization of adaptive VR learning environments. By providing real-time insights into learner behaviors and preferences, LA enables the creation of personalized and engaging educational experiences. The integration of advanced analytics techniques, ethical considerations, and interdisciplinary collaboration will further enhance these environments' effectiveness, ensuring their long-term impact on education.

The Potential of AI-VR Environments for Personalized Content Delivery

The integration of AI with VR presents transformative potential in delivering personalized educational content. This synergy between AI and VR creates highly customized learning experiences that cater to individual student needs, thereby enhancing engagement, motivation, and learning outcomes. This section explores the potential of AI-VR environments for personalized content delivery, highlighting current research, applications, and future directions.

The fusion of AI into VR environments facilitates the creation of adaptive learning systems that respond to the unique needs and preferences of each learner (McInnes et al., 2023). AI algorithms, particularly those based on ML and RL, can analyze extensive datasets to generate personalized educational content. This encompasses practice questions, quizzes, and interactive VR scenarios tailored to the learner's progress and areas requiring improvement. Such personalization ensures that each learner receives content that is optimally challenging and pertinent, fostering a more effective learning experience.

PCG methods, augmented by AI, are employed to automatically produce both textual and non-textual educational content. This approach not only enhances the efficiency of content creation but also ensures that the generated material is highly relevant to the learner's needs. Empirical studies have demonstrated the efficacy of AI-driven PCG in improving student engagement and learning outcomes in VR environments. AI-driven adaptive learning systems have been implemented across various educational contexts, offering real-time customization of the learning experience. For instance, AI can adjust the difficulty level of VR scenarios based on the learner's performance, ensuring an optimal challenge that promotes continuous learning and improvement. These systems have proven to significantly enhance learning efficiency and effectiveness.

In virtual museums, AI technologies have been utilized to personalize experiences, creating tailored educational tours that align with the visitor's interests and learning goals. This approach not only heightens user engagement but also provides a richer, more informative experience. The success of these implementations underscores the broader applicability of AI-driven personalization in educational VR environments. Despite the immense potential of AI-VR integration for personalized content delivery, several challenges must be addressed:

1. Quality and Effectiveness of AI Algorithms: Developing high-quality AI algorithms that can accurately analyze learner data and generate effective educational content remains a significant challenge. Continuous research and development are needed to refine these algorithms and ensure their reliability and effectiveness.
2. Ethical Considerations and Data Privacy: The use of AI in personalized learning raises ethical concerns, particularly regarding data privacy and the potential for algorithmic bias. It is crucial to implement robust data protection measures and ensure transparency in the use of AI technologies to address these concerns.
3. Integration with Educational Practices: Successfully integrating AI-driven personalized content into traditional educational practices requires careful planning and collaboration between educators, technologists, and researchers. This integration should focus on enhancing the educational experience while maintaining pedagogical integrity.

Future research in AI-VR personalized content delivery should focus on several key areas:

1. Advanced AI Techniques: Exploring advanced AI techniques, such as deep learning and natural language processing, can enhance the ability of AI systems to understand and respond to complex learner needs. These techniques can improve the quality of personalized content and make the learning experience more immersive and engaging.
2. Longitudinal Studies: Conducting longitudinal studies to assess the long-term impact of AI-driven personalized learning in VR environments is essential. These studies can provide insights into the sustainability and effectiveness of such approaches over time.
3. Cross-Disciplinary Applications: Expanding the use of AI-VR personalization beyond traditional educational fields into areas such as healthcare, engineering, and language learning can demonstrate the versatility and effectiveness of these technologies.

The potential of AI-VR environments for personalized content delivery is vast, offering opportunities to create highly tailored and effective learning experiences. By leveraging advanced AI algorithms and VR technologies, educators can enhance engagement, improve learning outcomes, and provide personalized support to learners. Addressing the challenges and exploring new research directions will be crucial in realizing the full potential of AI-VR integration in education.

Contributions of AI-VR in Achieving Learning Objectives

The integration of AI with VR environments offers transformative possibilities for enhancing educational experiences and achieving learning objectives. This section explores the contributions of AI-VR systems in education, focusing on their impact on learning outcomes, engagement, and the development of essential skills. AI-driven VR environments significantly improve learning outcomes by providing personalized, adaptive learning experiences tailored to individual student needs. ML and RL algorithms analyze learner data to customize content, ensuring that educational materials are relevant and appropriately challenging. This personalization enhances knowledge retention and understanding, making learning more effective.

Research indicates that AI-VR systems are particularly effective in complex subjects where traditional teaching methods fall short. For instance, in healthcare education, AI-VR simulations offer realistic, hands-on practice that substantially improves students' practical skills and knowledge retention compared to conventional methods. The immersive nature of VR, combined with AI's ability to adapt content in real-time, creates a dynamic learning environment conducive to deep learning and long-term retention. AI-VR environments also increase student engagement and motivation by creating immersive, interactive learning experiences. These environments leverage AI to adapt scenarios based on student interactions, providing immediate feedback and adjusting the difficulty level to maintain optimal challenge and interest. This adaptivity keeps students engaged and motivated, as the learning experience is continuously aligned with their capabilities and progress.

Studies have demonstrated that immersive VR environments significantly boost student engagement and motivation. For instance, research in language learning using AI-VR systems found that students were more motivated and engaged when learning in a VR environment compared to traditional classroom settings. The sense of presence and interaction in VR environments makes learning more enjoyable and stimulating, leading to better educational outcomes. Moreover, AI-VR systems are instrumental in developing essential skills such as problem-solving, critical thinking, and creativity. The interactive and immersive nature of VR, coupled with AI-driven personalization, provides a conducive environment for practicing and honing these skills. For example, in art education, AI-VR environments have significantly improved students' creativity and concentration by providing tailored, immersive learning experiences that encourage deep engagement with the subject matter.

Additionally, AI-VR systems facilitate the development of practical skills through realistic simulations. In medical training, for example, AI-VR environments enable students to practice surgical procedures in a risk-free setting, enhancing their practical skills and confidence. These systems provide immediate AI-driven feedback, allowing students to learn from their mistakes and improve their techniques in real-time. Several case studies highlight the successful implementation of AI-VR systems in achieving learning objectives across various educational fields:

1. Healthcare Education: AI-VR simulations provide realistic, hands-on practice, significantly improving practical skills and knowledge retention (Kyaw et al., 2019).
2. Language Learning: AI-driven VR environments enhance motivation and engagement, leading to better language acquisition and cultural understanding (Font de la Vall & González Araya, 2023).
3. Art Education: AI-VR systems improve creativity and concentration by providing immersive, personalized learning experiences (Rong et al., 2022).

Future research should focus on refining AI algorithms to further enhance the personalization and effectiveness of VR learning environments. Ethical considerations and data privacy must also be addressed to ensure the responsible use of AI in education. Interdisciplinary collaboration between educators, technologists, and researchers will be essential for advancing the field and exploring new applications of AI-VR in education.

The integration of AI and VR in educational settings offers significant contributions to achieving learning objectives. By providing personalized, adaptive, and immersive learning experiences, AI-VR systems enhance learning outcomes, increase engagement and motivation, and develop essential skills. Continued research and collaboration will be crucial for unlocking the full potential of AI-VR in education, ensuring that these technologies are effectively and ethically integrated into educational practices.

ETHICAL BIAS IN AI-SUPPORTED VR LEARNING ENVIRONMENTS

Data Privacy and Security

The integration of AI in VR learning environments presents significant opportunities for enhancing education, yet also introduces critical ethical concerns, particularly regarding data privacy and security. The collection of personal data within VR-based systems, coupled with its integration into deep learning frameworks, poses substantial ethical and security challenges (Soccini, 2021). This section explores these concerns, discussing current issues, mitigation strategies, and the imperative of addressing these challenges to ensure the safe and ethical deployment of AI in educational VR contexts.

The extensive collection and analysis of personal data in AI-VR environments introduce substantial privacy risks. Learner interactions, behaviors, and biometric data are frequently recorded to tailor learning experiences, which can lead to potential misuse if not properly managed (Li et al., 2022). Safeguarding the confidentiality of this sensitive data is paramount to prevent unauthorized access and breaches. AI-driven VR systems are vulnerable to various security threats, including cyber-attacks and data breaches, which can compromise the integrity and confidentiality of educational data, causing significant harm to learners and institutions alike (Baihakki & Ba Qutayan, 2023). It is essential to implement robust security measures to protect against such threats.

The opaque nature of AI algorithms can foster mistrust among users. Learners and educators may be apprehensive about how their data is being utilized and whether AI systems are making fair and unbiased decisions (Mooghali et al., 2023). Ensuring transparency in AI operations and data handling processes is crucial for building trust and maintaining ethical standards.

Developing and adhering to ethical frameworks that prioritize data privacy and security is essential. These frameworks should encompass guidelines for data collection, storage, and processing, alongside mechanisms for accountability and transparency (Klimova et al., 2023). Collaboration between educators and technologists is vital to ensure that ethical considerations are integrated into AI-VR systems from their inception. Additionally, educating users about the significance of data privacy and security, and involving them in decision-making processes related to their data, can enhance trust and compliance. Providing clear information about data usage and obtaining informed consent are critical steps in fostering a transparent and ethical AI-VR environment (Casas-Roma & Conesa, 2021).

Addressing data privacy and security concerns in AI-supported VR learning environments is crucial for ensuring ethical and safe educational experiences. By implementing advanced privacy-preserving techniques, developing robust ethical frameworks, and fostering transparency and user engagement, educators and technologists can mitigate the risks associated with data privacy and security. These efforts will contribute to building trust in AI-VR systems and ensuring their responsible and effective use in education.

Social Equity and Accessibility

The integration of AI and VR in educational settings holds transformative potential for creating personalized and immersive learning experiences. However, to ensure equitable benefits for all learners, it is imperative to address issues of social equity and accessibility. This section examines these concerns, highlighting key findings from the literature, current strategies to enhance accessibility, and future directions.

AI-supported VR learning environments have the potential to significantly expand educational opportunities for marginalized communities. By offering immersive and interactive learning experiences, these technologies can bridge educational gaps for students who lack access to traditional resources. For instance, extended reality (XR) vocational training programs have demonstrated success in improving soft skills development and enhancing workforce equity by providing on-demand accessibility options that support lifelong learning and career advancement (Boland, 2023).

These AI-VR environments can be customized to meet diverse learning needs, including those of students with disabilities. Customizable and adaptive learning experiences enable learners with special needs to engage more effectively with educational content. Participatory design (PD) approaches in developing VR platforms for individuals with autism, for example, have shown the potential to empower users by actively involving them in the customization process (Politis et al., 2019).

Ensuring that VR learning environments are accessible to all students necessitates various technological adaptations. VR systems can be designed to accommodate users with visual, auditory, and physical impairments by incorporating features such as voice commands, adjustable text sizes, and alternative input methods. Research indicates that effective feedback systems for hearing-impaired students in VR-supported distance learning environments significantly enhance the learning experience and accessibility (Teke et al., 2023). These adaptations are crucial for making VR technologies more inclusive and user-friendly.

Protecting the privacy and security of learner data is essential for building trust and ensuring equitable access to AI-VR technologies. Federated learning, which enables AI models to be trained across multiple decentralized devices without transferring raw data, enhances data privacy and reduces the risk of data breaches

(Dash et al., 2022). Ensuring transparency and security in AI algorithms is vital for maintaining user confidence and promoting wider adoption of these technologies.

Developing ethical frameworks that prioritize accessibility and equity is critical for the responsible implementation of AI-VR technologies in education. These frameworks should encompass guidelines for inclusive design, data protection, and user engagement to ensure all learners benefit from these innovations (Klimova et al., 2023). Collaboration between educators and technologists is necessary to integrate these ethical considerations into the development and deployment of AI-VR systems.

Longitudinal studies are needed to evaluate the long-term impacts of AI-VR learning environments on social equity and accessibility. These studies should assess not only immediate educational outcomes but also the sustained effects on learners' career prospects, social mobility, and overall well-being (Hamilton et al., 2020). Advancing the field of AI-VR in education requires interdisciplinary collaboration among educators, technologists, policymakers, and researchers. This collaboration can drive innovation and ensure the development of AI-VR technologies aligns with the needs and values of diverse learner populations (Kyaw et al., 2010). Emphasizing inclusive design practices in developing AI-VR environments can help address accessibility challenges and promote social equity. Engaging users from diverse backgrounds in the design process ensures that the technologies are responsive to their needs and preferences (Politis et al., 2019).

Addressing social equity and accessibility in AI-supported VR learning environments is essential for ensuring all learners can benefit from these technological advancements. By implementing inclusive design practices, protecting data privacy, and developing ethical frameworks, educators and technologists can create more equitable and accessible educational experiences. Continued research and interdisciplinary collaboration will be key to realizing the full potential of AI-VR technologies in promoting social equity in education.

Ethical Principles and Practices in AI and VR Integration

The integration of AI and VR in educational settings brings forth significant ethical considerations. Ensuring that these technologies are implemented in a manner that aligns with ethical principles is crucial for fostering trust, accountability, and equity in their use. Jia (2017) comprehensively examined the ethical dimensions of VR applications and users' reactions to these applications; in this context, he revealed that the situations that users encounter in the virtual world may conflict with ethical values in the real world, and the decisions users make and behaviours they exhibit in the virtual world may deviate from their ethical values in the real world. On the other hand, in the research on ethical decision-making processes in VR environments and how these processes can be optimised, the potential to provide students with ethical issues and ethical decision-making skills by using VR technology to increase ethical sensitivity and teach ethical decision-making processes was emphasised (Kang, 2019). Therefore, regarding the integration processes of AI and VR, which have great potential in both learning processes and ethical principles and practices in general, this section explores the ethical principles and practices necessary for responsible AI and VR integration, drawing on insights from current literature and best practices.

Ethical Principles in AI and VR Integration:

1. Transparency and Accountability: Transparency is crucial in AI and VR systems to ensure users comprehend how decisions are made and how their data is utilized. Accountability mechanisms must be established to hold developers and institutions responsible for the ethical deployment of these technologies (Khan et al., 2021). Clear communication regarding the functioning and limitations of AI-VR systems builds trust and fosters informed consent among users.
2. Privacy and Data Protection: Protecting the privacy and security of user data is paramount. AI-VR systems often collect and process substantial amounts of personal data, which must be safeguarded against unauthorized access and breaches. Implementing robust data protection measures, such as encryption and secure data storage, is essential (Jaiswal et al., 2023). Additionally, policies should limit data collection to what is necessary and ensure users have control over their data.
3. Fairness and Non-Discrimination: AI and VR technologies should be designed to be inclusive and free from biases that could lead to discrimination. Ensuring fairness involves rigorous testing and validation of AI algorithms to detect and mitigate biases. It also requires considering diverse user groups during the design and deployment phases to ensure the technology serves all users equitably (Taiwo et al., 2023).
4. Beneficence and Non-Maleficence: The principles of beneficence (doing good) and non-maleficence (avoiding harm) are foundational in the ethical use of AI and VR. These technologies should be deployed to enhance educational outcomes and well-being without causing harm. Continuous monitoring and evaluation are necessary to identify and address any unintended negative consequences (Leikas et al., 2019).

Ethical Practices for AI and VR Integration:

1. Ethical Design Frameworks: Adopting ethical design frameworks integrates ethical considerations into the development lifecycle of AI and VR systems. These frameworks provide guidelines for incorporating ethical principles at each stage, from initial design to deployment and maintenance. For example, the Responsible AI Pattern Catalogue offers systematic guidance for implementing ethical AI (Lu et al., 2022).
2. Stakeholder Engagement: Engaging stakeholders, including educators, students, policymakers, and technologists, in the design and implementation process ensures that the perspectives and needs of all affected parties are considered. This collaborative approach helps identify potential ethical issues early and fosters a sense of ownership and responsibility among all stakeholders (Stahl et al., 2021).
3. Ethics Training and Education: Providing ethics training for developers, educators, and users is crucial for fostering a culture of ethical awareness and responsibility. Training programs should cover key ethical principles, practical guidelines for ethical decision-making, and the importance of transparency and accountability in AI and VR technologies (Cihon et al., 2021).
4. Regulatory Compliance and Best Practices: Compliance with regulatory standards and adherence to best practices are essential for the ethical deployment of AI and VR systems. Regulatory frameworks often provide a baseline for ethical considerations, and adherence to these standards helps ensure that the technologies are used responsibly (Barletta et al., 2023). Best practices include regular audits, impact assessments, and the development of ethical guidelines tailored to specific use cases.

Integrating ethical principles and practices into the development and deployment of AI and VR technologies is essential for ensuring their responsible and equitable use in educational settings. By focusing on transparency, privacy, fairness, and beneficence, and by adopting ethical design frameworks, engaging stakeholders, providing ethics training, and ensuring regulatory compliance, educators and technologists can create AI-VR systems that enhance learning while safeguarding the rights and well-being of users.

CONCLUSION

Evaluating the Potential of AI and VR Technologies in Education

The integration of AI and VR technologies into educational frameworks holds substantial potential to transform conventional learning paradigms. These technologies provide personalized, immersive, and adaptive learning experiences that address the unique needs of individual students. By harnessing AI algorithms and VR simulations, educators can develop dynamic learning environments that significantly enhance student engagement, motivation, and knowledge retention. Empirical research demonstrates that AI-VR systems markedly improve learning outcomes across diverse educational domains, including healthcare, engineering, language acquisition, and the arts.

AI-VR environments facilitate the comprehension of complex concepts and offer hands-on practice in a secure, simulated setting, which is particularly advantageous for disciplines requiring practical skills and experiential learning. For example, VR simulations in medical education enable students to perform surgical procedures in a controlled virtual space, thereby refining their practical skills and boosting their confidence. Similarly, language learners benefit from immersive VR experiences that foster cultural understanding and language acquisition through interactive, context-rich scenarios.

Despite these advantages, the realization of AI and VR's full potential in education necessitates addressing several challenges. Ensuring accessibility and equity is paramount to guarantee that all students, irrespective of their backgrounds or abilities, can benefit from these technological advancements. Furthermore, the development and implementation of AI-VR systems must be guided by ethical principles to prevent misuse and protect user data. Establishing robust data privacy and security measures is essential for building trust and promoting the responsible use of these technologies.

Guidance for Ethical and Effective Use

Guidelines for the ethical and effective utilization of AI and VR technologies are crucial for their successful integration into educational settings. Ethical frameworks and best practices should be embedded in the design and deployment of these systems. Core ethical principles such as transparency, accountability, and fairness must guide the development of AI algorithms and VR content. Adhering to these principles ensures that AI-VR systems are employed responsibly and that the interests and rights of all users are safeguarded.

Stakeholder engagement plays a vital role in identifying potential ethical issues and collaboratively developing solutions. This involves including educators, students, technologists, and policymakers in the design and implementation processes. Such inclusive engagement ensures that diverse perspectives are considered and that AI-VR systems are tailored to meet the needs of all stakeholders. Additionally, providing ethics training for developers and users fosters a culture of responsibility and ethical awareness in the use of these technologies.

To further ensure ethical use, implementing ethical design frameworks and conducting regular audits and impact assessments are imperative. These practices help identify and mitigate potential ethical risks and ensure adherence to regulatory standards. By fostering a collaborative approach and prioritizing ethical considerations, educators and technologists can create AI-VR learning environments that are both effective and equitable.

Recommendations for Future Research and Applications

Future research and applications of AI and VR in education should focus on several key areas to enhance their effectiveness and ethical use. Advancements in AI techniques, such as deep learning and natural language processing, can further refine the personalization and adaptability of VR environments. These technologies can analyze complex learner behaviors and provide deeper insights into the learning process, thereby improving the quality of educational content and experiences.

Longitudinal studies are necessary to assess the long-term impacts of AI-VR systems on educational outcomes and student well-being. Such research should evaluate not only immediate learning gains but also the sustained effects on learners' career prospects, social mobility, and overall well-being. These studies will offer valuable insights into the effectiveness and sustainability of AI-VR technologies in education.

Interdisciplinary collaboration between educators, technologists, and researchers is essential for driving innovation and ensuring that the development of AI-VR technologies aligns with educational goals and ethical principles. By working together, these stakeholders can explore new applications and refine existing systems to address emerging challenges and opportunities. This collaborative approach will help unlock the full potential of AI and VR in education, ensuring that these technologies are used effectively and ethically to enhance learning experiences for all students.

IMPLICATIONS AND FUTURE DIRECTIONS

The Use of AI-Supported VR Technologies in Education

The integration of AI-supported VR technologies in education has the potential to fundamentally transform learning experiences. AI algorithms enhance VR environments by offering personalized learning tailored to individual student needs, thereby increasing engagement, motivation, and improving learning outcomes. Studies have demonstrated that AI-VR systems make complex subjects more accessible, providing hands-on practice in a risk-free setting, and enhancing practical skills and knowledge retention (Wang, 2023; Kyaw et al., 2019).

AI-VR environments also facilitate the development of critical skills such as problem-solving, creativity, and critical thinking. For instance, AI-VR applications in art education have been shown to improve students' creativity and concentration by offering immersive, interactive experiences that encourage deep engagement with the subject matter (Rong et al., 2022). Similarly, in medical training, VR simulations powered by AI create realistic scenarios that enhance students' practical skills and confidence, better preparing them for real-world challenges (Ghaednia et al., 2021).

However, implementing AI-supported VR technologies in education is not without challenges. Accessibility, equity, data privacy, and significant infrastructural investments are key issues that need to be addressed to ensure all students benefit equally from these advancements. Continuous research and development are also necessary to refine AI algorithms and VR technologies, enhancing their efficiency and effectiveness in diverse educational settings (Zhang & Aslan, 2021).

Strategic Recommendations for Technology Developers and Educators

For technology developers, it is essential to focus on creating robust, scalable, and user-friendly AI-VR systems. This involves developing sophisticated AI algorithms capable of analyzing complex learner data and generating high-quality educational content. Additionally, developers should prioritize ethical considerations such as data privacy and security by implementing advanced encryption techniques and federated learning approaches (Dash et al., 2022). Interdisciplinary collaboration with educators and policymakers can ensure that AI-VR systems are designed to meet the practical needs of the educational sector.

Educators, meanwhile, should proactively integrate AI-VR technologies into their teaching practices. This includes gaining familiarity with these technologies and understanding their potential benefits and limitations. Training programs and professional development initiatives can equip educators with the necessary skills to effectively use AI-VR systems in the classroom. Furthermore, educators should collaborate with technologists to provide feedback and insights that can help refine and improve these technologies (Tarabasz et al., 2018).

Both technology developers and educators must work together to address the challenges associated with AI-VR integration, such as ensuring accessibility and equity. Developing inclusive design frameworks that cater to diverse learning needs and backgrounds is crucial. Additionally, ongoing support and maintenance are necessary to ensure the sustainability and effectiveness of AI-VR systems in education (Kamalov et al., 2023).

Recommendations for Future Research and Applications

Future research in AI-supported VR technologies in education should concentrate on several key areas. Advanced AI techniques, such as deep learning and natural language processing, can enhance the personalization and adaptability of VR environments. These technologies can provide deeper insights into learner behaviors and preferences, leading to more effective educational interventions (Wang et al., 2023). Longitudinal studies are essential to assess the long-term impacts of AI-VR systems on educational outcomes and student well-being. These studies should evaluate not only immediate learning gains but also sustained effects on learners' career prospects and overall well-being (Hamilton et al., 2020).

Interdisciplinary collaboration between educators, technologists, and researchers is critical to drive innovation and ensure the development of AI-VR technologies aligns with educational goals and ethical principles. By working together, these stakeholders can explore new applications and refine existing systems to address emerging challenges and opportunities. Additionally, fostering a culture of continuous improvement and adaptation will help educators and technologists stay abreast of technological advancements and integrate them effectively into educational practices (Kyaw et al., 2019).

In conclusion, the integration of AI-supported VR technologies in education offers significant opportunities to enhance learning experiences and outcomes. By addressing challenges related to accessibility, equity, and ethics, and by fostering collaboration and innovation, educators and technologists can unlock the full potential of these technologies. Future research should continue to explore new applications and refine existing systems to ensure AI and VR are used effectively and ethically in education. This collaborative effort will create a future where AI and VR play a central role in providing high-quality, personalized, and immersive learning experiences for all students.

REFERENCES

Algerafi, M., Zhou, Y., Oubibi, M., & Wijaya, T. (2023). Unlocking the potential: A comprehensive evaluation of augmented reality and virtual reality in education. *Electronics (Basel)*, 12(18), 3953. Advance online publication. DOI: 10.3390/electronics12183953

Amin, S., Uddin, M., Mashwani, W., Alarood, A., Alzahrani, A., & Alzahrani, A. (2023). Developing a personalized e-learning and MOOC recommender system in IoT-enabled smart education. *IEEE Access : Practical Innovations, Open Solutions*, 11, 136437–136455. DOI: 10.1109/ACCESS.2023.3336676

Ausburn, L., Martens, J., Washington, A., Steele, D., & Washburn, E. (2009). A cross-case analysis of gender issues in desktop virtual reality learning environments. *Journal of Industrial Teacher Education*, 46, 51–89. https://ir.library.illinoisstate.edu/jste/vol46/iss3/6

Baihakki, M., & Qutayan, S. (2023). Ethical issues of artificial intelligence (AI) in the healthcare. *Journal of Science, Technology and Innovation Policy*. https://doi.org/DOI: 10.11113/jostip.v9n1.129

Barletta, V., Caivano, D., Gigante, D., & Ragone, A. (2023). A rapid review of responsible AI frameworks: How to guide the development of ethical AI. *Proceedings of the 27th International Conference on Evaluation and Assessment in Software Engineering*. https://doi.org/DOI: 10.1145/3593434.3593478

Bassyouni, Z., & Elhajj, I. (2021). Augmented reality meets artificial intelligence in robotics: A systematic review. *Frontiers in Robotics and AI*, 8, 724798. Advance online publication. DOI: 10.3389/frobt.2021.724798 PMID: 34631805

Boland, B. (2023). *Extended reality vocational training's ability to improve soft skills development and increase equity in the workforce*. AI, Computer Science and Robotics Technology., DOI: 10.5772/acrt.22

Casas-Roma, J., & Conesa, J. (2021). *A literature review on artificial intelligence and ethics in online learning*. Intelligent Systems and Learning Data Analytics in Online Education., DOI: 10.1016/B978-0-12-823410-5.00006-1

Cihon, P., Kleinaltenkamp, M., Schuett, J., & Baum, S. (2021). AI certification: Advancing ethical practice by reducing information asymmetries. *IEEE Transactions on Technology and Society*, 2(4), 200–209. DOI: 10.1109/TTS.2021.3077595

Cooper, N., Millela, F., Cant, I., White, M., & Meyer, G. (2021). Transfer of training—Virtual reality training with augmented multisensory cues improves user experience during training and task performance in the real world. *PLoS One*, 16(3), e0248225. Advance online publication. DOI: 10.1371/journal.pone.0248225 PMID: 33760859

Cukurbasi, B., & Kiyici, M. (2021). Instructional design and instructional effectiveness in virtual classrooms: Research trends and challenges: Instructional design and instructional effectiveness in virtual classroom. *Australasian Journal of Educational Technology*, 37(6), 156–174. DOI: 10.14742/ajet.6882

Dash, B., Sharma, P., & Ali, A. (2022). Federated learning for privacy-preserving: A review of PII data analysis in fintech. *International Journal of Software Engineering and Its Applications*, 13(4), 1–13. Advance online publication. DOI: 10.5121/ijsea.2022.13401

Dvareckienė, V., Kurilovas, E., & Jevsikova, T. (2016). Virtual, augmented, and mixed reality-based learning systems: Personalisation framework. *Lietuvos Matematikos Rinkinys, 57*(B), 1–6. https://doi.org/DOI: 10.15388/LMR.B.2016.01

Esposito, C., Siciliano, M., Persico, C., Carotenuto, M., Ricci, M., & Russo, M. (2023). Virtual reality and foreign language learning (short paper). *ICERI2023 Proceedings*. https://doi.org/DOI: 10.21125/iceri.2023.2364

Fox-Turnbull, W., & Snape, P. (2011). Technology teacher education through a constructivist approach. *Journal of Design and Technology Education*, 16(2), 45–56.

Geris, A., Cukurbasi, B., Kilinc, M., & Teke, O. (2024). Balancing performance and comfort in virtual reality: A study of FPS, latency, and batch values. *Software, Practice & Experience*, 54(12), 2336–2348. Advance online publication. DOI: 10.1002/spe.3356

Geriş, A., & Özdener, N. (2024). Design, development, and evaluation of educational virtual reality environment: EVRECA. *Educational Technology Research and Development*, 72(2), 915–945. DOI: 10.1007/s11423-023-10303-3

Ghaednia, H., Fourman, M., Lans, A., Detels, K., Dijkstra, H., Lloyd, S., Sweeney, A., Oosterhoff, J., & Schwab, J. (2021). Augmented and virtual reality in spine surgery, current applications and future potentials. *The Spine Journal*, 21(10), 1617–1625. Advance online publication. DOI: 10.1016/j.spinee.2021.03.018 PMID: 33774210

Hamilton, D., McKechnie, J., Edgerton, E., & Wilson, C. (2020). Immersive virtual reality as a pedagogical tool in education: A systematic literature review of quantitative learning outcomes and experimental design. *Journal of Computers in Education*, 8(1), 1–32. DOI: 10.1007/s40692-020-00169-2

Han, Y. (2023). Virtual reality in engineering education. *SHS Web of Conferences*. https://doi.org/DOI: 10.1051/shsconf/202315702001

Heinemann, B., Görzen, S., & Schroeder, U. (2022, July). Systematic design for effective learning in virtual reality. In *2022 International Conference on Advanced Learning Technologies (ICALT)* (pp. 341-343). IEEE. https://doi.org/DOI: 10.1109/ICALT55010.2022.00107

Inkarbekov, M., Monahan, R., & Pearlmutter, B. (2023). Visualization of AI systems in virtual reality: A comprehensive review. *ArXiv, abs/2306.15545*. https://doi.org/DOI: 10.14569/IJACSA.2023.0140805

Jaiswal, R., Sharma, S., & Kaushik, R. (2023). Ethics in AI and machine learning. *Journal of Nonlinear Analysis and Optimization*. https://doi.org/DOI: 10.36893/JNAO.2023.V14I1.0008-0012

Jeyaraman, M., Balaji, S., Jeyaraman, N., & Yadav, S. (2023). Unraveling the ethical enigma: Artificial intelligence in healthcare. *Cureus*, 15. Advance online publication. DOI: 10.7759/cureus.43262 PMID: 37692617

Jia, J., & Chen, W. (2017, July). The ethical dilemmas of virtual reality application in entertainment. In *2017 IEEE International Conference on Computational Science and Engineering (CSE) and IEEE International Conference on Embedded and Ubiquitous Computing (EUC) (Vol. 1, pp. 696-699)*. IEEE. https://doi.org/DOI: 10.1109/CSE-EUC.2017.134

Jiang, J., & Fryer, L. (2023). The effect of virtual reality learning on students' motivation: A scoping review. *Journal of Computer Assisted Learning*. Advance online publication. DOI: 10.1111/jcal.12885

Kamalov, F., Calonge, D., & Gurrib, I. (2023). New era of artificial intelligence in education: Towards a sustainable multifaceted revolution. *Sustainability (Basel)*, 15(16), 12451. Advance online publication. DOI: 10.3390/su151612451

Kang, S., Chanenson, J., Ghate, P., Cowal, P., Weaver, M., & Krum, D. M. (2019, March). Advancing ethical decision making in virtual reality. In *2019 IEEE Conference on Virtual Reality and 3D User Interfaces (VR) (pp. 1008-1009)*. IEEE. https://doi.org/DOI: 10.1109/VR.2019.8798151

Kayii, N., & Akpomi, M. (2022). Constructivist approaches: A budding paradigm for teaching and learning entrepreneurship education. *International Journal of Education, Teaching, and Social Sciences*. https://doi.org/DOI: 10.47747/ijets.v2i1.586

Khan, A., Badshah, S., Liang, P., Khan, B., Waseem, M., Niazi, M., & Akbar, M. (2021). Ethics of AI: A systematic literature review of principles and challenges. *Proceedings of the 26th International Conference on Evaluation and Assessment in Software Engineering*. https://doi.org/DOI: 10.1145/3530019.3531329

Kiourt, C., Koutsoudis, A., & Kalles, D. (2020). *Enhanced virtual reality experience in personalised virtual museums*. Natural Language Processing., DOI: 10.4018/978-1-7998-0951-7.ch065

Klimova, B., Pikhart, M., & Kacetl, J. (2023). Ethical issues of the use of AI-driven mobile apps for education. *Frontiers in Public Health*, 10, 1118116. Advance online publication. DOI: 10.3389/fpubh.2022.1118116 PMID: 36711343

Krikun, I. (2017). Applying learning analytics methods to enhance learning quality and effectiveness in virtual learning environments. *2017 5th IEEE Workshop on Advances in Information, Electronic and Electrical Engineering (AIEEE)*, 1-6. https://doi.org/DOI: 10.1109/AIEEE.2017.8270532

Kurilovas, E. (2016). Evaluation of quality and personalisation of VR/AR/MR learning systems. *Behaviour & Information Technology*, 35(11), 998–1007. DOI: 10.1080/0144929X.2016.1212929

Kyaw, B., Saxena, N., Posadzki, P., Všetečková, J., Nikolaou, C., George, P., Divakar, U., Masiello, I., Kononowicz, A., Zary, N., & Car, L. (2019). Virtual reality for health professions education: Systematic review and meta-analysis by the digital health education collaboration. *Journal of Medical Internet Research*, 21(1), e12959. Advance online publication. DOI: 10.2196/12959 PMID: 30668519

Lai, N., Wei, S., Halim, D., Fow, K., Kang, H., & Yu, L. (2021). Why not more virtual reality in higher ed teaching and learning? *2021 IEEE International Conference on Engineering, Technology & Education (TALE)*, 248-254. https://doi.org/DOI: 10.1109/TALE52509.2021.9678523

Leikas, J., Koivisto, R., & Gotcheva, N. (2019). Ethical framework for designing autonomous intelligent systems. *Journal of Open Innovation*, 5(1), 18. Advance online publication. DOI: 10.3390/joitmc5010018

Li, F., Ruijs, N., & Lu, Y. (2022). Ethics & AI: A systematic review on ethical concerns and related strategies for designing with AI in healthcare. *AI*, 4(1), 28–53. Advance online publication. DOI: 10.3390/ai4010003

Lim, T., Gottipati, S., & Cheong, M. L. (2023). Ethical considerations for artificial intelligence in educational assessments. In Keengwe, J. (Ed.), *Creative AI Tools and Ethical Implications in Teaching and Learning* (pp. 32–79). IGI Global., DOI: 10.4018/979-8-3693-0205-7.ch003

Lu, Q., Zhu, L., Xu, X., Whittle, J., Zowghi, D., & Jacquet, A. (2022). Responsible AI pattern catalogue: A collection of best practices for AI governance and engineering. *ACM Computing Surveys*. Advance online publication. DOI: 10.1145/3626234

Makransky, G., & Lilleholt, L. (2018). A structural equation modeling investigation of the emotional value of immersive virtual reality in education. *Educational Technology Research and Development*, 66(5), 1141–1164. DOI: 10.1007/s11423-018-9581-2

Marougkas, A., Troussas, C., Krouska, A., & Sgouropoulou, C. (2023). Virtual reality in education: A review of learning theories, approaches and methodologies for the last decade. *Electronics (Basel)*, 12(13), 2832. DOI: 10.3390/electronics12132832

Mavroudi, A., Giannakos, M., & Krogstie, J. (2018). Supporting adaptive learning pathways through the use of learning analytics: Developments, challenges and future opportunities. *Interactive Learning Environments*, 26(2), 206–220. DOI: 10.1080/10494820.2017.1292531

McInnes, R., Carandang, M., & Kulkarni, A. (2023). *Unleashing the power of gen-AI for digital education development*. ASCILITE Publications., DOI: 10.14742/apubs.2023.520

Mooghali, M., Stroud, A., Yoo, D., Barry, A., Grimshaw, A., Ross, J., Zhu, X., & Miller, J. (2023). Barriers and facilitators to trustworthy and ethical AI-enabled medical care from patient and healthcare provider perspectives: A literature review. https://doi.org/DOI: 10.1101/2023.10.02.23296447

Muravevskaia, E., & Gardner-Mccune, C. (2022). VR empathy game: Creating empathic VR environments for children based on a social constructivist learning approach. *2022 International Conference on Advanced Learning Technologies (ICALT)*, 360-362. https://doi.org/DOI: 10.1109/ICALT55010.2022.00112

Oliveira, T., Silva, M., Spinasse, R., Ludke, G., Gaudio, M., Gomes, G., Cotini, L., Vargens, D., Schimidt, M., Andreão, R., & Mestria, M. (2021). Systematic review of virtual reality solutions employing artificial intelligence methods. *Symposium on Virtual and Augmented Reality*. https://doi.org/DOI: 10.1145/3488162.3488209

Politis, Y., Olivia, L., & Olivia, T. (2019). Empowering autistic adults through their involvement in the development of a virtual world. *Advances in Autism*, 5(4), 303–317. Advance online publication. DOI: 10.1108/AIA-01-2019-0001

Prakash, A., & Rajendran, R. (2022). Mechanism to capture learners' interactions in virtual reality learning environment. *2022 International Conference on Advanced Learning Technologies (ICALT)*, 335-337. https://doi.org/DOI: 10.1109/ICALT55010.2022.00105

Pugachova, K. (2023). Transforming education with artificial intelligence: Challenges, opportunities, and future directions. *Вісник науки та освіти*, 11(17), 475-484. https://doi.org/DOI: 10.52058/2786-6165-2023-11(17)-475-484

Qin, H., & Hui, P. (2023). Empowering the metaverse with generative AI: Survey and future directions. *2023 IEEE 43rd International Conference on Distributed Computing Systems Workshops (ICDCSW)*, 85-90. https://doi.org/DOI: 10.1109/ICDCSW60045.2023.00022

Rakya, Z. (2023). Exploring the impact of artificial intelligence (AI) on learner-instructor interaction in online learning (literature review). *International Journal of Emerging Multidisciplinaries: Computer Science & Artificial Intelligence*. https://doi.org/DOI: 10.54938/ijemdcsai.2023.02.1.236

Rebolledo Font de la Vall, R., & González Araya, F. (2023). Exploring the benefits and challenges of AI-language learning tools. *International Journal of Social Sciences and Humanities Invention*, 10(01), 7569–7576. DOI: 10.18535/ijsshi/v10i01.02

Regal, G., Pretolesi, D., Schrom-Feiertag, H., Puthenkalam, J., Migliorini, M., De Maio, E., Scarrone, F., Nadalin, M., Guarneri, M., Xerri, G. P., Di Giovanni, D., Tessari, P., Genna, F., D'Angelo, A., & Murtinger, M. (2023). Challenges in virtual reality training for CBRN events. *Multimodal Technologies and Interaction*, 7(9), 88. DOI: 10.3390/mti7090088

Rong, Q., Lian, Q., & Tang, T. (2022). Research on the influence of AI and VR technology for students' concentration and creativity. *Frontiers in Psychology*, 13, 767689. Advance online publication. DOI: 10.3389/fpsyg.2022.767689 PMID: 35401322

Scott, E., Soria, A., & Campo, M. (2016). Adaptive 3D virtual learning environments—A review of the literature. *IEEE Transactions on Learning Technologies*, 10(3), 262–276. DOI: 10.1109/TLT.2016.2609910

Singh, G., Mantri, A., Sharma, O., & Kaur, R. (2020). Virtual reality learning environment for enhancing electronics engineering laboratory experience. *Computer Applications in Engineering Education*, 29(1), 229–243. DOI: 10.1002/cae.22333

Soccini, A. M., & Cena, F. (2021, November). The ethics of rehabilitation in virtual reality: The role of self-avatars and deep learning. In *2021 IEEE International Conference on Artificial Intelligence and Virtual Reality (AIVR)* (pp. 324-328). IEEE. https://doi.org/DOI: 10.1109/AIVR52153.2021.00068

Stahl, B., Antoniou, J., Ryan, M., Macnish, K., & Jiya, T. (2021). Organisational responses to the ethical issues of artificial intelligence. *AI & Society*, 37(1), 23–37. DOI: 10.1007/s00146-021-01148-6

Taiwo, E., Akinsola, A., Tella, E., Makinde, K., & Akinwande, M. (2023). A review of the ethics of artificial intelligence and its applications in the United States. *ArXiv, abs/2310.05751*. http://dx.doi.org/DOI: 10.5121/ijci.2023.120610

Tarabasz, A., Selaković, M., & Abraham, C. (2018). The classroom of the future: Disrupting the concept of contemporary business education. *Entrepreneurial Business and Economics Review*, 6(4), 231–245. DOI: 10.15678/EBER.2018.060413

Teke, O., Kilinc, M., Geris, A., & Cukurbasi, B. (2023). Feedback systems suitable for hearing impaired students in virtual reality supported distance learning environments in higher education: MetaCBU case. *BILTEVT2023: International Barrier-Free Informatics Technology Congress 2023*. Retrieved from https://engelsizbilisim.org/biltevt/wp-content/uploads/2024/02/A4-Olcusunde-BILTEVT2023_Program_ve_Bildiri_Ozetleri_Kitabi.pdf

Tiwari, R. (2023). *The integration of AI and machine learning in education and its potential to personalize and improve student learning experiences*. International Journal Of Scientific Research In Engineering And Management., DOI: 10.55041/IJSREM17645

Vall, R., & Araya, F. (2023). Exploring the benefits and challenges of AI-language learning tools. *International Journal of Social Sciences and Humanities Invention*. https://doi.org/DOI: 10.18535/ijsshi/v10i01.02

Van Mechelen, M., Smith, R. C., Schaper, M. M., Tamashiro, M., Bilstrup, K. E., Lunding, M., Graves Petersen, M., & Sejer Iversen, O. (2023). Emerging technologies in K–12 education: A future HCI research agenda. *ACM Transactions on Computer-Human Interaction*, 30(3), 1–40. DOI: 10.1145/3569897

Vassigh, S., Corrigan, S., Bogosian, B., & Peterson, E. (2023). *Adaptive immersive learning environments for teaching industrial robotics*. Emerging Technologies and Future of Work., DOI: 10.54941/ahfe1004411

Wang, Y. (2023). *Procedural content generation for VR educational applications: The investigation of AI-based approaches for improving learning experience*. Applied and Computational Engineering., DOI: 10.54254/2755-2721/17/20230905

Webster, R. (2015). Declarative knowledge acquisition in immersive virtual learning environments. *Interactive Learning Environments*, 24(6), 1319–1333. DOI: 10.1080/10494820.2014.994533

Xi, W. (2020). Research on application of artificial intelligence in VR games. In *Fuzzy Systems and Data Mining VI* (pp. 247–254). IOS Press., DOI: 10.3233/FAIA200704

Yin, J., Hinchet, R., Shea, H., & Majidi, C. (2020). Wearable soft technologies for haptic sensing and feedback. *Advanced Functional Materials*, 31(39), 2007428. Advance online publication. DOI: 10.1002/adfm.202007428

Yu, Z., & Xu, W. (2022). A meta-analysis and systematic review of the effect of virtual reality technology on users' learning outcomes. *Computer Applications in Engineering Education*, 30(5), 1470–1484. DOI: 10.1002/cae.22532

Zahabi, M., & Razak, A. (2020). Adaptive virtual reality-based training: A systematic literature review and framework. *Virtual Reality (Waltham Cross)*, 24(4), 1–28. DOI: 10.1007/s10055-020-00434-w

Zhang, K., & Aslan, A. (2021). AI technologies for education: Recent research & future directions. *Comput. Educ. Artif. Intell.*, 2, 100025. DOI: 10.1016/j.caeai.2021.100025

KEY TERMS AND DEFINITIONS

Artificial Intelligence (AI): The simulation of human intelligence processes by machines, especially computer systems, including learning, reasoning, and self-correction.

Data Privacy: The aspect of information technology that deals with the ability of an organization or individual to determine what data in a computer system can be shared with third parties.

Ethical Considerations: The principles and standards that guide behavior in the world of business, particularly concerning the moral implications of business decisions and actions.

Learning Analytics: The measurement, collection, analysis, and reporting of data about learners and their contexts, for the purpose of understanding and optimizing learning and the environments in which it occurs.

Personalized Learning: An educational approach that aims to customize learning for each student's strengths, needs, skills, and interests, often with the support of technology.

Privacy and Data Protection: Policies and procedures implemented to protect personal data from being accessed or disclosed without authorization.

Social Equity: The fair and just access to opportunities and resources for all individuals, particularly in the context of education, ensuring that every student has the support they need to succeed.

Virtual Reality (VR): A simulated experience that can be similar to or completely different from the real world, often used in educational settings to create immersive learning environments.

VR Learning Environments: Interactive digital spaces created using virtual reality technology, designed to facilitate and enhance the learning experience through immersive simulations.

VR Simulations: Digital recreations of real-world scenarios or environments using virtual reality technology, used for educational and training purposes to provide realistic practice opportunities.

Chapter 6
Exploring the Use of Virtual Reality Headsets as a Learning Tool for Classroom Instruction

James N. Oigara
SUNY Geneseo, USA

ABSTRACT

Continuing advancement in technology provides an opportunity for institutions of higher education to enhance electronic learning experiences for students. Virtual Reality (VR) technologies have been developed for a wide range of applications in education, but further research is needed to establish appropriate and effective learning techniques and practices to promote meaningful learning. By creating an immersive and interactive learning environment, VR offers a novel approach to education that can enhance engagement, improve understanding of abstract concepts, and provide teaching experiences that the traditional lecture method cannot. Using VR immerses the student in the topic at hand without distraction from real-world events. VR in the classroom can provide innovative and engaging learning experiences that encourage students to approach the subject matter from alternative perspectives. This chapter examines the potential use of VR systems for education, examining its benefits, applications, challenges and prospects.

DOI: 10.4018/979-8-3693-6030-9.ch006

INTRODUCTION

The past few decades have seen an acceleration in the use of technology to support teaching and learning, with new learning opportunities arising through the integration of interactive technology in the classroom. There have been numerous examples of hardware and software that have been successful in aiding educational processes, indicate that edtech industry can improve learning process for most students. Studies have indicated that integrating technology into education generally leads to positive outcomes on various issues faced by the education sector including increased student engagement, improved collaboration, and improved access to learning materials (Kalati & Kim, 2022). More and more educational institutions are starting to introduce powerful new technology tools to help meet the needs of diverse student populations (Collins & Halverson, 2018). Virtual Reality (VR) is an emerging technology that enables users to experience immersive, three-dimensional (3D) computer-generated simulations of real-world environments that are perceived as spatially realistic. VR utilizes a 3D computer-generated environment which can be interacted with and explored by the learner. VR experience is made possible through VR headset devices, controllers and custom software (Wonsick & Padir, 2020; Kaplan-Rakowski & Gruber, 2019). VR has already been integrated into various sectors and has recently attracted interest in education.

VR in education is a transformative approach that immerses students in interactive learning environments. By simulating real-world scenarios, VR enhances understanding and retention of complex concepts. VR allows instructors to immerse learners within authentic contexts, providing a safe, convenient, and low-cost environment in which to practice and develop new skills and knowledge (Lave & Wenger, 1991). The technology has become sufficiently inexpensive and accessible to consider VR educational content. Research shows that the emergence of educational software benefits the learning process and makes it more interesting for students (Donkin & Kynn, 2021; Chen & Teh, 2013). VR offers unique learning experiences through its ability to provide real-time 3D visualization and various types of interactivities within virtual learning environments (Chen & Teh, 2013). 3D images or environments can be experienced with a mouse and a keyboard, or with headsets designed to immerse the user in a virtual simulated environment. According to Clark (2006), VR can be used to make the learning experience more interesting and fun, thus improving student engagement. VR makes it possible to explore real world situations in various subjects that previously would have been dangerous, costly, or impossible to access. For instance, history students can use VR to explore ancient civilizations, virtual labs can be used to conduct science experiments in STEM education, and immersive environments can provide new language practice and cultural experiences.

The growing use of VR for education, and the theories that support its use, increasingly indicates the need for more insight into VR-based learning. VR technology has been named the learning aid of the 21st century (Rogers, 2019). The underlying reason for the rapid rise in its use for instruction is the unique way it offers enhancement of learners' cognitive skills, its ability to take students into places otherwise inaccessible, the high memory retention of VR experiences as opposed to passive observation, and its ability to induce greater user immersion and visualization (Merchant et al, 2014; Magdalene & Sridharan, 2018; Marougkas, et al., 2023; Kozinets, 2023). VR technology encourages student-centered active learning, simultaneously boosting memorization (Krokos et al., 2019), providing enjoyable learning experiences (Chen et al., 2017; Kaplan-Rakowski & Wojdynski, 2018), and reducing anxiety (Gruber & Kaplan-Rakowski, 2020; Kaplan-Rakowski et al., 2022). The research suggests that VR-based instruction is an effective means of enhancing learning outcomes (Merchant et al., 2014). VR can give students who require extra assistance the opportunities to build the skills they need to be successful in the classroom as their peers. This chapter explores the perception of the utility of VR to enhance teaching and learning of course materials. In this context, the chapter will explore the benefits, challenges, and future potential of VR in educational settings, highlighting its role in fostering creativity, critical thinking, and collaboration among learners.

BACKGROUND

Different terms are used to describe virtual worlds (Virtual Reality (VR), Augmented Reality (AR), and Mixed Reality (MR)), leading to confusion in discussion. Virtual reality (VR) is a purely synthetic, computer-generated environment with which the user interacts. AR mixes the physical world (real world) with synthetic computer-generated information. The virtual representations can give the user additional information about the physical world not accessible by unaided human senses. MR (sometimes referred to as hybrid reality) describes immersive experiences that blend AR and VR to produce new environments and visualizations of physical and digital objects interacting in real time.

Technological advances are evolving rapidly in VR, making it difficult to define. This chapter will utilize the definition used by practitioners and scholars. VR is the computer-generated simulation of 3D images or environments to enhance the participant's virtual world experience. VR is a medium that offers the user a simulated experience approaching that of the physical reality. VR also eliminates any danger in physical reality and can also create scenarios which are not possible in the real world. The VR system provides direct sensory feedback to the user based on their physical position. In most cases, it is the visual sense that receives feedback, although VR environments exist which use haptic experiences, sound experiences and so on. Achieving immediate interactive feedback requires a high-speed computer as a mediating device. The devices used in virtual environments play a significant role in the creation of successful virtual experiences.

According to the literature, technology can be distinguished as input and output devices (Bricken, 1991). Input devices allow the user to communicate with the virtual environment and can range from a simple joystick or keyboard to a glove that captures finger movements and a tracker able to capture body posture. Keyboard, mouse, trackball, and joystick are simple desktop input devices, which allow the user to launch continuous and discrete commands or movements to the environment. More complex input devices include bend-sensing gloves that capture hand movements, postures and gestures, or pinch gloves that detect finger movements, and trackers that follow the user's movements in the physical world and translate them to the virtual environment.

Output devices allow the user to see, hear, smell, or touch everything that happens in the virtual environment. As mentioned above, visual devices range from the simplest or least immersive (a computer monitor) to the most immersive (VR glasses or helmets), or head-mounted display (HMD) or cave automatic virtual environment (CAVE) systems. Furthermore, auditory speakers or haptic output devices can stimulate body senses to provide a more real virtual experience. For example, haptic devices can stimulate touch and feeling in the user.

In VR, the user is mentally immersed in the experience. This is often referred to as having 'a sense of presence' within an environment. Unlike more traditional media, VR allows participants to select their vantage point by positioning their body, and to affect events in the virtual world. These features help to make the reality more compelling than static, third-person media experiences.

THE HISTORY OF VIRTUAL REALITY

VR has existed since the 1960s. The first proper system was invented by Ivan Sutherland in 1965, who created a head-mounted system called the "The Sword of Damocles", to project 3D images on to a screen for users to experience a VR world in real time. This system was the first to allow users to experience a virtual world in real time and to interact with it (SPREE Interactive, 2024; Cross, 2023; Sutherland, 2001).

Since then, the technology has advanced rapidly. The first commercially available VR systems were introduced in the 1980s and 1990s. The most popular was the Virtuality arcade system, which allowed users to play games in a fully immersive virtual world. However, these systems were expensive and required powerful computers to run (Schmandt et al., 1983). In the mid-1990s, VPL Research introduced the DataGlove and the EyePhone, some of the first VR consumer peripherals. These devices allowed users to interact with virtual environments using their hands and eyes (Iwata & Fujii, 1996; SPREE Interactive, 2024).

In the early 2000s, companies like Sony, Samsung, HTC Vive, Oculus and Google made huge investments in VR to develop high-quality VR headsets that leveraged powerful graphics and motion tracking technology. Oculus began developing head-mounted displays with wider fields of view and better resolution. The Oculus Rift headset led to a surge of interest in VR and stimulated further industry innovations. The current generation of VR systems was brought about by advances in display, sensing, and computing technology from the smartphone industry (Sampaio et al., 2010). VR headsets are now mass-produced and in the hands of millions of people. In 2014, Facebook's acquisition of Oculus led to a significant increase in the popularity of VR devices for home use. Since then, VR has become more popular and accessible to the everyday consumer, with more VR headsets available on the market, such as the HTC Vive, Samsung VR, Oculus, Google Cardboard, and more.

While gaming has been a driving force behind VR's popularity, its uses are not limited to this, and various other fields have embraced it as a powerful tool. This trend is similar in many ways to the home computer and web browser revolutions; as a wider variety of people have access to VR technology, the range of its uses substantially broadens. With continued advancements in technology and affordability, the number of educational VR applications and experiences in education has also risen (Swapp et al., 2010; SPREE Interactive, 2024).

THEORETICAL FOUNDATIONS OF VIRTUAL REALITY LEARNING

The introduction of VR technology in education has generated excitement and high expectations of its capabilities. VR continues to advance rapidly and is providing possibilities to create new learning experiences and opportunities. However, the theoretical foundations of using VR in education have not been widely addressed. There is lack of theory-based research in the existing literature on VR based learning. Studies to gain more theoretical insights are critical to enable effective, efficient, and appropriate utilization of the technology for educational purposes.

The theoretical foundation of VR learning draws on several established educational theories and approaches. Learning theories provide valuable insights into the design and implementation of VR in education. They offer a theoretical framework that helps educators understand how learners engage with the virtual environment, process information and construct knowledge. By aligning VR experiences with learning theories, educators can optimize the effectiveness of VR in enhancing learning outcomes. One such theory is constructivism, which argues that knowledge is constructed through an individual's real-life experiences and reflection on those experiences. For proponents such as Jean Piaget and Lev Vygotsky (1980), constructivism as a learning theory emphasizes the combination of inputs from existing knowledge and new information gained, to develop new meaning and understanding through active, authentic, cooperative and reflective learning activities. Learners actively interact with the real world, applying their knowledge to daily life activities, thus increasing the effectiveness of the learning process (Chen, 2011; Chen & Tsai, 2012). Constructivism is applicable to VR learning as VR provides immersive, interactive environments where learners can experiment, make decisions, and experience scenarios in ways that support the active construction of knowledge. Meaningful VR experiences provide opportunities for students to construct and practice their own knowledge. Students can immersivity engage in educational activities and gain a better understanding of the topic at hand. Reeves (1993) suggested that well-designed simulated multimedia environments allow for the development of apprenticeship-type tasks to support real-life activities.

Research indicates that various capabilities of VR technologies support constructivist learning (Jonassen et al., 2000; Greening, 1998; Chen & The, 2000; Bricken, 1991). VR provides a controlled environment in which learners can navigate and manipulate the virtual objects found within and, importantly, the effects of such interaction can be observed in real time. Furthermore, VR also offers flexibility for repetition and self-pacing. All these factors contribute to motivation, which is a key component of learning. This complies with another principle of constructivism that specifies the need to grant learners responsibility for the learning process in order to create their own understanding (Jonassen et al., 2000). Dewey (1916) suggested that the main function of education was to enhance the learner's reasoning processes. A learner who is not motivated will not really perceive a problem, so problems selected for study should be derived from learner interests. VR is therefore very well suited for providing exploratory learning environments which enable learning through experimentation (Chen, 2000).

Constructivists believe that students can learn better when they are actively involved in constructing knowledge in a learning-by-doing situation. To engage the learner in meaningful learning, it must be an active process in which the learner uses sensory input and constructs meaning from it. A virtual environment allows the learner to control and interact directly with objects in the virtual world. Such control and interaction, together with free exploration, provide a greater sense of empowerment. A virtual environment provides a space for problem manipulation, allowing the learner to freely explore and manipulate virtual objects within the environment. Unlike many other educational tools, a virtual environment is designed without a specified sequence. Learners can learn from their own exploration of the virtual environment. Such navigation enables discovery and experiential learning. VR platforms that simulate historical events or scientific experiments provide contexts where learners can actively engage and construct their own understanding (Falk et al., 2022). VR devices has made it possible for students to experience their education in more immersive and engaging ways. VR can transport students from their desks to the ancient Roman ruins, let them mix volatile chemicals and see the reaction without being physically harmed, and allow them to not only see but interact with the virtual worlds.

Constructivism also asserts the importance of the collaborative nature of learning. Vygotsky (1980) proposed that learning is a socially mediated activity, occurring when learners work together to solve problems. This concept of social constructivism emphasizes the importance of interaction with other learners through teamwork and mutual exploration. When a collaborative task is completed successfully, each individual in the group has learnt to complete the task independently. Therefore, constructivist learning environments provide access to information and cognitive tools to assist learners to work collaboratively to achieve the learning goal. Collaborative VR environments support such social learning theories by enabling students to work together in virtual spaces, share knowledge, and solve problems collectively (Schroeder et al., 2021). The virtual learning environment provides an opportunity where a group can share the same experience of virtual learning or problem manipulation, and collaboratively construct new knowledge through conversations about the task. A group of learners may collaborate through synchronous and/or asynchronous communication. Examples of synchronous communication include real-time text and/or audio chatting and desktop video conferencing. Asynchronous communication includes written and/or auditory messages, or even virtual actions, left for later participants, as well as e-mails and newsgroups, where the conversations do not occur in real time (Chen, 2009). VR technologies can build synthetic 'real' worlds capable of simulating, representing, or recreating different facets of reality (Carmigniani et al., 2011; Sánchez et al., 2000).

Winn (1993) emphasized that thc characteristics of VR and the axioms of constructivist learning theory are entirely compatible, asserting that constructivism provides a valid and reliable basis for a theory of VR learning. Advanced VR learning environments could bridge the gap between the theoretical learning of formal instruction provided in traditional classrooms and the application of such knowledge in virtual environments. Along with the Internet and other innovative technological tools for communication, visualization, and simulation, VR provides important technological support for creating constructivist learning environments to provide learners with a more authentic learning experience (Changet al., 2010). The ability to integrate VR into lessons to achieve learning goals requires the teacher to be flexible and adaptive to harness the immersive nature of VR technologies, while ensuring that there is sufficient. Scaffolding of content effective lesson enactment strategies to enable students to have a clear. Understanding of the concepts.

Virtual reality has a rich history and a promising future. Its journey continues to unfold, unlocking new realms of experiences and possibilities. As an ever-evolving technology that has the power to transform the way we perceive and interact with the world, there are many opportunities to explore its application in education.

VIRTUAL REALITY APPLICATIONS

VR technology platforms can be grouped under three paradigms: head-mounted, hand based and stationary. Head-mounted devices (headsets) block the user from the outside world, as the user puts on a headset to become part of the VR environment. The VR experience can be enhanced by adding devices like voice recognition or a hand-held controller, to make it immersive: beyond simply looking around, the user interacts with the computer-generated environment. Hand-based VR involves the user holding a device like a smartphone or smart glasses which displays the information. The user then holds the device to their eyes to experience the VR environment. In the stationary VR paradigm, the device is not worn or carried by the user. The system uses large display screens or monitors to carry the visual information of the VR experience.

Since its appearance, VR has been used in different fields, including military training, medical simulations, architectural design, sports and gaming industry environments (Song et al., 2017; Zhang Ros et al., 2021; NMC, 2016; Chen & Denoyelles, 2013; Checa & Bustillo, 2020). The lifelike simulations provide authentic experiences for users. In engineering, mathematics, and the sciences, VR offers the chance to visualize geometric relations between concepts, or data that are difficult to interpret. Furthermore, VR is naturally suited to practical training, because skills developed in a realistic virtual environment can transfer naturally to the real environment. The motivation for use of VR is particularly high if the real environment is costly to provide or the experience poses health risks. One of the earliest and most common examples of training in VR is flight simulation. On an educational level, the greatest opportunities for VR lie in the humanities, including history, anthropology, geography and foreign language acquisition. Rather than simply reading a textbook on ancient Egyptian civilization, it is much more attractive to virtually visit ancient Egypt in a VR simulation. Viewing and experiencing VR simulations complements classroom instruction in many ways (Adam, 2016). For instance, a teacher sharing virtual experiences relevant to the subject being discussed in class can expect students to gain a deeper and richer understanding. To illustrate, prior to teaching a unit on volcanoes a teacher might show students a 360° video or VR environment on volcano eruption and flowing lava. This scaffolding technique is not only enjoyable and stimulating for the learner, but it also provides visuals of the erupting volcano in a much more authentic experience (Corporation for Public Broadcasting, 2004). The VR activity enables students to experience the volcano as if they were standing in the middle of flowing lava, providing a far more engaging and memorable learning experience.

VR in education can enhance collaborative learning. Learners can interact with their peers and the virtual environment, making the experience more active and memorable. It can additionally offer students a personalized learning experience by allowing them to explore the virtual world at their own pace and in the way they prefer. Students can improve their comprehension of the subject matter by using VR technology to deliver personalized feedback. VR technology is attractive to the education sector because of its adaptability to different learning styles. For visual learners who prefer graphics over explanations, VR provides highly visual aspects. For those who learn by exploration instead of lecture, VR can provide a detailed analysis of concepts that would not have been otherwise possible. For those who learn better by interacting with the environment, VR allows the direct manipulation of environmental elements that respond to the actions of the user in real time. VR creates environments, experiences and interactions that look and seem real. When users wear VR headsets, they are transported into a three-dimensional, interactive world that can be explored and manipulated. This digital environment is designed to engage multiple senses, including sight, sound, touch, and movement. This innovative form of simulation offers a unique and communal way to enjoy content, allowing learners to share the virtual space and collectively engage in the content.

BENEFITS OF VR IN EDUCATION

In recent years, significant technological improvements have made it possible for VR technologies to support many educational activities that integrate traditional classroom teaching and learning (Carmigniani et al., 2001; Dunleavy et al., 2009; Shim et al., 2003). Immersive VR applications offer numerous advantages, allowing multi-sensory interaction where learners can construct meaning from the experience. VR learning can engage students' attention, inspire creativity, and spark their imaginations. Traditional teaching methods can sometimes struggle to engage students, particularly with complex or abstract subjects.

VR provides an immersive experience that can make learning more dynamic and interactive, making difficult concepts accessible. Learning in a shared virtual reality can reveal ways in which collaboration and problem-solving work in practice (Reynard, 2017), thus promoting constructive learning. Students are encouraged to think actively and create their own learning experiences thus enhancing engagement and retention. For example, through VR geometry students can examine 3D geometric forms from multiple perspectives; they can rotate a shape to see it from different angles and even view it from the inside. Similarly, students exploring a 3D model of the solar system can experience the vastness of space and the scale of planets firsthand, which can be more engaging than a textbook description.

Studies show that students often find VR experiences more engaging than traditional learning methods. VR allows for experiential learning, where students can practice skills in safe, controlled environments. The benefits of VR in education go beyond academic subjects to include cultural competence, the ability to understand another person's culture and values an important skill in today's interconnected, global society. VR has the capacity to transport students to different environments, allowing them to learn and explore various concepts safely and efficiently, as when a VR field trip to another part of the world, near or far, exposes students to cultures other than their own. There are several engaging VR apps and projects that can be used in the classroom. A great example is Google Expeditions, which allows the teacher to take an entire class on virtual trip. The application recreates an immersive experience of a real-world with 360-degree videos shot of different locations such as an underwater exploration of a coral reef in the South Pacific, the Great Pyramid of Giza or Louvre Museum in Paris using Google Street View technology (Brown and Green, 2016).

Research indicate that VR can improve cognitive learning and problem-solving skills. The VR immersive nature can help in complex concept visualization. Growing evidence suggests that VR in education, as well as the combination of VR and AR technologies known as mixed reality (MR), can improve student outcomes. In a March 2019 report, EdTech cited a study showing that students in an MR biology classroom received higher scores than other students in a traditional learning environment. AR and VR can also help with memory retention and recall. EdTech reports on a recent study that showed an increase in retention of almost 9 percent for students who learned in an immersive VR environment over those in a traditional learning environment.

The literature is increasingly recognizing the potential benefits of VR as a tool supporting special needs students in the learning process. Research indicates the critical role of VR technology in improving the behavioral, communication and social skills of children who have autism spectrum disorder (ASD). The application of VR technology is being considered as the best method to monitor ASD intervention through VR-based human–computer for everyday tasks (Schultheis and Rizzo, 2001).

Despite the growing popularity and acceptance of VR, some reservations exist regarding its applications in education curricula (Pirker et al., 2020). Some VR-based research has furnished mixed findings, or even negative results for learning outcomes. Some obstacles to implementing VR technology learning include the cost of equipment or headsets, reports of motion sickness such as nausea or dizziness by some users, lack of technical (IT) support regarding the integration of VR into the teaching process, unequal access to VR among different demographic groups, and lack of teacher training on the technology (Alfalah, 2018; Pirker et al., 2020). VR use can also have detrimental effect in cases of severe anxiety. Due to these factors, an alternative solution must always be available when using VR learning for instruction. Lectures need to be present when using the VR applications to support students and possibly offer other tasks if the limitations cannot be overcome. Research is still limited on how VR can be integrated into the curriculum and how it can be part of a classroom experience.

With VR technology further advancing, it could also be used for live, synchronous classes where students can engage with classmates and teachers in real time from home. This would have been especially beneficial when schools were closed due to the Covid 19 pandemic, but it can also provide a way for students to attend classes during absence due to health issues, traveling, or distant living, etc. Even though live classes have not yet really been held using VR, such applications can be developed in the future, especially with some of the current developments being made in both asynchronous learning and social interaction.

LITERATURE REVIEW

The growing interest in VR has resulted in multiple literature reviews on the use of VR for learning (Dhimolea et al., 2022). Research show that educational media with a high degree of technological immersion positively influences the engagement, presence, and motivation of students. In order for the VR experience to be seen by students as more than a playful element, the immersive experience must be embedded in the instructional sequence. This can be achieved by aligning the virtual environment with learning objectives (Pirker et al., 2020). Discussions on the use of VR often focus on the concepts of immersion and the sense of presence. Immersion can be defined as "the involvement of a user in a virtual environment during which his or her awareness of time and the real world often becomes disconnected, thus providing a sense of 'being' in the task environment instead," (Radianti et al., 2020,

p. 2). VR increases the sense of presence, which is a feeling of being "there" in the VR environment, while simultaneously recognizing that one is not "there," but in the real world (Gruber & Kaplan-Rakowski, 2020). VR has the power of 'tricking' the user's brain into feeling that they are inside real VR experiences and can fully engage with the content. Given that high immersion and the sense of presence are factors contributing to high engagement, from the pedagogical point of view, VR should serve as an attractive platform to complement classroom instruction, which is often associated with relatively low engagement. The current literature indicates that VR holds substantial promise for enhancing educational experiences by increasing engagement, supporting experiential learning, and facilitating collaborative activities. It makes teaching complex topics accessible and easier as it provides a means of visualization (Christou, 2010). Use of immersive VR experiences helps students to learn better as learning activities do not feel like work and enjoy the learning process instead. Thus, VR increases student motivation. Motivation towards learning is not only closely related to academic achievement but also psychological well-being. Previous research has found that learning with VR could be very motivating for students, because of its unique features of navigating, interactivity, and immersion (Webster,2016). More specifically, studies have found that interactivity and content immersion were strongly related to *psychological presence* (Terkildsen & Makransky, 2019).

Immersive virtual environments support learning by diverse students, including academically weak students, who are more comfortable with learning from digital technology. VR proves useful in improving teachers' abilities to help students think differently about content (Cheng & Tsai, 2020; Winn, 1993; Psotka, 1995; Al-Amri et al., 2020).

Research shows that VR supports better learning outcomes in various subjects by providing opportunities for experiential learning that would be more difficult in real-world settings (Mikropoulos & Natsis, 2020). In science education, VR simulations allow students to explore complex systems, such as the human body or astronomical phenomena (Slater et al., 2021). Liu (2020) indicated that students who were taught science in immersive VR classrooms achieved better outcomes compared to traditional teaching methods with slides and video. Immersive experiences and interactive elements in VR environments capture students' attention more effectively than traditional methods (Huang et al., 2020). Research on VR in K-12 education demonstrates that VR can make abstract concepts more tangible and engaging, leading to improved learning outcomes (Bailenson, 2021). VR tools enable teachers to expand their students' learning experiences by providing 'virtual field trips' on topics of study. Parong (2020) stated that high school students in an immersive VR biology classroom achieved better learning than those in a traditional classroom. This indicates a positive impact of immersive VR technology experience in enhancing interest and achievement in science. Using tools such as Google Street View, teachers can provide students with an in-depth knowledge of cultures, places, and ideas. Research shows that students with prior knowledge of a topic are impacted by their understanding of concepts more than those with no prior knowledge (Richardson et al., 2012; Sousa, 2005; Marzano, 2004; Remolar et al., 2021). Students with considerable prior knowledge of a subject can use problem-solving strategies more effectively than those with little prior knowledge. Put simply, students who have been to a beach, and who are reading text about a beach, may better understand the topic than those who have never visited a beach.

Although there has been an increase in VR in education systems, challenges remain which hinder its comprehensive use across school systems. These relate to high cost, usability, and technical support. These problems need to be addressed to fully realize its potential. Increased accessibility, practical training, knowledge of one's field of study, and a closer link between VR use and higher education will help facilitators to access VR course-related content suitable for classroom use. Future research will benefit from focusing on long-term impacts, curriculum integration, and inclusivity, to advance the field further.

This brief literature review shows VR's potential to benefit a multitude of educational applications. VR as a technology is still in its infancy in education, but more people are becoming more interested in it and are optimistic about the changes VR can make in their everyday lives. With rapidly increased use of personal computers and smartphones, VR could be the next technological breakthrough to become common in most households. As VR becomes more popular, and more content is produced, many teachers are wondering how best to integrate it into the classroom. VR in education will aid the discovery, exploration and building of new knowledge about subjects, places, and situations that were previously remote.

RESEARCH HYPOTHESES

VR technology has been broadly accepted by researchers and educators as useful for creating an alternative learning environment to real life settings. It has the potential to increase learner engagement and motivation to explore interactions between instructional content and virtual objects. Hsiao and Rashvand (2011) proposed three important factors to motivate learners: intuitive interaction, a sense of physical imagination, and a feeling of immersion. Interactivity and environmental factors can improve learning motivation (Ryan & Deci, 2000). Based on these discussions and with reference to the conceptual model of this study, the following hypotheses are derived:

H1. Experience of using VR in learning will have a positive impact on perceived usefulness of VR in education.

H2. Using VR will have a positive impact on perceived ease of use of VR learning systems.

H3. Using VR will have a positive impact on motivation for VR learning systems.

METHODOLOGY

Both quantitative and qualitative research methods were used for the study as an effort to create a more comprehensive understanding of the problem under investigation. The use and analysis of both qualitative and quantitative methods allowed for neutralizing of the weaknesses in one method, by using the strength of the other method. Tobergte (2013) describes triangulation as the effort of combining both types of data that have been used within the mixed methods process, in the attempt to use one set to corroborate the other.The qualitative research techniques seek to provide explanations of attitudes and experiences rather than to quantify the degree to which a phenomenon exists. The researcher, through interaction with participants seeks their perspectives and meaning. The researcher starts the process by gathering detailed information and forming categories or themes as patterns emerge. An interpretive literature review method was selected for the present literature review following the framework described by Arksey and O'Malley (2005). The aims of conducting a literature review are to examine the extent, range, and the nature of research activity. The research gaps can be identified in the existing literature by summarizing and disseminating research findings of interest (Arksey & O'Malley, 2005). The framework of scoping reviews includes five stages in total: (1) identifying the research question; (2) identifying relevant literature; (3) selecting literature; (4) charting data; and (5) collating, summarizing and reporting the results.

The quantitative methods not only involve the use of numbers such as official statistics, but they also include the entire process in which data are collected. The quantitative data were compiled and analyzed using SPSS statistical software. This study surveyed learners' attitudes toward the use of VR learning environments. VR headsets were used as supplementary tools for instruction in a college-level social science course. Critical to this study was feedback about the VR application as a part of course content. Each VR headset contained ready-made curriculum content. All participants were undergraduates majoring in Elementary Education. A total of 120 students completed the study as well as a confidential questionnaire. The goal for this study was to observe students' attitudes to, and use of, immersive VR experiences related to social studies education, and then to reflect on specific learning objectives based on those experiences (Alhalabi, 2016). Students were asked about their experience of VR and how useful they thought it was. The project sought to determine whether immersive VR experience improved student engagement and interest. It also focused on the basic user experience of concepts (Reeves & Crippen, 2021). The independent variable was the teaching method: VR or the traditional approach. The dependent variable was the level of enjoyment in learning social studies.

Data were collected using a paper-and-pencil survey on a Likert scale (1-5) with close-ended questions, to discover whether the user felt that VR made a difference during instruction. A literature review of common journal search engines and websites, including peer-reviewed studies and articles provided relevant sources for the topic of VR technology applications. Sources are still limited, but there were promising examples of how VR could be beneficial in an educational environment.

Differing VR course-related activities were applied to various social studies concepts. Following a pre-test survey on ancient Egypt, students used VR headsets to learn about ancient Egyptian civilization by exploring virtual environments of the pyramids and the tombs of the kings, and then completed a post-learning survey. The two surveys were compared to determine if improvement was observable. The dependent variables were compared between the pre-test and post-test surveys. If the *p value* obtained is less than 0.05 it confirms that there is a significant difference in student performance between the learning modes. This concluded that VR resulted in greater enjoyment in learning social science concepts. With VR, students can visualize the tomb and the mummy of King Tutankhamun, making abstract concepts into concrete experiences.

VR learning promoted the activation of students through self-directed by means of interactions. During the VR course assignments students were asked to use the "Think Aloud" method to express their thoughts when interacting with the VR system (Shim et al., 2003), where the instructor typically prompts students to keep talking as they interact with the VR application. This helped to document student's perceptions of VR applications. With the use of VR, students interests are activated through collaborative learning, which can lead to a promotion intrinsic motivation.

RESULTS

Survey data were reviewed and analyzed to determine students' opinions towards the use of VR as an instructional tool. Overall, participants shared positive opinions towards their use of VR as a supplementary tool in the course (See Table1). Table 1 provides descriptive statistics of survey data of participants perceptions on use of VR as an instructional tool in the course. Descriptive statistics help describe and explain the features of a specific data set by giving short summaries about the sample and measures of the data.

Table 1. Students' perceptions of using VR as an instructional tool.

Survey Questions	Mean (M)	Statistics Std. Deviation
VR was easy to use	3.74	1.023
VR was fun to use	4.19	.622
Using VR increased my opportunity to interact with fellow students	3.67	.832
I felt more engaged in the class material using VR Cardboard compared to traditional lecture classes	3.81	.834
Using VR improved my interest in the geography course material	4.04	.759
Using VR helped me to understand the concepts better	4.19	.557
VR technology applications make things feel more real and thus easier to understand	4.04	.808
VR technology was effective in helping me understand a geography concept	3.59	.971

The mean(*M*), or the average, is calculated by adding all the figures within the data set and then dividing by the number of figures within the data set. The mean is the most stable and reliable central tendency measure. Table 1 mean scores are based on a "5-point Likert **type** scale with responses ranging from strongly disagree (1) to strongly agree" (5). The means scores range from 3.59 to the highest 4.19 indicating that the respondents perceived use of VR in the course to have a positive impact in their learning. For the first hypothesis, *H1. Experience of using VR in learning will have a positive impact on perceived usefulness of VR in education;* data show that students perceived VR as a useful tool to provide immersive and active learning experiences in the course. Participants stated that they had a feeling of being present in the exact environment provided to them. The participants stated that VR provided them opportunity to visit destinations where they could otherwise not go. VR made concepts easier to understand (*M* 4.19), VR improved interest in the course materials (*M* 4.04), and VR made the subject matter easier to understand compared to the traditional lecture method (*M* 3.81). For the second hypothesis, *H2. Using VR will have a positive impact on perceived ease of use of VR learning systems;* data show that participants responded positively indicating that the VR headsets effective, are fun to use (*M* 4.19), and easy to use (*M* 3.74). Participants shared that VR made the content more interesting and realistic. It was stated that the VR content created excitement in participants therefore the desire to was created for going to the VR environment in real life.

For the third hypothesis, *H3. Using VR will have a positive impact on motivation for VR learning systems*; students were asked to state their opinions towards use of technology in education. In this context, all participants positively felt that VR provided a helpful new way of learning that made class discussions more enjoyable and increased their interest in the course materials. It was stated that VR facilitated collaborative learning by allowing students to interact in virtual spaces and made the course materials more enjoyable. This can enhance communication and teamwork skills. Students felt more engaged in the class material using VR compared to traditional lecture classes (*M* 3.81). VR use increased opportunity for students to interact with fellow students (M 3.67) thus enhancing collaborative learning.

The use of VR added value and interest to the course in various ways. VR encouraged student participation in instructional goals. It increased student engagement, student attention, depth of knowledge of content, ability to grasp 3D visuals of content, and digital skills. Students agreed that VR experiences provided an ideal technology to make learning more interesting and fun. VR allowed students to explore, experience, and become immersed in virtual environments. In some instances, VR more accurately illustrated some features, processes, and environments, allowing extreme close-up examination of an object, and the observation and examination of environments and events unavailable by other instructional means. VR applications show a great potential for acquiring knowledge by having students shift from being viewers to being performers thus deepening the knowledge they have learned.

LIMITATIONS OF VR IN EDUCATION

This section will discuss VR advancements in education and summarize the challenges and drawbacks of using VR technology as an educational tool. Research show that VR has great potential for positive educational outcomes by providing more engaging learning environment stimulating various perception points. However, as it is a new delivery method for knowledge, VR lacks the in-depth research (Davis, Nesbitt, & Nalivaiko, 2015). Most modern existing VR solutions are based on HMDs, which provide a total immersion through 3D virtual environment imitating the reality.

According to Christou, 2010, one of the challenges that need be addressed is the lack of visual realism and realism of the dynamics and interaction. It can be concluded that existing techniques used to generate VR graphics and displaying technology are quite limited. Note that, psycho-visually, the human brain's construction allows us to detect even small unrealistic details, which can easily break the immersion. Thus, in the creation of the VR world, maximizing the appearance of reality is an ongoing challenge.

Another challenge is that realistic VR environments require computationally powerful hardware for rendering, which goes hand in hand with the high price. According to Christou, C. 2010, high costs of developing or purchasing a VR system is a significant hurdle to overcome. Currently, devices providing high-end VR experiences, such as Oculus Rift or HTC Vive cost approximately $400–$600, respectively; they should be supported by computationally powerful PC, which is still a relatively expensive alternative to conventional methods of teaching. VR technology is under constant development, seeking low-cost, wearable solutions for the mass market. Professional technology companies have provided products that incorporate mobile phones. For example, Samsung Gear VR, Google Daydream, or a more low-end Google Cardboard, are more accessible than the above-mentioned high-end solutions (e.g., HTC Vive or Oculus), they do not require an additional computer, only a low-cost headset with a phone. However, experiences or simulations generated on mobile may not match the ones generated on a PC concerning immersion. Additionally, the mobile solutions have minimal interactive capabilities in comparison with what is achievable with high-end solutions. Nonetheless, the trade-off between accessibility and price might be the key factor in using the low-end mobile solutions by a wider audience. Educational simulations might not require the highest available quality but are rather based on the content of the experience and possibility to provide many headsets for a class of students at a significantly lower cost compared to high-end HMDs.

Human factor and physical side effects are another issue (Christou, 2010). Recent reports suggested that the use of HMDs may have unwanted physical/physiological side effects such as anxiety, stress, addiction isolation and mood changes. Further, simulated motions can affect one perception of time and space, inducing dizziness and nausea, called VR sickness or cybersickness. HMD worn on the head, due to unnatural postural demands, may have a negative effect on dissociation of accommodation/convergence and cardiovascular change. However, there are only a few scientific studies presenting clinical trials on the effect of using HMDs. Notably, most of the scientific experiments were carried out using very early HMD technologies. Due to the technical advancements in HMD technology, new investigations are required in this domain. Furthermore, every man is unique and may have different perception; therefore, scenarios preparing for education, especially for kids or handicapped should be accurately examined and evaluated, consulted with professional psychologists and educators.

The present study provides insights into how VR-based learning in relation to impact on student learning. However, it should be noted that the present study has its limitations due to the small sample size and the selection of content and application strategies. Specifically, this study was limited to use of Cardboard VR headsets, which are of lower-end VR devices, compared to the Oculus Rift or the HTC Vive. Moreover, the study literature is limited to peer-reviewed journal articles only to ensure the quality of included articles. However, Conference proceedings and theses could also provide meaningful evidence if chosen carefully. Databases such as Springer and ERIC should also be used to search articles. Future reviews on this topic could extend the range of inclusion criteria to provide a broader picture of the issues that have been discussed in the present research.

DISCUSSION AND CONCLUSION

The use of VR can provide more varied and authentic experiences to enhance learning for all students. VR provides outstanding visualization of content, which cannot be obtained in traditional classroom. The technology offers immersive learning experiences to students that provide countless ways to experience the world around them, promoting collaboration and increasing engagement and motivation. The survey results show a positive perceived learning effect on using VR applications for instruction. It is a technology that proves useful in improving teachers' abilities to enhance content learning (Winn, 1993; Psotka, 1995; Mak, 2016). VR can provide innovative educational opportunities that encourage students to approach subject matter from alternative perspectives. Immersive VR technologies can bring about greater understanding of abstract concepts by an authentic presentation of educational content. One powerful feature of VR technology is that it allows users to intuitively interact with 3D objects in real-time (Thomassen & Rive, 2010). VR technology creates a highly intuitive and interactive user experience (Chittaro & Ranon, 2007), making the system easy to use. It gives students the ability to participate in virtual field trips, explore historical landmarks and connect their learning experience to the real world. However, these benefits to education are contingent upon the technology's successful integration into the classroom. The success on VR learning depends upon the technical knowledge of the instructor. VR application should not be seen as a replacement to traditional teaching methods but as a supplement to classic teaching methods. If VR applications are used this way, they can find great use in teaching the school curriculum.

The results support the hypothesis that 3D immersive VR learning environments increase learning motivation (Limniou & Papadopoulos, 2008; Ryan & Deci, 2000). Perceived ease of use, perceived usefulness, and learning motivation significantly affect learners' willingness to use the VR learning system in the classroom. Perceived usefulness has consistently been seen as the most influential predictor of intention to use virtual reality systems (Islam, 2013; Sun & Cheng, 2009; Verhagen et al., 2012). The immersive aspect of virtual learning environments is found to motivate learners; thus, use of virtual reality systems can improve knowledge acquisition and retention (Burdea & Coiffet, 2003) beyond what is possible with 2D animated environments (Limniou et al., 2008). Therefore, educators should seek to maximize learner motivation by increasing interactivity in learning activities by utilizing technology.

However, it is still the case that many teachers lack understanding of the immersive VR technologies and the pedagogical content knowledge to use them proficiently. This calls for strategic professional development opportunities by practitioners to support teachers in learning the use of immersive VR technologies.

Although using modern technology like VR in education is clearly beneficial, it is not without risks. One of the main issues is the lack of flexibility during instruction. During the traditional class session, a students may ask questions, receive answers, take part in discussion. Using a virtual reality headset with specific software, the students are restricted and must follow the rules, cannot do anything else except what they are supposed work on. Some educators are naturally resistant to change, and their involvement and active participation is crucial for successful introduction of VR technology into the classroom. Others might tend to over rely on technological developments, leading to lack of teacher–student interaction thus negatively impacting students' academic performance, social-emotional development, and sense of security.

Given the novelty of VR tools in education, there is limited research so far on the applied implementation of VR in classroom instruction. More research is needed to shed light on the effective learning strategies and pedagogy for integrating VR technologies into the school curricula. As technologies continue to evolve, the power of the VR experience will increase. In some cases, the priority will be the maximum realism of the environment; but in others, leaving some imagination to the users will also remain valuable. The technology surrounding VR has become both affordable and accessible to the point where it is now appropriate to an increasingly technology-rich classroom setting. Although technological design changes constantly, humans (users) are still designed the same way. Understanding how the human mind works is crucial to understanding the fundamentals of VR systems. Future research could focus on how VR learning influences the relationship between learning motivation and learning achievement, since this study focuses only on learner perceptions of perceived usefulness. It is important to evaluate actual learning outcomes based on the use of such learning systems.

REFERENCES

Adams, R. L. (2016). Five reasons why virtual reality is a game-changer. *Forbes*. Retrieved from https://www.forbes.com/sites/robertadams/2

Al Amri, A., Osman, M., & Musawi, A. A. (2020). The effectiveness of a 3D virtual reality learning environment (3D-VRLE) on Omani eighth grade students' achievement and motivation towards physics learning. *International Journal of Emerging Technologies in Learning*, 15(5), 1–16. DOI: 10.3991/ijet.v15i05.11890

Alfadil, M. (2020). Effectiveness of virtual reality games in foreign language vocabulary acquisition. *Computers & Education*, 153, 103893. Advance online publication. DOI: 10.1016/j.compedu.2020.103893

Arksey, H., & O'Malley, L. (2005). Scoping studies: Towards a methodological framework. *International Journal of Social Research Methodology*, 8(1), 19–32. DOI: 10.1080/1364557032000119616

Bédi, L., Bradley, K., Friðriksdóttir, H., Garðarsdóttir, H., Thouësny, S., & Whelpton, M. J. (2022) (Eds.). *Intelligent call, granular systems, and learner data: short papers from EUROCALL 2022*. Netútgáfa: Research-publishing.net. https://ritaskra.arnastofnun.is/media/skraning_pdf/Short_Papers_from_EUROCALL_2022.pdf

Beilenson, J., & Markowitz, D. (2021). Virtual reality and the psychology of climate change. *ScienceDirect*, 9(3), 23–64.

Bricken, M. (1991). Virtual Reality Learning Environments: Potentials and challenges. *Computer Graphics*, 25(3), 178–184. DOI: 10.1145/126640.126657

Brown, A., & Green, T. (2016). Virtual reality: Low-cost tools and resources for the classroom. *TechTrends*, 60(5), 517–519. DOI: 10.1007/s11528-016-0102-z

Campos, E., Hidrogo, I., & Zavala, G. (2022). Impact of virtual reality use on the teaching and learning of vectors. *Frontiers in Education*, 7, 965640. DOI: 10.3389/feduc.2022.965640

Carmigniani, J., Furht, B., Anisetti, M., Ceravolo, P., Damiani, E., & Ivkovic, M. (2011). Augmented reality technologies, systems and applications. *Multimedia Tools and Applications*, 51(1), 341–377. DOI: 10.1007/s11042-010-0660-6

Checa, D., & Bustillo, A. (2020). A review of immersive virtual reality serious games to enhance learning and training. *Multimedia Tools and Applications*, 79(9–10), 5501–5527. DOI: 10.1007/s11042-019-08348-9

Chen, B., & Denoyelles, A. (2013). Exploring students' mobile learning practices in higher education. *EDUCAUSE Review*, •••, 7.

Chen, C. J. (2009). Theoretical bases for using virtual reality in education. *Themes in Science and Technology Education*, 21, 71–90.

Chen, C. J., & Teh, C. S. 2000. An affordable virtual reality technology for constructivist learning environments. *4th Global Chinese Conference on Computers in Education*, 414-421.

Chen, C. J., & Teh, C. S. (2013). Enhancing an instructional design model for virtual reality-based learning. *Australasian Journal of Educational Technology*, 29(5), 699–714. DOI: 10.14742/ajet.247

Chen, C. J., Yun, H., Lin, K. Y., Chang, Y. S., Lin, H. C., Lin, C. Y., & Hsaio, H. S. (2019). Developing a hands-on activity using virtual reality to help students learn by doing. *Journal of Computer Assisted Learning*, 6(1), 46–60. DOI: 10.1111/jcal.12389

Cheng, K., & Tsai, C. (2020). Students' motivational beliefs and strategies, perceived immersion and attitudes towards science learning with immersive virtual reality: A partial least squares analysis. *British Journal of Educational Technology*, 51(5), 2139–2158. DOI: 10.1111/bjet.12956

Clark, R. E. (2006). Reconsidering the research on learning from media. *Review of Educational Research*, 53(4), 445–459. DOI: 10.3102/00346543053004445

Collins, A., & Halverson, R. (2018). *Rethinking Education in the Age of Technology: The Digital Revolution and Schooling in America*. Teachers College Press.

Cross, A. (2023). The evolution of virtual reality: Exploring the past, present and future. *Forbes*.https://www.forbes.com/sites/forbesbusinesscouncil/2023/11/09/the- evolution-of-virtual-reality-exploring-the-past-present-and- future/?sh=eaba2d72b70f

Davis, S., Nesbitt, K., & Nalivaiko, E. (2015). Comparing the onset of cybersickness using the Oculus Rift and two virtual roller coasters. In *Proceedings of the 11th Australasian Conference on Interactive Entertainment (IE)*, Sydney, Australia; Volume 27, p. 30.

Dewey, J. (1916). *Democracy and education*. The Free Press.

Dhimolea, T. K., Kaplan-Rakowski, R., & Lin, L. (2021). A systematic review of research on high-immersion virtual reality for language learning. *SSRN*. https://dx.doi.org/DOI: 10.2139/ssrn3863724

Donkin, R., & Kynn, M. (2021). Does the learning space matter? An evaluation of active learning in a purpose-built technology-rich collaboration studio. *Australasian Journal of Educational Technology*, 37(1), 133–146. DOI: 10.14742/ajet.5872

Dunleavy, M., Dede, C., & Mitchell, R. (2009). Affordances and limitations of immersive participatory augmented reality simulations for teaching and learning. *Journal of Science Education and Technology*, 18(1), 7–22. DOI: 10.1007/s10956-008-9119-1

Gruber, A., & Kaplan-Rakowski, R. (2020). User experience of public speaking practice in virtual reality. In Zheng, R. Z. (Ed.), *Cognitive and affective perspectives on immersive technology in education* (pp. 235–249). IGI Global., DOI: 10.4018/978-1-7998-3250-8.ch012

Gruber, A., & Kaplan-Rakowski, R. (2022). Verbal and nonverbal communication in high immersion virtual reality for language learners. In Arnbjörnsdóttir, B. (Eds.), *Intelligent CALL, granular systems, and learner data: short papers from EUROCALL 2022, 129-134*. DOI: 10.14705/rpnet.2022.61.1447

Hsiao, K. F., & Rashvand, H. F. (2011). Integrating body language movements in augmented reality learning environment. *Human-centric Computing and Information Sciences*, 1(1), 1–10. DOI: 10.1186/2192-1962-1-1

Huang, C. L., Luo, Y. F., Yang, S. C., Lu, C. M., & Chen, A. S. (2020). Influence of students' learning style, sense of presence, and cognitive load on learning outcomes in an immersive virtual reality learning environment. *Journal of Educational Computing Research*, 58(3), 596–615. DOI: 10.1177/0735633119867422

Interactive, S. P. R. E. E. (2024). The history of virtual reality and its impact on Gen Alpha. https://jointhespree.com/the-history-of-virtual-reality/ Retrieved 2021-01-22.

Jonassen, D. H., Hernandez-Serrano, J., & Choi, I. 2000. Integrating constructivism and learning technologies. In Spector, M. & Anderson, T.M. (Eds,), *Integrated and holistic perspectives on learning, instruction and technology: Understanding complexity,* 103-127. Springer.

Kalati, A. T., & Kim, M. S. (2022). What is the effect of touchscreen technology on young children's learning? A systematic review. *Education and Information Technologies*, •••, 1–19.

Kaplan-Rakowski, R., & Gruber, A. (2023). An experimental study on reading in high- immersion virtual reality. *SSRN*. https://ssrn.com/abstract=4262124

Kozinets, R. V. (2023). Immersive netnography: A novel method for service experience research in virtual reality, augmented reality and metaverse contexts. *Journal of Service Management*, 34(1), 100–125. DOI: 10.1108/JOSM-12-2021-0481

Krokos, E., Plaisant, C., & Varshney, A. (2019). Virtual memory palaces: Immersion aids recall. *Virtual Reality (Waltham Cross)*, 23(1), 1–15. DOI: 10.1007/s10055-018-0346-3

Lave, J., & Wenger, E. (1991). *Situated learning: Legitimate peripheral participation.* Cambridge University Press. DOI: 10.1017/CBO9780511815355

Liu, R., Wang, L., Lei, J., Wang, Q., & Ren, Y. (2020). Effects of an immersive virtual reality- based classroom on students' learning performance in science lesson. *British Journal of Educational Technology*, 51(6), 2034–2049. DOI: 10.1111/bjet.13028

Magdalene, R., & Sridharan, D. (2018). Powering E-Learning Through Technology: An Overview of Recent Trends in Educational Technologies. *The Online Journal of Distance Education and e-Learning : TOJDEL*, 6, 60.

Mak, J. (2016). Google Expeditions offers stunning field trips without leaving school. The International Society for Technology in Education. Retrieved from https://www.iste.org/explore/articleDetail?articleid=664&category=In-the- classroom&article.

Marougkas, A., Troussas, C., Krouska, A., & Sgouropoulou, C. (2023). Virtual Reality in Education: A Review of Learning Theories, Approaches and Methodologies for the Last Decade. *Electronics (Basel)*, 12(13), 28–32. DOI: 10.3390/electronics12132832

Marzano, R. J. (2004). *Building background knowledge for academic achievement: Research on what works in schools.* Association for Supervision and Curriculum Development.

Merchant, Z., Goetz, E. T., Cifuentes, L., Keeney-Kennicutt, W., & Davis, T. J. (2014). Effectiveness of virtual reality-based instruction on students' learning outcomes in K-12 and higher education: A meta-analysis. *Computers & Education*, 70, 29–40. DOI: 10.1016/j.compedu.2013.07.033

New Media Consortium (NMC). (2016). NMC/CoSN Horizon Report 2016 K-12 Edition. Retrieved from http://cdn.nmc.org/media/2016-nmc-cosn-horizon-report - k12- EN.pdf

Parong, J., & Mayer, R. (2021). Cognitive and affective processes for learning science in immersive virtual reality. *Journal of Computer Assisted Learning*, 37(1), 226–241. DOI: 10.1111/jcal.12482

Pirker, J., Lesjak, I., Kopf, J., Kainz, A., & Dini, A. (2020). Immersive learning in real VR. In Magnor, M., & Sorkine Hornung, A. (Eds.), *Real VR–Immersive Digital Reality* (pp. 321–336). Springer. DOI: 10.1007/978-3-030-41816-8_14

Psotka, J. (1995). Immersive training systems: Virtual reality and education in training. *Instructional Science*, 23(5-6), 405–431. DOI: 10.1007/BF00896880

Reeves, S., & Crippen, K. (2021). Virtual laboratories in undergraduate science and engineering courses: A systematic review 2009-2019. *Journal of Science Education and Technology*, 30(6), 16–30. DOI: 10.1007/s10956-020-09866-0

Reeves, T. C. (1993). Interactive learning systems as mindtools. In Newhouse, P. (Ed.), *Viewpoints 2, 2-11, 29*. ECAWA.

Remolar, I., Rebollo, C., & Fernández-Moyano, J. A. (2021). Learning history using virtual and augmented reality. *Computers*, 10(11), 146. DOI: 10.3390/computers10110146

Reynard, R., (2017). The impact of virtual reality on learning. *Campus Technology,* n.d.

Richardson, J. S., Morgan, R. F., & Fleener, C. (2012). *Reading to learn in the content areas*. Wadsworth.

Rogers, S. (2019). Virtual reality: THE learning aid of the 21st Century. *Forbes* .www.forbes.com/sites/solrogers/2019/03/15

Ryan, R. M., & Deci, E. L. (2000). Intrinsic and extrinsic motivations: Classic definitions and new directions. *Contemporary Educational Psychology*, 25(1), 54–67. DOI: 10.1006/ceps.1999.1020 PMID: 10620381

Sampaio, A. Z., Ferreira, M. M., Rosário, D. P., & Martins, O. P. (2010). 3D and VR models in civil engineering education: Construction, rehabilitation and maintenance. *Automation in Construction*, 19(7), 819–828. DOI: 10.1016/j.autcon.2010.05.006

Schneider, D., Biener, V., Otte, A., Gesslein, T., Gagel, P. & Campos, C., (2021). Accuracy evaluation of touch tasks in commodity virtual and augmented reality head-mounted displays. arxiv.org/pdf/2109.10607.

Schultheis, T., & Rizzo, A. (2001). The application of virtual reality technology in rehabilitation. *Rehabilitation Psychology*, 46(3), 296–311. DOI: 10.1037/0090-5550.46.3.296

Shim, C., Park, J., Kim, H., Kim, J., Park, Y., & Ryu, H. (2003). Application of virtual reality technology in biology education. *Journal of Biological Education*, 37(2), 71–74. DOI: 10.1080/00219266.2003.9655854

Slater, M. (2021). Beyond speculation about the ethics of virtual reality: The need for empirical results. *Frontiers in Virtual Reality*, 2, 687609. Advance online publication. DOI: 10.3389/frvir.2021.687609

Song, H., Chen, F., Peng, Q., Zhang, J., & Gu, P. (2017). Improvement of user experience using virtual reality in open-architecture product design. *Proceedings of the Institute of Mechanical Engineering*. 232.

Sousa, D. (2005). *How the brain learns to read*. Corwin Press.

Sutherland, I. E. (1965). The ultimate display. Paper presented at the IFIP Congress. www. papers.cumincad.org/cgi-bin/works/c58e. Retrieved April 22, 2019.

Swapp, D., Williams, J., & Steed, A. (2010). The implementation of a novel walking interface within an immersive display. *Institute of Electrical and Electronics Engineers (IEEE) Symposium on 3D User Interfaces* (3DUI).

Terkildsen, T., & Makransky, G. (2019). Measuring presence in video games: An investigation of the potential use of physiological measures as indicators of presence. *International Journal of Human-Computer Studies*, 126, 64–80. DOI: 10.1016/j.ijhcs.2019.02.006

Thomassen, A., & Rive, P. (2010). How to enable knowledge exchange in Second Life in design education? *Learning, Media and Technology*, 35(2), 155–169. DOI: 10.1080/17439884.2010.494427

Tobergte, D., & Curtis, S. (2013). Social research methods. *Journal of Chemical Information and Modeling*, 88, 327–342.

Van Krevelen, D. W. F., & Poelman, R. (2010). A survey of augmented reality technologies, applications and limitations. *The International Journal of Virtual Reality : a Multimedia Publication for Professionals*, 9(2), 1–20. DOI: 10.20870/IJVR.2010.9.2.2767

Vygotsky, L. S. (1980). *Mind in society: The development of higher psychological processes*. Harvard University Press. DOI: 10.2307/j.ctvjf9vz4

Webster, R. (2016). Declarative knowledge acquisition in immersive virtual learning environments. *Interactive Learning Environments*, 24(6), 1319–1333. DOI: 10.1080/10494820.2014.994533

Winn, W. (1993). A conceptual basis for educational applications of virtual reality. *Technical Report* TR-93-9, Human Interface Technology Laboratory, University of Washington.

Wonsick, M., & Padir, T. (2020). A Systematic Review of Virtual Reality Interfaces for Controlling and Interacting with Robots. *Applied Sciences (Basel, Switzerland)*, 10(24), 9051. DOI: 10.3390/app10249051

Yoo, J., & Brownlee, E. A. (2020). The past, present, and future of virtual reality in higher education. In Okojie, M. C. P. O., & Boulder, T. C. (Eds.), *Handbook of research on adult learning in higher education* (pp. 633–657). IGI Global. DOI: 10.4018/978-1-7998-1306-4.ch024

Zhang, X., Lo, P., So, S., Chiu, D., Leung, K., Ho, K., & Stark, A. (2021). Medical students' attitudes and perceptions towards the effectiveness of mobile learning: A comparative information-need perspective. *Journal of Librarianship and Information Science*, 53(1), 116–129. DOI: 10.1177/0961000620925547

KEY TERMS AND DEFINITIONS

Augmented Reality: A medium in which real-time interactive digital information is overlaid on the physical world in both spatial and temporal alignment.

Constructivism: An approach to learning that emphasizes the active role of learners in building their own knowledge. Rather than passively receiving information, learners reflect on their experiences to gain deeper learning and understanding.

Immersion: The sensation of being in an environment, whether a purely natural state or manipulated by physical means.

Mental Immersion: A state of being deeply engaged; a suspension of disbelief; a deep sense of involvement.

Simulation: A computer-based imitative representation of a process or system that could exist in the real world.:

Three-dimensional: **(3D)**: This refers to the three spatial dimensions of width, height and depth. The physical world and everything that is observed in it is three-dimensional.

Virtual: An indication that an entity mimics the characteristics of another; in the context of a virtual world, any object in that world is said to be virtual.

Virtual Reality: Immersion into an alternate reality or point of view.

Virtual World: An imaginary space often manifested through a medium.

Chapter 7
Augmented Reality Applications in Mathematics Education

Ibrahim Kepceoglu
Kastamonu University, Turkey

Mehmet Koray Serin
https://orcid.org/0000-0003-4104-5902
Kastamonu University, Turkey

ABSTRACT

The primary purpose of this book chapter is to examine the use of augmented reality applications in mathematics education from a general perspective. In this context, information about the use of technology in mathematics education is given first. In the following sections, the concept of augmented reality is explained, and the explanations are supported by sample applications of how augmented reality is used in educational processes. Then, by evaluating how augmented reality applications in mathematics education have been handled and used, especially in recent years, the reader is provided with both theoretical and practical information about augmented reality applications in mathematics learning-teaching processes.

USE OF TECHNOLOGY IN MATHEMATICS EDUCATION

Contemporarily, technology has a significant impact on people and society. This impact also affects education. The issue of how to effectively integrate digital technology into teaching and learning practices becomes critical in recent years. The use of modern equipment technology and tools, the learning and interactivity

DOI: 10.4018/979-8-3693-6030-9.ch007

of students increases and the transfer of knowledge becomes very easy and convenient, as well as effective (Raja & Nagasubmarini, 2018). As educational models should be more and more student-centered, more integration of new technologies into learning-teaching processes is necessary. For the past decades, scholars have stressed the potential of technological tools in combination with appropriate pedagogy to support learning of mathematics in education (Gómez-García et al., 2020). Technology integration has brought about a change in mathematics education starting from the 1970s (Engelbrecht et al., 2020). Following this process that started with programming, dynamic geometry systems (DGS) and computer algebra systems (CAS) were adopted as technology integration in mathematics teaching (Herfort et al., 2023). The emergence of computer algebra systems (Mathematica, Maple, etc.) running on personal computers in the late 1980s is seen as a significant technological advance in mathematics. Computer Algebra Systems (CAS), which emphasize the processing of symbolic expressions, and Dynamic Geometric Software (DGS), which focuses on the relationships between points, lines, circles, etc., can be stated as two main types of software that contribute to the teaching and learning of mathematics. With the publication of GeoGebra dynamic software by Markus Hohenwarter in 2001, these two software were combined into a single mathematics teaching software package (Hohenwater et al., 2009; Yohannes & Chen, 2021).

While traditional education is limited to the time when students are physically in the classroom, participation in discussions outside the classroom (e.g., on social online platforms) is prolonged and efficient. Noroozi et al. (2020) emphasize that today's topic in education is digitalization and the use of technology and that higher-order thinking skills can be gained not through traditional education processes but through technology integration. The introduction of technology in mathematics education transforms mathematics teaching and learning environments (Clements et al., 2013; Roschelle et al., 2017). Students could investigate conceptual knowledge, practice problems, justify mathematical ideas, and communicate with their peers and teachers using various technology tools (Higgins et al., 2019; Roschelle et al., 2017) In addition to the integration of technology into mathematics teaching-learning processes and the diversity of this integration, the effect of this technology on students' mathematics performance has also been an essential topic of discussion and research. In most studies, results have been reached that technology can improve students' mathematics performance. For example, Hillmayr et al. (2020) stated that technology-based learning activities such as gamification and interactive software led to a significant increase in students' mathematics performance. In addition, technology can provide students with immediate feedback on their work, allowing them to self-correct and adapt faster (Bright et al., 2024). However, technology in itself is not a sufficient factor to improve math performance (Gómez-García et al., 2020).

In some cases, technology may pose technical difficulties for students in terms of use or may become a distraction and distract them from learning goals. In addition, the unconditional and unprepared implementation of some technology-supported activities that need to be adapted to individual learning styles and abilities may only be suitable for some students in the classroom (Bright et al., 2024). It should be noted that teachers have an essential role in the successful integration of digital technologies into mathematics classrooms (Clark-Wilson et al., 2023). Teachers who 'strongly' believe in the potential and value of digital technologies to support teaching practices and students' learning and understanding use digital technologies much more effectively and efficiently (Crisan et al., 2023).

With an increasing number of digital applications and Web 2.0 tools readily available, technology has a vital role in the 21st-century classroom (Purcell et al., 2013). Current technological innovations such as wireless mobile devices and virtual or augmented reality offer additional opportunities to develop innovative learning environments in mathematics education (Tomaschko & Hohenwarter, 2019). Digital technology applications for mathematics have various purposes and design features. A number of mathematics-specific applications commonly used by students in schools or at home are listed in the table below (Crisan et al., 2023):

Table 1. Technological tools specific to mathematics (Crisan et al., 2023)

Categories	Use in Mathematics Education	Sample Tools/Applications
Tools for outsourcing the maths	Tools that can perform numerical calculations algorithmic processes, and quickly produce the correct answer.	• Four-function, Scientific, and Graphic calculators • Excel • CAS applications (Maple, Mathematica, Derive, Wolfram Alpha)
Dynamic Mathematical tools	Software with dynamically manipulable tools for drawing graphs or figures, writing algebraic expressions, representing data.	• GeoGebra, Geometer's Sketchpad, Cabri • Graph, Autograph, Omnigraph • Desmos, CAS with dynamic features
Data analysis software	Tools that allow data to be gathered and analyzed.	• Excel, Python, CODAP, R
Programming tools	Software programs that help users create, organize, and maintain any programming task.	• Scratch, Logo, 3D Logo, Python, MATLAB
Extended Reality (XR) technology tools	Tools that allow students to experience and interact with a 3D world virtually.	• Augmented reality such as GeoGebra's 3D • Calculator (with AR) • Virtual reality (VR) such as GeoGebra 3D

continued on following page

Table 1. Continued

Categories	Use in Mathematics Education	Sample Tools/Applications
Mathematics content learning platforms	Through learning platforms, students can access different worksheets, supporting information, and valuable resources. They are personalized and interactive tools.	• MyMaths, Dr Frost Maths, Hegarty Maths, Integral Maths, Purple Maths, Headstart, Times Tables Rock Stars, AtomLearning, Mathletics
AI tools	AI-based calculators that solve arithmetic operations or algebraic expressions that students struggle with, as well as ChatGPT applications that can improve mathematical reasoning skills.	• AI-based calculators (Photomath) • AI tutoring systems (Chat GPT)

WHAT IS AUGMENTED REALITY?

Augmented reality (AR) is a field of study that covers the combination of the real world and computer-generated data such as audio, video, graphics, GPS location information (Zachary et al., 1997). In this field of study, virtual objects are added to real images and simultaneous interaction between virtual and real objects is provided. AR is a technology with three basic features: 1) it combines real and virtual images, 2) it is interactive in real time, and 3) virtual images are recorded in three dimensions (Azuma, 1997). It is aimed to strengthen and support reality by providing information that is not normally detectable by people's senses and cognitive processes (Azuma, 1999). With AR applications that offer conceptual learning in an interactive way, users have the opportunity of real observation and perception through the virtual world. In a sense, they experience the feeling of being in a multimedia environment (Chen et al., 2013). An AR system aims to create an environment in which the user can have a sensory experience enriched with information and virtual elements and which allows the user to participate in certain applications. Therefore, AR is both a visual paradigm and an interface based on the combination of information generated by a computer (static and dynamic images, sounds, tactile sensations) with the real environment in which the user is located (figure 1) (Vertucci et al., 2023).

Figure 1. An example AR application (Garcia, 2022)

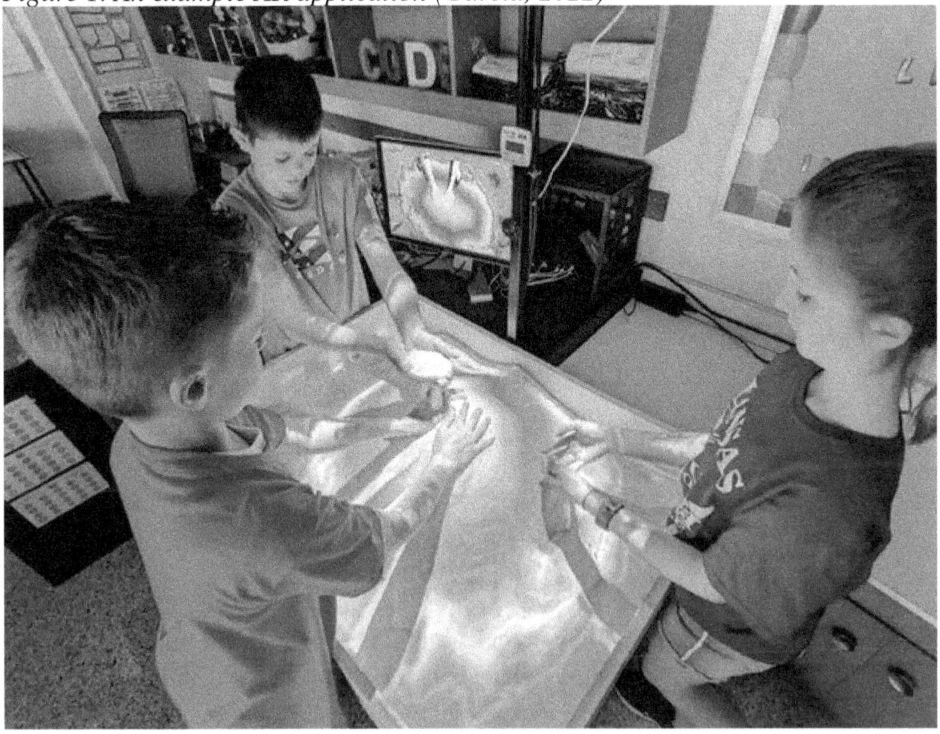

The term Augmented Reality (AR) was introduced in the early 90s. In 1992, Boeing researcher Thomas Preston Caudell developed an AR application for industrial use to display some assembly diagrams (Arena et al., 2022). Although definitions were made in the 90s, the first emergence of AR dates back to the 1950s when Morton Heilig, a cinematographer, thought that cinema was an activity that had the ability to draw the viewer into the activity on the screen by effectively involving all senses (Carmigniani and Furht, 2011). Heiling developed the Sensorama simulator to simulate a motorbike ride in New York City (Cazzola et al., 2019; Schmalstieg & Hollerer, 2016). Slightly larger than an Arcade Cabinet in a game room (Figure 2), this simulator allowed the user to see 3D stereo images enhanced with sensations such as vibrations, wind, feedback on the handlebars, stereo sound and a special system to reproduce odours (Arena et al., 2022; Kaminska et al., 2023).

Figure 2. Sensorama simulator

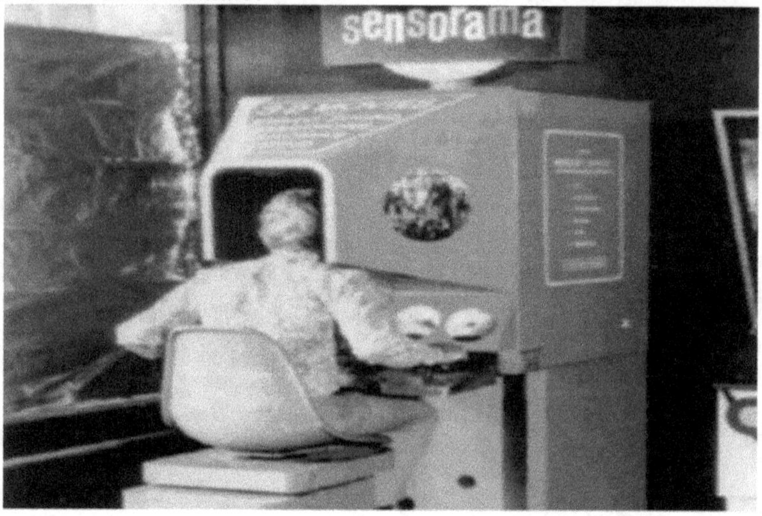

Later, Ivan Sutherland, in his 1965 article The Ultimate Display, talked about a future computer interface that blurs the distinction between the digital and physical worlds and invented the head-mounted display (HMD) in 1966 (Billinghurst, 2021). The so-called "Sword of Damocles" helmet (Figure 3) was equipped with lenses for AR and made it possible to view images superimposed on the real world. The helmet was developed to help helicopter pilots land at night by operating cameras with the movement of their head. Due to its extreme weight, this mechanism has been dubbed the Sword of Damocles as it is attached to the ceiling using a pivoting arm that aids head movement (Aschauer et al., 2021; Arena et al., 2022).

Figure 3. The first head-mounted display (Werner, 2024).

Like augmented reality (AR), virtual reality (VR) is another concept that is not very new in the literature but is very popular today. Both concepts are often confused by both media and users due to the increasing popularity of technological devices and the corresponding increasing interest and demand of consumers (Burdea & Coiffet, 2003). Although AR and VR technologies are closely related, they offer different approaches to interacting with reality and virtuality (Azuma, 1997; Cevikbas et al., 2023; Milgram & Kishino, 1994). In the traditional sense, virtual reality (VR) is a world in which one is completely immersed in a synthetic world and can interact with it. Such a world can mimic the characteristics of some existing or fictional real-world environments; however, it can also cross the boundaries of physical reality by creating a world where the physical laws govern space, time, mechanics, material properties, etc. No longer apply (Milgram & Kishino, 1994). Virtual reality refers to immersion in a completely virtual environment, usually or most easily achieved by capturing the entire peripheral field of view of a participant through a head-mounted display (HMD) (Sutherland et al., 2019). The aim of VR is to create three-dimensional and interactive virtual environments in which the real world is modelled. AR, on the other hand, aims to enrich the real world in real time and interactively with virtual data developed in a computer environment. In other words, VR aims to bring reality to the virtual world as it is, while AR focuses on enriching reality with virtual information (Somyürek, 2014). While VR is based on equipment that is relatively foreign to daily life and can be expensive, AR mostly uses smartphones as input devices to overlay digital content in the real world. Therefore, unlike VR, it does not require expensive hardware (Kaminska et al., 2023; Velarde-Camaqui et al., 2024).

Virtual objects used in AR systems can include text, still images, video clips, sounds, 3D models and animations. Ideally, these virtual objects will be perceived as coexisting in a real-world environment (Bower et al., 2014). In AR, virtual elements are overlaid on the surrounding real-world environment, usually using an HMD that does not obstruct the user's view. Modern AR systems range from simple, handheld displays that show models superimposed on real-world video images to head-mounted devices with clear goggles that allow users to visualise virtual elements with additive blending superimposed on the surrounding real-world environment (Figure 4) (Moro et al., 2017; Plasencia et al., 2015; Sutherland et al., 2019).

Figure 4. AR hardware interfaces: displays for the head and displays for the hand (Campbell, 2016).

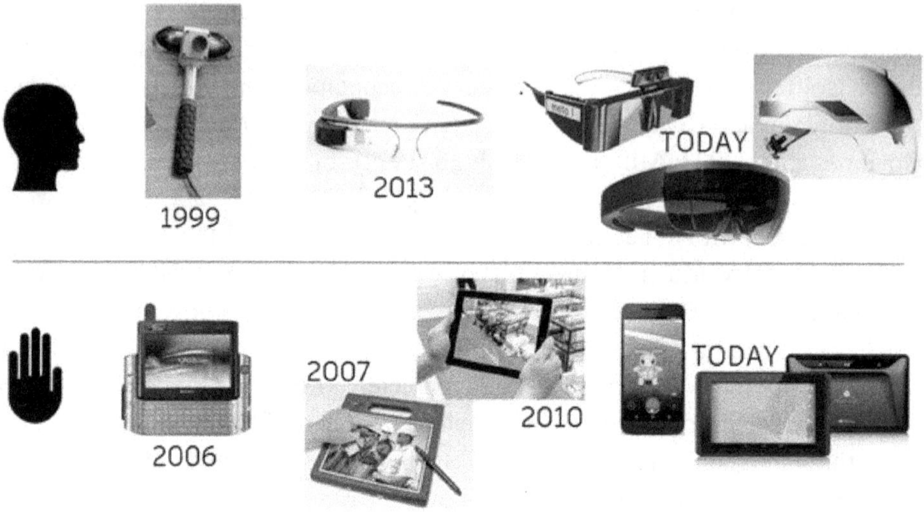

Given their common elements, the relationship between VR and AR can be better assessed through the concept of reality-virtuality continuum. Milgram and Kishino (1994) introduced the concept of mixed reality (MR), which blends both types of interaction into a single process. They proposed the reality-virtuality continuum, a central model that introduces the MR structure for understanding AR/VR. Figure 5 shows this continuum between two extremes, with the real world at one end and a completely virtual reality at the other. The space in between defines the mixed reality virtuality continuum, which includes a combination of both real and virtual elements. Augmented reality refers to a largely real environment with few virtual elements, while the less relevant concept of augmented virtuality (AV) consists of a predominantly virtual environment with elements of the real world (Sutherland et al., 2019).

Figure 5. Illustration of the reality-virtuality continuum (Sutherland et al., 2019).

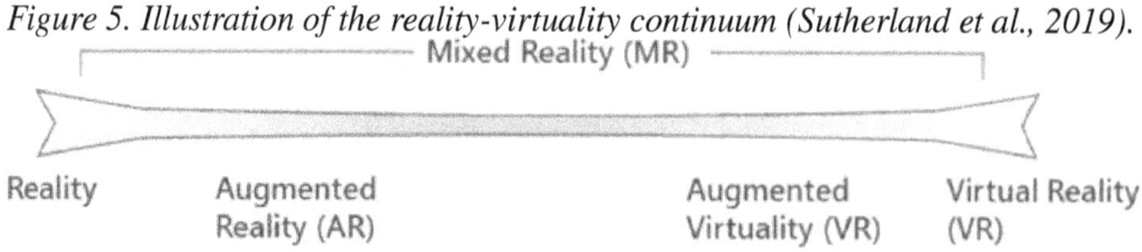

As a result, AR, VR and MR, which can be expressed as immersive technologies, enable users to have immersive experiences by integrating digital elements into the real world. These technologies are interconnected and take place along a continuum of virtuality extending from the real environment to the virtual environment as classified in the taxonomy of virtuality (Milgram & Kishino, 1994).

Figure 6. VR, AR and MR (URL-1)

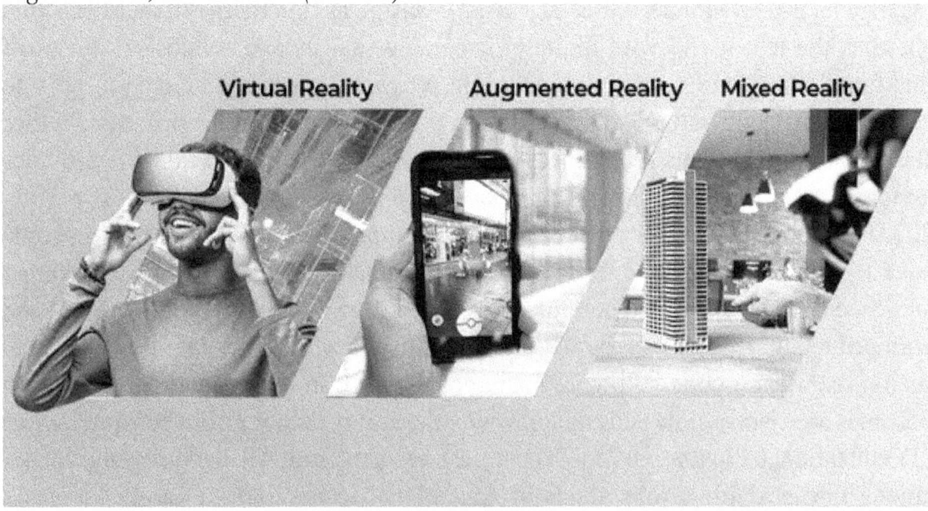

AUGMENTED REALITY APPLICATIONS IN EDUCATION

In Education 5.0-based learning processes, the interaction between teachers and students is no longer the main focus. Students have direct or indirect access to various sources of information through a manipulated interactive world. This process of education 5.0 has encouraged the development of a personalized learning process by emphasizing student individuality. Education 5.0 includes learning-teaching processes that can be adjusted according to the individual pace and interest of the student by using artificial intelligence, robotic process automation and extended reality (XR) in line with the developing fourth industrial revolution (Bhanu prasad et al., 2022). XR is an important component of education 5.0 in order to understand that individuals' learning needs and interests are not only unique but also their progress in the learning-teaching process and the learning outcomes they achieve and to adapt the learning process to bridge the gap between industry needs and academic learning (Liu et al., 2017). In the field of educational technology, there is a wide range of technologies and approaches used worldwide to support teaching and learning processes better (Avila-Garzon et al., 2021).

The idea that technological tools or applications can be utilised for the qualified human profile targeted to be achieved in line with educational policies is quite valid for all pedagogical processes of learning, including the use of feedback to inform student strategies and actions. In this direction, it can be said that augmented reality technologies can be used together with educational activities in a natural harmony (Marshall, 2023; Munnerley et al., 2012). AR is an interactive experience that enriches the real world with digitally generated images and sounds. The uses of this functionality are numerous, including providing a new and engaging way to acquire knowledge and information during a teaching or learning process. Studies show that most students remember AR-based lectures better and that AR provides a more memorable environment than lab-based demonstrations (Kaminska et al., 2023). According to the Pow Research Centre, approximately 70% of young people have access to a smartphone. Therefore, AR is available for the majority of the target audience (Lenhart, 2015). Therefore, this technology has great potential to be used with printed materials, such as AR-enabled illustrations in a textbook that come to life on the user's phone, allowing for interaction and in-depth analysis. Education becomes more accessible and engaging with the ability to move from non-interactive 2D educational illustrations to 3D interactive ones and AR becomes the leader among the most important trends in educational technologies (Kaminska et al., 2023). Dunleavy and Dede (2014) claim that AR is compatible with constructivist learning theory because it positions the learner in a real-world physical and social context while guiding, supporting and facilitating participatory and meta-cognitive learning processes such as authentic inquiry, active observation, peer coaching, reciprocal teaching, and legitimate environmental engagement with multiple modes of representation. In the field of education, content can be used and developed on mobile devices thanks to AR, which will enable students to interact with the virtual objects displayed. In this direction, 3D objects can be visualised, dynamic processes that are difficult to observe naturally can be presented as a simulation, and learning-teaching processes can be organised more efficiently by providing a high level of reality in general (Cerqueira et al., 2023; Goh et al., 2019; Wei et al., 2015). AR provides better visualization of scientific phenomena through the original interaction process it offers, thus reducing cognitive load. Many AR applications have been developed for a wide range of learning domains, such as science, engineering, and social sciences (Cipresso et al., 2018; Garzón & Acevedo, 2019).

When the devices designed for AR applications are analysed, it can be said that Microsoft HoloLens, Magic Leap One, Google Glass and Meta 2 (Figure 7) stand out. While mobile devices such as tablets and smartphones are most commonly used in education, HoloLens is the next choice of users (Kaminska et al., 2023).

Mobile AR is a technology that allows digital information to be superimposed on a real-world environment through a mobile device such as a smartphone or tablet. This technology uses the mobile device's camera and sensors to monitor the user's environment and overlay digital content in real time. Mobile augmented reality applications can range from simple experiences such as adding filters to a camera application to more complex experiences such as interactive games or educational tools that allow users to explore and learn about their environment in a new way (Koumpouros, 2024). While factors such as size, autonomous use, and relatively low purchase cost are considered as the reasons for more preference for mobile devices, the disadvantages of almost always requiring hand-holding and the use of static handles severely limit the functionality of AR applications. Looking at the external devices that support AR technology in education, users' AR experiences can be further improved with devices such as kinect, leap motion, projector, motion capture, magic mirror and microscope (Kaminska et al., 2023).

Figure 7. Devices designed for AR (McDowall, 2020).

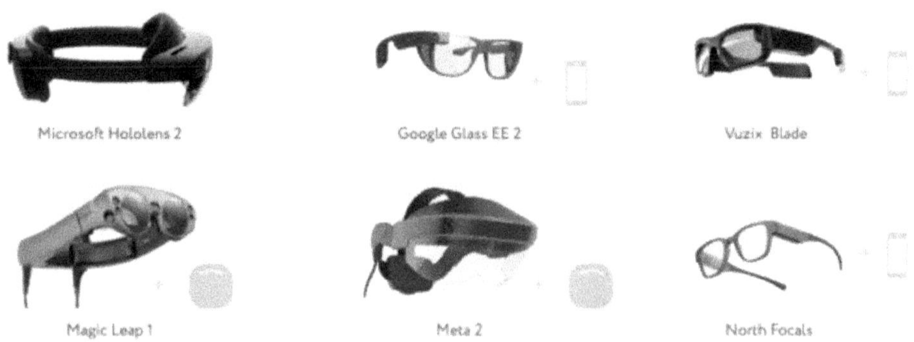

AR can be said to be an innovation that overlays intelligent segments such as content, images, video segments, sounds and 3D models on top of the real world. This innovation will not only enhance learning but also give students the freedom to shape their own education. In this context, some AR applications that can be used for education are as follows (Reddy, 2022):

- 3DBear
- Catchy Words AR
- CoSpacesEdu
- Froggipedia
- Jig Space
- Moat boat

- Orb
- World Brush

Maebell and Lawrence (2021) mentioned some AR/MR applications that can be used in education, emphasising that through AR, students can increase their knowledge and experience in various areas such as reading, arithmetic processing, real life environments and scenarios, spatial concepts, content creation and gaming:

- **Google Expeditions:** It is a virtual reality and augmented reality application that allows teachers to take their students on virtual trips to explore different parts of the world. With AR capabilities, students can bring distant landmarks and historical events directly into their classrooms and enhance their understanding of various subjects (URL-2).
- **SkyView:** Stars, planets and even satellites can be identified by pointing mobile devices at the sky. It helps students explore the universe.
- **Microsoft HoloLens:** Students can learn about anatomy by walking through the components of the human body.
- **ARKit:** Thanks to this library that offers augmented reality, many two-dimensional and 3D objects can be shown in the real world.
- **Quiver:** This application allows students to interact with three-dimensional figures in addition to the visuals in textbooks. For example, students can rotate a sphere in the air in the geography lesson, they can view the pictures on the marker papers in 3D according to the colours they paint (Figure 8).

Figure 8. Quiver app image (Uzun & Akın, 2022).

- **Elements 4D:** Especially in chemistry teaching, it enables the periodic table to be integrated into real life in blocks.
- **Blippar:** It is an application developed to improve children's reading experiences.
- **Arloon Plants:** In addition to presenting some basic science concepts related to the growth of plants, it allows students to observe plant growth and movement.
- **Math Alive:** Math Alive is an AR app that makes math fun and engaging for students by turning math problems into interactive games and puzzles. With features such as 3D graphics, geometric shapes and animated characters, Math Alive helps students visualize mathematical concepts and develop

problem-solving skills (URL-2). Teachers and students place the trigger card under a camera to practice counting and basic arithmetic skills.

With AR technology, students can be enabled to acquire the teaching content with 3D perspectives and in a collaborative manner in any suitable environment. In doing so, AR enhances students' sense of presence and proximity by visualising the invisible. Thus, a bridge is established between formal and non-formal learning. With these features, AR has created a new learning method and made the learning experience more fun and interesting (Blazauskas & Gudoniene, 2020; Masmuzidin & Aziz, 2018). When the relevant literature is examined, the benefits of using augmented reality applications in educational processes can be discussed under different headings. For example, it is stated that AR applications are more accepted compared to other pedagogical tools because they create a new way of interaction with real life, manipulate virtual objects, and allow observation or experimentation of phenomena that are difficult to observe or experience in the real world (Khan et al., 2019; Wu et al., 2013). The use of AR can provide students with additional information and facilitate the understanding of complex concepts. In addition to effectively attracting students' attention to the relevant concept or the subject to be taught, it also facilitates the explanation of abstract and difficult concepts (Huang et al., 2016; Sırakaya & Alsancak-Sırakaya, 2020). AR applications help students to organize and use their cognitive processes more efficiently by reducing their cognitive load (Bower et al., 2014; Kesim & Ozarslan, 2012) and transform the passive learning process into an active learning process by allowing them to interact with the teaching content, be creative and apply their knowledge in real time (Diegmann et al., 2015). In addition to the cognitive processes mentioned here, there are many studies in the literature that the use of AR applications in learning-teaching processes increases student motivation, positively affects students' learning outcomes, positively contributes to students' positive attitudes towards learning and the related course, and positively contributes to affective processes such as their perceptions of the relevance of what they learn to daily life (Billinghurst & Duenser, 2012; Gopalan et al, 2016; Jerry & Aaron, 2010; Khan et al., 2019; Lee, 2012; Rasimah et al., 2011; Tarng & Ou, 2012). Masmuzidin and Aziz (2018) stated that one of the biggest advantages of AR technology is to provide motivation and that students' (a) fun, interest and enjoyment; (b) participation; (c) satisfaction; (d) willingness to learn; (e) positive attitude; (f) attention; and (g) confidence level processes/statuses progress positively. Similarly, Akçayır and Akçayır (2017) stated that AR-based systems increase students' enjoyment, motivation and satisfaction with learning, even though their usability poses a great challenge. Chang and Hwang (2018) stated that AR-based systems have a positive impact on students' critical thinking skills as well as factors such as achievement, motivation, and attitude.

Avila-Garzon et al. (2021) state that the topics of education-centered studies using AR applications are mostly focused on special educational needs, Industry 4.0, storytelling, 3D printing, mobile applications and higher education. He emphasizes that in recent years, especially the concepts of 'gamification' and 'game-based learning' have been addressed together with AR applications. AR games have the potential to enable new forms of learning in the education sector and transform the learning experience. Below are some education-centered AR games (Weerasinghe et al., 2019):

- **Outbreak @ The Institute** (Rosenbaum et al. 2007): A simulation-based game that simulates the spread of an infectious disease on a university campus. Players take on various roles such as doctor, medical technician or public health expert and try to identify and control the source of the outbreak.
- **Astrid's Steps** (Nilsson et al., 2012): An outdoor mobile AR educational game that aims to enhance the experience of visiting a culturally significant place. Players activate the content by moving between locations and pointing their mobile devices at different landmarks and in different directions through various design concepts.
- **Amon Planet** (Hodhod, 2014): Aims to teach computational thinking skills through storytelling. The user is expected to perform a series of tasks embedded in the story at the center of the game. These tasks can be related to different courses and learning domains.
- **Monster Adventure** (Viinikkala et al. 2014): Aims to present the daily life of a 19th century city. The player is the protagonist who must solve a mysterious situation by performing various tasks. Players go through different experiences within the main story, developing new skills, new attitudes or new ways of thinking.

Avila-Garzon et al. (2021) state that the topics of education-centered studies using AR applications are mostly focused on special educational needs, Industry 4.0, storytelling, 3D printing, mobile applications and higher education. He emphasizes that in recent years, There is also growing interest in designing AR learning experiences for higher education. In the field of teacher education, AR has been used to facilitate the development of preservice teachers' proportional reasoning (Arican & Özçakir, 2021), the structuring of instructional materials (Chookaew et al., 2017), curriculum design (Nikimaleki & Rahimi, 2022), etc. Wang and Li (2024) systematically examined the research on the use of XR-based technologies (AR, VR, MR) in teacher education. According to the results obtained in the study, XR technologies are mostly used to improve teachers' procedural knowledge (e.g., classroom management processes). The studies were mostly conducted with preservice teachers, whereas there were not many studies on the in-service development of current teachers. VR was the most frequently used tool among XR technologies. Finally, the majority of studies reported that XR-based training positively affected teachers.

AUGMENTED REALITY APPLICATIONS IN MATHEMATICS EDUCATION

Advances in technology and ubiquitous access to mobile devices have increased the popularity of AR in recent years. By combining books or printed documents with immersive technology, teachers can provide students with access to digital content and extend learning in a 3D space. In addition, teachers can provide individualized instruction to students and place learning outside the classroom walls (Estapa & Nadolny, 2015). While significant strides have been made in educational technologies in line with technological advances, it is difficult to talk about a similar momentum in the use of advanced technologies in mathematics education. Although new technologies may not solve students' difficulties with mathematical problem solving skills, inactivity in the use of technology will continue to hold back advances in mathematics pedagogy. Therefore, educators need to create interactive environments to facilitate conceptual understanding, support learning, and solve mathematical problems based on real-life applications (Lai & Cheong, 2022).

It is stated that one of the negativities experienced in mathematics learning-teaching processes is that interactive learning cannot be realized sufficiently. The fact that the class size is higher than it should be or that students are forced to search for printed resources when they go out of the classroom can be shown as two simple examples that cause interactive learning not to be realized. At this point, AR applications contribute to the meaningful learning of mathematical topics or concepts by allowing students to work interactively both inside and outside the classroom (Cai et al., 2020; Koparan et al., 2023). Mathematics learning often requires the ability to construct mental models of abstract mathematical concepts that are drawn or verbally explained by teachers. This situation is also one of the factors that underlie the failure of students in mathematics learning processes (Quintero et al., 2015). At this point, AR applications both enable teachers to present these skills in a real-life based manner and allow students to experience them interactively. AR provides benefits especially for mathematics education in terms of visualization, manipulation and creating real contexts (Estapa & Nadolny, 2015), as well as providing opportunities to motivate students to explore virtual objects from various perspectives and to engage them interactively (Kerawalla et al., 2006).

Some mathematics applications in which AR technology is used in learning-teaching processes are as follows (Cerqueira et al., 2023):

- **Geometry AR** (https://www.venturaes.com/iosapps/geometryar.html)
- **GeoGebra Augmented Reality** (https://www.geogebra.org/)
- **Counting With Paula** (https://apk.support/developer/Omens+Studios)
- **AR Flashcards Addition** (https://arflashcards.com/)
- **Numbeanies Number Forest** (https://www.simoneinness.com/projects/numbeanies.html)

Among these applications, GeoGebra Augmented Reality can be used to place three-dimensional mathematical objects on the desktop, floor or any other flat surface. At the same time, since it is a dynamic geometry software, these objects can be resized, moved and calculations can be performed.

Figure 9. Geogebra AR app image.

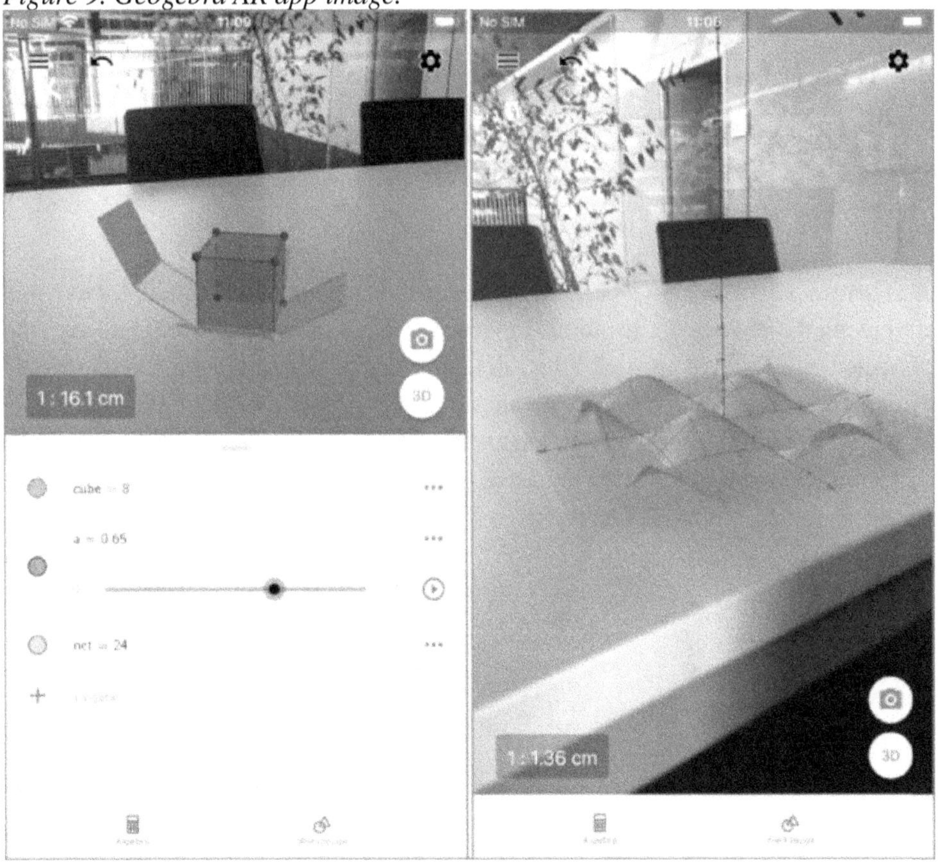

GeoGebra developers stated that they created this application to explore the potential of AR for mathematics education and training (Tomaschko & Hohenwarter, 2019). A sample application for teaching mathematics is given below. The aim of this activity is to model an object that students encounter in real life with GeoGebra AR. Then, by using this model, it will be possible to perform calculations on the object. In order to realize this activity, GeoGebra's 3D calculator tool must first be installed on the mobile device.

Figure 10. Geogebra 3D download image and main screen

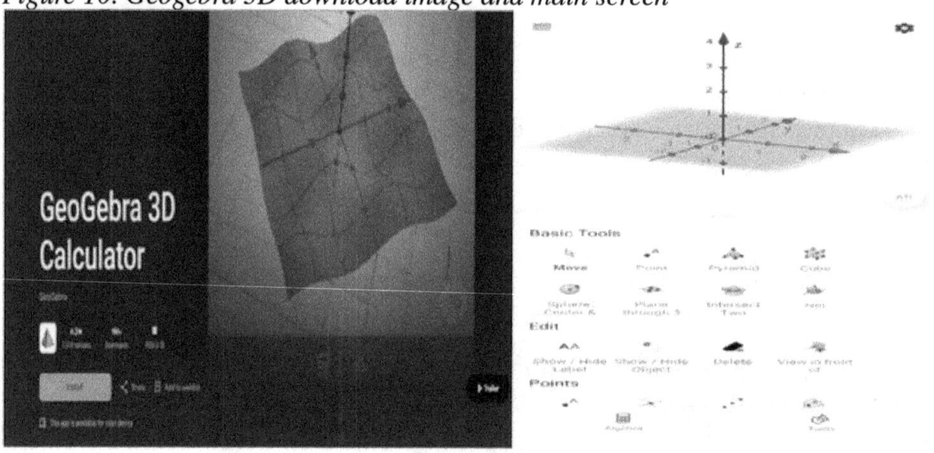

Then switch to the "AR" mode in the lower right corner of this calculator tool and start using the camera of the mobile device. With this mode, the coordinate axes are projected on a flat real ground. Thus, all operations performed on the GeoGebra 3D calculator can be simultaneously displayed on the ground on which the coordinate axes are projected. After the AR mode is turned on, the mathematical model of the dog kennel in front of the student in real life should be made on the mobile device.

Figure 11. Example of GeoGebra AR app

In this way, students can understand what geometric shapes real-life objects resemble and how they can be modeled. In addition, they can examine the details of this geometric model using the features of GeoGebra's 3D calculator. Within the scope of the activity, students can be asked calculation questions such as calculating the volume of the real object over the 3D model. Apart from this activity, the "Geometry AR" program, similar to the GeoGebra Augmented Reality program, enables the reflection of 3D predetermined objects on real grounds. Geometry AR is a tool for viewing and learning geometric shapes using Augmented Reality technology (AR).

Figure 12. Geometry AR app

With Geometry AR, students can view planar and solid shapes by moving around the shape to see all sides. Students use the slider or arrow buttons to move through a list of more than 25 shapes. As shapes are selected, they instantly appear in AR view and can be viewed by moving around the virtual object. Tapping the notepad icon displays information screens about the geometric shape. Text can be read aloud if audio is enabled by tapping the speaker icon. The limitation of this program is that the shapes are selected from a predefined list and there is no manipulation of these objects.

For students starting primary school, the "Counting with Paula" app can be used to teach numbers, basic operations and counting. The numbers and operations cards specific to this application can be activated with the camera of the mobile device.

Figure 13. Counting with Paula AR app

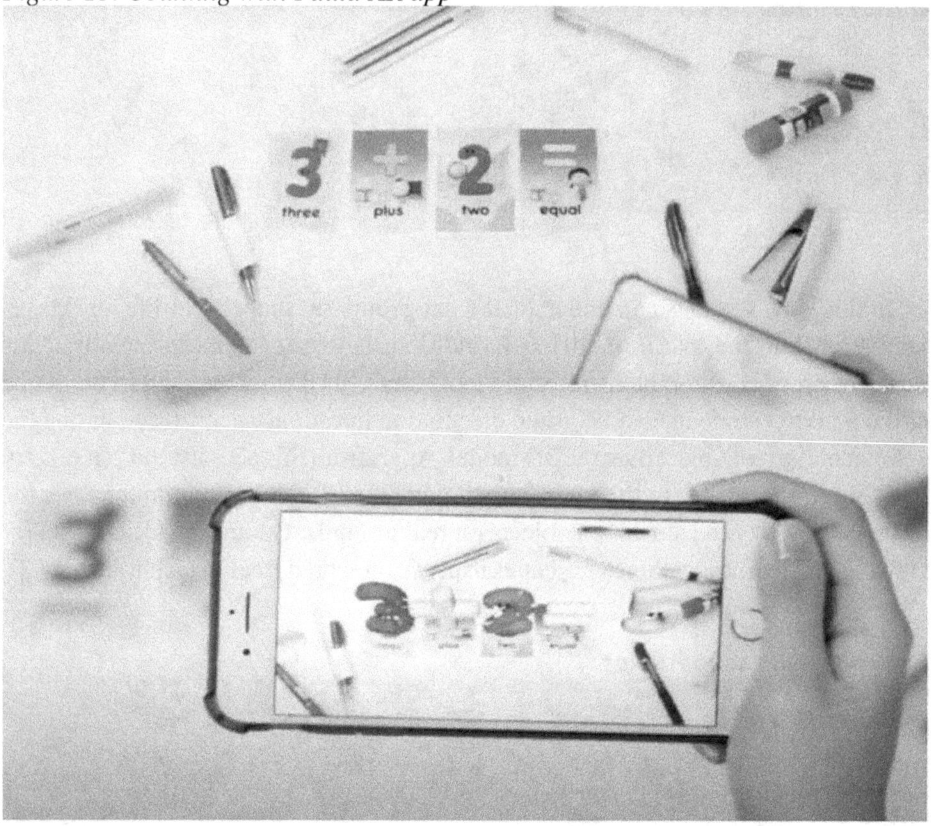

After the cards are activated, clicking on the "equals" icon on the mobile device automatically performs the operation and is reflected on the screen. When the transaction and number cards are actively changed, the augmented realities displayed on the mobile device can change.

CONCLUSION

As technological developments increasingly take place in our lives, it is seen that AR technology is used in many areas such as education, military, sports, health, design, and cultural areas. According to many studies conducted in this field, it is stated that AR will be a very important technology in the future and will become more prevalent in daily life. They stated that AR environments contribute to learning by doing and experiencing more through physical actions. Studies show that AR applications contribute positively to learning-teaching processes by revealing their importance in educational environments, especially in STEM education. For example, real life problems can be presented to students with 3D models through AR. Thus, STEM subjects or applications can become more relevant and meaningful for students (Cahyono et al., 2020; Hidayat & Wardat, 2024; Wang et al. 2024). Similarly, AR can attract students' attention more than other stimuli thanks to the computerized content it incorporates into the original image (Huang et al., 2021) and increase motivation as it enables students to participate in interactive learning experiences (Chang et al., 2022). AR applications offer an environment where students can learn knowledge and skills by doing and experiencing with the perfect combination of the real learning environment and the virtual environment. With the AR environment, an interactive environment is provided for the individuals to learn, and it provides communication where they share their knowledge and experiences face to face. The use of AR materials in mathematics teaching physically provides students with the opportunity to apply and use the information they have acquired in the real world, and with the increased 3D materials, making the learning environment attractive to students occurs as a result of natural interaction and reduces extraneous cognitive load. In addition, thanks to this natural interaction, learning becomes more controllable, increases the memorability of spatial concepts and learning content, and contributes to meaningful learning by encouraging learning by doing and experiencing. Especially considering that mathematics is a course consisting of abstract concepts, AR applications can be considered as important applications to eliminate the abstractness in question. Specifically, it has been stated in the literature that they have effects on developing students' spatial intelligence skills in geometry subjects. For example, Wang et al. (2024) state that AR has the potential to enhance visual cognition and promote math-related spatial skills through virtual object experiments and applications. Based on this, it can be said that AR applications bring learning and teaching processes more efficiently compared to traditional methods.

AR technologies allow holograms to be layered over the real world, "augmenting" human vision by adding technical information or illustrations to 3D space (Walkington et al., 2024). From a cognitive perspective, by establishing symbolic connections between abstract concepts that are difficult to understand and real objects, cognitive load is reduced, and meaningful learning with interactive 3D objects is improved. From a contextual perspective, creating environments where students can interact with the developed AR materials allows students to take control of these 3D objects from their own perspective and increases students' motivation due to its ease of use.

Since learning environments that stimulate students' senses and the materials used in these environments will facilitate the concretization of abstract thoughts during the learning process, their use in education is very important. Since learning environments and materials used in these environments that stimulate students' senses will facilitate the concretization of abstract thoughts in the learning process, the use of augmented reality applications can also increase students' multi-dimensional thinking skills. In this way, increasing students' multi-dimensional thinking skills positively affects their academic success and thus reduces their anxiety towards mathematics. It can be said that the use of AR increases students' motivation, and increased motivation increases performance. Therefore, it is expected that math anxiety will decrease at the end of this process (Chen, 2019).

Learning environments aimed at effective teaching and the methods and techniques applied in these environments should be equipped with concrete and highly visual tools and equipment. AR technology, which includes advantages such as enriching the learning environment, allowing the student to take an active role in the learning process, providing a realistic learning environment, eliminating material deficiencies due to security risks and cost problems and which students enjoy using, provides simultaneous use by adding virtual objects developed in a computer environment to the physical world environment. In this way, students can establish a connection between the real world and virtual objects without being isolated from the real environment they are in.

Nowadays, it is seen that the number of AR-supported games is increasing day by day. Considering these developments, it is thought that in the near future, the opportunity to experience AR games more effectively thanks to wearable equipment will become inevitable. Considering the fact that using games in mathematics teaching increases students' motivation towards lessons, it can be stated that the use of AR-supported games in mathematics lessons will be more attractive to students. For example, Huang et al. (2023) investigated the impact of AR board game on computational thinking and programming skills of elementary school students and stated that AR technology provided students with real-time simulation so that they could both practice programming skills and develop their computational thinking concepts. AR board games can provide learning scaffolds by enabling students to clearly understand the steps of operations and their consequences. In addition, AR games can be developed and offered for use in classes for students with special needs. In this way, it is thought that using AR-supported games during inclusive learning activities will also benefit students with special needs. AR content is mostly used to support effective teaching strategies. It is seen that the use of AR as a learning material yields positive results in the education of individuals with special needs (Köse & Güner-Yildiz, 2021; Wu, 2023). When collaborative learning environments, which are frequently used in mathematics teaching, are considered, it is seen in the literature that AR-supported applications encourage students' ability to work together. In learning environments where AR-supported applications are used, students' social skills are encouraged and supported. With the use of AR technology, which is being tried to be widespread in educational environments, AR technologies are being enriched in terms of quantity and quality day by day, but there is a need for scientific data to be obtained by using these enrichments in AR technology in educational environments.

REFERENCES

Akçayır, M., & Akçayır, G. (2017). Advantages and challenges associated with augmented reality for education: A systematic review of the literature. *Educational Research Review*, 20, 1–11. DOI: 10.1016/j.edurev.2016.11.002

Arena, F., Collotta, M., Pau, G., & Termine, F. (2022). An overview of augmented reality. *Computers*, 11(28), 1–15. DOI: 10.3390/computers11020028

Arican, M., & Özçakir, B. (2021). Facilitating the development of Preservice teachers' proportional reasoning in geometric similarity problems using augmented reality activities. *Education and Information Technologies*, 26(2), 2327–2353. DOI: 10.1007/s10639-020-10359-1

Aschauer, A., Reisner-Kollmann, I., & Wolfartsberger, J. (2021). Creating an open-source augmented reality remote support tool for industry: Challenges and learnings. *Procedia Computer Science*, 180, 269–279. DOI: 10.1016/j.procs.2021.01.164

Avila-Garzon, C., Bacca-Acosta, J., Duarte, J., & Betancourt, J. (2021). Augmented Reality in Education: An Overview of Twenty-Five Years of Research. *Contemporary Educational Technology*, 13(3), 1–30. DOI: 10.30935/cedtech/10865

Azuma, R. T. (1997). A survey of augmented reality. *Presence (Cambridge, Mass.)*, 6(4), 355–385. DOI: 10.1162/pres.1997.6.4.355

Azuma, R. T. (1999). The challenge of making augmented reality work outdoors. In Ohta, Y., & Tamura, H. (Eds.), *Mixed reality: Merging real and virtual worlds* (pp. 379–390). Springer. DOI: 10.1007/978-3-642-87512-0_21

Bhanu Prasad, P., Padmaja, N. B., Satish Kumar, B., & Aravind, A. (2022). Industry 4.0: Augmented and virtual reality in education. In Kaliraj, P., & Thirupati, D. (Eds.), *Innovating with augmented reality* (pp. 29–52). Auerbach Publications., DOI: 10.1201/9781003175896

Billinghurst, M. (2021). Grand challenges for augmented reality. *Frontiers in Virtual Reality*, 1–4. doi: 10.3389/frvir.2021.578080

Billinghurst, M., & Duenser, A. (2012). Augmented reality in the classroom. *Computer*, 45(7), 56–63. DOI: 10.1109/MC.2012.111

Blazauskas, T., & Gudoniene, D. (2020). Virtual reality and augmented reality in educational programs. In Linda, D. (Ed.), *New perspectives on virtual and augmented reality* (pp. 82–94). Routledge., DOI: 10.4324/9781003001874-6

Bower, M., Howe, C., McCredie, N., Robinson, A., & Grover, D. (2014). Augmented reality in Education cases, places, and potentials. *Educational Media International*, 51(1), 1–15. DOI: 10.1080/09523987.2014.889400

Bright, A., Welcome, N. B., & Arthur, Y. D. (2024). The effect of using technology in teaching and learning mathematics on student's mathematics performance: The mediation effect of students' mathematics interest. *Journal of Mathematics and Science Teacher*, 4(2), em059. DOI: 10.29333/mathsciteacher/14309

Burdea, G., & Coiffet, P. (2003). *Virtual reality technology*. Wiley-Interscience.

Cahyono, A. N., Sukestiyarno, Y. L., Asikin, M., Ahsan, M. G. K., & Ludwig, M. (2020). Learning Mathematical modelling with augmented reality Mobile Math trails program: How can it work? *Journal on Mathematics Education, 11*(2), 181–192. . 11.2. 10729. 181- 192DOI: 10. 22342/ jme

Cai, S., Liu, E., Shen, Y., Liu, C., Li, S., & Shen, Y. (2020). Probability learning in mathematics using augmented reality: Impact on student's learning gains and attitudes. *Interactive Learning Environments*, 28(5), 560–573. DOI: 10.1080/10494820.2019.1696839

Campbell, D. (2016). *Augmented reality: The next interface for design and making*. Retrieved August 1, 2024, from https://beyonddesign.typepad.com/posts/2016/10/augmented-reality-the-next-interface-for-design-and-making.html

Carmigniani, J., & Furht, B. (2011). Augmented reality: An overview. In Furht, B. (Ed.), *Handbook of augmented reality* (pp. 3–46). Springer., DOI: 10.1007/978-1-4614-0064-6_1

Cazzolla, A., Lanzilotti, R., Roselli, T., & Rossano, V. (2019). Augmented reality to support education in industry 4.0. In: *18th International Conference on Information Technology Based Higher Education and Training (ITHET)* (pp. 1–5). DOI: DOI: 10.1109/ITHET46829.2019.8937365

Cerqueira, J. M., Cleto, B., Moura, J. M., Sylla, C., & Ferreira, L. (2023). Potentiating learning through augmented reality and serious games. In Nee, C., & Ong, K. (Eds.), *Springer Handbook of Augmented Reality* (pp. 369–390). Springer., DOI: 10.1007/978-3-030-67822-7_15

Cevikbas, M., Bulut, N., & Kaiser, G. (2023). Exploring the benefits and drawbacks of AR and VR technologies for learners of mathematics: Recent developments. *Systems*, 11(5), 244. DOI: 10.3390/systems11050244

Chang, H. Y., Binali, T., Liang, J. C., Chiou, G. L., Cheng, K. H., Lee, S. W. Y., & Tsai, C. C. (2022). Ten years of augmented reality in education: A meta-analysis of (quasi-) experimental studies to investigate the impact. *Computers & Education, 191*, 104641. . compe du. 2022. 104641DOI: 10. 1016/j

Chang, S., & Hwang, G. (2018). Impacts of an augmented reality-based flipped learning guiding approach on students' scientific project performance and perceptions. *Computers & Education*, 125, 226–239. DOI: 10.1016/j.compedu.2018.06.007

Chen, D. R., Chen, M. Y., Huang, T. C., & Hsu, W. P. (2013). Developing a mobile learning system in augmented reality context. *International Journal of Distributed Sensor Networks*, 9(12), 594627. DOI: 10.1155/2013/594627

Chen, Y. (2019). Effect of mobile augmented reality on learning performance, motivation, and math anxiety in a math course. *Journal of Educational Computing Research*, 57(7), 1695–1722. DOI: 10.1177/0735633119854036

Chookaew, S., Howimanporn, S., Sootkaneung, W., & Wongwatkit, C. (2017). Motivating Pre-service Teachers with Augmented Reality to Developing Instructional Materials through Project-Based Learning Approach. *2017 6th IIAI International Congress on Advanced Applied Informatics (IIAI-AAI)*, 780–784. https://doi.org/ DOI: 10.1109/IIAI-AAI.2017.106

Cipresso, P., Giglioli, C., Raya, A., & Riva, G. (2018). The past, present, and future of virtual and augmented reality research: A network and cluster analysis of the literature. *Frontiers in Psychology*, 9, 2086. DOI: 10.3389/fpsyg.2018.02086

Clark-Wilson, A., Robutti, O., & Sinclair, N. (2023). *The mathematics teacher in the digital era. International Research on Professional Learning and Practice, 16.* Springer Nature.

Clements, M. A. K., Bishop, A. J., Keitel, C., Kilpatrick, J., & Leung, F. K. S. (Eds.). (2013). *Third international handbook of mathematics education.* Springer., DOI: 10.1007/978-1-4614-4684-2

Crisan, C., Geraniou, E., & Hodgen, J. (2023). Educational technologies in mathematics education. *The Royal Society: Mathematical Futures Programme*

Diegmann, P., Schmidt-Kraepelin, M., Van den Eynden, S. & Basten, D. (2015): Benefits of augmented reality in educational environments-A systematic literature review. *Wirtschaftsinformatik Proceedings*, 103.

Dunleavy, M., & Dede, C. (2014). Augmented reality teaching and learning. In Spector, J. M., Merrill, M. D., Elen, J., & Bishop, M. J. (Eds.), *Handbookof research on educational communications and technology* (pp. 735–745). Springer. DOI: 10.1007/978-1-4614-3185-5_59

Engelbrecht, J., Llinares, S., & Borba, M. C. (2020). Transformation of the mathematics classroom with the internet. *ZDM Mathematics Education*, 52(5), 825–841. DOI: 10.1007/s11858-020-01176-4

Estapa, A., & Nadolny, L. (2015). The effect of an augmented reality enhanced mathematics lesson on student achievement and motivation. *Journal of STEM Education: Innovations and Research*, 16(3), 40–48.

Garcia, R. (2022). *Homemade augmented reality sandbox brings mountains and more to this Kansas elementary school.* Retrieved August 1, 2024, from https://www.cjonline.com/story/news/education/2022/04/12/augmented-virtual-reality-ar-sandbox-kansas-school-silver-lake-elementary/9500440002/

Garzon, J., & Acevedo, J. (2019). Meta-analysis of the impact of augmented reality on students' learning gains. *Educational Research Review*, 27, 244–260. DOI: 10.1016/j.edurev.2019.04.001

Goh, E. S., Sunar, M. S., & Ismail, A. (2019). 3D object manipulation techniques in handheld mobile augmented reality interface: A review. *IEEE Access : Practical Innovations, Open Solutions*, 24(7), 40581–40601. Advance online publication. DOI: 10.1109/ACCESS.2019.2906394

Gómez-García, M., Hossein-Mohand, H., Trujillo-Torres, J. M., Hossein-Mohand, H., & Aznar-Díaz, I. (2020). Technological factors that influence the mathematics performance of secondary school students. *Mathematics*, 8(11), 1935. DOI: 10.3390/math8111935

Gopalan, V., Zulkifi, A. N., & Bakar, J. A. A. (2016, August). A study of students' motivation using the augmented reality science textbook. In *AIP Conference Proceedings, 1761*(1), 020040.

Herfort, J. D., Tamborg, A. L., Meier, F., Allsopp, B. B., & Misfeldt, M. (2023). Twenty years of research on technology in mathematics education at CERME: A literature review based on a data science approach. *Educational Studies in Mathematics*, 112(2), 309–336. DOI: 10.1007/s10649-022-10202-z

Hidayat, R., & Wardat, Y. (2024). A systematic review of augmented reality in science, technology, engineering and mathematics education. *Education and Information Technologies*, 29(8), 9257–9282. DOI: 10.1007/s10639-023-12157-x

Higgins, K., Huscroft-D'Angelo, J., & Crawford, L. (2019). Efects of technology in mathematics on achievement, motivation, and attitude: A meta-analysis. *Journal of Educational Computing Research*, 57(2), 283–319. DOI: 10.1177/0735633117748416

Hillmayr, D., Ziernwald, L., Reinhold, F., Hofer, S. I., & Reiss, K. M. (2020). The potential of digital tools to enhance mathematics and science learning in secondary schools: A context-specific meta-analysis. *Computers & Education*, 153, 103897. DOI: 10.1016/j.compedu.2020.103897

Hodhod, R., Fleenor, S., & Nabi, S. (2014). Adaptive augmented reality serious game to foster problem solving skills. In *Proceedings of the Workshop on Hyperrealistic Intelligent Environments*, Shanghai, China. IOS Press

Hohenwarter, M., Jarvis, D., & Lavicza, Z. (2009). Linking geometry, algebra, and mathematics teachers: GeoGebra soft-ware and the establishment of the International GeoGebra institute. *The International Journal for Technology in Mathematics Education*, 16(2), 83–86.

Huang, S. Y., Tarng, W., & Ou, K. L. (2023). Effectiveness of AR board game on computational thinking and programming skills for elementary school students. *Systems*, 11(25), 25. Advance online publication. DOI: 10.3390/systems11010025

Huang, X., Zou, D., Cheng, G., & Xie, H. (2021). A systematic review of AR and VR enhanced language learning. *Sustainability (Basel)*, 13(9), 4639. DOI: 10.3390/su13094639

Huang, Y. C., Backman, K. F., Backman, S. J., & Chang, L. L. (2016). Exploring the implications of virtual reality technology in tourism marketing: An integrated research framework. *International Journal of Tourism Research*, 18(2), 116–128. DOI: 10.1002/jtr.2038

Jerry, T., & Aaron, C. (2010). *The impact of augmented reality software with inquiry-based learning on students' learning of kinematics graph.* In 2nd International Conference on Education Technology and Computer (ICETC), (pp. V2-1–V2-5). Shanghai: IEEE. DOI: 10.1109/ICETC.2010.5529447

Kamińska, D., Zwoliński, G., Laska-Leśniewicz, A., Raposo, R., Vairinhos, M., Pereira, E., Urem, F., Ljubić Hinić, M., Haamer, R. E., & Anbarjafari, G. (2023). Augmented reality: Current and new trends in education. *Electronics (Basel)*, 12(16), 3531. DOI: 10.3390/electronics12163531

Kerawalla, L., Luckin, R., Seljeflot, S., & Woolard, A. (2006). "Making it real": Exploring the potential of augmented reality for teaching primary school science. *Virtual Reality (Waltham Cross)*, 10(3-4), 163–174. DOI: 10.1007/s10055-006-0036-4

Kesim, M., & Ozarslan, Y. (2012). Augmented reality in education: Current technologies and the potential for education. *Procedia: Social and Behavioral Sciences*, 47, 297–302. DOI: 10.1016/j.sbspro.2012.06.654

Khan, T., Johnston, K., & Ophoff, J. (2019). The impact of an augmented reality application on learning motivation of students. *Advances in Human-Computer Interaction*, 2019, 1–14. Advance online publication. DOI: 10.1155/2019/7208494

Khan, T., Johnston, K., & Ophoff, J. (2019). The impact of an augmented reality application on learning motivation of students. *Advances in Human-Computer Interaction*, 2019, 1–14. Advance online publication. DOI: 10.1155/2019/7208494

Koparan, T., Dinar, H., Koparan, E. T., & Haldan, Z. S. (2023). Integrating augmented reality into mathematics teaching and learning and examining its effectiveness. *Thinking Skills and Creativity*, 47, 101245. DOI: 10.1016/j.tsc.2023.101245

Köse, H., & Güner-Yildiz, N. (2021). Augmented reality (AR) as a learning material in special needs education. *Education and Information Technologies*, 26(2), 1921–1936. DOI: 10.1007/s10639-020-10326-w

Koumpouros, Y. (2024). Revealing the true potential and prospects of augmented reality in education. *Smart Learn. Environ.*, 11(2), 2. Advance online publication. DOI: 10.1186/s40561-023-00288-0

Lai, J. W., & Cheong, K. H. (2022). Adoption of virtual and augmented reality for mathematics education: A scoping review. [Crossref]. *IEEE Access : Practical Innovations, Open Solutions*, 10, 13693–13703. DOI: 10.1109/ACCESS.2022.3145991

Lee, K. (2012). Augmented reality in education and training. *TechTrends*, 56(2), 13–21. DOI: 10.1007/s11528-012-0559-3

Lenhart, A. (2015) *Teens, social media & technology overview 2015*. Retrieved 1 August, 2024 from https://www.pewresearch.org/internet/2015/04/09/teens-social-media-technology-2015/

Liu, D., Dede, C., Huang, R., & Richards, J. (Eds.). (2017). *Virtual, augmented, and mixed realities in education*. Springer. DOI: 10.1007/978-981-10-5490-7

Maebell, R., & Lawrence, A. S. A. (2021). Augmented reality and mixed reality in education. In *Proceedings of the 3rd International Conference on Virtual Reality* (pp. 119-122). Harran, Türkiye.

Marshall, S. (2023). Augmented reality's application in education and training. In Nee, C., & Ong, K. (Eds.), *Handbook of augmented reality* (pp. 335–353). Springer. DOI: 10.1007/978-3-030-67822-7_13

Masmuzidin, M. Z., & Aziz, N. A. A. (2018). The current trends of augmented reality in early childhood education. [IJMA]. *The International Journal of Multimedia & Its Applications*, 10(6), 47–58. DOI: 10.5121/ijma.2018.10605

McDowall, J. (2020). Charting a Path to Viable Consumer AR Glasses, Part I. Retrieved August 1, 2024, from https://arinsider.co/2020/10/22/charting-a-path-to-viable-consumer-ar-glasses-part-i/

Milgram, P., & Kishino, F. A. (1994). Taxonomy of mixed reality visual displays. *IEICE Transactions on Information and Systems*, 77, 1321–1329.

Moro, C., Štromberga, Z., Raikos, A., & Stirling, A. (2017). The effectiveness of virtual and augmented reality in health sciences and medical anatomy. *Anatomical Sciences Education*, 10(6), 549–559. DOI: 10.1002/ase.1696

Munnerley, D., Bacon, M., Wilson, A., Steele, J., Hedberg, J., & Fitzgerald, R. (2012). Confronting an Augmented Reality. *Research in Learning Technology*, 20(sup1), 39–48. DOI: 10.3402/rlt.v20i0.19189

Nikimaleki, M., & Rahimi, M. (2022). Effects of a collaborative AR-enhanced learning environment on learning gains and technology implementation beliefs: Evidence from a graduate teacher training course. *Journal of Computer Assisted Learning*, 38(3), 758–769. DOI: 10.1111/jcal.12646

Nilsson, S., Arvola, M., Szczepanski, A., & Bång, M. (2012). Exploring place and direction: mobile augmented reality in the Astrid Lindgren landscape. In: *Proceedings of the 24th Australian computer-human interaction conference*. ACM, pp 411–419. DOI: 10.1145/2414536.2414601

Noroozi, O., Dehghanzadeh, H., & Talaee, E. (2020). A systematic review on the impacts of game-based learning on argumentation skills. *Entertainment Computing*, 35, 100369. DOI: 10.1016/j.entcom.2020.100369

Plasencia, D. M. (2015). One step beyond virtual reality: connecting past and future developments. *XRDS: Crossroads. The ACM Magazine for Students*, 22(1), 18–23.

Purcell, K., Heaps, A., Buchanan, J., & Friedrich, L. (2013). *How teachers are using technology at home and in their classrooms*. Pew Research Center's Internet & American Life Project.

Quintero, E., Salinas, P., González-Mendívil, E., & Ramírez, H. (2015). Augmented reality app for calculus: A proposal for the development of spatial visualization. In E. G. Mendívil, P. G. Ramírez Flores, J. M. Gutiérrez, & E. Ginters (Eds.), *International Conference on virtual and augmented reality in education* (pp. 301–305). Elsevier B.V. DOI: 10.1016/j.procs.2015.12.251

Raja, R., & Nagasubramani, P. C. (2018). Impact of modern technology in education. *Journal of Applied and Advanced Research*, 3(1), 33–35. DOI: 10.21839/jaar.2018.v3iS1.165

Rasimah, C., Ahmad, A., & Zaman, H. (2011). Evaluation of user acceptance of mixed reality technology. *Australasian Journal of Educational Technology*, 27(8), 1369–1387. DOI: 10.14742/ajet.899

Reddy, P. (2022). New Horizons for learning: Augmented reality in education. In Kaliraj, P., & Thirupati, D. (Eds.), *Innovating with augmented reality* (pp. 100–120). Auerbach Publications., DOI: 10.1201/9781003175896

Roschelle, J., Noss, R., Blikstein, P., & Jackiw, N. (2017). Technology for learning mathematics. In Cai, J. (Ed.), *Compendium for research in mathematics education* (pp. 273–296). NCTM.

Rosenbaum, E., Klopfer, E., & Perry, J. (2007). On location learning: Authentic applied science with networked augmented realities. *Journal of Science Education and Technology*, 16(1), 31–45. DOI: 10.1007/s10956-006-9036-0

Schmalstieg, D., & Hollerer, T. (2016). *Augmented reality: principles and practice*. Addison-Wesley Professional.

Sırakaya, M., & Alsancak Sırakaya, D. (2020). Augmented reality in STEM education: A systematic review. *Interactive Learning Environments*, 30(8), 1556–1569. https://doi.org/10.1080/10494820.2020.1722713DOI: 10.1080/10494820.2020.1722713

Somyürek, S. (2014). Öğretim sürecinde z kuşağının dikkatini çekme: Artırılmış gerçeklik. *Eğitim Teknolojisi Kuram ve Uygulama*, 4(1), 63–80. DOI: 10.17943/etku.88319

Sutherland, J., Belec, J., Sheikh, A., Chepelev, L., Althobaity, W., Chow, B., Mitsouras, D., Christensen, A., Rybicki, F. J., & La Russa, D. J. (2019). Applying modern virtual and augmented reality technologies to medical ımages and models. *Journal of Digital Imaging*, 32(1), 38–53. DOI: 10.1007/s10278-018-0122-7

Tarng, W., & Ou, K. L. (2012). A study of campus butterfly ecology learning system based on augmented reality and mobile learning. In *IEEE Seventh International Conference on Wireless, Mobile and Ubiquitous Technology in Education (WMUTE)*, (pp. 62–66). Takamatsu: IEEE. DOI: 10.1109/WMUTE.2012.17

Tomaschko, M., & Hohenwarter, M. (2019). Augmented reality in mathematics education: The case of GeoGebra AR. In *Augmented reality in educational settings* (1st ed., pp. 325–346). Brill., DOI: 10.1163/9789004408845_014

URL-1. (2023). *Reality remix: Understanding the differences between VR, AR, and MR*. Retrieved August 1, 2024, from https://www.mirrar.com/blogs/reality-remix-understanding-the-differences-between-vr-ar-and-mr

URL-2. (2024). *Top augmented reality apps for classroom use*. Retrieved August 1, 2024, from https://moldstud.com/articles/p-top-augmented-reality-apps-for-classroom-use

Uzun, Y., & Akın, M. (2022). Virtual and augmented reality concepts. In Y. Uzun. & R. Butuner (Eds.), *Current studies in artificial ıntelligence, virtual reality and augmented reality* (pp. 57–73). ISRES Publishing

Velarde-Camaqui, D., Sanabria-Z, J., Ramírez-Montoya, M. S., & Cebral-Loureda, M. (2024). Augmented reality in educational innovation: A literature mapping review in D. B. Ibáñez, L. M. Castro, A. Espinosa, I. Puentes-Rivera, and P. C. López-López (Eds), *Communication and applied technologies*. Singapore: Springer.

Vertucci, R., D'Onofrio, S., Ricciardi, S., & Nino, M. D. (2023). History of augmented reality. In Nee, Y., & Ong, S. (Eds.), *Springer handbook of augmented reality*. Springer., DOI: 10.1007/978-3-030-67822-7_2

Viinikkala, L., Heimo, O. I., Korkalainen, T., Mäkilä, T., Helle, S., Pönni, V., & Lehtonen, T. (2014) The Luostarinmäki adventure–an augmented reality game in an open-air museum. In: *NODEM 2014 – Engaging Spaces – Interpretation, Design and Digital Strategies.*

Walkington, C., Nathan, M. J., Washington, J., Hunnicut, J., Darwin, T., Daughrity, L., & Schenck, K. (2024). Comparing learning geometry using a tablet to head-mounted display augmented reality: How and when dimensionality matters. *Education and Information Technologies*. Advance online publication. DOI: 10.1007/s10639-024-13008-z

Wang, L., Zhang, Q., & Sun, D. (2024). Exploring the impact of an augmented reality-integrated mathematics curriculum on students' spatial skills in elementary school. *International Journal of Science and Mathematics Education*. Advance online publication. DOI: 10.1007/s10763-024-10473-3

Wang, Q., & Li, Y. (2024). How virtual reality, augmented reality and mixed reality facilitate teacher education: A systematic review. *Journal of Computer Assisted Learning*, 40(3), 1276–1294. DOI: 10.1111/jcal.12949

Wang, X. M., Yu, D. D., Yu, X. H., Hwang, G.-J., & Li, F. (2024). Impacts of augmented reality-supported STEM education on students' achievement: A meta-analysis of selected SSCI publications from 2010 to 2023. *Education and Information Technologies*. Advance online publication. DOI: 10.1007/s10639-024-12641-y

Weerasinghe, M., Quigley, A., Ducasse, J., Pucihar, K., & Kljun, M. (2019). Educational augmented reality games. In Geroimenko, V. (Ed.), *Augmented reality games II: The gamification of education, medicine and art* (pp. 159–177). Springer Nature. DOI: 10.1007/978-3-030-15620-6_1

Wei, X., Weng, D., Liu, Y., & Wang, Y. (2015). Teaching based on augmented reality for a technical creative design course. *Computers & Education*, 81, 221–234. DOI: 10.1016/j.compedu.2014.10.017

Wu, C. L. (2023). Using video modeling with augmented reality to teach students with developmental disabilities to solve mathematical word problems. *Journal of Developmental and Physical Disabilities*, 35(3), 487–507. DOI: 10.1007/s10882-022-09862-9

Wu, H. K., Lee, S. W. Y., Chang, H. Y., & Liang, J. C. (2013). Current status, opportunities and challenges of augmented reality in education. *Computers & Education*, 62, 41–49. DOI: 10.1016/j.compedu.2012.10.024

Yohannes, A., & Chen, H. L. (2021). GeoGebra in mathematics education: A systematic review of journal articles published from 2010 to 2020. *Interactive Learning Environments*, 31(9), 5682–5697. DOI: 10.1080/10494820.2021.2016861

Zachary, W., Ryder, J., Hicinbothom, J., & Bracken, K. (1997). The use of executable cognitive models in simulation based ıntelligent embedded training. *Proceedings of Human Factors Society 41st Annual Meeting*. (pp. 1118-1122). Santa Monica, CA: Human Factors Society. DOI: 10.1177/107118139704100287

KEY TERMS AND DEFINITIONS

Augmented Reality: A field of study that covers the combination of the real world and computer-generated data such as audio, video, graphics, GPS location information.

Dynamic Geometry System: Computer programs which allow one to create and then manipulate geometric constructions, primarily in plane geometry.

GeoGebra: A dynamic mathematics software for all levels of education that brings together geometry, algebra, spreadsheets, graphing, statistics and calculus in one engine.

Information and Communication Technologies: The use of computers and other electronic equipment and systems to collect, store, use, and send data electronically

Mixed Reality: A world which blends both types of interaction (VR and AR) into a single process

Technology integration: The use of technology resources -- computers, mobile devices like smartphones and tablets, digital cameras, social media platforms and networks, software applications, the Internet, etc. -- in daily classroom practices, and in the management of a school.

Virtual Reality: A world in which one is completely immersed in a synthetic world and can interact with it

Chapter 8
Deployment of a Locally Developed Enterprise System for Local Requirements:
The Case of a Ghanaian Higher Education Institution

Zelda Arku
https://orcid.org/0000-0001-8045-9804
University of Mines and Technology, Ghana

John Effah
University of Ghana, Ghana

Stephen Boateng
University of Mines and Technology, Ghana

ABSTRACT

The purpose of this study is to understand how a Locally Developed Enterprise System (LDES) in a developing country can be deployed and used for local requirements. Research on Enterprise System (ES) has focused more on developed countries and less on developing countries. Within the limited developing country literature, the dominant focus has been on imported ES rather than locally developed ES. An interpretive case study using semi-structured interviews was applied as the methodological stance and affordance theory as an analytical lens of the research. The research highlights that to meet local requirement, the strategic alignment of ES with local regulatory frameworks and operational needs, compliance and oper-

DOI: 10.4018/979-8-3693-6030-9.ch008

ational continuity, customizability and adaptability are critical. However, network dependency and infrastructure compatibility, tension between maintaining data integrity and providing flexible access to users were constraints. The study provide recommendations for research, policy and practice.

1. INTRODUCTION

The digital economy has significantly transformed how business is conducted and the information is communicated in various sectors and industries. Organizations have phased out their stand-alone outmoded systems to a real-time Information System with great enthusiasm. The purpose of this study is to understand how a locally developed Enterprise System (ES) in a developing country's Higher Education Institutions (HEI) can be deployed and used for local requirements. ES is a fully integrated software that covers all the functional areas of an organization (Aral et al., 2024). As a modular application, ES integrates and coordinates organizational processes (Stonig et al., 2022). ES streamlines organizational activities to gain competitive advantage and customer loyalty (Almutairi et al., 2021). The developers of ES also play a vital role in the success of its deployment and use because they convert and mobilize business needs into technology. Concerning developing countries, examples of dominant imported ESs include Oracle, PeopleSoft, SAP, and Jenzabar. Organizations in developing countries mostly import ESs from the developed world. However, due to the advancement of technology in today's digital era, some organizations are acquiring ESs that are developed locally to use, especially in developing countries (Bahloul et al., 2024). With this development, HEIs are no exception as they have been steadily influenced by global trends, particularly in the perspective of the call by governments for HEIs globally to upsurge their performance, efficiency, and effectiveness (Roztocki et al., 2024). HEIs are striving to deliver an impeccable educational service and to be a state-of-the-art and socially advantageous institution that will be attractive to all and sundry. As such, Chofreh et al., (2018) stated that HEIs need multidisciplinary skills, coordinated efforts, and adequate knowledge to implement successful information systems.

For this research, Locally Developed Enterprise System (LDES) refers to ES developed by a Ghanaian-owned company. Organizations that import ES spend time and resources to customize the software to fit the local context. However, the customization often turns out to be problematic and unsuccessful due to contextual differences (Liu & Kara, 2023). Extant literature on ES is from developed countries (Abdulqader et al., 2024). Though developing countries are espousing ES, there is limited research on locally developed ES. Following this research gap, the research question for this paper is how a locally developed ES in a developing country HEI can be deployed and used for local requirements.

To address the research question, this paper used the affordance theory (Gibson, 1979) as an analytical lens and interpretive case study approach (Walsham, 1995) as a methodological stance to understand how an HEI in Ghana, a developing country in Africa deployed and used a locally developed ES for local requirements. The rest of the paper is organized as follows: Section 2 reviews relevant literature on ES deployment and use. Section 3 discusses the theoretical foundation. Section 4 describes the research methodology. Section 5 presents the case description and Section 6 presents the analysis of the case using affordance theory as an analytical lens. Then, Sections 7 and 8 present the discussion of the findings and conclusions of the paper respectively.

2. LITERATURE REVIEW

Based on the nature of the study, a literature review was conducted from three themes namely Evolution of ES, ES Definitions, ES deployment and use, Foreign ES deployment and use in developing countries, locally developed ES deployment and use in developing countries, ES in HEIs.

2.1 Evolution of ES

Understanding the evolution of enterprise systems is crucial for enhancing their future development. Pollock and Hyysalo, (2014) detail the hierarchical development of ES, starting from the manufacturing sector in the 1960s with material resource planning systems (MRP and MRP II) focused on inventory control. In the 1970s, MRP was used for managing manufacturing data streams, and by the late 1980s, MRP II addressed internal operations, production schedules, and material design. In the 1990s, ES emerged as an integrated package connecting internal and inter-organizational processes, such as supplier and customer relationship management. The term ES was coined by the Gartner Group in 1993. Abdulqader et al., (2024) noted that ES arose from large enterprises' need for seamless data integration and coordination between business units for higher efficiency.

2.2 ES Definitions

The digital economy has positioned ES at the core of firms that implement them, prompting extensive research by both scholars and practitioners (Javidroozi et al., 2018). This ongoing interest is fueled by recent trends in diverse work environments, leading to a proliferation of ES studies (Soliman & Karia, 2017). ES research is vast and well-established, not in its infancy, with contributions from various disciplines making it a multidisciplinary and interdisciplinary field. ES and ERP often used interchangeably, have been widely accepted across industries and companies of all sizes over the past few decades. Consequently, researchers have defined ES or ERP in various ways tailored to different sectors. While common characteristics like 'integration', functional support, ‘cross-organizational support’, competitive advantage, and 'centralization' are frequently mentioned in ES definitions, it is crucial to develop a more comprehensive definition to better represent contemporary systems.

The American Production and Inventory Control Society (APICS) definition of ES, as ‘an accounting-oriented information system for identifying and planning the enterprise-wide resources needed to take, make, ship, and account for customer orders (Hurbean & Fotache, 2014), is one of the most popularly-held definitions of these systems. Another popular definition of the ES as an ‘ERP system’ was presented by (Davenport, 1998), who explained: ‘as commercial software packages, ERP systems provide cross-organization integration through embedded business processes, generally comprising several modules, including logistics, procurement, sales, marketing, human resources, and finance’. Again, Almutairi et al., (2021) defined it as any software system that executes an organization’s business processes through the use of data and technology to achieve certain goals and enhance the competitive advantage of the organization. Moreover, Soliman and Karia, (2017) defined ES as a fully integrated business management system covering all the functional areas of an enterprise including Logistics, Production, Finance, Accounting, and Human Resources. In addition, to give a more detailed definition, Mahmud et al., (2017) added that ES is a functional software tool that supports the areas of logistics, planning, finance, manufacturing, procurement, human resource, project management, distribution, accounting, service maintenance, and transpiration. It is evident from the above definitions that the structure of an ES simplifies crystal clear amalgamation amongst all the various functions and it provides support for complete data flow within the enterprise. The evolution of ES started in the manufacturing sector and has now been applied in all sectors and industries. Table 1 outlines definitions of ES from four perspectives.

Table 1. Definitions of ES from Four Perspectives

Perspective	Definition	Source
Business Process Perspective	ES are instruments for enabling enterprises to manage and streamline business processes through cross-functional or cross-organizational integration.	(Wieder et al., 2006)
Technological/Technical Perspective	ES are configurable, online real-time interactive software packages, consisting of multiple modules that support information processing across enterprises using a single database and uniform operating platform.	(AlMuhayfith & Shaiti, 2020)
Communication Perspective	ES serves as enterprise-wide information systems that integrate all information flows and provide access to real-time information.	(Raja et al., 2020)
Functionality Perspective	ES are an integrated set of programs that automate various business procedures.	(Altamony et al., 2016)

2.1 ES Deployment and Use

Many institutions are acquiring ES solutions offered by commercial vendors in different contexts to support core business processes such as budgeting, accounting, procurement, performance, and HR management by integrating the data required for these processes into a single database (Javidroozi et al., 2018; Stonig et al., 2022). Deployment of ES is a challenging endeavor because it is costly, time-consuming, and complex to integrate into business operations (Jawad & Balázs, 2024). However, the benefits that are derived from the deployment of ESs outweigh the challenges (Singh & Pekkola, 2023). The advantages include real-time transactions, enhancing the integration between the institutions' functional units, achieving better efficiency by increasing income and decreasing expenses (Chofreh et al., 2018) gaining competitive advantage (Almutairi et al., 2021), and providing integrity of information (Rouhani & Mehri, 2018). Pakkala et al., (2024) argued that imported ES provides solutions to generic business problems applicable to a broader market. The developers of ES play a major role in its success or failure. The next section explains the deployment and use of both foreign and locally developed ES.

2.3 *ES Infrastructure*

The infrastructure behind an ES is critical to its success, encompassing hardware, software, network, and security systems that allow it to operate efficiently (Hamdani et al., 2021). Hardware is foundational, including servers and storage systems that must be scalable to handle growing data loads. While traditional on-premise ES demands significant hardware investments, cloud-based ES offers a flexible alternative by reducing the need for physical infrastructure (Prakash et al., 2022). This shift to cloud solutions enables organizations to manage ES without heavy upfront costs while ensuring scalability.

A reliable network is equally essential for ES, ensuring seamless communication between departments. Bandwidth, latency, and redundancy are key factors in network design (Ojugo & Eboka, 2020). Redundancy, through backup systems, protects against network downtime, which can disrupt ERP operations. Network challenges, particularly in regions with poor connectivity, often impede system performance and can slow down critical processes. Compatibility with existing software is another important aspect (Akpaku et al, 2023). Integrating an ES with legacy systems can be complex, as these older systems may lack the capacity to interact with modern ES (Dambrin & Grall, 2023). Customization needs often require adjustments to the software infrastructure, making integration more challenging. Ensuring that all components—databases, operating systems, and applications—are aligned is key to the smooth implementation of an ES.

Security remains a crucial component of ES infrastructure, especially given the sensitive data handled by these systems. Organizations must employ encryption, firewalls, and role-based access control to protect their data (Joshi et al., 2020). Compliance with regulatory frameworks further enhances data protection and prevents legal repercussions (Yanamala et al., 2023). Implementing ES infrastructure poses challenges, including high initial costs, the complexity of integrating with legacy systems, and scalability issues (Molina-Castillo et al., 2022). However, adopting cloud-based solutions and ensuring regular system upgrades can mitigate these issues, allowing organizations to maintain a flexible and secure ES that adapts to their evolving needs (Fianu et al, 2024). Overall, a well-structured ES infrastructure forms the backbone of an organization's operational efficiency, enabling the ES to deliver its full potential.

2.4 *Foreign ES Deployment and Use in Developing Countries*

Extant literature on ES in developing countries has been from developers such as Oracle, PeopleSoft, SAP, Jenzabar, and Datatel which have dominated in ES market over the years (Rasheed et al., 2024). Moreover, the literature on ES dominated in North America, Western Europe, Australia, China, Hong Kong, and Taiwan, where most ES developers are located; and hence have been imported from. Some ideologies of deploying foreign software in developing countries are that the stakeholders in the organizations believe that it was developed by experts with an excellent track record of high success rate (Abdellatif, 2014). It is believed that software imported from developed countries promotes organizational success in developing countries (Kamhawi, 2008).

2.5 *Locally Developed ES and Use in Developing Countries*

Though the deployment of locally developed ES in developing countries is in its infancy, a few authors have attempted to understand the phenomenon (Atieh et al., 2023). Institutions deploy these systems for several reasons including politics, legislation, culture, environment, finances, work demands, and the internal fragmentation that results in a constant change in users' needs (Irani et al., 2023). Organizations that use locally developed systems have greater flexibility for customization especially in terms of the laid down policies, regulations, and procedures in the respective context (Hansen et al., 2023). Again, it is imperative to implement a localized system because it fits the culture of the respective context. Sometimes, management stresses more on the technical aspects without focusing on local issues including regulations and laws, which can also be mainstream contributing factors to the system's success.

On the other hand, due to the contextual diversities, when organizations implement imported ES, they face challenges because of the culture, environment, and other related factors (Soliman & Karia, 2017). Most researchers focus on such systems without paying a closer look at the contextual factors that either afford or impede the implementation. Moreover, when there are no ES vendors in a given context and an organization cannot afford a foreign vendor, they tend to implement an in-house solution that has the potential to meet their needs (Leonardi, 2011). Limited research seeks to understand how a locally developed ES in a developing country could be deployed for local requirements; hence there is the need to address the discrepancy in this knowledge gap.

2.6 Enterprise Systems In HEI

The adoption of Enterprise Systems in Higher Education Institutions has been extensively researched, reflecting the sector's unique demands and challenges (Chofreh et al., 2018; Mahmud, Ramayah & Kurnia, 2017). HEIs, unlike profit-driven organizations, serve a broad spectrum of stakeholders, including students, faculty, and administrators, necessitating specialized software for academic purposes (Pollock & Cornford, 2004; Abugabah & Sanzogni, 2011). The impetus for ES adoption in HEIs is driven by factors such as evolving user needs, globalization, increasing competition, and government pressure for improved operational efficiency (Ahmed & Noaman, 2015; Chofreh et al., 2018). Research indicates that the primary goal of ES in HEIs is to unify information and processes, thereby improving service delivery across various academic and administrative functions (Soliman & Karia, 2015; Goel et al., 2012). ES systems integrate essential functions such as recruitment, admissions, financial aid, and student records, enhancing workflow efficiency and control (Rico, 2012). Additionally, ES facilitates better access to information and supports the lifecycle management of students, which is central to the operation of HEIs (Thelen, 2015).

Empirical studies have shown that ES adoption in HEIs leads to significant benefits, including improved administrative services, better integration of departments, and enhanced academic support (Chofreh et al., 2018). However, ES implementation in HEIs must address both academic and general administrative needs, such as HR, finance, and procurement, to ensure comprehensive institutional support (Panetto et al., 2016; Zdravkovic et al., 2015). Despite the challenges and complexities of implementing ES in the academic sector, there has been a marked global expansion of such systems, emphasizing their importance in modern educational environments (Panetto et al., 2016).

3. THEORETICAL FOUNDATION

The theoretical lens underpinning this study is affordance theory. Affordance theory was originated by (Gibson, 1979) in ecological psychology as the interaction between actor and environment. Affordance therefore refers to action possibilities available in the environment (Gibson, 1979). Over the years, the concept of affordance has been applied from environment to technologies (Hutchby, 2001). Affordance theory is then used to analyze interactions between actors and objects in a given setting (Wang et al., 2018). Basic concepts include actors, objects, and interactions. Objects include technological artifacts and actors are users who use technological artifacts (Bygstad et al., 2016). In effect, affordances are crucial for investigating actors with specific needs, goals, and practices in a particular historical, cultural, and social context. For this research, the object is locally developed ES used by the case institution; and actors are users of the system.

Affordance theory is still in use as researchers are exploring principles that underpin its use (Alshawmar, 2021). Affordance is neither the property of objects nor actors but emanates from their interaction (Wang et al., 2022). Affordance is subjective because actors perceive and actualize it based on their own goals to produce different effects based on their beliefs and interpretations (Pozzi et al., 2014). Affordance could also be an enabler or constraint (Volkoff & Strong, 2018). This is because affordance includes both the properties of enabling and constraining factors and has a strong explanatory power. When technology is in use, there will inevitably enabling and constraining possibility to act simultaneously. When actors interact with technology, they can be constrained by it depending on the type of technology and the skill level of the users. Affordance is also a relational concept because it does not exist on its own; rather its existence is actualized when actors interact with an object (Leonardi, 2011). When actors interact with objects, it can be used differently depending on the needs and beliefs of the actors. Affordances are also specific to one actor; hence, affordance for one actor may be completely useless for another. Perception and actualization of affordances are dependent on the relationship between system and user in the context in which IS are used; hence affordance can be actualized at both the organizational and individual level.

Affordance theory has also been used to study how users interact with technology in terms of what they can do with the system in a given situation (Pozzi et al., 2014; Leung et al., 2023). For instance, Koch, (2017) investigated affordances faced by functional departments implementing shadow analytics projects. They found out that both the vendor and the clients play a vital role in the success of the system and sometimes, the same factors can enable or constrain the various departments and stakeholders. In addition, Duan et al., (2024) found that using digital technologies can enhance job performance through improved coordination, communication, knowledge sharing, and decision-making. In HEI, the availability of a presentation package, access to ICT resources outside lessons by the students, room layout, and student allocation to computers could either afford or constrain the teacher-student-ICT triad relationship. Again, Dini et al., (2018) explored a government-developed social media project within a young democratic society. Their findings revealed that affordances are not predetermined but emerge from the practice of using the system.

Therefore, since this study is aimed at understanding how a locally developed ES could be deployed and used for local requirements, affordance theory provides a comprehensive insight concerning how the system could enable and constrain the case institution to meet the local requirements.

4. RESEARCH METHODOLOGY

The study employed a qualitative interpretive case study approach (Walsham, 2012). Interpretive studies largely seek to understand a phenomenon that is being studied through the meanings, understandings, norms, beliefs, and values that people associate with the phenomenon (Effah, 2019). The interpretive case study is most appropriate since this research seeks to understand how a locally developed ES in a developing country can be deployed and used for local requirements. This approach also helps the researchers to be a vital part of the study and consider the interviewees as participants and not objects (Walsham, 2012). Hence, each participant's opinions and perspectives were considered in detail. Moreover, this approach was chosen because the intention was to understand the subjective meanings that people associated with the phenomenon. The study was conducted in G-UNI (Pseudoname) because it is one of the institutions that has deployed and used a locally developed

ES successfully in Ghana. Ghana is a developing country in Africa and due to its sociotechnical context, it has its standards and laws when it comes to systems. It is therefore imperative to implement a system that meets these standards and laws. The study used a single holistic case study of G-UNI because the purpose of the paper sought to understand a unique case.

4.1 Data Collection

With the process of data collection, the aim was to find answers to the research questions and to establish the purpose of the study. The data used were interviews, direct observation, and documents (Boateng, 2016). Concerning the qualitative stance of the research, it was relevant to employ an in-depth semi-structured interview to get in-depth insights (Effah, 2012) into how the locally developed ES was deployed for the local requirement. Stakeholders who were actively involved in the implementation process; from the decision to acquire the software to the installation and training processes were interviewed to better understand the subjective meanings they associated with it. Notes were also made that gave direction on the follow-up questions to ask the respondents. Twenty interviewees were interviewed for the study from two institutions; Local Developer who is the vendor and developer of the software and G-UNI (the university deploying the locally developed ES). Table 2 below shows the list of interviewees.

Table 2. Summary of Interviewees

Institution	Functional Unit	No. of Interviewee
G-UNI	IT Department	3
	Accounts Module Users	3
	Human Resource Module Users	2
	Stock Management Module Users	2
	Account sub-module (Payroll)	1
	Top Management	2
	Lecturers	3
	Administrators	2
	Sub-Total	18
Local Developers	Software Implementers	1
	Technical Support	1
	Sub-Total	2
	Total Number of Interviewees:	**20**

Source: Fieldwork

The authors also sought the participants' consent and recorded the interviews which lasted for forty-five to ninety minutes. Based on the fact that the interviews were recorded, the interviewees were also assured of security with the tape recordings that they will never be played publicly. The interviews were then transcribed simultaneously with the data collection and the analysis. Moreover, during the data collection process, there were discussions with some staff, and notes were made on it to help accurately report on every piece of information that was encountered during the data collection. There were manual systems that were in use for some of the departments before the implementation of locally developed ES. Evidence of the former paper-based system as documents to provide further useful information was also used. Just to mention a few, there were some financial reports, files of faculties that were kept on shelves, pay slips of some employees, and annual reports of the university.

4.2 Data Analysis

The data collection and analysis were done simultaneously (Myers, 2015) and inductive as per the tradition of the interpretive paradigm. When data is collected and analysed concurrently, the main question is when to stop the process as this is done at a point of saturation (Boateng, 2016). The inductive nature of the analysis enabled the researchers to identify the themes from the data gathered. The themes were also developed using affordance theory as an analytical lens. Then, data was iteratively analysed according to the themes and research focus. Since the research was done inductively, more data were gathered from the field as analysis was being done to develop themes. The data collection and analysis ended when no new insights were emerging from the gathered data; hence it was at a point of saturation.

5. CASE DESCRIPTION

G-Uni is a public university in Ghana, established in October 1962 following the recommendation of an international commission appointed by the Ghanaian Government in December 1960. The university was founded to address the critical need for highly qualified professionals in the education sector. Over the years, G-Uni has trained numerous graduates for secondary schools, technical institutions, and teacher-training colleges. To adapt to the evolving needs of society and the Ghanaian education system, G-Uni has significantly expanded its academic offerings. It has restructured its degree programs, separating professional education courses from the main degree curricula. The university is organized into five Colleges and fourteen Faculties/Schools, each headed by Provosts and Deans. Currently, G-Uni offers a range of degree programs, including bachelor's, master's, and doctoral levels.

The student population at G-Uni has grown steadily over the years, driven by the increasing demand for professionals across various sectors in Ghana. As of the 2023/2023 academic year, the university had 60,406 undergraduate students 5648 graduate students and 578 PhD students encompassing regular, distance, and sandwich programs. G-Uni's staff capacity includes 5,073 members, comprising both teaching and non-teaching staff across senior and junior levels. To maintain international standards and enhance operational efficiency, G-Uni has integrated modern technology into its administrative processes, reflecting its commitment to innovation and excellence in higher education.

5.1 Traditional System in Use

Before the locally developed ES was deployed, the administrative work was generally done using a manual approach from its inception till 2015. In the respective administrative units, users work either using a silo system or a paper-based approach. The various offices especially the human resource (HR) and stock management units were filled with a heap of files, folders, and documents. The users in the human resource unit are in charge of employee well-being in terms of managing their data, processing leave requests, pensions, and promotions among many others. They added that they have to look through over 5000 folders to make an update or edit an employee's biodata. The HR officer explained that

This was time-consuming and tedious and sometimes there would be duplication of work. When the staff capacity was less than 1000, we did not experience these challenges, but now, the staff capacity has increased so the work is difficult.

Employees always complain that there is a delay in processing their claims and requests. Moreover, keeping the data in folders and shelves posed security threats. Intruders can easily gain access to the data, also they could lose everything when a natural disaster befalls them. Likewise, the users in the stock management unit professed that they had similar challenges with the manual approach to work. They are in charge of supplying the entire university with stationery, computing, and electronic devices every month and when needed. The manual approach made work tedious, ineffective, and inefficient. Also, there were inconsistencies with the stock-taking due to the nature of it. The university account was prepared using an outmoded software called Topnic. The users stated that, since G-UNI is a public institution, they have to send their reports to the Local Regulator (LR). Some documents observed were some of the reports that will be sent manually by some of the accounting staff to be delivered. One of the account officers stated that

There are so many challenges with this because we incur extra costs in submitting, and the report is also exposed to a lot of unauthorised people who can easily gain access. The software itself was giving us challenges.

Again, the accounting unit was also experiencing challenges with the silo system they were using. The users explained that the system was a legacy system; hence it was slow to work and it became incompatible with the current hardware and software in use. Further, one of the accounting staff proclaimed that

After going through the tedious process of preparing the payslip, the distribution is another hard nut to crack. We had to manually share these payslips with over 5000 staff and we had to make sure we didn't do any wrong deliveries.

In a discussion with the accounting staff, they added that they had to print all these payslips which was time-wasting and not the best approach. Many challenges existed with how these administrative roles were carried out.

5.2 Decision to Migrate to Locally Developed ES

The challenges that emanated from the silo and manual era required that G-UNI migrate to a digital environment. So, there was a need to digitize these administrative roles. Aside from these challenges, the LR also presented local regulatory standards that the software should meet. They also wanted the reports in a format that meets their local standards. The manual approach and legacy software could not meet the standards so they had to get software that meets the standards of their regulators. According to the principal ICT assistant, the requirements of LR were a system that contains the local currency symbol (cedi sign), local terminologies understood by both the users and themselves (LR), and readily available support in terms of customization, updates, upgrades, and maintenance. Further, in a discussion with some of the users of the account module, they explained that as per the requirement of LR and themselves, they wanted a system that meets the local standards in terms of payroll calculations, taxation, pensions, and other statutory deductions, they wanted the software to fit all these local standards as explained by the users of the finance department. The locally developed ES was selected based on the recommendation from LR; hence the software had to meet the aforementioned requirements. The LR recommended LDES by LD to G-UNI because it meets their requirement and other public universities have been able to deploy it successfully. G-UNI was on the edge of migrating their account activities to the regulators if they didn't implement a system that met their standards so they had no option but to select what had been proposed to them.

5.3 Deployment of Locally Developed ES

The locally developed proprietary software was called LDES; developed by LD in Ghana and the license is renewable on an annual basis based on the end user license agreement (EULA). The vendors explained that the users were ready for the system as they used it without feeling they were being coerced or forced to use it though they did not choose the system themselves. The main purpose of the system was to meet the requirements of LR and to curb the challenges of the traditional approaches. To begin the process, there were several meetings between the stakeholders involved and they formed a five-member implementation team that comprised of technical people from both LD and G-UNI. The G-UNI representatives were trained on the software before it was implemented so that they could provide additional support for the users during the implementation phase. In 2015, the implementation commenced as they expanded the university network bandwidth since the system ran on the network. They also made available backup and replication servers and other IT infrastructure to ensure that everything was effective. Again, they acquired new backup generators to ensure constant power supply.

The installation process began and lasted for a month; then the system was tested to ensure that everything worked effectively. The data was then mounted onto the locally developed ES. The first module to be implemented was the account module since they were under pressure. They used the parallel approach; that is both the old and new systems were used together for two months to ensure that everything worked perfectly before they rolled out the old system. The payslip was sent electronically to the users as well as the report to the local regulator. This was repeated for all the modules as they were installed. The modules were the human resource module followed by the stock management module deployed in 2016. The principal ICT assistant explained that

We were indirectly involved in the customization, modification, installation and setup of the system. However, we provide support for the users; the whole thing was planned, and the requirement was analyzed, and it was developed.

During this transitioning process, the respective users were trained by the implementation team for two weeks when the module was implemented. The implementation team also provided support to the users during the implementation phase. This was very effective because the developers and implementers are in the same context so they clearly understood how the software would suit the users. Moreover, since the implementation team comprised both people from LD and G-UNI, the users were able to clearly state any challenges that had to be addressed. The team also understood the modus operandi of G-UNI since some of the team members were from G-UNI. One of the users in the account section added that

The LDES ES fit our local business model and our culture. We understand the terminologies that were used in it too. Again, it is not difficult to calculate the payroll and other deductions since it has already been configured to fit the local payroll regulation.

In an interview with some of the users, one of them proclaimed that

One interesting thing about the ES was the fact that when I opened it, they used the local cedi sign. Also, we are happy because we will no longer migrate our account procedures to LR.

Further, one of the technical team members explained that

When we downloaded the monthly report to be sent to LR, it was a very exciting moment when we realised that it meets the local reporting standards.

Though there was some level of excitement with how the ES met the national requirements and organizational needs, they had some challenges at the initial phase which were stated by the technical team as

The configuration of the system was conflicting with eset antivirus on some old machines. The machines were changed in order to rectify these problems. We had network challenges because the system was sometimes slow.

5.4 LDES in Use

LDES was used in 2015 which enabled the case institution to meet the requirements of LR. For the first time, they were able to generate the required reports in the required format which was sent via email. When asked for further details on the report submission, one of the stakeholders at the account section explained that

We no longer submit the report manually, we generate the report electronically from the system. It does not go through bureaucracies for any delays and we are able to reduce the human intervention with the reports before it gets to LR. Also, the mode of submission which is email has also made it safe and faster.

When asked about the issues of ensuring system security, a member of the technical team stated that they are not allowed to have access to the system outside campus. Hence they can access only the system when they are on campus. Though LDES was fully rolled out, some of the units like the human resources used a hybrid approach whereby the university staff had to manually submit their claims which are electronically processed. So, the use of the system did not include all the business processes at the start. In a discussion with some of the lecturers, they asserted that they felt they had been left out of the system because they still had to send their claims manually. With respect to the account module, they were able to send the payslips to the employees through their institutional emails for the first two months. However, the employees complained that they do not access their emails so they required alternatives to send their payslips. The technical team developed a web portal whereby they could easily upload the payslips so that the users could easily download them. The website contains the necessary security features to ensure that the data is protected. This approach worked better for them as the rate of complaints was reduced.

When asked about the downtimes and support issues after the digitization process, the technical team explained that sometimes they can rectify the issues that come up; however, sometimes they have to consult the developers to either log in remotely and rectify it or they had to be present to rectify the issue depending on the level of the issue at hand. After the implementation, although they encountered some challenges with the system, there were many benefits accrued. Work done was faster and more effective since it runs on a network and the users can work simultaneously. Further, the users added that since the system meets the requirement of LR, they are able to work with great commitment.

6. ANALYSIS OF FINDINGS

This section uses affordance theory as a theoretical lens to analyze the affordances of the locally developed ES that can be deployed for local requirements. This section explains the affordances of the locally developed ES.

6.1 Enabling Affordances of LDES

One of the primary enabling affordances of the locally developed ES was its strategic alignment with the local context and regulatory requirements. The system was specifically designed to integrate local currency symbols, comply with national payroll and tax regulations, and use familiar terminologies that resonated with the institution's operational framework. This alignment was critical for G-UNI, as it allowed the institution to seamlessly meet the demands of its regulatory environment while maintaining operational continuity. As one respondent noted, *"LDES was therefore recommended by LR because it fits their requirements. These requirements included a system that has the local currency symbol (cedi sign), meeting the local payroll and tax regulation, terminologies and the reporting standards."* This quote highlights how the system's design catered specifically to local needs, making it an effective tool for ensuring compliance and enhancing administrative efficiency.

Figure 1. Data Structure Related to Strategic Alignment with Local Context and Regulatory Needs

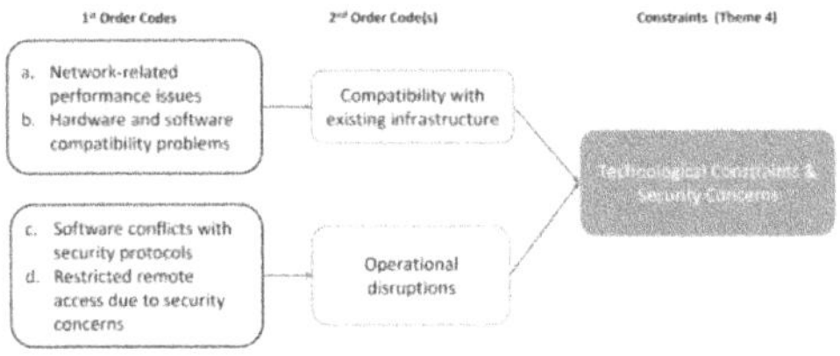

The system's flexibility and the availability of immediate support from local developers were other significant affordances that facilitated its successful implementation. The ability to customize the ES to meet the evolving needs of the institution was particularly crucial. This adaptability ensured that the system could be continuously tailored to fit G-UNI's unique operational requirements. One respondent emphasized this point, stating, *"The customization of the system took into consideration the needs of G-UNI because it was crucial for them to have a system that affords them to meet the requirements of their regulators."* The fact that the system was developed by local experts who were part of the same environment as G-UNI meant that support was readily available and contextually relevant. This facilitated a smoother implementation process and minimized disruptions. Another respondent highlighted, *"The system was developed locally, and the developers were available to provide support whenever necessary, making real-time adjustments possible."* The proximity of the developers enabled rapid implementation and adjustment capabilities, which were vital for staying compliant with evolving local regulations, as noted by another respondent: *"Having the developers in the same context allowed us to implement necessary changes quickly, which was vital for staying compliant with evolving local regulations."*

Figure 2. Data Structure Related to Customization and Support Flexibility

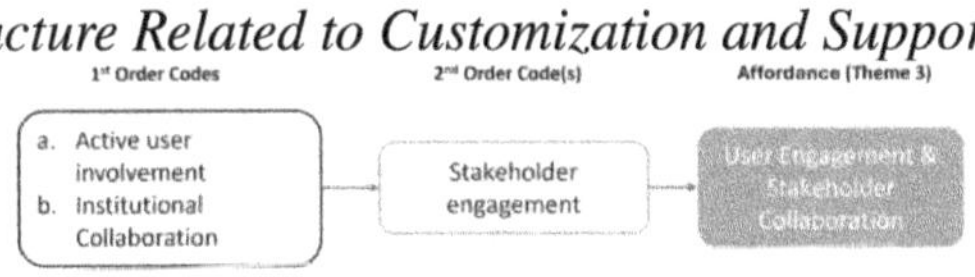

Additionally, the implementation process was characterized by significant user engagement and stakeholder collaboration. The involvement of G-UNI's staff in the customization and deployment of the system ensured that the ES was not only technically sound but also culturally aligned with the institution's operations. One respondent mentioned, *"We were indirectly involved in the customization, modifi-*

cation, installation and setup of the system." This participatory approach fostered a sense of ownership among the users, which is crucial for the successful adoption of new technologies. By actively engaging with the system and its developers, the stakeholders at G-UNI were able to ensure that the system met their specific needs, thereby reducing resistance to change and facilitating a more effective transition.

Figure 3. Data Structure Related to User Engagement & Stakeholder Collaboration

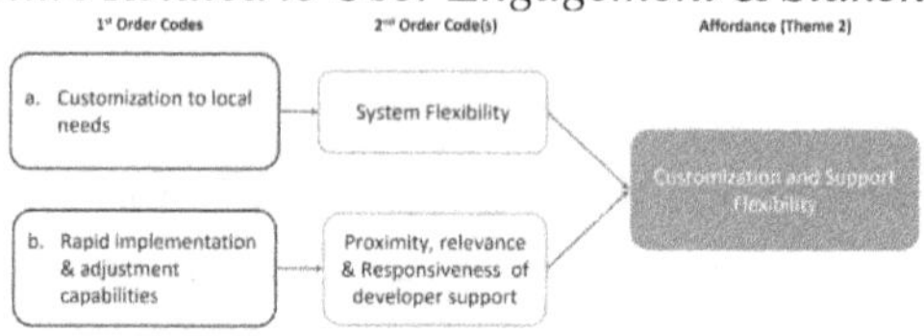

6.2 Constraining Affordances of the Locally Developed ES

Despite the enabling affordances, the implementation of the ES also revealed several constraints, particularly related to technological infrastructure. The system's reliance on network connectivity became a significant challenge, as any disruptions in the network adversely affected its performance. This issue was noted by one respondent who mentioned, *"Due to the fact that the system runs on a network, the system use is sometimes very slow because of network challenges."* Such network-related performance issues highlighted the need for robust infrastructure to support the ES effectively.

Compatibility issues with existing hardware and software at G-UNI posed further challenges. Some of the institution's computers were outdated or incompatible with the new system, necessitating reconfiguration or replacement to function properly. A respondent described this situation by saying, *"Some of the computers had to be changed and others too had to be reconfigured before it worked."* Moreover, the presence of antivirus software like ESET caused operational disruptions, with pop-up messages interfering with the system's smooth operation and slowing down the pace of work. This was highlighted by another respondent: *"The presence of antivirus software like ESET caused operational disruptions, with pop-up messages slowing down the pace of work."* These technical challenges underscored the constraints imposed by the existing technological ecosystem, which required adjustments to accommodate the new system.

Another significant constraint was the restricted accessibility of the system due to security concerns. The system's affordance of enhanced security also led to a limitation: it was designed to be accessible only on the premises of G-UNI, preventing remote access. As described in the case study, *"The system does not permit off campus, so users are constrained with working at leisure hours when they are not on campus."* This restriction limited the flexibility of the system, as users were unable to work from home or other locations outside the campus, which could have enhanced productivity and convenience. This constraint was a direct consequence of the system's security affordance, demonstrating how certain affordances can simultaneously enable and restrict system use.

Figure 4. Data Structure Related to Technological Constraints & Security Concerns

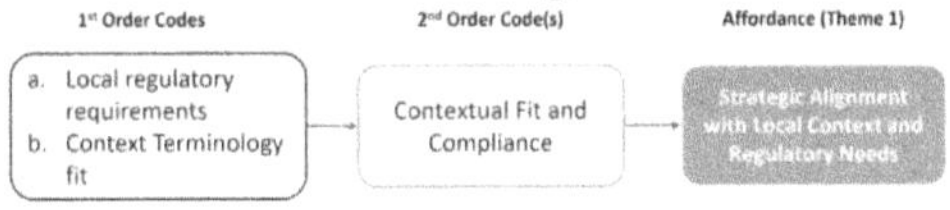

7. DISCUSSION

To answer the research question, this section discusses the research findings with respect to why the locally developed ES was deployed for local requirements. Locally developed ES addresses local requirement problems related to local regulatory reporting standards, national payroll and tax regulations and local system terminologies. Also, LDES incorporated the exact needs of the case institution and the users in terms of the provision of readily available support and customization when the need be.

7.1 Alignment with Local Regulatory and Institutional Needs

The alignment of the ES with local regulatory frameworks and institutional needs is crucial for ensuring compliance and operational continuity in HEIs (Fianu et al, 2022). The system's design, which integrated local currency symbols, payroll and tax regulations, and familiar terminologies, exemplifies the importance of tailoring information systems to meet specific regulatory requirements. This finding aligns with existing literature that highlights the necessity of contextual relevance in information systems for achieving institutional goals (Alotaibi & Liu, 2017). However, it also contrasts with the challenges faced by imported systems that often fail to meet local standards, leading to compliance issues and user dissatisfaction. As such, tailoring ES to local contexts enhances compliance, effectiveness, and user satisfaction.

7.2 Customizability and Adaptability to Institutional Dynamics

The study found that the ES's flexibility and adaptability were critical to its successful implementation. The system's ability to be customized to meet evolving institutional demands ensured its continued relevance and effectiveness in the dynamic environment of HEIs. This aligns with literature emphasizing the importance of system flexibility to accommodate changes in regulatory frameworks, academic policies, and administrative needs (Saade & Nijher, 2016). The finding also supports the view that locally developed systems offer greater customization potential compared to generic off-the-shelf solutions. Hence, flexibility in system design is essential for supporting the evolving needs of higher education institutions.

7.3 Engaged Stakeholder Participation and Collaborative Implementation

Active engagement of stakeholders and users during the system's customization and deployment was a key factor in its successful implementation. This participatory approach ensured that the ES was not only technically sound but also culturally aligned with the institution's operations. The involvement of diverse user groups, including administrative staff and faculty, facilitated the tailoring of the system to meet specific needs and fostered a sense of ownership, reducing resistance to change. This finding is consistent with the literature on information systems implementation, which explains the importance of user engagement for successful adoption and effective utilization (Jo & Park, 2023). Therefore, engaging stakeholders early in the process fosters system ownership and smooth implementation.

7.4 Technological Constraints and Infrastructure Limitations

The study highlighted the technological constraints that emerged during the implementation, particularly related to network dependency and compatibility with existing hardware. These challenges are reflective of infrastructural limitations that can impede the successful adoption of advanced enterprise systems in HEIs, particularly in contexts where technological infrastructure may be underdeveloped. This finding resonates with other studies that have identified infrastructure limitations as a common barrier to successful system implementation in educational institutions, especially in developing countries (Mahmood et al., 2020). In essence, a robust technological infrastructure is a prerequisite for the successful deployment of enterprise systems.

7.5 Security Considerations and Accessibility Trade-offs

The implementation of the ES also revealed significant trade-offs between security and accessibility. While the system's security features were robust, these measures sometimes restricted flexibility, such as limiting remote access for users. This finding highlights the ongoing challenge of balancing data security with user convenience, particularly in HEIs where staff and faculty may need access to systems outside of campus environments. This balance is crucial in maintaining both the integrity of sensitive data and the operational flexibility of the institution, as discussed in the existing literature (Chatterjee et al., 2015). It can therefore be stated that balancing security and accessibility is crucial to support both data integrity and operational flexibility.

8. CONCLUSION

The study explored the implementation of an LDES within HEI, applying affordance theory to analyze both enabling and constraining factors. The findings revealed that the ES was effectively aligned with local regulatory frameworks and operational needs, ensuring compliance and operational continuity. Again, the system's customizability and adaptability emerged as critical success factors, allowing it to respond to evolving institutional demands. Further, active stakeholder engagement and user collaboration played a significant role in the system's successful adoption and integration. Also, technological constraints, particularly related to network dependency and infrastructure compatibility, posed challenges that required careful management. Lastly, the balance between security and accessibility highlighted the tension between maintaining data integrity and providing flexible access to users. These findings highlight the importance of context-specific customization, stakeholder involvement, and robust infrastructure in the successful implementation of information systems in HEIs. Finally, although the LDES primarily manages administrative tasks like payroll and resource management, it indirectly enhances teaching and learning. By ensuring timely and accurate compensation, the system fosters a more motivated and focused workforce, allowing faculty and staff to concentrate on their core educational responsibilities. This improved focus and job satisfaction lead to more effective teaching, ultimately benefiting students. Additionally, streamlined administrative processes free up resources and reduce operational inefficiencies, creating a more supportive environment for academic activities.

8.1 Implications to Research, Policy, and Practice

The study's findings have significant implications for research, policy, and practice within the field of higher education and information systems.

For research, the application of affordance theory in this study contributes to the broader understanding of how technological affordances are actualized in institutional settings. It provides a framework for analyzing both the enabling and constraining aspects of technology implementation, offering insights that can inform future research on information systems in educational environments.

For policymakers within HEIs, the study emphasizes the importance of aligning technology implementations with local regulatory and operational requirements. It suggests that policies should encourage the development or customization of systems that are tailored to specific institutional contexts, thereby enhancing compliance and operational efficiency.

Practitioners involved in the implementation of information systems in HEIs can draw from the study's findings to prioritize stakeholder engagement and system flexibility. By involving users in the customization and deployment processes, institutions can reduce resistance to change and ensure that systems are better suited to meet their specific needs. Additionally, the study highlights the need for investment in robust technological infrastructure to support system performance and reliability.

8.2 Limitations and Future Research Directions

While this study provides valuable insights into the implementation of a locally developed ES in an HEI, it is not without limitations. The research is based on a single case study, which may limit the generalizability of the findings to other contexts. Additionally, the study primarily focuses on the perspectives of the users and stakeholders within the institution, which may not fully capture the broader systemic challenges or successes experienced by similar institutions.

Future research should explore multiple case studies across different HEIs to validate and extend the findings of this study. Comparative studies between locally developed and off-the-shelf systems could also provide deeper insights into the advantages and challenges associated with each approach. Moreover, research could investigate the long-term impact of system customization and stakeholder engagement on the sustainability and effectiveness of information systems in higher education. Finally, examining the role of technological infrastructure in greater detail, particularly in developing countries, could offer a further understanding of the challenges and solutions related to information system implementations in educational institutions.

REFERENCES

Abdellatif, H. J. (2014). ERP in higher education: a deeper look on developing countries. *2014 International Conference on Education Technologies and Computers (ICETC)*, 73–78. DOI: 10.1109/ICETC.2014.6998905

Abdulqader, Z. R., Abdulqader, D. M., Ahmed, O. M., Ismael, H. R., Ahmed, H., & Haji, L. (2024). *Responsible AI Development for Sustainable Enterprises A Review of Integrating Ethical AI with IoT and Enterprise Systems. 03*(02), 129–156.

Akpaku, E., Arku, Z., & Boateng, S. (2023). Global perspective of the effects of digital financial inclusion and ICT intensity on socio-economic development. *International Journal of Business Forecasting and Marketing Intelligence*, 8(1), 13–34. DOI: 10.1504/IJBFMI.2023.127699

AlMuhayfith, S., & Shaiti, H. (2020). The impact of enterprise resource planning on business performance: With the discussion on its relationship with open innovation. *Journal of Open Innovation*, 6(3), 87. DOI: 10.3390/joitmc6030087

Almutairi, A., Naeem, M. A., & Weber, G. (2021). Assessing User Satisfaction of Current Enterprise Systems and Their Adaptability from the Perspective of Top Management. *IEEE Access : Practical Innovations, Open Solutions*, 9, 153442–153455. DOI: 10.1109/ACCESS.2021.3127950

Alotaibi, Y., & Liu, F. (2017). Survey of business process management: Challenges and solutions. *Enterprise Information Systems*, 11(8), 1119–1153. DOI: 10.1080/17517575.2016.1161238

Alshawmar, M. (2021). A review of the applications of affordance theory in mHealth app research. *Proceedings of the Annual Hawaii International Conference on System Sciences, 2020-January*, 3595–3604. DOI: 10.24251/HICSS.2021.437

Altamony, H., Al-Salti, Z., Gharaibeh, A., & Elyas, T. (2016). The relationship between change management strategy and successful enterprise resource planning (ERP) implementations: A theoretical perspective. *International Journal of Business Management and Economic Research*, 7(4), 690–703.

Aral, S., Brynjolfsson, E., Gu, C., Wang, H., & Wu, D. J. (2024). Understanding the returns from integrated enterprise systems: The impacts of agile and phased implementation strategies. *Management Information Systems Quarterly*, 48(2), 749–774. DOI: 10.25300/MISQ/2023/17420

Atieh, A. M., Cooke, K. O., & Osiyevskyy, O. (2023). The role of intelligent manufacturing systems in the implementation of Industry 4.0 by small and medium enterprises in developing countries. *Engineering Reports*, 5(3), 1–21. DOI: 10.1002/eng2.12578

Bahloul, M., Trivedi, R., Cardo-Miota, J., Papadimitriou, C., Efthymiou, V., Nouri, A., & Khadem, S. (2024). Analysis of barriers and key enablers toward citizen ESS successful integration. *Journal of Energy Storage, 86*(PA), 111166. DOI: 10.1016/j.est.2024.111166

Boateng, R. (2016). *Research made easy*. CreateSpace Independent Publishing Platform.

Bygstad, B., Munkvold, B. E., & Volkoff, O. (2016). Identifying generative mechanisms through affordances: A framework for critical realist data analysis. *Journal of Information Technology*, 31(1), 83–96. DOI: 10.1057/jit.2015.13

Chatterjee, S., Sarker, S., & Valacich, J. S. (2015). The behavioral roots of information systems security: Exploring key factors related to unethical IT use. *Journal of Management Information Systems*, 31(4), 49–87. DOI: 10.1080/07421222.2014.1001257

Chofreh, A. G., Goni, F. A., & Klemeš, J. J. (2018). Sustainable enterprise resource planning systems implementation: A framework development. *Journal of Cleaner Production*, 198, 1345–1354. DOI: 10.1016/j.jclepro.2018.07.096

Dambrin, C., & Grall, B. (2023). Long-term alterations of ERP systems: Lasting through relinquishment and regeneration. *Qualitative Research in Accounting & Management*, 20(2), 169–200. DOI: 10.1108/QRAM-03-2022-0043

Davenport, T. H. (1998). Putting the enterprise into the enterprise system. *Harvard Business Review*, 76(4), 121–131. PMID: 10181586

Dini, A. A., Sæbo, Ø., & Wahid, F. (2018). Affordances and effects of introducing social media within eParticipation—Findings from government-initiated Indonesian project. *The Electronic Journal on Information Systems in Developing Countries*, 84(4), 1–14. DOI: 10.1002/isd2.12035

Duan, S. X., Deng, H., & Wibowo, S. (2024). Technology Affordances for Enhancing Job Performance in Digital Work. *Journal of Computer Information Systems*, 64(2), 232–244. DOI: 10.1080/08874417.2023.2188497

Effah, J. (2012). Mobilizing culture for e-business in developing countries: An actor network theory account. *The Electronic Journal on Information Systems in Developing Countries*, 52(1), 1–18. DOI: 10.1002/j.1681-4835.2012.tb00370.x

Effah, J. (2019). *Digital Process Virtualization : An Action Case Study in Ghana John Effah To cite this version : HAL Id : hal-02294701 Brightening Physical University Admission through Digital Process Virtualization : An Action Case Study in*.

Fianu, E., Boateng, S., & Arku, Z. (2024). Revisiting Automated Essay Scoring via the GPT Artificial Intelligence Chatbot: A Mixed Methods Study. In *Reshaping Learning with Next Generation Educational Technologies* (pp. 116–135). IGI Global. DOI: 10.4018/979-8-3693-1310-7.ch008

Fianu, E. E., Arku, Z., Affum, E. K., Boateng, S., & Boateng, F. (2022, November). Investigating Zoom Continuance Use by Ghanaian University Students in Blended Learning Arrangements in the Post-Covid Era. In *Proceedings of the 2022 6th International Conference on Education and E-Learning* (pp. 95-100). DOI: 10.1145/3578837.3578851

Gibson, J. J. (1979). The Theory of Affordances. *The Ecological Approach to Visual Perception*, 127–137.

Hamdani, S. W. A., Abbas, H., Janjua, A. R., Shahid, W. B., Amjad, M. F., Malik, J., Murtaza, M. H., Atiquzzaman, M., & Khan, A. W. (2021). Cybersecurity standards in the context of operating system: Practical aspects, analysis, and comparisons. *ACM Computing Surveys*, 54(3), 1–36. DOI: 10.1145/3442480

Hansen, H. F., Haddara, M., & Langseth, M. (2023). Investigating ERP system customization: A focus on cloud-ERP. *Procedia Computer Science*, 219, 915–923. DOI: 10.1016/j.procs.2023.01.367

Hurbean, L., & Fotache, D. (2014). ERP III: The promise of a new generation. *Conference on Informatics in Economy ASE Bucarest Romania*.

Hutchby, I. (2001). Technologies, Texts and Affordances Author (s): Ian Hutchby Published by : Sage Publications, Ltd. Stable URL : https://www.jstor.org/stable/42856294 JSTOR is a not-for-profit service that helps scholars, researchers, and students discover, use, a. *Sociology, 35*(2), 441–456.

Irani, Z., Abril, R. M., Weerakkody, V., Omar, A., & Sivarajah, U. (2023). The impact of legacy systems on digital transformation in European public administration: Lesson learned from a multi case analysis. *Government Information Quarterly*, 40(1), 101784. DOI: 10.1016/j.giq.2022.101784

Javidroozi, V., Shah, H., & Feldman, G. (2018). Qualitative Critical Realism in Information Systems Research. *UK Academy for Information Systems Conference Proceedings 2018*, 24. https://aisel.aisnet.org/ukais2018/24

Jawad, Z. N., & Balázs, V. (2024). Machine learning-driven optimization of enterprise resource planning (ERP) systems: A comprehensive review. *Beni-Suef University Journal of Basic and Applied Sciences*, 13(1), 4. Advance online publication. DOI: 10.1186/s43088-023-00460-y

Jo, H., & Park, D.-H. (2023). Mechanisms for successful management of enterprise resource planning from user information processing and system quality perspective. *Scientific Reports*, 13(1), 12678. DOI: 10.1038/s41598-023-39787-y PMID: 37542092

Joshi, K. P., Elluri, L., & Nagar, A. (2020). An integrated knowledge graph to automate cloud data compliance. *IEEE Access : Practical Innovations, Open Solutions*, 8, 148541–148555. DOI: 10.1109/ACCESS.2020.3008964

Kamhawi, E. M. (2008). Enterprise resource-planning systems adoption in Bahrain: Motives, benefits, and barriers. *Journal of Enterprise Information Management*, 21(3), 310–334. DOI: 10.1108/17410390810866655

Koch, H. (2017). Shadow Analytics Full Paper. *Amercan Conferences on Information Systems*, 2012, 1–10.

Leonardi, P. M. (2011). When flexible routines meet flexible technologies: Affordance, constraint, and the imbrication of human and material agencies. *Management Information Systems Quarterly*, 35(1), 147–167. DOI: 10.2307/23043493

Leung, X. Y., Zhang, H., Lyu, J., & Bai, B. (2023). Why do hotel frontline employees use service robots in the workplace? A technology affordance theory perspective. *International Journal of Hospitality Management, 108*(November 2022), 103380. DOI: 10.1016/j.ijhm.2022.103380

Liu, A., & Kara, S. (2023). Constructing product usage context knowledge graph using user-generated content for user-driven customization. *Journal of Mechanical Design*, 145, 41401–41403.

Mahmood, F., Khan, A. Z., & Bokhari, R. H. (2020). ERP issues and challenges: A research synthesis. *Kybernetes*, 49(3), 629–659. DOI: 10.1108/K-12-2018-0699

Mahmud, I., Ramayah, T., & Kurnia, S. (2017). To use or not to use: Modelling end user grumbling as user resistance in pre-implementation stage of enterprise resource planning system. *Information Systems*, 69, 164–179. DOI: 10.1016/j.is.2017.05.005

Molina-Castillo, F. J., Rodríguez, R., López-Nicolas, C., & Bouwman, H. (2022). The role of ERP in business model innovation: Impetus or impediment. *Digital Business*, 2(2), 100024. DOI: 10.1016/j.digbus.2022.100024

Myers, M. (2015). Ten years of Qualitative Research in Organizations and Management: Some reflections. *Qualitative Research in Organizations and Management*, 10(4), 337–339. DOI: 10.1108/QROM-07-2015-1307

Ojugo, A. A., & Eboka, A. O. (2020). Mitigating technical challenges via redesigning campus network for greater efficiency, scalability and robustness: A logical view. *International Journal of Modern Education and Computer Science*, 11(6), 29–45. DOI: 10.5815/ijmecs.2020.06.03

Pakkala, D., Kääriäinen, J., & Mätäsniemi, T. (2024). Improving efficiency and quality of operational industrial production assets information management in customer–vendor interaction. *Journal of Industrial Information Integration*, 41, 100644. DOI: 10.1016/j.jii.2024.100644

Pollock, N., & Hyysalo, S. (2014). The business of being a user. *Management Information Systems Quarterly*, 38(2), 473–496. DOI: 10.25300/MISQ/2014/38.2.07

Pozzi, G., Pigni, F., & Vitari, C. (2014). Affordance theory in the IS discipline: A review and synthesis of the literature. *20th Americas Conference on Information Systems, AMCIS 2014.*

Prakash, V., Savaglio, C., Garg, L., Bawa, S., & Spezzano, G. (2022). Cloud-and edge-based ERP systems for industrial internet of things and smart factory. *Procedia Computer Science*, 200, 537–545. DOI: 10.1016/j.procs.2022.01.251

Raja, S. L. N., Joseph, N., & Totawar, A. (2020). Analysing ERP implementations from organizational change perspective: an exploratory study. *International Working Conference on Transfer and Diffusion of IT*, 674–678. DOI: 10.1007/978-3-030-64861-9_58

Rasheed, H. H., Salih, A. A., Ahmed, O. M., Yazdeen, A. A., Majeed, R., Mohammed, T., & Sami, G. (2024). Consideration of Cloud-Web-Concepts for Standardization and Interoperability : A Comprehensive Review for Sustainable Enterprise Systems. *AI, and IoT Integration.*, 03(02), 20–38.

Rouhani, S., & Mehri, M. (2018). Empowering benefits of ERP systems implementation: Empirical study of industrial firms. *Journal of Systems and Information Technology*, 20(1), 54–72. DOI: 10.1108/JSIT-05-2017-0038

Roztocki, N., Strzelczyk, W., & Weistroffer, H. R. (2024). Enterprise Systems in the Public Sector: Current Research Landscape. *Information Systems Management*, •••, 1–28. DOI: 10.1080/10580530.2024.2361617

Saade, R. G., & Nijher, H. (2016). Critical success factors in enterprise resource planning implementation: A review of case studies. *Journal of Enterprise Information Management*, 29(1), 72–96. DOI: 10.1108/JEIM-03-2014-0028

Singh, C., & Pekkola, S. (2023). Reasons for customizing packaged enterprise systems: A case study on an enterprise asset management system. *Journal of Information Technology Case and Application Research*, 25(2), 159–186. DOI: 10.1080/15228053.2023.2223464

Soliman, M., & Karia, N. (2017). Antecedents for the success of the adoption of organizational ERP among higher education institutions and competitive advantage in Egypt. *Engineering, Technology &. Applied Scientific Research*, 7(3), 1719–1724.

Stonig, J., Schmid, T., & Müller-Stewens, G. (2022). From product system to ecosystem: How firms adapt to provide an integrated value proposition. *Strategic Management Journal*, 43(9), 1927–1957. DOI: 10.1002/smj.3390

Volkoff, O., & Strong, D. M. (2018). The Routledge Companion to Management Information Systems. *The Routledge Companion to Management Information Systems*, 232–246.

Walsham, G. (1995). Interpretive case studies in IS research: Nature and method. *European Journal of Information Systems*, 4(2), 74–81. DOI: 10.1057/ejis.1995.9

Walsham, G. (2012). Are we making a better world with ICTs? Reflections on a future agenda for the IS field. *Journal of Information Technology*, 27(2), 87–93. DOI: 10.1057/jit.2012.4

Wang, H., Wang, J., & Tang, Q. (2018). A Review of Application of Affordance Theory in Information Systems. *Journal of Service Science and Management*, 11(01), 56–70. DOI: 10.4236/jssm.2018.111006

Wieder, B., Booth, P., Matolcsy, Z. P., & Ossimitz, M. (2006). The impact of ERP systems on firm and business process performance. *Journal of Enterprise Information Management*, 19(1), 13–29. DOI: 10.1108/17410390610636850

Yanamala, A. K. Y., Suryadevara, S., & Kalli, V. D. R. (2023). Evaluating the Impact of Data Protection Regulations on AI Development and Deployment. *International Journal of Advanced Engineering Technologies and Innovations*, 1(01), 319–353.

Yu Chung Wang, W., Pauleen, D., & Taskin, N. (2022). Enterprise systems, emerging technologies, and the data-driven knowledge organisation. *Knowledge Management Research and Practice*, 20(1), 1–13. DOI: 10.1080/14778238.2022.2039571

KEY TERMS AND DEFINITIONS

Affordance Theory: A theoretical framework that examines the potential actions or uses an environment or technology enables for its users, based on the interaction between actors and objects.

Customization: The process of modifying software or systems to fit specific user or organizational requirements, ensuring that it meets unique operational, regulatory, or cultural needs.

Enterprise System (ES): An integrated software platform designed to streamline and manage an organization's core business processes by facilitating information flow across all functional areas.

Higher Education Institution (HEI): An organization that provides post-secondary education, such as colleges and universities, often involving complex administrative processes requiring specialized information systems.

Locally Developed Enterprise System (LDES): A custom-built Enterprise System designed by local developers, tailored to meet the specific needs, regulations, and cultural context of a particular region or institution.

Network Connectivity: The technological infrastructure, such as internet or intranet connections, required for an information system to function efficiently across different departments or locations

Chapter 9

The Rapid Transition to Online Learning During the Pandemic: Challenges and Implications for Digital Transformation in Higher Education

Mahir Tonga
https://orcid.org/0000-0002-5540-3021
İncirli Şehit Hüdai Arslan Vocational and Technical Anatolian High School, Turkey

Mehmet Kara
https://orcid.org/0000-0003-2758-2015
Amasya University, Turkey

ABSTRACT

Digital transformation is a requisite for dealing with equity, access, quality, and sustainability issues in higher education. Understanding the challenges faced during the rapid transition to online learning amid the pandemic would provide valuable insights into digital transformation in higher education. Therefore, this chapter presents the challenges faced during the rapid transition to online learning, the first year of the pandemic, and the implications for digital transformation. The synthesized findings from the reviewed articles published during the rapid transition period were presented and discussed with the example empirical studies. The identified challenges were classified into four categories: (1) challenges faced by learners, (2) challenges faced by instructors, (3) challenges faced in online teaching, and (4) challenges faced in management and organization. Based on these challenges,

DOI: 10.4018/979-8-3693-6030-9.ch009

the implications for digital transformation in higher education, a requisite for the institutions' resilience for equity, access, quality, and sustainability, were presented.

INTRODUCTION AND BACKGROUND

The rapid transition to online learning at all educational levels, including higher education, was a requisite for the continuity of education all around the world during the pandemic period. In these crisis times, online learning was considered an alternative to traditional face-to-face education due to the pandemic restrictions despite the weaknesses observed during this period (Fernandez-Batanero et al., 2022). The higher education institutions responded to this crisis depending on the degree to which they achieved digital transformation, which determined their resilience. Regardless of the institutional resilience, all higher education institutions moved to online learning by using online platforms, web conferencing systems, videos, and open educational resources (Rodríguez & Pulido-Montes, 2022) and are forced to adopt online assessment strategies (Chan, 2023). Although this rapid transition showed the importance of online learning with the need for alternative educational strategies (Pokhrel & Chhetri, 2021), the development of online learning and digital transformation depends on our understanding of the challenges faced in the rapid transition process.

This crisis and the need for a rapid transition revealed several challenges together with good practices. Different stakeholders of higher education, including learners, instructors, and administrators, faced several challenges (Zarei & Mohammadi, 2022), some of which were common for both learners and instructors (Hamad, 2022). The foremost concerns regarding the rapid transition were access and equity issues. Within a country, particularly learners from rural areas and low-income families face access-related challenges in addition to other associated challenges such as inadequate skills to use online tools and mental health problems (e.g. depression, anxiety, and stress) (Mseleku, 2020). These challenges led to inequalities among learners in participating in quality education at the same level (Sonn et al., 2021). Besides, inadequate internet connection and technological infrastructure were observed as a challenge (Hamad, 2022) as well as insufficient or lack of technological resources (Ozdamli & Karagozlu, 2022). Financial problems were also encountered as a major problem for managers and policymakers in addition to the technological infrastructure problems (Zarei & Mohammadi, 2022). As for between the countries, a review study conducted by Zarei and Mohammadi (2022) concludes that developing countries did not have the readiness or resilience for this rapid transition while developed countries established and adapted their systems to the transition to online learning.

In addition to the access and equity issues, the stakeholders of higher education faced several other challenges. On the part of learners, the challenges can be categorized as technological, educational, social, and individual challenges (Shazli et al., 2023). Weak internet connection and access to technological resources were encountered as the challenges faced by learners (Zarei & Mohammadi, 2022). Although learners have equal access to technology and online and offline tools, their readiness for online learning, including digital literacy, self-directed learning, and motivation, played a significant role in their engagement (Kara, 2022). This means that access to digital resources does not necessarily provide learners with self-directed learning skills (Koh & Daniel, 2022). For this reason, learners' readiness for online learning also gained more importance in accessing the desired learning outcomes. Similar challenges were also observed for the instructors. Their readiness for online teaching gained a more significant role in excelling in educational practices. Inadequate readiness for both online learning and teaching causes additional pedagogical challenges. In the same vein, insufficient competencies, training, and lack of learner engagement and feedback were reported as the main pedagogical challenges (Hamad, 2022). Besides, poor interaction with learners and peers, instructors' inability to motivate learners, and lack of technical competency were reported as other pedagogical challenges (Zarei & Mohammadi, 2022). Montenegro-Rueda et al. (2021) further documented that the lack of training for instructors on online assessment was a challenging factor during emergency remote teaching. Therefore, a review study conducted by Koh and Daniel (2022) concludes that both learners and instructors are required to improve their competencies for online learning and teaching. The requisite calls for training for the professional development of instructors (Fernandez-Batanero et al., 2022; Salas-Pilco, Yang, & Zhang, 2022).

Even though both learners and instructors have readiness for online learning and teaching, they still faced challenges in applied fields such as sports and health as it is very difficult for them to practice. In their review study, Ozdamli and Karagozlu (2022) showed that the lack of practice in applied fields posed a major challenge in emergency remote teaching. In the same vein, Zarei and Mohammadi (2022) listed the difficulties of practice in the sports and health disciplines as a challenge faced by the instructors. Cheating and academic dishonesty were another challenge stemming from the nature of online learning. Preventing cheating was reported as a major pedagogical challenge in several review studies (e.g. Montenegro-Rueda et al., 2021; Zarei & Mohammadi, 2022).

Apart from the pedagogical issues, both learners and instructors faced other challenges relevant to their home environment and work conditions. The inappropriate home environment for participating in the learning activities was shown as a challenge for learners (Koh & Daniel, 2022; Zarei & Mohammadi, 2022). On the part of instructors, the increasing workload and stress they experienced owing to this workload challenged their teaching practices (Zarei & Mohammadi, 2022). Similar mental health problems such as stress, anxiety, and depression were also observed in learners (Mseleku, 2020). However, even the mental health problems varied depending on the characteristics of the higher education learners. For example, a review study conducted by Jehi et al. (2023) showed that learners, who have demographic characteristics such as being female, living in rural areas of a country, having financial problems, or having poor sleep quality, experienced increasing levels of anxiety in the pandemic period.

While some of these challenges were specific to the rapid transition to online learning during the pandemic, many of the challenges were observed before the rapid transition period. For example, a review study conducted Kara et al. (2019), reporting the challenges faced by adult learners in online learning before the pandemic, revealed similar challenges for learners. These challenges included an inappropriate home environment, limited interaction with instructors and peers, social isolation, lack of institutional support, technical and financial problems, and inappropriate learning materials. This implies that there are still major problems to be overcome in online learning in the post-pandemic world. Dealing with the challenges of online learning is a requisite for all higher education institutions as online learning has been an integrated part of higher education in the form of blended learning. The degree to which higher education institutions deal with these challenges depends on how they achieve digital transformation and become resilient to the global crisis as experienced in the pandemic period, and local crisis as experienced in the emergency remote teaching due to the earthquake disasters in Türkiye.

Higher education institutions can be more resilient against global and local crises through digital transformation. The challenges faced during the rapid transition to online learning are the best starting points for this aim. Transforming higher education is a necessity to deal with the faced challenges (Salas-Pilco et al., 2022). Understanding these challenges and implementing the required transformation will enable the equity, quality, and sustainability of higher education (Chans et al., 2023). Higher education institutions are required to develop long-term strategies to deal with these challenges and achieve digital transformation for quality education (García-Morales, Garrido-Moreno, & Martín-Rojas, 2021). This is also a necessity for dealing with a similar crisis in the future for the sustainability of education (Ngoatle, Mothiba, & Ngoepe, 2022).

The sustainability of online learning in the post-pandemic period depends on understanding of these challenges and converting them into opportunities (Adedoyin & Soykan, 2023). Therefore, the papers published in the first year of the pandemic were reviewed regarding the challenges experienced during the rapid transition to emergency remote teaching. Based on this review, the implications for sustainable online learning and digital transformation in higher education were proposed, accordingly.

SELECTION OF THE REVIEWED ARTICLES

The content of the empirical research studies conducted and published in the first year of the pandemic period (2020 and 2021) and available on the Web of Science (WoS) database were reviewed to synthesize the challenges faced during the emergency remote teaching in higher education. The search was delimited with the journal articles available on WoS database. The publications in English including "COVID-19" and "Higher Education" in their abstract and keywords were included in the review. Only the journal articles reporting empirical studies on online/distance learning during the COVID-19 pandemic were included in the review. The journal articles included in the Social Sciences Citation Index (SSCI), Science Citation Index-Expanded (SCI-E), Arts and Humanities Citation Index (AHCI), and Emerging Sources Citation Index (ESCI) were included in the review. Finally, the articles included in the "Education & Educational Research" category of WoS were included in the review.

The journal articles reporting the studies conducted before the pandemic were excluded from the review. The ones that do not include either "COVID-19" or "Higher Education" were excluded from the review. Thirdly, the non-empirical documents (e.g. book reviews, literature reviews, editorials, letters to the editor, and so on) and conference proceedings were excluded. The journal articles included in other indexes (e.g. Book Citation Index, Russian Science Citation Index) than the specified ones above were excluded from the review. The articles reporting the design and development procedure of software were excluded. Finally, the articles that are not included in the "Education & Educational Research" category of WoS and written in other languages than English were excluded from this chapter. The synthesis was begun with the database search on WoS through the keywords of "COVID-19" and "Higher Education". The full text of the accessed journal articles was comprehensively reviewed based on the goal of synthesizing the challenges.

CHALLENGES FACED DURING THE RAPID TRANSITION TO ONLINE LEARNING AMID PANDEMIC

The synthesized findings from the reviewed articles published in the first year of the pandemic were presented in this part. The identified challenges were classified into four categories: (1) Challenges faced by Learners, (2) Challenges faced by

Instructors, (3) Challenges Faced in Online Teaching, and (4) Challenges Faced in Management and Organization.

Challenges Faced by Learners

Learner-related challenges were categorized as (1) Psychological challenges, (2) Access-related challenges, (3) Competency-related challenges, (4) Domestic challenges, and (5) Support-related challenges. These categories and the obtained concepts are presented in Table 1.

Table 1. Challenges Faced by Learners

Category	Challenges
Psychological challenges	Mental health problems
	Social isolation
Access-related challenges	Technical issues
	Challenges on the access to technology
	Challenges on the access to library resources
Readiness-related challenges	Inadequate motivation or interest
	Inadequate digital competency
Domestic challenges	Inappropriate home environment for online learning
	Increasing workload
	Increasing expenses on education
Support-related challenges	Inadequate learner support services
	Challenges in interaction with university and instructors

The first category includes the psychological challenges experienced by the learners during the pandemic such as fear (Al-Maroof et al., 2023), stress, depression (Raja & Kallarakal, 2021), anxiety (Marshalsey & Sclater, 2020), and loneliness (Händel et al., 2020). Several studies revealed that learners experienced these psychological challenges, and they negatively influenced the rapid transition to online distance learning. Dogar et al. (2020), for instance, reported that the first challenge was the panic atmosphere caused by the pandemic and this atmosphere resulted in a major level of anxiety felt by the learners. Several other studies reported feelings of social isolation as another challenge during the transition to online distance learning (Raza et al., 2020; Wilson et al., 2020). In the relevant articles, it was observed that these psychological challenges negatively influenced online education during the pandemic.

The second category encompasses access-related challenges including technical issues and the challenges on the access to both technology and library resources. The first challenge inhibiting learner access to education was the technical problems they experienced. These technical issues include problems with the internet connection or speed, electricity cuts (Abou-Khalil, et al., 2021), old computers (Prokes & Housel, 2021), difficulties in the use of online tools (Elfirdoussi vd., 2020), and other technological flaws (Raja & Kallarakal, 2021). The challenges in access to technology include difficulties in accessing the required software and hardware (e.g. Kabir, Islam, & Deena, 2020) and the internet (e.g. Dogar et al., 2020) to engage in online learning. The final access-related challenge was difficulties in accessing library resources (e.g. Khan et al., 2020). These access-related challenges caused social and educational inequalities (Shin & Hickey, 2021).

The third learner-related challenge was observed as a readiness-related challenge. These challenges included inadequate motivation or interest and inadequate digital competency for online learning. Several studies reported decrease in or lack of student motivation (Abou-Khalil et al., 2021; Gonçalves, Sousa, & Pereira, 2020; Nenko, Kybalna, & Snisarenko, 2020; Prokes & Housel, 2021; Shin & Hickey, 2021) and low interest or enthusiasm in online learning (Arribathi et al., 2021; Elfirdoussi et al., 2020) as an obstacle experienced in emergency remote teaching. The reason behind this challenge was also reported as less interaction (Väljataga et al., 2020) and lack of face-to-face interaction opportunities (Dogar et al., 2020). The other readiness-related challenge is the inadequate or lack of digital competency of students attending online courses (Elfirdoussi et al., 2020; Khan et al., 2020; Nenko et al., 2020). A study by Händel et al. (2020) also revealed that lack of digital competencies for online learning is also an antecedent of mental problems such as stress and loneliness.

Another learner-related challenge category emerged as domestic challenges, which is about learners' conditions in their daily life during the pandemic period. The first challenge is the inappropriate home environment for online learning or difficulty in creating an appropriate study environment at home (Chattaraj & Vijayaraghavan, 2021; García-Alberti et al., 2021; Gelles et al., 2020; Khalaf et al., 2020) due to such factors as noise and space for study. The second domestic challenge was observed as the increase in learners' workloads. Relevant studies reported that learners' workloads increased due to their increased responsibilities at home and work (Chattaraj & Vijayaraghavan, 2021; Prokes & Housel, 2021). The final domestic challenge was reported as increasing expenses on education. The reason behind this challenge is the requirement for some learners to buy extra internet packages (Dogar et al., 2020).

The final category in learner-related challenges emerged as support-related challenges, which include both academic and other support services. For this category, relevant studies indicated that inadequate learner support services were observed as a major barrier to online learning during the pandemic including communication challenges with the instructors (Gelles et al., 2020) and the need for other services such as advising, technology, and mental health supports (Prokes & Housel, 2021).

Challenges Faced by Instructors

The similar challenges experienced by the learners were also observed for the instructors. Like learners, the challenges faced by the instructors were (1) Psychological challenges, (2) Access-related challenges, (3) Competency-related and instructional challenges, (4) Domestic challenges, and (5) Support-related challenges. These categories and the observed challenges are presented in Table 2.

Table 2. Challenges Faced by Instructors

Category	Challenges
Psychological challenges	Mental health problems
	Negative attitude toward or low motivation for online teaching
Access-related challenges	Inadequate/Inappropriate technological solutions
	Inadequate technological support
	Difficulty in accessing online learning materials
Competency-related and instructional challenges	Inadequate readiness for online teaching
	Need for in-service training
	Increased workload
Domestic challenges	Difficulty in work-life balance
	Inappropriate home environment for online teaching
Support-related challenges	Inadequate technical support
	Inadequate support for online teaching practices

Similar to learners, the first psychological challenge faced by the instructors was mental health problems. These mental health problems included stress (Khan et al., 2020; Marek, Chew, & Wu, 2021) and anxiety (Khan et al., 2020). The second challenge in this category was negative attitude toward or low motivation for online teaching. In the study conducted by Marek et al. (2021), it was stated that instructors experienced stress due to the increasing workload in teaching practices while Watermeyer et al. (2021) revealed instructors' negative attitude towards online teaching.

The second category regarding the challenges faced by the instructors is the access-related challenges, including access to technology, support for technology, and access to digital instructional materials. In their study, Joshi, Vinay, and Bhaskar (2020) showed the technology-related challenges experienced by instructors including inadequate technological infrastructure, inappropriate online platforms for online teaching, and security concerns in addition to insufficient technical support for the technical problems. In addition to these problems, Khan et al. (2020) stated that instructors had challenges in accessing materials for online teaching and this caused additional workload. Likewise, Xie, Gulinna, and Rice (2021) reported that finding and distributing instructional materials to the instructors was a challenge for instructional designers.

The third category is the challenges regarding instructor competencies and online teaching. Considering that online teaching was a novel experience for most of the instructors, it is apparent that they needed further in-service training and professional development to be ready for online teaching. Particularly inadequate instructor competency or readiness for online teaching emerged as a major barrier to online teaching (Almazova et al., 2020; Nenko et al., 2020). The readiness for online teaching covers inadequate digital competencies (Almazova et al., 2020; Elfirdoussi et al., 2020), inadequate pedagogy, materials (Khan et al., 2020), and assessment (Sharadgah & Sa'di, 2020). The need for instructor readiness necessitated in-service training or professional development programs regarding online teaching and technology integration, the lack of which posed barriers to moving to online education (Joshi et al., 2020). These challenges required instructors to spend more effort on their teaching practices, which in turn increased their workload. Therefore, the workload of the instructors was reported as a major challenge in moving to online education (Marek et al., 2021; Väljataga et al., 2020).

As learners did, instructors also had domestic challenges including work-life balance and appropriate home environment for online teaching. As stated, instructors had stressful times under the conditions of the pandemic, and this created a challenge of establishing a balance between their life conditions and teaching responsibilities (Ramlo, 2021). Setting a home environment suitable for online teaching was a part of their stressful life conditions such as unavailability of basic resources and external issues in the home environment (Joshi et al., 2020).

As implied in the access-related challenges, the lack of or inadequate support for teachers also caused major challenges including insufficient technical or professional support. The need for technical support and the support for technology integration to online courses was reported as the major challenges faced by teachers (Joshi et al., 2020). Ramlo (2021) also reported the need for universities' support for instructors to access the required tools to teach online in their home environments.

Challenges Faced in Online Teaching

Several challenges regarding the instructional processes during the transition to online education were experienced. The challenges are classified as the challenges regarding (1) online teaching process, (2) learning outcomes, and (3) online assessment (see Table 3).

Table 3. Challenges Faced in Online Teaching

Category	Challenges
Online teaching process	Lack of or decrease in interaction/collaboration
	Inability of practices in applied courses
	Inadequate learner motivation for or interest in online learning
	Inability to use diverse instructional methods and materials appropriate with the learning objectives
Accessing learning outcomes	Low learner engagement
	Low learner satisfaction
	Low learner achievement
Online assessment	Difficulties in the design and implementation of online assessments
	Cheating/academic dishonesty
	Inappropriate online assessment platforms

The first category is the challenges associated with the online teaching process, which is more about the implementation of instructional planning. Many of the studies reported a lack of or decrease in interaction in teaching and learning activities. For example, Wut and Xu (2021) reported that there were challenges in establishing adequate learner-instructor and learner-learner interactions in online learning environments. Other studies additionally revealed the lack of individual interaction (Hussein et al., 2020), the difficulties in accessing social, cognitive, and affective engagement (Müller et al., 2020), and difficulty in the implementation of group works (Abou-Khalil et al., 2021). These findings indicated that the inability to create a classroom environment suitable for social collaborative learning was a major challenge in accessing the desired learning outcomes.

One of the major concerns in emergency remote teaching was the implementation of the applied courses, which can also require team or collaborative activities. Thus, it posed another major challenge in especially applied courses. According to a study conducted by Gonçalves et al. (2020), learners needed face-to-face environments for the courses in which learning objectives require practical and laboratory activities, which would cause major deficiencies in developing learner competencies.

Gonçalves and Capucha (2020) further documented that the stakeholders view the lack of applied courses as the worst aspect of emergency remote teaching due to the pandemic. This was a major problem for especially the higher education programs such as studio education (Marshalsey & Sclater, 2020), physical education (O'Brien et al., 2020), and medical education (Ahmed et al., 2020) as the learning objectives in the curriculum require practical and collaborative activities or tasks.

Inadequate learner motivation or interest posed another challenge in the implementation of online teaching. The difficulty in enhancing learner motivation to actively participate in online learning was observed as a challenge in achieving learning outcomes. From the instructors' perspective, learners' lack of motivation was shown as an external challenge to using Google Classroom as an online learning environment (Hussein et al., 2020). Other studies also revealed boredom or low learner motivation as a challenge in low-resource contexts (Abou-Khalil et al., 2021) and civil engineering courses (García-Alberti et al., 2021).

The reason behind learner motivation might be the inability to use diverse instructional methods appropriate to the learning objectives. This challenge and previously mentioned challenges likely led to another challenge, the inability to access the desired learning outcomes. In this sense, Müller et al. (2021) revealed meeting learners' diverse needs and delivering satisfactory learning experiences as the key challenges. There are several challenges behind these key challenges such as the size of the online classrooms, inadequate collaborative activities, and inappropriate learning materials (Khan et al., 2020).

The challenges in the implementation of online teaching unsurprisingly resulted in low outcomes such as low learner engagement, satisfaction, and achievement. Müller et al. (2021) showed that achieving cognitive, social, and affective learner engagement was a key challenge. Wilson et al. (2020) pointed out the relationships between social isolation and engagement as well as motivation. A study conducted by Elfirdoussi et al. (2020) also showed that learners are dissatisfied with the learning materials and the delivery of online courses during emergency remote teaching. All these challenges obviously led to low outcomes or a decrease in learning outcomes (Arribathi et al., 2021; Marshalsey & Sclater, 2020; Shin & Hickey, 2021).

The final category regarding the challenges of the instructional processes during the transition to online education is online assessment. The focus of the challenges in this category is more on the design and implementation of online assessment and cheating issues or academic dishonesty. In this regard, Khan et al. (2020) reported the difficulties in the design and implementation of the online assessment, including the validity and reliability of the online exams and cheating or academic dishonesty. Hussein et al. (2020) likewise pointed out the challenges of exam management and precluding cheating. On the other hand, Kabir et al. (2020) reported that online assessment platforms negatively influenced learners' acceptance of online learning. Sharadgah and Sa'di (2020) further elaborated on the challenges of online assessment including higher education institutions' inadequate readiness for online assessment, lack of satisfactory systems to block academic dishonesty, inadequate instructor readiness for online assessment, and paying less attention to formative assessment. In addition to academic dishonesty, the limitations of the online platforms, and the validity of the assessments with the full inclusion of the learning objectives, Guangul et al. (2020) also revealed learners' commitment to submitting their assignments as another challenge. Khalaf et al. (2020) additionally determined such challenges from learners' and instructors' standpoints as insufficient time for the exam questions, navigating among the questions, exam preparation and grading by the instructors, and technological problems.

Challenges Faced in Management and Organization

In addition to the micro challenges mentioned in the prior parts, the macro challenges at the management and organizational levels were also experienced. These challenges were categorized as (1) technological infrastructure and support, (2) management, and (3) quality issues (see Table 4).

Table 4. Challenges Faced in Management and Organization

Category	Challenges
Technological infrastructure and support	Inappropriate technological infrastructure/solutions
	Inadequate technological support
Management issues	Inability to allocate funding
	Difficulties in change management
	Need for the revision in the regulations and policies
Quality	Quality concerns for online learning experience

The first category in the faced macro challenges is, as implied previously, inadequate technological infrastructure, including inappropriate technological solutions with the goals and inadequate support for technology. Insufficient technological infrastructure posed one of the main challenges in emergency remote teaching (Dogar et al., 2020; Guangul et al., 2020; Joshi et al., 2020; Väljataga et al., 2020). Hussein et al. (2020) specifically reported problems such as low internet speed or bandwidth, laboratory activities, and interface design. The inadequate institutional support for technology was also an underlined challenge (Joshi et al., 2020). These identified challenges imply that technological infrastructure and support mechanisms were a foremost priority for the resilience of higher education institutions in times of crisis.

Another challenge lies behind the management issues, including budget, change management, bureaucracy, and rules and regulations. The establishment of the required technological infrastructure and support mechanisms is surely possible only through the allocation of a sufficient budget for these purposes. Therefore, many studies documented the difficulties in allocating sufficient financial funding or budget to overcome the macro and micro challenges (Almaiah et al., 2020; Joshi et al., 2020; Nenko et al., 2020). Almaiah et al. (2020) distinctively revealed that change management issues were also one of the major barriers as it requires the inclusion of governmental legislations and policies and other stakeholders including learners and instructors. In the same vein, Nenko et al. (2020) indicated excessive bureaucracy for online learning as a challenge in addition to other mentioned issues. For this reason, Almaiah et al., (2020) underlined the need for revision in the regulations and policies to facilitate the adoption of online learning.

As the final macro issue, all these faced challenges posed an outcome, quality concerns in higher education during emergency remote teaching as also implied while explaining learner dissatisfaction, which is a quality indicator in both regular times and emergency remote teaching (Gantasala et al., 2022). Dogar et al. (2020) stated that emergency remote teaching practices had negative influences on the quality of education due to factors such as instructor readiness for online teaching, technological infrastructure, and mental health. Similarly, Eringfeld (2021) pointed out quality as a dystopian fear by the learners. A study conducted during emergency remote teaching (Elumalai et al., 2020) showed that the factors such as administrative support, course design, social and technical support, and learner and instructor characteristics are significantly associated with the quality of online learning experience. Therefore, the quality concerns as a challenge faced during the emergency remote teaching is a consequence of all other challenges and providing quality online learning experience is possible through dealing holistically with all identified challenges.

CONCLUSION AND IMPLICATIONS FOR DIGITAL TRANSFORMATION IN HIGHER EDUCATION

The empirical studies reporting the challenges faced during the rapid transition to online learning and published in the first year of the pandemic were reviewed and their findings were synthesized. The review resulted in four main categories of the faced challenges: (1) challenges faced by Learners, (2) challenges faced by Instructors, (3) challenges Faced in Online Teaching, and (4) challenges Faced in Management and Organization. The main aim of the review on the challenges is to determine the implications for digital transformation in higher education as these challenges are the best starting points towards this goal.

Although the review covered only the first year of the pandemic, the rapid transition period, the emerged challenges were quite similar to the findings of the relevant review studies. For example, the review study conducted by Zarei and Mohammadi (2022) revealed similar challenges for learners, instructors, and management. As the prior review studies offered implications for digital transformation in higher education (e.g. García-Morales et al., 2021; Ngoatle et al., 2022), the presented challenges faced in the rapid transition to online learning period also have several implications for digital transformation in higher education. Since the higher education institutions are not expected to deal with all identified challenges such as inappropriate home environments of both learners and instructors or low-speed internet connection in rural areas, they can deal with other challenges with the digital transformation policies and practices. The institutions capable of dealing with these challenges would demonstrate effective online learning and teaching practices in the post-pandemic period.

The first implication for digital transformation in higher education is to provide learners with a curriculum from K12 to higher education that supports the development of their digital literacy or digital competencies. Digital literacy is a competency that facilitates learners' self-directed learning skills and motivation in online learning (Kara, 2022). The digitally competent learners would accelerate digital transformation efforts by dealing with learners' readiness-related challenges, and the challenges in both the online teaching process and online learning outcomes. The studies conducted during the rapid transition period (Händel et al., 2020) and later during the pandemic (Kara, 2022) also revealed that learners' digital skills facilitated online teaching and learning practices. Including learners' digital skills, their readiness for online learning was also a critical factor for acceptance of online learning during the pandemic (Kabir, 2020; Kabir et al., 2020; Thongsri et al., 2020). Another learner-related implication is that online learning and relevant online environments are required to be an integral part of higher education in the post-pandemic world. The relevant studies during the rapid transition likewise demonstrated that learners' and instructors' prior online learning and teaching experience facilitated the transition process (Khalaf et al., 2020; Prokes & Housel, 2021).

On the part of the instructors, the integration of online learning modalities into higher education practices in the post-pandemic period would enable them to gain further professional experience. The relevant studies during the pandemic indicated that previous instructor experience in online learning and technology substantially influenced their practices during the pandemic (Marek et al., 2021; Martinho, Sobreiro, & Vardasca, 2021; Ramlo, 2021). Instructor characteristics also influenced the quality of online learning during the pandemic (Elumalai et al., 2020). Besides, in-service training or professional development programs for online teaching is a required aspect of digital transformation in higher education. In the same vein, the relevant studies conducted during the rapid transition period demonstrated that online instructor readiness is a critical factor for online education acceptance (Kabir, 2020; Kabir et al., 2020). These programs are necessary to improve instructor readiness in terms of using appropriate teaching and evaluation strategies, instructional design and material development, and improvement of digital competencies. The studies reported that the use of appropriate teaching methods (Abou-Khalil et al., 2021; Gonçalves et al., 2020), diverse evaluation strategies (Gonçalves et al., 2020; Guangul et al., 2020), and course design (Elumalai et al., 2020; Patwardhan et al., 2020) enabled successful online teaching and learning practices. For this reason, the competency of instructors for online teaching would contribute to their rapid adaptation to the digital transformation by dealing with the challenges such as competency-related and instructional challenges and other challenges faced in online teaching. The professional development programs and the ongoing support for both technical and pedagogical issues would decrease their resistance to change, improve their motivation for online teaching practices, including blended teaching, and manage their workloads.

The final implication is the enhancement of the technological and organizational infrastructure of the universities and integration of online learning modalities, including the use of appropriate digital platforms for online teaching, assessment, required support mechanisms, and professional development programs. A study conducted during the pandemic revealed that trust in the technological infrastructure including regulations, online learning culture, the quality of the online learning systems, and learners' self-efficacy are influential on the acceptance of online learning (Almaiah et al., 2020). The integration of online learning modalities with the required technological and organizational infrastructure is only possible through the development of the digital transformation vision, the required policies, strategic planning, and allocating financial funding for these goals, including the professional development of the relevant stakeholders and the introduction of the required support mechanisms. This sort of action at the macro level would contribute to dealing with the challenges identified in all categories, and ensure equity, access, quality, and sustainability in higher education.

ACKNOWLEDGMENT

This chapter was derived from the graduate study of the first author supervised by the second author. Both of the authors equally contributed to the chapter.

REFERENCES

Abou-Khalil, V., Helou, S., Khalifé, E., Chen, M. A., Majumdar, R., & Ogata, H. (2021). Emergency online learning in low-resource settings: Effective student engagement strategies. *Education Sciences*, 11(1), 1–18. DOI: 10.3390/educsci11010024

Adedoyin, O. B., & Soykan, E. (2023). Covid-19 pandemic and online learning: The challenges and opportunities. *Interactive Learning Environments*, 31(2), 863–875. DOI: 10.1080/10494820.2020.1813180

Ahmed, S. A., Hegazy, N. N., Abdel Malak, H. W., Cliff Kayser, W.III, Elrafie, N. M., Hassanien, M., Al-Hayani, A. A., El Saadany, S. A., AI-Youbi, A. O., & Shehata, M. H. (2020). Model for utilizing distance learning post COVID-19 using (PACT)™ a cross sectional qualitative study. *BMC Medical Education*, 20(1), 1–13, 400. DOI: 10.1186/s12909-020-02311-1 PMID: 33138818

Al-Maroof, R. S., Salloum, S. A., Hassanien, A. E., & Shaalan, K. (2023). Fear from COVID-19 and technology adoption: The impact of Google Meet during Coronavirus pandemic. *Interactive Learning Environments*, 31(3), 1293–1308. DOI: 10.1080/10494820.2020.1830121

Almaiah, M. A., Al-Khasawneh, A., & Althunibat, A. (2020). Exploring the critical challenges and factors influencing the e-learning system usage during COVID-19 pandemic. *Education and Information Technologies*, 25(6), 5261–5280. DOI: 10.1007/s10639-020-10219-y PMID: 32837229

Almazova, N., Krylova, E., Rubtsova, A., & Odinokaya, M. (2020). Challenges and opportunities for Russian higher education amid COVID-19: Teachers' perspective. *Education Sciences*, 10(12), 1–11. DOI: 10.3390/educsci10120368

Arribathi, A. H., Suwarto, , Miftakhu Rosyad, A., Budiarto, M., Supriyanti, D., & Mulyati, . (2021). An analysis of student learning anxiety during the COVID-19 pandemic: A study in higher education. *The Journal of Continuing Higher Education*, 69(3), 192–205. DOI: 10.1080/07377363.2020.1847971

Chan, C. K. Y. (2023). A review of the changes in higher education assessment and grading policy during covid-19. *Assessment & Evaluation in Higher Education*, 48(6), 874–887. DOI: 10.1080/02602938.2022.2140780

Chans, G. M., Orona-Navar, A., Orona-Navar, C., & Sánchez-Rodríguez, E. P. (2023). Higher education in Mexico: The effects and consequences of the COVID-19 pandemic. *Sustainability (Basel)*, 15(12), 1–22, 9476. DOI: 10.3390/su15129476

Chattaraj, D., & Vijayaraghavan, A. P. (2021). Why learning space matters: A script approach to the phenomena of learning in the emergency remote learning scenario. *Journal of Computers in Education*, 8(3), 343–364. DOI: 10.1007/s40692-021-00182-z

Dogar, A. A., Shah, I., Ali, S. W., & Ijaz, A. (2020). Constraints to online teaching in institutes of higher education during pandemic COVID-19: A case study of CUI, Abbottabad Pakistan. *Revista Romaneasca Pentru Educatie Multidimensionala, 12*(2Sup1), 12-24. https://doi.org/DOI: 10.18662/rrem/12.2Sup1/285

Elfirdoussi, S., Lachgar, M., Kabaili, H., Rochdi, A., Goujdami, D., & El Firdoussi, L. (2020). Assessing distance learning in higher education during the COVID-19 pandemic. *Education Research International*, 2020, 1–13, 8890633. DOI: 10.1155/2020/8890633

Elumalai, K. V., Sankar, J. P., Kalaichelvi, R., John, J. A., Menon, N., Alqahtani, M. S. M., & Abumelha, M. A. (2021). Factors affecting the quality of e-learning during the COVID-19 pandemic from the perspective of higher education students. *Journal of Information Technology Education*, 19, 731–753. DOI: 10.28945/4628

Fernández-Batanero, J. M., Montenegro-Rueda, M., Fernández-Cerero, J., & Tadeu, P. (2022). Online education in higher education: Emerging solutions in crisis times. *Heliyon*, 8(8), 1–9. DOI: 10.1016/j.heliyon.2022.e10139 PMID: 35965985

Gantasala, V. P., Gantasala, S. B., Al Tawil, T. N. E., & Prasad, P. (2022). Quality of learning experience, student satisfaction and perceived overall experience in the COVID-19 context. *Journal of Applied Research in Higher Education*, 14(1), 507–520. DOI: 10.1108/JARHE-12-2020-0440

García-Morales, V. J., Garrido-Moreno, A., & Martín-Rojas, R. (2021). The transformation of higher education after the COVID disruption: Emerging challenges in an online learning scenario. *Frontiers in Psychology*, 12, 1–6, 616059. DOI: 10.3389/fpsyg.2021.616059 PMID: 33643144

Gelles, L. A., Lord, S. M., Hoople, G. D., Chen, D. A., & Mejia, J. A. (2020). Compassionate flexibility and self-discipline: Student adaptation to emergency remote teaching in an integrated engineering energy course during COVID-19. *Education Sciences*, 10(11), 1–23. DOI: 10.3390/educsci10110304

Gonçalves, E., & Capucha, L. (2020). Student-centered and ICT-enabled learning models in veterinarian programs: What changed with COVID-19? *Education Sciences*, 10(11), 1–17. DOI: 10.3390/educsci10110343

Gonçalves, S. P., Sousa, M. J., & Pereira, F. S. (2020). Distance learning perceptions from higher education students—The case of Portugal. *Education Sciences*, 10(12), 1–15. DOI: 10.3390/educsci10120374

Guangul, F. M., Suhail, A. H., Khalit, M. I., & Khidhir, B. A. (2020). Challenges of remote assessment in higher education in the context of COVID-19: A case study of Middle East College. *Educational Assessment, Evaluation and Accountability*, 32(4), 519–535. DOI: 10.1007/s11092-020-09340-w PMID: 33101539

Hamad, W. (2022). Understanding the foremost challenges in the transition to online teaching and learning during COVID-19 pandemic: A systematic literature review. *Journal of Educational Technology and Online Learning*, 5(2), 393–410. DOI: 10.31681/jetol.1055695

Händel, M., Stephan, M., Gläser-Zikuda, M., Kopp, B., Bedenlier, S., & Ziegler, A. (2020). Digital readiness and its effects on higher education students' socio-emotional perceptions in the context of the COVID-19 pandemic. *Journal of Research on Technology in Education*, 54(2), 267–280. DOI: 10.1080/15391523.2020.1846147

Hussein, M. H., Ow, S. H., Ibrahim, I., & Mahmoud, M. A. (2021). Measuring instructors continued intention to reuse Google Classroom in Iraq: A mixed-method study during COVID-19. *Interactive Technology and Smart Education*, 18(3), 380–402. DOI: 10.1108/ITSE-06-2020-0095

Jehi, T., Khan, R., Dos Santos, H., & Majzoub, N. (2023). Effect of COVID-19 outbreak on anxiety among students of higher education; A review of literature. *Current Psychology (New Brunswick, N.J.)*, 42(20), 17475–17489. DOI: 10.1007/s12144-021-02587-6 PMID: 35018081

Joshi, A., Vinay, M., & Bhaskar, P. (2021). Impact of coronavirus pandemic on the Indian education sector: Perspectives of teachers on online teaching and assessments. *Interactive Technology and Smart Education*, 18(2), 205–226. DOI: 10.1108/ITSE-06-2020-0087

Kabir, M. R. (2020). Impact of faculty and student readiness on virtual learning adoption amid Covid-19. *Revista Internacional de Educacion Para La Justicia Social*, 9(3), 387–414. DOI: 10.15366/riejs2020.9.3.021

Kabir, M. R., Islam, M. A., & Deena, S. A. (2020). Explaining the adoption of technology-based design of higher education during and after COVID 19 period from a developing country perspective. *Interaction Design and Architecture(s). Journal*, 46(46), 88–119. DOI: 10.55612/s-5002-046-005

Kara, M. (2022). Revisiting online learner engagement: Exploring the role of learner characteristics in an emergency period. *Journal of Research on Technology in Education, 54*(sup1), S236-S252. https://doi.org/DOI: 10.1080/15391523.2021.1891997

Kara, M., Erdogdu, F., Kokoç, M., & Cagiltay, K. (2019). Challenges faced by adult learners in online distance education: A literature review. *Open Praxis*, 11(1), 5–22. DOI: 10.5944/openpraxis.11.1.929

Khalaf, K., El-Kishawi, M., Moufti, M. A., & Al Kawas, S. (2020). Introducing a comprehensive high-stake online exam to final-year dental students during the COVID-19 pandemic and evaluation of its effectiveness. *Medical Education Online*, 25(1), 1–10, 1826861. DOI: 10.1080/10872981.2020.1826861 PMID: 33000704

Khan, R., Bashir, A., Basu, B. L., & Uddin, M. E. (2020). Emergency online instruction at higher education in Bangladesh during COVID-19: Challenges and suggestions. *Journal of Asia TEFL*, 17(4), 1497–1506. DOI: 10.18823/asiatefl.2020.17.4.26.1497

Koh, J. H. L., & Daniel, B. K. (2022). Shifting online during COVID-19: A systematic review of teaching and learning strategies and their outcomes. *International Journal of Educational Technology in Higher Education*, 19(1), 1–23, 56. DOI: 10.1186/s41239-022-00361-7 PMID: 36404984

Marek, M. W., Chew, C. S., & Wu, W. C. V. (2021). Teacher experiences in converting classes to distance learning in the COVID-19 pandemic. *International Journal of Distance Education Technologies*, 19(1), 89–109. DOI: 10.4018/IJDET.20210101.oa3

Marshalsey, L., & Sclater, M. (2020). Together but apart: Creating and supporting online learning communities in an era of distributed studio education. *International Journal of Art & Design Education*, 39(4), 826–840. DOI: 10.1111/jade.12331

Martinho, D., Sobreiro, P., & Vardasca, R. (2021). Teaching sentiment in emergency online learning—a conceptual model. *Education Sciences, 11*(2), 53, 1-16. https://doi.org/DOI: 10.3390/educsci11020053

Montenegro-Rueda, M., Luque-de la Rosa, A., Sarasola Sánchez-Serrano, J. L., & Fernández-Cerero, J. (2021). Assessment in higher education during the COVID-19 pandemic: A systematic review. *Sustainability (Basel)*, 13(19), 1–13, 10509. DOI: 10.3390/su131910509

Mseleku, Z. (2020). A literature review of e-learning and e-teaching in the era of Covid-19 pandemic. *International Journal of Innovative Science and Research Technology*, 5(10), 588–597. https://www.ijisrt.com/a-literature-review-of-elearning-and-eteaching-in-the-era-of-covid19-pandemic

Müller, A. M., Goh, C., Lim, L. Z., & Gao, X. (2021). Covid-19 emergency elearning and beyond: Experiences and perspectives of university educators. *Education Sciences*, 11(1), 1–15. DOI: 10.3390/educsci11010019

Nenko, Y., Kybalna, N., & Snisarenko, Y. (2020). The COVID-19 distance learning: Insight from Ukrainian students. *Revista Brasileira de Educação do Campo, 5*, 1-19, e8925. https://doi.org/DOI: 10.20873/uft.rbec.e8925

Ngoatle, C., Mothiba, T. M., & Ngoepe, M. A. (2022). Navigating through COVID-19 pandemic period in implementing quality teaching and learning for higher education programmes: A document analysis study. *International Journal of Environmental Research and Public Health*, 19(17), 1–8, 11146. DOI: 10.3390/ijerph191711146 PMID: 36078862

Ozdamli, F., & Karagozlu, D. (2022). Online education during the pandemic: A systematic literature review. [iJET]. *International Journal of Emerging Technologies in Learning*, 17(16), 167–193. DOI: 10.3991/ijet.v17i16.32287

Patwardhan, V., Rao, S., Thirugnanasambantham, C., & Prabhu, N. (2020). Community of Inquiry (CoI) framework and course design as predictors of satisfaction in emergency remote teaching: Perspectives of hospitality management students. *Journal of E-learning and Knowledge Society*, 16(4), 94–103. DOI: 10.20368/1971-8829/1135315

Pokhrel, S., & Chhetri, R. (2021). A literature review on impact of COVID-19 pandemic on teaching and learning. *Higher Education for the Future*, 8(1), 133–141. DOI: 10.1177/2347631120983481

Prokes, C., & Housel, J. (2021). Community college student perceptions of remote learning shifts due to COVID-19. *TechTrends*, 65(4), 576–588. DOI: 10.1007/s11528-021-00587-8 PMID: 33585838

Raja, M. A. S., & Kallarakal, T. K. (2021). "COVID-19 and students perception about MOOCs" a case of Indian higher educational institutions. *Interactive Technology and Smart Education*, 18(3), 450–474. DOI: 10.1108/ITSE-07-2020-0106

Ramlo, S. (2021). The coronavirus and higher education: Faculty viewpoints about universities moving online during a worldwide pandemic. *Innovative Higher Education*, 46(3), 241–259. DOI: 10.1007/s10755-020-09532-8 PMID: 33437113

Raza, S. A., Qazi, W., Khan, K. A., & Salam, J. (2021). Social isolation and acceptance of the learning management system (LMS) in the time of COVID-19 pandemic: An expansion of the UTAUT model. *Journal of Educational Computing Research*, 59(2), 183–208. DOI: 10.1177/0735633120960421

Rodríguez, M. L., & Pulido-Montes, C. (2022). Use of digital resources in higher education during COVID-19: A literature review. *Education Sciences*, 12(9), 612. DOI: 10.3390/educsci12090612

Salas-Pilco, S. Z., Yang, Y., & Zhang, Z. (2022). Student engagement in online learning in Latin American higher education during the COVID-19 pandemic: A systematic review. *British Journal of Educational Technology*, 53(3), 593–619. DOI: 10.1111/bjet.13190 PMID: 35600418

Sharadgah, T. A., & Sa'di, R. A. (2020). Preparedness of institutions of higher education for assessment in virtual learning environments during the Covid-19 lockdown: Evidence of bona fide challenges and pragmatic solutions. *Journal of Information Technology Education*, 19, 755–774. DOI: 10.28945/4615

Shazli, I. F. A., Che Lah, N. H., Hashim, M., Mailok, R., Saad, A., & Hamid, S. (2023). A comprehensive study of students' challenges and perceptions of emergency remote education during the early COVID-19 pandemic: A systematic literature review. *SAGE Open*, 13(4), 1–20. DOI: 10.1177/21582440231219152

Shin, M., & Hickey, K. (2021). Needs a little TLC: Examining college students' emergency remote teaching and learning experiences during COVID-19. *Journal of Further and Higher Education*, 45(7), 973–986. DOI: 10.1080/0309877X.2020.1847261

Sonn, I. K., Du Plessis, M., Jansen Van Vuuren, C. D., Marais, J., Wagener, E., & Roman, N. V. (2021). Achievements and challenges for higher education during the COVID-19 pandemic: A rapid review of media in Africa. *International Journal of Environmental Research and Public Health*, 18(24), 1–14, 12888. DOI: 10.3390/ijerph182412888 PMID: 34948499

Stanković, M., Nejić, K., & Stojiljković, N. (2020). Level of fear, opinion and quality of study during the coronavirus pandemic (COVID-19). How hard is it to get back to daily commitments? *Pedagogika-Pedagogy*, 92(7), 176–183.

Thongsri, N., Chootong, C., Tripak, O., Piyawanitsatian, P., & Saengae, R. (2021). Predicting the determinants of online learning adoption during the COVID-19 outbreak: A two-staged hybrid SEM-neural network approach. *Interactive Technology and Smart Education*, 18(3), 362–379. DOI: 10.1108/ITSE-08-2020-0165

Väljataga, T., Poom-Valickis, K., Rumma, K., & Aus, K. (2020). Transforming higher education learning ecosystem: Teachers' perspective. *Interaction Design and Architecture(s). Journal*, 46, 47–69. DOI: 10.55612/s-5002-046-003

Watermeyer, R., Crick, T., Knight, C., & Goodall, J. (2021). COVID-19 and digital disruption in UK universities: Afflictions and affordances of emergency online migration. *Higher Education*, 81(3), 623–641. DOI: 10.1007/s10734-020-00561-y PMID: 32836334

Wilson, S., Tan, S., Knox, M., Ong, A., Crawford, J., & Rudolph, J. (2020). Enabling cross-cultural student voice during COVID-19: A collective autoethnography. *Journal of University Teaching & Learning Practice*, 17(5), 1–21. DOI: 10.53761/1.17.5.3

Wut, T. M., & Xu, J. (2021). Person-to-person interactions in online classroom settings under the impact of COVID-19: A social presence theory perspective. *Asia Pacific Education Review*, 22(3), 371–383. DOI: 10.1007/s12564-021-09673-1

Xie, J., & Rice, M. F. (2021). Instructional designers' roles in emergency remote teaching during COVID-19. *Distance Education*, 42(1), 70–87. DOI: 10.1080/01587919.2020.1869526

Zarei, S., & Mohammadi, S. (2022). Challenges of higher education related to e-learning in developing countries during COVID-19 spread: A review of the perspectives of students, instructors, policymakers, and ICT experts. *Environmental Science and Pollution Research International*, 29(57), 85562–85568. DOI: 10.1007/s11356-021-14647-2 PMID: 34100207

KEY TERMS AND DEFINITIONS

Digital Transformation: The process of information technology integration into the works and/or services of an organization.

Higher Education: Formal education provided by institutions such as universities and colleges beyond secondary education.

Online Learning: Learning activities in synchronous and/or asynchronous online environments.

Rapid Transition during the Pandemic: The process of moving face-to-face education to online environments during the COVID-19 pandemic period.

Chapter 10
Virtual Mobility:
A New Pathway to Foster Internationalization of Higher Education

Rashim Wadhwa
Akal University, India

ABSTRACT

In recent times, with the advent of digitalization of higher education virtual mobility has emerged more clearly as a new model in the domain of internationalization of higher education. This more inclusive mobility model offers meaningful and multilateral interaction for the wider youth and offers the opportunity to build greater intercultural understanding of different societies and thus expands their worldwide view. However, despite the growth in virtual mobility opportunities in the current scenario, there is sparse research on the theoretical and empirical analysis of such programmes on human capital or career development outcomes. In this context, the prime aim of this article is to provide the conceptual underpinning of Virtual mobility. The strengths and weaknesses of virtual mobility model have been analyzed in contrast to traditional physical mobility model. Lastly, this paper sheds light on the potential effects of this new model of mobility and thus raised important concerns.

SETTING THE CONTEXT

Majority of the higher education institutions across the globe have internationalization high on their strategic agenda (Bruhn-Zass, 2023). An analytic perspective of the literature within the domain of internationalization of higher education revealed that the organic composition of internationalization of higher education has changed

DOI: 10.4018/979-8-3693-6030-9.ch010

significantly from last two decades and brought new complexity in the internationalization discourse (Bruhn-Zass, 2023; Wadhwa, 2019; Wadhwa 2016b). Specifically, in the recent years internationalization is often seen as a transversal concept and this notion of transversality is very well articulated in the new model of comprehensive internationalization (Bruhn-Zass, 2023; Helms & Brajkovic, 2017; Hudzik, 2011; Crowther et al., 2000). Now a day, the Internationalization at home movement has left its mark and the credit goes to Covid-19 pandemic. The outbreak of the Covid-19 pandemic has altered the landscape of internationalization of higher education and a major hit was on student mobility due to international travel restrictions (IEASA, 2020). The global climate crisis under the realm of covid-19 pandemic has made the traditional model of physical student mobility[1] unsustainable (UNESCO IESALC, 2022). But the consistent and continued demand for international education has led to an astonishing transition from physical mobility towards virtual mobility (Carr & Beaudry, 2023; Faek, 2023; Mason, 2021). This is confirmed by the findings of an IAU survey which highlighted that 60 percent of higher education institutions reported that Covid-19 has increased virtual mobility and/or collaborative online learning as alternatives to physical student mobility (Marinoni & Jensen, 2020, p. 12). Similarly, the findings of a global survey of college and university leadership revealed that 63 percent of higher education institution leadership worldwide was planning to engage in more virtual mobility post Covid-19 (International Association of University Presidents & Santander Universidades, 2020, p. 54).Moreover, in one recent survey report conducted in European higher education institutions (Gaebel et al., 2021), it is found that 25% from the universities participated in the study offer virtual mobility for their students, without replacing the physical mobility, and stressed about the "strong consensus" on keeping the two concepts separated. These facts reveal that students and teachers became more exposed to online teaching and learning during this pandemic period (Wadhwa et al., 2024). However, despite the growth in virtual mobility opportunities in the current scenario, there is sparse research on the theoretical and empirical analysis of such programmes influence on human capital or career development outcomes. An extensive literature is available to understand the trends and scenarios of physical student mobility but the understanding and comparable baseline of virtual student mobility in higher education institutions across the globe is miniscule (Faek, 2023; UNESCO IESALC, 2022). In this context, the prime aim of this article is to provide the conceptual underpinning of Virtual mobility. In the next section, different forms of mobility are discussed in general with a special focus on virtual mobility by critically analyzing from the lens of different scholars along with its types and how it is different from related concepts. The third section sheds light on the strengths and weaknesses of the physical and virtual mobility model. The fourth section analyses the opportunities and challenges of virtual mobility specifically in the context of teachers. Lastly, in the conclusion this paper sheds light on the potential effects of this new model of mobility and thus raised important concerns.

DIFFERENT FORMS OF MOBILITY

The discourse on internationalization in higher education has traditionally been focused on physical student mobility[2] as this form of mobility is the heart of the internationalization and has long been recognized as one of the strongest pillars of the internationalization of higher education in the literature (UNESCO IESALC, 2022; Tan et al. 2021; Teichler, 2017; Wadhwa, 2016a, Wadhwa, 2019).Though the number has jumped to 200% with the turn of the century but the prevailing statistics highlights the uneven global growth and unequal access in student mobility as it has just reached to 2.6% of the world's tertiary population (UNESCO IESALC, 2022; Shields, 2013). The number of physically mobile students has increased from 0.3 million in 1963 to 6.4 million in 2021(UNESCO IESALC, 2022; Project Atlas, 2023). The literature recognised that due to cost in finances (travel, housing) and time the rate of physical student mobility is low and the benefits of physical mobility can only be exploited by the miniscule students and can only be affordable for the privileged class (Tan et al. 2021; Brandenburg et al.,2014). Though the prevailing trends are highly imbalanced across the globe as one third of all international students were studying in just three Anglophone destinations i.e. the United States, the United Kingdom and Canada. In total, just around 70% of all international students were located in one of the top ten international student destination countries in 2022 (Project Atlas, 2023). Moreover, the patterns of physical mobility are driven by the imperatives of competition. With the advent of the digitalization of higher education, new forms of mobility i.e. virtual mobility[3] and hybrid mobility[4] has gained pace.

CONCEPTUAL UNDERPINNING OF VIRTUAL MOBILITY

The conceptual notions of 'Virtual Mobility' have emerged in the literature in the beginning of twenty first century with the advent of the internet and the development of information and communication technologies (UNESCO IESALC, 2022). Prior to pandemic, virtual mobility has played a peripheral role in the internationalization of higher education (ibid). Literature highlights that though the term has emerged in the 1990s (Wende, 1998) but no numbers are currently available to measure global participation in this form of student mobility (ibid). The 'Virtual Mobility' is a combination of two words: 'Virtual' + 'Mobility'. The word 'Virtual' referred to information and communication technology and 'Mobility' means movement. The most commonly used and quoted definition of Virtual Mobility is provided by elearningeuropa.info portal and is defined as "*the use of information and communication technologies (ICT) to obtain the same benefits as one would have with physical mobility but without the need to travel*".Bunt-Kokhuis (1996, 2001) creates a rather interesting though specific definition of Virtual Mobility as "*the collaborative communication between a faculty member and his/her counterpart(s) mediated by a computer. More often, these meetings will be interactive and take place across national borders and across time zones*". Boninsegna and Dondi (1998) has characterized virtual mobility as "Trans-national lectures and/or learning materials, cross-border recruitment of students, intensity of communication flows, international accreditation of achievements, multilingualism, complementarities to both physical mobility and conventional teaching". In the Humanities project (1995), the concept of virtual mobility is considered broad and constitutes elements like: Transnational lectures and/or learning materials; Cross-border recruitment of students; Intensity of communication flows; International accreditation of achievements; Multilingualism; complementarily between virtual mobility activities, traditional lectures, and physical mobility to be "effective networking". As it was one of the first projects on 'Virtual Mobility', the definition is quite broad and tried to cover different aspects and activities of higher education institutions. On the other hand, "Spot plus" project team (2001) widened the understanding of this concept and presented two forms of mobility – physical and virtual. In the training material (Spot+ project team, 2001, p. 10), virtual mobility is defined as a situation within university which implies a "*possibility to attend classes, seminars and other events held in a place located anywhere in the world; the possibility to access reference materials and contents at a distance, by using ICT-based solutions; the possibility to communicate with other people located anywhere*".

In the context of emerging form of Internationalization, Wende (1998) defined virtual mobility as "*where students follow courses offered by institutions abroad and interact with students and teachers, libraries and databases in other countries. She explicated the use of information and communication technology (ICT) in expanding the possibilities for cooperation and competition between institutions, and providing students and academic teachers that are not able to travel extensively with opportunities to benefit from internationalization*".

A new approach appeared in 2003-2005, where virtual mobility is described in virtual space. Silvio (2003) defined virtual mobility as a movement "*from one place to another in a new space called virtual space <...> enabled by computer mediated communication*" (Silvio, 2003, p. 3). Similarly to Silvio (2003), Vilhelmson & Thulin (2005) defined Virtual Mobility as "*physical transportation and face-to-face contacts, replaced, complemented or even generated by virtual ones*". Pursuea et al. (2005) see virtual mobility "*as a tool that fosters the use of e-learning*". Another more extensive definition of virtual mobility which covered intercultural aspect is given in the framework of the Being Mobile project as "*Virtual Mobility is a form of learning which consists of virtual components through a fully ICT supported learning environment that includes cross-border collaboration with people from different backgrounds and cultures working and studying together, having, as its main purpose, the enhancement of intercultural understanding and the exchange of knowledge*" (Bijnens et al., 2006). However, Schreurs et al. (2006) find this kind of Virtual Mobility definition too narrow and proposed a definition which is broader in scope. Virtual Mobility was defined as "*Virtual student exchange allows collaboration with foreign students and teachers that are no longer location dependent. The exchange might range from a single course to a full academic year. Through Virtual Mobility a university can also offer international experience for students and staff through an international discussion group, an international seminar an international learning community with regard to a theme of a course or a cluster of courses.*" Poulová et al. (2007) states that virtual mobility is "*the opportunity for collaboration of people from different backgrounds and cultures, who are working and studying together and are not placed in the same country*". In the Move-IT project Virtual Mobility has been defined "*as a set of ICT-supported activities that realize cross-border, collaborative experiences in a context of teaching and/or learning. These activities can take place in a fully ICT supported learning environment or as a complement to physical mobility (before, during and after). They can be aimed at the (practical) organization of the learning process or they can consist of actual teaching and/or learning activities. Virtual Mobility activities can cross borders between regions, countries, cultures and languages, but also between disciplines. Virtual mobility activities enable collaborative learning (i.e. learning from and with each other) and are always aimed at inter-cultural experiences*" (cited in Vriens et al., 2010, pp. 1-2).

In the Lifelong learning programme (2007-2013), Virtual Mobility is defined as "*a complement; or as a substitute to physical mobility in addition to a type of independent mobility which builds on the specific potentials of on-line learning and network communication. It may prepare and extend physical mobility, and/or offer new opportunities for students/academic staff who are unwilling or unable to take advantage of physical mobility*". Virtual mobility is defined as a compliment to physical mobility by Op de Beeck et al. (2007) as "*virtual mobility can be used to prepare, support and follow-up physical mobility to enrich the latter and to make it even more effective and fruitful*".

Vriens et al. (2010) defined virtual mobility as *the set of ICT-supported activities that realize cross-border, collaborative experiences in a context of teaching and/ or learning*.

In the Tea Camp project partnership (2010), Virtual Mobility at higher education is defined as "*an activity or form of learning, research, communication and collaboration, based on the following characteristics: cooperation of at least 2 higher education institutions (HEI); virtual components through ICT supported learning environment; collaboration of people from different background and cultures working and studying together, creating a virtual community; having a clear goal and clearly defined learning outcomes; having, as its main purpose, the exchange of knowledge and improvement of intercultural competences; as a result of which the participants may obtain ECTS credits and/or its academic recognition will be assumed by the home university; providing visibility of university in higher education area, capitalization of educational process; leading to integration of ICT into their mainstream academic and business processes.*"

Engineering mobility in Europe (EMEU, 2019) highlighted that with Virtual Mobility the aim is '*to create an educational context where students and staff in country A communicate with their peers in country B to acquire knowledge, skills and attitudes (competences) which makes them more competitive and employable on an increasingly international labour market.*'

According to UNESCO IESALC (2022) virtual student mobility is "*a form of mobility that uses information and communication technologies to facilitate cross-border and/or inter-institutional academic, cultural, and experiential exchanges and collaboration which may be credit-bearing or not for credit.*"

Below table 1 have provided the summary of the definitions of virtual mobility. The concept of virtual mobility has been addressed in the literature in two ways: (i) as an alternative to physical mobility (ii) a way to prepare, support and followup physical mobility (Op de Beeck et al., 2007)

Table 1. Summary of Definitions of Virtual Mobility in the Literature

Authors	Definition
Bunt-Kokhuis (1996, 2001)	*"the collaborative communication between a faculty member and his/her counterpart(s) mediated by a computer. More often, these meetings will be interactive and take place across national borders and across time zones"*
Boninsegna and Dondi (1998)	*"Trans-national lectures and/or learning materials, Cross-border recruitment of students, Intensity of communication flows, International accreditation of achievements, Multilingualism, complementarities to both physical mobility and conventional teaching"*
Van Wende (1998)	*"An emerging form of internationalization where students follow courses offered by institutions abroad and interact with students and teachers, libraries and databases in other countries".*
Silvio (2003)	*"Virtual mobility is a movement "from one place to another in a new space called virtual space enabled by computer-mediated communication"*

continued on following page

Table 1. Continued

Authors	Definition
Vilhelmson and Thulin (2005)	*"Physical transportation and face-to-face contacts, replaced, complemented or even generated by virtual ones"*
Virtual Mobility Best-Practice Manual (2006)	*"Virtual Mobility is a form of learning which consists of virtual components through an ICT supported learning environment that includes cross-border collaboration with people from different backgrounds and cultures working and studying together, having, as its main purpose, the enhancement of intercultural understanding and the exchange of knowledge"*
VICTORIOUS project (2007)	*"use of the internet to enable learners to take courses and participate in local communities at a remote physical university without need to go to it directly. It often implies more than just taking courses but being able to access some of the cultural aspects"*
Move-IT project	*"as a set of ICT-supported activities that realize cross-border, collaborative experiences in a context of teaching and/or learning. These activities can take place in a fully ICT supported learning environment or as a complement to physical mobility (before, during and after). They can be aimed at the (practical) organization of the learning process or they can consist of actual teaching and/or learning activities. Virtual Mobility activities can cross borders between regions, countries, cultures and languages, but also between disciplines. Virtual mobility activities enable collaborative learning (i.e. learning from and with each other) and are always aimed at inter-cultural experiences"*
Op de Beeck et al. (2007)	*"Virtual mobility can be used to prepare, support and follow-up physical mobility to enrich the latter and to make it even more effective and fruitful".*
Lifelong learning Programme (2007-2013)	*"acomplement; or as a substituteto physical mobility in addition to a type of independent mobility which builds on the specific potentials of on-line learning and network communication. It may prepare and extend physical mobility, and/or offer new opportunities for students/academic staff who are unwilling or unable to take advantage of physical mobility"*
UNESCO IESALC (2022)	*a form of mobility that uses information and communication technologies to facilitate cross-border and/or inter-institutional academic, cultural, and experiential exchanges and collaboration which may be credit-bearing or not for credit*

Source: Compiled by author

Characteristics of Virtual Mobility

Different definitions of virtual mobility pointed out a series of common characteristics with the passage of time. After analyzing the different activities described in the definitions of virtual mobility, some of the pertinent characteristics of virtual mobility are:

(i) The communication, discussion and/or interaction between participants is no longer location restricted (Bunt-Kokhuis, 1996, 2001), (Spot+ project team, 2001), (Schreurs, et al., 2006), (Vilhelmson and Thulin, 2008)

(ii) Enhancement of intercultural understanding (Van der Wende, M. (Ed.), 1998), (The Scottish Centre for research into On-Line Learning & Assessment, 2007), (Op de Beeck et al., 2008), (Pigliapoco and Bogliolo, 2007)
(iii) Attendance of classes, seminars, courses, other events held in a place located anywhere in the world (Spot+ project team, 2001), (Schreurs, et al, 2006), (BEST Educational Commitee, 2006), (The Scottish Centre for research into On-Line Learning & Assessment, 2007) as well as participation in local communities (The Scottish Centre for research into On-Line Learning & Assessment, 2007)
(iv) A form of learning or exchange of knowledge (Eds. Op de Beeck, I. et al, 2008)
(v) Full academic recognition of the acquired competences (EC Glossary on the LLP 2007-2013, 2010) or a possibility to earn ECTS-points based on co-operation of – at least two – Higher Education-institutions (Brey, et al., 2007)
(vi) A possibility to access reference materials and contents at a distance by using information and communication technology (Spot+ project team, 2001), (Bacsich, P. et al, 2009).

Green Paper of the Commission of the European Communities (2009) also described some of the characteristics of Virtual Mobility:

(i) An activity conveying at least some of the benefits of physical mobility in its own right
(ii) The use of the internet and other electronic forms of information and communication is often a catalyst for embarking on a period of physical mobility
(iii) It enables young people to prepare for a stay abroad and can create conditions for future physical mobility by facilitating friendships, contacts and social networking, etc., although it is not a substitute for physical mobility
(iv) May be an appropriate and practical form of mobility for young pupils, where travelling abroad may not be an option
(v) Provides a means to keep in contact with the host country once the mobility period is over
(vi) Provides an international dimension to those learners who, for different reasons, are not able or willing to go abroad. In that context, ICT can be used for "electronic twinning" and for virtual platforms, for teachers, other "multipliers", interested individuals, interactive communities, open source initiatives, etc.

Types and Tools for Virtual Mobility

Various types of Virtual Mobility have been identified in the literature: Student Virtual Mobility (SVM); Teacher Virtual Mobility (TVM) or the combination of two is also possible in the higher education institutions. Both types of mobility are of equal importance from the institutional context. Virtual mobility may have other two forms – fully virtual mobility or a part of blended mobility (Dauksiene, 2013). Fully virtual mobility may be an alternative to physical mobility or a motivator for physical mobility and may be combined with physical mobility. Virtual mobility as a part of blended mobility aims to enrich the physical mobility experience. Though the different authors have documented separate activities under the domain of virtual mobility. Beeck and Petegem (2013) categorized virtual mobility as international students or staff exchange; international internships and internationalized curriculum. Fuente et al. (2011) categorized virtual mobility by keeping in mind the academic purpose of the visit as virtual mobility for studies; virtual mobility for placements and virtual mobility for shorter academic activities. From the teacher virtual mobility perspective, shorter academic activities could include research and participation at various professional development events.

Tools and technologies that can be used to support virtual mobility are increasingly becoming larger in number and more diverse in their application. Generally, these tools are categorized into two large categories:

- (I) Synchronous tools facilitate communication between users at the same time. The interesting feature of synchronous tools lies in the direct contact between users and thus decreasing the feeling of distance between the users. Synchronous tools play a very important role when the goal is on language learning. For example: chat, videoconferencing, web conferencing, audio conferencing.
- (II) Asynchronous tools facilitate communication between users independent of time i.e. instruction can be provided through this tool at anytime and anywhere. For example: e-mail, online discussion forums, eportfolio.

Irrespective of the above distinction, there are reflective tools (e-portfolio, weblog), non-interactive tools (streaming media, informational website), collaborative tools (wiki, group blog, discussion forum), communication tools (e-mail, chat, video-, audio-, and web conferencing), and social networking tools (social networking, shared media, social bookmarking). Below table 2 provides the descriptions of different tool categories.

Table 2. Different Tool Categories

	Synchronous	Asynchronous
Instruction	Once only online instruction e.g. web or video conference	Accessible anytime, anywhere.
	Examples of web conferencing tools: Skype, Adobe Connect, Microsoft Lync, Google Hangout	Example: instructional videos, accessible via an online platform
Communication	Video conferencing is mostly used for lectures and live discussions between larger groups. Web conferencing is mostly used for one on one communication or communication between small groups.	Email-use is very widespread and effective tool of communication between teachers and students. Social networking platforms are used for establishing informal coordination between different international group members. More official tools like learning management systems "LMS" have been used to complete academic tasks.
	Examples: Skype, Adobe Connect, Lync, Google Hangout, chat	Examples: email, discussion fora, facebook, Multiply, Myspace
Collaboration	Collaborative tools allows students to work together on a product like a collaborative paper or a presentation. These tools are of much significance when the focus is on to analyze the contribution of everyone in the given task rather than on the product.	
	Examples: voicethread, wiki technology, prezi, Google docs, Sharepoint, Dropbox	
Reflection		Tools like blogging and portfolio help students to reflect on their learning. Tools: Blogger, wordpress

Source: https://teacamp.vdu.lt/mod/book/view.php?id=2958&chapterid=28

The tools used for virtual mobility are increasing becoming larger and more diverse in their application in the current scenario under the realm of information and communication technology. Diversified tools used in the educational process range from Custom Built Learning Platform, open-source platforms (Moodle, edX, ILIAS), cloud-based platforms (Microsoft Teams), in addition with video conferencing tools. Video-conferencing platforms such as Zoom, WebEx, and Microsoft Teams have been used initially for team activities. Now days, with the development of the metaverse environment, educational activities using the metaverse have increased recently. Gather.Town, Roblox, iFlands etc. have been used as alternative platforms for team activities. The metaverse platform allows participants to communicate with others verbally and non-verbally in the virtual world through their avatars thus provides an environment that enhances the sense of reality with the distinctive characteristics of video-conferencing platforms.

Virtual mobility activities are categorized in the following way:

(1) **A virtual course or seminar** -(a) courses or seminars at a foreign education providing institution while staying at home and vice-versa; (b) joint courses development and/or delivery by two or more education providing institutions or their group of teachers.
(2) **A virtual study programme** -(a)a study programme provided by virtual education providing institution; (b) joint curricular development and/or delivery by two or more institutions/ inter-institutional group of teachers.
(3) **Virtual student placements/internships**
(4) **Virtual support activities to physical exchange**

In the context of teacher virtual mobility (TVM), Joint course development by teachers of two or more institutions broadens the areas of expertise offered to the learners (EuroPACE, 2010). It enhances the quality of courses and curricula (EADTU network, 2007) and contributes to the quality of the academic education (Brey and e-move project partners, 2007). At the institutional level, Virtual Mobility initiatives enhance sound competition between institutions and thus contribute to the competitiveness and attractiveness of the educational offer in general (Bijnens, et al., 2006).

Difference Between Virtual Mobility and Other Related Concepts

Virtual mobility is not a standalone concept and it shares commonalities with other virtual learning experiences like MOOCs (massive open online learning courses), virtual exchanges, e-learning, and distance learning). Generally virtual mobility concept is often confused and conceived as distance learning and e-learning. Distance learning is part of the most virtual mobile activities and thus shares some of the same benefits. Salandin et al. (2010) differentiates virtual mobility from eLearning by 'internationalization and interculturality' because interculturality is the foundation of virtual mobility. In virtual mobility collaboration takes place with other learners and teachers which lead towards the building of intercultural competence. Whereas e-learning and distance education do not necessarily imply internationalization of learning/knowledge, intercultural dialogue and cross-border academic cooperation <...> which are, in turn, the major virtual mobility drivers" (Dondi &Salandin, 2010).

Both phenomena i.e. '*Internationalization at Home*' and 'Virtual Mobility' contribute towards the internationalization of higher education and the development of intercultural competence of teachers and students. The phenomenon of 'Internationalization at Home' is broader in scope and involves various activities where the concept of virtual mobility focuses on the activities that support to physical mobility and development of intercultural competence among teachers and students. Virtual mobility may be a way to contribute towards 'Internationalization at Home' in the institutional context but there may be other ways to realize the 'Internationalization at Home' (Dauksiene, 2013). In below table3, a comparative picture of virtual mobility characteristics with other elated concepts is highlighted. In this table white areas indicate similarities and light grey areas highlight small differences where as dark areas indicate that virtual mobility feature is not required in other forms of learning.

Table 3. Differences of Virtual Mobility from other related concepts

Feature	Virtual Mobility	Distance Education	Internationalization at Home	Physical Mobility
Main aim	Learning and teaching in multicultural environment	Learning on selected place in own pace time, and preferred way	Acquire internationally oriented competencies	Different aims; possibility to experience cultural differences
International student groups	For cooperation and intercultural competence development	Not required	For development to internationally oriented competencies	Student learning in different cultural environment
Interactivityandcommunication betweenstudentsofdifferentcountriesthroughICT	Must be present at SVM	Different countries are not required	ICT are not required	ICT are not required
International teaching groups	Must be present at TVM	Not required	Notrequired	International from the point of view of travelling person
Multicultural exchange	Intercultural or multicultural depend on VM model (No. of participating countries)	Not required	Not required	Cultural exchange
Use of appropriate technological solutions	Must be present	Must be present	Not required	Not required
Joint choice of the subject to be studied	An option at SVM	Not required	Not required	Not required
Joint curricula design	Ano ption at TVM	Not required	Not required	Not required
Joint production of learning resources	An option at SVM or TVM	Not required	Not required	Not required

continued on following page

Table 3. Continued

Feature	Virtual Mobility	Distance Education	Internationalization at Home	Physical Mobility
Recognition	Still an option at SVM or TVM	Must be present	Not required	Must be present
Mutual confidence relationships between different HEI	Must be present at SVM or TVM	Not required	Not required	Must be present

Source:Dauksiene (2013)

PHYSICAL MOBILITY VERSUS VIRTUAL MOBILITY

Physical mobility and virtual mobility are two different forms of mobility. Each form of mobility has its own characteristics and legitimacy. Both form of mobility i.e. physical mobility and virtual mobility compliment and reinforce each other. However,geographic and administrative restrictions along with the cost involved in the traditional physical mobility model refrain majority of students and staff to access such an international experience as part of their study and training pertinently who come from less affluent or disenfranchised background and thus raised an important concern within the purview of inequality in higher education (Wadhwa et al., 2024; UNESCO IESALC, 2022; Tan et al., 2021; Dauksiene, 2009). So the emergence of virtual mobility which has gained pace in the recent time is more inclusive mobility model for connecting a greater number of students and staff and thus offers a wider space for dialogue and relationship building with their global peers (Buchem, 2019). Thus, the main benefit of virtual mobility is to offer both students and teachers the opportunity to work in an international environment, even if they were unable to take part in physical mobility programmes, in line with the concept of the internationalized curriculum (Beelen & Jones, 2015). Virtual mobility offers meaningful and multilateral interaction for the wider youth and offers opportunity to build greater intercultural understanding of different societies and thus expands their worldwide view.

Virtual Mobility arises due to the development of new structural models like virtual campuses at higher education level across the globe with the incorporation and development of information and communication technology.Thus in virtual mobility, as a result of information and communication technologies, it is possible to study part of our degree in a different higher education centre without actually having to move. Virtual mobility thus strengthens and compliments physical mobility. At the same time, it is also really effective and efficient in terms of time and costs (Guide for Virtual Mobility, 2010).In the European context, virtual mobility complements already existing mobility programmes, such as Erasmus or Erasmus-Mundus, where students physically transfer to another university in order to complete part of their studies. In this way, virtual mobility is compatible with physical mobility, e.g. virtual preparatory work or the follow-up on studies carried out at the host university, or provided as an alternative. Below table 4highlights the difference between Physical and Virtual Mobility

Table 4. Difference between Physical and Virtual mobility

Physical Mobility	**Virtual Mobility**
In a different physical location which implies travel and stay in another country. For a limited period of time A considerable effort in time Extra economic cost Based on on-campus activities and meetings, face-to-face teaching and immersion in the country's daily life Social, cultural and educational enrichment	Study is carried out at home, at university, and at work. No restrictions as to the time invested in the course Balanced time and cost Access to the courses and programmes of the host country; communications with teachers and fellow students through ICT Acquisition of educational, intercultural and technological skills

Source: Guide for Virtual Mobility (2010)

The traditional mobility model i.e. physical mobility is an important way to provide international and intercultural experiences to individuals. In the physical mobility, the advantage is that incoming international students can very easily establish direct contact with teachers and teachers can keep an eye on their successful integration in the courses. The strength of physical mobility is that international students get a greater chance to foster the intercultural learning in the host universities and host countries(Tan et al., 2021). A comparative picture of strengths and weakness of physical and virtual mobility model has been highlighted in table 5 and 6.

Table 5. Strengths and Weaknesses of Physical Mobility

Weaknesses	Strengths
A break-off from daily responsibilities. Limited period of time. High cost (registration, accommodation, etc.) Many steps to be completed as foreign residents (visa, insurance, resident permit, etc.) Required adjustment to the group's activity. Acessed by a small number of students. Access restricted to especific educational offer. Initial training proposals only.	Learning of academic, social and intercultural skills. Learning with an international perspective. A stay in another country. Direct intercultural experience. Social and cultural enrichment. Experience in other learning styles. Access to other fields of learning. Synchronous education. Learning another language.

Source: Garcia et al. (2008)

But this traditional model of physical mobility can only be accessed by the individuals from the high socio-economic background (López-Duarte et al., 2021) which makes this mobility unattainable for the individuals who belong to lower socio-economic and underprivileged background. In contrast to the traditional physical mobility model, the emergence of the new form of mobility i.e. virtual mobility has an advantage in terms of its availability and accessibility, as virtual mobility is based on digital communication technologies. Many hurdles of the physical mobility do not occur in the virtual setting. Therefore, virtual mobility is more accessible to many more people (Guimarães et al., 2019). Yet, at the same time, other hurdles like lack of social contact with the host students will probably be pronounced, as informal meetings, informal communication and extra-curricular activities are not available. In addition to that, international students can hardly establish relationships with other international students or with people outside of the university, it is unlikely that they discover the city life of the respective university location. Spontaneous forms of intercultural learning are therefore limited which were the strengths of the physical mobility.

Table 6. Strengths and Weaknesses of Virtual Mobility

Weaknesses	Strengths
Demand for a high level of linguistic and ICT communication skills. More restricted intercultural experience. Limitations of new learning environments. Solitude when completing the course Demand for accurate course planning. Lack of flexibility in administrative proceedings. Difficult accessibility of virtual platforms. Demand for a highly technological infrastructure. Greater attention from tutors. Higher rates of uncompleted studies.	Learning of academic skills Learning of an international perspective. The stay does not involve abandoning daily responsibilities. No particular time restrictions. Flexibility in course arrangements. Medium cost (registration and Internet connection) Experience of other learning style. More individualised learning. Synchronous and asynchronous education. Learning of abilities demanded by current society. Accessibility to a large number of students. Unrestricted access to education at any stage of life. More variety of training possibilities (stay at another university, joint programmes, joint seminars, teaching provided partly on-site, etc.) Proposals for initial training and lifelong education.

Source: Garcia et al. (2008) cited in Wadhwa et al. (2024)

The goal set by the EU for 20% of the European Higher Education Area graduates to have experience of a study or training period abroad by 2020 (Commission of the European Communities, 2009, p. 20) may not be reached easily, although more and "more traditional universities open their borders, collaborate supra/intra-institutionally and often (inter)nationally, and/or involve non-traditional students in their traditional learning environment. In this way every campus becomes a virtual campus, and all mobility has now some form of virtual mobility included" (Van Petegem, 2010, p. 1).Though, virtual mobility phenomenon is rather new in higher education institutions which lead to different interpretations and uncertainty of its benefits and needs. However, new forms of mobility are not intended in any way to replace traditional physical mobility. Rather, they are designed to be a useful addition and permit the involvement of people at higher education institutions who are unable to be mobile for whatever reason. With the advent of Internationalization of Higher Education and development of ICT, the teaching paradigm has changed from knowledge transfer to knowledge sharing and role of teacher has changed from being an authority to being flexible and the new model of virtual mobility fits well in this changing paradigm. In sum, both the models of mobility are complimentary to each other as it has been rightly pointed as, "*Virtual and physical mobility are two different sides of the same coin, although they were both conceived as different educational methods, and they both have their own future. However, neither one is less important than the other. Each one has its own characteristics and legitimacy. Furthermore, they both complement and reinforce each other in different ways"* (Ruiz-Corbella& Álvarez-González, 2014, p. 167 cited in UNESCO, 2022).

OPPORTUNITIES AND CHALLENGES OF VIRTUAL MOBILITY SPECIFICALLY IN THE CONTEXT OF TEACHERS

Both models of mobility *i.e.* Physical and Virtual mobility improve the educational environment of higher education institutions. Teachers and students benefit culturally, linguistically and educationally from the experience of other countries and institutions (UNESCO IESALC, 2022; Vriens, 2010; Dauksiene, 2013). Benefits specifically in the context of Virtual Mobility in the context of teachers, trainers and curriculum developers are highlighted below:

Virtual mobility unwrapped the opportunities for teachers to collaborate and work with geographically disparate teams.

Virtual mobility offers the teachers from different institutions across the globe not only on the design and development of courses but also on the delivery of courses.

The collaboration across the globe with other colleagues helps teachers to reconsider their routine practice and to add innovative and quality elements in their courses to match the requests of international standards.

Virtual mobility provides an international platform to teachers and trainers for the exchange of ideas and information and thus learns from each other.

Virtual mobility helps in expanding the global view and gaining a broader perspective on a specific subject as well as on the world in general for teachers and trainers. Working in cross-border teams can develop a true sense of global citizenship.

Virtual mobility allows flexibility to teachers in teaching and learning process, even a-synchronously, from any place and within smaller personalized learning spaces and communities.

Teachers and trainers, who due to socio-economic and personal reasons don't want to be involved in physical mobility, can be involved in Virtual Mobility and thus this model of mobility is more inclusive.

The international cooperation and partnership among different teachers and trainers across the institutions enhanced the quality of the study programmes and thus instills the competition among higher education institutions. Many teachers claim that they have found greater satisfaction in virtual interaction with their students, due to the greater quality and depth of their contributions (Mason &Rennie, 2006).

Online teachers play a key role in the creation and consolidation of virtual learning environments, and in influencing a change of attitude further to the training provided. It is also clear that teachers need greater technological support from their institutions as, in general, students are more skilled in this regard than their own teachers.

Every teacher should have are, at least, three fields of literacy, essential in any virtual environment and which are clearly valued in today's society (i) Technological literacy or the ability to use these means (ii) Literacy for information, or the ability to find, analyze, use and reuse information (iii) Educational literacy or the ability to work in an intercultural and collaborative manner (iv) Teaching innovation, introducing new methodologies in virtual scenarios

Irrespective of the advantages which Virtual Mobility offers, it also brings some challenges for all the stakeholders who include students, teachers and higher education institutions. There are some of the conditions and requirements which need to be fulfilled before the implementation of the Virtual Mobility model. Specifically in the context of the teachers, they need to be trained with appropriate techniques and tools in order to prepare the courses that are implemented virtually. The knowledge of foreign language is one of the biggest challenges not only for teachers but also for students in the context of Virtual mobility (Opde Beeck& Mazar, 2005). Irrespective of that, the stable information technologies, system compatibility and consideration of standards are some of the technical challenges which need to be taken care of before the implementation of Virtual Mobility programme (Macek &Ritoneja, 2016). The teacher's role significantly changes by becoming a guide and learning support in the new model of mobility i.e. Virtual Mobility (Guide for VM in higher education). Below table 7 has summarized the advantages and challenges of teacher virtual mobility (TVM).

Table 7: Advantages and Challenges of Teacher Virtual Mobility (TVM)

Advantages of TVM	Challenges of TVM
1. Professional networking	1. Teacher training
2. Exchange of good practices	2. Mobility assessment
3. Enhanced employability	3. Workload
4. Research enhancement	4. Cultural identity
5. Transparency and recognition of teaching	5. Legal framework
6. Rich experience	6. Academic recognition

continued on following page

Table 7: Advantages and Challenges of Teacher Virtual Mobility (TVM)

Advantages of TVM	Challenges of TVM
7. More career opportunities	7. Coordination
8. Upgrade of skills and competencies (a) Intercultural (b) Personal, social (c) Linguistic (d) ICT related (e) Joint curricula design	8. Quality 9. Blended Mobility

Source: Dauksiene (2013) cited in Wadhwa et al. (2024)

Characteristics of a Virtual Mobile Teacher

(i)Virtual mobile teacher needs to have a good insight about the level of the students involved i.e. what are the characteristics of the students have at different levels?

(ii) Virtual mobile teacher need to choose the activities, skills and associated knowledge according to the level of the students involved in the Virtual mobile programme.

(iii) Virtual mobile teacher need to prepare the virtual mobile activities with the other colleagues and institutions involved. The start, middle and end should be made clear to the students from the beginning.

(iv)Virtual mobile teacher need to incorporate appropriate strategies to introduce students to each other.

(v)Virtual mobile teacher needs to know the different user-friendly techniques and tools of ICT

(vi) Virtual mobile teacher needs to be enthusiastic, honest and flexible. More enthusiastic a teacher is, the higher the chance of a successful experience

(vii) Virtual mobile teacher needs to be ready to act as coaches and counselors for the students

(viii) Virtually mobile teacher needs to be open to digital skills and training

CONCLUSION

Internationalization, being high on the agenda of various political documents, fosters collaborations of higher education institutions. However, physical mobility of students and researchers is sometimes not enough or possible at all times. Thus, the need for virtual mobility arises; however, limited availability of practices asks for in-depth research and guidance for virtual mobility implementation. From the last one decade, with the development of information and communication technology, students and teachers became more exposed to blended and online learning during. So a shift from traditional mobility to virtual mobility is significant. Virtual mobility has started as a complement for physical mobility and in recent times it is the key trend of collaboration development between higher education institutions across the globe. Virtual mobility promotes cooperation and collaboration among higher education institutions and thus leads towards quality enhancement and transparency in educational processes. Some of the significant benefits of Virtual mobility are that it leads towards openness, flexibility, visibility, exposure to different points of view on the subject, more experienced and qualifies staff and development of virtual mobility competences. Moreover, the concept of virtual mobility changed over time due to the important developments in the arena of communication and technology and with the evolution of new educational policies and resources. In the current scenario of changing landscape of internationalization of higher education, it is the high time that higher education institutions need to think seriously about the ways and means through which virtual mobility cab be integrated in order to meet the internationalization goals. Despite the numerous benefits of virtual mobility in terms of flexibility, inclusivity and diversity there remains a need for further efforts to overcome certain obstacles and establish virtual mobility as a crucial component of international education (Faek, 2023). Higher educational institutions need to invest in resources, training and faculty support in order to integrate virtual mobility into their curricula (ibid). With the meaningful use of digital technology, virtual mobility is giving a boost to internationalization at home by opening a wider range of educational offers with the use of educational technology. Montes et al. (2011) highlights that Virtual Mobility is still an underestimated tool and there is a strong need to promote its usage at higher education level due to its significant benefits. Virtual mobility can enhance traditional learning activities by the use of collaborative and learning activities. Virtual mobility allows students who would not be able to participate in exchange mobilities, for various reasons like due to different forms of disabilities, students with children, fully employed students, or other such categories to be part of an international academic community and to be more connected with their peers through digitally mediated learning opportunities.

With in the context of Teacher Virtual Mobility, many teachers claim that they have found greater satisfaction in virtual interaction with their students, due to the greater quality and depth of their contributions (Mason&Rennie, 2006). With in this new era of globaloization and information and communication technology, teaching paradigm has changed from knowledge tranfer to knowledge-sharing and thus role of teacher has changed from being an authoritative to being flexible and as guidance provider. Thus, there is a strong need to adopt new teaching, learning and assessment methods in our teaching learning process. Therefore, virtual mobility in general and teacher virtual mobility (TVM) specifically is a significant tool which contributes to the internationalization of Higher Education (EuroPACE, 2010). So some of the pertinent questions needs to be answered before this new model of mobility i.e. Virtual mobility could be strengthened: are the teachers already prepared for this new change? Have they acquired necessary competences for Virtual mobility implementation? How to prepare curriculum to get the most of this virtual exchange? Coherent long term policy support at Government and Institutional level remains a key factor to be considered if the potential impact of virtual mobility has to be achieved across the globe.

REFERENCES

Bacsich, P., Bastiaens, T., Bristow, S. F., Op de Beeck, I., Reynolds, S., & Schreurs, B. (2009). *Reviewing the Virtual Campus* from The Rise of Large-Scale E-learning Initiatives Worldwide http://revica.europace.org/Re.ViCa%20Online%20Handbook.pdf

Beeck, I. op de, & van Petegem, W. (2013). *Virtual mobility: An alternative or complement to physical mobility?* ERACON 2011 & 2012 Dual Year Proceedings. https://lirias.kuleuven.be/retrieve/237431

Beelen, J., & Jones, E. (2015). Redefining internationalization at home. In Curai, A., Matei, L., Pricopie, R., Salmi, J., & Scott, P. (Eds.), *The European higher education area: Between critical reflections and future policies* (pp. 67–80). Springer. DOI: 10.1007/978-3-319-20877-0_5

Being-mobile project network. Retrieved from http://www.being-mobile.net/

Bijnens, H., Boussemaere, M., & Rajagopal, K. (2006). European Cooperation in Education through Virtual Mobility- A Best Practice Manual, retrieved from https://www.eurashe.eu/library/modernising- phe/mobility/virtual/WG4%20R%20Virtual%20Mobility%20Best%20Practice%20Manual.pdf

Bijnens, H., & Op de Beeck, I. (2006). Virtual Mobility in Europe from Pilot Level Towards Integration in Mainstream Education. *Bridging the gap between business and business schools - Being Mobile* -, (psl. 39-44). Vilnius.

Board of European Students of Technology (BEST) Educational Commitee. *Virtual Mobility – The educational challenge of the future*. BEST Symposium on Education, 23-29 July 2006, Retrieved from https://www.best.eu.org/download/edu/Bucharest_EoE_report.pdf

Boninsegna, A. & Dondi, C. (1998). Humanities Guidelines for the implementation of ODL and a virtual mobility approach in Conventional Universities. DG XXII SOCRATES ODL Programme, Humanities project result.

Brandenburg, U., Berghoff, S., & Taboadela, O. (2014). *The Erasmus impact study: Effects of mobility on the skills and employability of students and the internationalisation of higher education institutions*. Publications Office.

Brey, C. and e-move project partners (2007). EADTU. From Guide to Virtual Mobility. http://145.20.178.4/Portals/0/documents/The_Guide_to_Virtual_Mobility.pdf

Bruhn-Zass, E. (2023). Virtual Internationalization as a Concept for Campus-Based and Online and Distance Higher Education. In: Zawacki-Richter, O., Jung, I. (eds) Handbook of Open, Distance and Digital Education. Springer, Singapore. Retrieved from file:///C:/Users/Lenovo/Downloads/978-981-19-2080-6.pdf DOI: 10.1007/978-981-19-2080-6_23

Buchem, I. (2019). Digital Impact: How is International Student and Staff Mobility Changing in Higher Education? Retrieved from https://oeb.global/oeb-insights/digital-impact-how-is-international-student-and-staff-mobility-changing-in-higher-education

Bunt-Kokhuis, S. G. (1996). 2001). *Academic Pilgrims: Faculty Mobility in the Virtual World.On the Horizon*, 9(1), 1–6. DOI: 10.1108/10748120110803626

Carr, A., & Beaudry, A. (2023). Effectiveness of in-person and virtual international mobility scholars programme on career and professional development. *Journal of Learning for Development*, 10(3), 333–345. DOI: 10.56059/jl4d.v10i3.722

Commision of the European communities. *Green paper: Promoting the learning mobility of young people*, 2009.07.08, Brussels, COM (2009) 329 final, Retrieved from https://ec.europa.eu/education/lifelong-learningpolicy/doc/mobility/com329_en.pdf

Crowther, P., Joris, M., Otten, M., Nilsson, B., Teekens, H., & Wächter, B. (2000). *Internationalisationat home. A position paper*. EAIE.

Dauksien, E., Teresevicien, M., & Volungevicien, A. (2009), Teacher Virtual Mobility for research and practice, retrieved from https://www.researchgate.net/publication/317549364_TEACHER_VIRTUAL_MOBILITY_FOR_RESEARCH_AND_PRACTICE

Dauksiene, E. (2013). Virtual mobility in higher education. Doctoral dissertation, VytautasMagnus University. http://talpykla.elaba.lt/elaba-edora/objects/elaba:1915200/datastreams/MAIN/content

EADTU network. (2007). from an operational conception of virtual mobility:http://www.eadtu.nl/e-move/

Elearningeurope.info. (2009). *Glossary: Virtual Mobility*. Retrieved fromhttp://www.elearningeuropa.info/main/index.php?page=glossary&abc=V

EMEU - Engineering Mobility in Europe Erasmus+ Project. (2019). Virtual Mobility Manual. Retrieved from https://www.emeu.eu/media/1478/final_emeu4all_virtualmobility-manualmarch-2019.pdf

EuroPACE. (2010). Virtual mobility, Retrieved from http://www.europace.org/interest3.php

European Commission Glossary on the Lifelong Learning Programme 2007-2013. http://ec.europa.eu/education/programmes/llp/guide/glossary_en.html#117

Faek, R. (2023) Shifting Tides: Exploring the rise of virtual student mobility in international education, retrieved from https://wenr.wes.org/2023/11/shifting-tides-exploring-the-rise-of-virtual-student-mobility-in-international-education

Fuente, A. A., & Menendez Ferreira, R. (2011). *TeaCamp Scenario and Barriers.* WP7: TeaCamp Exploitation, TeaCamp project.

Fuente, A. A. J., Fueyo, A., & Menendez, R. (2011). Virtual Mobility Tools. In Tereseviien, M., Volungeviien, A., & Daukšien, E. (Eds.), *Virtual mobility forteachers and students*. Vytautas Magnus University.

Gaebel, M., Zhang, T., Stoeber, H. & Morrisroe, A. (2021). Digitally enhanced learning and teaching in European higher education institutions. European University Association absl.

García-A, L., Álvarez-González, B., & Ruiz-Corbella, M. (2008). *NetActive: Basesand proposals for good practices in virtual academic mobility (an intercontinentalapproach)*. UNED. Glossary: Virtual Mobility. Elearningeurope.info, Retrieved from https://www.elearningeuropa.info/main/index.php?page=glossary&abc=V

Guimarães, F. F., Mendes, A. R. M., Rodrigues, L. M., Paiva, R. S. d. S., & Finardi, K. R. (2019). Internationalization at home, coil and intercomprehension: for more inclusive activieties in the global south. SFU Educational Review, 12(3), 90–109. Retieved from DOI: 10.21810/sfuer.v12i3.1019

Helms, R. M., & Brajkovic, L. (2017). *Mapping internationalization on U.S. campuses* (2017edition). ACE.

Hudzik, J. K. (2011). Comprehensive internationalization. From concept to action. Washington,DC: NAFSA: Association of International Educators.

Humanities project report. (1995). Retrieved from https://tecfa.unige.ch/tecfa/research/humanities/humanities-report.html

IEASA. (2020). Higher Education Internationalisation in South Africa in the Context of the COVID-19 Pandemic: Impact on International Students, retrieved from https://ieasa.studysa.org/wp-content/uploads/2020/05/IEASA-position-paper_COVID-19_May2020_Final.pdf

International Association of University Presidents & Santander Universidades. (2020). Leadership Responses to COVID-19: A Global Survey of College and University Leadership. Retrieved from: https://www.iaup.org/wpcontent/uploads/2020/11/IAUP-Survey-2020- ExecutiveSummary.pdf

López-Duarte, C., Maley, J. F., & Vidal-Suárez, M. M. (2021). Main challenges to international student mobility in the European arena. *Scientometrics*, 126(11), 8957–8980. DOI: 10.1007/s11192-021-04155-y PMID: 34602676

Maček, A., & Ritonija, N. (2016). Virtual mobility in higher Education–the case of DOBA Faculty. *Studies from Education and Society*, 98-106. https://doi.org/DOI: 10.18427/iri-2016-0089

Marinoni, G., van't Land, H., & Jensen, T. (2020). *The impact of Covid-19 on Higher Education Around the World: IAU Global Survey Report*. International Association of Universities.

Mason, L. (2021). *International Student MobilityFlows and COVID-19 Realities*. Institute of InternationalEducation. Retrieved from https://www.iie.org:443/en/Research-and-Insights/Publications/IntlStudent-Mobility-Flows-and-C19-Realities

Mason, R., & Rennie, F. (2006). *E-Learning: The Key Concepts*. Routlege. DOI: 10.4324/9780203099483

Montes, R., Gea, M., Dondi, C., & Salandin, T. (2011). Virtualmobility: The value of inter-cultural exchange, eLearning Papers,ISSN: 1887-1542, https://www.elearningpapers.eu

Move-IT - Seminars Promoting Virtual Support For Mobile Students. retrieved from http://move-it.europace.org

Op de Beeck, I. (2008). VM-BASE: Virtual Mobility Before and After Student Exchanges. Retrieved from http://vm-base.europace.org/

Op de Beeck, I., Bijnens, H., Michielsens, C., & Van Petegem, W. *Extending and supporting physical student mobility through virtual mobility*. 18th SPACE Conference, Nicosia (Cyprus), 23-24 February 2007. Retrieved from http://www.eunis.org/events/congresses/eunis2007/CD/pdf/papers/p121.pdf

Op de Beeck, I., Bijnens, H., Michielsens, C., & Van Petegem, W. (2007). *Extending and supporting physical student mobility through virtual mobility*.

Op de Beeck, I., & Mazar, I. (2005). *Reve-real virtual Erasmus: opportunities andchallenges*. Retrieved fromhttp://www.beingmobile.net/pdf/Vilnius_2006_new_brochure.pdf

Pigliapoco, E., & Bogliolo, A. (2007, November 8-9). *Accessible virtual mobility*. Retrieved from EADTU's 20th Anniversary Conference 2007 "Internationalcources and services online: Virtual Erasmus and a new generation of Open Educational Resources for a European and global outreach: http://www.eadtu.nl/conference-2007/iles/I6.pdf

Poulová, P., Černá, M., & Svobodová, L. (2009). *University Network – Efficiencyof Virtual Mobility*. In *Proceedings of the 5th WSEAS/IASME InternationalConference on educational technologies (EDUTE' 09)* (pp. 87-92).

Poulová, P.; Janeček, V., Černá, M. (2007). Reasons Of Failing In Interuniversity Study. Information and Communication Technology in Education, 37-40.

Project Atlas. (2023). Project Atlas [Dataset]. Institute of International Education. https://www.iie.org/Research-and-Insights/Project-Atlas

Pursuea, M., Warsta, M., & Laaksonen, I. (2005). Virtual University: A Vehicle forDevelopment, Cooperation and Internationalisation in Teaching and Learning. *European Journal of Engineering Education*, 30(4), 439–446. DOI: 10.1080/03043790500213201

ReVe project Virtual Mobility Manual. 2006. Retrieved from http://reve.europace.org/drupal

Ruiz-Corbella, M., & Álvarez-González, B. (2014). Virtual Mobility as an Inclusion Strategy inHigher Education: Research on Distance EducationMaster Degrees in Europe, Latin Americaand Asia. *Research in Comparative and International Education*, 9(2), 165–180. DOI: 10.2304/rcie.2014.9.2.165

Schreurs, B., Verjans, S., & Van Petegem, W. (2006). *Towards SustainableVirtual Mobility in Higher Education Institutions*. EADTU Annual Conference2006.

Shields, R. (2013). Globalization and InternationalStudent Mobility: A Network Analysis. *Comparative Education Review*, 57(4), 609–636. DOI: 10.1086/671752

Silvio, J. (2003). Global Learning and Virtual Mobility. (T. Varis, T. Utsumi, & W. R. Klemm, Eds.) Retrieved from http://www.friends-partners.org/glosas/Global_University/Global%20University%20 System/ UNESCO_ Chair_Book/Manuscripts/Part_IV_Global_Collaboration/Silvio,%20Jose/Silvio_web/SilvioD9.html

Spot+ project team. (2001). *Training Module 2: A Virtual Erasmus Student*. Retrieved from http://www.spotplus.odl.org/downloads/Training_module_2.pdf

Tan, A. E., Schiffmann, L., & Salden, P. (2021). Handbook on Physical and Virtual Mobility. Teaching and Learning in Intercultural Settings. Retrieved from file:///C:/Users/Lenovo/Downloads/D%203.5%20UNIC%20Handbook%20on%20Physical%20and%20Virtual%20Mobility.pdf

TeaCamp project partnership. (2010). Here from E. Dauksiene, M. Tereseviciene, A. Volungeviciene. Virtual Mobility Creates Opportunities. In Conference Proceedings "Application of ICT in Education 2010: experience, issues and perspectives of e-studies", 18 November 2010, ISSN 1822-7244, p. 30-35.

Teichler, U. (2017). Internationalisation Trends inHigher Education and the Changing Role ofInternational Student Mobility. *Journal of InternationalMobility*, 5(1), 177–216.

The Scottish Centre for research into On-Line Learning & Assessment. (2007). *Student Mobility in a Digital World*. Retrieved November 21, 2010, from Victorious Final Report, retrieved from http://www.coimbra-group.eu/victorious/VIC%20Final%20Report%20print%20version.pdf

UNESCO International Institute for Higher Education in Latin America and the Caribbean (IESALC). (2022). Moving minds: Opportunities and challenges for virtual student mobility (VSM) in a post-pandemic world. UNESCO IESALC. Petegem, W. (2010). *Virtual Mobility and International Networking*. VirtualCampus conference, Granada (Spain).

van der Wende, M. C. (Ed.). (1998). *Virtual Mobility: New Technologies and Internationalisation. Nuffic Paperback no. 10*. Nuffic.

VICTORIOUS - Virtual Curricula Through Reliable Interoperating University Systems. retrieved from http://www.coimbra-group.eu/victorious/

Vilhelmson, B., & Thulin, E. (2005). Virtual Mobility of Urban Youth: ICT-basedCommunication in Sweden. *Journal ofEconomic & Social Geography*, 96(5), 477–487.

Vilhelmson, B., & Thulin, E. (2008). Virtual mobility, time use and the place of the home. *Tijdschrift voor Economische en Sociale Geografie*, 99(5), 602–618. DOI: 10.1111/j.1467-9663.2008.00494.x

Vriens, M., Achten, M., Op de Beeck, I., & Van Petegem, W. (2010,). Virtual mobility as an alternative or complement to physical mobility. Retrieved from http://move-it.europace.org/kfm/uploads/Edulearn_Move-IT_VM.pdf

Vriens, M., & VanPetegem, W. (Eds.). (2012). *Make it work! Integrating virtualmobility in international work placements*. Education and Culture DG; LifelongLearningProgramme. Retrieved from https://www.efmd.org/projectstest?'

Wadhwa, R. (2016). Students on move: Understanding decision making process and destination choice of Indian students. *Higher Education for the Future*, 3(1), 54–75. DOI: 10.1177/2347631115610221

Wadhwa, R. (2016b). New phase of internationalization of higher education and institutional change. *Higher Education for the Future*, 3(2), pp-227-246.

Wadhwa, R. (2019). Pathways to Internationalization in Indian Higher Education: Reflections on Policy Options. In Bhushan, S. (Ed.), *The future of Higher Education in India*. Springer. DOI: 10.1007/978-981-32-9061-7_19

Wadhwa, R., Shcheglova, D., Opfer, E., & Garmonova, A. (2024). Teachers on the Move: Understanding the New Model of Virtual Mobility Through the Case Study of a Russian University. *Higher Education for the Future*, 11(1), 90–108. DOI: 10.1177/23476311231222965

KEY TERMS AND DEFINITIONS

Digitalization in Higher Education: The use of technology to improve the educational experience for students and teachers.

Hybrid Mobility: In hybrid mobility, the elements of both physical and virtual mobility has been combined. Hybrid mobility has been considered as an in-between approach across the two extremes of Physical mobility and virtual mobility. Hybrid mobility combines the elements of both physical and virtual mobility and has been considered as an in-between approach across the two extremes of Physical mobility and virtual mobility. Scholars argue that hybrid mobility will increase in near future with the rise of virtual mobility due to its flexibility approach in recent times (UNESCO, 2022).

International Mobility: Has generally been conceptualized as the cross-border movement of students and scholars based on the assumption that the individual is physically mobile (UIS, 2006; OECD, 2009).

Internationalization of Higher Education: The process of integrating an international, intercultural, or global dimension into the purpose, functions or delivery of higher education.

Physical Mobility: Staying in another country for academic, professional or cultural reasons relating to higher education with varying duration. Physical mobility refers to a staying in another country for academic, professional or cultural reasons relating to higher education with varying duration. This form of mobility has always been at the forefront to promote internationalization in higher education institutions.

Virtual Mobility: The use of information and communication technologies (ICT) to obtain the same benefits as one would have with physical mobility but without the need to travel. Virtual mobility covers a comprehensive range of higher educational activities and has gained pace after pandemic. UNESCO IESALC defines VSM as a "form of mobility that uses information and communication technologies to facilitate cross-border and/or inter-institutional academic, cultural, and experiential exchanges and collaboration which may be credit-bearing or not for credit".

Chapter 11
Objective Measurement and Evaluation in Virtual Technology-Driven Environments:
Methods, Applications, and Future Directions

Şeyma Çağlar Özhan
https://orcid.org/0000-0002-0106-6285
Bartın University, Turkey

Perihan Tekeli
https://orcid.org/0000-0001-7831-9693
Hacettepe University, Turkey

ABSTRACT

Virtual technology-driven environments (VTD) are widely used in education and training due to their positive impact on cognitive, affective, and psychomotor skills. However, measuring and evaluating the effectiveness of these environments poses challenges, including technological complexity, diverse user behavior, and data collection methods. Researchers and practitioners employ various methods to address these issues, such as self-report measurements and objective methods that assess user experiences during system interactions. This book chapter examines physiological, physical and behavioural measures used to assess user responses, cognitive competencies and task performance in VTDs. The chapter offers an overview of existing methods, discusses their applications across different fields, and highlights future developments. The aim is to provide a comprehensive perspective on the challenges

DOI: 10.4018/979-8-3693-6030-9.ch011

of measurement and evaluation in virtual environments.

INTRODUCTION

Virtual technology-driven environments (VTD) are often preferred in the fields of education and training due to their positive effects on cognitive, affective and psychomotor skills. However, there are various challenges in measuring and evaluating the effectiveness of these environments. These include the complexity of the technology, the diversity of user behavior and data collection methodologies (Suh & Lee, 2021). In these environments, which are characterized by dynamic and ever-changing conditions, it is possible to encounter measurement and evaluation challenges. Various methods are employed by researchers and practitioners in order to overcome these difficulties and to accurately evaluate the effectiveness of the environments (Suh & Lee, 2021). These are self-report measurements, whereby user reports are received, and objective measurement methods are employed to assess the user's experiences during their interaction with the system (Radianti et al, 2020). In this study, a variety of measurement techniques were employed to gain insight into the user's physiological responses, physical expressions, and behavioral tendencies within virtual technology-driven environments. These techniques included physiological measurements, which explore the user's body response patterns, physical measurements that capture the user's expressive components, and behavioral measurement methods and applications that reveal the user's behavioral tendencies.

Figure 1. Distribution of studies in which objective measurement was carried out in VTD in the last five years

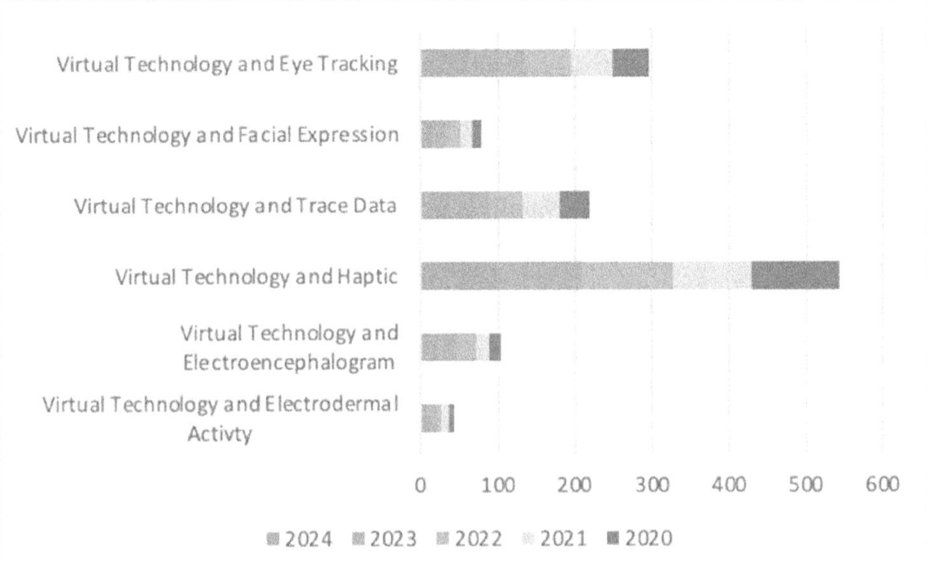

Figure 1 illustrates the distribution of studies conducted with the keywords identified in Web of Science by year. As illustrated in the presented graph, studies employing objective measurement methods in VTD have been a prevalent approach over the past five years. The measurement of physiological signals plays an important role in the perception of user physiological states in VTD environment, with techniques such as electrodermal activity (EDA) and electroencephalogram (EEG) being employed (Nokelainen et al., 2024; Wu et al., 2024). It is possible to design systems that are appropriate for individuals' cognitive, motivational and attention networks by developing a comprehensive understanding of how users interact with these signals. The measurement of physical responses is an invaluable tool for understanding the immediate reactions and attention of users, as evidenced by techniques such as facial expression analysis and eye tracking. Facial expressions permit the identification of emotional responses to stimuli in the VTD environment, thereby facilitating the organization of VTD according to the emotional states of users (D'Mello & Kory, 2015). Eye tracking is a frequently employed tool in VTD, offering a powerful means of analyzing where users focus their attention and how they interact with virtual elements (Holmqvist et al., 2011). Furthermore, behavioral measurement methods, such as haptic and trace data, are of significant importance as non-invasive techniques. Haptic interaction performance can be evaluated using this method during interaction (Amirabdollahian et al., 2018). Additionally, trace data reveals users' navigation patterns and interactions within the environment (Hou et al., 2020), thus facilitating a comprehensive understanding of user behavior and preferences. The utilization of these methodologies, either in conjunction or as standalone techniques, enables researchers to ascertain insights pertaining to affect, cognitive abilities, behavioral tendencies, and task execution. Nevertheless, the utilization of these techniques is not without its own set of limitations and challenges.

Figure 2. Google Ngram viewer trend graph

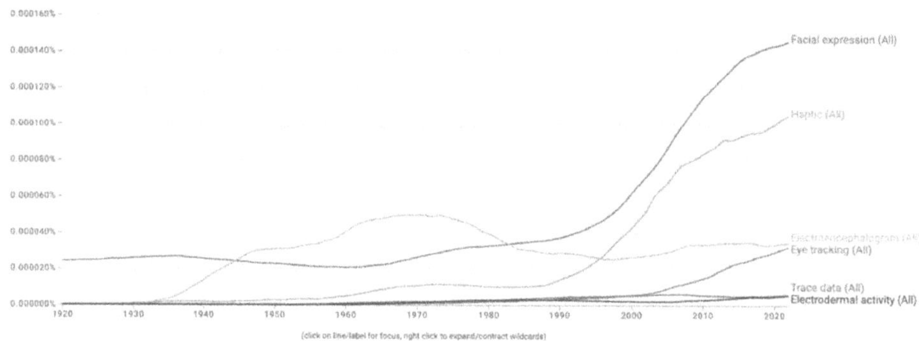

Figure 2 shows that Google Ngram Viewer is a visualization tool that uses text mining techniques in the background to show how words and phrases used in books have changed over a period of time. Figure 2 shows the change in the frequency of use of the terms “Facial expression”, “Haptic”, “Electroencephalogram”, “Eye tracking”, “Trace data” and “Electrodermal activity” between 1920 and 2022. These numbers are percentages and represent the ratio of the word to the number of occurrences of the word in all books in the specified time period. For example, the expression “0.000160%” indicates that this term was used at a frequency of 0.000160% of all printed words in a given year. In other words, this word was used approximately 1.6 times per million words. The horizontal axis (x-axis) of the graph represents years. While the term “facial expression” had a very low usage rate from the 1920s to the 1960s, it started to gain popularity from the 1990s onwards, with a significant increase in usage especially from the early 2000s. By 2022, it reached its highest frequency of use. The term “haptic” which has shown a great upward trend after the 2000s, shows an increase in research on haptic feedback and interactions. As of the 2010s, the frequency of use has steadily increased. The frequency of use of the term “electroencephalogram” has increased since the 1940s and peaked in the 1960s. It then followed a downward trend, but has been on an upward trend since the 2000s. This may indicate that EEG has started to be used more in scientific studies. The term “eye tracking” has increased steadily since the 1980s. In the 2000s, the frequency of use increased significantly. The term "trace data" started to be used especially in the 2000s and has followed a slight upward trend since then. Although the frequency of use is low, it shows an interest in modern data analysis methods and digital monitoring studies. Finally, the term "Electrodermal activity" has shown a very low increase in usage since the 1980s. This term is usually associated with physiological measurements and mood analysis, and its popularity has been limited due to the difficult data collection process and analysis.

The objective of this chapter is to present measurement and evaluation methods in virtual technology-driven environments. The applications of these methods in a variety of domains and future developments in this field are explained in detail. In this context, the objective is to present an overview of the existing methods, illustrate their applications, and provide a comprehensive analysis of the challenges encountered and the strategies employed to overcome them.

Keywords: physical measurements, behavioral measures, physiological measurements, virtual technology-driven environments

BACKGROUND

Subjective measures are based on individuals' personal experiences, feelings and interpretations. Data collected through methods such as questionnaires, self-report scales and interviews are shaped by the individual's own perceptions and evaluations. Since these reports reflect the participants' own emotional experiences, researchers need to interpret and categorize them. Subjective data collection tools can offer possible explanations for learning activities, but are less successful in documenting temporal fluctuations, unconscious reactions and hidden changes in affective state variables (Deng & Gao, 2023). Thus, there is a need for measures that directly capture individuals' immediate learning processes.

The term 'objective measurement' refers to assessments conducted using data that are observable, quantifiable, and repeatable. These measurements are free from any form of bias or personal interpretation. The application of objective measurements enables the precise measurement, analysis and repetition of phenomena. When the experimental context is repeated, different researchers may observe the same results (Gardhouse & Anderson, 2013). These measurements are based on observable phenomena and entail the gathering of raw, uninterpreted data through the utilization of technological tools. Objective data can provide direct, objective information about specific aspects of students' behavioral and mental processes that correlate with factors such as study choices, confusion, and changes in effort or attention in a learning situation that are otherwise difficult to capture (Henriques, Paiva, & Antunes, 2013). This type of measurement is designed to objectively monitor and analyze physiological, behavioral and digital responses to external stimuli. To illustrate, eye-tracking devices quantify how individuals interact with their environment and their attentional orientations (Bulling et al., 2011), whereas methods such as galvanic skin response (GSR) assess individuals' engagement (Barrow et al., 2024), stress (Kerous et al., 2020), anxiety (Simoes et al., 2018), and emotional arousal.

In contrast, multimodal data seeks to gain a more profound understanding of the user experience by gathering data from a range of sources. Multimodal data is derived from disparate data channels that encompass both subjective and objective elements (Järvelä et al., 2021). The utilization of representative, objective, diverse and accurate data facilitates a more profound comprehension of users and the design of meaningful experiences for them (Giannakos et al., 2018). Giannakos et al. (2019) demonstrated that the utilization of multimodal data (including eye-tracking, EEG and facial expression) resulted in considerably enhanced skill acquisition predictions in comparison to those derived from a single data stream. The utilization of multimodal data represents an efficacious methodology for the comprehension of cognitive and emotional processes, as well as the engineering of bespoke learning experiences, particularly within the context of learning environments. Moreover, no single component can fully capture the essence of an emotional experience, given that emotions are inherently multifaceted. It is therefore important to use objective and subjective measures together in order to reveal correlations between the neurocognitive, physiological, behavioral and phenomenological reality of emotional events (Gardhouse & Anderson, 2013). It is also important to note that the seamless integration of different devices and the interpretation of multimodal data streams represents a significant challenge in supporting the learning experience (Lahat et al., 2015).

MAIN FOCUS OF THE CHAPTER

This section will present a summary of studies conducted with objective measurement and evaluation methods in virtual reality, educational simulations, games and digital learning environments. Additionally, it will address the integration of multimodal data in these studies, as well as the challenges and limitations encountered in understanding participant experiences.

The Utilisation of Physical Measurements in Virtual Technology-Driven Environments

Facial expressions

The objective of acquiring facial expressions from users is to comprehend their affective states, with the aim of enhancing products or services based on this information (McDuff, Czerwinski, & Rowan, 2018). In facial expression analyses, the emotional states on the face can be considered alongside other variables, such as Action Units (AU) and gaze durations (Ekman, Friesen, & Hager, 2002).

The methods used to obtain data on facial expression can be examined in three categories (Bastida et al., 2024). (1) Facial electromyography (fEMG), which enables the tracking of facial muscles with skin-mounted electrodes. (2) The collection of facial expressions via a camera and the subsequent automatic analysis of these expressions using machine learning methods. It is acknowledged that these methods possess a range of advantages and disadvantages. While it is possible to collect data in a more sensitive but invasive manner with fEMG (Maity & Veer, 2024), it has been stated that facial expression analysis software is non-invasive, although the accuracy of the results may vary depending on the context (Banerjee et al., 2023). Although the coding of facial action units by experts is both a non-invasive and sensitive method, it is disadvantageous in terms of time and cost (Di Mitri et al., 2018).

Facial expression analysis is a technique employed in a number of fields, including user experience research, education, marketing, psychological testing and medical research. The present study is concerned with the utilization of facial expressions in the VTD environments.

The objective of the study conducted by Bastida et al. (2024) was to examine the emotional states of 49 participants using psychophysiological signals and facial expressions in a virtual reality (VR) environment. The study revealed that a combined technique utilizing facial expressions could effectively determine emotional states, although certain emotions, such as fear and trust, remained challenging to identify. It was highlighted that identifying emotions based on facial expressions represented a significant challenge, particularly when utilizing VR equipment, given the inability to accurately recognize the eye region of participants.

In a digital game-based learning environment prepared for teaching mathematics, Zhang et al. (2023) examined the differentiation of cognitive, motivational and emotional factors according to gender. Facial expression detection software was employed for the purpose of evaluating emotions. In the study conducted with 269 middle school students, fourth-grade girls exhibited significantly higher levels of anger than boys. The study reported that the facial expressions of all participants could not be recorded due to a lack of appropriate equipment and that data loss occurred due to the low video quality.

Dubovi (2022) sought to examine the cognitive and emotional engagement of individuals in a virtual reality-based simulation. A multimodal data analysis was conducted on the aforementioned application, which was completed by 61 university students. The data were collected via eye tracking, electrodermal activity (EDA) measurement, facial expression analysis, and self-report. Facial expressions were employed as a means of ascertaining the emotional states of the participants. In the procedural learning phase, it was determined from the analysis of facial expressions that the participants experienced a greater sense of joy. However, it was observed that participants who experienced joy exhibited higher levels of mental effort, as indicated by EDA and eye tracking data.

In conclusion, the results of studies conducted in VTD environment and measuring facial expression indicate that emotion (Zhang et al., 2024; Zhang et al., 2023) and engagement (Dubovi, 2022) variables were predicted. It is worth noting that the majority of studies employed automatic facial recognition systems. It has been asserted that a number of limitations are encountered in accordance with the characteristics of VTD. In this context, it has been emphasized that in environments such as VR that cause the eye area to be closed (Bastida et al., 2024) and in situations where equipment such as cameras is scarce (Zhang et al., 2024), the accuracy rate of automatic facial recognition systems may decrease. Furthermore, it has been suggested that emotions such as anger and fear may be confused with other emotions. (Bastida et al., 2024; Zhang et al., 2024). In studies employing facial expression as a multi-modal data collection tool, findings were obtained for cognitive and emotional variables (Bastida et al., 2024).

Eye Tracking

Eye tracking methods and tools are employed in a multitude of domains, including education, marketing, and human-computer interaction. These techniques facilitate the examination of human eye movements and the distribution of attention. The objective of eye tracking is to gain insight into the manner in which users direct their gaze on specific area or object, the duration of their focus, and the cognitive processes underlying these focusing behaviors. Eye tracking is a technology that records an individual's eye movements, viewing angle, speed, and duration of eye movements, pupil size, and other relevant eye parameters (Duchowski, 2007). This technology enables the objective detection of where users direct their gaze, the duration of their gaze, and the sequence in which they direct their gaze (Jacob & Karn, 2003). It thereby provides information about visual attention, information processing, and other psychological processes (Rayner, 1998). Consequently, eye tracking technologies facilitate communication between the user and the computer. In the context of eye tracking, fixation refers to the act of focusing the eyes on a specific object or point for a fixed period of time. The frequency and intensity of fixation, duration, and the peak speed and amplitude of eye movements are critical indicators for understanding attentional intensity and information processing (Negi & Mitra, 2020). Furthermore, they can be employed to evaluate the intricacy of a given problem (Maggio et al., 2019). The metrics of gaze fixation, fixation duration, and the number and duration of visits are of significant importance in decision-making estimations (Spinks & Mortimer, 2015). A saccade is defined as the movement of the eye from one point to another. The gaze path illustrates the sequence of points traversed by the user's gaze and the order in which these points are visited. In other words, gaze paths encompass both saccades and fixations, thereby illustrating which areas a user's eyes direct their attention towards and the manner in which they transition between these areas. In the context of eye-tracking studies, the term “Areas of Interest” (AOI) refers to the specific regions that are subjected to analysis. These regions determine whether a gaze point or a fixation is directed to a predefined region around the target point (Vehlen et al., 2022). The utilization of AOIs facilitates a more profound comprehension of attention allocation and cognitive processing procedures (Muthumanickam et al., 2018). The use of AOIs is frequently employed in conjunction with metrics such as heat maps, fixations, and gaze paths, with the objective of demonstrating how users allocate their attention intensity over specific regions (Holmqvist et al., 2011; Hessels et al., 2016). In eye-tracking studies, heatmaps are used to visualize where participants' gaze is concentrated. In these heat maps, concentrated areas are shown in warm colors such as red or orange, while less concentrated areas are shown in cool colors such as blue (Figure 3).

Figure 3. Heatmap showing where the gaze is concentrated during eye tracking according to color intensity

It can be stated that the utilization of eye tracking to examine the distribution of user attention, cognitive processes and interactions in Virtual Technology-Driven (VTD) environments represents a novel approach. In VTD environments, particularly in three-dimensional settings such as virtual reality (VR), eye tracking is employed to investigate which elements students direct their attention towards, the duration of their gaze, their responses to visual stimuli, and the strategies they utilize. The observation of eye movements in different regions and changes in visual attention can facilitate the acquisition of valuable insights into cognitive processing. The monitoring of students' visual behaviors, particularly in digital environments such as video-based learning, multimedia content and virtual reality, provides invaluable data that can be used to enhance the effectiveness of instructional design. Consequently, eye tracking technologies can be employed as a predictive instrument when examining the decision-making process concerning an individual's necessity for social and cognitive interactions in a virtual environment.

The use of eye tracking in virtual reality (VR) environments is a relatively straightforward process. The flexibility and potential of VR environments make them an attractive option for a wide range of scientific fields, as the areas of interest can be clearly defined, designed, and reconfigured. Furthermore, data collection, environmental settings and stimuli can be controlled, and the user experience can be made more natural (Mikhailenko et al., 2022). Virtual environments are particularly suited to the eye-tracking process and are also well-suited to research focusing on human cognition and behavior. Immersive educational application environments may be preferred for the learning process and evaluation, with the aim of determining any distracting elements or cues. These can then be reflected in the design, using eye-tracking technologies.

In a recent study, Bacca-Acosta et al. (2022) presented a design proposal based on eye tracking data. The aim was to assess the effectiveness of different types of scaffolding in VR environments for English language education. The researchers examined how students' visual attention patterns differed based on the type of scaffolding employed. Four distinct types of scaffolding were implemented within VR environments, with the subject of English prepositions of place being addressed. A total of 41 university students participated in the study, which employed an experimental design and eye-tracking methodology. The findings indicated that both static and dynamic VR learning environments had a beneficial impact on students' learning outcomes. However, the dynamic VR environment demonstrated a more pronounced effect. The second result demonstrated that scaffolds that were naturally integrated into the VR environment in terms of visual attention and in closer proximity to the objects with which students were required to interact were more effective in enhancing their learning performance.

In a similar vein, Liu et al. (2022) employed 360-degree video, which is regarded as an immersive virtual reality, to investigate the impact of textual and visual cues on learning and attention in immersive 360-degree video. The research was conducted using a mixed-methods approach, combining experimental research with semi-structured interviews. In this study, 110 undergraduate students were randomly assigned to one of four experimental conditions. The four experimental conditions were as follows: a control group, a group receiving textual cues within the initial field of view, a group receiving textual cues outside the initial field of view, and a group receiving both textual and visual cues outside the initial field of view. In the eye-tracking process, data were collected on total fixation time, fixation time by AOIs, fixation time on initial field of view AOIs, and heat maps. The results demonstrated that visual cues had a significant guiding effect on students' attention. In immersive 360-degree videos, cues were found to guide attention and improve students' learning performance. Additionally, it was observed that students allocated a greater proportion of their attention to the initial object.

The general challenges associated with eye-tracking tools can be broadly categorized as follows: calibration issues; data accuracy issues resulting from head movements; and individual differences. Such challenges have the potential to impact the accuracy of the data obtained and, consequently, the reliability of the subsequent analysis. A substantial body of research has demonstrated the necessity for supplementary verbal data to achieve a comprehensive understanding of the outcomes yielded by eye tracking. In order to supplement the data, Liu et al. (2022) employed post-experiment semi-structured interview questions. A further limitation of eye-tracking research is the difficulty of determining area of interest (AOI) when comparing different training designs that include both moving and static images. It is regrettable that there is a paucity of guidance available for the generation of AOIs or for the comparison of AOI generation methods (Hessels et al., 2016). One significant challenge in the field of eye tracking is the accurate interpretation of gaze data. The majority of studies did not cross-validate their eye-tracking data with other data sources (Bendall et al., 2019). However, it is proposed that eye tracking can be interpreted with greater accuracy if it is employed for cross-validation in conjunction with other neuroimaging, psychometric, and behavioral measures (Ke et al., 2024). While eye-tracking technology can effectively capture participants' eye movements during learning, it is recommended that eye-tracking findings be complemented with supporting evidence from different types of measurements to ensure correct interpretation of eye movement data and to fully utilize the eye-tracking process in measuring cognitive processes during learning. In conclusion, eye-tracking technology presents a significant opportunity for the analysis of user attention, cognitive processes, and interactions within virtual environments. Nevertheless, it is advised that it be corroborated by supplementary data sources and that the eye-tracking process be reinforced through cross-validation for accurate interpretation.

The Utilisation of Behavioural Measurements in Virtual Technology-Driven Environments

Trace data

The term 'trace data' is defined as the behavioral residues left by individuals when they interact online (Hinds & Joinson, 2018). This record data presents researchers with novel opportunities to examine social and behavioral phenomena through the utilization of diverse metrics, including the timing, frequency, duration and sequence of user behaviors and interactions within the digital environment. This data is derived from a multitude of systems, including websites, commercial transaction platforms, telecommunication networks, social media applications, smartphone applications, sensors integrated into wearable devices, and smart meters (Stier, Breuer, Siegers, & Thorson, 2019). The advantage of trace data is that it allows for more objective measurement, as it records users' actual behaviors and is less subjective and more accurate than self-report methods (Fitzpatrick et al., 2017). Furthermore, it offers the potential for a comprehensive examination of user interactions, which may elucidate behavioral patterns, preferences and potential impediments. Nevertheless, the recording of users' interaction data gives rise to a number of ethical concerns and potential privacy issues (Fitzpatrick et al., 2017). It is imperative that the steps to be taken for the management and preliminary analysis of large data sets are implemented meticulously (Siemens and Baker, 2012).

Wearable technology, such as trackers worn on the wrist or waist that track physical activity and, depending on the model, additional data such as heart rate and geolocation, can also yield digital traces (Keusch & Kreuter, 2021). The potential applications of trace data in learning scenarios are numerous. These include the development of educational games and apps, the creation of real-time learning dashboards, the use of predictive analytics to assess learner performance, and the implementation of data-driven decision-making in educational institutions (Hakimi et al., 2021).

In a recent study, Ye and Pennisi (2022) sought to ascertain whether self-reported data on self-regulated learning (SRL) among students could be corroborated by trace data collected from the learning management system. The study encompasses data pertaining to learner-content interactions, learner-learner interactions, and learner-instructor interactions. The study employed a combination of quantitative and qualitative research methods. A total of 65 students participated in the study. Consequently, the researchers concluded that trace data is an accurate reflection of students' learning. In this study, all trace data were anonymized and stored in password-protected files in accordance with ethical standards and the confidentiality of participants.

Verma et al. (2024) conducted an investigation into the factors influencing the happiness and satisfaction of informatics students engaged in hybrid learning, utilizing statistical and machine learning algorithms with trace data within the learning environment. The study examines the factors affecting student happiness, with a particular focus on hybrid learning environments, utilizing statistical and machine learning algorithms. The findings indicated that students expressed a preference for future hybrid learning modes, with the perception that they would be more beneficial for theoretical courses than practical laboratories. The findings of the study indicate that hybrid learning environments have a considerable impact on student happiness, with younger students perceiving these environments as more secure and conducive to productivity. Furthermore, it was emphasized that the provision of robust technical support and the implementation of enhanced security protocols in online examinations are essential.

The data in question, which we and other parties refer to as “trace data,” can also be designated as “Big Data.” The term “trace data” is typically used to describe data sets that are both voluminous and multi-layered (Hakimi et al., 2021). The analysis of these data sets necessitates the utilization of data mining and learning analytics techniques, in particular. The analysis of trace data collected at different points in time presents a significant challenge due to the intricate interactions and relationships inherent in such data sets. These complexities can be overcome through the utilization of advanced data analysis methodologies, such as machine learning and deep learning algorithms, in conjunction with Big Data analysis tools. Furthermore, another controversial issue pertaining to trace data is that of ethical violations. There is a significant gap in the existing literature on the ethical considerations associated with the study and processing of trace data (Hakimi et al., 2021). The ethical implications are contingent upon the methodology employed. The debate surrounding ethics and big data is contingent upon the definition of ethics itself (Herschel & Miori, 2017). The aforementioned studies demonstrate that trace data offers extensive volumes and multi-layered data, and that its analysis can significantly impact learning processes and experiences. It can be argued that trace data has the potential to provide meaningful insights in learning environments. However, it is essential to consider the ethical implications and the challenges associated with data processing.

Haptic

Haptic technologies are systems that provide physical feedback to the user, thereby simulating tactile perception. The hardware comprising these systems contains motors and sensors. Such technologies provide feedback to the user in response to their movements, utilizing techniques such as vibration, force feedback, and other physical sensations (Srinivasan and Basdogan, 1997). These technologies are predominantly employed in the domains of virtual reality, medical simulations, and robotic systems (Figure 4). The objective of haptic technologies is to provide a more realistic experience by enhancing users' tactile perception in virtual or remote-controlled environments. This technology is employed particularly in the fields of education, simulation, robotic surgery and user interface design, facilitating more effective and natural interactions for users (Amirabdollahian et al., 2018). Haptic technologies are also employed for performance evaluation, with metrics typically encompassing response time, force accuracy, tactile resolution perceived by the user, and system stability (Salisbury, 1997). The requisite equipment for haptic systems includes haptic gloves, wearable devices, and force-feedback joysticks. These devices are designed with the specific purpose of providing physical feedback to users (Burdea & Coiffet, 2003).

Figure 4. Haptic VR gloves

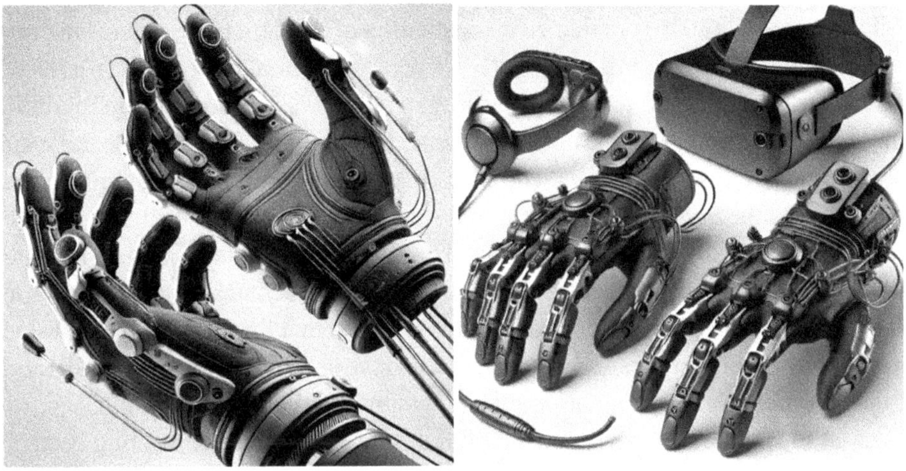

A number of studies have concentrated on the beneficial effects of incorporating haptic interactions into virtual reality environments or simulations, with a particular focus on students' learning outcomes, performance, and sense of presence. The utilization of haptic technologies has been demonstrated to enhance user engagement and performance, facilitating the provision of more realistic and effective feedback in both educational and virtual environment experiences. To illustrate, Zohar and Levy (2021) devised a tangible learning environment for chemistry instruction. The authors posit that students' conceptual understanding is enhanced as the degree of physical interaction with tools such as movies, simulations, joysticks, and haptic devices increases. Furthermore, they assert that haptic interactions encompassing a broader range of movements and forces yield higher learning gains.

In their study, Qi et al. (2024) investigate the potential of 3D simulations supported by virtual and haptic technologies in museum learning environments to enhance students' engagement in the learning process. A total of 40 undergraduate students participated in the study. The experiment comprised a three-dimensional artefact simulation and four distinct tasks, namely contour (shape), colour, volume, and material interaction tasks. The haptic interaction group utilized devices that provided haptic feedback, whereas the non-haptic group employed only a mouse and keyboard. Consequently, the implementation of haptic-supported interaction led to a notable enhancement in students' learning performance and engagement in museum learning tasks involving 3D collections. The study concluded that haptic feedback was more pronounced, particularly in the context of volume and material tasks. Furthermore, students demonstrated a greater capacity to acquire detailed information through tactile feedback.

Thawani et al. (2016) conducted an evaluation of resident performance in endoscopic endonasal surgery utilizing the NeuroTouch VR simulation platform as haptic technology. The specific focus of their investigation was the impact of simulation training on performance in the operating room. In this study, the experimental method was employed, with students who participated in the simulation training group designated as the experimental group and students who did not receive simulation training designated as the control group. The findings indicated that the simulated training sessions, specifically those involving the experimental group of students, led to enhanced task performance. The findings revealed that the subjects in the trained group exhibited higher mean scores than those in the untrained group. The utilization of the NeuroTouch VR simulation platform, supported by haptic technology, was observed to enhance the performance of young residents in the operating room.

In another study conducted by Luciano and colleagues (2009), the authors focused on researching and developing a prototype dental simulator for training in periodontal procedures. A periodontal simulator incorporating virtual reality and haptic technology was employed. In this haptics-based virtual reality periodontal training simulator, the objective was to facilitate the acquisition of competencies related to the diagnosis and treatment of periodontal diseases through the experience of a tangible sensation while interacting with virtual dental instruments. The results demonstrated that tactile feedback not only facilitates the learning process but is also a crucial component of the periodontal simulator, enabling the reproduction of the authentic conditions encountered by a dentist examining actual patients.

The extant literature identifies a number of different classifications of haptic technology. In their 2021 study, Wee and colleagues categorise these technologies as handheld devices, wearable devices, devices encountered in situ, physical props, and mid-air approaches. Although handheld haptic devices are typically straightforward to operate, they do present certain challenges. Handheld haptic devices should be sufficiently flexible to accommodate a range of hand sizes (Wee et al., 2021). This may be achieved by the application of adjustable hinges along the controller. Wearable haptic interfaces are typically designed to be compact and comfortable, with the objective of not impeding the user's movement (Prattichizzo et al., 2019). In the development of new wearable systems or actuators, factors such as weight must be considered without compromising functionality and with the capacity for adaptation (Wee et al., 2021). Mid-air interfaces are of significant interest due to their capacity to provide haptic sensations without direct contact. In the case of airborne haptic interfaces, vibrating haptic feedback is transmitted to users via an ultrasonic transducer panel. A further challenge is to enable users to move freely while still processing the required data (Wee et al., 2021).

The Utilisation of Physiological Measurements in Virtual Technology-Driven Environments

Galvanic Skin Response (GSR)- Electrodermal Activity (EDA)

It measures changes in heat and electricity in the skin through the processes of sweating and nerve conduction. The galvanic skin response is a consequence of alterations in the electrical characteristics of the skin that occur when individuals engage with external stimuli (phasic) and when there is no stimulation (tonic) (Rosenzweig, 2015). For this reason, it is also referred to as electrodermal activity (EDA). The data obtained from the dermis via electrodermal measurement may be compromised by the use of various cosmetic products, which could affect the quality of the data collected. The electrodermal activity (EDA) is essentially associated with the level of arousal and vitality of the sympathetic nervous system. An increase in arousal indicates that an individual is experiencing excitement, attention, anxiety, fear, or anger (Blikstein et al., 2017). A reduction in arousal is indicative of a state of boredom or relaxation (Burt & Obradovic, 2013).

Galvanic skin response (GSR) devices can be examined in four categories: (1) professional devices suitable for use in laboratory environments, (2) wearable and wireless measurement devices, (3) wearable devices in the form of a wristband, and (4) devices designed for biofeedback applications that can be used with smartphones. It is notable that different types of devices are employed in the studies reviewed here, in accordance with the specific aims and methods of the research. Wearable GSR devices are particularly prevalent, reflecting the nature of virtual technology-driven environments (Nokelainen et al., 2024; Liberman & Dubovi, 2023; Caglar-Ozhan et al., 2022).

In the study conducted by Barrow et al. (2024), the electrodermal activity (EDA) of 10 participants was measured while they interacted with a virtual reality (VR) environment designed for the purpose of teaching complex biochemical processes. The study, which employed a mixed-methods approach, revealed that the increase in skin conductance during virtual reality activities indicated an increase in autonomic arousal and engagement among the participants. However, the study indicates that a novel technology such as VR may influence arousal due to its intrinsic novelty and potentially impede the accurate measurement of EDA. It is therefore recommended that long-lasting applications be designed for the use of EDA in virtual technology-driven environments.

The study by Hakami et al. (2024) sought to determine whether EDA has an impact on teachers' assessment of orchestration load in collaborative learning activities. The study employed a single-subject research design. A total of five teachers participated in the study. The application process was conducted five to seven times for each teacher, with each session lasting between 10 and 35 minutes. The variable designated as "orchestration load" was derived by conducting a separate evaluation and interpretation of the variables "self-report stress," "cognitive-mental demand," and "EDA peaks." The results demonstrated that the specific task, the number of students involved, and the duration of the activity had a significant impact on the orchestration load.

In a longitudinal study, Nokelainen et al. (2024) examined the self-report emotions and electrodermal activities of 22 teachers in teaching-related situations. The experience sampling method with event-contingent sampling was employed via a mobile application. In this process, measurements were also taken with a wearable electrodermal activity (EDA) device, and the process spanned a two-week period. The findings indicated that the prospective and retrospective emotional states of teachers in teaching-related activities were characterized by positivity. The greatest degree of positive affect was reported in the aftermath of interactive teaching tasks. The occurrence of high levels of electrodermal activity (EDA) was associated with a slight increase in the intensity of positive emotional states. No significant difference was identified in terms of EDA across the teaching, tutoring, planning, and assessment stages. Furthermore, the highest levels of negative affect and EDA were observed during the teaching planning stage.

The objective of Pavic et al. (2023) was to develop a model that would explain how factors such as immersion, environmental contents and sense of presence affect emotion. The study employed an experimental design with two video conditions, one presented on a head-mounted display and the other on a computer screen. A total of 26 participants were recruited for the study and completed a questionnaire before being instructed to view the videos. In order to ascertain the emotions experienced, self-report data, electrodermal activity and heart rate data were employed. The researchers calculated the arousal levels of the participants by analyzing the skin conductance levels (measured by EDA data). The findings indicated that, irrespective of content, immersion resulted in the experience of more positive emotions and higher levels of arousal. The results of the structural equation modelling indicated that the indirect effect of immersion on arousal was accompanied by a sense of presence. It was noted in the study that the videos watched in VR were relatively short, and that longer materials should be used in order to obtain more reliable physiological responses.

Simoes et al. (2018) conducted an experiment with 20 participants in a serious game designed to teach bus-taking routines to individuals with Autism Spectrum Disorder. During the course of the application, the electrodermal activity peaks exhibited by the participants were interpreted as indicative of anxiety. The findings indicated a reduction in electrodermal activity over time, which was associated with a decrease in anxiety.

EDA is employed in VTD environments, particularly to ascertain individuals' cognitive states, including orchestration load (Crespi et al., 2022), engagement (Barrow et al., 2024), cognitive load (Liberman & Dubovi, 2023), and stress (Kerous et al., Furthermore, it is used to assess and regulate emotional states, including anxiety (Simoes et al., 2018) and various categories of emotional states (Nokelainen et al., 2024). The research methods employed in the studies were identified as experimental (Hakami et al., 2024; Liberman & Dubovi, 2023), relational (Pavic et al., 2023) and mixed method (Barrow et al., 2024). It has been observed that small groups are preferred in terms of the number of participants. It has been observed that the measurement of skin conductance level (Pavic et al., 2023; Liberman & Dubovi, 2023) and EDA peaks (Liberman & Dubovi, 2023) are the preferred metrics for measurement. Although studies emphasize that electrodermal activity (EDA) is a powerful tool for measuring physiological responses, it is highlighted that the novelty effect (Barrow et al., 2024) and the brief duration of applications (Nokelainen et al., 2024) can influence arousal and result in inaccurate measurements. It is indicated by the studies that these limitations can be overcome with the use of long-lasting applications.

EEG

An electroencephalogram (EEG) allows for the observation and measurement of electrical processes occurring in the vicinity of the brain surface (Bayazıt, 2018). The cerebral cortex, which is the outer shell of the brain, plays a pivotal role in cognitive processes such as perception, memory, thinking, emotion and therefore action. This non-invasive method exhibits a markedly inferior spatial resolution in comparison to functional imaging techniques (Nunez & Srinivasan, 2006). In cognitive and behavioral studies, significant findings are derived from the examination of time-based and frequency-based electrical currents produced in cortical tissue in response to a stimulus through electrodes placed on specific regions of the scalp (Luck, 2014). The main challenges associated with this technique are the potential for data corruption due to the collection of data from sources such as head and body movements, and the complexity of data analysis.

EEG devices can be employed in three distinct forms: as professional tools suitable for clinical laboratories, as mobile tools, and as EEG devices with electrodes that can transmit data wirelessly. Moreover, EEG electrodes, which are instrumental in transmitting electrical signals, can be selected as gel systems or dry electrodes (Figure 5). The choice of both the EEG device and the electrode type is dependent on the specific research area under consideration. The following section presents a selection of studies on the use of EEG in VTD environment.

Figure 5. An example of an EEG device

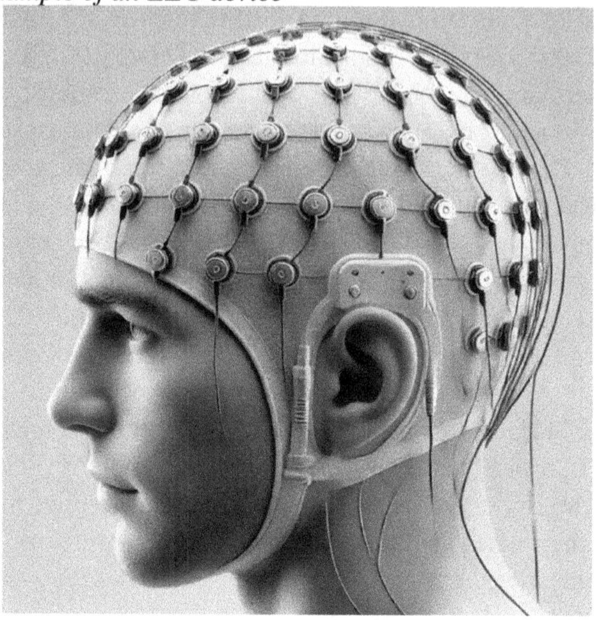

In a study by Wu et al. (2024), the impact of integrating vibrotactile feedback into VR on the creativity, attention, and cognitive load of university students was investigated. The researchers employed a headband EEG to assess the participants' attention levels, and provided vibrotactile feedback when their attention levels were found to be below the desired threshold during the VR experience. A total of 149 students participated in this study, which employed an experimental methodology. The findings indicated that the experimental group, which received vibrotactile feedback, exhibited elevated levels of creativity and attention compared to the control group, which did not receive feedback. Individuals with high spatial ability demonstrated a reduced cognitive load, along with elevated levels of attention and creativity. The study's limitations included the potential for novelty effects associated with the use of VR and EEG, which may have influenced attention levels.

The objective of the study conducted by Sumardani and Lin (2023) was to undertake a comparative analysis of the cognitive processes underlying learning and reading activities performed in a virtual reality (VR) environment, as reflected in the patterns of brain waves. The researchers employed a mobile EEG in order to ascertain whether attention and meditation could be predicted. A total of nine graduate students participated in the study. The findings revealed that reading elicited a heightened level of attention, whereas learning in VR resulted in a considerable cognitive load. Furthermore, the study revealed that the levels of meditation exhibited during learning activities in VR and reading were comparable. In light of the physiological findings obtained in the study, it was recommended that VR environments be structured in a more organized manner.

Zhao et al. (2023) examined the impact of augmented reality (AR)-based mobile photography applications on learning and cognitive load. In addition to self-report measurements, the study employed EEG measurements to ascertain the participants' engagement, relaxation, interest, and focus states. A total of 28 participants were included in this study, which was conducted using an experimental methodology. The findings indicated that the AR-based application yielded superior learning outcomes and reduced cognitive load in comparison to the mobile application. Furthermore, a positive correlation was identified between the emotional state index and learning gains. The relatively small number of participants was identified as a limitation of the study.

The objective of the study conducted by Parong and Mayer (2021) was to compare the affective-cognitive effects of VR and 3D interactive video in an educational context. The study was conducted with an experimental method and involved the participation of 80 university students. The emotional state of the participants was determined through the analysis of EDA, heart rate, and self-report data. Cognitive engagement was measured using mobile EEG. The results indicated that the participants in the VR application exhibited a heightened level of emotional arousal compared to those in the 3D interactive video environment. However, they demonstrated a diminished level of cognitive engagement and performance. The limitations of the study include the potential influence of the measurement devices worn by the participants and the need for further investigation into the underlying cognitive processes.

In conclusion, it is notable that the utilization of EEG in VTD environments is preferred for the measurement of variables such as cognitive load (Sumardani & Lin, 2023), emotion (Parong & Mayer, 2021), and engagement (Zhao et al., 2023). It has been observed that studies have employed relatively small participant groups, which has been identified as a potential limitation (Zhao et al., 2023). It has been posited that the EEG cap and associated apparatus may engender a novelty effect (Wu et al., 2024).

FUTURE RESEARCH DIRECTIONS

The majority of studies in the literature highlight the challenges associated with the capture, processing, analysis and interpretation of objective data. It is advised that machine learning techniques be employed for the automatic analysis of these processes. Consequently, the utilization of multimodal data sources derived from subjective and objective data facilitates a more precise interpretation of the predicted variable.

It is worthy of note that the studies in question have been conducted in the context of online learning environments, VR, and digital games. In this context, interdisciplinary studies can be conducted in collaboration with experts from the fields of cognitive sciences, computer science, and neuroscience. In the context of the VTD environment, recommendation systems that are capable of understanding user experiences in a cognitive, affective, and motivational context, and of providing feedback to users in accordance with these experiences, can be integrated into the VTD environment, and their effects can be investigated.

In addition, the objective measurement of variables is believed to be an effective method of enhancing the adaptability and responsiveness of the VTD environment within the context of artificial intelligence. Furthermore, it is hypothesized that self-report data can be employed as a supplementary measure, thereby enhancing the interpretation of variables. In conclusion, it is proposed that a range of machine learning and artificial intelligence algorithms be employed to automate processes such as multimodal data collection and analysis. It is important to note that cognitive, affective, and motivational variables can be predicted with greater accuracy when all their dimensions are considered, particularly when data diversification is employed. It is proposed that future studies should focus on the design and effects of an adaptive VTD environment that can change according to the data obtained from objective sources. This would provide visual, auditory, and tactile feedback to the user in a manner that is responsive to the data.

CONCLUSION

The necessity for objective measurement and evaluation in VTD environments is made evident by the direct and dependable data provided, which facilitates a comprehensive understanding of the cognitive, behavioral and emotional processes of users. Individual performance and experiences in virtual environments can be obtained and evaluated in real-time through the use of physical, physiological, and behavioral measurements. Among these methods, facial expression and electrodermal activity (EDA) are typically employed to assess affective variables, such as emotion. Conversely, inferences may be drawn regarding cognitive variables, such as attention, cognitive load and engagement, through the use of eye tracking and EEG. Similarly, behavioral variables, including participation, can be inferred through the analysis of trace data.

It is important to note that there are several challenges associated with the utilization of these measurements. Therefore, it is essential to organize research within this context to ensure the integrity and reliability of the findings. Data can be lost as a result of calibration issues in eye tracking and an insufficient number and quality of hardware being used in the measurement of facial expressions. It is important to note that the accuracy of automatic facial expression identification software may be influenced by contextual factors, potentially leading to decreased accuracy rates. Conversely, given that GSR primarily captures data pertaining to arousal status, it is challenging to forecast the impact of cognitive variables and the use of cosmetics by participants on skin conductance. Such factors may potentially lead to data loss or inaccuracies in the data. In studies employing EEG, the relatively small number of participants is highlighted as a potential limitation. This may be attributed to the challenging nature of the data collection process and the intricate analysis of the data. The potential for ethical and privacy violations in trace data is a topic of ongoing debate. It is generally acknowledged that the use of wearable devices, such as EEG and GSR, may have an impact on the data collected due to the unfamiliarity and novelty effect. It is currently believed that it would be beneficial to prepare protocols that will inform participants before the application is conducted. These protocols should take into account the characteristics of each of the measurement methods in question, familiarize participants with the equipment used through preliminary applications and carry out long-term applications in the VTD environment.

Although there are ethical, practical, and methodological challenges regarding objective measurement, it is seen that these measurements provide advantages in terms of understanding the effectiveness of these environments used in various fields such as education, health, marketing by monitoring and interpreting user experiences in VTD environment and optimizing the environments. In particular, understanding the experiences of individuals in VTD environment in terms of affective, cognitive, and motivational context can make serious contributions to preparing personalized environments.

REFERENCES

Amirabdollahian, F., Livatino, S., Vahedi, B., Gudipati, R., Sheen, P., Gawrie-Mohan, S., & Vasdev, N. (2018). Prevalence of haptic feedback in robot-mediated surgery: A systematic review of literature. *Journal of Robotic Surgery*, 12(1), 11–25. DOI: 10.1007/s11701-017-0763-4 PMID: 29196867

Bacca-Acosta, J., Tejada, J., Fabregat, R., Kinshuk, , & Guevara, J. (2022). Scaffolding in immersive virtual reality environments for learning English: An eye tracking study. *Educational Technology Research and Development*, 70(1), 1–24. DOI: 10.1007/s11423-021-10068-7

Barrow, J., Hurst, W., Edman, J., Ariesen, N., & Krampe, C. (2024). Virtual reality for biochemistry education: The cellular factory. *Education and Information Technologies*, 29(2), 1647–1672. DOI: 10.1007/s10639-023-11826-1 PMID: 37361784

Bastida, L., Sillaurren, S., Loizaga, E., Tomé, E., & Moya, A. (2024). Exploring human emotions: A virtual reality-based experimental approach integrating physiological and facial analysis. *Multimodal Technologies and Interaction*, 8(6), 47. DOI: 10.3390/mti8060047

Bayazıt, T. (2018). Event related potentials (ERP). *Journal of Medical Clinics*, 1(1), 59–65. https://dergipark.org.tr/tr/pub/atk/issue/38771/451155

Bendall, R. C., Lambert, S., Galpin, A., Marrow, L. P., & Cassidy, S. (2019). Psychophysiological indices of cognitive style: A triangulated study incorporating neuroimaging, eye-tracking, psychometric and behavioral measures. *Personality and Individual Differences*, 144, 68–78. DOI: 10.1016/j.paid.2019.02.034

Blikstein, P., Gomes, J. S., Akiba, H. T., & Schneider, B. (2017). The effect of highly scaffolded versus general instruction on students' exploratory behavior and arousal. *Technology. Knowledge and Learning*, 22(1), 105–128. DOI: 10.1007/s10758-016-9291-y

Bulling, A., Ward, J. A., Gellersen, H., & Troster, G. (2011). Eye movement analysis for activity recognition using electrooculography. *IEEE Transactions on Pattern Analysis and Machine Intelligence*, 33(4), 741–753. DOI: 10.1109/TPAMI.2010.86 PMID: 20421675

Burdea, G. C., & Coiffet, P. (2003). *Virtual reality technology*. John Wiley & Sons.

Burt, K. B., & Obradovic, J. (2013). The construct of psychophysiological reactivity: Statistical and psychometric issues. *Developmental Review*, 33(1), 29–57. DOI: 10.1016/j.dr.2012.10.002

Caglar-Ozhan, S., Altun, A., & Ekmekcioglu, E. (2022). Emotional patterns in a simulated virtual classroom supported with an affective recommendation system. *British Journal of Educational Technology*, 53(6), 1724–1749. DOI: 10.1111/bjet.13209

Crespi, F., Amarasinghe, I., Vujovic, M., & Hernández-Leo, D. (2022, July). *Estimating orchestration load in CSCL situations using EDA. In 2022.international conference on advanced learning technologies (icalt)*. IEEE.

D'Mello, S., & Kory, J. (2015). A review and meta-analysis of multimodal affect detection systems. *ACM Computing Surveys*, 47(3), 1–36. DOI: 10.1145/2682899

Deng, R., & Gao, Y. (2023). A review of eye tracking research on video-based learning. *Education and Information Technologies*, 28(6), 7671–7702. DOI: 10.1007/s10639-022-11486-7 PMID: 36532792

Di Mitri, D., Schneider, J., Specht, M., & Drachsler, H. (2018). From signals to knowledge: A conceptual model for multimodal learning analytics. *Journal of Computer Assisted Learning*, 34(4), 338–349. DOI: 10.1111/jcal.12288

Dubovi, I. (2022). Cognitive and emotional engagement while learning with VR: The perspective of multimodal methodology. *Computers & Education*, 183, 104495. DOI: 10.1016/j.compedu.2022.104495

Duchowski, A., & Duchowski, A. (2007). Eye tracking techniques. *Eye tracking methodology. Theory into Practice*, •••, 51–59.

Ekman, P., Friesen, W. V., & Hager, J. C. (2002). The Facial Action Coding System. *Research Nexus division of Network Information Research Corporation.*

Fitzpatrick, G., Ellingsen, G., & Bellotti, V. (2017). Instrumenting the interaction: HCI and the sense of measurement. *InProceedings of the 2017 CHI Conference on Human Factors in Computing Systems.* DOI: 10.1145/3025453.3025709

Gardhouse, K., & Anderson, A. K. (2013). Objective and subjective measurements in affective science. In *The Cambridge handbook of human affective neuroscience* (pp. 57-81). DOI: 10.1017/CBO9780511843716.005

Giannakos, M., Sharma, K., Martinez-Maldonado, R., Dillenbourg, P., & Rogers, Y. (2018, September). Learner-computer interaction. *InProceedings of the 10th Nordic Conference on Human-Computer Interaction* (pp. 968-971). DOI: 10.1145/3240167.3240259

Giannakos, M. N., Sharma, K., Pappas, I. O., Kostakos, V., & Velloso, E. (2019). Multimodal data as a means to understand the learning experience. *International Journal of Information Management*, 48, 108–119. DOI: 10.1016/j.ijinfomgt.2019.02.003

Google. (2024). Google Books Ngram Viewer: Facial expression, Haptic, Electroencephalogram, Eye tracking, Trace data, Electrodermal activity.

Hahn, L., & Klein, P. (2022). Eye tracking in physics education research: A systematic literature review. *Physical Review. Physics Education Research*, 18(1), 013102. DOI: 10.1103/PhysRevPhysEducRes.18.013102

Hakami, L., Hernández-Leo, D., Amarasinghe, I., & Sayis, B. (2024). Investigating teacher orchestration load in scripted CSCL: A multimodal data analysis perspective. *British Journal of Educational Technology*, 55(5), 1926–1949. DOI: 10.1111/bjet.13500

Hakimi, L., Eynon, R., & Murphy, V. A. (2021). The ethics of using digital trace data in education: A thematic review of the research landscape. *Review of Educational Research*, 91(5), 671–717. DOI: 10.3102/00346543211020116

Henriques, R., Paiva, A., & Antunes, C. (2012, June). On the need of new methods to mine electrodermal activity in emotion-centered studies. In *International Workshop on Agents and Data Mining Interaction* (pp. 203-215). Berlin, Heidelberg: Springer Berlin Heidelberg.

Herschel, R., & Miori, V. M. (2017). Ethics & big data. *Technology in Society*, 49, 31–36. DOI: 10.1016/j.techsoc.2017.03.003

Hessels, R. S., Kemner, C., van den Boomen, C., & Hooge, I. T. (2016). The area-of-interest problem in eye-tracking research: A noise-robust solution for face and sparse stimuli. *Behavior Research Methods*, 48(4), 1694–1712. DOI: 10.3758/s13428-015-0676-y PMID: 26563395

Hinds, J., & Joinson, A. N. (2018). What demographic attributes do our digital footprints reveal? A systematic review. *PLoS One*, 13(11), e0207112. DOI: 10.1371/journal.pone.0207112 PMID: 30485305

Holmqvist, K., Nyström, M., Andersson, R., Dewhurst, R., Jarodzka, H., & Van de Weijer, J. (2011). *Eye tracking: A comprehensive guide to methods and measures*. Oxford University Press.

Jacob, R. J., & Karn, K. S. (2003). Eye tracking in human-computer interaction and usability research: Ready to deliver the promises. In *The mind's eye* (pp. 573–605). North-Holland. DOI: 10.1016/B978-044451020-4/50031-1

Järvelä, S., Malmberg, J., Haataja, E., Sobocinski, M., & Kirschner, P. A. (2021). What multimodal data can tell us about the students' regulation of their learning process? *Learning and Instruction*, 72, 101203. DOI: 10.1016/j.learninstruc.2019.04.004

Ke, F., Liu, R., Sokolikj, Z., Dahlstrom-Hakki, I., & Israel, M. (2024). Using eye-tracking in education: Review of empirical research and technology. *Educational Technology Research and Development*, 72(3), 1–36. DOI: 10.1007/s11423-024-10342-4

Kerous, B., Barteček, R., Roman, R., Sojka, P., Bečev, O., & Liarokapis, F. (2020). Examination of electrodermal and cardio-vascular reactivity in virtual reality through a combined stress induction protocol. *Journal of Ambient Intelligence and Humanized Computing*, 11(12), 6033–6042. DOI: 10.1007/s12652-020-01858-7

Keusch, F., & Kreuter, F. (2021). Digital trace data: Modes of data collection, applications, and errors at a glance. In *Handbook of Computational Social Science* (Vol. 1). Taylor & Francis.

Lahat, D., Adali, T., & Jutten, C. (2015). Multimodal data fusion: An overview of methods, challenges, and prospects. *Proceedings of the IEEE*, 103(9), 1449–1477. DOI: 10.1109/JPROC.2015.2460697

Liu, R., Xu, X., Yang, H., Li, Z., & Huang, G. (2022). Impacts of cues on learning and attention in immersive 360-degree video: An eye-tracking study. *Frontiers in Psychology*, 12, 792069. DOI: 10.3389/fpsyg.2021.792069 PMID: 35153916

Luciano, C., Banerjee, P., & DeFanti, T. (2009). Haptics-based virtual reality periodontal training simulator. *Virtual Reality (Waltham Cross)*, 13(2), 69–85. DOI: 10.1007/s10055-009-0112-7

Luck, S. J. (2014). *An introduction to the event-related potential technique*. MIT press.

Maggio, M. G., Maresca, G., De Luca, R., Stagnitti, M. C., Porcari, B., Ferrera, M. C., Galletti, F., Casella, C., Manuli, A., & Calabrò, R. S. (2019). The growing use of virtual reality in cognitive rehabilitation: Fact, fake or vision? A scoping review. *Journal of the National Medical Association*, 111(4), 457–463. DOI: 10.1016/j.jnma.2019.01.003 PMID: 30739728

Maity, S., & Veer, K. (2024). An approach for evaluation and recognition of facial emotions using EMG signal. *International Journal of Sensors, Wireless Communications and Control*, 14(2), 113–121. DOI: 10.2174/0122103279260571231213053403

McDuff, D., Czerwinski, M., & Rowan, K. (2018). Measuring emotions in the user experience. *International Journal of Human-Computer Studies*, 120, 56–67.

Mikhailenko, M., Maksimenko, N., & Kurushkin, M. (2022, March). Eye-tracking in immersive virtual reality for education: A review of the current progress and applications. [). Frontiers Media SA.]. *Frontiers in Education*, 7, 697032. DOI: 10.3389/feduc.2022.697032

Muthumanickam, P. K., Vrotsou, K., Nordman, A., Johansson, J., & Cooper, M. (2018). Identification of temporally varying areas of interest in long-duration eye-tracking data sets. *IEEE Transactions on Visualization and Computer Graphics*, 25(1), 87–97. DOI: 10.1109/TVCG.2018.2865042 PMID: 30183636

Negi, S., & Mitra, R. (2020). Fixation duration and the learning process: An eye tracking study with subtitled videos. *Journal of Eye Movement Research*, 13(6). Advance online publication. DOI: 10.16910/jemr.13.6.1 PMID: 33828811

Nokelainen, P., Pylväs, L., & Hartikainen, S. (2024). University teachers' self-reported emotions and electrodermal activity during teaching-related working events. *Studies in Higher Education*, •••, 1–20. DOI: 10.1080/03075079.2024.2387750

Parong, J., & Mayer, R. E. (2021). Learning about history in immersive virtual reality: Does immersion facilitate learning? *Educational Technology Research and Development*, 69(3), 1433–1451. DOI: 10.1007/s11423-021-09999-y

Pavic, K., Chaby, L., Gricourt, T., & Vergilino-Perez, D. (2023). Feeling virtually present makes me happier: The influence of immersion, sense of presence, and video contents on positive emotion induction. *Cyberpsychology, Behavior, and Social Networking*, 26(4), 238–245. DOI: 10.1089/cyber.2022.0245 PMID: 37001171

Prattichizzo, D., Otaduy, M., Kajimoto, H., & Pacchierotti, C. (2019). Wearable and hand-held haptics. *IEEE Transactions on Haptics*, 12(3), 227–231. DOI: 10.1109/TOH.2019.2936736

Qi, B., Zhang, M., Zhu, X., Jiang, Y., & Xiang, X. (2024). Effects of haptic interaction on learning performance and satisfaction with 3D collections. *Education and Information Technologies*, 29(7), 7793–7811. DOI: 10.1007/s10639-023-11921-3

Radianti, J., Majchrzak, T. A., Fromm, J., & Wohlgenannt, I. (2020). A systematic review of immersive virtual reality applications for higher education: Design elements, lessons learned, and research agenda. *Computers & Education*, 147, 103778. DOI: 10.1016/j.compedu.2019.103778

Rosenzweig, E. (2015). *Successful user experience: Strategies and roadmaps*. Morgan Kaufmann.

Salisbury, J. K. (1997). Design, measurement and evaluation of haptic interfaces. *Basic Research in Computer Science*, 26(3), 1–18.

Siemens, G., & Baker, R. S. D. (2012, April). Learning analytics and educational data mining: towards communication and collaboration. In *Proceedings of the 2nd international conference on learning analytics and knowledge* (pp. 252-254). DOI: 10.1145/2330601.2330661

Spinks, J., & Mortimer, D. (2015). Lost in the crowd? Using eye-tracking to investigate the effect of complexity on attribute non-attendance in discrete choice experiments. *BMC Medical Informatics and Decision Making*, 16(1), 1–13. DOI: 10.1186/s12911-016-0251-1 PMID: 26842646

Srinivasan, M. A., & Basdogan, C. (1997). Haptics in virtual environments: Taxonomy, research status, and challenges. *Computers & Graphics*, 21(4), 393–404. DOI: 10.1016/S0097-8493(97)00030-7

Stier, S., Breuer, J., Siegers, P., & Thorson, K. (2020). Integrating survey data and digital trace data: Key issues in developing an emerging field. *Social Science Computer Review*, 38(5), 503–516. DOI: 10.1177/0894439319843669

Suh, A., & Lee, H. (2021). Challenges in measuring effectiveness of virtual reality environments. *Journal of Virtual Worlds Research*, 14(1), 1–15. DOI: 10.1111/jvw.12112

Sumardani, D., & Lin, C. H. (2023). Cognitive processes during virtual reality learning: A study of brain wave. *Education and Information Technologies*, 28(11), 14877–14896. DOI: 10.1007/s10639-023-11788-4

Thawani, J. P., Ramayya, A. G., Abdullah, K. G., Hudgins, E., Vaughan, K., Piazza, M., & Grady, M. S. (2016). Resident simulation training in endoscopic endonasal surgery utilizing haptic feedback technology. *Journal of Clinical Neuroscience*, 34, 112–116. DOI: 10.1016/j.jocn.2016.05.036 PMID: 27473019

Vehlen, A., Standard, W., & Domes, G. (2022). How to choose the size of facial areas of interest in interactive eye tracking. *PLoS One*, 17(2), e0263594. DOI: 10.1371/journal.pone.0263594 PMID: 35120188

Verma, C., Illés, Z., & Kumar, D. (2024). An investigation of novel features for predicting student happiness in hybrid learning platforms–An exploration using experiments on trace data. *International Journal of Information Management Data Insights*, 4(1), 100219. DOI: 10.1016/j.jjimei.2024.100219

Wee, C., Yap, K. M., & Lim, W. N. (2021). Haptic interfaces for virtual reality: Challenges and research directions. *IEEE Access : Practical Innovations, Open Solutions*, 9, 112145–112162. DOI: 10.1109/ACCESS.2021.3103598

Wu, L., Chau, K. T., Wan Yahaya, W. A. J., Wang, S., & Wu, X. (2024). The Effect of Electroencephalogram Feedback in Virtual Reality Interactive System on Creativity Performance, Attention Value, and Cognitive Load. *International Journal of Human-Computer Interaction*, •••, 1–18. DOI: 10.1080/10447318.2024.2371692

Ye, D., & Pennisi, S. (2022). Using trace data to enhance students' self-regulation: A learning analytics perspective. *The Internet and Higher Education*, 54, 100855. DOI: 10.1016/j.iheduc.2022.100855

Zhao, G., Zhang, L., Chu, J., Zhu, W., Hu, B., He, H., & Yang, L. (2023). An augmented reality-based mobile photography application to improve learning gain, decrease cognitive load, and achieve better emotional state. *International Journal of Human-Computer Interaction*, 39(3), 643–658. DOI: 10.1080/10447318.2022.2041911

KEY TERMS AND DEFINITIONS

Behavioral Measurements: Measurement methods that address behavioral metrics such as trace data and haptic technologies.

Physical Measurements: Physical measurements covering measurement methods such as facial expressions and eye tracking.

Physiological Measurements: Physiological measurement methods such as EEG, GSR, EDA are measurements that explore body response patterns.

Virtual Technology-Driven Environments: Virtual Technology-Driven Environments (VTD) are digitally created spaces that use advanced computing technologies.

Chapter 12
The Use of Artificial Intelligence in History Education

Yasin Özkan
https://orcid.org/0000-0002-2029-0856
Zonguldak Bulent Ecevit University, Turkey

Mustafa Samur
Zonguldak Bulent Ecevit University, Turkey

ABSTRACT

Artificial intelligence is also used to transfer knowledge and culture about the past to future generations. Thus, the improvement of students' history education processes and the innovations that artificial intelligence can bring to history education can be discussed. Historical research is an important discipline that helps us understand the evolution of humanity by examining past events. Traditionally, historians access and interpret information by manually analyzing documents, archives and other sources. However, with the development of artificial intelligence technologies in recent years, new possibilities in historical research are emerging, and AI has great potential in historical research. In the future, AI technologies are expected to help us understand our historical knowledge in a deeper and more comprehensive way. In this study, as well as answering the question of what artificial intelligence is, the question of how artificial intelligence can be used in history education is also answered.

DOI: 10.4018/979-8-3693-6030-9.ch012

INTRODUCTION

The Importance of History Education

The concept of intelligence has been defined in a multitude of ways by various academic disciplines, yet a universally accepted definition remains elusive. Furthermore, there are categorized definitions of intelligence according to different disciplines (Legg & Hutter, 2007). While intelligence can be quantified using the traditional approach, the approach initiated by Piaget posits that intelligence can be evaluated through a test, undergo renewal, and adapt (Selçuk, 2012). In the view of Gardner, the pioneer of the theory of intelligence, which has been the subject of much research, intelligence is a network associated with the brain and nervous system, and is defined as having the ability to solve problems (Arslan, 2020). If we proceed from the definition of intelligence and arrive at the concept of artificial intelligence, it is notable that although the concept was first expressed in a letter of proposal presented by John McCarthy, Marvin L. Minsky, Nathaniel Rochester and Claude E. Shannon at the Dortmund Conference in 1956, the sources indicate that John McCarthy is regarded as the pioneer of this concept (Alpaydın, 2013). McCarthy defined intelligence as 'a calculative aspect of the capacity to achieve goals in the world'. The concept of artificial intelligence encompasses the development of intelligent machines, particularly computer programs, that exhibit capabilities analogous to those of humans. This field of study recognizes the existence of diverse forms and levels of intelligence in humans, animals, and even some machines. As the definition indicates, the objective is to develop human-made hardware tools that can perform high-level cognitive functions, such as reasoning, analytical thinking, and problem-solving. The concept of artificial intelligence is currently employed in numerous disciplines across a range of fields, resulting in a multitude of definitions (Arslan, 2020). It is evident that artificial intelligence is being employed extensively, and is being increasingly sought to be employed, in the field of education. It can be argued that artificial intelligence is employed in the field of education at both the level of knowledge and in applications that facilitate high-level cognition. In particular, a number of areas can be identified for consideration, including individual and personalised education, data mining in education, article analysis, and mutual dialogue training. Furthermore, educational institutions can benefit from artificial intelligence in administrative support roles. For example, the contributions of artificial intelligence can be identified in numerous areas, including course and personnel programmes, facility and school management (Holmes, Bialik, & Fadel, 2019). In order to gain a respected place in the developing world, it has become imperative that the quality of education should be of a high standard (Samur & Sofuoğlu, 2022). In the contemporary era, the education and training system is undergoing a period of constant transformation and renewal, with the advent of artificial intelligence playing a pivotal role. Furthermore, the Ministry of National Education of the Republic of Turkey has set forth the objective of expanding the scope of artificial intelligence applications in education through research into the potential benefits and applications of AI in the field of education (İşler, Kılıç, 2021). One of the most significant challenges in the education system is the recognition that individuals have varying learning styles and abilities, with different subjects requiring different approaches and rates of acquisition (Sarıbaş & Babadağ, 2015: 18-34). In this context, the objective is to facilitate interactive learning through the integration of artificial intelligence and modern technologies, such as virtual reality, to engage individuals in the educational process (Kuprenko, 2020). Furthermore, the potential for teachers and classes to enhance learning outcomes through the utilisation of artificial intelligence technologies is being explored (İşler & Kılıç, 2021).

The utilisation of artificial intelligence-supported applications enables the analysis of students' knowledge (Kuprenko, 2020) and facilitates the provision of appropriate and personalised solutions by teachers (Fahimirad & Kotamjani, 2018).

The most significant factor in the existence and survival of a nation is a national historical consciousness. Every nation that has survived from the past to the present has had a unifying ideal, a national history and a language. It is inconceivable that a nation can possess its own culture and maintain its independence in the absence of a language and historical consciousness. Furthermore, Mustafa Kemal Pasha asserted in his speeches that the continued existence of the Republic would be contingent upon the preservation of an authentic language and a national history. The existence of a national culture is contingent upon the nation in question having an independent history (Turan, 2006). The formation of an independent nation is contingent upon the protection of historical and moral values (Samur, 2022). She asserted that her historical knowledge proved invaluable during the National Struggle and the Republic (İnan, 1939). In her 1939 publication, İnan states that Pasha began a comprehensive investigation into the role of Turks in global history and civilisation in 1929. In this year, Mustafa Kemal Pasha undertook a comprehensive study of Turkish history, engaging in discourse with scientists and parliamentarians on the subject (İnan, 1939). His objective was to establish cultural independence, charting a course towards the future without forsaking the legacy of the past (Kodaman, 1981).

During the Republican period, which saw the inception of a cultural revolution, it became imperative to reveal the Turkish identity through national unity and to transmit a national history from generation to generation (Turan, 1997). In the view of Atatürk, a fundamental aspect of nationhood is the coherence of historical narrative (Şıvgın, 2009). In the context of globalisation, history textbooks have assumed an even greater significance. The principal objective of history education is to instill in individuals a sense of national identity and an awareness of their citizenship. In the context of globalisation, which entails the transcending of nation-states, the reorganisation of history teaching is a topic of discussion (Şıvgın, 2009). Furthermore, an analysis of the overarching objectives of the history curriculum reveals that one of the primary concerns is to facilitate an understanding of the processes involved in the formation of national identity, the constituent elements of this identity and the necessity to safeguard national identity (Şıvgın, 2009).

As is the case in all branches of science, concepts occupy a significant position and are of great consequence in the fields of history writing, history education and teaching (Özkan & Toz, 2022). It is therefore crucial to utilise historical terminology accurately in order to facilitate an accurate understanding and effective teaching of history (Köstüklü, 2019). In accordance with the educational objectives of the 21st century, history teaching has evolved to encompass a broader scope than the mere recitation of historical facts. In lieu of mere memorization of past events, students should engage in the analysis and interpretation of historical occurrences, employing critical thinking skills. However, the efficacy of history teaching is contingent upon the methodologies and pedagogical tools employed (Uluçay & Küçük, 2023). The incorporation of technology into history teaching provides students with a more engaging, interactive and realistic learning experience. By way of illustration, the utilisation of interactive software, virtual history museums and online history resources affords students the opportunity to explore and interact with historical events, people and periods. Such technologies facilitate meaningful learning by offering visual and audio content in lieu of the conventional text-based format. The pervasive integration of technology in the domain of historical education serves to bolster students' advanced cognitive capabilities. The utilisation of artificial intelligence and visual aids can facilitate a more comprehensive understanding of historical events (Uluçay, Küçük 2023). The utilisation of artificial intelligence facilitates a more profound comprehension of historical events and historical figures by enabling interactive experiences with fellow students in the context of history teaching (Uluçay, Küçük 2023).

WHAT IS ARTIFICIAL INTELLIGENCE?

In order to understand the current place of artificial intelligence, its position in human life and its possible effects, artificial intelligence must first be defined. Without knowing where artificial intelligence is used, what it is and where it can be used, it is extremely difficult to encourage or prevent its current effects. Artificial intelligence is the closest invention to humans throughout history. In the inventions made up to the present day, machines have been produced that utilize the physical characteristics of humans, thus reducing the physical burden on humans. Another stage has been passed by reducing the computational burden with computers. But artificial intelligence aims to reduce the mental fatigue of humans. Artificial intelligence is able to alleviate the aforementioned burden through the coding of software developers. Again, artificial intelligence imitates the human brain with the aforementioned coding and continues to do more by improving itself (Doğan, 2021, p. 83).

If it is necessary to define artificial intelligence, it is first necessary to examine the words intelligence and artificial. TDK (Turkish Language Association) defines the word artificial as "Made or produced by human hands by resembling the examples in nature, artificial, artificial and unnatural". On the other hand, the word intelligence is defined as "All of human's abilities of thinking, reasoning, perceiving objective facts, judging and drawing conclusions from them, dirayet, anlak, feraset and zeyreklik" (TDK, 2023). Utilizing these, it is possible to define artificial intelligence as "the transfer of the ability to imitate human intelligence to computers". The important points here are that the powers specific to intelligence are transferred to the computer through human beings and that intelligence is specific to humans.

Say (2020) defines artificial intelligence as "the branch of science that examines how we can make artificial systems perform every cognitive activity that natural systems can do at even higher levels of achievement." To give an example of a higher level of achievement, when humans aim to solve a problem that they do not already know the solutions to through a program they will write, they cannot write the program because they do not know the solution. But with existing programs, they can reach the solution as a result of different trials. This shows that programs are basically fed by humans, but after a while they can also develop without the need for human support. Humans can solve any problem that they do not know the solution to thanks to artificial intelligence. This makes artificial intelligence a self-developed program that can achieve high success in solving problems and evolves on its own, not by humans (Say, 2020, pp. 83-97).

The word "Artificial" was first used in Old French in the late 14th century to mean spontaneous and unnatural. Its more distant origins are the Latin words "artificialis" meaning artistic, "Artificium" meaning theory, skill and work of art, and "Artifex" meaning artist. The first use of the word "Artificial" in English occurred in the 15th and 16th centuries, and the word was first used in the term "Artificial day", i.e. "artificial day", which refers to the period from sunrise to sunset in a different way from the natural 24-hour day, and later to express "what is made by human skill and labor, imitation and substitution of the natural" The word "Intelligence" was first used in Old French in the 21st century as "the ability to understand, comprehension". In the 14th century it came to mean "the highest faculty of the intellect, the ability to grasp general truths". In the distant past of the word, the word "intelligentia" was derived from the Latin verb "intelligere" meaning "to understand", which means "comprehension, reasoning, intelligence, science, knowledge, skill, thought, idea and art" (Kabaağaç and Alova, 1995, p.54).

The products produced with artificial intelligence techniques are, on the one hand, the result of human labor, and on the other hand, an imitation of human understanding, thinking, comprehension and designing abilities. The creation of a mental mechanism that is similar to the human being itself reveals its creative and artistic identity and therefore shows compatibility with the meanings of words. The Turkish equivalent of the word "artificial intelligence", which is one of the concepts popularly used in computer sciences, mathematics and logic in our period, is called "artificial intelligence". In particular, its use in relation to information technologies is indicated by the letters AI as an acronym.

First of all, when the term intelligence is examined in the word group structure, it is known that intelligence is understood as a whole of analyzing, perceiving and reacting behaviors and is understood as a desired ability to show rational behavior (Chowdhary, 2020, p.45). For this reason, it has always been one of the basic images that humanity has always dreamed of, and even in ancient Greek and Egyptian mythologies, there are many myths about objects being able to show human-like behaviors. The current use of artificial intelligence to express the imitation of the intelligence of individuals was first developed by Alan Turing, a British computer scientist and mathematician, to indicate the situation in which a computer can communicate with humans in a limited way through a chat box (Shawar & Atwell, 2007, p.34; Landgrebe & Smith, 2019, p.58). In the aforementioned modeling, people thought that the other system was a real person with intelligence (Larson, 2021, p.45). In this context, according to Joshi (2020), who is considered the pioneer of computer science, Alan Turing defined artificial intelligence as "If there is a machine behind the curtain and a human interacts with it (e.g. through voice or writing, etc.) and the human feels that he is interacting with another human, that machine is artificial intelligence." The concept of artificial intelligence is defined as the simulation of human actions and ideas, and it is defined in different sources as a term that supports the ability to automate business phases, gain insights through data analysis, gain insights through data analysis, and support the ability to create interaction with customers, especially in our time, in order to simulate the basic discipline, creativity and cognitive field in automation-based processes, and in a comprehensive sense (Mainzer, 2020, p.64)

As can be understood from the aforementioned definitions, artificial intelligence is understood to be a structure that shows human-like behavior, as opposed to a machine that produces incredible results. This is the most confusing aspect of artificial intelligence, and it can make models to solve problems like humans.

History and Development of Artificial Intelligence

Artificial intelligence is most simply defined as systems that mimic human intelligence to perform specific tasks and can improve themselves by iterating the information they gather. Important periods and development process in this field:

1. Early Period (1950s - 1960s)

- Formation of the field: The study of artificial intelligence was initiated in the mid-1950s by the founders of the field. It was pioneered by Alan McCarthy, John McCarthy, Marvin Minsky, Nathaniel Rochester and Claude Shannon.
- Dartmouth Conference (1956): The term artificial intelligence and the cornerstones of the discipline were laid at a conference held at Dartmouth College in 1956. John McCarthy, Marvin Minsky, Nathaniel Rochester and Claude Shannon were key participants who shaped and advanced the field of artificial intelligence.

2. First Steps of Artificial Intelligence (1960s - 1970s)

- Logical Thinking and Relationships between Symbols: Early AI projects focused on simulating the logical thinking of computers and understanding relationships between symbols. For example, the "Logic Theorist" (1956) program aimed to prove mathematical theorems.
- Eliza (1966): One of the first speech simulations, Eliza was able to communicate with humans at a basic level in natural language.

3. Increase in Computer Power and Crisis Period (1980s - 1990s)

- Expert Systems: In the 1980s and 1990s, artificial intelligence applications began to be used in the business world with the development of expert systems. Expert systems are systems that model knowledge in a specific field and are used in decision-making processes.
- Artificial Intelligence Crisis: Contrary to initial expectations, progress in the field of artificial intelligence was slower than expected, leading to the so-called "artificial intelligence crisis" in the late 1980s. The field declined somewhat during this period, as the promised successes of AI did not materialize.

4. Machine Learning and Deep Learning Era (2000s - Present)

- Machine Learning: Since the 2000s, with the use of large data sets and more powerful computers, great progress has been made in the field of machine learning. In this process, the performance of algorithms was improved and they started to be used effectively in applications such as spam filters.
- Deep Learning: The development of deep learning techniques since the 2010s revolutionized the field of artificial intelligence. Deep neural networks are used in many application areas with their ability to recognize and predict complex patterns in large data sets. For example, image recognition, natural language processing and autonomous vehicles.

The development of artificial intelligence continues today. Current research is being conducted in areas such as reinforcement learning, generative models and the ethical dimensions of these technologies. The field is dynamic and advances will shape the future direction of AI.

Basic Concepts of Artificial Intelligence

- Machine Learning: Machine learning is a sub-branch of artificial intelligence that enables computer systems to learn through experience or data. Unlike traditional programming, machine learning models learn patterns from data and use these patterns to make future decisions.
- Deep Learning: Deep learning is a sub-branch of machine learning that consists of multi-layered structures called artificial neural networks. This technology is used to develop algorithms that can recognize and learn complex patterns from large amounts of data (Ozkan & Erdogmus, 2024).
- Natural Language Processing (NLP): NLP is the field of artificial intelligence used for computers to understand, interpret, produce and process human language. This technology enables computers to work with text data and perform various tasks on human language.
- Image Processing: Image processing refers to the process of extracting or enhancing information by performing various operations on digital images. These processes include operations to detect, analyze, interpret or better present an image. Image processing is a field in which techniques related to computer vision, computer analysis and machine vision are usually applied.

Artificial Intelligence Application Areas

Artificial intelligence is a technology that has developed rapidly in recent years and has led to significant changes in many sectors. Artificial intelligence is a discipline that aims to give computer systems human-like intelligence and learning capabilities. The application areas of this technology are quite wide and are used for different purposes in various sectors. Here are some of the main application areas of artificial intelligence discussed in detail:

1. Healthcare and Medicine

- Medical Imaging and Diagnostics: Artificial intelligence diagnoses diseases and accelerates the diagnostic process by analyzing data obtained through imaging methods such as MRI and CT. For example, deep learning models play an important role in cancer screening and diagnosis.
- Personalized Treatment Plans: Using information such as the patient's genetic data and medical history, it can help create individualized treatment plans.
- Health Care Management: AI can be used to provide better healthcare management by analyzing data about patients' health status.

2. Automotive Sector

- Autonomous Vehicles: Artificial intelligence and machine learning are used in the environmental sensing, traffic management and decision-making processes of autonomous vehicles. In this way, vehicles can understand their surroundings and move safely.
- Traffic Forecasting and Management: By analyzing traffic flow, AI can create traffic prediction models and develop strategies to reduce traffic jams.

3. Financial Services

- Risk Assessment: Banks and financial institutions can perform credit risk assessment using AI models and develop fraud detection systems to prevent fraud.
- Investment and Trading: AI supports investment decision-making by analyzing the market and enables the creation of automated trading systems.

4. Retail and E-Commerce

- Personalized Marketing: By analyzing customer behavior, AI can deliver personalized recommendations and ads.
- Inventory Management: With advanced forecasting models, inventory management can be optimized and demand forecasts can be made more accurately.

5. Education

- Student Performance Analysis: AI can monitor students' learning processes, identify their educational needs and provide teachers with personalized teaching strategies.
- Educational Material Development: AI can support teaching processes by recommending student-appropriate materials and content (Çevik & Barın, 2015).

6. Production and Industrial Processes

- Smart Manufacturing: AI can increase efficiency in production processes, enable maintenance planning and error prediction.
- Quality Control: Product quality can be controlled automatically using image processing and AI.

7. Media and Entertainment

- Content Recommendation: AI can offer personalized experiences by recommending content such as movies, music or news based on users' preferences.
- Language Processing and Voice Recognition: Voice assistants and natural language processing techniques can increase engagement with users and make media content easier to access.

Artificial intelligence is a rapidly developing and advancing technology in these and many other areas. It offers solutions for different needs and applications in every sector, optimizing business processes and creating new opportunities. These application areas show how artificial intelligence has an impact on our daily lives and how it can transform the future.

Artificial Intelligence Applications Used in Education

Artificial intelligence applications in education are used in a variety of ways to support students' learning processes, enable teachers to teach more effectively, and optimize the management of educational institutions. Here are some of these applications:

1. Adaptive Learning Systems: These systems customize teaching materials based on students' individual characteristics and previous learning experiences. For example, data analytics and recommendation systems used to identify student strengths and weaknesses have been extensively researched in this area (Koedinger et al., 2015).
2. Predicting Student Success: Artificial intelligence is used to predict students' academic success. Models created by taking into account students' past performance data, demographic characteristics and other factors are used to develop strategies to improve achievement (Romero & Ventura, 2010).
3. Natural Language Processing (NLP) Based Educational Tools: Language processing techniques are used to improve students' language skills. For example, text analysis and synthesis are effectively used in language learning applications (Graesser et al., 2004).
4. Educational Management and Planning: AI can help school administrators to optimize educational resources. Prediction models and optimization algorithms enable more efficient use of resources (Aydin et al., 2019).
5. Teacher Assistants: AI can help teachers with tasks such as lesson planning, monitoring student performance and assignment evaluation. Automated assessment systems and analysis of student interaction are used in this field (Koedinger et al., 2012).
6. Virtual Learning Environments and Simulations: AI-based virtual environments enable students to practice and simulate real-life scenarios. This is an important application area in vocational training and skills development (Berg, 2017).
7. Autonomous Learning Systems: Autonomous learning systems are designed to increase students' capacity to learn on their own. Artificial intelligence helps students optimize their motivation and learning strategies (Vygotsky, 1978).

These examples illustrate how AI applications in education are used in various fields and research in the academic literature. Each application area offers different approaches to improve student achievement, increase teachers' effectiveness, and optimize the overall efficiency of educational institutions.

Future Perspectives and Impact of AI on Society

Artificial intelligence is a technology that is expected to have profound impacts on society in many aspects in the future. These impacts can manifest themselves in a variety of areas, such as the development of technology, the economy, the workforce, social structures and ethical issues. Here are some important thoughts on the future perspectives of AI and its impact on society:

1. Labor and the Economy

- Job Transformation and Automation: AI and automation technologies can transform business processes in many industries and perform some jobs with AI instead of human labor. This may lead to the disappearance or change of some occupational groups.
- New Job Opportunities: Artificial intelligence can also create new business areas and job opportunities. In particular, people specialized in areas such as artificial intelligence development, data analysis and system integration will be needed.

2. Healthcare

- Personalized Medicine: AI can offer personalized medical treatment and healthcare using data such as patients' genetic profiles, medical histories and lifestyles. This has great potential for early detection of diseases and improving treatment processes.
- Medical Imaging and Diagnostics: Artificial intelligence can perform faster and more accurate analysis than humans in medical imaging techniques (MRI, CT, X-ray, etc.), which can greatly improve medical diagnosis processes.

3. Education

- Learning Management and Customized Education: By analyzing students' learning styles and needs, AI can help personalize teaching materials and methods. This can improve student achievement and contribute to achieving equity in education (Yıldız, Yağcı, & Özkan, 2023).

4. Transportation and Urban Planning

- Autonomous Vehicles and Traffic Management: AI can be used to ensure the safe integration of autonomous vehicles into traffic. It can also play an important role in traffic flow optimization and urban transport planning.

5. Security and Defense

- Cyber Security: AI can be used to detect cyber attacks and develop defense strategies. It can also be used as surveillance and decision support systems in military applications.

6. Societal and Ethical Impacts

- Data Privacy and Ethical Issues: Issues such as data privacy, data security and algorithmic fairness related to the use of AI are gaining importance. How to manage data collection, storage and use is an important ethical debate.
- Human-Rights Protection: AI systems need to respect human rights and promote social justice. Otherwise, problems such as discrimination and prejudice may arise.

Artificial intelligence can revolutionize many areas in the future and significantly improve human life. However, there are many ethical, legal and social issues related to the widespread use of this technology that need to be carefully managed. Therefore, it is important to establish a strong regulatory and ethical framework to maximize societal benefits and minimize potential risks in the development and application of AI technologies (Ozkan & Erdogmus, 2020).

Application

The present study employs visual examples and artificial intelligence to elucidate the significance of the Çanakkale Victory, a pivotal event in recent history. In this context, Mustafa Kemal's words, "Bayonet on, bayonet on the ground," which represent a pivotal moment in the Battle of Çanakkale, and the Nusret Mine Ship were rendered through the use of artificial intelligence. Consequently, this approach offers a novel perspective on historical events and provides a model for future research. Furthermore, it has been demonstrated that historical events can be visualised with artificial intelligence, thereby providing a rationale for the incorporation of visual materials in history teaching.

The Battle of Çanakkale represents a seminal victory for the Turkish nation and has left an indelible mark on history, serving as irrefutable evidence that the Turkish people's profound attachment to their homeland surpasses the might of military weaponry. Sir Edward Grey, the British Foreign Secretary of the period, offered the following description of the Çanakkale Victory: 'No event in history has so frustrated the plans and predictions made, confused the decisions taken and disrupted the strategic rules determined as in the Çanakkale Battles.' (Ünalp, 2015).

The Çanakkale Victory is currently examined under two principal headings: naval and land battles. On 19 February 1915, an armada of Allied Powers initiated an offensive with the objective of entering the Dardanelles and occupying Istanbul. The naval battle concluded with a victory for the Turkish nation on 18 March 1915. In consequence of this, land battles commenced (Yazıcı, 2013).

Churchill was of the opinion that it would be possible to reach Istanbul in a relatively short period of time by crossing the Dardanelles. He was therefore able to persuade the war council of the merits of this course of action. He did not perceive the Turkish Navy as a significant competitor to the Allied Navy. On 15 January 1915, the War Council convened in London and the invasion plan for the Dardanelles was accepted (Yazıcı, 2013). The finalised plan was presented to France and Russia, where it was approved. The French government declared its intention to dispatch a naval force, while Russia pledged to provide the cruiser Askold for the combined fleet and to participate in the occupation of Istanbul (Atabey, 2010). Until 18 March, despite intermittent invasion attempts, the United Navy was on the verge of defeat (Ünalp, 2015). In the context of the defence of the Dardanelles, the Nusret Mineship laid 26 mines at intervals of 100 metres in Eren Bay Dark Harbour in the hours connecting the night of 7 March to 8 March. This event will be forever etched in the annals of history. This testimony represents a pivotal moment in both Turkish and global history. The laying of mines in this bay was a mandatory and historically significant undertaking. The Nusret Mineship was responsible for the completion of this task (Ünalp, 2015).

Figure 1.

Figure 2.

In his account of 18 March, British General Oglander observed that the day, which had begun auspiciously, ultimately concluded in a resounding failure, largely attributable to the extraordinary and calamitous success of the hitherto unknown mine line. The impact of these twenty mines on the course of the campaign is incalculable. While emphasising the remarkable success of the Nusret Mineship, he acknowledged that the Dardanelles could not be traversed by the United Fleet (Ünalp, 2015). In consequence of the unsuccessful invasion attempt of the Entente States through the strait, the Mediterranean Expeditionary Force was activated, as was the land invasion movement. The 5th Army was constituted for the purpose of defending the straits, and German General Liman von Sanders was appointed as commander. Lieutenant Colonel Mustafa Kemal was the commander of the 19th Infantry Division in the Bigalı region (Erkal, 2002).

With the entry of the Ottoman Empire into the First World War, Lieutenant Colonel Mustafa Kemal, who was serving as a military attaché in Sofia, was assigned to the 19th Division Command in Çanakkale (Çeliker, 1994). Lieutenant Colonel Mustafa Kemal's actions during the Çanakkale Campaign were instrumental in altering the course of the war. To illustrate, he postulated that the invading forces would enter Çanakkale from Kocaçimen and Conkbayırı. Mustafa Kemal proceeded to mobilise the 57th Regiment in the direction of Kocaçimen, while he himself advanced to Conkbayırı. He observed that the Turkish troops he encountered on Conkbayırı had exhausted their ammunition reserves and issued the following directive: "If you have no ammunition, you have a bayonet, put on a bayonet and lie down." Subsequently, he stated, "I do not order you to attack; I order you to die." In issuing this command, he played a pivotal role in the eventual victory at Çanakkale (Saygılı, 2022).

Lieutenant Colonel Mustafa Kemal articulated the significance of Çanakkale as follows:

'...' This is not a conventional military operation; it is an offensive in which all parties are prepared to act with the determination to succeed or perish. Furthermore, I supplemented the orders I had previously conveyed to the commanders in person with the following additional instructions. It is not my intention to order an attack; rather, it is to order the sacrifice of your lives. "In the interim period prior to our demise, alternative forces and commanders may assume our roles."

British General Lan Hamilton, who was in command of the Mediterranean Expeditionary Force, observed the situation from the ship Queen Elizabeth in Arıburnu and subsequently recorded his recollections in the form of memoirs pertaining to the Gallipoli campaign.

Despite the significant blows inflicted by our forces, the mountainous terrain continued to yield Turkish combatants. Lines of communication are established between locations, with dots indicating the movement of personnel across the green terrain. On the ridge of Sarıbayır, successive dots are visible on a wide red earthen surface, akin to a battle scar. They advance, become obscured, and then re-emerge. The highest and most central part of our position is subjected to successive waves of loading. In addition to the thunderous roar of the artillery, the incessant clatter of machine guns and rifles reverberates, akin to the sound of hail striking the roof of a lemonade stand amidst the tumultuous thunder. Subsequently, the intensity of the fire abates. The assault was successfully repelled. Our troops were able to maintain their position. A small number of dots were observed to return over the green grass. The others had entered the realm of darkness (Ünalp, 2015).

The following is an excerpt from the diaries of an Australian soldier who perished during the Gallipoli Campaign:

On Tuesday, 27 April 1915, the night was marked by a series of unfortunate events. The Turks advanced to within twenty paces of our position on occasion, whereupon we returned fire. However, the Turks, who were adept at combat, were undeterred by this and continued to attack us. The machine guns used by the Turks were particularly lethal. The enemy forces consistently disrupted the soldiers' ability to rest. The day was particularly lengthy.

On Wednesday, 28 April 1915, the situation on the battlefield was described as "hell on earth." The enemy launched a sustained assault throughout the night. At what point would supplies and reinforcements be forthcoming to enable a reciprocal attack? Somehow, we managed to survive the day. It is imperative that we maintain our position until such time as ammunition becomes available. A significant quantity of ammunition was expended during the night (Ünalp, 2015).

Figure 3.

Figure 4.

Mustafa Kemal described the moment of the attack to retake Conkbayırı on August 10, 1915 as follows:

"... The dark curtain of the night had completely lifted. It was now the moment of attack. I looked at my watch. It was almost four-thirty. In a few minutes it would be completely light and the enemy would be able to see our soldiers. If the enemy's infantry and machine gun fire started, and the land and naval guns' shells exploded once on our soldiers standing in this tight formation, I had no doubt that the attack would be impossible. I ran forward immediately. I came across the division commander. He and the people accompanying us both moved to the front of the attack line. I made a very quick and brief inspection. I passed in front of him and saluted the soldiers loudly. I said:

Soldiers! There is no doubt that we will defeat the enemy in front of us. But don't rush. I will go forward first. You will all attack when I give the signal with my whip.

I also ordered the commander and officers to draw the soldiers' attention to my signal. After that, we advanced to a point in front of the attack line and from there I raised my whip into the air and gave the attack signal.

All the soldiers and officers had forgotten everything and were directing their eyes and hearts to the signal to be given. Our soldiers with their bayonets and one leg extended forward and our officers with their pistols and swords in front of them, rushed forward in a lion-like charge as my whip came down. A second later, nothing could be heard except the shouts of Allah, Allah rising to the sky from the enemy trenches. The enemy did not have time to use their weapons. As a result of the heroic struggle from the straits to the throats, the enemy in the first line was completely destroyed."

"After the Conkbayırı Hill fell into the hands of our soldiers, the enemy turned Conkbayırı into hell with the rapid and intense artillery fire they directed from land and sea. Shrapnel and iron pieces were raining down from the sky. The accurate shells of large-caliber naval guns were exploding after consuming the ground, and large sewers were opening up next to us. Everyone was resigned to their fate and waiting for their fate. Our surroundings were filled with martyrs and wounded. While I was watching the situation on the battlefield, a piece of shrapnel hit the right side of my chest. It shattered the watch in my pocket. It could not enter my body. It only left a deep blood stain. It was approaching noon. My soldiers were exhausted from fighting death for eight hours. The terrain made it impossible for our soldiers, who were struggling with the enemy's unyielding and intense fire, to receive any kind of help from the rear. Our losses were also important. I appreciated that it was not our superiority that defeated the enemy, but our attack, which was carried out in a terrific series of blows. Therefore, at 12:15, I gave the following order to the 8th Division Commander: Stop the attack. Reinforce the line you have occupied with your troops so that the most dominant point of Conkbayırı and Şahinsırt to the west will always be in hand. / Anafartalar Group Commander Mustafa Kemal" (Ünalp, 2010). The Çanakkale Victory, which took place between March 18, 1915 and January 9, 1916, is an indicator of the Turkish nation's love for the country as well as an epic of the heroism of the Turkish soldiers. The Turkish nation repelled the enemy by shielding them against the invading forces equipped with the most advanced weapons of the period. At the end of the Çanakkale War, the attempt of the United Fleet to cross the Bosphorus, occupy Istanbul and help Russia was destroyed, while the Tsarist Regime in Russia fell into difficulty and World War I was prolonged for approximately 2 more years. Lieutenant Colonel Mustafa Kemal proved himself as a successful and talented commander and the way was opened for him to become the leader of the National Struggle (Aytepe, 2000). The Çanakkale Victory stands out as an indescribable and unprecedented victory in Turkish history, and the national unity that emerged was an important force in winning the War of Independence (Şahin, 2009).

CONCLUSION

First mentioned in 1956 by John McCarthy, the concept of artificial intelligence is still the subject of significant research today. The history of artificial intelligence represents an important evolution in the history of computer science and technology. Efforts to imitate and understand human intelligence have been supported by technological advances and scientific discoveries. This process has led to artificial intelligence playing an important role in many industries and sectors, with profound technological and societal implications, and in this context, many companies around the world are making significant investments in the field of artificial intelligence. The popularity and use of artificial intelligence, which has a very important place in the field of education and training, is increasing day by day. In this context, artificial intelligence is directly involved in the learning and teaching process as well as supporting it with important applications in different areas of educational management in the field of education and training. When artificial intelligence is used effectively in the field of education, it is seen that it increases student success and supports the student cognitively. Today, as artificial intelligence is used in many fields, permanent learning is tried to be realized by producing the necessary materials for a correct education. Artificial intelligence is also used to transfer knowledge and culture about the past to future generations. In addition to transferring historical information, artificial intelligence can be utilized in learning national and spiritual values that can reach analytical and critical thinking skills that will learn the past correctly. Through artificial intelligence, permanent learning can be achieved by creating advanced materials about heroes and events that have left a mark in history. Thus, the improvement of students' history education processes and the innovations that artificial intelligence can bring to history education can be discussed. Historical research is an important discipline that helps us understand the evolution of humanity by examining past events. Traditionally, historians access and interpret information by manually analyzing documents, archives and other sources. However, with the development of artificial intelligence technologies in recent years, new possibilities in historical research are emerging, and AI has great potential in historical research. However, issues such as selecting the right data sets, training algorithms correctly, and integrating with human expertise are important considerations. In the future, AI technologies are expected to help us understand our historical knowledge in a deeper and more comprehensive way. In this study, as well as answering the question of what artificial intelligence is, the question of how artificial intelligence can be used in history education is also answered.

REFERENCES

Aydın, İ., Toptaş, B., Güner Demir, T. U. Ğ. B. A., & Erdemli, Ö. (2019). Being an expatriate teacher in Turkish private schools: Opinions on education, teaching, and administration processes. *Education in Science*, 44(200). Advance online publication. DOI: 10.15390/EB.2019.8105

Beck, J. E., & Woolf, B. P. (2000, May). Reasoning from Data Rather than Theory. In FLAIRS (pp. 34-39).

Berg, H. E. (2017). Will intelligent machine learning revolutionize orthopedic imaging? *Acta Orthopaedica*, 88(6), 577–577. DOI: 10.1080/17453674.2017.1387732 PMID: 29106336

Blikstein, P., & Wilensky, U. (2007, April). Bifocal modeling: a framework for combining computer modeling, robotics and real-world sensing. In *Annual Meeting of the American Educational Research Association (AERA 2007)*, Chicago, USA.

Chen, Z., & Klahr, D. (1999). All other things being equal: Acquisition and transfer of the control of variables strategy. *Child Development*, 70(5), 1098–1120. DOI: 10.1111/1467-8624.00081 PMID: 10546337

Chowdhary, K. R. (2020). Introducing artificial intelligence. In *Fundamentals of Artificial Intelligence* (pp. 1–23). Springer.

De Freitas, S. I. (2006). Using games and simulations for supporting learning. *Learning, Media and Technology*, 31(4), 343–358. DOI: 10.1080/17439880601021967

Doğan, M. (2021). *Artificial intelligence and free will: The possibility of artificial free will.* TRT Academy.

Graesser, A. C., Lu, S., Jackson, G. T., Mitchell, H. H., Ventura, M., Olney, A., & Louwerse, M. M. (2004). AutoTutor: A tutor with dialogue in natural language. *Behavior Research Methods, Instruments, & Computers*, 36(2), 180–192. DOI: 10.3758/BF03195563 PMID: 15354683

Holmes, W., & Bialik, M. ve Fadel, C. (2019). Artificial intelligence in education: Promises and implications for teaching and learning. Boston, MA: Center for Curriculum Redesign.

1. Afet İnan, "Atatürk ve Tarih Tezi", Belleten, C.III, S.10, 1 Nisan 1939, s. 244.

İşler, B., & Kılıç, M. (2021). Eğitimde yapay zekâ kullanımı ve gelişimi. *Yeni Medya Elektronik Dergisi*, 5(1), 1–11.

Kabaağaç, S., & Alova, E. (1995). *Latin-Turkish dictionary*. Social Publications.

Koedinger, K. R., D'Mello, S., McLaughlin, E. A., Pardos, Z. A., & Rosé, C. P. (2015). Data mining and education. *Wiley Interdisciplinary Reviews: Cognitive Science*, 6(4), 333–353. DOI: 10.1002/wcs.1350 PMID: 26263424

Koedinger, K. R., McLaughlin, E. A., & Stamper, J. C. (2012). *Automated Student Model Improvement*. International Educational Data Mining Society.

Kuprenko, V. (2020). Artificial intelligence in education: Benefits, challenges, and use cases. https://medium.com/towards-artificial-intelligence/artificial-intelligence-in-education-benefits-challenges-and-use-cases-db52d8921f7a

Landgrebe, J., & Smith, B. (2019). There is no general AI: why Turing machines cannot pass the Turing test. arXiv preprint arXiv:1906.05833.

Larson, E. J. (2021). *The Myth of Artificial Intelligence: Why Computers Can't Think the Way We Do*. Harvard University Press.

Legg, S. ve Hutter, M. (2007). A collection of definitions of intelligence. Frontiers in artificial ıntelligence and applications, 7(157), 17-24.

Mainzer, K. (2019). *Artificial intelligence-When do machines take over?* Springer Nature.

Mitrovic, A., Martin, B., Suraweera, P., Zakharov, K., Milik, N., Holland, J., & McGuigan, N. (2009). ASPIRE: An authoring system and deployment environment for constraint-based tutors. *International Journal of Artificial Intelligence in Education*, 19(2), 155–188.

Özkan, S. B., & Toz, M. (2022). A review study on the investigation of the effects of using robots in education on metacognitive behaviors. *Computer Applications in Engineering Education*, 30(4), 1277–1288. DOI: 10.1002/cae.22508

Özkan, Y., & Erdoğmuş, P. (2020). Generative Networks and Royalty-Free Products. *Sakarya University Journal of Computer and Information Sciences*, 3(3), 309–324. DOI: 10.35377/saucis.03.03.724645

Ozkan, Y., & Erdogmus, P. (2024). Evaluation of Classification Performance of New Layered Convolutional Neural Network Architecture on Offline Handwritten Signature Images. *Symmetry*, 16(6), 649. DOI: 10.3390/sym16060649

Romero, C., & Ventura, S. (2010). Educational data mining: A review of the state of the art. IEEE Transactions on Systems, Man, and Cybernetics [applications and reviews]. *Part C*, 40(6), 601–618.

Şahin, E. (2009, March). Kronolojik Çanakkale Savaşları Tarihi (3 Kasım 1914 - 9 Ocak 1916). *Atatürk Araştırma Merkezi Dergisi*, 25(73), 107–164.

Samur, M., & Sofuoğlu, A. (2022). TÜRK MİLLİ BASINI EKSENİNDE DARÜLFÜNUN'UN KAPATILMASI MESELESİ. *Atatürk Yolu Dergisi*, (70), 379–394.

Say, C. (2020). 50 questions about artificial intelligence. 7 Renk Basım.

Selçuk, Z. (2012). *Eğitim Psikolojisi*. Nobel.

Shawar, B. A., & Atwell, E. (2007). Chatbots: are they really useful? In *LDV Forum*, 22(1), 29-49.

Turkish Language Association (TDK). (2023). Turkish Dictionary. sozluk.gov.tr

Vygotsky, L. S., & Cole, M. (1978). *Mind in society: Development of higher psychological processes*. Harvard University Press.

Yazıcı, N. (2013). Lise Müfredat Programlarında ve Ders Kitaplarında Çanakkale Savaşı'nın Öğretimi Üzerine Eleştirel Bir Yaklaşım. Hacettepe Üniversitesi Eğitim Fakültesi Dergisi, 28(28-2), 535-550.

Yıldız, T. A., Yağcı, Ş. Ç., & Özkan, Y. (2023). Developing Augmented Reality Learning Material in Professional English Teaching and Examining Its Effect on Academic Success. E-International Journal of Educational Research, 14(6).

KEY TERMS AND DEFINITIONS

Artificial Intelligence (AI): A branch of computer science focused on creating systems capable of performing tasks that typically require human intelligence, such as learning, reasoning, and problem-solving.

Educational Technology: The use of technology tools and resources in educational settings to enhance learning and teaching processes.

History Education: The field of education focused on teaching and learning about historical events, contexts, and critical thinking skills related to historical inquiry.

Interactive Learning: A pedagogical approach that encourages active participation from students, often through the use of digital tools and resources.

Machine Learning: A subset of AI that enables systems to learn from data and improve their performance over time without being explicitly programmed.

Chapter 13
Metacognitive Strategies in Artificial Neural Networks

Sibel Barın Özkan
Zonguldak Bülent Ecevit University, Turkey

Yasin Özkan
Zonguldak Bülent Ecevit University, Turkey

ABSTRACT

This chapter explores the synergies between artificial neural networks (ANNs) and metacognition, highlighting how these two fields can inform and enhance each other. Metacognition, the awareness and regulation of one's own cognitive processes, plays a critical role in human learning and decision-making. Similarly, ANNs are computational models inspired by the human brain, designed to recognize patterns, make decisions, and learn from data.The chapter delves into the theoretical foundations of both ANNs and metacognition, drawing parallels between human cognitive functions and machine learning algorithms. It discusses how incorporating metacognitive strategies into ANNs can lead to more adaptive and robust models. For instance, metacognitive layers within neural networks can help in dynamically adjusting learning rates, selecting optimal network architectures, and improving generalization by preventing overfitting.

DOI: 10.4018/979-8-3693-6030-9.ch013

INTRODUCTION

1.1 Overview of Artificial Neural Networks

Artificial neural networks (ANNs) are computational models inspired by the working principles of the human brain. These networks have attracted a great deal of attention in recent years for their ability to extract meaning from complex data and make predictions. In this section, we will provide an overview of the basics, history and application areas of artificial neural networks.

1.2 Definition of Artificial Neural Networks

Artificial neural networks are composed of simple computational units (neurons) in a multi-layered structure. These networks are designed to process input data to produce a specific output. Each neuron takes the sum of the inputs multiplied by a given weight and passes this sum through an activation function to generate the output.

1.3 History of Artificial Neural Networks

The development of artificial neural networks has gone through several critical phases. Starting in the 1950s and 1960s, with McCulloch and Pitts describing artificial neurons and the first neural network models, Rosenblatt's Perceptron model introduced the first learning algorithm. These early developments laid the foundation for neural networks. In the 1970s and 1980s, multilayer neural networks and back-propagation algorithms were developed, making it possible to solve more complex problems. This phase significantly expanded the capabilities of neural networks. Throughout the 1990s and 2000s, the increase in computing power and the explosion in the amount of data fueled the rapid development of deep learning and large-scale neural networks. Finally, in the 2010s and beyond, deep learning revolutionized many fields such as computer vision and natural language processing, and major technology companies and research institutions began to use neural networks in a variety of applications. This evolution has led to a wide range of applications for neural networks.

1.4 Application Areas

Artificial neural networks offer a wide range of applications:

- Image Recognition: Recognizing objects and faces.
- Natural Language Processing: Text and speech analysis.

- Gaming and Simulation: Game playing and strategy development.
- Health: Disease diagnosis and treatment recommendations.
- Finance: Stock forecasting and risk analysis.

What is Metacognition?

Metacognition can be defined as the ability to recognize, understand and control one's own thinking processes. First conceptualized by Flavell (1979), metacognition plays a critical role in learning and problem solving processes. In this section, we will examine the basic concepts, components and importance of metacognition.

Definition and Components of Metacognition

Metacognition consists of two main components: metacognitive knowledge and metacognitive regulation. Metacognitive knowledge refers to an individual's understanding of their own cognitive processes and includes three subcomponents. The first is personal knowledge, which encompasses awareness of one's cognitive capacities and limitations. The second is task knowledge, relating to the understanding of the difficulty and feasibility of specific tasks. The third is strategy knowledge, which involves awareness of various strategies that can be employed to accomplish tasks (Flavell, 1979). On the other hand, metacognitive regulation pertains to an individual's ability to plan, monitor, and evaluate cognitive processes. This component also comprises three subcomponents: planning, which involves devising strategies and making decisions for task performance; monitoring, which refers to the ongoing assessment of cognitive processes during a task, allowing for necessary adjustments; and evaluation, which entails assessing the processes and outcomes once a task is completed (Schraw & Dennison, 1994).

The Importance of Metacognition

Metacognition plays a critical role in learning and problem-solving processes, enabling individuals with metacognitive awareness to manage their learning more effectively and tackle problems with greater efficiency. One key aspect is the efficiency in learning, as metacognition aids individuals in better managing their learning processes and utilizing learning strategies effectively, which results in improved performance and knowledge retention. In terms of problem-solving, metacognition facilitates more strategic and conscious decision-making, allowing individuals to resolve challenges more quickly and effectively. Additionally, it fosters self-regulation by helping individuals organize and manage their learning, making it easier to achieve goals and promoting independence in the learning process. Finally, metacognition enhances adaptability, enabling individuals to adjust to various learning and problem-solving situations by identifying and employing the most effective strategies for different tasks and contexts.

Developing Metacognition

Developing metacognitive skills can significantly enhance an individual's ability to learn and solve problems more effectively and efficiently. One important strategy is learning strategies training, which involves teaching individuals effective learning techniques and demonstrating how to apply them. Self-reflection is another key approach, encouraging individuals to think critically about their own learning processes and evaluate their effectiveness. Additionally, monitoring and feedback play crucial roles by enabling individuals to track their learning progress and providing constructive feedback on their methods. Lastly, planning and goal setting help guide individuals in establishing clear learning objectives and creating actionable plans to achieve these goals, fostering a more structured and self-directed approach to learning.

Intersection of Neural Networks and Metacognition

Artificial neural networks (ANNs) and metacognition are two fundamental concepts that have important roles in learning and problem solving processes. Neural networks are computational models inspired by biological neural networks and used in tasks such as data processing, pattern recognition and learning. Metacognition is the ability to understand, monitor and control one's own cognitive processes. The combination of these two concepts enables the development of more intelligent and effective artificial intelligence systems. In this chapter, we will explore how neural networks and metacognition come together and the potential benefits of this combination.

Artificial Neural Networks and Metacognition

Artificial Neural Networks (ANN): ANN is a multilayer computational model that mimics the structure and functioning of biological neural networks. ANNs consist of an input layer, hidden layers and an output layer. Neurons in each layer are connected to neurons in the previous layer and process data through these connections. ANNs gain the ability to learn by training on large datasets, and this learning process is accomplished by adjusting and optimizing weights.

Metacognition: Metacognition is the ability to understand, monitor and control one's own thinking processes. Metacognitive awareness includes the individual's ability to plan, monitor and evaluate learning strategies. Metacognition plays an important role in learning and problem solving processes and helps individuals process information more effectively and efficiently.

The Role of Metacognition in Artificial Neural Networks

The combination of neural networks and metacognition has the potential to enhance the performance and efficiency of AI systems in several ways. One significant benefit is adaptive learning, where metacognitive mechanisms enable artificial neural networks (ANNs) to continuously monitor and evaluate their learning processes. This allows ANNs to identify the most suitable learning strategies for various datasets and tasks, adapting these strategies dynamically. Additionally, metacognition aids in error analysis and correction, helping ANNs analyze mistakes and take necessary corrective actions, thus enabling rapid identification and resolution of issues encountered during learning. Moreover, metacognitive mechanisms facilitate better resource management, allowing ANNs to utilize computational resources more efficiently, which leads to quicker and more effective performance on complex tasks. Finally, metacognition enhances learning transfer, enabling ANNs to apply knowledge and strategies acquired in one task to different tasks, thereby increasing their generalization capabilities and overall performance across diverse challenges.

Developing Metacognitive Neural Networks

Integrating metacognitive mechanisms into artificial neural networks can be achieved through various methods, one of which is the implementation of metacognitive layers. By adding these layers to ANNs, the network gains the ability to monitor and control its own learning processes, continuously evaluating performance and making necessary adjustments as needed. Another approach involves teaching ANNs different learning strategies while using metacognitive mechanisms to monitor the effectiveness of these strategies. This enables the networks to select and apply the most appropriate strategies for diverse tasks, enhancing their overall adaptability and performance in complex learning environments.

Fundamentals of Artificial Neural Networks

Artificial neural networks (ANNs) are computational models inspired by biological nervous systems and used to solve complex problems. These models are particularly effective in tasks such as learning, pattern recognition and classification on large datasets. In this section, we will examine the basic concepts, structure and operation of artificial neural networks.

History of Artificial Neural Networks

Artificial neural networks originated in the 1940s with the work of McCulloch and Pitts to model the functioning of nerve cells (neurons). In the 1950s, the perceptron model developed by Rosenblatt is considered the first practical application of ANNs. However, the limitations of this model became apparent in the 1960s and the development of ANNs stalled for a while. In the 1980s, with the development of techniques such as the multilayer perceptron (MLP) and backpropagation algorithm, ANNs started to gain interest again (Rosenblatt, 1958).

Structure of Artificial Neural Networks

Artificial neural networks are composed of interconnected artificial neurons and have a basic structure consisting of three main layers. The input layer is the first layer, receiving the data that is fed into the network, with each neuron representing an individual input feature. Following this, hidden layers exist between the input and output layers; these layers are crucial for processing the data and enhancing the learning capacity of the network through complex transformations. Finally, the output layer generates the results predicted or classified by the network, providing the final output based on the learned patterns from the input data.

Artificial Neurons and Activation Functions

Artificial neurons process data by following a series of steps that culminate in producing an output. Initially, each input is multiplied by a specific weight, with these weights being adjusted throughout the learning process to optimize the network's performance. Next, the weighted inputs are summed to yield a total value. This total is then passed through an activation function, which determines the neuron's output based on the computed value. Common activation functions include sigmoid, tanh, and ReLU, each serving different purposes in shaping the behavior of the neuron (Nair & Hinton, 2010). This structured approach allows artificial neurons to learn complex patterns and make predictions based on the input data.

Training and Learning Process

Training neural networks involves optimizing the weights based on a given dataset, typically through a series of steps. The process begins with a forward pass, where input data is fed into the network, and the outputs are calculated. Following this, the error calculation step determines the difference between the predicted output and the actual output, quantifying the error. This error is then backpropagated through the network in the backpropagation step, which updates the weights to minimize the error. During this phase, the weights are optimized using error derivatives, allowing the network to adjust and improve its predictions over time (Rumelhart, Hinton & Williams, 1986). This iterative process is crucial for enabling neural networks to learn from data and enhance their performance on various tasks.

Common Neural Network Architectures

Neural networks come in various architectures tailored for specific applications. Fully connected networks, where each neuron is interconnected with all neurons in the previous layer, are commonly used for basic classification and regression tasks. Convolutional neural networks (CNNs) are particularly effective in image processing and pattern recognition, incorporating convolutional layers and pooling layers to capture spatial hierarchies in data (LeCun et al., 1998). Recurrent neural networks (RNNs) are designed for tasks involving time series data and language processing, utilizing feedback loops that allow them to remember previous inputs (Hochreiter & Schmidhuber, 1997). Long short-term memory networks (LSTMs) are an advanced version of RNNs, specifically engineered to better learn long-term dependencies in sequential data, making them highly effective for complex tasks that require retaining information over extended periods.

Applications of Artificial Neural Networks

Artificial neural networks are applied across a wide range of fields due to their versatility and effectiveness. In image recognition, ANNs excel in tasks such as object and face recognition, as well as medical image analysis, allowing for accurate identification and classification of visual data. In the realm of natural language processing, they are employed for various tasks, including text classification, translation, sentiment analysis, and language modeling, enabling machines to understand and generate human language. Additionally, ANNs are utilized in gaming and simulation to enhance decision-making in strategy games and complex simulations, improving the overall user experience. In finance, they play a crucial role in applications like stock prediction, credit risk analysis, and algorithmic trading, providing insights that drive investment strategies and financial decision-making (Goodfellow, Bengio & Courville, 2016).

Training Neural Networks and Metacognitive Strategies

Training and Learning Strategies

Training and learning strategies encompass methods and techniques that aim to optimize individuals' processes of acquiring, processing, storing and retrieving information. These strategies include deliberate and planned approaches used to enable individuals to learn more effectively and efficiently. Using these strategies in education helps students improve their academic achievement and lifelong learning skills (Pressley & Harris, 2006).

Types of Learning Strategies

Learning strategies are generally divided into three main categories: cognitive, metacognitive and motivational strategies.

1. Cognitive Strategies:
    - Repetition: Repetitive practice to memorize and recall information.
    - Note Taking: Noting down information learned, summarizing important points.
    - Making Sense: Associating learned information with existing knowledge and making it meaningful (Weinstein & Mayer, 1986).
2. Metacognitive Strategies:
    - Planning: Determining learning goals and planning the necessary steps to reach these goals.
    - Monitoring: Continuously monitoring the learning process and changing strategies when necessary.
    - Evaluation: Evaluating success and the effectiveness of learning strategies at the end of the learning process (Schraw & Dennison, 1994).
3. Motivational Strategies:
    - Goal setting: Setting specific and achievable goals in the learning process.
    - Self-regulation: Controlling and motivating one's own learning processes.
    - Self-reward: Rewarding oneself when certain learning goals are achieved (Pintrich, 2000).

Importance of Learning Strategies in Education

Learning strategies enable students to acquire knowledge and skills, process this knowledge effectively and retain it in the long term. These strategies provide students with independent learning skills and increase their academic achievement. By encouraging students to use these strategies, teachers can make their learning processes more effective (Boekaerts, 1997).

Application of Learning Strategies in Education

Effective implementation of learning strategies in the classroom can be supported by a variety of methods and techniques. First, teachers can use direct teaching methods to help students learn and use strategies. This involves explaining the basic principles of strategies and how to apply them. Also, teachers can model by providing examples that show students how to use the strategies, which helps students to better understand the strategies. Finally, self-reflection and feedback processes should be encouraged; students have the opportunity to continuously improve their learning strategies by evaluating their own learning processes and analyzing what works or does not work (Hattie & Timperley, 2007). These methods ensure that learning strategies are implemented effectively and students become more aware of their own learning processes.

Hyperparameter Optimization and Metacognition

Hyperparameter Optimization

In machine learning, hyperparameter optimization plays a critical role to maximize the performance of the model. Hyperparameters are parameters that remain constant during model training and are usually determined empirically (Bergstra & Bengio, 2012). These parameters include variables that affect the structure of the model and the training process, such as the learning rate, the number of layers connected to the network, and the number of nodes.

Hyperparameter optimization is usually performed by various techniques such as grid search, random search, and more advanced methods such as Bayesian optimization (Snoek, Larochelle, & Adams, 2012). Grid search is a method of systematically testing hyperparameters over a given range. However, this method can be time-consuming over a large hyperparameter space. Random search works by selecting random values within a given range and can cover a larger search space (Bergstra et al., 2012).

Bayesian optimization uses a model to predict the performance of hyperparameters and searches for the best hyperparameters through this model (Snoek et al., 2012). This method offers a more efficient search strategy and generally yields better results.

Metacognition (Meta Learning)

Metacognition or meta-learning is a method used to optimize learning processes and algorithms (Schmidhuber, 1987). Meta-learning allows a model to learn from experience gained from various learning tasks and apply this knowledge to new tasks. In this context, meta-learning can make hyperparameter optimization more effective.

Meta-learning methods can speed up the hyperparameter search process and increase the ability to find better hyperparameter settings (Ruder, 2016). In particular, metacognitive strategies can be used to speed up the learning process of hyperparameters and make it more efficient. These approaches leverage past experience to improve the overall learning ability of the model, leading to better results.

Integrating Metacognition into Artificial Neural Networks

1 Metacognitive Agents

Metacognitive agents are systems that can regulate and improve their own learning processes and cognitive strategies. These agents have knowledge about how to learn in the learning process and use this knowledge to customize and optimize their learning strategies (Brown, 1987). Metacognition can be defined as a system's awareness of its own cognitive processes and its ability to manage these processes (Flavell, 1979).

Metacognitive agents generally have two basic components: metacognition and self-regulation. Metacognition is an agent's awareness of his/her thought processes and the ability to evaluate these processes (Schraw & Moshman, 1995). Self-regulation is the capacity of agents to dynamically change their learning processes, goals and strategies (Zimmerman, 2002). These features allow metacognitive agents to adapt their learning strategies according to the information coming from their environment.

2 Automated Learning

Automated learning means that a system can automatically manage and optimize its own learning processes. Such systems can independently perform learning and adaptation on data using machine learning algorithms (Mitchell, 1997). Automated learning involves tuning the hyperparameters of the model, automating model selection processes and implementing performance improvement strategies.

Automated learning generally covers two main areas: hyperparameter optimization and model selection. Hyperparameter optimization involves the automatic determination of the best hyperparameters to improve model performance (Bergstra & Bengio, 2012). Model selection, on the other hand, involves automated decision-making processes to select the most appropriate model among different models (Hutter, Kotthoff, & Vanschoren, 2019).

3 Relationship between Metacognitive Agents and Automated Learning

The relationship between metacognitive agents and automated learning is important for the ability of systems to optimize their learning processes. Metacognitive agents can improve the effectiveness of automated learning algorithms through their capacity to evaluate and manage learning processes (Kluwe & Renkl, 2006). For example, a metacognitive agent can analyze the difficulties encountered in the learning process and develop strategies to overcome these difficulties. This can include valuable information that automated learning systems can use to adapt more quickly and effectively.

Furthermore, metacognitive agents can enable the model to better understand and optimize its own learning processes, thus improving the success of automated learning algorithms (Aleven & Koedinger, 2002). The combination of these two areas can improve both individual learning processes and overall model performance.

Adaptive Learning Systems

Definition of Adaptive Learning Systems

Adaptive learning systems are systems that provide educational experiences customized to the needs and learning styles of individual learners. These systems monitor student performance and use the data to dynamically adjust learning materials and strategies (Brusilovsky & Millán, 2007). The aim is to increase learning effectiveness by providing the most appropriate learning experience for each student.

These systems typically collect and analyze student data. This data includes factors such as the student's knowledge level, learning speed, and interest in the subject matter. Based on the analysis, the system can tailor learning materials, tests, and teaching methods to the individual needs of the student (Kerr, 2007).

Basic Components

Adaptive Learning Systems Usually Consist of Several Key Components:

Adaptive learning systems incorporate key components to enhance the learning experience. The first component is student profiling, which involves a data collection process aimed at identifying individual student characteristics and needs. This profiling gathers information about a student's abilities, prior knowledge, and learning style, enabling a deeper understanding of how each student learns best (Woolf, 2009). The second component is content adaptation, which personalizes learning materials and activities based on the collected learner data. This includes adjusting the difficulty level of instructional materials and selecting content that aligns with the student's unique learning process, ensuring that the educational experience is both relevant and effective (Brusilovsky & Millán, 2007). Together, these components create a tailored learning environment that fosters student engagement and success.

Application Areas

Adaptive learning systems can be applied in a variety of educational settings. These areas include:

Adaptive learning systems offer significant advantages across various educational contexts. In personal education, they provide customized learning materials tailored to the needs of individual learners, supporting their personal development and enhancing engagement (Jiang, 2017). In corporate training, organizations can leverage these systems to facilitate the skills development of their employees, enabling continuous training and upskilling of the workforce to keep pace with changing demands (Pappano, 2012). Additionally, in distance learning environments, adaptive learning technologies can monitor student interactions and performance, allowing for the personalization of training materials and ultimately increasing the effectiveness of online learning processes (Siemens, 2013). This adaptability makes learning more relevant and impactful across different settings.

Current Approaches

Adaptive learning systems utilize various approaches to customize educational experiences for students. One approach is rule-based strategies, where content and activities are modified based on predefined rules that correlate with the learner's performance (Brusilovsky & Millán, 2007). Another method involves data mining and machine learning, which leverage big data analysis to gain deep insights into a student's learning habits and performance, allowing for real-time adaptations based on this information (Romero & Ventura, 2013). Additionally, cognitive modeling offers a sophisticated technique that involves modeling the cognitive processes of students, enabling the adaptation of learning strategies and materials to align with each student's cognitive structure (Woolf, 2009). These approaches work together to create a more personalized and effective learning environment.

Metacognitive Monitoring and Model Updates

Metacognitive Monitoring

Metacognitive monitoring is the ability of individuals to evaluate and manage their own cognitive processes and learning strategies. This process involves individuals recognizing and evaluating their own thinking and learning processes and making adjustments when necessary (Flavell, 1979). Metacognitive monitoring allows individuals to consciously control their problem solving and learning strategies and therefore can increase the effectiveness of learning processes (Schraw, 1998).

Metacognitive monitoring has two main components: metacognitive knowledge and metacognitive control. Metacognitive knowledge includes individuals' knowledge about their own learning processes and strategies. Metacognitive control is the ability of individuals to regulate their learning strategies and processes using this knowledge (Schraw & Moshman, 1995).

Model Updates

Model updating refers to the continuous improvement of the model in dynamic systems based on available data and observations. Especially in the fields of machine learning and artificial intelligence, this process plays a critical role in improving the performance of systems and adapting to changing conditions (Mitchell, 1997). Model updates usually consist of two main phases: data collection and model retraining. First, in the data collection phase, data is continuously collected and analyzed from the system or environment; this process is important to assess the current performance of the model and identify shortcomings (Bishop, 2006). Then, in the model retraining phase, the model is retrained to improve its performance in light of the collected data. This involves updating the model's parameters or retraining it with new data (Goodfellow, Bengio, & Courville, 2016). These two stages support the model to adapt to dynamic conditions and continuously improve its performance.

Relationship between Metacognitive Monitoring and Model Updates

Metacognitive monitoring can play an important role in the process of model updates. In particular, metacognitive monitoring can be used to assess the effectiveness of the model's learning process and make strategic changes when necessary. This is true both in individual learning processes and in machine learning systems.

For example, a metacognitive mechanism that monitors the performance of a machine learning model can evaluate various performance metrics of the model and update its parameters or structure based on these evaluations (Kuhn & Johnson, 2013). Such metacognitive monitoring ensures that the model is continuously optimized and increases its ability to adapt to changing conditions.

Application Areas

In educational technologies, metacognitive monitoring plays an important role in systems that monitor student performance and personalize learning strategies. These technologies make the learning process more effective by dynamically adjusting the model and teaching strategies according to the needs of the student (Aleven, McLaren, Sewall, & Koedinger, 2009). Similarly, in artificial intelligence and machine learning systems, model updates are applied to improve the performance of the system and adapt to changing data conditions. Metacognitive monitoring can make these updates more effective and efficient, thus improving the adaptation processes of machine learning systems (Cheng, Yang, & Rusu, 2018). This integration contributes to improving performance in both training and data analysis.

Metacognitive Responsiveness and Error Management

Metacognitive Sensitivity

Metacognitive sensitivity is the ability of individuals to be aware of and evaluate their own cognitive processes and strategies. This concept helps individuals to understand which strategies to use in learning and problem solving processes, when to change their strategies and which errors to correct (Flavell, 1979; Schraw, 1998). Metacognitive sensitivity enables individuals to be aware of their own thought processes and actively manage these processes.

Metacognitive sensitivity includes two main components: metacognitive knowledge and metacognitive regulation. Metacognitive knowledge is the knowledge and understanding that individuals have about their own learning processes. Metacognitive regulation is the ability of individuals to adjust their learning strategies and processes using this knowledge (Schraw & Moshman, 1995). These components help individuals to develop more effective learning and problem solving strategies.

Error Management

Error management involves the processes of analyzing errors and failures, developing strategies to cope with these situations and preventing future errors. Effective error management can help individuals understand the challenges they face in their learning process and develop appropriate strategies to cope with these challenges (Hattie & Timperley, 2007).

Error management usually involves the following steps:

The defect management process involves several critical stages. First, in the defect identification phase, the types and causes of defects are identified; this is a necessary step to understand the root causes of defects and possible solutions (Reason, 1990). Next, error analysis is performed, which involves conducting an in-depth investigation to identify the root causes of errors (James, 2011). Once the errors have been identified and analyzed, we move on to the error correction phase, where errors are corrected and lessons learned from these errors are applied to improve future performance (Guskey, 2002). Finally, preventive measures are developed and implemented, where systems or processes are improved to prevent future mistakes (Senge, 1990). This holistic approach provides a strategic framework for both effectively managing errors and improving future performance.

Relationship between Metacognitive Sensitivity and Error Management

Metacognitive sensitivity plays an important role in error management processes. Individuals' awareness of their own learning processes and strategies can help them develop more effective strategies during error management. Metacognitive sensitivity allows individuals to better understand the likelihood of making errors and the causes of errors (Flavell, 1979; Schraw, 1998).

For example, when an error is made, a student or employee can analyze the error, review their own learning processes and develop strategies to avoid similar errors in the future. Such metacognitive monitoring can increase the effectiveness of error management processes and improve individuals' learning and performance (Hattie & Timperley, 2007).

Application Areas

1. Education: Educational programs and strategies that help students develop error management and metacognitive sensemaking skills. These programs can enable students to better understand and manage their own learning processes (Aleven, McLaren, Sewall, & Koedinger, 2009).
2. The World of Work: Strategies used to improve employees' error management and metacognitive sensemaking skills. These strategies can improve employee performance and make business processes more effective (Senge, 1990).
3. Health: Applications that enable healthcare professionals to reduce error rates by using metacognitive sensemaking in error management processes (Reason, 1990).

Application Areas and Examples

Metacognitive Sensemaking and Error Management in Education

Metacognitive sensemaking and error management in education are critical for improving students' learning processes. Metacognitive sensemaking allows students to evaluate their own learning processes and adjust their strategies, while error management enables students to learn from mistakes and improve their performance (Schraw, 1998; Hattie & Timperley, 2007).

Examples:

1. Personal Learning Plans: Students can develop personal learning plans to assess their own learning process and achieve their goals. These plans can help students identify their learning strategies and correct their mistakes (Aleven, McLaren, Sewall, & Koedinger, 2009).
2. Error Analysis Activities: In education, students can try to understand the reasons for their errors by participating in various error analysis activities. These activities can help students learn from mistakes and improve their learning strategies (Guskey, 2002).

Metacognitive Sensitivity and Error Management in Business

In business, metacognitive sensemaking and error management can be used to enhance employee performance and improve business processes. Metacognitive sensemaking allows employees to evaluate their own work processes and strategies, while error management helps them improve performance by analyzing and correcting errors (Senge, 1990).

Examples:

1. Performance Evaluation and Feedback: Using metacognitive sensemaking, employees can evaluate their own performance and adjust their strategies based on feedback from managers. This process can help employees to continuously improve and correct their mistakes (James, 2011).
2. Error Management Systems: In workplaces, error management systems can be developed to enable employees to quickly identify, analyze and correct their mistakes. These systems can make business processes more efficient (Senge, 1990).

Metacognitive Sensitivity and Error Management in Healthcare

In the healthcare sector, metacognitive sensitivity and error management are important to improve patient safety and reduce medical errors. Healthcare professionals can assess their own cognitive processes and decision-making strategies and develop various strategies to prevent errors (Reason, 1990).

Examples are:

1. Error Reporting Systems: In the healthcare sector, medical errors can be quickly detected and analyzed using error reporting systems. These systems can help healthcare professionals learn from errors and prevent future errors (Reason, 1990).
2. Simulation Trainings: Healthcare professionals can reduce the risk of making errors and improve their metacognitive sensitivity through simulation trainings. These trainings can be used to improve medical decision-making processes and error management (Gordon et al., 2010).

Metacognitive Sensemaking and Error Management in Scientific Research and Technology

In the fields of scientific research and technology, metacognitive sensemaking and error management are critical for enhancing the quality of research processes and improving the performance of technological systems. Researchers and engineers can evaluate their own processes and achieve more effective results by applying error management strategies (Bishop, 2006).

Examples:

1. Error Analysis for Research Projects: Researchers can evaluate the effectiveness of scientific methods by analyzing the errors encountered in projects. These analyses can provide important information to improve research processes (Bishop, 2006).
2. Testing and Updating Technological Systems: Technological systems can be tested and their performance analyzed using metacognitive sensemaking. When errors are identified and corrected, the reliability and effectiveness of systems can be increased (Goodfellow, Bengio, & Courville, 2016).

Future Directions and Ethical Issues

Future Directions

Future directions in educational technologies, neural networks and metacognition are being shaped to reflect the rapid advances in technology and education. Emerging trends in these areas aim to make educational processes more effective and personalized.

1. Personalized Learning

In the future, personalized learning experiences are expected to become even more prevalent in educational technologies. Artificial neural networks have the capacity to provide personalized educational materials and strategies by analyzing student performance and trying to understand learning styles. Personalized learning can make the learning process more effective by providing solutions tailored to student needs (Heffernan & Heffernan, 2014).

2. Adaptive Learning Systems

Adaptive learning systems are technologies that adjust learning materials and pathways according to learners' performance and needs. Artificial neural networks play an important role in the development of such systems. These systems can meet individual learning needs by identifying students' weaknesses and providing them with appropriate support (VanLehn, 2011).

3. Artificial Intelligence and Metacognition Integration

The integration of artificial intelligence (AI) and metacognition could usher in a new era in education. AI can develop intelligent systems and tools that support metacognition strategies. Such systems can monitor students' learning processes, help them evaluate their own cognitive processes, and provide feedback (Mouza et al., 2016).

4. Data Security and Privacy

Data security and privacy in educational technologies will be a critical issue, especially in terms of protecting student data. With the proliferation of educational technologies, stricter regulations and security measures will be required for how student data is collected, stored and used (Zuboff, 2019).

Ethical Issues

Ethical issues related to educational technologies, neural networks and metacognition address the problems encountered during the implementation and use of these technologies. These issues aim to ensure that technologies are used fairly, safely and effectively.

1. Data Use and Privacy

The use, privacy and security of data collected in educational technologies are important ethical issues. Unauthorized use or misuse of student data can threaten the privacy of individuals. Educational institutions and technology providers must comply with data protection laws and ensure the security of students' data (Cummings & Ferris, 2021).

2. Access and Justice in Education

Neural networks and other educational technologies can make learning opportunities more accessible. However, it is important to ensure that these technologies are accessible and that every student can benefit equally. Educational technologies need to be designed in a way that prevents discrimination and is inclusive (Gillard, 2020).

3. Artificial Intelligence and Decision Making

The use of artificial intelligence systems in education raises the need for transparency and fairness in decision-making processes. It is important that the algorithms used in the decision-making processes of artificial neural networks are transparent and produce fair results. In addition, these systems need to be managed in an understandable and accurate way by instructors and students (O'Neil, 2016).

4. Metacognition and Autonomy

Metacognitive strategies can help students manage their own learning processes. However, students' autonomy and decision-making authority should also be taken into consideration in the implementation of these strategies. Educational technologies should be designed to support students' independent thinking and learning skills (Zimmerman, 2002).

Metacognition and Social Impacts of Artificial Intelligence

Metacognition and Social Dynamics

Metacognition is the ability of individuals to recognize and manage their own thinking processes. This ability allows individuals to manage their own learning processes and decisions more effectively. At the societal level, the effects of metacognition can improve the learning and problem solving skills of individuals, thereby increasing the general level of education and the quality of decision-making in society (Flavell, 1979; Schraw, 1998).

Societal Effects

The social effects of metacognition strategies cover a wide range. The effective use of metacognitive strategies in education can increase student achievement and improve the overall quality of education, as well as reduce social educational inequalities (Zimmerman, 2002). In terms of labor productivity, metacognition can improve employees' ability to evaluate and improve work processes, which can contribute to economic development (Schraw, 1998). Furthermore, metacognition supports the personal development of individuals, allowing them to evaluate their own thinking processes and learning strategies; this can lead to more informed and educated individuals in society (Flavell, 1979). Thus, metacognitive strategies can provide significant benefits at both individual and societal levels.

Social Impacts of Artificial Intelligence

Artificial intelligence (AI), with its vast data analysis capacities and learning capabilities, is significantly affecting societal dynamics. The societal impacts of AI are evident in economic, social and cultural spheres (Brynjolfsson & McAfee, 2014).

Societal Impacts

The societal impacts of artificial intelligence (AI) are broad and multifaceted. The automation capabilities of AI can directly affect the workforce in many sectors; the automation of some jobs can lead to job losses, while on the other hand, it can create new job opportunities, which may require retraining and skill development of the workforce (Bessen, 2019). Furthermore, AI systems can both increase and decrease social inequalities; when algorithms reflect social biases, they can lead to discrimination, so it is important that AI applications are designed in a fair and inclusive manner (O'Neil, 2016). AI's big data analytics have the capacity to collect and use individuals' personal information, which can raise privacy concerns and security risks, making data security and privacy protection critical (Zuboff, 2019). Moreover, AI-based applications can affect individuals' social behaviors and interactions, especially AI algorithms used on social media platforms can shape the way individuals acquire information and their social interactions (Tufekci, 2018).

Social Impacts of Metacognition and Artificial Intelligence Together

The societal implications of metacognition and AI can vary depending on how these two fields combine and interact. Some societal implications of these interactions include the following:

Innovative approaches in education emphasize how metacognition strategies can be used in artificial intelligence (AI)-based education systems. While AI has the capacity to deliver personalized learning experiences, metacognition strategies can help learners make the most of these experiences, resulting in more effective and accessible solutions in education (Heffernan & Heffernan, 2014). Similarly, AI's powerful tools for data analysis and prediction, coupled with metacognition strategies, can enable individuals to evaluate this information more effectively and make more informed decisions (Mouza et al., 2016). Moreover, the integration of AI and metacognition strategies can enhance the ability to adapt to societal changes; these approaches in education can help individuals better adapt to changing societal conditions (Zimmerman, 2002). These combinations can play an important role in improving educational and social adaptation processes.

Conclusions and Discussion

Results

In this study, the relationships between neural networks, metacognition and educational technologies and the social effects of these interactions are examined in detail. The findings highlight the potential of educational technologies to provide personalized learning experiences and the role of neural networks in these processes. Furthermore, how metacognition strategies can be used effectively in education and artificial intelligence systems and the effects of these two areas on societal dynamics are discussed.

Main Findings:

1. The Role of Artificial Neural Networks in Educational Technologies: Artificial neural networks are effectively used in areas such as analyzing student performance, providing personalized learning experiences, and creating automated assessment systems (Bishop, 2006; Zhang et al., 2018). These technologies make educational processes more efficient and student-centered.
2. Metacognition and its place in education: Metacognitive strategies increase students' ability to evaluate and manage their own learning processes (Flavell, 1979; Schraw, 1998). Effective use of these strategies in education can increase student achievement and support personal development.
3. Societal Impacts: The societal impacts of AI are evident in many areas such as labor, equality, privacy, and social interactions (Brynjolfsson & McAfee, 2014; Zuboff, 2019). The integration of metacognition and AI can help individuals make informed decisions and adapt to societal changes (Zimmerman, 2002; Mouza et al., 2016).

Discussion

1. Neural Networks and Metacognition in Educational Technology:

While neural networks have the capacity to provide personalized learning experiences and effective assessment systems in education, metacognition strategies can help to use these experiences more effectively. The data and feedback provided by neural networks can be integrated with metacognition strategies that allow students to monitor and manage their own learning processes. This integration can offer more customized and effective solutions in education, but it also raises ethical issues such as data security and privacy (Heffernan & Heffernan, 2014).

2. Societal Impacts and Ethical Issues:

The integration of metacognition strategies and AI can play an important role in adapting to societal changes. However, these processes need to be managed in a fair and inclusive manner. Assessing the societal impact of metacognition and AI applications in education can help to make the most of the potential of these technologies and minimize their negative effects (Zimmerman, 2002).

3. Future Directions:

In the future, the impact of artificial neural networks and metacognition on education and society will become even more evident. The potential of these technologies to provide more personalized and effective solutions may lead to significant changes in education and the workforce. However, the ethical and social aspects of these changes will need to be carefully considered. Issues such as data protection, social equity and transparency are important for the sustainable use of these technologies (Zuboff, 2019; Tufekci, 2018).

REFERENCES

Aleven, V., Rowe, J., Huang, Y., & Mitrovic, A. (2023). Domain modeling for AIED systems with connections to modeling student knowledge: A review. *Handbook of Artificial Intelligence in Education*, 127-169.

Bergstra, J., & Bengio, Y. (2012). Random search for hyper-parameter optimization. *Journal of Machine Learning Research*, 13(2).

Bessen, J. (2018). *AI and jobs: The role of demand* (No. w24235). National Bureau of Economic Research.

Boekaerts, M. (1997). Self-regulated learning: A new concept embraced by researchers, policy makers, educators, teachers, and students. *Learning and Instruction*, 7(2), 161–186. DOI: 10.1016/S0959-4752(96)00015-1

Brown, A. (1987). Metacognition, executive control, self-regulation, and other more mysterious mechanisms. *Metacogniton, motivation, and understanding/Lawrence Erlbaum Associates.*

Brynjolfsson, E., & McAfee, A. (2014). *The second machine age: Work, progress, and prosperity in a time of brilliant technologies.* WW Norton & company.

Goodfellow, I., Bengio, Y., & Courville, A. (2016). *Deep learning*. The MIT Press.

Guskey, T. R. (2002). Professional development and teacher change. *Teachers and Teaching*, 8(3), 381–391. DOI: 10.1080/135406002100000512

Hattie, J., & Timperley, H. (2007). The power of feedback. *Review of Educational Research*, 77(1), 81–112. DOI: 10.3102/003465430298487

Heffernan, N. T., & Heffernan, C. L. (2014). The ASSISTments ecosystem: Building a platform that brings scientists and teachers together for minimally invasive research on human learning and teaching. *International Journal of Artificial Intelligence in Education*, 24(4), 470–497. DOI: 10.1007/s40593-014-0024-x

Hochreiter, S. (1997). *Long Short-term Memory.* Neural Computation MIT-Press. DOI: 10.1162/neco.1997.9.8.1735

Hofmann, D. A., & Frese, M. (Eds.). (2011). *Error in organizations.* Routledge. DOI: 10.4324/9780203817827

Hutter, F., Kotthoff, L., & Vanschoren, J. (2019). *Automated machine learning: methods, systems, challenges.* Springer Nature. DOI: 10.1007/978-3-030-05318-5

Kerns, B. R. (2019). *A case study of A flipped curriculum using collaborative and active learning with an adaptive learning system* (Doctoral dissertation, Indiana State University).

LeCun, Y., Bottou, L., Bengio, Y., & Haffner, P. (1998). Gradient-based learning applied to document recognition. *Proceedings of the IEEE*, 86(11), 2278–2324. DOI: 10.1109/5.726791

Liu, T. (2024). Assessing implicit computational thinking in game-based learning: A logical puzzle game study. *British Journal of Educational Technology*, 55(5), 2357–2382. DOI: 10.1111/bjet.13443

Mitchell, T. M., & Mitchell, T. M. (1997). [). New York: McGraw-hill.]. *Machine Learning*, 1(9), •••.

Nair, V., & Hinton, G. E. (2010). Rectified linear units improve restricted boltzmann machines. In *Proceedings of the 27th international conference on machine learning (ICML-10)* (pp. 807-814).

O'neil, C. (2017). *Weapons of math destruction: How big data increases inequality and threatens democracy*. Crown.

Pappano, L. (2012). The year of the MOOC. *The New York Times, November, 2.*

Pintrich, P. R. (2000). The role of goal orientation in self-regulated learning. *Handbook of self-regulation/Academic.*

Pressley, M., & Harris, K. R. (2009). Cognitive strategies instruction: From basic research to classroom instruction. *Journal of Education*, 189(1-2), 77–94. DOI: 10.1177/0022057409189001-206

Rauner, M. S., & Haunschmied, J. (2010). *A ustrian Society of Operations Research (O esterreichische G esellschaft für Operations Research, O egor).* Wiley Encyclopedia of Operations Research and Management Science.

Reason, J. (1990). *Human error.* Cambridge university press. DOI: 10.1017/CBO9781139062367

Rosenblatt, F. (1958). The perceptron: A probabilistic model for information storage and organization in the brain. *Psychological Review*, 65(6), 386–408. DOI: 10.1037/h0042519 PMID: 13602029

Rumelhart, D. E., Hinton, G. E., & Williams, R. J. (1986). Learning representations by back-propagating errors. *nature, 323*(6088), 533-536.

Schraw, G. (1998). Promoting general metacognitive awareness. *Instructional Science*, 26(1), 113–125. DOI: 10.1023/A:1003044231033

Schraw, G., & Dennison, R. S. (1994). Assessing metacognitive awareness. *Contemporary Educational Psychology*, 19(4), 460–475. DOI: 10.1006/ceps.1994.1033

Shaun, R., De Baker, J., & Inventado, P. S. (2014). *Educational Data Mining and Learning Analytics*.

Siemens, G. (2013). Learning analytics: The emergence of a discipline. *The American Behavioral Scientist*, 57(10), 1380–1400. DOI: 10.1177/0002764213498851

Tufekci, Z. (2017). *Twitter and tear gas: The power and fragility of networked protest*. Yale University Press.

VanLehn, K. (2011). The relative effectiveness of human tutoring, intelligent tutoring systems, and other tutoring systems. *Educational Psychologist*, 46(4), 197–221. DOI: 10.1080/00461520.2011.611369

Weinstein, C. E., & Mayer, R. E. (1983, November). The teaching of learning strategies. In *Innovation abstracts* (Vol. 5, No. 32, p. n32).

Woolf, B. P. (2010). *Building intelligent interactive tutors: Student-centered strategies for revolutionizing e-learning*. Morgan Kaufmann.

Zhang, W., & Duan, C. (2017). Construction and implementation of institutional e-learning development framework in continuing higher education. [JETDE]. *Journal of Educational Technology Development and Exchange*, 10(1), 2. DOI: 10.18785/jetde.1001.02

Zimmerman, B. J. (2002). Becoming a self-regulated learner: An overview. *Theory into Practice*, 41(2), 64–70. DOI: 10.1207/s15430421tip4102_2

Zuboff, S. (2023). The age of surveillance capitalism. In *Social theory re-wired* (pp. 203–213). Routledge. DOI: 10.4324/9781003320609-27

KEY TERMS AND DEFINITIONS

Cognitive Processes: Mental activities involved in gaining knowledge and comprehension, including thinking, knowing, remembering, and problem-solving.

Deep Learning: A subset of machine learning involving neural networks with many layers, capable of handling large datasets and complex tasks.

Metacognition: The awareness and understanding of one's own thought processes, encompassing both knowledge about cognition and regulation of cognitive activities.

Metacognitive Regulation: The ability to plan, monitor, and evaluate one's cognitive processes during task performance.

Chapter 14
Forging the Path: A Journey Through the Historical Evolution of Virtual Technology in Education

Gurtek Singh
https://orcid.org/0009-0008-4207-176X
Akal University, India

Tabish Hashmi
Lovely Professional University, India

ABSTRACT

This chapter delves into the history of virtual technology and its transformative impact on education. It examines its origins in academia, its gradual integration, and the pivotal moments that have shaped its evolution. The chapter also discusses the role of technological advancements, research breakthroughs, and educational initiatives in shaping virtual education. It highlights early adopters and pioneers who have played instrumental roles in championing virtual technology in education, highlighting their contributions and trailblazing efforts.

INTRODUCTION

The fast progress of virtual technology has caused a seismic upheaval in the educational environment in recent decades. The development of virtual technology in education has been nothing short of transformative, spanning from the early phases of computer-assisted learning in the late 20th century to the immersive experiences provided by virtual reality (VR) and augmented reality (AR) platforms

DOI: 10.4018/979-8-3693-6030-9.ch014

of contemporary times (Azuma, 1997). This chapter, "Forging the Path: Journey Through the Historical Evolution of Virtual Technology in Education" delves into the transformative journey of these technologies, exploring how they have reshaped pedagogical approaches, enhanced student engagement, and broadened access to educational resources. Virtual technology in education has a history of constant invention and modification. Subsequent versions of educational technology, including basic computer programs and virtual courses, established the foundation for the advanced virtual worlds of today (Johnso et al., 2015). These initial steps, although modest by current standards, marked the beginning of a paradigm shift in how education could be delivered and experienced . As technology evolved, so did its applications in education, moving from simple digital aids to complex, interactive learning ecosystems .This chapter examines key milestones in this journey, highlighting significant technological breakthroughs and their impact on educational practices. From the introduction of multimedia elements in the classroom to the advent of distance learning platforms, and from the integration of simulations and educational games to the rise of VR and AR, each development has contributed to a richer, more dynamic learning experience (Garris, 2002) . Present chapter considers the sociocultural and economic factors that have influenced the adoption and integration of virtual technologies in various educational contexts . By tracing the historical trajectory of virtual technology in education, this chapter not only celebrates the achievements of the past but also provides insights into current trends and future possibilities. As we stand at the cusp of a new era in education, understanding this evolution is crucial for educators, technologists, policymakers, and students alike . It enables us to appreciate the transformative power of technology in learning and to harness its potential to create more inclusive, engaging, and effective educational environments . In "Forging the Path: Journey Through the Historical Evolution of Virtual Technology in Education" readers will embark on a comprehensive journey through time, witnessing the pivotal moments and innovations that have shaped the educational landscape. This exploration underscores the ongoing dialogue between technology and pedagogy, emphasizing the importance of continual adaptation and innovation in the quest to enhance learning experiences. As we navigate this complex and exciting terrain, we are reminded that the journey is far from over indeed, it is just beginning.

Methodology

This chapter employs a secondary research methodology, relying on the critical analysis of existing literature, studies, and data related to "Forging the Path: Journey Through the Historical Evolution of Virtual Technology in Education." The methodology involves a systematic review and synthesis of scholarly articles, books, reports, and other reputable sources to address the central research topic.

1. Research Design

The research design is based on a literature review approach, aimed at gathering and synthesizing knowledge from various existing studies. This method was chosen to provide a comprehensive overview of "Forging the Path: Journey Through the Historical Evolution of Virtual Technology in Education." without the need for primary data collection. By drawing on previously published work, this chapter provides a well-rounded understanding of the research theme.

2. Data Collection: Literature Review

The data for this research was sourced from peer-reviewed academic papers, books, and reports published by credible institutions. The following steps were involved in the data collection process: Source Selection Criteria: Sources were selected based on their relevance, credibility, and contribution to the understanding of "Forging the Path: Journey Through the Historical Evolution of Virtual Technology in Education." Priority was given to peer-reviewed journal articles. Books authored by recognized experts in the field. -Reports published by international organizations, governmental agencies, or well-established think tanks.

1. **Search Strategy:** The literature search was conducted using academic databases such as (e.g., Google Scholar, JSTOR, PubMed, etc.), focusing on keywords such as [list relevant keywords]. The search included studies from (specific time frame, if applicable) and articles that directly addressed (specific aspects of the topic).
2. **Inclusion and Exclusion Criteria:** Articles and studies were included if they - Directly examined the phenomena that provided empirical or theoretical insights relevant to the research question. Studies were excluded if they were outdated, not peer-reviewed, or lacked sufficient methodological rigor.
3. **Analytical Techniques** Once the relevant literature was gathered, a thematic analysis was conducted to identify key patterns, trends, and findings across different studies.

This involved- Comparative Analysis: Examining the similarities and differences in findings across various sources.

Synthesis of Evidence: Combining insights from multiple studies to form a cohesive narrative that addresses the research questions.

Critical Evaluation: Assessing the strengths and limitations of each study, considering the methodology, scope, and findings of the original research.

4. **Ethical Considerations** Since this chapter relies solely on secondary data, no direct interaction with human participants or collection of primary data was involved. However, ethical standards were upheld in the following ways: -
    - All sources were properly cited to give credit to the original authors.
    - Care was taken to ensure that only reputable and ethically conducted studies were included in the analysis.
5. **Limitations** While this research provides a comprehensive overview of the literature on "Forging the Path: Journey Through the Historical Evolution of Virtual Technology in Education", it is limited by its reliance on secondary data. The availability of existing studies may limit the scope of analysis to the perspectives or regions covered in prior research. Additionally, the conclusions drawn are dependent on the quality and reliability of the sources used.
    A. Definition of virtual technology in education

Virtual technology in education refers to the use of advanced computer-generated environments, digital tools, and online platforms to facilitate and enhance the learning process. It encompasses a wide array of applications, ranging from simple digital aids to immersive, interactive simulations that transform traditional educational approaches (De & Jarvis, 2006). The integration of these technologies allows educators and students to explore new methods of teaching and learning, which are increasingly becoming essential in today's fast-paced, digitally driven world. Below are several definitions that capture the breadth and depth of virtual technology in the educational context:

Digital Learning Environments

Virtual technology includes online learning environments where students use computers, tablets, and other electronic devices to access resources and instructional materials (Cuban, 2001). These digital learning environments provide a platform for students to engage with content beyond the confines of a traditional classroom. Examples of these environments include digital libraries that offer vast collections of books and research materials, instructional websites with interactive content, and online courses that facilitate distance learning. Students can participate in lessons, complete assignments, and collaborate with their peers regardless of geographic location. This flexibility supports a variety of learning styles and ensures accessibility for students who might otherwise face barriers to traditional education.

Virtual Reality (VR)

Virtual reality (VR) in education involves the use of computer-generated simulations that immerse students in fully interactive environments. These virtual worlds simulate real-life situations or entirely new realms that learners can explore, manipulate, and interact with, offering a rich, experiential learning process. For instance, medical students can use VR to practice surgical procedures, allowing them to gain practical skills without the risks associated with real-life surgery. Similarly, students in environmental sciences can explore ecosystems or geographical locations through VR, giving them an understanding of these places without the need to travel. The experiential aspect of VR makes it an incredibly effective tool for hands-on learning, enabling students to practice, experiment, and gain a deep understanding of concepts that would otherwise be difficult to access in a traditional classroom setting.

Augmented Reality (AR)

Augmented reality (AR) technology overlays digital information onto the physical world, enriching the learning experience by adding layers of interactive and contextual elements to the environment. This can include the use of 3D models, animations, and interactive activities that students view on their device screens while looking at real-world objects. For example, AR can be used in biology classes to overlay anatomical models on a real skeleton or in history classes to project historical events onto present-day landmarks (Azuma, 1997). The combination of real-world interaction with digital enhancements makes AR a powerful educational tool, offering students an engaging, multisensory experience that can improve comprehension and retention of complex subjects. The hands-on, visual nature of AR also makes it particularly beneficial for kinaesthetic and visual learners (Milgram, 1994; Ercan, 2010).

E-Learning Platforms

E-learning platforms are another integral component of virtual technology in education, serving as a bridge between students and instructors via the internet. These platforms deliver educational content through a variety of media, including video lectures, digital textbooks, quizzes, and interactive assignments. Additionally, they often include features that facilitate communication and collaboration, such as discussion forums, live chats, and virtual group projects. Popular examples of e-learning platforms include Moodle, Canvas, and Google Classroom, which allow educators to organize their lessons, assess student progress, and provide feedback in real-time. These platforms also support a blended learning approach, combining online and face-to-face instruction to offer students greater flexibility and control over their learning experience. As the demand for remote education continues to rise, e-learning platforms have become essential in ensuring continuity and access to quality education for students worldwide.

Simulations and Serious Games

Educational simulations and serious games represent a significant application of virtual technology in education, especially in fields where real-life practice is either too dangerous or too costly (De Freitas & Jarvis, 2006). Simulations provide a safe, controlled environment where learners can practice complex tasks, such as piloting an aircraft, performing a medical procedure, or managing a business. Serious games, on the other hand, are designed to teach concepts and problem-solving skills through interactive gameplay. These applications combine the entertainment value of gaming with educational objectives, making learning more engaging and effective (Ibid). In disciplines like engineering, military training, or healthcare, simulations and serious games allow students to gain practical experience and build competency in scenarios that closely mimic real-world challenges, ensuring they are well-prepared for their professional roles (Squire & Jenkins, 2003).

Mixed Reality (MR)

Mixed reality (MR) integrates both virtual reality and augmented reality to create hybrid environments where physical and digital objects coexist and interact in real-time. MR allows students to engage with virtual content while still remaining aware of and interacting with the physical world around them. For example, a student studying architecture could use MR to visualize and manipulate a 3D model of a building within their physical environment, giving them a better sense of space, structure, and design. This technology also supports collaborative learning, as multiple users can interact with the same digital content simultaneously, regardless of their physical location (Milgram & Kishino, 1994). By blending the virtual and real worlds, MR offers a unique and immersive learning experience that enhances practical applications of knowledge and encourages interactive, hands-on learning.

Cloud-Based Learning Tools

Cloud-based tools and services are a vital aspect of virtual technology in education, providing platforms that facilitate remote access to educational resources and promote collaboration between students and teachers (Kirschner & Selinger, 2003). These tools allow users to store and share files, access software applications, and work together on projects from any location with an internet connection (Dede,2009; Devlin,2023). Examples of cloud-based learning tools include Google Drive, Microsoft OneDrive, and collaborative applications like Slack or Zoom. In the context of education, cloud computing enables students and educators to participate in remote learning, access course materials, submit assignments, and communicate in real-time (Ercan,2010). The cloud-based infrastructure also supports scalability, ensuring that educational institutions can expand their digital offerings without significant investments in hardware or IT infrastructure (Ibid).

B. Importance of understanding the historical evolution

Understanding the historical evolution of virtual technology in education is crucial for several reasons. First, it provides context for current practices and innovations. By tracing the development of these technologies, educators and technologists can appreciate the incremental advancements and the significant leaps that have shaped educational landscape of contemporary times. This historical perspective helps in recognizing the foundational elements that continue to influence modern educational tools and methodologies. The journey from basic computer-assisted instruction to sophisticated virtual and augmented reality environments reveals how educational goals and technological capabilities have co-evolved. Early innovations, such as the introduction of personal computers and the internet into classrooms, set the stage for more complex developments like online learning platforms and immersive simulations. Each phase in this evolution reflects broader trends in technology adoption, pedagogical theory, and societal needs (Harris et al., 2009). Understanding these phases enables educators to build on proven strategies and avoid past mistakes (Wegerif,2013).

Moreover, examining the historical trajectory of virtual technology in education highlights the role of innovation in addressing educational challenges. For example, the rise of distance learning technologies was significantly accelerated by the need for flexible learning solutions, a trend that was particularly evident during the COVID-19 pandemic. Historical analysis shows how crises and opportunities have driven technological adoption and adaptation, offering lessons on how to navigate future disruptions and leverage emerging technologies effectively (Devlin,2023). Understanding the historical progression emphasizes the significance of ongoing professional development for educators. As new technologies develop, educators must adapt in order to successfully integrate these tools into their teaching practices. Historical awareness fosters a culture of lifelong learning and adaptability among educators, ensuring they remain responsive to technological advancements and changing educational paradigms (Freina & Ott, 2015). Additionally, this historical perspective reveals the socio-economic factors that have influenced the development and adoption of virtual technologies in education. Issues such as digital divide, access to resources, and funding for technological infrastructure have historically impacted how and when schools and institutions adopt new technologies. By understanding these factors, policymakers and educational leaders can devise strategies to mitigate disparities and promote equitable access to technological advancements. Finally, recognizing the historical evolution of virtual technology in education can inspire future innovations (Freina & Ott, 2015). By studying past successes and failures, current developers and educators can identify gaps in existing technologies and explore new possibilities for enhancing the learning experience (Diner, 2015). This forward-thinking approach ensures that the integration of virtual technology in education continues to evolve in ways that are pedagogically sound and responsive to the needs of learners (Harris et al., 2009).

II. EARLY BEGINNINGS: FOUNDATIONS OF VIRTUAL TECHNOLOGY IN EDUCATION

A. Pre-Digital Era: Origins of Virtual Learning Environments

The roots of virtual learning environments (VLEs) extend deep into the history of education, long before the digital age. While modern VLEs rely on digital tools and platforms, early attempts to extend learning beyond the traditional classroom and make education more accessible laid the groundwork for the sophisticated VLEs we see today. These early efforts focused on bridging geographical and temporal barriers to education, providing alternative ways for students to engage with learning. This section explores the pre-digital origins of virtual learning environments, highlighting key developments and innovations that set the stage for the evolution of modern educational technology.

Correspondence Courses

One of the earliest forms of distance education emerged in the mid-19th century with the development of correspondence courses. Sir Isaac Pitman, an English educator and the developer of shorthand, is widely credited with launching the first formal distance education course in 1840. Pitman taught shorthand by mailing assignments to students, who would complete the tasks and return them for feedback. This method allowed learners to study at their own pace and location, removing the geographical constraints of traditional face-to-face education. The success of Pitman's model led to the rapid spread of correspondence courses across different subjects, providing educational opportunities to people who were otherwise unable to attend conventional schools due to distance, work commitments, or financial limitations. As these programs grew, they began to include exams and certifications, further legitimizing distance education as a viable alternative to traditional schooling.

Extension Programs

In the late 19th and early 20th centuries, universities began establishing extension programs to reach adult learners and working professionals who sought to further their education without enrolling in full-time courses. These programs often included evening and weekend classes, as well as correspondence courses, giving individuals more flexibility in their studies. One notable example is the University of Chicago, which established one of the first university extension programs in 1892. This initiative offered a wide variety of courses to students who could not attend the university full-time, making higher education more accessible to a broader population. The goal of extension programs was not only to expand the reach of formal education but also to cater to lifelong learners, emphasizing the importance of continuing education for personal and professional development. These early initiatives laid the foundation for modern online education and demonstrated the growing demand for flexible learning options that cater to diverse student needs (Garrison & Vaughan, 2008; Selwyn, 2011; Selwyn,2020).

Radio and Television

The invention of radio and television in the early 20th century significantly expanded the possibilities of virtual learning environments, offering new ways to deliver educational content to students across wide geographic areas. Educational radio broadcasts began in the 1920s, providing instruction in a variety of subjects, particularly to students in remote or rural areas who lacked access to traditional educational institutions. For instance, the University of Wisconsin began offering instructional radio broadcasts as early as 1921, delivering courses in subjects such as agriculture, history, and literature. These programs aimed to bring high-quality educational content to learners regardless of their location, demonstrating the potential of mass communication technologies to democratize education.

In the 1950s, the advent of television further revolutionized educational delivery. Educational television programs, such as "Sesame Street," which premiered in 1969, played a crucial role in bringing instructional content directly into homes and classrooms. Produced by the Television Workshop of Children (now Sesame Workshop), "Sesame Street" used television as an engaging medium to teach young children basic literacy and numeracy skills, as well as social and emotional lessons. The success of "Sesame Street" demonstrated the power of television as an educational tool capable of reaching millions of children worldwide, and it paved the way for the development of other educational programming aimed at various age groups (Gergen, 2022; Goldman-Segall & Goldman, 2014).

Teaching Machines

In the 1950s and 1960s, the concept of teaching machines, pioneered by B.F. Skinner and other behaviourist psychologists, introduced an early form of interactive learning. Teaching machines were mechanical devices that presented instructional material in a systematic and structured manner, allowing students to receive immediate feedback based on their responses. Skinner's teaching machines were grounded in the principles of operant conditioning, which emphasized reinforcement and repetition as key elements of learning. These devices were an early attempt to tailor education to individual learners, allowing students to progress through material at their own pace based on their unique responses. While the capabilities of teaching machines were limited compared to today's educational technology, they represented a significant step toward more individualized and interactive learning experiences, foreshadowing the personalized learning platforms that would emerge in later decades.

Language Laboratories

Language laboratories, which emerged in the mid-20th century, were another important precursor to modern virtual learning environments. These labs utilized audio equipment to provide language instruction, enabling students to listen to and practice speaking foreign languages in a controlled environment. Language laboratories offered learners the opportunity to study at their own pace, receive immediate feedback on their pronunciation, and practice language skills in a way that was difficult to replicate in a traditional classroom setting. The use of technology in language labs helped pave the way for more advanced language learning tools and software in the digital age, such as Rosetta Stone and Duolingo. These early technological innovations demonstrated the potential of using machines and media to enhance language learning and laid the groundwork for future advancements in educational technology.

B. Early Experiments with Educational Technology

As digital technology began to emerge in the mid-20th century, educational technologists started to explore its potential to transform teaching and learning. The early experiments with instructional technology, though rudimentary by today's standards, laid the foundation for the development of the complex virtual learning environments that exist today. These early initiatives demonstrated that computers and other digital tools could enhance the learning experience, leading to further innovations in educational technology.

Computer-Assisted Instruction (CAI)

Computer-assisted instruction (CAI) emerged in the 1960s and 1970s as a major leap forward in educational technology. Early CAI systems utilized mainframe computers to deliver instructional content and facilitate interactive learning experiences. One of the most notable CAI systems of this era was PLATO (Programmed Logic for Automatic Teaching Operations), which was developed in 1960 at the University of Illinois. PLATO was an innovative system that offered a diverse range of educational content, from basic reading and math skills to advanced scientific and technical subjects. It featured various novel components, such as graphical displays, touch screens, and online forums, to enhance user interaction and collaboration. PLATO was used by schools, universities, and corporate training programs, showcasing the potential of computer technology to revolutionize education. Another significant CAI system was TICCIT (Time-shared, Interactive, Computer-Controlled Information Television), developed by MIT and Brigham Young University in the 1970s. TICCIT focused on providing individualized instruction in subjects like mathematics and language arts, utilizing television monitors and computer terminals to deliver content. The system made learning more accessible and user-friendly for students, demonstrating the potential of multimedia technology to enhance education.

Inception of the Internet

The late 20th century saw the emergence of the internet, which revolutionized educational technology and opened up new possibilities for virtual learning environments. Early adopters of the internet recognized its potential to connect learners and educators across the globe. The creation of the World Wide Web in the early 1990s enabled the development of online educational platforms, allowing students to access course materials, participate in discussions, and complete assignments electronically. The University of Phoenix was a pioneer in online education, offering online degree programs as early as 1989. Similarly, The Open University in the United Kingdom made significant contributions to the development of online education, launching its first internet-based courses in the mid-1990s. These early online programs demonstrated the feasibility and effectiveness of delivering education via the internet, paving the way for the rapid growth of online learning in the 21st century.

Multimedia and Interactive Learning

The 1980s and 1990s saw the rise of multimedia educational tools, such as CD-ROMs and educational software, which combined text, images, sound, and video to create rich, interactive learning experiences. These tools allowed for the development of simulations, virtual labs, and educational games, making learning more engaging and effective (De Freitas & Jarvis, 2006). One of the most notable examples was the development of HyperCard by Apple in 1987. HyperCard enabled educators to design multimedia lessons and activities using a simple, user-friendly interface, making it a powerful tool for creating customized educational content. Educational games also gained popularity during this period, with titles like "The Oregon Trail" and "Math Blaster" combining entertainment with education to provide immersive learning experiences for students. These early educational games laid the foundation for the growing field of educational gaming, which continues to evolve with advancements in technology (Psotka, 2013).

Learning Management Systems (LMS)

The development of learning management systems (LMS) in the late 1990s and early 2000s marked a significant milestone in educational technology. LMS platforms, such as Blackboard and Moodle, provided a centralized system for managing and delivering online courses. These systems offered tools for creating and organizing course content, facilitating communication and collaboration, and tracking student progress (Brown & Mbati, 2015). LMS platforms made it easier for educators to design and deliver online courses, while providing students with a structured and organized learning environment. The widespread adoption of LMS platforms in schools, universities, and corporate training programs highlighted the growing importance of digital technology in education and set the stage for the continued expansion of online learning.

Conclusion

The early beginnings of virtual technology in education were characterized by innovative attempts to overcome the limitations of traditional classroom instruction. From correspondence courses to educational radio and television, and from teaching machines to early computer-assisted instruction, each invention built on the one before it, paving the way for the digital era of education. The introduction of the internet and multimedia technologies in the late twentieth century hastened this progression, paving the way for the sophisticated virtual learning environments that are now standard in modern education. These early experiments and innovations laid a strong foundation for the ongoing development and expansion of virtual technology in education, promising even greater possibilities for the future. The history of virtual learning environments is a testament to the enduring human desire to make education more accessible, flexible, and effective. As technology continues to advance, the potential for virtual learning environments to transform education remains boundless. The early pioneers of educational technology, from Sir Isaac Pitman to the developers of PLATO and beyond, have left a lasting legacy that continues to inspire and shape the future of education (Saler, 2012).

C. Development of Early Virtual Reality Systems and Simulations

The development of early virtual reality (VR) systems and simulations marks a fascinating chapter in the history of technology, blending advancements in computer graphics, human-computer interaction, and immersive experiences (Garris et al., 2002). From the initial conceptualizations in the mid-20th century to the practical implementations in the 1980s and 1990s, the journey of VR has been driven by visionary thinkers, pioneering researchers, and groundbreaking innovations.

Conceptual Foundations

The roots of virtual reality can be traced back to the mid-20th century when visionary thinkers motivated to imagine immersive environments that could replicate or enhance the real world. One of the primary conceptualizations of VR was presented by Morton Heilig, who in the 1950s created the Sensorama, a multi-sensory simulator. The Sensorama was created to provide users an immersive experience by merging stereoscopic 3D images, stereo sound, sensations, and even fragrances. Although it was not interactive in the modern sense, it laid the groundwork for the idea of multisensory virtual experiences.

Early Prototypes and Military Applications

The 1960s and 1970s saw significant advancements in VR technology, largely driven by military research. Ivan Sutherland, often considered as the pioneer of computer graphics, made significant advances to the discipline with the design of the"Sword of Damocles" in 1968. This was the first head-mounted display (HMD) device, with a stereoscopic screen that tracked the user's head motions. Though bulky and primitive by standards of present time, it represented a major leap toward immersive virtual environments. Simultaneously, the U.S. military explored VR for training and simulation purposes. Flight simulators, which had been in development since World War II, began to incorporate computer-generated imagery (CGI) to create more realistic and varied training scenarios. These simulators allowed pilots to practice manoeuvres and experience different flight conditions in a safe and controlled environment, highlighting the practical applications of VR technology.

The Rise of Computer Graphics

A period of rapid development the 1980s and 1990s marked in computer graphics, which in turn propelled the advancement of VR systems. Companies like Atari and NASA were at the forefront of this movement. Research lab of Atari, for instance, developed the first data glove, which could capture hand movements and translate them into digital commands. Ames Research Centre of NASA explored the use of VR for telepresence and remote manipulation of robotic systems. One of the most influential figures during this era was Jaron Lanier, who coined the term "virtual reality" and founded VPL Research in 1985. VPL developed several key technologies, including the Data Glove and the Eyephone, an HMD (Lanier, 2017). Work of Lanier popularized the concept of VR and helped garner interest from both the public and private sectors.

Commercial and Academic Exploration

By the early 1990s, VR had captured the imagination of a broader audience, and both commercial and academic institutions began to explore its potential applications. Virtual reality arcades, such as those featuring the Virtuality system, offered the public a taste of immersive gaming experiences. These systems used HMDs and tracked controllers to allow players to interact with 3D environments in real-time. Academically, universities and research institutions delved into VR for various purposes, from psychological studies to architectural visualization. The University of North Carolina at Chapel Hill, for example, became a leading centre for VR research, developing advanced techniques for rendering and interaction.

Challenges and Limitations

Despite the excitement, early VR systems faced significant challenges. Technical limitations, such as low resolution, high latency, and limited computational power, hindered the realism and responsiveness of virtual environments. Additionally, the cost of VR equipment was prohibitive for many, restricting its accessibility.

Legacy and Impact

The early development of virtual reality systems and simulations laid the foundation for the complicated VR technologies we are having in present. The pioneering efforts of researchers, coupled with advancements in computer graphics and human-computer interaction, have led to the creation of immersive experiences that span entertainment, education, healthcare, and beyond. While the road was fraught with challenges, the visionaries of the past set the stage for the vibrant and rapidly evolving field of virtual reality.

III. PIONEERING INNOVATIONS: ADVANCEMENTS IN VIRTUAL TECHNOLOGY FOR EDUCATION

The integration of virtual technology into education has transformed traditional learning methods, offering students immersive and interactive experiences that enhance engagement and comprehension. This section explores the evolution of virtual technology in education, from the emergence of computer-based learning systems to the introduction of online learning platforms and virtual classrooms (Means etal., 2010).

A. Beginning of Computer-Based Learning Systems

The early stages of virtual technology in education can be traced back to the emergence of computer-based learning systems in the 1960s and 1970s. These systems, which used mainframe computers, enabled students to engage with instructional content in digital form. One of the first instances of computer-based learning was PLATO (Programmed Logic for Automated Teaching Operations), which was created at the University of Illinois in 1960. PLATO was a revolutionary system that provided a variety of educational modules, including mathematics, science, and language arts (Brown et al.,2015). Computer-based learning systems continued to evolve throughout the 1980s and 1990s, with the development of more sophisticated software and hardware. Companies like Apple and IBM played a significant role in advancing the field, introducing computers and software programs specifically designed for educational purposes (Wang & Hannafin, 2005). These advancements paved the way for the integration of multimedia and interactive content into educational materials, setting the stage for the next wave of virtual technology in education.

B. Expansion of Multimedia and Interactive Educational Content

The expansion of multimedia and interactive educational content in the 1990s marked a significant milestone in the evolution of virtual technology for education. The prevalent availability of personal computers and the internet enabled educators to create and distribute digital learning materials that incorporated text, images, audio, and video. CD-ROMs, in particular, became a popular medium for delivering multimedia educational content, offering students a more engaging and dynamic learning experience. One notable example of multimedia educational content from this era is the Encarta encyclopaedia, launched by Microsoft in 1993. Encarta revolutionized the way students accessed and interacted with information, providing a comprehensive multimedia resource that included articles, videos, animations, and interactive maps. Success of Encarta demonstrated the potential of multimedia technology to enhance learning and laid the foundation for the development of more advanced educational tools and platforms.

C. Evolution of Virtual Reality Technology in Educational Settings

The evolution of virtual reality (VR) technology has had a profound impact on education, offering students immersive and interactive experiences that transcend traditional classroom boundaries. VR technology allows students to explore virtual environments, manipulate objects, and engage with complex concepts in ways that are not possible with traditional educational materials. One of the earliest applications of VR in education was the development of virtual reality modelling language (VRML) in the 1990s, which allowed educators to create and share 3D models of objects and environments. This technology paved the way for the development of more advanced VR educational applications, such as virtual laboratories, simulations, and field trips. Today, VR technology is being used in a wide range of educational settings, from K-12 schools to universities and professional training programs. Educators are leveraging VR to create immersive learning experiences that cater to diverse learning styles and abilities, enabling students to visualize abstract concepts, explore complex environments, and collaborate with peers in virtual space.

D. Introduction of Online Learning Platforms and Virtual Classrooms

The emergence of online learning systems and virtual classrooms has transformed how education is given and accessible, especially in the aftermath of the COVID-19 epidemic. Online learning platforms such as Coursera, Udemy, and Khan Academy provide students with access to a diverse choice of courses and instructional resources from anywhere in the globe. These platforms use virtual technology to provide interactive courses, evaluations, and collaborative activities that are similar to those found in traditional classroom settings. Virtual classrooms, on the other hand, offer a more immersive and interactive learning environment by enabling students and teachers to connect in real time via video conferencing and chat tools. Platforms like as Zoom, Google Meet, and Microsoft Teams have become indispensable tools for instructors trying to provide interesting and successful online training (Kirschner & Selinger, 2003).

In conclusion, the amalgamation of virtual technology into education has opened up new possibilities for teaching and learning, offering students immersive and interactive experiences that enhance engagement and comprehension. From computer-based learning systems to online learning platforms and virtual classrooms, virtual technology has transformed the educational environment, making learning more accessible, interesting, and successful for students all over the world.

IV. MAINSTREAM INTEGRATION: VIRTUAL TECHNOLOGY IN CONTEMPORARY EDUCATION

The use of virtual technology into modern education has grown increasingly common, influencing how students learn and instructors teach. This section looks at the evolution of online education and distance learning programs, the use of virtual reality (VR) and augmented reality (AR) in educational settings, the incorporation of gamification and immersive learning experiences, and the impact of virtual technology on teaching methodologies and student engagement (Wu et al., 2013).

A. Growth of Online Education and Distance Learning Programs

Online education and distance learning programs have experienced noteworthy growth in latest years, driven by advancements in technology and the increasing demand for flexible and accessible learning opportunities. Institutions around the world are offering a extensive range of online courses and degree programs, allowing students to learn from anywhere at any time. One of the key advantages of online education is its accessibility. Students who may not have access to traditional educational institutions due to geographic or time constraints can now pursue their education online. This has opened up new opportunities for lifelong learning and professional development (Schlager & Fusco, 2003). Additionally, Online education is flexible and convenient, allowing students to mix their studies with jobs and other responsibilities. Online courses frequently make use of virtual technologies, such as video lectures, online forums, and interactive assignments, to offer interesting and dynamic learning experiences.

B. Adoption of Virtual Reality and Augmented Reality in Educational Contexts

The adoption of virtual reality (VR) and augmented reality (AR) in learning contexts has transformed the way students learn and educators teach. VR and AR technologies offer immersive and interactive experiences that can enhance understanding and engagement. In the field of medicine, VR simulations are being used to train medical students in surgical procedures and patient care. These simulations provide students with realistic scenarios to practice their skills in a safe and controlled environment. In the field of history, AR applications are being used to bring historical events and artifacts to life. Students can explore ancient ruins or witness key moments in history through their smartphones or AR glasses, enhancing their understanding of the past.

C. Integration of Gamification and Immersive Learning Experiences

Gamification and immersive learning experiences are growing popular in education, especially in K-12 settings. Gamification is the use of gaming components like points, badges, and leaderboards to engage and inspire pupils. Immersive learning activities, such as virtual field excursions and simulations, enable students to explore and engage with virtual worlds in ways not feasible with traditional instructional resources. These encounters help improve comprehension and recall of complicated subjects (Bucher, 2017). For example, a history lesson on the Roman Empire could be gamified by allowing students to earn points for correctly answering questions about key events and figures. An immersive experience could then allow students to explore a virtual recreation of ancient Rome, giving them a firsthand glimpse into life in the empire (Jarmon et al., 2009).

D. Impact of Virtual Technology on Teaching Methodologies and Student Engagement

The effect of virtual technology on teaching methodologies and student engagement has been profound. Virtual technology has enabled educators to create more interactive and personalized learning experiences, catering to diverse learning styles and abilities. For educators, virtual technology has opened up new possibilities for teaching. VR simulations, for example, can be used to build realistic scenarios that allow students to apply their knowledge in practical settings. AR applications can provide real-time feedback and guidance, helping students learn at their own pace. For students, virtual technology has made learning more engaging and accessible. Virtual field trips may bring students to distant locales, allowing them to discover new cultures and settings. Gamified classes may make learning more enjoyable and rewarding, encouraging students to remain interested and focused.

Conclusion

The mainstream integration of virtual technology into contemporary education has revolutionized the way students learn and educators teach. From the growth of online education and distance learning programs to the adoption of VR and AR in educational contexts, virtual technology has opened up new possibilities for teaching and learning. By integrating gamification and immersive learning experiences, educators can create more engaging and personalized learning experiences that cater to the diverse needs of students. Overall, the impact of virtual technology on teaching methodologies and student engagement has been profound, shaping the future of education in exciting and innovative ways.

V. CHALLENGES AND OPPORTUNITIES: NAVIGATING THE FUTURE OF VIRTUAL TECHNOLOGY IN EDUCATION

As virtual technology becomes increasingly integrated into education systems around the world, it offers a myriad of opportunities for innovation, transformation, and advancement. However, the expansion of virtual learning also presents several challenges that need to be carefully addressed. Educators, policymakers, and learners are at a crossroads, where the need to balance the benefits of technological advancement with the ethical, logistical, and social concerns of implementing these tools has become paramount. This section explores key issues such as accessibility, equity, ethical considerations, the potential advantages and limitations of virtual technology, and the future trends shaping the landscape of virtual education. By examining both the opportunities and the obstacles, we can gain a clearer understanding of the path forward in utilizing virtual technology to enhance education on a global scale.

A. Accessibility and Equity Issues in Virtual Education

One of the foremost challenges associated with integrating virtual technology into education is ensuring that all students, regardless of their socio-economic background, geographic location, or personal circumstances, have equal access to these tools. For students in rural, low-income, or underserved communities, access to reliable internet connections, up-to-date devices, and technical support can be substantial barriers. Without these essential resources, virtual education becomes difficult or even impossible, exacerbating existing educational inequalities. Equity concerns extend beyond mere access to technology. There is also a gap in the quality of virtual learning experiences offered across different schools, districts, and regions. Well-funded institutions may have the financial means to invest in advanced virtual platforms, tools, and educator training, whereas schools with limited resources may struggle to provide even the most basic virtual learning environments. These disparities can lead to a significant gap in educational outcomes, with students in under-resourced schools receiving suboptimal virtual education compared to their peers in wealthier districts.

B. Ethical Considerations in the Use of Virtual Technology in Learning

The increased use of virtual technology in education raises significant ethical considerations that must be addressed to ensure responsible use. One of the primary ethical concerns involves student privacy and data security. Virtual learning environments collect a vast amount of data on student behavior, performance, and interaction patterns. While this data can be useful for improving educational outcomes, it also raises questions about how the information is stored, used, and protected. Data privacy becomes even more concerning when considering the growing use of artificial intelligence and machine learning algorithms that analyze student data to personalize learning experiences. Who has access to this data, and how it is being utilized, remains a critical question. There are also concerns about whether students and their families are fully aware of the extent to which their data is being tracked and whether they have given informed consent.

In addition to privacy, there are ethical concerns surrounding the potential for virtual technology to be used for surveillance and monitoring of students. Some virtual platforms have built-in monitoring tools that allow educators to track student engagement, monitor behavior, and even observe students through their webcams during virtual classes or exams. While these tools can help ensure academic integrity and keep students on task, they also raise significant concerns about student autonomy, freedom, and trust.

C. Potential Benefits and Limitations of Virtual Technology in Education

The integration of virtual technology in education offers numerous benefits that have the potential to enhance the learning experience for students at all levels. One of the most significant advantages is the ability to create more engaging and interactive learning environments. Virtual technology, including simulations, games, and multimedia content, can make complex concepts more accessible and help students develop critical thinking and problem-solving skills in ways that traditional classroom methods may not. Moreover, virtual technology provides opportunities for personalized learning, allowing educators to tailor instruction to meet the individual needs and learning styles of each student. This can be particularly beneficial for students who require additional support or those who excel and need more challenging material. By adapting to the pace and preferences of the learner, virtual technology can improve student engagement, motivation, and outcomes. However, despite these benefits, there are also limitations to virtual technology in education. Not all students thrive in virtual learning environments, and some may struggle with the lack of face-to-face interaction with teachers and peers. The absence of social interaction and hands-on learning experiences can be a significant drawback for students who learn best through collaborative or tactile methods. Additionally, the effectiveness of virtual education is often dependent on external factors, such as access to reliable internet and suitable devices. Students who do not have these resources may find themselves at a disadvantage, further exacerbating educational inequalities.

Furthermore, virtual technology can sometimes lead to a more passive learning experience if not implemented thoughtfully. For example, merely watching video lectures or clicking through online materials may not provide the same depth of learning as active participation in classroom discussions or hands-on activities. To maximize the benefits of virtual technology and mitigate its limitations, educators should consider adopting a blended learning approach, combining virtual and traditional teaching methods to provide a more balanced and comprehensive educational experience. By doing so, students can benefit from the flexibility and personalization of virtual learning while still engaging in face-to-face interactions and hands-on experiences when appropriate.

D. Future Trends and Directions in Virtual Education Research and Practice

As virtual technology continues to evolve, several trends are likely to shape the future of education. One of the most promising developments is the increasing use of immersive technologies, such as virtual reality (VR) and augmented reality (AR). These technologies have the potential to revolutionize the way students learn by creating realistic, interactive simulations that allow them to engage with content in a more hands-on and experiential manner. For example, VR can be used to take students on virtual field trips to historical sites or provide them with simulated lab experiences in subjects like biology or chemistry. In addition to immersive technologies, there is also a growing emphasis on personalized learning. Virtual platforms that use artificial intelligence and data analytics to customize educational experiences for individual learners are becoming more prevalent. This trend aligns with the broader shift toward student-cantered education, where the focus is on meeting the unique needs of each student rather than following a one-size-fits-all approach. Personalized learning has the potential to improve student outcomes by providing tailored support, resources, and challenges based on each student's strengths and weaknesses. Another important trend is the increasing recognition of the need for digital literacy and citizenship education. As students spend more time in virtual learning environments, it becomes essential to teach them how to navigate the digital world responsibly. This includes understanding online safety, recognizing misinformation, practicing ethical online behavior, and developing critical thinking skills for evaluating digital content. Educators are placing a growing emphasis on these skills to ensure that students are not only proficient in using technology but also prepared to handle the ethical and practical challenges of the digital age. In conclusion, while virtual technology offers immense potential to transform education, it also presents significant challenges that must be addressed. By focusing on issues of accessibility, equity, ethics, and innovation, educators and policymakers can navigate the future of virtual technology in education in a way that ensures all students have access to high-quality, engaging, and effective learning experiences.

VI. CASE STUDIES: EXEMPLARS OF VIRTUAL TECHNOLOGY IN EDUCATION

This section presents case studies that illustrate the diverse applications and benefits of virtual technology in education. From virtual reality simulations for medical education to online learning platforms for K-12 education, these case studies showcase how virtual technology is transforming the way students learn and educators teach.

A. Case Study 1: Virtual Reality Simulations for Medical Education

Virtual reality (VR) simulations have revolutionized medical education by providing students with realistic and immersive learning experiences that simulate clinical environments. One notable example is the use of VR simulations to train medical students in surgical procedures. Companies like Osso VR and Precision OS offer VR simulations that allow students to practice surgeries in a virtual operating room, providing a safe and controlled environment to develop and refine their skills. These simulations not only improve students' surgical skills but also enhance their understanding of anatomy and physiology. By allowing students to interact with virtual patients and medical equipment, VR simulations help bridge the gap between theory and practice, enabling students to apply their knowledge in a realistic setting. Another application of VR in medical education is the use of simulations to train students in patient care and communication skills. SimX, for example, offers VR scenarios that simulate interactions with virtual patients, allowing students to practice empathy, communication, and decision-making in a realistic and immersive environment.

B. Case Study 2: Online Learning Platforms for K-12 Education

Online learning platforms have transformed K-12 education by providing students with access to a wide range of educational resources and opportunities. One notable example is Khan Academy, which offers a comprehensive library of video lessons, practice exercises, and assessments across various subjects and grade levels.

Interactive lessons of Khan Academy and personalized learning features allow students to learn at their own pace and track their progress, making learning more engaging and effective (Reeves & Hedberg, 2003). Additionally, Khan Academy provides teachers with tools to monitor students' progress and tailor instruction to meet individual learning needs. Another example of an online learning platform for K-12 education is Google Classroom, which provides teachers with a digital platform to manage assignments, communicate with students, and collaborate with colleagues. Google Classroom's integration with other Google services, such as Google Docs and Google Drive, allows for seamless sharing and collaboration on assignments and projects.

C. Case Study 3: Virtual Laboratories for Science Education

Virtual laboratories have transformed science education by providing students with hands-on learning experiences that simulate real laboratory environments. One notable example is Labster, which offers a library of virtual labs covering a wide range of scientific disciplines, including biology, chemistry, and physics. Virtual labs of Labster allow students to conduct experiments, analyze data, and draw conclusions in a realistic and immersive environment. By providing students with access to virtual labs, Labster enhances their understanding of scientific concepts and processes, while also promoting critical thinking and problem-solving skills. Another application of virtual laboratories is the use of simulations to teach complex scientific concepts. For example, PhET Interactive Simulations offers a collection of interactive simulations that allow students to explore physics, chemistry, biology, and earth science concepts in a virtual environment.

D. Case Study 4: Augmented Reality Applications in Language Learning

Augmented reality (AR) applications have transformed language learning by providing students with immersive and interactive experiences that enhance their language skills and cultural understanding. One notable example is the use of AR applications to teach vocabulary and grammar. Apps like Mondley AR and Hello Talk use AR technology to superimpose virtual objects and characters into the real world, creating a fun and engaging learning environment. These AR applications allow students to interact with virtual objects and characters in real-time, providing contextualized learning experiences that enhance their understanding and retention of language concepts (Brown & Mbati, 2015). By combining visual, auditory, and kinaesthetic learning modalities, AR applications make language learning more engaging and effective. Another application of AR in language learning is the use of AR-enhanced textbooks and materials. For example, publishers like Pearson and Cambridge University Press are integrating AR technology into their textbooks, allowing students to access additional multimedia content, such as videos, audio clips, and interactive exercises, that enhance their learning experience.

Conclusion

The case studies presented in this section highlight the diverse applications and benefits of virtual technology in education. From virtual reality simulations for medical education to online learning platforms for K-12 education, these case studies showcase how virtual technology is transforming the way students learn and educators teach. By providing students with realistic and immersive learning experiences, virtual technology is revolutionizing education and opening up new possibilities for teaching and learning.

A. Recap of Key Points and Insights from the Chapter

Throughout this chapter, we have explored the historical evolution of virtual technology in education, highlighting key advancements, case studies, and implications for the future. Here are some key points and insights:

Emergence of Computer-Based Learning Systems: The development of computer-based learning systems in the 1960s and 1970s laid the foundation for the integration of technology into education. These systems, such as PLATO, offered interactive and multimedia learning experiences.

Expansion of Multimedia and Interactive Educational Content: The 1990s saw a significant expansion of multimedia and interactive educational content, with the introduction of CD-ROMs and platforms like Encarta. These technologies enhanced learning by providing students with engaging and dynamic educational materials.

Evolution of Virtual Reality Technology: The evolution of virtual reality (VR) technology has transformed education by providing students with immersive and interactive learning experiences. VR simulations for medical education, virtual laboratories for science education, and AR applications for language learning are examples of how VR technology is being used to enhance education (Song et al., 2023).

Introduction of Online Learning Platforms: Online learning platforms have transformed education by giving students access to a diverse set of educational resources and possibilities. Platforms like as Khan Academy and Google Classroom have made education more accessible and interesting for students all around the world.

B. Reflections on the Historical Evolution of Virtual Technology in Education

The historical evolution of virtual technology in education reflects a continuous quest to enhance the teaching and learning process. From the early experiments with computer-based learning systems to the sophisticated VR simulations and online learning platforms of today, educators and technologists have sought to leverage technology to improve educational outcomes. One of the key insights from this evolution is the importance of immersive and interactive experiences in education (George & Wooden, 2023). Virtual technology has the unique ability to transport students to different environments and contexts, allowing them to explore and learn in ways that were previously unimaginable. This immersive nature of virtual technology has the potential to significantly enhance student engagement and understanding, particularly in subjects that are traditionally challenging or abstract. Another reflection is the democratizing effect of virtual technology on education. Online learning platforms and virtual classrooms have made education more accessible to students around the world, breaking down barriers of time and space. This democratization of education has the potential to empower learners from diverse backgrounds and regions, opening up new opportunities for personal and professional growth.

C. Implications for Future Research, Practice, and Policy

The evolution of virtual technology in education has several implications for future research, practice, and policy:

Research: Future research should continue to explore the effectiveness of virtual technology in education and identify best practices for integrating virtual technology into teaching and learning. Research should also focus on addressing issues of equity and accessibility to ensure that all students have access to virtual learning experiences.

Practice: Educators should embrace virtual technology as a tool to enhance their teaching practices and engage students in new and innovative ways. Educators should also receive training and support to effectively integrate virtual technology into their classrooms.

Policy: Policymakers should support the integration of virtual technology into education by investing in infrastructure, providing funding for research and development, and creating policies that promote equitable access to virtual learning experiences.

D. Closing Remarks on the Transformative Potential of Virtual Technology in Shaping the Future of Education

In conclusion, virtual technology has the transformative potential to reshape the future of education. By providing immersive and interactive learning experiences, virtual technology has the power to engage students, enhance understanding, and democratize access to education. As we continue to explore the possibilities of virtual technology in education, it is essential to remember that technology is a tool, and its effectiveness ultimately depends on how it is used. By embracing virtual technology thoughtfully and purposefully, we can create a future where education is more engaging, accessible, and effective for all learners.

REFERENCES

Azuma, R. T. (1997). A survey of augmented reality. *Presence (Cambridge, Mass.)*, 6(4), 355–385. DOI: 10.1162/pres.1997.6.4.355

Brown, T. H., & Mbati, L. S. (2015). Mobile learning: Moving past the myths and embracing the opportunities. *International Review of Research in Open and Distance Learning*, 16(2), 115–135. DOI: 10.19173/irrodl.v16i2.2071

Bucher, J. (2017). *Storytelling for virtual reality: Methods and principles for crafting immersive narratives*. Routledge. DOI: 10.4324/9781315210308

Cuban, L. (2001). *Oversold and underused: Computers in the classroom*. Harvard University Press. DOI: 10.4159/9780674030107

De Freitas, S., & Jarvis, S. (2006). *A framework for developing serious games to meet learner needs. Interservice/Industry Training, Simulation & Education Conference*. I/ITSEC.

Dede, C. (2009). Immersive interfaces for engagement and learning. *Science*, 323(5910), 66–69. DOI: 10.1126/science.1167311 PMID: 19119219

Devlin, M. (2023). *2035 AND BEYOND. A GUIDE TO THRIVING IN THE FUTURE WORKPLACE.: Unleash Your Potential in a Futuristic Career Landscape*. Virtual Worlds, Skills Mastery, and Success. Little Fish Big Impact.

Diner, H. R. (2015). *Roads taken: The great Jewish migrations to the new world and the peddlers who forged the way*. Yale University Press. DOI: 10.12987/yale/9780300178647.001.0001

Ercan, T. (2010). Effective use of cloud computing in educational institutions. *Procedia: Social and Behavioral Sciences*, 2(2), 938–942. DOI: 10.1016/j.sbspro.2010.03.130

Freina, L., & Ott, M. (2015). A literature review on immersive virtual reality in education: State of the art and perspectives. eLearning & Software for Education (eLSE), (1), 133-141.

Garris, R., Ahlers, R., & Driskell, J. E. (2002). Games, motivation, and learning: A research and practice model. *Simulation & Gaming*, 33(4), 441–467. DOI: 10.1177/1046878102238607

Garrison, D. R., & Vaughan, N. D. (2008). *Blended learning in higher education: Framework, principles, and guidelines*. John Wiley & Sons.

George, B., & Wooden, O. (2023). Managing the strategic transformation of higher education through artificial intelligence. *Administrative Sciences*, 13(9), 196. DOI: 10.3390/admsci13090196

Gergen, K. J. (2022). An invitation to social construction: Co-creating the future.

Goldman-Segall, R., & Goldman, R. (2014). *Points of viewing children's thinking*. Psychology Press. DOI: 10.4324/9781315805818

Harris, J., Mishra, P., & Koehler, M. (2009). Teachers' technological pedagogical content knowledge and learning activity types: Curriculum-based technology integration reframed. *Journal of Research on Technology in Education*, 41(4), 393–416. DOI: 10.1080/15391523.2009.10782536

Jarmon, L., Traphagan, T., Mayrath, M., & Trivedi, A. (2009). Virtual world teaching, experiential learning, and assessment: An interdisciplinary communication course in Second Life. *Computers & Education*, 53(1), 169–182. DOI: 10.1016/j.compedu.2009.01.010

Kirschner, P., & Selinger, M. (2003). The state of affairs of teacher education with respect to information and communications technology. *Technology, Pedagogy and Education*, 12(1), 5–17. DOI: 10.1080/14759390300200143

Lanier, J. (2017). *Dawn of the new everything: A journey through virtual reality*. Random House.

Means, B., Toyama, Y., Murphy, R., Bakia, M., & Jones, K. (2010). *Evaluation of evidence-based practices in online learning: A meta-analysis and review of online learning studies*. US Department of Education.

Milgram, P., & Kishino, F. (1994). A taxonomy of mixed reality visual displays. *IEICE Transactions on Information and Systems*, 77(12), 1321–1329.

Psotka, J. (2013). Educational games and virtual reality as disruptive technologies. *Journal of Educational Technology & Society*, 16(2), 69–80.

Reeves, T. C., & Hedberg, J. G. (2003). Interactive learning systems evaluation. *Educational Technology*.

Saler, M. (2012). *As if: Modern enchantment and the literary prehistory of virtual reality*. Oxford University Press.

Schlager, M. S., & Fusco, J. (2003). Teacher professional development, technology, and communities of practice: Are we putting the cart before the horse? *The Information Society*, 19(3), 203–220. DOI: 10.1080/01972240309464

Selwyn, N. (2011). *Education and technology: Key issues and debates*. Bloomsbury Publishing.

Selwyn, N. (2020). *Telling tales on technology: Qualitative studies of technology and education*. Routledge. DOI: 10.4324/9781138368736

Song, C., Shin, S. Y., & Shin, K. S. (2023). Optimizing Foreign Language Learning in Virtual Reality: A Comprehensive Theoretical Framework Based on Constructivism and Cognitive Load Theory (VR-CCL). *Applied Sciences (Basel, Switzerland)*, 13(23), 12557. DOI: 10.3390/app132312557

Squire, K., & Jenkins, H. (2003). Harnessing the power of games in education. *Insight (American Society of Ophthalmic Registered Nurses)*, 3(1), 5–33. PMID: 12703249

Wang, F., & Hannafin, M. J. (2005). Design-based research and technology-enhanced learning environments. *Educational Technology Research and Development*, 53(4), 5–23. DOI: 10.1007/BF02504682

Wegerif, R. (2013). *Dialogic: Education for the internet age*. Routledge. DOI: 10.4324/9780203111222

Wu, H. K., Lee, S. W. Y., Chang, H. Y., & Liang, J. C. (2013). Current status, opportunities and challenges of augmented reality in education. *Computers & Education*, 62, 41–49. DOI: 10.1016/j.compedu.2012.10.024

KEY TERMS AND DEFINITIONS

Augmented Reality (AR): Technology that overlays digital information onto the real world, enhancing educational experiences by adding interactive elements to real-life settings.

Computer-Assisted Learning: Early educational programs that used computers to supplement teaching, marking the beginning the role of virtual technology in education.

Distance Learning Platforms: Online education tools that facilitate learning outside traditional classrooms, such as video conferencing and e-learning systems.

Educational Games: Digital or virtual games created for educational purposes, which enhance learning through interactive, game-based experiences.

Immersive Learning: An approach to education that deeply engages students in the learning material through interactive and engaging digital technologies.

Literature Review: A comprehensive survey of scholarly articles, books, and reports to gather insights on a specific topic, employed in this chapter to analyze the history of virtual technology in education.

Pedagogical Approaches: Methods and practices of teaching, which have evolved with the integration of virtual technologies to enhance learning outcomes.

Secondary Research: Research method that involves reviewing existing literature and data, which this chapter uses to explore the evolution of virtual technology in education.

Simulations: Virtual environments that replicate real-world scenarios for training or educational purposes, often used in fields like medicine, engineering, and social sciences.

Sociocultural Factors: Social and cultural influences that affect the adoption of technology in education, such as societal attitudes toward technology and access to resources.

Virtual Reality (VR): A technology that immerses users in a fully digital environment, often used in education for creating experiential learning opportunities.

Virtual Technology: Technology that enables digital simulations and interactions, including VR and AR, which transform traditional educational practices into interactive experiences.

Compilation of References

Abbad, M. M. M. (2021). Using the UTAUT model to understand students' usage of e-learning systems in developing countries. *Education and Information Technologies*, 26(6), 7205–7224. DOI: 10.1007/s10639-021-10573-5 PMID: 34025204

Abbas, A., Ar, A. Y., & Hosseini, S. (2024). A global perspective of government initiatives to support higher education during the COVID-19 pandemic: A systematic review of literature. *Research in Globalization*, 8, 100202. DOI: 10.1016/j.resglo.2024.100202

Abdellatif, H. J. (2014). ERP in higher education: a deeper look on developing countries. *2014 International Conference on Education Technologies and Computers (ICETC)*, 73–78. DOI: 10.1109/ICETC.2014.6998905

Abdulqader, Z. R., Abdulqader, D. M., Ahmed, O. M., Ismael, H. R., Ahmed, H., & Haji, L. (2024). *Responsible AI Development for Sustainable Enterprises A Review of Integrating Ethical AI with IoT and Enterprise Systems. 03*(02), 129–156.

Abou-Khalil, V., Helou, S., Khalifé, E., Chen, M. A., Majumdar, R., & Ogata, H. (2021). Emergency online learning in low-resource settings: Effective student engagement strategies. *Education Sciences*, 11(1), 1–18. DOI: 10.3390/educsci11010024

About | buX. (n.d.). Retrieved June 30, 2024, from https://bux-home.bracu.ac.bd/about

Ackermann, E. (2001). Piaget's constructivism, Papert's constructionism: What's the difference. *Future of Learning Group Publication*, 5(3), 438.

Adams, R. L. (2016). Five reasons why virtual reality is a game-changer. *Forbes*. Retrieved from https://www.forbes.com/sites/robertadams/2

Adedoyin, O. B., & Soykan, E. (2023). Covid-19 pandemic and online learning: The challenges and opportunities. *Interactive Learning Environments*, 31(2), 863–875. DOI: 10.1080/10494820.2020.1813180

Agbo, F. J., Sanusi, I. T., Oyelere, S. S., & Suhonen, J. (2021). Application of Virtual Reality in Computer Science Education: A Systemic Review Based on Bibliometric and Content Analysis Methods. *Education Sciences*, 11(142), 1–23. DOI: 10.3390/educsci11030142

Ahmed, M. T. (2021). Online education in Bangladesh during Covid-19: An empirical study. *The International Journal of Social Sciences (Islamabad)*, 4(5), 172–188.

Ahmed, M., Hasan, M., & Haque, A. (2021). Exploring the Challenges and Opportunities of E-Learning Platforms in Bangladesh. *Asian Journal of Multidisciplinary Studies*, 9(1), 111–120.

Ahmed, S. A., Hegazy, N. N., Abdel Malak, H. W., Cliff Kayser, W.III, Elrafie, N. M., Hassanien, M., Al-Hayani, A. A., El Saadany, S. A., AI-Youbi, A. O., & Shehata, M. H. (2020). Model for utilizing distance learning post COVID-19 using (PACT)™ a cross sectional qualitative study. *BMC Medical Education*, 20(1), 1–13, 400. DOI: 10.1186/s12909-020-02311-1 PMID: 33138818

Akbıyık, N. (2019, October*).The effects of using Arduino microcontroller in programming education on high school student's self-efficacy and problem solving skills.In* SETSCI-Conference Proceedings (pp. 99-105).

Akçayır, M., & Akçayır, G. (2017). Advantages and challenges associated with augmented reality for education: A systematic review of the literature. *Educational Research Review*, 20, 1–11. DOI: 10.1016/j.edurev.2016.11.002

Akpaku, E., Arku, Z., & Boateng, S. (2023). Global perspective of the effects of digital financial inclusion and ICT intensity on socio-economic development. *International Journal of Business Forecasting and Marketing Intelligence*, 8(1), 13–34. DOI: 10.1504/IJBFMI.2023.127699

Akter, A., Munira, S., & Amin, K. (2017). Key influencing factors for adopting e-learning platforms of private University Students' in Bangladesh. *Journal of Business and Economic Development*, 2, 94–98.

Al Amri, A., Osman, M., & Musawi, A. A. (2020). The effectiveness of a 3D virtual reality learning environment (3D-VRLE) on Omani eighth grade students' achievement and motivation towards physics learning. *International Journal of Emerging Technologies in Learning*, 15(5), 1–16. DOI: 10.3991/ijet.v15i05.11890

Al Lily, A. E.. (2020). Academic domains as political battlegrounds: A global enquiry by ninety-nine academics in the fields of education and technology. *Information Development*, 36(2), 198–223.

Al Lily, A. E., Ismail, A. F., Abunasser, F. M., Alqahtani, R., & Alabdulkareem, S. A. (2020). Distance education as a response to pandemics: Coronavirus and Arab culture. *Technology in Society*, 63, 101317. DOI: 10.1016/j.techsoc.2020.101317 PMID: 32836570

Al-Emran, M. A. Al-Sharafi, & K. Shaalan (Eds.), *International Conference on Information Systems and Intelligent Applications* (pp. 227–242). Cham: Springer International Publishing. https://doi.org/DOI: 10.1007/978-3-031-16865-9_19

Aleven, V., Rowe, J., Huang, Y., & Mitrovic, A. (2023). Domain modeling for AIED systems with connections to modeling student knowledge: A review. *Handbook of Artificial Intelligence in Education*, 127-169.

Alfadil, M. (2020). Effectiveness of virtual reality games in foreign language vocabulary acquisition. *Computers & Education*, 153, 103893. Advance online publication. DOI: 10.1016/j.compedu.2020.103893

Alfalah, S. F. (2018). Perceptions toward adopting virtual reality as a teaching aid in information technology. *Education and Information Technologies*, 23(6), 2633–2653. DOI: 10.1007/s10639-018-9734-2

Algerafi, M., Zhou, Y., Oubibi, M., & Wijaya, T. (2023). Unlocking the potential: A comprehensive evaluation of augmented reality and virtual reality in education. *Electronics (Basel)*, 12(18), 3953. Advance online publication. DOI: 10.3390/electronics12183953

Ali, A. F., Abdullah, R. H., Hassan, A. A., Abdullahi, H. O., & Mohamed, M. M. (2024). COVID-19 Pandemic Impact on E-Learning Adoption and Its Utilization at Higher Education: A Comparative Analysis of Institutions and Students' Perspectives. *Ingénierie Des Systèmes d Information*, 29(2), 447–457. DOI: 10.18280/isi.290206

Alimisis, D. (2013). Educational robotics: Open questions and new challenges. *Themes in Science and Technology Education*, 6(1), 63–71.

Allcoat, D., & von Mühlenen, A. (2018). Learning in virtual reality: Efects on performance, emotion and engagement. *Research in Learning Technology*, 26(0). Advance online publication. DOI: 10.25304/rlt.v26.2140

Almaiah, M. A., Al-Khasawneh, A., & Althunibat, A. (2020). Exploring the critical challenges and factors influencing the e-learning system usage during COVID-19 pandemic. *Education and Information Technologies*, 25(6), 5261–5280. DOI: 10.1007/s10639-020-10219-y PMID: 32837229

Al-Maroof, R. S., Alhumaid, K., Akour, I., & Salloum, S. (2021). Factors That Affect E-Learning Platforms after the Spread of COVID-19: Post Acceptance Study. *Data*, 6(5), 49. DOI: 10.3390/data6050049

Al-Maroof, R. S., Salloum, S. A., Hassanien, A. E., & Shaalan, K. (2023). Fear from COVID-19 and technology adoption: The impact of Google Meet during Coronavirus pandemic. *Interactive Learning Environments*, 31(3), 1293–1308. DOI: 10.1080/10494820.2020.1830121

Almazova, N., Krylova, E., Rubtsova, A., & Odinokaya, M. (2020). Challenges and opportunities for Russian higher education amid COVID-19: Teachers' perspective. *Education Sciences*, 10(12), 1–11. DOI: 10.3390/educsci10120368

AlMuhayfith, S., & Shaiti, H. (2020). The impact of enterprise resource planning on business performance: With the discussion on its relationship with open innovation. *Journal of Open Innovation*, 6(3), 87. DOI: 10.3390/joitmc6030087

Almutairi, A., Naeem, M. A., & Weber, G. (2021). Assessing User Satisfaction of Current Enterprise Systems and Their Adaptability from the Perspective of Top Management. *IEEE Access : Practical Innovations, Open Solutions*, 9, 153442–153455. DOI: 10.1109/ACCESS.2021.3127950

Alotaibi, Y., & Liu, F. (2017). Survey of business process management: Challenges and solutions. *Enterprise Information Systems*, 11(8), 1119–1153. DOI: 10.1080/17517575.2016.1161238

Alsaffar, M. J. (2021). Virtual reality software as preparation tools for oral presentations: Perceptions from the classroom. *Theory and Practice in Language Studies*, 11(10), 1146–1160. DOI: 10.17507/tpls.1110.02

Al-Samarraie, H., Ghazal, S., & Saeed, N. (2021). Mobile Learning Applications: A Systematic Literature Review. *Education Sciences*, 11(1), 12.

Alshawmar, M. (2021). A review of the applications of affordance theory in mHealth app research. *Proceedings of the Annual Hawaii International Conference on System Sciences, 2020-January*, 3595–3604. DOI: 10.24251/HICSS.2021.437

Alsoliman, B. S. H. (2022, July). Virtual robotics in education: The experience of eighth grade students in STEM. [). Frontiers Media SA.]. *Frontiers in Education*, 7, 950766. DOI: 10.3389/feduc.2022.950766

Altamony, H., Al-Salti, Z., Gharaibeh, A., & Elyas, T. (2016). The relationship between change management strategy and successful enterprise resource planning (ERP) implementations: A theoretical perspective. *International Journal of Business Management and Economic Research*, 7(4), 690–703.

Amin, S., Uddin, M., Mashwani, W., Alarood, A., Alzahrani, A., & Alzahrani, A. (2023). Developing a personalized e-learning and MOOC recommender system in IoT-enabled smart education. *IEEE Access : Practical Innovations, Open Solutions*, 11, 136437–136455. DOI: 10.1109/ACCESS.2023.3336676

Amirabdollahian, F., Livatino, S., Vahedi, B., Gudipati, R., Sheen, P., Gawrie-Mohan, S., & Vasdev, N. (2018). Prevalence of haptic feedback in robot-mediated surgery: A systematic review of literature. *Journal of Robotic Surgery*, 12(1), 11–25. DOI: 10.1007/s11701-017-0763-4 PMID: 29196867

Aral, S., Brynjolfsson, E., Gu, C., Wang, H., & Wu, D. J. (2024). Understanding the returns from integrated enterprise systems: The impacts of agile and phased implementation strategies. *Management Information Systems Quarterly*, 48(2), 749–774. DOI: 10.25300/MISQ/2023/17420

Arena, F., Collotta, M., Pau, G., & Termine, F. (2022). An overview of augmented reality. *Computers*, 11(28), 1–15. DOI: 10.3390/computers11020028

Arican, M., & Özçakir, B. (2021). Facilitating the development of Preservice teachers' proportional reasoning in geometric similarity problems using augmented reality activities. *Education and Information Technologies*, 26(2), 2327–2353. DOI: 10.1007/s10639-020-10359-1

Arksey, H., & O'Malley, L. (2005). Scoping studies: Towards a methodological framework. *International Journal of Social Research Methodology*, 8(1), 19–32. DOI: 10.1080/1364557032000119616

Arribathi, A. H., Suwarto, , Miftakhu Rosyad, A., Budiarto, M., Supriyanti, D., & Mulyati, . (2021). An analysis of student learning anxiety during the COVID-19 pandemic: A study in higher education. *The Journal of Continuing Higher Education*, 69(3), 192–205. DOI: 10.1080/07377363.2020.1847971

Aschauer, A., Reisner-Kollmann, I., & Wolfartsberger, J. (2021). Creating an open-source augmented reality remote support tool for industry: Challenges and learnings. *Procedia Computer Science*, 180, 269–279. DOI: 10.1016/j.procs.2021.01.164

Ashtari, N., Bunt, A., McGrenere, J., Nebeling, M., & Chilana, P. K. (2020, April). Creating augmented and virtual reality applications: Current practices, challenges, and opportunities. In *Proceedings of the 2020 CHI conference on human factors in computing systems* (pp. 1-13). DOI: 10.1145/3313831.3376722

Atieh, A. M., Cooke, K. O., & Osiyevskyy, O. (2023). The role of intelligent manufacturing systems in the implementation of Industry 4.0 by small and medium enterprises in developing countries. *Engineering Reports*, 5(3), 1–21. DOI: 10.1002/eng2.12578

Atmatzidou, S., & Demetriadis, S. (2016). Advancing students' computational thinking skills through educational robotics: A study on age and gender relevant differences. *Robotics and Autonomous Systems*, 75, 661–670. DOI: 10.1016/j.robot.2015.10.008

Ausburn, L., Martens, J., Washington, A., Steele, D., & Washburn, E. (2009). A cross-case analysis of gender issues in desktop virtual reality learning environments. *Journal of Industrial Teacher Education*, 46, 51–89. https://ir.library.illinoisstate.edu/jste/vol46/iss3/6

Avila-Garzon, C., Bacca-Acosta, J., Duarte, J., & Betancourt, J. (2021). Augmented Reality in Education: An Overview of Twenty-Five Years of Research. *Contemporary Educational Technology*, 13(3), 1–30. DOI: 10.30935/cedtech/10865

Aydın, İ., Toptaş, B., Güner Demir, T. U. Ğ. B. A., & Erdemli, Ö. (2019). Being an expatriate teacher in Turkish private schools: Opinions on education, teaching, and administration processes. *Education in Science*, 44(200). Advance online publication. DOI: 10.15390/EB.2019.8105

Azuma, R. T. (1997). A survey of augmented reality. *Presence (Cambridge, Mass.)*, 6(4), 355–385. DOI: 10.1162/pres.1997.6.4.355

Azuma, R. T. (1999). The challenge of making augmented reality work outdoors. In Ohta, Y., & Tamura, H. (Eds.), *Mixed reality: Merging real and virtual worlds* (pp. 379–390). Springer. DOI: 10.1007/978-3-642-87512-0_21

Babalola, A., Manu, P., Cheung, C., Yunusa-Kaltungo, A., & Bartolo, P. (2023). A systematic review of the application of immersive technologies for safety and health management in the construction sector. *Journal of Safety Research*, 85, 66–85. DOI: 10.1016/j.jsr.2023.01.007 PMID: 37330902

Bacca-Acosta, J., Tejada, J., Fabregat, R., Kinshuk, , & Guevara, J. (2022). Scaffolding in immersive virtual reality environments for learning English: An eye tracking study. *Educational Technology Research and Development*, 70(1), 1–24. DOI: 10.1007/s11423-021-10068-7

Bacsich, P., Bastiaens, T., Bristow, S. F., Op de Beeck, I., Reynolds, S., & Schreurs, B. (2009). *Reviewing the Virtual Campus* from The Rise of Large-Scale E-learning Initiatives Worldwide http://revica.europace.org/Re.ViCa%20Online%20Handbook.pdf

Bahloul, M., Trivedi, R., Cardo-Miota, J., Papadimitriou, C., Efthymiou, V., Nouri, A., & Khadem, S. (2024). Analysis of barriers and key enablers toward citizen ESS successful integration. *Journal of Energy Storage, 86*(PA), 111166. DOI: 10.1016/j.est.2024.111166

Baihakki, M., & Qutayan, S. (2023). Ethical issues of artificial intelligence (AI) in the healthcare. *Journal of Science, Technology and Innovation Policy*. https://doi.org/DOI: 10.11113/jostip.v9n1.129

Barletta, V., Caivano, D., Gigante, D., & Ragone, A. (2023). A rapid review of responsible AI frameworks: How to guide the development of ethical AI. *Proceedings of the 27th International Conference on Evaluation and Assessment in Software Engineering*. https://doi.org/DOI: 10.1145/3593434.3593478

Baroroh, D. K., & Agarwal, A. (2022). Immersive Technologies in Indonesia Faces "New Normal" COVID-19. *International Journal of Technology*, 13(3), 633–642. DOI: 10.14716/ijtech.v13i3.5220

Barrow, J., Hurst, W., Edman, J., Ariesen, N., & Krampe, C. (2024). Virtual reality for biochemistry education: The cellular factory. *Education and Information Technologies*, 29(2), 1647–1672. DOI: 10.1007/s10639-023-11826-1 PMID: 37361784

Barteit, S., Lanfermann, L., Bärnighausen, T., Neuhann, F., & Beiersmann, C. (2021). Augmented, mixed, and virtual reality-based head-mounted devices for medical education: Systematic review. *JMIR Serious Games*, 9(3), e29080. DOI: 10.2196/29080 PMID: 34255668

Başaran, B. (2018*). Investigation of the effect of integration of arduino to electrical experiments and preparation of experiment reports in poster type on the attitudes of science teacher candidates towards physics laboratories, technology and information and communication tecnology* (Unpublished Master's thesis). Kocaeli University, Institute of Science and Technology, Kocaeli.

Bassyouni, Z., & Elhajj, I. (2021). Augmented reality meets artificial intelligence in robotics: A systematic review. *Frontiers in Robotics and AI*, 8, 724798. Advance online publication. DOI: 10.3389/frobt.2021.724798 PMID: 34631805

Bastida, L., Sillaurren, S., Loizaga, E., Tomé, E., & Moya, A. (2024). Exploring human emotions: A virtual reality-based experimental approach integrating physiological and facial analysis. *Multimodal Technologies and Interaction*, 8(6), 47. DOI: 10.3390/mti8060047

Bates, A. W. (2015). *Teaching in a digital age: Guidelines for designing teaching and learning*. BCcampus. Retrieved from https://openlibrary-repo.ecampusontario.ca/jspui/handle/123456789/276

Bayazıt, T. (2018). Event related potentials (ERP). *Journal of Medical Clinics*, 1(1), 59–65. https://dergipark.org.tr/tr/pub/atk/issue/38771/451155

Bazavan, L. C., Roibu, H., Petcu, F. B., Cismaru, S. I., & George, B. N. (2021, September). Virtual reality and augmented reality in education. In 2021 30th Annual Conference of the European Association for Education in Electrical and Information Engineering (EAEEIE) (pp. 1-4). IEEE. DOI: 10.1109/EAEEIE50507.2021.9531005

Beck, J. E., & Woolf, B. P. (2000, May). Reasoning from Data Rather than Theory. In FLAIRS (pp. 34-39).

Becker, S. A., Cummins, M., Davis, A., Freeman, A., Hall, C. G., & Ananthanarayanan, V. (2017). *NMC horizon report: 2017 higher education edition*. The New Media Consortium.

Bédi, L., Bradley, K., Friðriksdóttir, H., Garðarsdóttir, H., Thouësny, S., & Whelpton, M. J. (2022) (Eds.). *Intelligent call, granular systems, and learner data: short papers from EUROCALL 2022*. Netútgáfa: Research-publishing.net. https://ritaskra.arnastofnun.is/media/skraning_pdf/Short_Papers_from_EUROCALL_2022.pdf

Beeck, I. op de, & van Petegem, W. (2013). *Virtual mobility: An alternative or complement to physical mobility?* ERACON 2011 & 2012 Dual Year Proceedings. https://lirias.kuleuven.be/retrieve/237431

Beelen, J., & Jones, E. (2015). Redefining internationalization at home. In Curai, A., Matei, L., Pricopie, R., Salmi, J., & Scott, P. (Eds.), *The European higher education area: Between critical reflections and future policies* (pp. 67–80). Springer. DOI: 10.1007/978-3-319-20877-0_5

Beilenson, J., & Markowitz, D. (2021). Virtual reality and the psychology of climate change. *ScienceDirect*, 9(3), 23–64.

Being-mobile project network. Retrieved from http://www.being-mobile.net/

Bendall, R. C., Lambert, S., Galpin, A., Marrow, L. P., & Cassidy, S. (2019). Psychophysiological indices of cognitive style: A triangulated study incorporating neuroimaging, eye-tracking, psychometric and behavioral measures. *Personality and Individual Differences*, 144, 68–78. DOI: 10.1016/j.paid.2019.02.034

Benitti, F. B. V. (2012). Exploring the educational potential of robotics in schools: A systematic review. *Computers & Education*, 58(3), 978–988. DOI: 10.1016/j.compedu.2011.10.006

Berg, H. E. (2017). Will intelligent machine learning revolutionize orthopedic imaging? *Acta Orthopaedica*, 88(6), 577–577. DOI: 10.1080/17453674.2017.1387732 PMID: 29106336

Bergstra, J., & Bengio, Y. (2012). Random search for hyper-parameter optimization. *Journal of Machine Learning Research*, 13(2).

Berland, M., & Wilensky, U. (2015). Comparing virtual and physical robotics environments for supporting complex systems and computational thinking. *Journal of Science Education and Technology*, 24(5), 628–647. DOI: 10.1007/s10956-015-9552-x

Bessen, J. (2018). *AI and jobs: The role of demand* (No. w24235). National Bureau of Economic Research.

Bhanu Prasad, P., Padmaja, N. B., Satish Kumar, B., & Aravind, A. (2022). Industry 4.0: Augmented and virtual reality in education. In Kaliraj, P., & Thirupati, D. (Eds.), *Innovating with augmented reality* (pp. 29–52). Auerbach Publications., DOI: 10.1201/9781003175896

Bijnens, H., & Op de Beeck, I. (2006). Virtual Mobility in Europe from Pilot Level Towards Integration in Mainstream Education. *Bridging the gap between business and business schools - Being Mobile* -, (psl. 39-44). Vilnius.

Bijnens, H., Boussemaere, M., & Rajagopal, K. (2006). European Cooperation in Education through Virtual Mobility- A Best Practice Manual, retrieved from https://www.eurashe.eu/library/modernising- phe/mobility/virtual/WG4%20R%20 Virtual%20Mobility%20Best%20Practice%20Manual.pdf

Billinghurst, M. (2021). Grand challenges for augmented reality. *Frontiers in Virtual Reality*, 1–4. doi: 10.3389/frvir.2021.578080

Billinghurst, M., & Duenser, A. (2012). Augmented reality in the classroom. *Computer*, 45(7), 56–63. DOI: 10.1109/MC.2012.111

Biswas, B., Roy, S. K., & Roy, F. (2020, June 13). *Students Perception of Mobile Learning During COVID-19 in Bangladesh: University Student Perspective* [SSRN Scholarly Paper]. Rochester, NY. Retrieved from https://papers.ssrn.com/abstract =3667908

Blazauskas, T., & Gudoniene, D. (2020). Virtual reality and augmented reality in educational programs. In Linda, D. (Ed.), *New perspectives on virtual and augmented reality* (pp. 82–94). Routledge., DOI: 10.4324/9781003001874-6

Blikstein, P., Gomes, J. S., Akiba, H. T., & Schneider, B. (2017). The effect of highly scaffolded versus general instruction on students' exploratory behavior and arousal. *Technology. Knowledge and Learning*, 22(1), 105–128. DOI: 10.1007/s10758-016-9291-y

Blikstein, P., & Wilensky, U. (2007, April). Bifocal modeling: a framework for combining computer modeling, robotics and real-world sensing. In *Annual Meeting of the American Educational Research Association (AERA 2007)*, Chicago, USA.

Board of European Students of Technology (BEST) Educational Commitee. *Virtual Mobility – The educational challenge of the future*. BEST Symposium on Education, 23-29 July 2006, Retrieved from https://www.best.eu.org/download/edu/Bucharest _EoE_report.pdf

Boateng, R. (2016). *Research made easy*. CreateSpace Independent Publishing Platform.

Bocconi, S., Chioccariello, A., Dettori, G., Ferrari, A., Engelhardt, K., Kampylis, P., & Punie, Y. (2016). *Developing computational thinking in compulsory education* (Policy Report). Spain: European Commission

Boekaerts, M. (1997). Self-regulated learning: A new concept embraced by researchers, policy makers, educators, teachers, and students. *Learning and Instruction*, 7(2), 161–186. DOI: 10.1016/S0959-4752(96)00015-1

Boland, B. (2023). *Extended reality vocational training's ability to improve soft skills development and increase equity in the workforce*. AI, Computer Science and Robotics Technology., DOI: 10.5772/acrt.22

Bonetti, F., Warnaby, G., & Quinn, L. (2018). Augmented reality and virtual reality in physical and online retailing: A review, synthesis and research agenda. In *Augmented reality and virtual reality* (pp. 119–132). Springer., DOI: 10.1007/978-3-319-64027-3_9

Boninsegna, A. & Dondi, C. (1998). Humanities Guidelines for the implementation of ODL and a virtual mobility approach in Conventional Universities. DG XXII SOCRATES ODL Programme, Humanities project result.

Bower, M., DeWitt, D., & Lai, J. W. (2020). Reasons associated with preservice teachers' intention to use immersive virtual reality in education. *British Journal of Educational Technology*, 51(6), 2215–2233. DOI: 10.1111/bjet.13009

Bower, M., Howe, C., McCredie, N., Robinson, A., & Grover, D. (2014). Augmented reality in Education cases, places, and potentials. *Educational Media International*, 51(1), 1–15. DOI: 10.1080/09523987.2014.889400

Brandenburg, U., Berghoff, S., & Taboadela, O. (2014). *The Erasmus impact study: Effects of mobility on the skills and employability of students and the internationalisation of higher education institutions*. Publications Office.

Brennan, K., & Resnick, M. (2012, April). New frameworks for studying and assessing the development of computational thinking. In Levine, F. J. (Ed.), *Proceedings of the 2012 Annual Meeting of the American Educational Research Association* (pp. 1-25). Vancouver: The University of British Columbia.

Brey, C. and e-move project partners (2007). EADTU. From Guide to Virtual Mobility. http://145.20.178.4/Portals/0/documents/The_Guide_to_Virtual_Mobility.pdf

Bricken, M. (1991). Virtual Reality Learning Environments: Potentials and challenges. *Computer Graphics*, 25(3), 178–184. DOI: 10.1145/126640.126657

Bright, A., Welcome, N. B., & Arthur, Y. D. (2024). The effect of using technology in teaching and learning mathematics on student's mathematics performance: The mediation effect of students' mathematics interest. *Journal of Mathematics and Science Teacher*, 4(2), em059. DOI: 10.29333/mathsciteacher/14309

Brown, A. (1987). Metacognition, executive control, self-regulation, and other more mysterious mechanisms. *Metacogniton, motivation, and understanding/Lawrence Erlbaum Associates*.

Brown, A. (2019). *Personalized e-learning: The future of education*. Routledge.

Brown, A., & Green, T. (2016). Virtual reality: Low-cost tools and resources for the classroom. *TechTrends*, 60(5), 517–519. DOI: 10.1007/s11528-016-0102-z

Brown, T. H., & Mbati, L. S. (2015). Mobile learning: Moving past the myths and embracing the opportunities. *International Review of Research in Open and Distance Learning*, 16(2), 115–135. DOI: 10.19173/irrodl.v16i2.2071

Bruhn-Zass, E. (2023). Virtual Internationalization as a Concept for Campus-Based and Online and Distance Higher Education. In: Zawacki-Richter, O., Jung, I. (eds) Handbook of Open, Distance and Digital Education. Springer, Singapore. Retrieved from file:///C:/Users/Lenovo/Downloads/978-981-19-2080-6.pdf DOI: 10.1007/978-981-19-2080-6_23

Brynjolfsson, E., & McAfee, A. (2014). *The second machine age: Work, progress, and prosperity in a time of brilliant technologies*. WW Norton & company.

Buchem, I. (2019). Digital Impact: How is International Student and Staff Mobility Changing in Higher Education? Retrieved from https://oeb.global/oeb-insights/digital-impact-how-is-international-student-and-staff-mobility-changing-in-higher-education

Bucher, J. (2017). *Storytelling for virtual reality: Methods and principles for crafting immersive narratives*. Routledge. DOI: 10.4324/9781315210308

Bulling, A., Ward, J. A., Gellersen, H., & Troster, G. (2011). Eye movement analysis for activity recognition using electrooculography. *IEEE Transactions on Pattern Analysis and Machine Intelligence*, 33(4), 741–753. DOI: 10.1109/TPAMI.2010.86 PMID: 20421675

Bunt-Kokhuis, S. G. (1996). 2001). *Academic Pilgrims: Faculty Mobility in the Virtual World.On the Horizon*, 9(1), 1–6. DOI: 10.1108/10748120110803626

Burdea, G., & Coiffet, P. (2003). *Virtual reality technology*. Wiley-Interscience.

Burt, K. B., & Obradovic, J. (2013). The construct of psychophysiological reactivity: Statistical and psychometric issues. *Developmental Review*, 33(1), 29–57. DOI: 10.1016/j.dr.2012.10.002

Bygstad, B., Munkvold, B. E., & Volkoff, O. (2016). Identifying generative mechanisms through affordances: A framework for critical realist data analysis. *Journal of Information Technology*, 31(1), 83–96. DOI: 10.1057/jit.2015.13

Caglar-Ozhan, S., Altun, A., & Ekmekcioglu, E. (2022). Emotional patterns in a simulated virtual classroom supported with an affective recommendation system. *British Journal of Educational Technology*, 53(6), 1724–1749. DOI: 10.1111/bjet.13209

Cahyono, A. N., Sukestiyarno, Y. L., Asikin, M., Ahsan, M. G. K., & Ludwig, M. (2020). Learning Mathematical modelling with augmented reality Mobile Math trails program: How can it work? *Journal on Mathematics Education, 11*(2), 181–192. . 11.2. 10729. 181- 192DOI: 10. 22342/ jme

Cai, S., Liu, E., Shen, Y., Liu, C., Li, S., & Shen, Y. (2020). Probability learning in mathematics using augmented reality: Impact on student's learning gains and attitudes. *Interactive Learning Environments*, 28(5), 560–573. DOI: 10.1080/10494820.2019.1696839

Calabuig-Moreno, F., González-Serrano, M. H., Fombona, J., & García-Tascón, M. (2020). The emergence of technology in physical education: A general bibliometric analysis with a focus on virtual and augmented reality. *Sustainability (Basel)*, 12(7), 2728. DOI: 10.3390/su12072728

Cameron, R. G. (2005). *Mindstorms robolab: Developing science concepts during a problem based learning club (Yayımlanmamış yüksek lisans tezi)*. The University of Toronto.

Campbell, D. (2016). *Augmented reality: The next interface for design and making*. Retrieved August 1, 2024, from https://beyonddesign.typepad.com/posts/2016/10/augmented-reality-the-next-interface-for-design-and-making.html

Campos, E., Hidrogo, I., & Zavala, G. (2022). Impact of virtual reality use on the teaching and learning of vectors. *Frontiers in Education*, 7, 965640. DOI: 10.3389/feduc.2022.965640

Carmigniani, J., & Furht, B. (2011). Augmented reality: An overview. In Furht, B. (Ed.), *Handbook of augmented reality* (pp. 3–46). Springer., DOI: 10.1007/978-1-4614-0064-6_1

Carmigniani, J., Furht, B., Anisetti, M., Ceravolo, P., Damiani, E., & Ivkovic, M. (2011). Augmented reality technologies, systems and applications. *Multimedia Tools and Applications*, 51(1), 341–377. DOI: 10.1007/s11042-010-0660-6

Carr, A., & Beaudry, A. (2023). Effectiveness of in-person and virtual international mobility scholars programme on career and professional development. *Journal of Learning for Development*, 10(3), 333–345. DOI: 10.56059/jl4d.v10i3.722

Casas-Roma, J., & Conesa, J. (2021). *A literature review on artificial intelligence and ethics in online learning*. Intelligent Systems and Learning Data Analytics in Online Education., DOI: 10.1016/B978-0-12-823410-5.00006-1

Cazzolla, A., Lanzilotti, R., Roselli, T., & Rossano, V. (2019). Augmented reality to support education in industry 4.0. In: *18th International Conference on Information Technology Based Higher Education and Training (ITHET)* (pp. 1–5). DOI: DOI: 10.1109/ITHET46829.2019.8937365

Cecotti, H., Huisinga, L., & Peláez, L. G. (2024). Fully immersive learning with virtual reality for assessing students in art history. *Virtual Reality (Waltham Cross)*, 28(33), 1–15. DOI: 10.1007/s10055-023-00920-x

Cerqueira, J. M., Cleto, B., Moura, J. M., Sylla, C., & Ferreira, L. (2023). Potentiating learning through augmented reality and serious games. In Nee, C., & Ong, K. (Eds.), *Springer Handbook of Augmented Reality* (pp. 369–390). Springer., DOI: 10.1007/978-3-030-67822-7_15

Cevikbas, M., Bulut, N., & Kaiser, G. (2023). Exploring the benefits and drawbacks of AR and VR technologies for learners of mathematics: Recent developments. *Systems*, 11(5), 244. DOI: 10.3390/systems11050244

Chan, C. K. Y. (2023). A review of the changes in higher education assessment and grading policy during covid-19. *Assessment & Evaluation in Higher Education*, 48(6), 874–887. DOI: 10.1080/02602938.2022.2140780

Chang, H. Y., Binali, T., Liang, J. C., Chiou, G. L., Cheng, K. H., Lee, S. W. Y., & Tsai, C. C. (2022). Ten years of augmented reality in education: A meta-analysis of (quasi-) experimental studies to investigate the impact. *Computers & Education, 191*, 104641. . compe du. 2022. 104641DOI: 10. 1016/j

Chang, S., & Hwang, G. (2018). Impacts of an augmented reality-based flipped learning guiding approach on students' scientific project performance and perceptions. *Computers & Education*, 125, 226–239. DOI: 10.1016/j.compedu.2018.06.007

Chans, G. M., Orona-Navar, A., Orona-Navar, C., & Sánchez-Rodríguez, E. P. (2023). Higher education in Mexico: The effects and consequences of the COVID-19 pandemic. *Sustainability (Basel)*, 15(12), 1–22, 9476. DOI: 10.3390/su15129476

Chao, L. N.. (2021). Digital literacy and the digital divide: The role of organizational digital citizenship and social support. *Computers in Human Behavior*, 115, 106637.

Chattaraj, D., & Vijayaraghavan, A. P. (2021). Why learning space matters: A script approach to the phenomena of learning in the emergency remote learning scenario. *Journal of Computers in Education*, 8(3), 343–364. DOI: 10.1007/s40692-021-00182-z

Chatterjee, S., Sarker, S., & Valacich, J. S. (2015). The behavioral roots of information systems security: Exploring key factors related to unethical IT use. *Journal of Management Information Systems*, 31(4), 49–87. DOI: 10.1080/07421222.2014.1001257

Checa, D., & Bustillo, A. (2020). A review of immersive virtual reality serious games to enhance learning and training. *Multimedia Tools and Applications*, 79(9–10), 5501–5527. DOI: 10.1007/s11042-019-08348-9

Chen, B., & Denoyelles, A. (2013). Exploring students' mobile learning practices in higher education. *EDUCAUSE Review*, •••, 7.

Chen, C. J. (2009). Theoretical bases for using virtual reality in education. *Themes in Science and Technology Education*, 21, 71–90.

Chen, C. J., & Teh, C. S. (2013). Enhancing an instructional design model for virtual reality-based learning. *Australasian Journal of Educational Technology*, 29(5), 699–714. DOI: 10.14742/ajet.247

Chen, C. J., & Teh, C. S. 2000. An affordable virtual reality technology for constructivist learning environments. *4th Global Chinese Conference on Computers in Education*, 414-421.

Chen, C. J., Yun, H., Lin, K. Y., Chang, Y. S., Lin, H. C., Lin, C. Y., & Hsaio, H. S. (2019). Developing a hands-on activity using virtual reality to help students learn by doing. *Journal of Computer Assisted Learning*, 6(1), 46–60. DOI: 10.1111/jcal.12389

Chen, D. R., Chen, M. Y., Huang, T. C., & Hsu, W. P. (2013). Developing a mobile learning system in augmented reality context. *International Journal of Distributed Sensor Networks*, 9(12), 594627. DOI: 10.1155/2013/594627

Chen, G., Shen, J., Barth-Cohen, L., Jiang, S., Huang, X., & Eltoukhy, M. (2017). Assessing elementary students' computational thinking in everyday reasoning and robotics programming. *Computers & Education*, 109, 162–175. DOI: 10.1016/j.compedu.2017.03.001

Cheng, K., & Tsai, C. (2020). Students' motivational beliefs and strategies, perceived immersion and attitudes towards science learning with immersive virtual reality: A partial least squares analysis. *British Journal of Educational Technology*, 51(5), 2139–2158. DOI: 10.1111/bjet.12956

Chen, L.. (2022). The impacts of e-learning on social interactions among students: A systematic review. *Computers & Education*, 174, 104345.

Chen, Y. (2019). Effect of mobile augmented reality on learning performance, motivation, and math anxiety in a math course. *Journal of Educational Computing Research*, 57(7), 1695–1722. DOI: 10.1177/0735633119854036

Chen, Y. L., & Hsu, C. C. (2020). Self-regulated mobile game-based English learning in a virtual reality environment. *Computers & Education*, 154, 103910. DOI: 10.1016/j.compedu.2020.103910

Chen, Z., & Klahr, D. (1999). All other things being equal: Acquisition and transfer of the control of variables strategy. *Child Development*, 70(5), 1098–1120. DOI: 10.1111/1467-8624.00081 PMID: 10546337

Chimakurthi, V. N. S. S. (2018). Emerging of Virtual Reality (VR) Technology in Education and Training. *Asian Journal of Humanity. Art and Literature*, 5(2), 157–166. Advance online publication. DOI: 10.18034/ajhal.v5i2.606

Chofreh, A. G., Goni, F. A., & Klemeš, J. J. (2018). Sustainable enterprise resource planning systems implementation: A framework development. *Journal of Cleaner Production*, 198, 1345–1354. DOI: 10.1016/j.jclepro.2018.07.096

Chookaew, S., Howimanporn, S., Sootkaneung, W., & Wongwatkit, C. (2017). Motivating Pre-service Teachers with Augmented Reality to Developing Instructional Materials through Project-Based Learning Approach. *2017 6th IIAI International Congress on Advanced Applied Informatics (IIAI-AAI)*, 780–784. https://doi.org/ DOI: 10.1109/IIAI-AAI.2017.106

Chowdhary, K. R. (2020). Introducing artificial intelligence. In *Fundamentals of Artificial Intelligence* (pp. 1–23). Springer.

Chowdhury, N. H., Hossain, M. S., & Ahmed, S. (2019). Challenges of E-Learning in Higher Education: Evidence from Bangladesh. *International Journal of Education and Development Using Information and Communication Technology*, 15(3), 144–155.

Cihon, P., Kleinaltenkamp, M., Schuett, J., & Baum, S. (2021). AI certification: Advancing ethical practice by reducing information asymmetries. *IEEE Transactions on Technology and Society*, 2(4), 200–209. DOI: 10.1109/TTS.2021.3077595

Cipresso, P., Giglioli, C., Raya, A., & Riva, G. (2018). The past, present, and future of virtual and augmented reality research: A network and cluster analysis of the literature. *Frontiers in Psychology*, 9, 2086. DOI: 10.3389/fpsyg.2018.02086

Clark, R. E. (2006). Reconsidering the research on learning from media. *Review of Educational Research*, 53(4), 445–459. DOI: 10.3102/00346543053004445

Clark-Wilson, A., Robutti, O., & Sinclair, N. (2023). *The mathematics teacher in the digital era. International Research on Professional Learning and Practice, 16.* Springer Nature.

Clements, M. A. K., Bishop, A. J., Keitel, C., Kilpatrick, J., & Leung, F. K. S. (Eds.). (2013). *Third international handbook of mathematics education*. Springer., DOI: 10.1007/978-1-4614-4684-2

Cochrane, T. (2016). Mobile VR in education: From the fringe to the mainstream. *International Journal of Mobile and Blended Learning*, 8(4), 44–60. DOI: 10.4018/IJMBL.2016100104

Collins, A., & Halverson, R. (2018). *Rethinking Education in the Age of Technology: The Digital Revolution and Schooling in America.* Teachers College Press.

Commision of the European communities. *Green paper: Promoting the learning mobility of young people*, 2009.07.08, Brussels, COM (2009) 329 final, Retrieved from https://ec.europa.eu/education/lifelong-learningpolicy/doc/mobility/com329_en.pdf

Cooper, N., Millela, F., Cant, I., White, M., & Meyer, G. (2021). Transfer of training—Virtual reality training with augmented multisensory cues improves user experience during training and task performance in the real world. *PLoS One*, 16(3), e0248225. Advance online publication. DOI: 10.1371/journal.pone.0248225 PMID: 33760859

Crespi, F., Amarasinghe, I., Vujovic, M., & Hernández-Leo, D. (2022, July). *Estimating orchestration load in CSCL situations using EDA. In 2022.international conference on advanced learning technologies (icalt).* IEEE.

Crisan, C., Geraniou, E., & Hodgen, J. (2023). Educational technologies in mathematics education. *The Royal Society: Mathematical Futures Programme*

Cross, A. (2023). The evolution of virtual reality: Exploring the past, present and future. *Forbes.*https://www.forbes.com/sites/forbesbusinesscouncil/2023/11/09/the- evolution-of-virtual-reality-exploring-the-past-present-and- future/?sh=eaba2d72b70f

Crowther, P., Joris, M., Otten, M., Nilsson, B., Teekens, H., & Wächter, B. (2000). *Internationalisationat home. A position paper*. EAIE.

Cruz-Neira, C., Fernández, M., & Portalés, C. (2018). Virtual Reality and Games. *Multimodal Technologies and Interaction*, 2018(2), 8. DOI: 10.3390/mti2010008

Cs2n.org. (2020). The CS-STEM Network. Retrieved from https://www.cs2n.org/

Cuban, L. (2001). *Oversold and underused: Computers in the classroom.* Harvard University Press. DOI: 10.4159/9780674030107

Cukurbasi, B., & Kiyici, M. (2021). Instructional design and instructional effectiveness in virtual classrooms: Research trends and challenges: Instructional design and instructional effectiveness in virtual classroom. *Australasian Journal of Educational Technology*, 37(6), 156–174. DOI: 10.14742/ajet.6882

D'Mello, S., & Kory, J. (2015). A review and meta-analysis of multimodal affect detection systems. *ACM Computing Surveys*, 47(3), 1–36. DOI: 10.1145/2682899

Daltoè, T., Ruth-Herbein, E., Brucker, B., Jaekel, A. K., Trautwein, U., Fauth, B., Gerjets, P., & Göllner, R. (2024). Immersive insights: Unveiling the impact of 360-degree videos on preservice teachers' classroom observation experiences and teaching-quality ratings. *Computers & Education*, 213, 104976. Advance online publication. DOI: 10.1016/j.compedu.2023.104976

Dambrin, C., & Grall, B. (2023). Long-term alterations of ERP systems: Lasting through relinquishment and regeneration. *Qualitative Research in Accounting & Management*, 20(2), 169–200. DOI: 10.1108/QRAM-03-2022-0043

Dash, B., Sharma, P., & Ali, A. (2022). Federated learning for privacy-preserving: A review of PII data analysis in fintech. *International Journal of Software Engineering and Its Applications*, 13(4), 1–13. Advance online publication. DOI: 10.5121/ijsea.2022.13401

Dauksien, E., Teresevicien, M., & Volungevicien, A. (2009), Teacher Virtual Mobility for research and practice, retrieved from https://www.researchgate.net/publication/317549364_TEACHER_VIRTUAL_MOBILITY_FOR_RESEARCH_AND_PRACTICE

Dauksiene, E. (2013). Virtual mobility in higher education. Doctoral dissertation, VytautasMagnus University. http://talpykla.elaba.lt/elaba-edora/objects/elaba:1915200/datastreams/MAIN/content

Davenport, T. H. (1998). Putting the enterprise into the enterprise system. *Harvard Business Review*, 76(4), 121–131. PMID: 10181586

Davis, S., Nesbitt, K., & Nalivaiko, E. (2015). Comparing the onset of cybersickness using the Oculus Rift and two virtual roller coasters. In *Proceedings of the 11th Australasian Conference on Interactive Entertainment (IE)*, Sydney, Australia; Volume 27, p. 30.

Davydova, D., Gil'vanov, R., Kukushkina, Y., & Romanova, I. (2023). Immersive Technologies in Higher Education. *Proceedings of Petersburg Transport University*, 20(1), 120–132. DOI: 10.20295/1815-588X-2023-1-120-132

Dawson, S. (2006). A study of the relationship between student communication interaction and sense of community. *The Internet and Higher Education*, 9(3), 153–162. DOI: 10.1016/j.iheduc.2006.06.007

De Freitas, S. I. (2006). Using games and simulations for supporting learning. *Learning, Media and Technology*, 31(4), 343–358. DOI: 10.1080/17439880601021967

De Freitas, S., & Jarvis, S. (2006). *A framework for developing serious games to meet learner needs. Interservice/Industry Training, Simulation & Education Conference.* I/ITSEC.

Dede, C. (2009). Immersive interfaces for engagement and learning. *Science*, 323(5910), 66–69. DOI: 10.1126/science.1167311 PMID: 19119219

DeLone, W., & McLean, E. (2003). The DeLone and McLean Model of Information Systems Success: A Ten-Year Update. *Journal of Management Information Systems*, 19(4), 9–30. DOI: 10.1080/07421222.2003.11045748

Deng, R., & Gao, Y. (2023). A review of eye tracking research on video-based learning. *Education and Information Technologies*, 28(6), 7671–7702. DOI: 10.1007/s10639-022-11486-7 PMID: 36532792

Devlin, M. (2023). *2035 AND BEYOND. A GUIDE TO THRIVING IN THE FUTURE WORKPLACE.: Unleash Your Potential in a Futuristic Career Landscape.* Virtual Worlds, Skills Mastery, and Success. Little Fish Big Impact.

Dewey, J. (1916). *Democracy and education.* The Free Press.

Dhimolea, T. K., Kaplan-Rakowski, R., & Lin, L. (2021). A systematic review of research on high-immersion virtual reality for language learning. *SSRN.* https://dx.doi.org/DOI: 10.2139/ssrn3863724

Di Mitri, D., Schneider, J., Specht, M., & Drachsler, H. (2018). From signals to knowledge: A conceptual model for multimodal learning analytics. *Journal of Computer Assisted Learning*, 34(4), 338–349. DOI: 10.1111/jcal.12288

Díaz, L. M., Hernández, C. M., Ortiz, A. V., & Gaytán-Lugo, L. S. (2019, October). *Tinkercad and Codeblocks in a summer course: An attempt to explain observed engagement and enthusiasm. In 2019 IEEE Blocks and Beyond Workshop (B&B).* IEEE.

Diegmann, P., Schmidt-Kraepelin, M., Van den Eynden, S. & Basten, D. (2015): Benefits of augmented reality in educational environments-A systematic literature review. *Wirtschaftsinformatik Proceedings*, 103.

Diner, H. R. (2015). *Roads taken: The great Jewish migrations to the new world and the peddlers who forged the way.* Yale University Press. DOI: 10.12987/yale/9780300178647.001.0001

Dini, A. A., Sæbo, Ø., & Wahid, F. (2018). Affordances and effects of introducing social media within eParticipation—Findings from government-initiated Indonesian project. *The Electronic Journal on Information Systems in Developing Countries*, 84(4), 1–14. DOI: 10.1002/isd2.12035

Doğan, M. (2021). *Artificial intelligence and free will: The possibility of artificial free will.* TRT Academy.

Dogar, A. A., Shah, I., Ali, S. W., & Ijaz, A. (2020). Constraints to online teaching in institutes of higher education during pandemic COVID-19: A case study of CUI, Abbottabad Pakistan. *Revista Romaneasca Pentru Educatie Multidimensionala, 12*(2Sup1), 12-24. https://doi.org/DOI: 10.18662/rrem/12.2Sup1/285

Donkin, R., & Kynn, M. (2021). Does the learning space matter? An evaluation of active learning in a purpose-built technology-rich collaboration studio. *Australasian Journal of Educational Technology*, 37(1), 133–146. DOI: 10.14742/ajet.5872

Drigas, A., Mitsea, E., & Skianis, C. (2021). Neuro-Linguistic Programming, Positive Psychology & VR in Special Education. *Scientific Electronic Archives*, 15(1), 31–39. DOI: 10.36560/15120221497

Duan, S. X., Deng, H., & Wibowo, S. (2024). Technology Affordances for Enhancing Job Performance in Digital Work. *Journal of Computer Information Systems*, 64(2), 232–244. DOI: 10.1080/08874417.2023.2188497

Dubovi, I. (2022). Cognitive and emotional engagement while learning with VR: The perspective of multimodal methodology. *Computers & Education*, 183, 104495. DOI: 10.1016/j.compedu.2022.104495

Duchowski, A., & Duchowski, A. (2007). Eye tracking techniques. *Eye tracking methodology. Theory into Practice*, •••, 51–59.

Dunleavy, M., & Dede, C. (2014). Augmented reality teaching and learning. In Spector, J. M., Merrill, M. D., Elen, J., & Bishop, M. J. (Eds.), *Handbookof research on educational communications and technology* (pp. 735–745). Springer. DOI: 10.1007/978-1-4614-3185-5_59

Dunleavy, M., Dede, C., & Mitchell, R. (2009). Affordances and limitations of immersive participatory augmented reality simulations for teaching and learning. *Journal of Science Education and Technology*, 18(1), 7–22. DOI: 10.1007/s10956-008-9119-1

Du, W., & Liang, R. Y. (2024). Teachers' Continued VR Technology Usage Intention: An Application of the UTAUT2 Model. *SAGE Open*, 14(1), 1–17. DOI: 10.1177/21582440231220112

Dvareckienė, V., Kurilovas, E., & Jevsikova, T. (2016). Virtual, augmented, and mixed reality-based learning systems: Personalisation framework. *Lietuvos Matematikos Rinkinys, 57*(B), 1–6. https://doi.org/DOI: 10.15388/LMR.B.2016.01

EADTU network. (2007). from an operational conception of virtual mobility:http://www.eadtu.nl/e-move/

Effah, J. (2019). *Digital Process Virtualization : An Action Case Study in Ghana John Effah To cite this version : HAL Id : hal-02294701 Brightening Physical University Admission through Digital Process Virtualization : An Action Case Study in.*

Effah, J. (2012). Mobilizing culture for e-business in developing countries: An actor network theory account. *The Electronic Journal on Information Systems in Developing Countries*, 52(1), 1–18. DOI: 10.1002/j.1681-4835.2012.tb00370.x

Eguchi, A. (2010, March). What is educational robotics? Theories behind it and practical implementation. In D. Gibson (Ed.), *In Society for Information Technology & Teacher Education İnternational Conference* (pp. 4006-4014). Waynesville: Association for the Advancement of Computing in Education Foss, A., Wilcoxen, C., & Rasmus, J. (2019). The academic and behavioral implications of robotics in the classroom: An elementary case study. *Technology & Innovation, 20*(3), 321-332. DOI: 10.21300/20.3.2019.321

Ekman, P., Friesen, W. V., & Hager, J. C. (2002). The Facial Action Coding System. *Research Nexus division of Network Information Research Corporation.*

Elearningeurope.info. (2009). *Glossary: Virtual Mobility*. Retrieved fromhttp://www.elearningeuropa.info/main/index.php?page=glossary&abc=V

Elfirdoussi, S., Lachgar, M., Kabaili, H., Rochdi, A., Goujdami, D., & El Firdoussi, L. (2020). Assessing distance learning in higher education during the COVID-19 pandemic. *Education Research International*, 2020, 1–13, 8890633. DOI: 10.1155/2020/8890633

Eltahir, M. E. (2019). E-Learning in developing countries: Is it a panacea? A case study of Sudan. *IEEE Access : Practical Innovations, Open Solutions*, 7, 97784–97792. DOI: 10.1109/ACCESS.2019.2930411

Elumalai, K. V., Sankar, J. P., Kalaichelvi, R., John, J. A., Menon, N., Alqahtani, M. S. M., & Abumelha, M. A. (2021). Factors affecting the quality of e-learning during the COVID-19 pandemic from the perspective of higher education students. *Journal of Information Technology Education*, 19, 731–753. DOI: 10.28945/4628

EMEU - Engineering Mobility in Europe Erasmus+ Project. (2019). Virtual Mobility Manual. Retrieved from https://www.emeu.eu/media/1478/final_emeu4all_virtualmobility-manualmarch-2019.pdf

Engelbrecht, J., Llinares, S., & Borba, M. C. (2020). Transformation of the mathematics classroom with the internet. *ZDM Mathematics Education*, 52(5), 825–841. DOI: 10.1007/s11858-020-01176-4

Ercan, T. (2010). Effective use of cloud computing in educational institutions. *Procedia: Social and Behavioral Sciences*, 2(2), 938–942. DOI: 10.1016/j.sbspro.2010.03.130

Esposito, C., Siciliano, M., Persico, C., Carotenuto, M., Ricci, M., & Russo, M. (2023). Virtual reality and foreign language learning (short paper). *ICERI2023 Proceedings*. https://doi.org/DOI: 10.21125/iceri.2023.2364

Estapa, A., & Nadolny, L. (2015). The effect of an augmented reality enhanced mathematics lesson on student achievement and motivation. *Journal of STEM Education: Innovations and Research*, 16(3), 40–48.

EuroPACE. (2010). Virtual mobility, Retrieved from http://www.europace.org/interest3.php

European Commission Glossary on the Lifelong Learning Programme 2007-2013. http://ec.europa.eu/education/programmes/llp/guide/glossary_en.html#117

Faek, R. (2023) Shifting Tides: Exploring the rise of virtual student mobility in international education, retrieved from https://wenr.wes.org/2023/11/shifting-tides-exploring-the-rise-of-virtual-student-mobility-in-international-education

Fernández-Batanero, J. M., Montenegro-Rueda, M., Fernández-Cerero, J., & Tadeu, P. (2022). Online education in higher education: Emerging solutions in crisis times. *Heliyon*, 8(8), 1–9. DOI: 10.1016/j.heliyon.2022.e10139 PMID: 35965985

Fiani, B., De Stefano, F., Kondilis, A., Covarrubias, C., Reier, L., & Sarhadi, K. (2020). Virtual reality in neurosurgery:"can you see it?"–a review of the current applications and future potential. *World Neurosurgery*, 141, 291–298. DOI: 10.1016/j.wneu.2020.06.066 PMID: 32561486

Fianu, E. E., Arku, Z., Affum, E. K., Boateng, S., & Boateng, F. (2022, November). Investigating Zoom Continuance Use by Ghanaian University Students in Blended Learning Arrangements in the Post-Covid Era. In *Proceedings of the 2022 6th International Conference on Education and E-Learning* (pp. 95-100). DOI: 10.1145/3578837.3578851

Fianu, E., Boateng, S., & Arku, Z. (2024). Revisiting Automated Essay Scoring via the GPT Artificial Intelligence Chatbot: A Mixed Methods Study. In *Reshaping Learning with Next Generation Educational Technologies* (pp. 116–135). IGI Global. DOI: 10.4018/979-8-3693-1310-7.ch008

Fitzpatrick, G., Ellingsen, G., & Bellotti, V. (2017). Instrumenting the interaction: HCI and the sense of measurement. *InProceedings of the 2017 CHI Conference on Human Factors in Computing Systems.* DOI: 10.1145/3025453.3025709

Fox-Turnbull, W., & Snape, P. (2011). Technology teacher education through a constructivist approach. *Journal of Design and Technology Education*, 16(2), 45–56.

Freina, L., & Ott, M. (2015). A literature review on immersive virtual reality in education: State of the art and perspectives. eLearning & Software for Education (eLSE), (1), 133-141.

Fuente, A. A., & Menendez Ferreira, R. (2011). *TeaCamp Scenario and Barriers.* WP7: TeaCamp Exploitation, TeaCamp project.

Fuente, A. A. J., Fueyo, A., & Menendez, R. (2011). Virtual Mobility Tools. In Tereseviien, M., Volungeviien, A., & Daukšien, E. (Eds.), *Virtual mobility forteachers and students.* Vytautas Magnus University.

Furse, J. S. (2019). Measuring the self-efficacy of students participating in VEX robotics competitions (Doctoral dissertation, Utah State University).

Gaebel, M., Zhang, T., Stoeber, H. & Morrisroe, A. (2021). Digitally enhanced learning and teaching in European higher education institutions. European University Association absl.

Gandedkar, N. H., Wong, M. T., & Darendeliler, M. A. (2021, June). Role of virtual reality (VR), augmented reality (AR) and artificial intelligence (AI) in tertiary education and research of orthodontics: An insight. [). WB Saunders.]. *Seminars in Orthodontics*, 27(2), 69–77. DOI: 10.1053/j.sodo.2021.05.003

Gantasala, V. P., Gantasala, S. B., Al Tawil, T. N. E., & Prasad, P. (2022). Quality of learning experience, student satisfaction and perceived overall experience in the COVID-19 context. *Journal of Applied Research in Higher Education*, 14(1), 507–520. DOI: 10.1108/JARHE-12-2020-0440

Garcia, R. (2022). *Homemade augmented reality sandbox brings mountains and more to this Kansas elementary school.* Retrieved August 1, 2024, from https://www.cjonline.com/story/news/education/2022/04/12/augmented-virtual-reality-ar-sandbox-kansas-school-silver-lake-elementary/9500440002/

García-A, L., Álvarez-González, B., & Ruiz-Corbella, M. (2008). *NetActive: Basesand proposals for good practices in virtual academic mobility (an intercontinentalapproach).* UNED. Glossary: Virtual Mobility. Elearningeurope.info, Retrieved from https://www.elearningeuropa.info/main/index.php?page=glossary&abc=V

Garcia, M. (2020). Addressing the digital divide: Strategies for equitable access to e-learning. *Journal of Educational Technology & Society*, 23(3), 179–191.

Garcia, M. (2020). Collaborative Approaches to Online Education: Lessons from the COVID-19 Pandemic. *Higher Education Research & Development*, 39(5), 987–995.

García-Morales, V. J., Garrido-Moreno, A., & Martín-Rojas, R. (2021). The transformation of higher education after the COVID disruption: Emerging challenges in an online learning scenario. *Frontiers in Psychology*, 12, 1–6, 616059. DOI: 10.3389/fpsyg.2021.616059 PMID: 33643144

García-Tudela, P. A., & Marín-Marín, J. A. (2023). Use of Arduino in Primary Education: A systematic review. *Education Sciences*, 13(2), 134. DOI: 10.3390/educsci13020134

Gardhouse, K., & Anderson, A. K. (2013). Objective and subjective measurements in affective science. In *The Cambridge handbook of human affective neuroscience* (pp. 57-81). DOI: 10.1017/CBO9780511843716.005

Garrison, D. R., & Vaughan, N. D. (2008). *Blended learning in higher education: Framework, principles, and guidelines*. John Wiley & Sons.

Garris, R., Ahlers, R., & Driskell, J. E. (2002). Games, motivation, and learning: A research and practice model. *Simulation & Gaming*, 33(4), 441–467. DOI: 10.1177/1046878102238607

Garzon, J., & Acevedo, J. (2019). Meta-analysis of the impact of augmented reality on students' learning gains. *Educational Research Review*, 27, 244–260. DOI: 10.1016/j.edurev.2019.04.001

Gelles, L. A., Lord, S. M., Hoople, G. D., Chen, D. A., & Mejia, J. A. (2020). Compassionate flexibility and self-discipline: Student adaptation to emergency remote teaching in an integrated engineering energy course during COVID-19. *Education Sciences*, 10(11), 1–23. DOI: 10.3390/educsci10110304

Geng, J., Chai, C. S., Jong, M. S. Y., & Luk, E. T. H. (2021). Understanding the pedagogical potential of Interactive Spherical Video-based Virtual Reality from the teachers' perspective through the ACE framework. *Interactive Learning Environments*, 29(4), 618–633. DOI: 10.1080/10494820.2019.1593200

George, B., & Wooden, O. (2023). Managing the strategic transformation of higher education through artificial intelligence. *Administrative Sciences*, 13(9), 196. DOI: 10.3390/admsci13090196

Gerecke, U., & Wagner, B. (2007). The challenges and benefits of using robots in higher education. *Intelligent Automation & Soft Computing*, 13(1), 29–43. DOI: 10.1080/10798587.2007.10642948

Gergen, K. J. (2022). An invitation to social construction: Co-creating the future.

Geris, A., Cukurbasi, B., Kilinc, M., & Teke, O. (2024). Balancing performance and comfort in virtual reality: A study of FPS, latency, and batch values. *Software, Practice & Experience*, 54(12), 2336–2348. Advance online publication. DOI: 10.1002/spe.3356

Geriş, A., & Özdener, N. (2024). Design, development, and evaluation of educational virtual reality environment: EVRECA. *Educational Technology Research and Development*, 72(2), 915–945. DOI: 10.1007/s11423-023-10303-3

Ghaednia, H., Fourman, M., Lans, A., Detels, K., Dijkstra, H., Lloyd, S., Sweeney, A., Oosterhoff, J., & Schwab, J. (2021). Augmented and virtual reality in spine surgery, current applications and future potentials. *The Spine Journal*, 21(10), 1617–1625. Advance online publication. DOI: 10.1016/j.spinee.2021.03.018 PMID: 33774210

Giannakos, M. N., Sharma, K., Pappas, I. O., Kostakos, V., & Velloso, E. (2019). Multimodal data as a means to understand the learning experience. *International Journal of Information Management*, 48, 108–119. DOI: 10.1016/j.ijinfomgt.2019.02.003

Giannakos, M., Sharma, K., Martinez-Maldonado, R., Dillenbourg, P., & Rogers, Y. (2018, September). Learner-computer interaction. *InProceedings of the 10th Nordic Conference on Human-Computer Interaction* (pp. 968-971). DOI: 10.1145/3240167.3240259

Gibson, J. J. (1979). The Theory of Affordances. *The Ecological Approach to Visual Perception*, 127–137.

Gilleard, C. (2020). Bourdieu's forms of capital and the stratification of later life. *Journal of Aging Studies*, 53, 100851. DOI: 10.1016/j.jaging.2020.100851 PMID: 32487342

Goh, E. S., Sunar, M. S., & Ismail, A. (2019). 3D object manipulation techniques in handheld mobile augmented reality interface: A review. *IEEE Access : Practical Innovations, Open Solutions*, 24(7), 40581–40601. Advance online publication. DOI: 10.1109/ACCESS.2019.2906394

Goldman-Segall, R., & Goldman, R. (2014). *Points of viewing children's thinking*. Psychology Press. DOI: 10.4324/9781315805818

Gómez-García, M., Hossein-Mohand, H., Trujillo-Torres, J. M., Hossein-Mohand, H., & Aznar-Díaz, I. (2020). Technological factors that influence the mathematics performance of secondary school students. *Mathematics*, 8(11), 1935. DOI: 10.3390/math8111935

Gonçalves, E., & Capucha, L. (2020). Student-centered and ICT-enabled learning models in veterinarian programs: What changed with COVID-19? *Education Sciences*, 10(11), 1–17. DOI: 10.3390/educsci10110343

Gonçalves, S. P., Sousa, M. J., & Pereira, F. S. (2020). Distance learning perceptions from higher education students—The case of Portugal. *Education Sciences*, 10(12), 1–15. DOI: 10.3390/educsci10120374

Goodfellow, I., Bengio, Y., & Courville, A. (2016). *Deep learning*. The MIT Press.

Google. (2024). Google Books Ngram Viewer: Facial expression, Haptic, Electroencephalogram, Eye tracking, Trace data, Electrodermal activity.

Gopalan, V., Zulkifi, A. N., & Bakar, J. A. A. (2016, August). A study of students' motivation using the augmented reality science textbook. In *AIP Conference Proceedings, 1761*(1), 020040.

Gorla, N., Somers, T. M., & Wong, B. (2010). Organizational impact of system quality, information quality, and service quality. *The Journal of Strategic Information Systems*, 19(3), 207–228. DOI: 10.1016/j.jsis.2010.05.001

Graesser, A. C., Lu, S., Jackson, G. T., Mitchell, H. H., Ventura, M., Olney, A., & Louwerse, M. M. (2004). AutoTutor: A tutor with dialogue in natural language. *Behavior Research Methods, Instruments, & Computers*, 36(2), 180–192. DOI: 10.3758/BF03195563 PMID: 15354683

Greig, J. A., Colclasure, B., Rampold, S., Ruth, T., & Granberry, T. (2024). Enhancing agricultural education through virtual reality: Facilitation, application, reflection, and measurement in the classroom. *Advancements in Agricultural Development*, 5(2), 64–80. DOI: 10.37433/aad.v5i2.353

Gruber, A., & Kaplan-Rakowski, R. (2020). User experience of public speaking practice in virtual reality. In Zheng, R. Z. (Ed.), *Cognitive and affective perspectives on immersive technology in education* (pp. 235–249). IGI Global., DOI: 10.4018/978-1-7998-3250-8.ch012

Gruber, A., & Kaplan-Rakowski, R. (2022). Verbal and nonverbal communication in high immersion virtual reality for language learners. In Arnbjörnsdóttir, B. (Eds.), *Intelligent CALL, granular systems, and learner data: short papers from EUROCALL 2022, 129-134*. DOI: 10.14705/rpnet.2022.61.1447

Guangul, F. M., Suhail, A. H., Khalit, M. I., & Khidhir, B. A. (2020). Challenges of remote assessment in higher education in the context of COVID-19: A case study of Middle East College. *Educational Assessment, Evaluation and Accountability*, 32(4), 519–535. DOI: 10.1007/s11092-020-09340-w PMID: 33101539

Guimarães, F. F., Mendes, A. R. M., Rodrigues, L. M., Paiva, R. S. d. S., & Finardi, K. R. (2019). Internationalization at home, coil and intercomprehension: for more inclusive activieties in the global south. SFU Educational Review, 12(3), 90–109. Retieved from DOI: 10.21810/sfuer.v12i3.1019

Guskey, T. R. (2002). Professional development and teacher change. *Teachers and Teaching*, 8(3), 381–391. DOI: 10.1080/135406002100000512

Güven, E. (2020). *Using of Arduino assisted robotics coding activities in science teaching on 5th grade secondary school* (Unpublished Master's thesis). Muğla Sıtkı Koçman University, Institute of Educational Sciences, Muğla.

Hahn, L., & Klein, P. (2022). Eye tracking in physics education research: A systematic literature review. *Physical Review. Physics Education Research*, 18(1), 013102. DOI: 10.1103/PhysRevPhysEducRes.18.013102

Hakami, L., Hernández-Leo, D., Amarasinghe, I., & Sayis, B. (2024). Investigating teacher orchestration load in scripted CSCL: A multimodal data analysis perspective. *British Journal of Educational Technology*, 55(5), 1926–1949. DOI: 10.1111/bjet.13500

Hakimi, L., Eynon, R., & Murphy, V. A. (2021). The ethics of using digital trace data in education: A thematic review of the research landscape. *Review of Educational Research*, 91(5), 671–717. DOI: 10.3102/00346543211020116

Hamad, W. (2022). Understanding the foremost challenges in the transition to online teaching and learning during COVID-19 pandemic: A systematic literature review. *Journal of Educational Technology and Online Learning*, 5(2), 393–410. DOI: 10.31681/jetol.1055695

Hämäläinen, T., & Vähäkangas, M. (2021). Creating Interactive Video Lectures with H5P: A Tool for Enhancing Active Learning in Online Courses. *International Journal of Information and Communication Technology Education*, 17(1), 32–43.

Hamdani, S. W. A., Abbas, H., Janjua, A. R., Shahid, W. B., Amjad, M. F., Malik, J., Murtaza, M. H., Atiqzzaman, M., & Khan, A. W. (2021). Cybersecurity standards in the context of operating system: Practical aspects, analysis, and comparisons. *ACM Computing Surveys*, 54(3), 1–36. DOI: 10.1145/3442480

Hamilton, D., McKechnie, J., Edgerton, E., & Wilson, C. (2020). Immersive virtual reality as a pedagogical tool in education: A systematic literature review of quantitative learning outcomes and experimental design. *Journal of Computers in Education*, 8(1), 1–32. DOI: 10.1007/s40692-020-00169-2

Han, Y. (2023). Virtual reality in engineering education. *SHS Web of Conferences*. https://doi.org/DOI: 10.1051/shsconf/202315702001

Händel, M., Stephan, M., Gläser-Zikuda, M., Kopp, B., Bedenlier, S., & Ziegler, A. (2020). Digital readiness and its effects on higher education students' socio-emotional perceptions in the context of the COVID-19 pandemic. *Journal of Research on Technology in Education*, 54(2), 267–280. DOI: 10.1080/15391523.2020.1846147

Hansen, H. F., Haddara, M., & Langseth, M. (2023). Investigating ERP system customization: A focus on cloud-ERP. *Procedia Computer Science*, 219, 915–923. DOI: 10.1016/j.procs.2023.01.367

Haque, M. Z., Sadeek, M. A., & Rahman, M. M. (2020). Online Learning Amidst COVID-19 Pandemic: A Case Study of Higher Education in Bangladesh. *Journal of Education and e-learning Research*, 7(3), 247–258.

Harris, J., Mishra, P., & Koehler, M. (2009). Teachers' technological pedagogical content knowledge and learning activity types: Curriculum-based technology integration reframed. *Journal of Research on Technology in Education*, 41(4), 393–416. DOI: 10.1080/15391523.2009.10782536

Harter, L., McKenna, J., & Van Campenhout, R. (2023, March). Teacher Perceptions of an Educational Robotics Professional Development Program. In *Society for Information Technology & Teacher Education International Conference* (pp. 2062-2068). Association for the Advancement of Computing in Education (AACE).

Hasan, M. M., Hossain, M. S., & Rahman, M. M. (2020). E-Learning Platforms in Higher Education: A Case Study of Bangladesh. *Journal of Management and Science*, 7(2), 98–107.

Hattie, J., & Timperley, H. (2007). The power of feedback. *Review of Educational Research*, 77(1), 81–112. DOI: 10.3102/003465430298487

Heffernan, N. T., & Heffernan, C. L. (2014). The ASSISTments ecosystem: Building a platform that brings scientists and teachers together for minimally invasive research on human learning and teaching. *International Journal of Artificial Intelligence in Education*, 24(4), 470–497. DOI: 10.1007/s40593-014-0024-x

Heinemann, B., Görzen, S., & Schroeder, U. (2022, July). Systematic design for effective learning in virtual reality. In *2022 International Conference on Advanced Learning Technologies (ICALT)* (pp. 341-343). IEEE. https://doi.org/DOI: 10.1109/ICALT55010.2022.00107

Helms, R. M., & Brajkovic, L. (2017). *Mapping internationalization on U.S. campuses* (2017edition). ACE.

Henriques, R., Paiva, A., & Antunes, C. (2012, June). On the need of new methods to mine electrodermal activity in emotion-centered studies. In *International Workshop on Agents and Data Mining Interaction* (pp. 203-215). Berlin, Heidelberg: Springer Berlin Heidelberg.

Herfort, J. D., Tamborg, A. L., Meier, F., Allsopp, B. B., & Misfeldt, M. (2023). Twenty years of research on technology in mathematics education at CERME: A literature review based on a data science approach. *Educational Studies in Mathematics*, 112(2), 309–336. DOI: 10.1007/s10649-022-10202-z

Herschel, R., & Miori, V. M. (2017). Ethics & big data. *Technology in Society*, 49, 31–36. DOI: 10.1016/j.techsoc.2017.03.003

Hessels, R. S., Kemner, C., van den Boomen, C., & Hooge, I. T. (2016). The area-of-interest problem in eye-tracking research: A noise-robust solution for face and sparse stimuli. *Behavior Research Methods*, 48(4), 1694–1712. DOI: 10.3758/s13428-015-0676-y PMID: 26563395

Hidayat, R., & Wardat, Y. (2024). A systematic review of augmented reality in science, technology, engineering and mathematics education. *Education and Information Technologies*, 29(8), 9257–9282. DOI: 10.1007/s10639-023-12157-x

Higgins, K., Huscroft-D'Angelo, J., & Crawford, L. (2019). Efects of technology in mathematics on achievement, motivation, and attitude: A meta-analysis. *Journal of Educational Computing Research*, 57(2), 283–319. DOI: 10.1177/0735633117748416

Hillmayr, D., Ziernwald, L., Reinhold, F., Hofer, S. I., & Reiss, K. M. (2020). The potential of digital tools to enhance mathematics and science learning in secondary schools: A context-specific meta-analysis. *Computers & Education*, 153, 103897. DOI: 10.1016/j.compedu.2020.103897

Hinds, J., & Joinson, A. N. (2018). What demographic attributes do our digital footprints reveal? A systematic review. *PLoS One*, 13(11), e0207112. DOI: 10.1371/journal.pone.0207112 PMID: 30485305

Hochreiter, S. (1997). *Long Short-term Memory*. Neural Computation MIT-Press. DOI: 10.1162/neco.1997.9.8.1735

Hodges, C. B., Moore, S., Lockee, B. B., Trust, T., & Bond, M. A. (2020). *The difference between emergency remote teaching and online learning*.

Hodhod, R., Fleenor, S., & Nabi, S. (2014). Adaptive augmented reality serious game to foster problem solving skills. In *Proceedings of the Workshop on Hyperrealistic Intelligent Environments*, Shanghai, China. IOS Press

Hofmann, D. A., & Frese, M. (Eds.). (2011). *Error in organizations*. Routledge. DOI: 10.4324/9780203817827

Hohenwarter, M., Jarvis, D., & Lavicza, Z. (2009). Linking geometry, algebra, and mathematics teachers: GeoGebra soft-ware and the establishment of the International GeoGebra institute. *The International Journal for Technology in Mathematics Education*, 16(2), 83–86.

Holmes, W., & Bialik, M. ve Fadel, C. (2019). Artificial intelligence in education: Promises and implications for teaching and learning. Boston, MA: Center for Curriculum Redesign.

Holmqvist, K., Nyström, M., Andersson, R., Dewhurst, R., Jarodzka, H., & Van de Weijer, J. (2011). *Eye tracking: A comprehensive guide to methods and measures*. Oxford University Press.

Hong, C., & Wang, L. (2023). Virtual Reality Technology in Nursing Professional Skills Training: Bibliometric Analysis. *JMIR Serious Games*, 11(e44766), 1–15. DOI: 10.2196/44766 PMID: 37603389

Hrastinski, S. (2009). A theory of online learning as online participation. *Computers & Education*, 52(1), 78–82. DOI: 10.1016/j.compedu.2008.06.009

Hsiao, K. F., & Rashvand, H. F. (2011). Integrating body language movements in augmented reality learning environment. *Human-centric Computing and Information Sciences*, 1(1), 1–10. DOI: 10.1186/2192-1962-1-1

Huang, C. L., Luo, Y. F., Yang, S. C., Lu, C. M., & Chen, A. S. (2020). Influence of students' learning style, sense of presence, and cognitive load on learning outcomes in an immersive virtual reality learning environment. *Journal of Educational Computing Research*, 58(3), 596–615. DOI: 10.1177/0735633119867422

Huang, S. Y., Tarng, W., & Ou, K. L. (2023). Effectiveness of AR board game on computational thinking and programming skills for elementary school students. *Systems*, 11(25), 25. Advance online publication. DOI: 10.3390/systems11010025

Huang, X., Zou, D., Cheng, G., & Xie, H. (2021). A systematic review of AR and VR enhanced language learning. *Sustainability (Basel)*, 13(9), 4639. DOI: 10.3390/su13094639

Huang, Y. C., Backman, K. F., Backman, S. J., & Chang, L. L. (2016). Exploring the implications of virtual reality technology in tourism marketing: An integrated research framework. *International Journal of Tourism Research*, 18(2), 116–128. DOI: 10.1002/jtr.2038

Hudzik, J. K. (2011). Comprehensive internationalization. From concept to action. Washington,DC: NAFSA: Association of International Educators.

Humanities project report. (1995). Retrieved from https://tecfa.unige.ch/tecfa/research/humanities/humanities-report.html

Hurbean, L., & Fotache, D. (2014). ERP III: The promise of a new generation. *Conference on Informatics in Economy ASE Bucarest Romania*.

Hussein, M. H., Ow, S. H., Ibrahim, I., & Mahmoud, M. A. (2021). Measuring instructors continued intention to reuse Google Classroom in Iraq: A mixed-method study during COVID-19. *Interactive Technology and Smart Education*, 18(3), 380–402. DOI: 10.1108/ITSE-06-2020-0095

Hutchby, I. (2001). Technologies, Texts and Affordances Author (s): Ian Hutchby Published by : Sage Publications, Ltd. Stable URL : https://www.jstor.org/stable/42856294 JSTOR is a not-for-profit service that helps scholars, researchers, and students discover, use, a. *Sociology, 35*(2), 441–456.

Hutter, F., Kotthoff, L., & Vanschoren, J. (2019). *Automated machine learning: methods, systems, challenges*. Springer Nature. DOI: 10.1007/978-3-030-05318-5

IEASA. (2020). Higher Education Internationalisation in South Africa in the Context of the COVID-19 Pandemic: Impact on International Students, retrieved from https://ieasa.studysa.org/wp-content/uploads/2020/05/IEASA-position-paper_COVID-19_May2020_Final.pdf

Inkarbekov, M., Monahan, R., & Pearlmutter, B. (2023). Visualization of AI systems in virtual reality: A comprehensive review. *ArXiv, abs/2306.15545*. https://doi.org/ DOI: 10.14569/IJACSA.2023.0140805

Interactive, S. P. R. E. E. (2024). The history of virtual reality and its impact on Gen Alpha. https://jointhespree.com/the-history-of-virtual-reality/ Retrieved 2021-01-22.

International Association of University Presidents & Santander Universidades. (2020). Leadership Responses to COVID-19: A Global Survey of College and University Leadership. Retrieved from: https://www.iaup.org/wpcontent/uploads/2020/11/IAUP-Survey-2020- ExecutiveSummary.pdf

Irani, Z., Abril, R. M., Weerakkody, V., Omar, A., & Sivarajah, U. (2023). The impact of legacy systems on digital transformation in European public administration: Lesson learned from a multi case analysis. *Government Information Quarterly*, 40(1), 101784. DOI: 10.1016/j.giq.2022.101784

Islam, R., Hossen, M. M., & Ali, S. Y. (2022). STUDENTS'PERCEPTION ABOUT ONLINE LEARNING IN THE EDUCATION SECTOR DURING COVID-19: A STUDY ON THE DIFFERENT EDUCATIONAL INSTITUTIONS OF BANGLADESH. *Journal of Business Studies*, 199.

Islam, M. R., & Haque, M. M. (2020). Integrating Microsoft Teams in Higher Education: An Experience from Bangladesh. *Journal of Education and Practice*, 11(15), 19–27.

İşler, B., & Kılıç, M. (2021). Eğitimde yapay zekâ kullanımı ve gelişimi. *Yeni Medya Elektronik Dergisi*, 5(1), 1–11.

Jacob, R. J., & Karn, K. S. (2003). Eye tracking in human-computer interaction and usability research: Ready to deliver the promises. In *The mind's eye* (pp. 573–605). North-Holland. DOI: 10.1016/B978-044451020-4/50031-1

Jaiswal, R., Sharma, S., & Kaushik, R. (2023). Ethics in AI and machine learning. *Journal of Nonlinear Analysis and Optimization*. https://doi.org/DOI: 10.36893/JNAO.2023.V14I1.0008-0012

Jarmon, L., Traphagan, T., Mayrath, M., & Trivedi, A. (2009). Virtual world teaching, experiential learning, and assessment: An interdisciplinary communication course in Second Life. *Computers & Education*, 53(1), 169–182. DOI: 10.1016/j.compedu.2009.01.010

Järvelä, S., Malmberg, J., Haataja, E., Sobocinski, M., & Kirschner, P. A. (2021). What multimodal data can tell us about the students' regulation of their learning process? *Learning and Instruction*, 72, 101203. DOI: 10.1016/j.learninstruc.2019.04.004

Javidroozi, V., Shah, H., & Feldman, G. (2018). Qualitative Critical Realism in Information Systems Research. *UK Academy for Information Systems Conference Proceedings 2018*, 24. https://aisel.aisnet.org/ukais2018/24

Jawad, Z. N., & Balázs, V. (2024). Machine learning-driven optimization of enterprise resource planning (ERP) systems: A comprehensive review. *Beni-Suef University Journal of Basic and Applied Sciences*, 13(1), 4. Advance online publication. DOI: 10.1186/s43088-023-00460-y

Jehi, T., Khan, R., Dos Santos, H., & Majzoub, N. (2023). Effect of COVID-19 outbreak on anxiety among students of higher education; A review of literature. *Current Psychology (New Brunswick, N.J.)*, 42(20), 17475–17489. DOI: 10.1007/s12144-021-02587-6 PMID: 35018081

Jensen, L., & Konradsen, F. (2018). A review of the use of virtual reality head-mounted displays in education and training. *Education and Information Technologies*, 23(4), 1515–1529. DOI: 10.1007/s10639-017-9676-0

Jent, J. F., St. George, S. M., Agosto, Y., Rothenberg, W. A., Howe, E., Velasquez, C., & Natale, R. (2024). Virtual robotic telepresence early childhood mental health consultation to childcare centers in the aftermath of COVID-19: Training approaches and perceived acceptability and usefulness. *Frontiers in Psychology*, 15, 1339230. DOI: 10.3389/fpsyg.2024.1339230 PMID: 38903468

Jerry, T., & Aaron, C. (2010). *The impact of augmented reality software with inquiry-based learning on students' learning of kinematics graph.* In 2nd International Conference on Education Technology and Computer (ICETC), (pp. V2-1–V2-5). Shanghai: IEEE. DOI: 10.1109/ICETC.2010.5529447

Jeyaraman, M., Balaji, S., Jeyaraman, N., & Yadav, S. (2023). Unraveling the ethical enigma: Artificial intelligence in healthcare. *Cureus*, 15. Advance online publication. DOI: 10.7759/cureus.43262 PMID: 37692617

Jia, J., & Chen, W. (2017, July). The ethical dilemmas of virtual reality application in entertainment. In *2017 IEEE International Conference on Computational Science and Engineering (CSE) and IEEE International Conference on Embedded and Ubiquitous Computing (EUC) (Vol. 1, pp. 696-699)*. IEEE. https://doi.org/DOI: 10.1109/CSE-EUC.2017.134

Jiang, J., & Fryer, L. (2023). The effect of virtual reality learning on students' motivation: A scoping review. *Journal of Computer Assisted Learning*. Advance online publication. DOI: 10.1111/jcal.12885

Jin, Q., Liu, Y., Yarosh, S., Han, B., & Qian, F. (2022). How Will VR Enter University Classrooms? Multi-stakeholders Investigation of VR in Higher Education. *CHI Conference on Human Factors in Computing Systems*, 1–17. DOI: 10.1145/3491102.3517542

Jo, H., & Park, D.-H. (2023). Mechanisms for successful management of enterprise resource planning from user information processing and system quality perspective. *Scientific Reports*, 13(1), 12678. DOI: 10.1038/s41598-023-39787-y PMID: 37542092

Jonassen, D. H., Hernandez-Serrano, J., & Choi, I. 2000. Integrating constructivism and learning technologies. In Spector, M. & Anderson, T.M. (Eds,), *Integrated and holistic perspectives on learning, instruction and technology: Understanding complexity,* 103-127. Springer.

Jones, R. (2021). Cost-effectiveness analysis of e-learning versus traditional classroom learning. *International Journal of Educational Technology in Higher Education*, 18(1), 1–15.

Joshi, A., Vinay, M., & Bhaskar, P. (2021). Impact of coronavirus pandemic on the Indian education sector: Perspectives of teachers on online teaching and assessments. *Interactive Technology and Smart Education*, 18(2), 205–226. DOI: 10.1108/ITSE-06-2020-0087

Joshi, K. P., Elluri, L., & Nagar, A. (2020). An integrated knowledge graph to automate cloud data compliance. *IEEE Access : Practical Innovations, Open Solutions*, 8, 148541–148555. DOI: 10.1109/ACCESS.2020.3008964

Juanda, E. A., & Khairullah, F. (2021, February). Tinkercad Application Software to Optimize Teaching and Learning Process in Electronics and Microprocessors Subject. In *6th UPI International Conference on TVET 2020 (TVET 2020)* (pp. 124-128). Atlantis Press. DOI: 10.2991/assehr.k.210203.101

Junior, L. A., Neto, O. T., Hernandez, M. F., Martins, P. S., Roger, L. L., & Guerra, F. A. (2013). A low-cost and simple Arduino-based educational robotics kit. Cyber Journals: Multidisciplinary Journals in Science and Technology. [JSRC]. *Journal of Selected Areas in Robotics and Control*, 3(12), 1–7.

Kabaağaç, S., & Alova, E. (1995). *Latin-Turkish dictionary*. Social Publications.

Kabir, M. H., Chowdhury, M. T., & Roy, M. K. (2019). Exploring the Role of Khan Academy in Improving E-Learning in Bangladesh. International Journal of Management. *IT and Engineering*, 9(3), 401–414.

Kabir, M. R. (2020). Impact of faculty and student readiness on virtual learning adoption amid Covid-19. *Revista Internacional de Educacion Para La Justicia Social*, 9(3), 387–414. DOI: 10.15366/riejs2020.9.3.021

Kabir, M. R., Islam, M. A., & Deena, S. A. (2020). Explaining the adoption of technology-based design of higher education during and after COVID 19 period from a developing country perspective. *Interaction Design and Architecture(s). Journal*, 46(46), 88–119. DOI: 10.55612/s-5002-046-005

Kafai, Y. B., & Resnick, M. (2012). *Constructionism in practice: Designing, thinking, and learning in a digital world*. Routledge. DOI: 10.4324/9780203053492

Kalati, A. T., & Kim, M. S. (2022). What is the effect of touchscreen technology on young children's learning? A systematic review. *Education and Information Technologies*, •••, 1–19.

Kamalov, F., Calonge, D., & Gurrib, I. (2023). New era of artificial intelligence in education: Towards a sustainable multifaceted revolution. *Sustainability (Basel)*, 15(16), 12451. Advance online publication. DOI: 10.3390/su151612451

Kamhawi, E. M. (2008). Enterprise resource-planning systems adoption in Bahrain: Motives, benefits, and barriers. *Journal of Enterprise Information Management*, 21(3), 310–334. DOI: 10.1108/17410390810866655

Kamińska, D., Zwoliński, G., Laska-Leśniewicz, A., Raposo, R., Vairinhos, M., Pereira, E., Urem, F., Ljubić Hinić, M., Haamer, R. E., & Anbarjafari, G. (2023). Augmented reality: Current and new trends in education. *Electronics (Basel)*, 12(16), 3531. DOI: 10.3390/electronics12163531

Kang, S., Chanenson, J., Ghate, P., Cowal, P., Weaver, M., & Krum, D. M. (2019, March). Advancing ethical decision making in virtual reality. In *2019 IEEE Conference on Virtual Reality and 3D User Interfaces (VR) (pp. 1008-1009)*. IEEE. https://doi.org/DOI: 10.1109/VR.2019.8798151

Kaplan-Rakowski, R., & Gruber, A. (2023). An experimental study on reading in high- immersion virtual reality. *SSRN*. https://ssrn.com/abstract=4262124

Kara, M. (2022). Revisiting online learner engagement: Exploring the role of learner characteristics in an emergency period. *Journal of Research on Technology in Education, 54*(sup1), S236-S252. https://doi.org/DOI: 10.1080/15391523.2021.1891997

Kara, M., Erdogdu, F., Kokoç, M., & Cagiltay, K. (2019). Challenges faced by adult learners in online distance education: A literature review. *Open Praxis*, 11(1), 5–22. DOI: 10.5944/openpraxis.11.1.929

Karim, M. E., Lemaignan, S., & Mondada, F. (2015, June). A review: Can robots reshape K-12 STEM education? In O. SwanteeIn (Ed.), *International Workshop on Advanced Robotics and its Social Impacts (ARSO)* (pp. 1-8). London: Institute of Electrical and Electronics Engineers.

Kaur, D. P., Kumar, A., Dutta, R., & Malhotra, S. (2022). The Role of Interactive and Immersive Technologies in Higher Education: A Survey. *Journal of Engineering Education Transformations*, 36(2), 79–86. DOI: 10.16920/jeet/2022/v36i2/22156

Kayii, N., & Akpomi, M. (2022). Constructivist approaches: A budding paradigm for teaching and learning entrepreneurship education. *International Journal of Education, Teaching, and Social Sciences*. https://doi.org/DOI: 10.47747/ijets.v2i1.586

Ke, F., Liu, R., Sokolikj, Z., Dahlstrom-Hakki, I., & Israel, M. (2024). Using eye-tracking in education: Review of empirical research and technology. *Educational Technology Research and Development*, 72(3), 1–36. DOI: 10.1007/s11423-024-10342-4

Kerawalla, L., Luckin, R., Seljeflot, S., & Woolard, A. (2006). "Making it real": Exploring the potential of augmented reality for teaching primary school science. *Virtual Reality (Waltham Cross)*, 10(3-4), 163–174. DOI: 10.1007/s10055-006-0036-4

Kerns, B. R. (2019). *A case study of A flipped curriculum using collaborative and active learning with an adaptive learning system* (Doctoral dissertation, Indiana State University).

Kerous, B., Barteček, R., Roman, R., Sojka, P., Bečev, O., & Liarokapis, F. (2020). Examination of electrodermal and cardio-vascular reactivity in virtual reality through a combined stress induction protocol. *Journal of Ambient Intelligence and Humanized Computing*, 11(12), 6033–6042. DOI: 10.1007/s12652-020-01858-7

Kersting, M., Bondell, J., Steier, R., & Myers, M. (2023). Virtual reality in astronomy education: Reflecting on design principles through a dialogue between researchers and practitioners. *International Journal of Science Education. Part B. Communication and Public Engagement*. Advance online publication. DOI: 10.1080/21548455.2023.2238871

Kesim, M., & Ozarslan, Y. (2012). Augmented reality in education: Current technologies and the potential for education. *Procedia: Social and Behavioral Sciences*, 47, 297–302. DOI: 10.1016/j.sbspro.2012.06.654

Keusch, F., & Kreuter, F. (2021). Digital trace data: Modes of data collection, applications, and errors at a glance. In *Handbook of Computational Social Science* (Vol. 1). Taylor & Francis.

Khalaf, K., El-Kishawi, M., Moufti, M. A., & Al Kawas, S. (2020). Introducing a comprehensive high-stake online exam to final-year dental students during the COVID-19 pandemic and evaluation of its effectiveness. *Medical Education Online*, 25(1), 1–10, 1826861. DOI: 10.1080/10872981.2020.1826861 PMID: 33000704

Khan, A., Badshah, S., Liang, P., Khan, B., Waseem, M., Niazi, M., & Akbar, M. (2021). Ethics of AI: A systematic literature review of principles and challenges. *Proceedings of the 26th International Conference on Evaluation and Assessment in Software Engineering*. https://doi.org/DOI: 10.1145/3530019.3531329

Khan, R., Bashir, A., Basu, B. L., & Uddin, M. E. (2020). Emergency online instruction at higher education in Bangladesh during COVID-19: Challenges and suggestions. *Journal of Asia TEFL*, 17(4), 1497–1506. DOI: 10.18823/asiatefl.2020.17.4.26.1497

Khan, T., Johnston, K., & Ophoff, J. (2019). The impact of an augmented reality application on learning motivation of students. *Advances in Human-Computer Interaction*, 2019, 1–14. Advance online publication. DOI: 10.1155/2019/7208494

Khatun, F. (2020, July 27). Making Online Education Effective. The Daily Star.

Kılıç, S., & Çakıroğlu, Ü. (2023). Design, implementation, and evaluation of a professional development program for teachers to teach computational thinking via robotics. *Technology. Knowledge and Learning*, 28(4), 1539–1569. DOI: 10.1007/s10758-022-09629-3

Kılıç, S., & Gökoğlu, S. (2022). Exploring the usability of virtual robotics programming curriculum for robotics programming teaching. *Informatics in Education*, 21(3), 523–540. DOI: 10.15388/infedu.2022.20

Kiourt, C., Koutsoudis, A., & Kalles, D. (2020). *Enhanced virtual reality experience in personalised virtual museums*. Natural Language Processing., DOI: 10.4018/978-1-7998-0951-7.ch065

Kirschner, P., & Selinger, M. (2003). The state of affairs of teacher education with respect to information and communications technology. *Technology, Pedagogy and Education*, 12(1), 5–17. DOI: 10.1080/14759390300200143

Klimova, B., Pikhart, M., & Kacetl, J. (2023). Ethical issues of the use of AI-driven mobile apps for education. *Frontiers in Public Health*, 10, 1118116. Advance online publication. DOI: 10.3389/fpubh.2022.1118116 PMID: 36711343

Koch, H. (2017). Shadow Analytics Full Paper. *Amercan Conferences on Information Systems*, 2012, 1–10.

Koedinger, K. R., D'Mello, S., McLaughlin, E. A., Pardos, Z. A., & Rosé, C. P. (2015). Data mining and education. *Wiley Interdisciplinary Reviews: Cognitive Science*, 6(4), 333–353. DOI: 10.1002/wcs.1350 PMID: 26263424

Koedinger, K. R., McLaughlin, E. A., & Stamper, J. C. (2012). *Automated Student Model Improvement*. International Educational Data Mining Society.

Koh, J. H. L., & Daniel, B. K. (2022). Shifting online during COVID-19: A systematic review of teaching and learning strategies and their outcomes. *International Journal of Educational Technology in Higher Education*, 19(1), 1–23, 56. DOI: 10.1186/s41239-022-00361-7 PMID: 36404984

Koparan, T., Dinar, H., Koparan, E. T., & Haldan, Z. S. (2023). Integrating augmented reality into mathematics teaching and learning and examining its effectiveness. *Thinking Skills and Creativity*, 47, 101245. DOI: 10.1016/j.tsc.2023.101245

Köse, H., & Güner-Yildiz, N. (2021). Augmented reality (AR) as a learning material in special needs education. *Education and Information Technologies*, 26(2), 1921–1936. DOI: 10.1007/s10639-020-10326-w

Koumpouros, Y. (2024). Revealing the true potential and prospects of augmented reality in education. *Smart Learn. Environ.*, 11(2), 2. Advance online publication. DOI: 10.1186/s40561-023-00288-0

Kozinets, R. V. (2023). Immersive netnography: A novel method for service experience research in virtual reality, augmented reality and metaverse contexts. *Journal of Service Management*, 34(1), 100–125. DOI: 10.1108/JOSM-12-2021-0481

Krikun, I. (2017). Applying learning analytics methods to enhance learning quality and effectiveness in virtual learning environments. *2017 5th IEEE Workshop on Advances in Information, Electronic and Electrical Engineering (AIEEE)*, 1-6. https://doi.org/DOI: 10.1109/AIEEE.2017.8270532

Krokos, E., Plaisant, C., & Varshney, A. (2019). Virtual memory palaces: Immersion aids recall. *Virtual Reality (Waltham Cross)*, 23(1), 1–15. DOI: 10.1007/s10055-018-0346-3

Kumar, S., & Daniel, B. K. (2016). Integration of learning technologies into teaching within Fijian Polytechnic Institutions. *International Journal of Educational Technology in Higher Education*, 13(1), 36. DOI: 10.1186/s41239-016-0036-8

Kuna, P., Hašková, A., & Borza, Ľ. (2023). Creation of virtual reality for education purposes. *Sustainability (Basel)*, 15(9), 7153. DOI: 10.3390/su15097153

Kuprenko, V. (2020). Artificial intelligence in education: Benefits, challenges, and use cases. https://medium.com/towards-artificial-intelligence/artificial-intelligence-in-education-benefits-challenges-and-use-cases-db52d8921f7a

Kurilovas, E. (2016). Evaluation of quality and personalisation of VR/AR/MR learning systems. *Behaviour & Information Technology*, 35(11), 998–1007. DOI: 10.1080/0144929X.2016.1212929

Kyaw, B., Saxena, N., Posadzki, P., Všetečková, J., Nikolaou, C., George, P., Divakar, U., Masiello, I., Kononowicz, A., Zary, N., & Car, L. (2019). Virtual reality for health professions education: Systematic review and meta-analysis by the digital health education collaboration. *Journal of Medical Internet Research*, 21(1), e12959. Advance online publication. DOI: 10.2196/12959 PMID: 30668519

Lahat, D., Adali, T., & Jutten, C. (2015). Multimodal data fusion: An overview of methods, challenges, and prospects. *Proceedings of the IEEE*, 103(9), 1449–1477. DOI: 10.1109/JPROC.2015.2460697

Lai, J. W., & Cheong, K. H. (2022). Adoption of virtual and augmented reality for mathematics education: A scoping review. [Crossref]. *IEEE Access : Practical Innovations, Open Solutions*, 10, 13693–13703. DOI: 10.1109/ACCESS.2022.3145991

Lai, N., Wei, S., Halim, D., Fow, K., Kang, H., & Yu, L. (2021). Why not more virtual reality in higher ed teaching and learning? *2021 IEEE International Conference on Engineering, Technology & Education (TALE)*, 248-254. https://doi.org/ DOI: 10.1109/TALE52509.2021.9678523

Landgrebe, J., & Smith, B. (2019). There is no general AI: why Turing machines cannot pass the Turing test. arXiv preprint arXiv:1906.05833.

Lanier, J. (2017). *Dawn of the new everything: A journey through virtual reality*. Random House.

Larson, E. J. (2021). *The Myth of Artificial Intelligence: Why Computers Can't Think the Way We Do*. Harvard University Press.

Lave, J., & Wenger, E. (1991). *Situated learning: Legitimate peripheral participation*. Cambridge University Press. DOI: 10.1017/CBO9780511815355

LeCun, Y., Bottou, L., Bengio, Y., & Haffner, P. (1998). Gradient-based learning applied to document recognition. *Proceedings of the IEEE*, 86(11), 2278–2324. DOI: 10.1109/5.726791

Lee, K. (2012). Augmented reality in education and training. *TechTrends*, 56(2), 13–21. DOI: 10.1007/s11528-012-0559-3

Lee, Y. W., Strong, D. M., Kahn, B. K., & Wang, R. Y. (2002). AIMQ: A methodology for information quality assessment. *Information & Management*, 40(2), 133–146. DOI: 10.1016/S0378-7206(02)00043-5

Lege, R., & Bonner, E. (2020). Virtual reality in education: The promise, progress, and challenge. *The JALT CALL Journal*, 16(3), 167–180. DOI: 10.29140/jaltcall.v16n3.388

Legg, S. ve Hutter, M. (2007). A collection of definitions of intelligence. Frontiers in artificial ıntelligence and applications, 7(157), 17-24.

Leikas, J., Koivisto, R., & Gotcheva, N. (2019). Ethical framework for designing autonomous intelligent systems. *Journal of Open Innovation*, 5(1), 18. Advance online publication. DOI: 10.3390/joitmc5010018

Lenhart, A. (2015) *Teens, social media & technology overview 2015*. Retrieved 1 August, 2024 from https://www.pewresearch.org/internet/2015/04/09/teens-social-media-technology-2015/

Leonardi, P. M. (2011). When flexible routines meet flexible technologies: Affordance, constraint, and the imbrication of human and material agencies. *Management Information Systems Quarterly*, 35(1), 147–167. DOI: 10.2307/23043493

Leung, X. Y., Zhang, H., Lyu, J., & Bai, B. (2023). Why do hotel frontline employees use service robots in the workplace? A technology affordance theory perspective. *International Journal of Hospitality Management, 108*(November 2022), 103380. DOI: 10.1016/j.ijhm.2022.103380

Li, C., & Li, Y. (2020). Feasibility Analysis of VR Technology in Physical Education and Sports Training. *IEEE Access : Practical Innovations, Open Solutions*, 20, 1–8. DOI: 10.1109/ACCESS.2020.2995063

Li, F., Ruijs, N., & Lu, Y. (2022). Ethics & AI: A systematic review on ethical concerns and related strategies for designing with AI in healthcare. *AI*, 4(1), 28–53. Advance online publication. DOI: 10.3390/ai4010003

Li, K., & Wang, S. (2021). Development and application of VR course resources based on embedded system in open education. *Microprocessors and Microsystems*, 83(103989), 1–6. DOI: 10.1016/j.micpro.2021.103989

Lim, T., Gottipati, S., & Cheong, M. L. (2023). Ethical considerations for artificial intelligence in educational assessments. In Keengwe, J. (Ed.), *Creative AI Tools and Ethical Implications in Teaching and Learning* (pp. 32–79). IGI Global., DOI: 10.4018/979-8-3693-0205-7.ch003

Lin, X., Li, R., Chen, Z., & Xiong, J. (2024). Design strategies for VR science and education games from an embodied cognition perspective: A literature-based meta-analysis. *Frontiers in Psychology*, 14(January), 1–14. DOI: 10.3389/fpsyg.2023.1292110 PMID: 38259582

Lin, Y., Weintrop, D., & Mckenna, J. (2023, June). Switch Mode: Building a middle ground between Block-based and Text-based programming. In *Proceedings of the 2023 Symposium on Learning, Design and Technology* (pp. 114-118). DOI: 10.1145/3594781.3594803

Liu, A., & Kara, S. (2023). Constructing product usage context knowledge graph using user-generated content for user-driven customization. *Journal of Mechanical Design*, 145, 41401–41403.

Liu, D., Dede, C., Huang, R., & Richards, J. (Eds.). (2017). *Virtual, augmented, and mixed realities in education*. Springer. DOI: 10.1007/978-981-10-5490-7

Liu, R., Wang, L., Lei, J., Wang, Q., & Ren, Y. (2020). Effects of an immersive virtual reality- based classroom on students' learning performance in science lesson. *British Journal of Educational Technology*, 51(6), 2034–2049. DOI: 10.1111/bjet.13028

Liu, R., Xu, X., Yang, H., Li, Z., & Huang, G. (2022). Impacts of cues on learning and attention in immersive 360-degree video: An eye-tracking study. *Frontiers in Psychology*, 12, 792069. DOI: 10.3389/fpsyg.2021.792069 PMID: 35153916

Liu, T. (2024). Assessing implicit computational thinking in game-based learning: A logical puzzle game study. *British Journal of Educational Technology*, 55(5), 2357–2382. DOI: 10.1111/bjet.13443

Liu, Z., Gong, S., Tan, Z., & Demian, P. (2023). Immersive Technologies-Driven Building Information Modeling (BIM) in the Context of Metaverse. *Buildings*, 13(1559), 1–30. DOI: 10.3390/buildings13061559

Loades, M. E., Chatburn, E., Higson-Sweeney, N., Reynolds, S., Shafran, R., Brigden, A., Linney, C., McManus, M. N., Borwick, C., & Crawley, E. (2020). Rapid systematic review: The impact of social isolation and loneliness on the mental health of children and adolescents in the context of COVID-19. *Journal of the American Academy of Child and Adolescent Psychiatry*, 59(11), 1218–1239. DOI: 10.1016/j.jaac.2020.05.009 PMID: 32504808

López-Duarte, C., Maley, J. F., & Vidal-Suárez, M. M. (2021). Main challenges to international student mobility in the European arena. *Scientometrics*, 126(11), 8957–8980. DOI: 10.1007/s11192-021-04155-y PMID: 34602676

Luciano, C., Banerjee, P., & DeFanti, T. (2009). Haptics-based virtual reality periodontal training simulator. *Virtual Reality (Waltham Cross)*, 13(2), 69–85. DOI: 10.1007/s10055-009-0112-7

Luck, S. J. (2014). *An introduction to the event-related potential technique*. MIT press.

Luo, J., Deng, L., & Wan, J. (2021). The Influence of COVID-19 on Chinese College Students' Attitudes toward Online Learning. *Educational Technology Research and Development*, 69(2), 783–803.

Lu, Q., Zhu, L., Xu, X., Whittle, J., Zowghi, D., & Jacquet, A. (2022). Responsible AI pattern catalogue: A collection of best practices for AI governance and engineering. *ACM Computing Surveys*. Advance online publication. DOI: 10.1145/3626234

Mabey, C., & Ramsey, J. (2020). Teaching and Learning Online with Zoom. *Journal of Chemical Education*, 97(9), 3257–3259.

Maček, A., & Ritonija, N. (2016). Virtual mobility in higher Education–the case of DOBA Faculty. *Studies from Education and Society*, 98-106. https://doi.org/DOI: 10.18427/iri-2016-0089

Maebell, R., & Lawrence, A. S. A. (2021). Augmented reality and mixed reality in education. In *Proceedings of the 3rd International Conference on Virtual Reality* (pp. 119-122). Harran, Türkiye.

Magdalene, R., & Sridharan, D. (2018). Powering E-Learning Through Technology: An Overview of Recent Trends in Educational Technologies. *The Online Journal of Distance Education and e-Learning : TOJDEL*, 6, 60.

Maggio, M. G., Maresca, G., De Luca, R., Stagnitti, M. C., Porcari, B., Ferrera, M. C., Galletti, F., Casella, C., Manuli, A., & Calabrò, R. S. (2019). The growing use of virtual reality in cognitive rehabilitation: Fact, fake or vision? A scoping review. *Journal of the National Medical Association*, 111(4), 457–463. DOI: 10.1016/j.jnma.2019.01.003 PMID: 30739728

Mahardika, H., Thomas, D., Ewing, M. T., & Japutra, A. (2019). Experience and facilitating conditions as impediments to consumers' new technology adoption. *International Review of Retail, Distribution and Consumer Research*, 29(1), 79–98. DOI: 10.1080/09593969.2018.1556181

Mahmood, F., Khan, A. Z., & Bokhari, R. H. (2020). ERP issues and challenges: A research synthesis. *Kybernetes*, 49(3), 629–659. DOI: 10.1108/K-12-2018-0699

Mahmud, I., Ramayah, T., & Kurnia, S. (2017). To use or not to use: Modelling end user grumbling as user resistance in pre-implementation stage of enterprise resource planning system. *Information Systems*, 69, 164–179. DOI: 10.1016/j.is.2017.05.005

Mainzer, K. (2019). *Artificial intelligence-When do machines take over?* Springer Nature.

Maisha, K., & Shetu, S. N. (2023). Influencing factors of e-learning adoption amongst students in a developing country: The post-pandemic scenario in Bangladesh. *Future Business Journal*, 9(1), 37. DOI: 10.1186/s43093-023-00214-3

Maity, S., & Veer, K. (2024). An approach for evaluation and recognition of facial emotions using EMG signal. *International Journal of Sensors, Wireless Communications and Control*, 14(2), 113–121. DOI: 10.2174/0122103279260571231213053403

Mak, J. (2016). Google Expeditions offers stunning field trips without leaving school. The International Society for Technology in Education. Retrieved from https://www.iste.org/explore/articleDetail?articleid=664&category=In-the- classroom&article.

Makeblock. (2024). About. Retrieved from https://www.makeblock.com/

Makransky, G., & Lilleholt, L. (2018). A structural equation modeling investigation of the emotional value of immersive virtual reality in education. *Educational Technology Research and Development*, 66(5), 1141–1164. DOI: 10.1007/s11423-018-9581-2

Makransky, G., Petersen, G. B., & Klingenberg, S. (2020). Can an immersive virtual reality simulation increase students' interest and career aspirations in science? *British Journal of Educational Technology*, 51(6), 2079–2097. DOI: 10.1111/bjet.12954

Marek, M. W., Chew, C. S., & Wu, W. C. V. (2021). Teacher experiences in converting classes to distance learning in the COVID-19 pandemic. *International Journal of Distance Education Technologies*, 19(1), 89–109. DOI: 10.4018/IJDET.20210101.oa3

Marinoni, G., van't Land, H., & Jensen, T. (2020). *The impact of Covid-19 on Higher Education Around the World: IAU Global Survey Report*. International Association of Universities.

Marks, B., & Thomas, J. (2022). Adoption of virtual reality technology in higher education: An evaluation of five teaching semesters in a purpose-designed laboratory. *Education and Information Technologies*, 27(1), 1287–1305. DOI: 10.1007/s10639-021-10653-6 PMID: 34257511

Marougkas, A., Troussas, C., Krouska, A., & Sgouropoulou, C. (2023). Virtual reality in education: A review of learning theories, approaches and methodologies for the last decade. *Electronics (Basel)*, 12(13), 2832. DOI: 10.3390/electronics12132832

Marougkas, A., Troussas, C., Krouska, A., & Sgouropoulou, C. (2024). How personalized and effective is immersive virtual reality in education? A systematic literature review for the last decade. *Multimedia Tools and Applications*, 83(6), 18185–18233. DOI: 10.1007/s11042-023-15986-7

Marshalsey, L., & Sclater, M. (2020). Together but apart: Creating and supporting online learning communities in an era of distributed studio education. *International Journal of Art & Design Education*, 39(4), 826–840. DOI: 10.1111/jade.12331

Martinho, D., Sobreiro, P., & Vardasca, R. (2021). Teaching sentiment in emergency online learning—a conceptual model. *Education Sciences, 11*(2), 53, 1-16. https://doi.org/DOI: 10.3390/educsci11020053

Marzano, R. J. (2004). *Building background knowledge for academic achievement: Research on what works in schools*. Association for Supervision and Curriculum Development.

Masmuzidin, M. Z., & Aziz, N. A. A. (2018). The current trends of augmented reality in early childhood education. [IJMA]. *The International Journal of Multimedia & Its Applications*, 10(6), 47–58. DOI: 10.5121/ijma.2018.10605

Mason, L. (2021). *International Student MobilityFlows and COVID-19 Realities*. Institute of InternationalEducation. Retrieved from https://www.iie.org:443/en/Research-and-Insights/Publications/IntlStudent-Mobility-Flows-and-C19-Realities

Mason, R., & Rennie, F. (2006). *E-Learning: The Key Concepts*. Routlege. DOI: 10.4324/9780203099483

Mavroudi, A., Giannakos, M., & Krogstie, J. (2018). Supporting adaptive learning pathways through the use of learning analytics: Developments, challenges and future opportunities. *Interactive Learning Environments*, 26(2), 206–220. DOI: 10.1080/10494820.2017.1292531

McDowall, J. (2020). Charting a Path to Viable Consumer AR Glasses, Part I. Retrieved August 1, 2024, from https://arinsider.co/2020/10/22/charting-a-path-to-viable-consumer-ar-glasses-part-i/

McDuff, D., Czerwinski, M., & Rowan, K. (2018). Measuring emotions in the user experience. *International Journal of Human-Computer Studies*, 120, 56–67.

McGovern, E., Moreira, G., & Luna-Nevarez, C. (2020). An application of virtual reality in education: Can this technology enhance the quality of students' learning experience? *Journal of Education for Business*, 95(7), 490–496. DOI: 10.1080/08832323.2019.1703096

McInnes, R., Carandang, M., & Kulkarni, A. (2023). *Unleashing the power of gen-AI for digital education development*. ASCILITE Publications., DOI: 10.14742/apubs.2023.520

Means, B., & Neisler, J. (2020). *Suddenly online: A national survey of undergraduates during the COVID-19 pandemic*. Digital Promise. Retrieved from Digital Promise website:https://digitalpromise.dspacedirect.org/bitstream/20.500.12265/98/3/DPSuddenlyOnlineReportJuly2020.pdf

Means, B., Toyama, Y., Murphy, R., Bakia, M., & Jones, K. (2010). *Evaluation of evidence-based practices in online learning: A meta-analysis and review of online learning studies*. US Department of Education.

Means, B., Toyama, Y., Murphy, R., Bakia, M., & Jones, K. (2013). *Evaluation of Evidence-Based Practices in Online Learning: A Meta-Analysis and Review of Online Learning Studies*. US Department of Education.

Mercer, N. (1995). *The guided construction of knowledge: Talk amongst teachers and learners*. Multilingual matters. DOI: 10.21832/9781800418288

Merchant, Z., Goetz, E. T., Cifuentes, L., Keeney-Kennicutt, W., & Davis, T. J. (2014). Effectiveness of virtual reality-based instruction on students' learning outcomes in K-12 and higher education: A meta-analysis. *Computers & Education*, 70, 29–40. DOI: 10.1016/j.compedu.2013.07.033

Mesjar, L., Cross, K., Jiang, Y., & Steed, J. (2023). The Intersection of Fashion, Immersive Technology, and Sustainability: A Literature Review. *Sustainability (Basel)*, 15(3761), 1–22. DOI: 10.3390/su15043761

Mikhailenko, M., Maksimenko, N., & Kurushkin, M. (2022, March). Eye-tracking in immersive virtual reality for education: A review of the current progress and applications. [). Frontiers Media SA.]. *Frontiers in Education*, 7, 697032. DOI: 10.3389/feduc.2022.697032

Milgram, P., & Kishino, F. (1994). A taxonomy of mixed reality visual displays. *IEICE Transactions on Information and Systems*, 77(12), 1321–1329.

Milgram, P., & Kishino, F. A. (1994). Taxonomy of mixed reality visual displays. *IEICE Transactions on Information and Systems*, 77, 1321–1329.

Mistretta, S. (2022). Virtual robotics in hybrid teaching and learning. *New Updates in E-Learning*, 1-15.

Mitchell, T. M., & Mitchell, T. M. (1997). [). New York: McGraw-hill.]. *Machine Learning*, 1(9), •••.

Mitrovic, A., Martin, B., Suraweera, P., Zakharov, K., Milik, N., Holland, J., & McGuigan, N. (2009). ASPIRE: An authoring system and deployment environment for constraint-based tutors. *International Journal of Artificial Intelligence in Education*, 19(2), 155–188.

Molina-Castillo, F. J., Rodríguez, R., López-Nicolas, C., & Bouwman, H. (2022). The role of ERP in business model innovation: Impetus or impediment. *Digital Business*, 2(2), 100024. DOI: 10.1016/j.digbus.2022.100024

Montenegro-Rueda, M., Luque-de la Rosa, A., Sarasola Sánchez-Serrano, J. L., & Fernández-Cerero, J. (2021). Assessment in higher education during the COVID-19 pandemic: A systematic review. *Sustainability (Basel)*, 13(19), 1–13, 10509. DOI: 10.3390/su131910509

Montes, R., Gea, M., Dondi, C., & Salandin, T. (2011). Virtualmobility: The value of inter-cultural exchange, eLearning Papers,ISSN: 1887-1542, https://www.elearningpapers.eu

Mooghali, M., Stroud, A., Yoo, D., Barry, A., Grimshaw, A., Ross, J., Zhu, X., & Miller, J. (2023). Barriers and facilitators to trustworthy and ethical AI-enabled medical care from patient and healthcare provider perspectives: A literature review. https://doi.org/DOI: 10.1101/2023.10.02.23296447

Moore, M. G. (1989, January 1). Editorial: Three types of interaction [Editorial]. DOI: 10.1080/08923648909526659

Moro, C., Štromberga, Z., Raikos, A., & Stirling, A. (2017). The effectiveness of virtual and augmented reality in health sciences and medical anatomy. *Anatomical Sciences Education*, 10(6), 549–559. DOI: 10.1002/ase.1696

Move-IT - Seminars Promoting Virtual Support For Mobile Students. retrieved from http://move-it.europace.org

Mozo, J. R., Quintero, H. M., & Ariza, H. M. (2017). Educational robotics: Algorithm logic learning comparison. *International Journal of Applied Engineering Research: IJAER*, 12(24), 15470–15474.

Mseleku, Z. (2020). A literature review of e-learning and e-teaching in the era of Covid-19 pandemic. *International Journal of Innovative Science and Research Technology*, 5(10), 588–597. https://www.ijisrt.com/a-literature-review-of-elearning-and-eteaching-in-the-era-of-covid19-pandemic

Müller, A. M., Goh, C., Lim, L. Z., & Gao, X. (2021). Covid-19 emergency elearning and beyond: Experiences and perspectives of university educators. *Education Sciences*, 11(1), 1–15. DOI: 10.3390/educsci11010019

Munnerley, D., Bacon, M., Wilson, A., Steele, J., Hedberg, J., & Fitzgerald, R. (2012). Confronting an Augmented Reality. *Research in Learning Technology*, 20(sup1), 39–48. DOI: 10.3402/rlt.v20i0.19189

Muravevskaia, E., & Gardner-Mccune, C. (2022). VR empathy game: Creating empathic VR environments for children based on a social constructivist learning approach. *2022 International Conference on Advanced Learning Technologies (ICALT)*, 360-362. https://doi.org/DOI: 10.1109/ICALT55010.2022.00112

Muthumanickam, P. K., Vrotsou, K., Nordman, A., Johansson, J., & Cooper, M. (2018). Identification of temporally varying areas of interest in long-duration eye-tracking data sets. *IEEE Transactions on Visualization and Computer Graphics*, 25(1), 87–97. DOI: 10.1109/TVCG.2018.2865042 PMID: 30183636

Myers, M. (2015). Ten years of Qualitative Research in Organizations and Management: Some reflections. *Qualitative Research in Organizations and Management*, 10(4), 337–339. DOI: 10.1108/QROM-07-2015-1307

Nair, V., & Hinton, G. E. (2010). Rectified linear units improve restricted boltzmann machines. In *Proceedings of the 27th international conference on machine learning (ICML-10)* (pp. 807-814).

Negi, S., & Mitra, R. (2020). Fixation duration and the learning process: An eye tracking study with subtitled videos. *Journal of Eye Movement Research*, 13(6). Advance online publication. DOI: 10.16910/jemr.13.6.1 PMID: 33828811

Nenko, Y., Kybalna, N., & Snisarenko, Y. (2020). The COVID-19 distance learning: Insight from Ukrainian students. *Revista Brasileira de Educação do Campo, 5*, 1-19, e8925. https://doi.org/DOI: 10.20873/uft.rbec.e8925

New Media Consortium (NMC). (2016). NMC/CoSN Horizon Report 2016 K-12 Edition. Retrieved from http://cdn.nmc.org/media/2016-nmc-cosn-horizon-report - k12- EN.pdf

Ngoatle, C., Mothiba, T. M., & Ngoepe, M. A. (2022). Navigating through COVID-19 pandemic period in implementing quality teaching and learning for higher education programmes: A document analysis study. *International Journal of Environmental Research and Public Health*, 19(17), 1–8, 11146. DOI: 10.3390/ijerph191711146 PMID: 36078862

Nikimaleki, M., & Rahimi, M. (2022). Effects of a collaborative AR-enhanced learning environment on learning gains and technology implementation beliefs: Evidence from a graduate teacher training course. *Journal of Computer Assisted Learning*, 38(3), 758–769. DOI: 10.1111/jcal.12646

Nilsson, S., Arvola, M., Szczepanski, A., & Bång, M. (2012). Exploring place and direction: mobile augmented reality in the Astrid Lindgren landscape. In: *Proceedings of the 24th Australian computer-human interaction conference*. ACM, pp 411–419. DOI: 10.1145/2414536.2414601

Noghabaei, M., Heydarian, A., Balali, V., & Han, K. (2020). Trend analysis on adoption of virtual and augmented reality in the architecture, engineering, and construction industry. *Data*, 5(1), 26. DOI: 10.3390/data5010026

Nokelainen, P., Pylväs, L., & Hartikainen, S. (2024). University teachers' self-reported emotions and electrodermal activity during teaching-related working events. *Studies in Higher Education*, •••, 1–20. DOI: 10.1080/03075079.2024.2387750

Noroozi, O., Dehghanzadeh, H., & Talaee, E. (2020). A systematic review on the impacts of game-based learning on argumentation skills. *Entertainment Computing*, 35, 100369. DOI: 10.1016/j.entcom.2020.100369

Numanoğlu, M., & Keser, H. (2017). Robot usage in programmıng teachıng - mBot example. *Bartın University Journal of Faculty of Education*, 6(2), 497–515.

O'neil, C. (2017). *Weapons of math destruction: How big data increases inequality and threatens democracy*. Crown.

Ocak, M. A., & Efe, A. (2018). *Coding and microcontroller applications with Arduino*. Anı Publishing.

Ojugo, A. A., & Eboka, A. O. (2020). Mitigating technical challenges via redesigning campus network for greater efficiency, scalability and robustness: A logical view. *International Journal of Modern Education and Computer Science*, 11(6), 29–45. DOI: 10.5815/ijmecs.2020.06.03

Oliveira, T., Silva, M., Spinasse, R., Ludke, G., Gaudio, M., Gomes, G., Cotini, L., Vargens, D., Schimidt, M., Andreão, R., & Mestria, M. (2021). Systematic review of virtual reality solutions employing artificial intelligence methods. *Symposium on Virtual and Augmented Reality*. https://doi.org/DOI: 10.1145/3488162.3488209

Oluk, A., & Korkmaz, Ö. (2018). Opinions of information technology teachers on the use of educational robots [Bilişim teknolojileri öğretmenlerinin eğitsel robotların kullanımına yönelik görüşleri]. *Pegem Citation Index*, 0, 215–224.

Op de Beeck, I. (2008). VM-BASE: Virtual Mobility Before and After Student Exchanges. Retrieved from http://vm-base.europace.org/

Op de Beeck, I., & Mazar, I. (2005). *Reve-real virtual Erasmus: opportunities andchallenges*. Retrieved fromhttp://www.beingmobile.net/pdf/Vilnius_2006_new_brochure.pdf

Op de Beeck, I., Bijnens, H., Michielsens, C., & Van Petegem, W. *Extending and supporting physical student mobility through virtual mobility*. 18th SPACE Conference, Nicosia (Cyprus), 23-24 February 2007. Retrieved from http://www.eunis.org/events/congresses/eunis2007/CD/pdf/papers/p121.pdf

Op de Beeck, I., Bijnens, H., Michielsens, C., & Van Petegem, W. (2007). *Extending and supporting physical student mobility through virtual mobility.*

Osti, F., de Amicis, R., Sanchez, C. A., Tilt, A. B., Prather, E., & Liverani, A. (2021). A VR training system for learning and skills development for construction workers. *Virtual Reality (Waltham Cross)*, 25(2), 523–538. DOI: 10.1007/s10055-020-00470-6

Ozdamli, F., & Karagozlu, D. (2022). Online education during the pandemic: A systematic literature review. [iJET]. *International Journal of Emerging Technologies in Learning*, 17(16), 167–193. DOI: 10.3991/ijet.v17i16.32287

Özkan, S. B., & Toz, M. (2022). A review study on the investigation of the effects of using robots in education on metacognitive behaviors. *Computer Applications in Engineering Education*, 30(4), 1277–1288. DOI: 10.1002/cae.22508

Özkan, Y., & Erdoğmuş, P. (2020). Generative Networks and Royalty-Free Products. *Sakarya University Journal of Computer and Information Sciences*, 3(3), 309–324. DOI: 10.35377/saucis.03.03.724645

Ozkan, Y., & Erdogmus, P. (2024). Evaluation of Classification Performance of New Layered Convolutional Neural Network Architecture on Offline Handwritten Signature Images. *Symmetry*, 16(6), 649. DOI: 10.3390/sym16060649

Pakkala, D., Kääriäinen, J., & Mätäsniemi, T. (2024). Improving efficiency and quality of operational industrial production assets information management in customer–vendor interaction. *Journal of Industrial Information Integration*, 41, 100644. DOI: 10.1016/j.jii.2024.100644

Papert, S. (1993). *The children's machine: Rethinking school in the age of the computer*. Basic Books, Inc.

Papert, S., & Harel, I. (1991). Situating constructionism. *Constructionism*, 36(2), 1–11.

Pappano, L. (2012). The year of the MOOC. *The New York Times, November, 2.*

Parong, J., & Mayer, R. (2021). Cognitive and affective processes for learning science in immersive virtual reality. *Journal of Computer Assisted Learning*, 37(1), 226–241. DOI: 10.1111/jcal.12482

Parong, J., & Mayer, R. E. (2021). Learning about history in immersive virtual reality: Does immersion facilitate learning? *Educational Technology Research and Development*, 69(3), 1433–1451. DOI: 10.1007/s11423-021-09999-y

Paszkiewicz, A., Salach, M., Dymora, P., Bolanowski, M., Budzik, G., & Kubiak, P. (2021). Methodology of implementing virtual reality in education for industry 4.0. *Sustainability (Basel)*, 13(9), 5049. DOI: 10.3390/su13095049

Patwardhan, V., Rao, S., Thirugnanasambantham, C., & Prabhu, N. (2020). Community of Inquiry (CoI) framework and course design as predictors of satisfaction in emergency remote teaching: Perspectives of hospitality management students. *Journal of E-learning and Knowledge Society*, 16(4), 94–103. DOI: 10.20368/1971-8829/1135315

Pavic, K., Chaby, L., Gricourt, T., & Vergilino-Perez, D. (2023). Feeling virtually present makes me happier: The influence of immersion, sense of presence, and video contents on positive emotion induction. *Cyberpsychology, Behavior, and Social Networking*, 26(4), 238–245. DOI: 10.1089/cyber.2022.0245 PMID: 37001171

Piaget, J. (1974). The future of developmental child psychology. *Journal of Youth and Adolescence*, 3(2), 87–93. DOI: 10.1007/BF02215168 PMID: 24414238

Pigliapoco, E., & Bogliolo, A. (2007, November 8-9). *Accessible virtual mobility*. Retrieved from EADTU's 20th Anniversary Conference 2007 "Internationalcources and services online: Virtual Erasmus and a new generation of Open Educational Resources for a European and global outreach: http://www.eadtu.nl/conference-2007/iles/I6.pdf

Pintrich, P. R. (2000). The role of goal orientation in self-regulated learning. *Handbook of self-regulation/Academic*.

Pirker, J., Lesjak, I., Kopf, J., Kainz, A., & Dini, A. (2020). Immersive learning in real VR. In Magnor, M., & Sorkine Hornung, A. (Eds.), *Real VR–Immersive Digital Reality* (pp. 321–336). Springer. DOI: 10.1007/978-3-030-41816-8_14

Pisarov, J., & Mester, G. (2019, December). Programming the mbot robot in school. In *Proceedings of the International Conference and Workshop Mechatronics in Practice and Education, MechEdu* (pp. 45-48).

Plasencia, D. M. (2015). One step beyond virtual reality: connecting past and future developments. *XRDS: Crossroads. The ACM Magazine for Students*, 22(1), 18–23.

Poddubnaya, T. N., Zadneprovskaya, E. L., Voevodina, S. S., Ilyinova, N. A., Khatit, F. R., & Panina, E. A. (2021). Distance Learning Experience in the Context of Globalization of Education. *Journal of Educational Psychology - Propositos y Representaciones, 9.* Retrieved from https://eric.ed.gov/?id=EJ1299286

Pokhrel, S., & Chhetri, R. (2021). A literature review on impact of COVID-19 pandemic on teaching and learning. *Higher Education for the Future*, 8(1), 133–141. DOI: 10.1177/2347631120983481

Politis, Y., Olivia, L., & Olivia, T. (2019). Empowering autistic adults through their involvement in the development of a virtual world. *Advances in Autism*, 5(4), 303–317. Advance online publication. DOI: 10.1108/AIA-01-2019-0001

Pollock, N., & Hyysalo, S. (2014). The business of being a user. *Management Information Systems Quarterly*, 38(2), 473–496. DOI: 10.25300/MISQ/2014/38.2.07

Poulová, P.; Janeček, V., Černá, M. (2007). Reasons Of Failing In Interuniversity Study. Information and Communication Technology in Education, 37-40.

Poulová, P., Černá, M., & Svobodová, L. (2009). *University Network – Efficiencyof Virtual Mobility*. In *Proceedings of the 5th WSEAS/IASME InternationalConference on educational technologies (EDUTE' 09)* (pp. 87-92).

Pozzi, G., Pigni, F., & Vitari, C. (2014). Affordance theory in the IS discipline: A review and synthesis of the literature. *20th Americas Conference on Information Systems, AMCIS 2014.*

Prakash, A., & Rajendran, R. (2022). Mechanism to capture learners' interactions in virtual reality learning environment. *2022 International Conference on Advanced Learning Technologies (ICALT)*, 335-337. https://doi.org/DOI: 10.1109/ICALT55010.2022.00105

Prakash, V., Savaglio, C., Garg, L., Bawa, S., & Spezzano, G. (2022). Cloud-and edge-based ERP systems for industrial internet of things and smart factory. *Procedia Computer Science*, 200, 537–545. DOI: 10.1016/j.procs.2022.01.251

Pratisto, E. H., Thompson, N., & Potdar, V. (2022). Immersive technologies for tourism: a systematic review. In *Information Technology and Tourism* (Vol. 24, Issue 2). Springer Berlin Heidelberg. DOI: 10.1007/s40558-022-00228-7

Prattichizzo, D., Otaduy, M., Kajimoto, H., & Pacchierotti, C. (2019). Wearable and hand-held haptics. *IEEE Transactions on Haptics*, 12(3), 227–231. DOI: 10.1109/TOH.2019.2936736

Pressley, M., & Harris, K. R. (2009). Cognitive strategies instruction: From basic research to classroom instruction. *Journal of Education*, 189(1-2), 77–94. DOI: 10.1177/0022057409189001-206

Project Atlas. (2023). Project Atlas [Dataset]. Institute of International Education. https://www.iie.org/Research-and-Insights/Project-Atlas

Prokes, C., & Housel, J. (2021). Community college student perceptions of remote learning shifts due to COVID-19. *TechTrends*, 65(4), 576–588. DOI: 10.1007/s11528-021-00587-8 PMID: 33585838

Psotka, J. (1995). Immersive training systems: Virtual reality and education in training. *Instructional Science*, 23(5-6), 405–431. DOI: 10.1007/BF00896880

Psotka, J. (2013). Educational games and virtual reality as disruptive technologies. *Journal of Educational Technology & Society*, 16(2), 69–80.

Pugachova, K. (2023). Transforming education with artificial intelligence: Challenges, opportunities, and future directions. *Вісник науки та освіти*, 11(17), 475-484. https://doi.org/DOI: 10.52058/2786-6165-2023-11(17)-475-484

Purcell, K., Heaps, A., Buchanan, J., & Friedrich, L. (2013). *How teachers are using technology at home and in their classrooms*. Pew Research Center's Internet & American Life Project.

Pursuea, M., Warsta, M., & Laaksonen, I. (2005). Virtual University: A Vehicle forDevelopment, Cooperation and Internationalisation in Teaching and Learning. *European Journal of Engineering Education*, 30(4), 439–446. DOI: 10.1080/03043790500213201

Qi, B., Zhang, M., Zhu, X., Jiang, Y., & Xiang, X. (2024). Effects of haptic interaction on learning performance and satisfaction with 3D collections. *Education and Information Technologies*, 29(7), 7793–7811. DOI: 10.1007/s10639-023-11921-3

Qin, H., & Hui, P. (2023). Empowering the metaverse with generative AI: Survey and future directions. *2023 IEEE 43rd International Conference on Distributed Computing Systems Workshops (ICDCSW)*, 85-90. https://doi.org/DOI: 10.1109/ICDCSW60045.2023.00022

Quintero, E., Salinas, P., González-Mendívil, E., & Ramírez, H. (2015). Augmented reality app for calculus: A proposal for the development of spatial visualization. In E. G. Mendívil, P. G. Ramírez Flores, J. M. Gutiérrez, & E. Ginters (Eds.), *International Conference on virtual and augmented reality in education* (pp. 301–305). Elsevier B.V. DOI: 10.1016/j.procs.2015.12.251

Radianti, J., Majchrzak, T. A., Fromm, J., & Wohlgenannt, I. (2020). A systematic review of immersive virtual reality applications for higher education: Design elements, lessons learned, and research agenda. *Computers & Education*, 147, 103778. DOI: 10.1016/j.compedu.2019.103778

Rafa, A. T. (2024, February 18). Paving way for a more inclusive Bangladesh. Retrieved May 4, 2024, from The Daily Star website: https://www.thedailystar.net/anniversary-supplement-2024/innovate-educate-elevate/news/paving-the-way-more-inclusive-bangladesh-3545126

Rahman, M. M., Hossain, M. S., & Islam, M. R. (2017). An Assessment of E-Learning Readiness in Higher Education: Evidence from Bangladesh. *International Journal of Engineering and Science Invention*, 6(3), 30–35.

Raja, M. A. S., & Kallarakal, T. K. (2021). "COVID-19 and students perception about MOOCs" a case of Indian higher educational institutions. *Interactive Technology and Smart Education*, 18(3), 450–474. DOI: 10.1108/ITSE-07-2020-0106

Raja, R., & Nagasubramani, P. C. (2018). Impact of modern technology in education. *Journal of Applied and Advanced Research*, 3(1), 33–35. DOI: 10.21839/jaar.2018.v3iS1.165

Raja, S. L. N., Joseph, N., & Totawar, A. (2020). Analysing ERP implementations from organizational change perspective: an exploratory study. *International Working Conference on Transfer and Diffusion of IT*, 674–678. DOI: 10.1007/978-3-030-64861-9_58

Rakya, Z. (2023). Exploring the impact of artificial intelligence (AI) on learner-instructor interaction in online learning (literature review). *International Journal of Emerging Multidisciplinaries: Computer Science & Artificial Intelligence*. https://doi.org/DOI: 10.54938/ijemdcsai.2023.02.1.236

Ramlo, S. (2021). The coronavirus and higher education: Faculty viewpoints about universities moving online during a worldwide pandemic. *Innovative Higher Education*, 46(3), 241–259. DOI: 10.1007/s10755-020-09532-8 PMID: 33437113

Rasheed, H. H., Salih, A. A., Ahmed, O. M., Yazdeen, A. A., Majeed, R., Mohammed, T., & Sami, G. (2024). Consideration of Cloud-Web-Concepts for Standardization and Interoperability : A Comprehensive Review for Sustainable Enterprise Systems. *AI, and IoT Integration.*, 03(02), 20–38.

Rasimah, C., Ahmad, A., & Zaman, H. (2011). Evaluation of user acceptance of mixed reality technology. *Australasian Journal of Educational Technology*, 27(8), 1369–1387. DOI: 10.14742/ajet.899

Rauner, M. S., & Haunschmied, J. (2010). *A ustrian Society of Operations Research (O esterreichische G esellschaft für Operations Research, O egor).* Wiley Encyclopedia of Operations Research and Management Science.

Ravichandran, R. R., & Mahapatra, J. (2023). Virtual Reality in Vocational Education and Training: Challenges and Possibilities. *Journal of Digital Learning and Education*, 3(1), 25–31. DOI: 10.52562/jdle.v3i1.602

Raza, S. A., Qazi, W., Khan, K. A., & Salam, J. (2021). Social isolation and acceptance of the learning management system (LMS) in the time of COVID-19 pandemic: An expansion of the UTAUT model. *Journal of Educational Computing Research*, 59(2), 183–208. DOI: 10.1177/0735633120960421

Reason, J. (1990). *Human error.* Cambridge university press. DOI: 10.1017/CBO9781139062367

Rebolledo Font de la Vall, R., & González Araya, F. (2023). Exploring the benefits and challenges of AI-language learning tools. *International Journal of Social Sciences and Humanities Invention*, 10(01), 7569–7576. DOI: 10.18535/ijsshi/v10i01.02

Reeves, S., & Crippen, K. (2021). Virtual laboratories in undergraduate science and engineering courses: A systematic review 2009-2019. *Journal of Science Education and Technology*, 30(6), 16–30. DOI: 10.1007/s10956-020-09866-0

Reeves, T. C. (1993). Interactive learning systems as mindtools. In Newhouse, P. (Ed.), *Viewpoints 2, 2-11, 29.* ECAWA.

Reeves, T. C., & Hedberg, J. G. (2003). Interactive learning systems evaluation. *Educational Technology.*

Regal, G., Pretolesi, D., Schrom-Feiertag, H., Puthenkalam, J., Migliorini, M., De Maio, E., Scarrone, F., Nadalin, M., Guarneri, M., Xerri, G. P., Di Giovanni, D., Tessari, P., Genna, F., D'Angelo, A., & Murtinger, M. (2023). Challenges in virtual reality training for CBRN events. *Multimodal Technologies and Interaction*, 7(9), 88. DOI: 10.3390/mti7090088

Remolar, I., Rebollo, C., & Fernández-Moyano, J. A. (2021). Learning history using virtual and augmented reality. *Computers*, 10(11), 146. DOI: 10.3390/computers10110146

Resnick, M., Martin, F., Sargent, R., & Silverman, B. (1996). Programmable bricks: Toys to think with. *IBM Systems journal, 35*(3.4), 443-452.

ReVe project Virtual Mobility Manual. 2006. Retrieved from http://reve.europace.org/drupal

Reynard, R., (2017). The impact of virtual reality on learning. *Campus Technology*, n.d.

Richardson, J. S., Morgan, R. F., & Fleener, C. (2012). *Reading to learn in the content areas*. Wadsworth.

Robot Virtual Worlds. (2024). Robot virtual worlds. Retrieved from https://www.robotvirtualworlds.com/

Robotics, V. E. X. (2024). The VEX ecosystem. Retrieved from https://www.vexrobotics.com/

Rodríguez, M. L., & Pulido-Montes, C. (2022). Use of digital resources in higher education during COVID-19: A literature review. *Education Sciences*, 12(9), 612. DOI: 10.3390/educsci12090612

Rogers, S. (2019). Virtual reality: THE learning aid of the 21st Century. *Forbes*.www.forbes.com/sites/solrogers/2019/03/15

Rogers, C., & Portsmore, M. (2004). Bringing engineering to elementary school. *Journal of STEM Education: Innovations and Research*, 5(3), 17–28.

Rojas-Sánchez, M. A., Palos-Sánchez, P. R., & Folgado-Fernández, J. A. (2023). Systematic literature review and bibliometric analysis on virtual reality and education. *Education and Information Technologies*, 28(1), 155–192. DOI: 10.1007/s10639-022-11167-5 PMID: 35789766

Romero, C., & Ventura, S. (2010). Educational data mining: A review of the state of the art. IEEE Transactions on Systems, Man, and Cybernetics [applications and reviews]. *Part C*, 40(6), 601–618.

Rong, Q., Lian, Q., & Tang, T. (2022). Research on the influence of AI and VR technology for students' concentration and creativity. *Frontiers in Psychology*, 13, 767689. Advance online publication. DOI: 10.3389/fpsyg.2022.767689 PMID: 35401322

Roschelle, J., Noss, R., Blikstein, P., & Jackiw, N. (2017). Technology for learning mathematics. In Cai, J. (Ed.), *Compendium for research in mathematics education* (pp. 273–296). NCTM.

Rosenbaum, E., Klopfer, E., & Perry, J. (2007). On location learning: Authentic applied science with networked augmented realities. *Journal of Science Education and Technology*, 16(1), 31–45. DOI: 10.1007/s10956-006-9036-0

Rosenblatt, F. (1958). The perceptron: A probabilistic model for information storage and organization in the brain. *Psychological Review*, 65(6), 386–408. DOI: 10.1037/h0042519 PMID: 13602029

Rosenzweig, E. (2015). *Successful user experience: Strategies and roadmaps*. Morgan Kaufmann.

Rospigliosi, P. A. (2022). Metaverse or Simulacra? Roblox, Minecraft, Meta and the turn to virtual reality for education, socialisation and work. *Interactive Learning Environments*, 30(1), 1–3. DOI: 10.1080/10494820.2022.2022899

Rouhani, S., & Mehri, M. (2018). Empowering benefits of ERP systems implementation: Empirical study of industrial firms. *Journal of Systems and Information Technology*, 20(1), 54–72. DOI: 10.1108/JSIT-05-2017-0038

Roztocki, N., Strzelczyk, W., & Weistroffer, H. R. (2024). Enterprise Systems in the Public Sector: Current Research Landscape. *Information Systems Management*, •••, 1–28. DOI: 10.1080/10580530.2024.2361617

Ruan, B. (2022). VR-Assisted Environmental Education for Undergraduates. *Advances in Multimedia*, 2022, 1–8. DOI: 10.1155/2022/3721301

Ruiz-Corbella, M., & Álvarez-González, B. (2014). Virtual Mobility as an Inclusion Strategy inHigher Education: Research on Distance EducationMaster Degrees in Europe, Latin Americaand Asia. *Research in Comparative and International Education*, 9(2), 165–180. DOI: 10.2304/rcie.2014.9.2.165

Rumelhart, D. E., Hinton, G. E., & Williams, R. J. (1986). Learning representations by back-propagating errors. *nature, 323*(6088), 533-536.

Ryan, R. M., & Deci, E. L. (2000). Intrinsic and extrinsic motivations: Classic definitions and new directions. *Contemporary Educational Psychology*, 25(1), 54–67. DOI: 10.1006/ceps.1999.1020 PMID: 10620381

Saade, R. G., & Nijher, H. (2016). Critical success factors in enterprise resource planning implementation: A review of case studies. *Journal of Enterprise Information Management*, 29(1), 72–96. DOI: 10.1108/JEIM-03-2014-0028

Sáez-López, J. M., Sevillano-García, M. L., & Vazquez-Cano, E. (2019). The effect of programming on primary school students' mathematical and scientific understanding: Educational use of mBot. *Educational Technology Research and Development*, 67(6), 1405–1425. DOI: 10.1007/s11423-019-09648-5

Şahin, E. (2009, March). Kronolojik Çanakkale Savaşları Tarihi (3 Kasım 1914 - 9 Ocak 1916). *Atatürk Araştırma Merkezi Dergisi*, 25(73), 107–164.

Salas-Pilco, S. Z., Yang, Y., & Zhang, Z. (2022). Student engagement in online learning in Latin American higher education during the COVID-19 pandemic: A systematic review. *British Journal of Educational Technology*, 53(3), 593–619. DOI: 10.1111/bjet.13190 PMID: 35600418

Saler, M. (2012). *As if: Modern enchantment and the literary prehistory of virtual reality*. Oxford University Press.

Salisbury, J. K. (1997). Design, measurement and evaluation of haptic interfaces. *Basic Research in Computer Science*, 26(3), 1–18.

Sampaio, A. Z., Ferreira, M. M., Rosário, D. P., & Martins, O. P. (2010). 3D and VR models in civil engineering education: Construction, rehabilitation and maintenance. *Automation in Construction*, 19(7), 819–828. DOI: 10.1016/j.autcon.2010.05.006

Samur, M., & Sofuoğlu, A. (2022). TÜRK MİLLİ BASINI EKSENİNDE DARÜLFÜNUN'UN KAPATILMASI MESELESİ. *Atatürk Yolu Dergisi*, (70), 379–394.

Sarker, M. F. H., Mahmud, R. A., Islam, M. S., & Islam, M. K. (2019). Use of e-learning at higher educational institutions in Bangladesh: Opportunities and challenges. *Journal of Applied Research in Higher Education*, 11(2), 210–223. DOI: 10.1108/JARHE-06-2018-0099

Say, C. (2020). 50 questions about artificial intelligence. 7 Renk Basım.

Schlager, M. S., & Fusco, J. (2003). Teacher professional development, technology, and communities of practice: Are we putting the cart before the horse? *The Information Society*, 19(3), 203–220. DOI: 10.1080/01972240309464

Schmalstieg, D., & Hollerer, T. (2016). *Augmented reality: principles and practice*. Addison-Wesley Professional.

Schmidt, M., & Glaser, N. (2021). Investigating the usability and learner experience of a virtual reality adaptive skills intervention for adults with autism spectrum disorder. *Educational Technology Research and Development*, 69(3), 1–35. DOI: 10.1007/s11423-021-10005-8

Schneider, D., Biener, V., Otte, A., Gesslein, T., Gagel, P. & Campos, C., (2021). Accuracy evaluation of touch tasks in commodity virtual and augmented reality head-mounted displays. arxiv.org/pdf/2109.10607.

Schraw, G. (1998). Promoting general metacognitive awareness. *Instructional Science*, 26(1), 113–125. DOI: 10.1023/A:1003044231033

Schraw, G., & Dennison, R. S. (1994). Assessing metacognitive awareness. *Contemporary Educational Psychology*, 19(4), 460–475. DOI: 10.1006/ceps.1994.1033

Schreurs, B., Verjans, S., & Van Petegem, W. (2006). *Towards SustainableVirtual Mobility in Higher Education Institutions.* EADTU Annual Conference2006.

Schultheis, T., & Rizzo, A. (2001). The application of virtual reality technology in rehabilitation. *Rehabilitation Psychology*, 46(3), 296–311. DOI: 10.1037/0090-5550.46.3.296

Scott, E., Soria, A., & Campo, M. (2016). Adaptive 3D virtual learning environments—A review of the literature. *IEEE Transactions on Learning Technologies*, 10(3), 262–276. DOI: 10.1109/TLT.2016.2609910

Selçuk, Z. (2012). *Eğitim Psikolojisi*. Nobel.

Selwyn, N. (2020). The digital divide: Beyond access. The International Encyclopedia of Digital Communication and Society, 1-11.

Selwyn, N. (2011). *Education and technology: Key issues and debates.* Bloomsbury Publishing.

Selwyn, N. (2020). *Telling tales on technology: Qualitative studies of technology and education.* Routledge. DOI: 10.4324/9781138368736

Shahryar, S. S. (2021, April 21). The realities of online education in Bangladesh. The Daily Star.

Shalannanda, W. (2020, November). Digital Logic Design Laboratory using Autodesk Tinkercad and Google Classroom. In *2020 14th International Conference on Telecommunication Systems, Services, and Applications (TSSA* (pp. 1-5). IEEE. DOI: 10.1109/TSSA51342.2020.9310842

Sharadgah, T. A., & Sa'di, R. A. (2020). Preparedness of institutions of higher education for assessment in virtual learning environments during the Covid-19 lockdown: Evidence of bona fide challenges and pragmatic solutions. *Journal of Information Technology Education*, 19, 755–774. DOI: 10.28945/4615

Shaun, R., De Baker, J., & Inventado, P. S. (2014). *Educational Data Mining and Learning Analytics.*

Shawar, B. A., & Atwell, E. (2007). Chatbots: are they really useful? In *LDV Forum*, 22(1), 29-49.

Shazli, I. F. A., Che Lah, N. H., Hashim, M., Mailok, R., Saad, A., & Hamid, S. (2023). A comprehensive study of students' challenges and perceptions of emergency remote education during the early COVID-19 pandemic: A systematic literature review. *SAGE Open*, 13(4), 1–20. DOI: 10.1177/21582440231219152

Shields, R. (2013). Globalization and InternationalStudent Mobility: A Network Analysis. *Comparative Education Review*, 57(4), 609–636. DOI: 10.1086/671752

Shim, C., Park, J., Kim, H., Kim, J., Park, Y., & Ryu, H. (2003). Application of virtual reality technology in biology education. *Journal of Biological Education*, 37(2), 71–74. DOI: 10.1080/00219266.2003.9655854

Shin, M., & Hickey, K. (2021). Needs a little TLC: Examining college students' emergency remote teaching and learning experiences during COVID-19. *Journal of Further and Higher Education*, 45(7), 973–986. DOI: 10.1080/0309877X.2020.1847261

Shoop, R., Flot, J., Friez, T., Schunn, C., & Witherspoon, E. (2016). Can computational thinking practices be taught in robotics classrooms. Retrieved from https://www.cmu.edu/roboticsacademy/PDFs/Research/CTP_RoboticsClassrooms.pdf

Siemens, G. (2013). Learning analytics: The emergence of a discipline. *The American Behavioral Scientist*, 57(10), 1380–1400. DOI: 10.1177/0002764213498851

Siemens, G., & Baker, R. S. D. (2012, April). Learning analytics and educational data mining: towards communication and collaboration. In *Proceedings of the 2nd international conference on learning analytics and knowledge* (pp. 252-254). DOI: 10.1145/2330601.2330661

Silvio, J. (2003). Global Learning and Virtual Mobility. (T. Varis, T. Utsumi, & W. R. Klemm, Eds.) Retrieved from http://www.friends-partners.org/glosas/Global_University/Global%20University%20 System/ UNESCO_ Chair_Book/Manuscripts/Part_IV_Global_Collaboration/Silvio,%20Jose/Silvio_web/SilvioD9.html

Şimşek, K. (2019). *Investigation of the effects of robotic coding application on science achievement and scientific process skills of 6th grade students in science course matter and heat unit* (Unpublished master's thesis). Marmara Üniversity, İstanbul.

Simulator MBot. (2024). About us. Retrieved from https://en.iraifrance.com/a-propos-de-nous

Singh, C., & Pekkola, S. (2023). Reasons for customizing packaged enterprise systems: A case study on an enterprise asset management system. *Journal of Information Technology Case and Application Research*, 25(2), 159–186. DOI: 10.1080/15228053.2023.2223464

Singh, G., Mantri, A., Sharma, O., & Kaur, R. (2020). Virtual reality learning environment for enhancing electronics engineering laboratory experience. *Computer Applications in Engineering Education*, 29(1), 229–243. DOI: 10.1002/cae.22333

Sırakaya, M., & Alsancak Sırakaya, D. (2020). Augmented reality in STEM education: A systematic review. *Interactive Learning Environments*, 30(8), 1556–1569. https://doi.org/10.1080/10494820.2020.1722713DOI: 10.1080/10494820.2020.1722713

Siron, Y., Wibowo, A., & Narmaditya, B. S. (2020). Factors affecting the adoption of e-learning in Indonesia: Lesson from Covid-19. *Journal of Technology and Science Education*, 10(2), 282. DOI: 10.3926/jotse.1025

Slater, M. (2021). Beyond speculation about the ethics of virtual reality: The need for empirical results. *Frontiers in Virtual Reality*, 2, 687609. Advance online publication. DOI: 10.3389/frvir.2021.687609

Smith, J. (2020). The benefits of online learning: A comparative analysis. *Journal of Online Learning and Teaching*, 16(2), 1–12.

Soccini, A. M., & Cena, F. (2021, November). The ethics of rehabilitation in virtual reality: The role of self-avatars and deep learning. In *2021 IEEE International Conference on Artificial Intelligence and Virtual Reality (AIVR)* (pp. 324-328). IEEE. https://doi.org/DOI: 10.1109/AIVR52153.2021.00068

Soliman, M., & Karia, N. (2017). Antecedents for the success of the adoption of organizational ERP among higher education institutions and competitive advantage in Egypt. *Engineering, Technology &. Applied Scientific Research*, 7(3), 1719–1724.

Soliman, M., Pesyridis, A., Dalaymani-Zad, D., Gronfula, M., & Kourmpetis, M. (2021). The application of virtual reality in engineering education. *Applied Sciences (Basel, Switzerland)*, 11(6), 1–14. DOI: 10.3390/app11062879

Somyürek, S. (2014). Öğretim sürecinde z kuşağının dikkatini çekme: Artırılmış gerçeklik. *Eğitim Teknolojisi Kuram ve Uygulama*, 4(1), 63–80. DOI: 10.17943/etku.88319

Song, C., Shin, S. Y., & Shin, K. S. (2023). Optimizing Foreign Language Learning in Virtual Reality: A Comprehensive Theoretical Framework Based on Constructivism and Cognitive Load Theory (VR-CCL). *Applied Sciences (Basel, Switzerland)*, 13(23), 12557. DOI: 10.3390/app132312557

Song, H., Chen, F., Peng, Q., Zhang, J., & Gu, P. (2017). Improvement of user experience using virtual reality in open-architecture product design. *Proceedings of the Institute of Mechanical Engineering*. 232.

Sonn, I. K., Du Plessis, M., Jansen Van Vuuren, C. D., Marais, J., Wagener, E., & Roman, N. V. (2021). Achievements and challenges for higher education during the COVID-19 pandemic: A rapid review of media in Africa. *International Journal of Environmental Research and Public Health*, 18(24), 1–14, 12888. DOI: 10.3390/ijerph182412888 PMID: 34948499

Sood, S. K., & Singh, K. D. (2018). An Optical-Fog assisted EEG-based virtual reality framework for enhancing E-learning through educational games. *Computer Applications in Engineering Education*, 26(5), 1565–1576. DOI: 10.1002/cae.21965

Sousa, D. (2005). *How the brain learns to read*. Corwin Press.

Souza, J. D., Silva, P. J., Pinto, A. H., Monteiro, F. F., & Teixeira, J. M. (2020, November). Assessing the reality gap of robotic simulations with educational purposes. In *2020 Latin American Robotics Symposium (LARS), 2020 Brazilian Symposium on Robotics (SBR) and 2020 Workshop on Robotics in Education (WRE)* (pp. 1-6). IEEE. DOI: 10.1109/LARS/SBR/WRE51543.2020.9306947

Spinks, J., & Mortimer, D. (2015). Lost in the crowd? Using eye-tracking to investigate the effect of complexity on attribute non-attendance in discrete choice experiments. *BMC Medical Informatics and Decision Making*, 16(1), 1–13. DOI: 10.1186/s12911-016-0251-1 PMID: 26842646

Spot+ project team. (2001). *Training Module 2: A Virtual Erasmus Student*. Retrieved from http://www.spotplus.odl.org/downloads/Training_module_2.pdf

Squire, K., & Jenkins, H. (2003). Harnessing the power of games in education. *Insight (American Society of Ophthalmic Registered Nurses)*, 3(1), 5–33. PMID: 12703249

Srikong, M., & Wannapiroon, P. (2020). Immersive technology for medical education: Technology enhance immersive learning experiences. In *Siriraj Medical Journal* (Vol. 72, Issue 3, pp. 265–271). DOI: 10.33192/Smj.2020.36

Srinivasan, M. A., & Basdogan, C. (1997). Haptics in virtual environments: Taxonomy, research status, and challenges. *Computers & Graphics*, 21(4), 393–404. DOI: 10.1016/S0097-8493(97)00030-7

Stahl, B., Antoniou, J., Ryan, M., Macnish, K., & Jiya, T. (2021). Organisational responses to the ethical issues of artificial intelligence. *AI & Society*, 37(1), 23–37. DOI: 10.1007/s00146-021-01148-6

Stanković, M., Nejić, K., & Stojiljković, N. (2020). Level of fear, opinion and quality of study during the coronavirus pandemic (COVID-19). How hard is it to get back to daily commitments? *Pedagogika-Pedagogy*, 92(7), 176–183.

Steinbauer, R. (2024). Teaching Students About Workplace Harassment by Letting Them Experience it in a Virtual Reality Environment. *Journal of Management Education*, 48(4), 671–707. DOI: 10.1177/10525629231225735

Stewardson, G. A., Robinson, T. P., Furse, J. S., & Pate, M. L. (2019). Investigating the relationship between VEX robotics and student self-efficacy: An initial look. *International Journal of Technology and Design Education*, 29(4), 877–896. DOI: 10.1007/s10798-018-9461-4

Stier, S., Breuer, J., Siegers, P., & Thorson, K. (2020). Integrating survey data and digital trace data: Key issues in developing an emerging field. *Social Science Computer Review*, 38(5), 503–516. DOI: 10.1177/0894439319843669

Stoffova, V., & Hyksova, H. (2023, October). Education Robotics in Virtual Environment. In *Proceedings of the Future Technologies Conference* (pp. 479-496). Cham: Springer Nature Switzerland.

Stonig, J., Schmid, T., & Müller-Stewens, G. (2022). From product system to ecosystem: How firms adapt to provide an integrated value proposition. *Strategic Management Journal*, 43(9), 1927–1957. DOI: 10.1002/smj.3390

Suh, A., & Lee, H. (2021). Challenges in measuring effectiveness of virtual reality environments. *Journal of Virtual Worlds Research*, 14(1), 1–15. DOI: 10.1111/jvw.12112

Suh, A., & Prophet, J. (2018). The state of immersive technology research: A literature analysis. *Computers in Human Behavior*, 86, 77–90. DOI: 10.1016/j.chb.2018.04.019

Sullivan, A., & Bers, M. U. (2019). VEX Robotics Competitions: Gender differences in student attitudes and experiences. *Journal of Information Technology Education*, 18, 18. DOI: 10.28945/4193

Sumardani, D., & Lin, C. H. (2023). Cognitive processes during virtual reality learning: A study of brain wave. *Education and Information Technologies*, 28(11), 14877–14896. DOI: 10.1007/s10639-023-11788-4

Sutherland, I. E. (1965). The ultimate display. Paper presented at the IFIP Congress. www. papers.cumincad.org/cgi-bin/works/c58e. Retrieved April 22, 2019.

Sutherland, J., Belec, J., Sheikh, A., Chepelev, L., Althobaity, W., Chow, B., Mitsouras, D., Christensen, A., Rybicki, F. J., & La Russa, D. J. (2019). Applying modern virtual and augmented reality technologies to medical ımages and models. *Journal of Digital Imaging*, 32(1), 38–53. DOI: 10.1007/s10278-018-0122-7

Swapp, D., Williams, J., & Steed, A. (2010). The implementation of a novel walking interface within an immersive display. *Institute of Electrical and Electronics Engineers (IEEE) Symposium on 3D User Interfaces* (3DUI).

Taiwo, E., Akinsola, A., Tella, E., Makinde, K., & Akinwande, M. (2023). A review of the ethics of artificial intelligence and its applications in the United States. *ArXiv, abs/2310.05751*. http://dx.doi.org/DOI: 10.5121/ijci.2023.120610

Tan, A. E., Schiffmann, L., & Salden, P. (2021). Handbook on Physical and Virtual Mobility. Teaching and Learning in Intercultural Settings. Retrieved from file:///C:/Users/Lenovo/Downloads/D%203.5%20UNIC%20Handbook%20on%20Physical%20and%20Virtual%20Mobility.pdf

Tan, Y., Xu, W., Li, S., & Chen, K. (2022). Augmented and virtual reality (AR/VR) for education and applications. *Buildings*, 12(10), 1529–1553. DOI: 10.3390/buildings12101529

Tarabasz, A., Selaković, M., & Abraham, C. (2018). The classroom of the future: Disrupting the concept of contemporary business education. *Entrepreneurial Business and Economics Review*, 6(4), 231–245. DOI: 10.15678/EBER.2018.060413

Tarng, W., & Ou, K. L. (2012). A study of campus butterfly ecology learning system based on augmented reality and mobile learning. In *IEEE Seventh International Conference on Wireless, Mobile and Ubiquitous Technology in Education (WMUTE)*, (pp. 62–66). Takamatsu: IEEE. DOI: 10.1109/WMUTE.2012.17

Taylor, S., & Todd, P. (1995). Decomposition and crossover effects in the theory of planned behavior: A study of consumer adoption intentions. *International Journal of Research in Marketing*, 12(2), 137–155. DOI: 10.1016/0167-8116(94)00019-K

TeaCamp project partnership. (2010). Here from E. Dauksiene, M. Tereseviciene, A. Volungeviciene. Virtual Mobility Creates Opportunities. In Conference Proceedings "Application of ICT in Education 2010: experience, issues and perspectives of e-studies", 18 November 2010, ISSN 1822-7244, p. 30-35.

Teichler, U. (2017). Internationalisation Trends inHigher Education and the Changing Role ofInternational Student Mobility. *Journal of InternationalMobility*, 5(1), 177–216.

Teke, O., Kilinc, M., Geris, A., & Cukurbasi, B. (2023). Feedback systems suitable for hearing impaired students in virtual reality supported distance learning environments in higher education: MetaCBU case. *BILTEVT2023: International Barrier-Free Informatics Technology Congress 2023*. Retrieved from https://engelsizbilisim.org/biltevt/wp-content/uploads/2024/02/A4-Olcusunde-BILTEVT2023_Program_ve_Bildiri_Ozetleri_Kitabi.pdf

Terkildsen, T., & Makransky, G. (2019). Measuring presence in video games: An investigation of the potential use of physiological measures as indicators of presence. *International Journal of Human-Computer Studies*, 126, 64–80. DOI: 10.1016/j.ijhcs.2019.02.006

Thawani, J. P., Ramayya, A. G., Abdullah, K. G., Hudgins, E., Vaughan, K., Piazza, M., & Grady, M. S. (2016). Resident simulation training in endoscopic endonasal surgery utilizing haptic feedback technology. *Journal of Clinical Neuroscience*, 34, 112–116. DOI: 10.1016/j.jocn.2016.05.036 PMID: 27473019

The Scottish Centre for research into On-Line Learning & Assessment. (2007). *Student Mobility in a Digital World*. Retrieved November 21, 2010, from Victorious Final Report, retrieved from http://www.coimbra-group.eu/victorious/VIC%20Final%20Report%20print%20version.pdf

Thomassen, A., & Rive, P. (2010). How to enable knowledge exchange in Second Life in design education? *Learning, Media and Technology*, 35(2), 155–169. DOI: 10.1080/17439884.2010.494427

Thongsri, N., Chootong, C., Tripak, O., Piyawanitsatian, P., & Saengae, R. (2021). Predicting the determinants of online learning adoption during the COVID-19 outbreak: A two-staged hybrid SEM-neural network approach. *Interactive Technology and Smart Education*, 18(3), 362–379. DOI: 10.1108/ITSE-08-2020-0165

Tinkercad. (2024). About. Retrieved from https://www.tinkercad.com/

Tiwari, R. (2023). *The integration of AI and machine learning in education and its potential to personalize and improve student learning experiences*. International Journal Of Scientific Research In Engineering And Management., DOI: 10.55041/IJSREM17645

Tobergte, D., & Curtis, S. (2013). Social research methods. *Journal of Chemical Information and Modeling*, 88, 327–342.

Tom Dieck, M. C., & Han, D. (2022). The role of immersive technology in Customer Experience Management. *Journal of Marketing Theory and Practice*, 30(1), 108–119. Advance online publication. DOI: 10.1080/10696679.2021.1891939

Tomaschko, M., & Hohenwarter, M. (2019). Augmented reality in mathematics education: The case of GeoGebra AR. In *Augmented reality in educational settings* (1st ed., pp. 325–346). Brill., DOI: 10.1163/9789004408845_014

Tufekci, Z. (2017). *Twitter and tear gas: The power and fragility of networked protest*. Yale University Press.

Turkish Language Association (TDK). (2023). Turkish Dictionary. sozluk.gov.tr

Tyagi, S. K., & Krishankumar, R. (2023). Examining interactions of factors affecting e-learning adoption in higher education: Insights from a fuzzy set qualitative and comparative analysis. *Journal of Science and Technology Policy Management, ahead-of-print*(ahead-of-print). https://doi.org/DOI: 10.1108/JSTPM-02-2023-0022

Uddin, M. M., Ghosh, A., & Isaac, O. (2019). Impact of the system, information, and service quality of online learning on user satisfaction among public universities students in Bangladesh. [IJMHS]. *International Journal of Management and Human Science*, 3(2), 1–10.

UNESCO International Institute for Higher Education in Latin America and the Caribbean (IESALC). (2022). Moving minds: Opportunities and challenges for virtual student mobility (VSM) in a post-pandemic world. UNESCO IESALC. Petegem, W. (2010). *Virtual Mobility and International Networking*. VirtualCampus conference, Granada (Spain).

UNESCO. (2020). COVID-19 Educational Disruption and Response. Retrieved from https://en.unesco.org/covid19/educationresponse

UNESCO. (2021). Education in the time of COVID-19—UNESCO Digital Library. Retrieved April 23, 2024, from https://unesdoc.unesco.org/ark:/48223/pf0000374075_eng

URL-1. (2023). *Reality remix: Understanding the differences between VR, AR, and MR*. Retrieved August 1, 2024, from https://www.mirrar.com/blogs/reality-remix-understanding-the-differences-between-vr-ar-and-mr

URL-2. (2024). *Top augmented reality apps for classroom use*. Retrieved August 1, 2024, from https://moldstud.com/articles/p-top-augmented-reality-apps-for-classroom-use

Utomo, P., Kurniasari, F., & Purnamaningsih, P. (2021). The effects of performance expectancy, effort expectancy, facilitating condition, and habit on behavior intention in using mobile healthcare application. *International Journal of Community Service & Engagement*, 2(4), 183–197. DOI: 10.47747/ijcse.v2i4.529

Uzun, Y., & Akın, M. (2022). Virtual and augmented reality concepts. In Y. Uzun. & R. Butuner (Eds.), *Current studies in artificial intelligence, virtual reality and augmented reality* (pp. 57–73). ISRES Publishing

Väljataga, T., Poom-Valickis, K., Rumma, K., & Aus, K. (2020). Transforming higher education learning ecosystem: Teachers' perspective. *Interaction Design and Architecture(s). Journal*, 46, 47–69. DOI: 10.55612/s-5002-046-003

van der Linde-van den Bor, M., Slond, F., Liesdek, O. C. D., Suyker, W. J., & Weldam, S. W. M. (2022). The use of virtual reality in patient education related to medical somatic treatment: A scoping review. In *Patient Education and Counseling* (Vol. 105, Issue 7). DOI: 10.1016/j.pec.2021.12.015

van der Wende, M. C. (Ed.). (1998). *Virtual Mobility: New Technologies and Internationalisation. Nuffic Paperback no. 10.* Nuffic.

Van Krevelen, D. W. F., & Poelman, R. (2010). A survey of augmented reality technologies, applications and limitations. *The International Journal of Virtual Reality : a Multimedia Publication for Professionals*, 9(2), 1–20. DOI: 10.20870/IJVR.2010.9.2.2767

Van Mechelen, M., Smith, R. C., Schaper, M. M., Tamashiro, M., Bilstrup, K. E., Lunding, M., Graves Petersen, M., & Sejer Iversen, O. (2023). Emerging technologies in K–12 education: A future HCI research agenda. *ACM Transactions on Computer-Human Interaction*, 30(3), 1–40. DOI: 10.1145/3569897

VanLehn, K. (2011). The relative effectiveness of human tutoring, intelligent tutoring systems, and other tutoring systems. *Educational Psychologist*, 46(4), 197–221. DOI: 10.1080/00461520.2011.611369

Vassigh, S., Corrigan, S., Bogosian, B., & Peterson, E. (2023). *Adaptive immersive learning environments for teaching industrial robotics*. Emerging Technologies and Future of Work., DOI: 10.54941/ahfe1004411

Vehlen, A., Standard, W., & Domes, G. (2022). How to choose the size of facial areas of interest in interactive eye tracking. *PLoS One*, 17(2), e0263594. DOI: 10.1371/journal.pone.0263594 PMID: 35120188

Velarde-Camaqui, D., Sanabria-Z, J., Ramírez-Montoya, M. S., & Cebral-Loureda, M. (2024). Augmented reality in educational innovation: A literature mapping review in D. B. Ibáñez, L. M. Castro, A. Espinosa, I. Puentes-Rivera, and P. C. López-López (Eds), *Communication and applied technologies*. Singapore: Springer.

Verma, C., Illés, Z., & Kumar, D. (2024). An investigation of novel features for predicting student happiness in hybrid learning platforms–An exploration using experiments on trace data. *International Journal of Information Management Data Insights*, 4(1), 100219. DOI: 10.1016/j.jjimei.2024.100219

Vertucci, R., D'Onofrio, S., Ricciardi, S., & Nino, M. D. (2023). History of augmented reality. In Nee, Y., & Ong, S. (Eds.), *Springer handbook of augmented reality*. Springer., DOI: 10.1007/978-3-030-67822-7_2

VEXcode VR. (2024). Expanding the VEXcode VR universe. Retrieved from https://www.vexrobotics.com/vexcode/vr

VICTORIOUS - Virtual Curricula Through Reliable Interoperating University Systems. retrieved from http://www.coimbra-group.eu/victorious/

Viinikkala, L., Heimo, O. I., Korkalainen, T., Mäkilä, T., Helle, S., Pönni, V., & Lehtonen, T. (2014) The Luostarinmäki adventure–an augmented reality game in an open-air museum. In: *NODEM 2014 – Engaging Spaces – Interpretation, Design and Digital Strategies.*

Vilhelmson, B., & Thulin, E. (2005). Virtual Mobility of Urban Youth: ICT-basedCommunication in Sweden. *Journal of Economic & Social Geography*, 96(5), 477–487.

Vilhelmson, B., & Thulin, E. (2008). Virtual mobility, time use and the place of the home. *Tijdschrift voor Economische en Sociale Geografie*, 99(5), 602–618. DOI: 10.1111/j.1467-9663.2008.00494.x

Virtual Robotics Toolkit. (2024). About. Retrieved from https://www.virtualroboticstoolkit.com/discover

Volkoff, O., & Strong, D. M. (2018). The Routledge Companion to Management Information Systems. *The Routledge Companion to Management Information Systems*, 232–246.

Vriens, M., & VanPetegem, W. (Eds.). (2012). *Make it work! Integrating virtualmobility in international work placements*. Education and Culture DG; LifelongLearningProgramme. Retrieved from https://www.efmd.org/projectstest?'

Vriens, M., Achten, M., Op de Beeck, I., & Van Petegem, W. (2010,). Virtual mobility as an alternative or complement to physical mobility. Retrieved from http://move-it.europace.org/kfm/uploads/Edulearn_Move-IT_VM.pdf

Vygotsky, L. S. (1978). *Mind in society: The development of higher psychological processes* (Vol. 86). Harvard university press.

Vygotsky, L. S., & Cole, M. (1978). *Mind in society: Development of higher psychological processes*. Harvard University Press.

Wadhwa, R. (2016b). New phase of internationalization of higher education and institutional change. *Higher Education for the Future*, 3(2), pp-227-246.

Wadhwa, R. (2016). Students on move: Understanding decision making process and destination choice of Indian students. *Higher Education for the Future*, 3(1), 54–75. DOI: 10.1177/2347631115610221

Wadhwa, R. (2019). Pathways to Internationalization in Indian Higher Education: Reflections on Policy Options. In Bhushan, S. (Ed.), *The future of Higher Education in India*. Springer. DOI: 10.1007/978-981-32-9061-7_19

Wadhwa, R., Shcheglova, D., Opfer, E., & Garmonova, A. (2024). Teachers on the Move: Understanding the New Model of Virtual Mobility Through the Case Study of a Russian University. *Higher Education for the Future*, 11(1), 90–108. DOI: 10.1177/23476311231222965

Walkington, C., Nathan, M. J., Washington, J., Hunnicut, J., Darwin, T., Daughrity, L., & Schenck, K. (2024). Comparing learning geometry using a tablet to head-mounted display augmented reality: How and when dimensionality matters. *Education and Information Technologies*. Advance online publication. DOI: 10.1007/s10639-024-13008-z

Walsham, G. (1995). Interpretive case studies in IS research: Nature and method. *European Journal of Information Systems*, 4(2), 74–81. DOI: 10.1057/ejis.1995.9

Walsham, G. (2012). Are we making a better world with ICTs? Reflections on a future agenda for the IS field. *Journal of Information Technology*, 27(2), 87–93. DOI: 10.1057/jit.2012.4

Wang, F., & Hannafin, M. J. (2005). Design-based research and technology-enhanced learning environments. *Educational Technology Research and Development*, 53(4), 5–23. DOI: 10.1007/BF02504682

Wang, H., Wang, J., & Tang, Q. (2018). A Review of Application of Affordance Theory in Information Systems. *Journal of Service Science and Management*, 11(01), 56–70. DOI: 10.4236/jssm.2018.111006

Wang, L., Zhang, Q., & Sun, D. (2024). Exploring the impact of an augmented reality-integrated mathematics curriculum on students' spatial skills in elementary school. *International Journal of Science and Mathematics Education*. Advance online publication. DOI: 10.1007/s10763-024-10473-3

Wang, Q., & Li, Y. (2024). How virtual reality, augmented reality and mixed reality facilitate teacher education: A systematic review. *Journal of Computer Assisted Learning*, 40(3), 1276–1294. DOI: 10.1111/jcal.12949

Wang, R., Bush-Evans, R., Arden-Close, E., Bolat, E., McAlaney, J., Hodge, S., Thomas, S., & Phalp, K. (2023). Transparency in persuasive technology, immersive technology, and online marketing: Facilitating users' informed decision making and practical implications. *Computers in Human Behavior*, 139(October), 1–15. DOI: 10.1016/j.chb.2022.107545

Wang, X. M., Yu, D. D., Yu, X. H., Hwang, G.-J., & Li, F. (2024). Impacts of augmented reality-supported STEM education on students' achievement: A meta-analysis of selected SSCI publications from 2010 to 2023. *Education and Information Technologies*. Advance online publication. DOI: 10.1007/s10639-024-12641-y

Wang, X., Young, G. W., Plechatá, A., Mc Guckin, C., & Makransky, G. (2023). Utilizing virtual reality to assist social competence education and social support for children from under-represented backgrounds. *Computers & Education*, 201(104815), 1–18. DOI: 10.1016/j.compedu.2023.104815

Wang, Y. (2023). *Procedural content generation for VR educational applications: The investigation of AI-based approaches for improving learning experience*. Applied and Computational Engineering., DOI: 10.54254/2755-2721/17/20230905

Watermeyer, R., Crick, T., Knight, C., & Goodall, J. (2021). COVID-19 and digital disruption in UK universities: Afflictions and affordances of emergency online migration. *Higher Education*, 81(3), 623–641. DOI: 10.1007/s10734-020-00561-y PMID: 32836334

Webster, R. (2015). Declarative knowledge acquisition in immersive virtual learning environments. *Interactive Learning Environments*, 24(6), 1319–1333. DOI: 10.1080/10494820.2014.994533

Wee, C., Yap, K. M., & Lim, W. N. (2021). Haptic interfaces for virtual reality: Challenges and research directions. *IEEE Access : Practical Innovations, Open Solutions*, 9, 112145–112162. DOI: 10.1109/ACCESS.2021.3103598

Weerasinghe, M., Quigley, A., Ducasse, J., Pucihar, K., & Kljun, M. (2019). Educational augmented reality games. In Geroimenko, V. (Ed.), *Augmented reality games II: The gamification of education, medicine and art* (pp. 159–177). Springer Nature. DOI: 10.1007/978-3-030-15620-6_1

Wegerif, R. (2013). *Dialogic: Education for the internet age*. Routledge. DOI: 10.4324/9780203111222

Weinstein, C. E., & Mayer, R. E. (1983, November). The teaching of learning strategies. In *Innovation abstracts* (Vol. 5, No. 32, p. n32).

Wei, X., Weng, D., Liu, Y., & Wang, Y. (2015). Teaching based on augmented reality for a technical creative design course. *Computers & Education*, 81, 221–234. DOI: 10.1016/j.compedu.2014.10.017

Westphal, A., Richter, E., Lazarides, R., & Huang, Y. (2024). More I-talk in student teachers' written reflections indicates higher stress during VR teaching. *Computers & Education*, 212, 1–15. DOI: 10.1016/j.compedu.2024.104987

Wieder, B., Booth, P., Matolcsy, Z. P., & Ossimitz, M. (2006). The impact of ERP systems on firm and business process performance. *Journal of Enterprise Information Management*, 19(1), 13–29. DOI: 10.1108/17410390610636850

Wilson, S., Tan, S., Knox, M., Ong, A., Crawford, J., & Rudolph, J. (2020). Enabling cross-cultural student voice during COVID-19: A collective autoethnography. *Journal of University Teaching & Learning Practice*, 17(5), 1–21. DOI: 10.53761/1.17.5.3

Winn, W. (1993). A conceptual basis for educational applications of virtual reality. *Technical Report* TR-93-9, Human Interface Technology Laboratory, University of Washington.

Witherspoon, E. B., Higashi, R. M., Schunn, C. D., Baehr, E. C., & Shoop, R. (2017). Developing computational thinking through a virtual robotics programming curriculum. [TOCE]. *ACM Transactions on Computing Education*, 18(1), 4–24.

Witherspoon, E. B., & Schunn, C. D. (2019). Teachers' goals predict computational thinking gains in robotics. *Information and Learning Science*, 120(5/6), 308–326. DOI: 10.1108/ILS-05-2018-0035

Wonsick, M., & Padir, T. (2020). A Systematic Review of Virtual Reality Interfaces for Controlling and Interacting with Robots. *Applied Sciences (Basel, Switzerland)*, 10(24), 9051. DOI: 10.3390/app10249051

Woolf, B. P. (2010). *Building intelligent interactive tutors: Student-centered strategies for revolutionizing e-learning*. Morgan Kaufmann.

Wu, C. L. (2023). Using video modeling with augmented reality to teach students with developmental disabilities to solve mathematical word problems. *Journal of Developmental and Physical Disabilities*, 35(3), 487–507. DOI: 10.1007/s10882-022-09862-9

Wu, H. K., Lee, S. W. Y., Chang, H. Y., & Liang, J. C. (2013). Current status, opportunities and challenges of augmented reality in education. *Computers & Education*, 62, 41–49. DOI: 10.1016/j.compedu.2012.10.024

Wu, L., Chau, K. T., Wan Yahaya, W. A. J., Wang, S., & Wu, X. (2024). The Effect of Electroencephalogram Feedback in Virtual Reality Interactive System on Creativity Performance, Attention Value, and Cognitive Load. *International Journal of Human-Computer Interaction*, •••, 1–18. DOI: 10.1080/10447318.2024.2371692

Wut, T. M., & Xu, J. (2021). Person-to-person interactions in online classroom settings under the impact of COVID-19: A social presence theory perspective. *Asia Pacific Education Review*, 22(3), 371–383. DOI: 10.1007/s12564-021-09673-1

Xie, J., & Rice, M. F. (2021). Instructional designers' roles in emergency remote teaching during COVID-19. *Distance Education*, 42(1), 70–87. DOI: 10.1080/01587919.2020.1869526

Xi, W. (2020). Research on application of artificial intelligence in VR games. In *Fuzzy Systems and Data Mining VI* (pp. 247–254). IOS Press., DOI: 10.3233/FAIA200704

Yanamala, A. K. Y., Suryadevara, S., & Kalli, V. D. R. (2023). Evaluating the Impact of Data Protection Regulations on AI Development and Deployment. *International Journal of Advanced Engineering Technologies and Innovations*, 1(01), 319–353.

Yazıcı, N. (2013). Lise Müfredat Programlarında ve Ders Kitaplarında Çanakkale Savaşı'nın Öğretimi Üzerine Eleştirel Bir Yaklaşım. Hacettepe Üniversitesi Eğitim Fakültesi Dergisi, 28(28-2), 535-550.

Ye, D., & Pennisi, S. (2022). Using trace data to enhance students' self-regulation: A learning analytics perspective. *The Internet and Higher Education*, 54, 100855. DOI: 10.1016/j.iheduc.2022.100855

Yıldız, T. A., Yağcı, Ş. Ç., & Özkan, Y. (2023). Developing Augmented Reality Learning Material in Professional English Teaching and Examining Its Effect on Academic Success. E-International Journal of Educational Research, 14(6).

Yildiz, T., & Seferoğlu, S. S. (2021). The effect of robotic programming on coding attitude and computational thinking skills toward self-efficacy perception. *Journal of Learning and Teaching in Digital Age*, 6(2), 101–116.

Yin, J., Hinchet, R., Shea, H., & Majidi, C. (2020). Wearable soft technologies for haptic sensing and feedback. *Advanced Functional Materials*, 31(39), 2007428. Advance online publication. DOI: 10.1002/adfm.202007428

Yohannes, A., & Chen, H. L. (2021). GeoGebra in mathematics education: A systematic review of journal articles published from 2010 to 2020. *Interactive Learning Environments*, 31(9), 5682–5697. DOI: 10.1080/10494820.2021.2016861

Yoo, J., & Brownlee, E. A. (2020). The past, present, and future of virtual reality in higher education. In *Handbook of Research on Adult Learning in Higher Education* (pp. 633–657). IGI Global. DOI: 10.4018/978-1-7998-1306-4.ch024

Yu Chung Wang, W., Pauleen, D., & Taskin, N. (2022). Enterprise systems, emerging technologies, and the data-driven knowledge organisation. *Knowledge Management Research and Practice*, 20(1), 1–13. DOI: 10.1080/14778238.2022.2039571

Yu, Z., & Xu, W. (2022). A meta-analysis and systematic review of the effect of virtual reality technology on users' learning outcomes. *Computer Applications in Engineering Education*, 30(5), 1470–1484. DOI: 10.1002/cae.22532

Zachary, W., Ryder, J., Hicinbothom, J., & Bracken, K. (1997). The use of executable cognitive models in simulation based ıntelligent embedded training. *Proceedings of Human Factors Society 41st Annual Meeting*. (pp. 1118-1122). Santa Monica, CA: Human Factors Society. DOI: 10.1177/107118139704100287

Zahabi, M., & Razak, A. (2020). Adaptive virtual reality-based training: A systematic literature review and framework. *Virtual Reality (Waltham Cross)*, 24(4), 1–28. DOI: 10.1007/s10055-020-00434-w

Zarei, S., & Mohammadi, S. (2022). Challenges of higher education related to e-learning in developing countries during COVID-19 spread: A review of the perspectives of students, instructors, policymakers, and ICT experts. *Environmental Science and Pollution Research International*, 29(57), 85562–85568. DOI: 10.1007/s11356-021-14647-2 PMID: 34100207

Zhang, K., & Aslan, A. (2021). AI technologies for education: Recent research & future directions. *Comput. Educ. Artif. Intell.*, 2, 100025. DOI: 10.1016/j.caeai.2021.100025

Zhang, M., Ding, H., Naumceska, M., & Zhang, Y. (2022). Virtual reality technology as an educational and intervention tool for children with autism spectrum disorder: Current perspectives and future directions. *Behavioral Sciences (Basel, Switzerland)*, 12(5), 138. DOI: 10.3390/bs12050138 PMID: 35621435

Zhang, M., Zhang, Z., Chang, Y., Aziz, E. S., Esche, S., & Chassapis, C. (2018). Recent developments In game-based virtual reality educational laboratories using the microsoft kinect. [IJET]. *International Journal of Emerging Technologies in Learning*, 13(1), 138–159. DOI: 10.3991/ijet.v13i01.7773

Zhang, W., & Duan, C. (2017). Construction and implementation of institutional e-learning development framework in continuing higher education. [JETDE]. *Journal of Educational Technology Development and Exchange*, 10(1), 2. DOI: 10.18785/jetde.1001.02

Zhang, X., Lo, P., So, S., Chiu, D., Leung, K., Ho, K., & Stark, A. (2021). Medical students' attitudes and perceptions towards the effectiveness of mobile learning: A comparative information-need perspective. *Journal of Librarianship and Information Science*, 53(1), 116–129. DOI: 10.1177/0961000620925547

Zhao, G., Zhang, L., Chu, J., Zhu, W., Hu, B., He, H., & Yang, L. (2023). An augmented reality-based mobile photography application to improve learning gain, decrease cognitive load, and achieve better emotional state. *International Journal of Human-Computer Interaction*, 39(3), 643–658. DOI: 10.1080/10447318.2022.2041911

Zimmerman, B. J. (2002). Becoming a self-regulated learner: An overview. *Theory into Practice*, 41(2), 64–70. DOI: 10.1207/s15430421tip4102_2

Zuboff, S. (2023). The age of surveillance capitalism. In *Social theory re-wired* (pp. 203–213). Routledge. DOI: 10.4324/9781003320609-27

About the Contributors

Seyfullah Gökoğlu is a researcher and faculty member at Bartın University, Türkiye. With MA and PhD degrees in computer education and instructional technologies, Dr. Gökoğlu focuses on empirical studies in virtual reality, online learning, programming education, and educational technology. He applies critical theories like constructivism, experiential learning, and social learning to his research. Dr. Gökoğlu is also interested in emerging research paradigms, including topic modeling, sentiment analysis, and meta-analysis. Dr. Gökoğlu's studies also cover integrating artificial intelligence technologies into educational processes in the axis of human-computer interaction. His dedication to advancing the field is reflected in his publications in leading journals in the instructional technology field, such as Computers & Education, Journal of Educational Computing Research, The International Review of Research in Open and Distributed Learning, and Online Information Review.

Fatih Erdoğdu is an Associate Professor of Computer Technologies at Zonguldak Bülent Ecevit University in Türkiye. He graduated with a bachelor's degree from the Middle East Technical University. He graduated from Computer Education and Instructional Technology at Gazi University with the degree of master in 2015. Dr. Erdoğdu gained his PhD in Computer Education and Instructional Technology at Karadeniz Technical University. His academic interest areas are instructional technology, distance learning, teacher training and humorous learning. He conducted over 30 scientific studies. He has also been serving as the head of the Department of Computer Technologies at Zonguldak Bülent Ecevit University for four years.

***

Nurul Ajleaa binti Abdul Rahman is a Head Centre of Studies at the Academy of Language Studies, Universiti Teknologi MARA (Terengganu). She received the Ph.D degree in TESL from Universiti Kebangsaan Malaysia (UKM), in 2017. She has more than 15 years of teaching experience. She is currently teaching several English language proficiency courses. Her interests are ESL Writing Skills, ESL Oral Communication Skills, Education, Social Sciences and Innovative Teaching and Learning.

Vichayanan Rattanawiboonsom is an Associate Professor at Naresuan University in Thailand. Currently, she is working as a Dean of the Faculty of Business Economics and Communications at Naresuan University, Thailand. Her research interests include tourism, foreign direct investment, technology transfer, and economic growth. She has conducted studies on topics such as the motivational factors for adopting augmented reality applications in tourism and the relationship between foreign direct investment, technology transfer, and economic growth in the Lower Northern Region of Thailand. Dr. Rattanawiboonsom has also presented her research at conferences and has been involved in the academic community.

Md. Khaled Amin is an Assistant Professor of marketing in the Faculty of Business Administration (FBA) at American International University-Bangladesh. Before joining the institution, Mr. Amin worked as a senior lecturer for Daffodil International University (DIU) and as a lecturer for Northern University Bangladesh (NUB). Mr. Amin also worked as a part-time faculty member for universities such as Zhejiang Shuren University, Zhejiang Gongshang University, and Uttara University (UU). He holds a master's degree and a bachelor's degree in business administration with a concentration in marketing from the American International University-Bangladesh and completed his doctorate degree in management science with a concentration in marketing and innovation management at the Zhejiang Gongshang University , China. Mr. Amin also has a Post Graduate Diploma (PGDipHET) with a focus in Higher Education Teaching which he earned from the Bangladesh University of Professionals (BUP). His academic research interest encompasses a broad spectrum of areas such as consumer psychology, e-commerce, social media, e-learning, consumer technology, and innovation. He is particularly concerned with the acceptance and adoption of various information and communications technology-driven products and services by rural consumers in Bangladesh. He has published several research papers, business cases, and notes both in local and foreign journals and conferences. Some of his contributions are available on SAGE Knowledge, IEEE Xplore, ACM Digital Library, AIS eLibrary, etc. Aside from being a faculty member, he has been serving as an active reviewer and editorial member for several journals from renowned publishers: Inderscience, Emerald, and Taylor &

Francis, and conferences. He has been actively participating in various conferences, workshops, and symposiums both at home and abroad.

Zelda Arku is a lecturer at the University of Mines and Technology and a PhD student in information systems at the University of Ghana. She holds an MPhil in Management Information Systems from the University of Ghana. Her research interest are electronic learning, cloud computing, enterprise resource planning, internet of things and digitalization.

Sibel Barın Özkan holds a Bachelor's and Master's degree in Computer Education and Instructional Technology (CEIT), as well as a Ph.D. in Computer Engineering. She is currently serving as a Lecturer in the Department of Computer Technology at Zonguldak Bülent Ecevit University (BEUN). Dr. Sibel's academic and professional expertise bridges the fields of educational technology and computer science, allowing her to contribute significantly to interdisciplinary research and teaching.

Stephen Boateng is a Lecturer, specializing in Management Information Systems. With a focus on digital transformation and the integration of emerging technologies, his research explores the impact of digitalization on business processes within developing economies. Stephen is also the Digital Lead at Digital Reach Limited, where he drives innovative digital strategies for businesses, and serves as a tutor at BuildUp Academy, imparting practical digital skills to the next generation of business leaders.

Şeyma Çağlar-Özhan completed her PhD in 2023 in the Department of Computer Education and Instructional Technology at Hacettepe University, Turkey. She is currently an assistant professor at Bartın University. Her research focuses on cognitive and emotional processes in teaching, educational games and simulations, and human-computer interaction. She is also a member of the Educational Ontology and Cognition Laboratory, where interdisciplinary research contributes to the design and development of e-learning environments by exploring cognition and information technologies.

Barış Çukurbaşı, is an Associate Professor in Computer and Instructional Technologies. After graduating from the Computer Department of Buca Technical High School in 2004, he completed my undergraduate studies in Computer Education and Instructional Technologies at Dokuz Eylül University in 2010. He earned my master's degree from Balıkesir University in 2012 and his doctorate from Sakarya University in 2016. He has served as a Lecturer at Dokuz Eylül University and as a Research Assistant at Bartın University, where he played an active role in establishing the Distance Education Application and Research Center and the Faculty of Education. In 2017, he was appointed as an Assistant Professor at Bartın University and directed the Distance Education Application and Research Center during the onset of the COVID-19 pandemic. Since September 2020, he has been working at Manisa Celal Bayar University as the Head of the Computer Technology Department and Director of the Computer Research and Application Center. On August 29, 2022, he became a founding partner and Chairman of Extensa Digital Solutions Software Industry and Trade Inc., established within the MCBÜ Technopark. His academic interests include open and distance learning, flipped classroom applications, educational technologies, technology integration in education, 21st-century skills, lifelong learning, internet technologies, robotic teaching applications, and three-dimensional virtual environments.

John Effah is an Associate Professor of Information Systems at the Department of Operations and Management Information Systems, University of Ghana Business School. His publications focus on design, development, implementation, and evaluation of digitally enabled information systems in developing countries.

Ali Geris is a Ph.D. in Computer Education & Instructional Technologies. As a Research Assistant i'm working at Department of CEIT, Education Faculty, Manisa Celal Bayar University, Turkey. He is additionally a member of MCBU Extended Reality Laboratory (XRLab). His researches focuses on Virtual Reality (VR), Extended Reality (XR) and Digital Twins. Specifically: developing VR/XR environments with Unity, learning in VR, technical specifications of VR/XR envrionments and creating digital twins.

Zhang Haiyan holds a master's degree from Inner Mongolia University and is a lecturer at Jining Normal University.

Mehmet Kara, PhD, is an Associate Professor at the Department of Educational Sciences, Amasya University, Türkiye. He received a PhD in Computer Education and Instructional Technology. His research interests include open and distance learning, instructional design and technology, and teacher education.

İbrahim Kepceoğlu is an associate professor doctor in Mathematics Education at Kastamonu University. He received the Bachelor of Science degree in Mathematics in 2009 from Bogazici University, İstanbul, Türkiye. He held the doctor of education degree in mathematics education from Marmara University in 2015. He has been lecturing at Elementary Mathematics Education Department at Kastamonu University, Kastamonu, Türkiye from 2016. He is the author of numerous papers in refereed journals, book chapters, and conference proceedings.

His research interests are teacher education, elementary mathematics education, and educational technology.

Servet Kılıç provides training as a lecturer in the Department of Computer Technologies at Ordu University on programming, three-dimensional object design, educational robotics applications, testing and automation, and graphic analysis. In the field of computer education and educational technologies,Dr. Kılıç conducts studies as an associate professor on topics such as educational technologies, distance education, teacher education, programming, robotics, virtual education technologies, STEM, and artificial intelligence technologies.

James Oigara currently works as an Associate Professor of Education. James does research in Pedagogic Theory, Teacher Education, Educational Technology, Active Learning and Teaching Methods. His current project is 'Preparing pre-service teachers to integrate emerged and emerging technologies and primary source documents for instruction to enhance active learning.'

Yasin Özkan received the M.S. degree in Electrical Electronics and Computer Engineering from Düzce University, Düzce, Turkey, in 2017 and 2019. He completed his PhD in the same department in 2024. He is currently working as a Lecturer at Zonguldak Bülent Ecevit University. His research interests include image processing, machine learning, and optimization.

Mustafa Samur graduated from Süleyman Demirel University, Faculty of Arts and Sciences, Department of History in 2005. He completed his master's degree in 2010 at Gazi Osmanpaşa University in the Department of Turkish Republic History and received his doctorate from Hacettepe University in the Department of Atatürk's Principles and History of Turkish Revolution in 2022. He began working at Bülent Ecevit University in 2015. Dr. Samur was appointed as a history teacher to Hürriyet Vocational and Technical Anatolian High School in Osmangazi, Bursa, under the Ministry of National Education in 2007. He continued his career as a history teacher at Sapanca Vocational and Technical Anatolian High School in Sapanca, Sakarya, in 2010. Between 2010 and 2015, he served as a history teacher at Aziz Altınpınar High School in Çankaya, Ankara. Currently, he works at Bülent Ecevit University in the Directorate of Atatürk's Principles and History of Turkish Revolution and at Karadeniz Ereğli Vocational School. His primary research areas include the History of the Turkish Republic and Political History.

Mehmet Koray Serin is an associate professor at Kastamonu University, Department of Primary School Education. He received his PhD in Primary School Education from Necmettin Erbakan University in 2015. Dr. Serin conducts research in the field of primary school mathematics education, especially in the areas of problem solving, problem posing, teacher education, content knowledge and metacognition.

Perihan Tekeli completed her PhD in 2024 in the Department of Computer Education and Instructional Technology at Hacettepe University, Turkey. She is currently a lecturer at Distance Education Application and Research Center at Hacettepe University, Turkey. In her doctoral study, she examined the effect of mental rotation and visual spatial memory on retrieval performance in different virtual reality environments. She is currently continuing her postdoctoral research. Her research interests; medical education, spatial memory, virtual reality, human-computer interaction, embodied cognition, e-learning, instructional design, digital storytelling and artificial intelligence. She is also a member of the Educational Ontology and Cognition Laboratory, where interdisciplinary research contributes to the design and development of e-learning environments by exploring cognition and information technologies.

Mahir Tonga received his MS degree in Instructional Technology and BS degree in Electronics and Computer Education. He currently works as an IT teacher in the Ministry of National Education. He has publications on Industry 4.0 and IT education. His research interests include computing education and online learning.

Rashim Wadhwa is working as an Associate Professor in the department of education at Akal University, India. She is working in the arena of higher education from last one decade. She has published extensively in various reputed international journals.

Seema Yadav has academic qualifications of M. Sc. (Chemistry), M Ed (RIE), UGC-NET, and PhD in Education. Presently she is working as an Assistant Professor, in the Department of Education at The Bhopal School of Education, Bhopal. She has almost 18 years of teaching experience. Her area of specialization is educational psychology, environmental education, and curriculum development.

Goh Ying Soon is a senior lecturer and he currently teaches Mandarin as the third language to non-native learners in MARA University of Technology, Malaysia. He is a member of the International Society for Chinese Language Teaching. He has experiences in teaching Mandarin at primary, secondary and tertiary level for more than 25 years. He has been actively presenting papers in national and international conferences. His research interests are on the use of educational technology in Mandarin teaching and learning, web-based instruction, translation, and etc. Updated resume: click here (dropbox). Google Scholar record. researchgate, academia.edu, cnki, scopus (Author ID: 25925392000).

Index

Symbols

A

B

C

D

E

F

H

I

L

M

O

P

R

T

V

www.ingramcontent.com/pod-product-compliance
Lightning Source LLC
LaVergne TN
LVHW060007031026
849161LV00025B/2243